Fundamentals of
Psychology

Josh R. Gerow
Indiana University—
Purdue University at Fort Wayne

Thomas Brothen
University of Minnesota

Jerry D. Newell
Citrus College

Scott, Foresman and Company
Glenview, Illinois   London, England

Cover and chapter opener illustrations by Guy
Billout.

Credit lines for photos, illustrations, and other
copyrighted materials appearing in this book are in
the *Acknowledgments* section beginning on page A1.
This section is to be considered an extension of the
copyright page.

Library of Congress Cataloging-in-Publication Data

Gerow, Joshua R.
  Fundamentals of psychology.

  "Based on the second edition of Psychology: an
introduction, by Josh R. Gerow"—Pref.
  Bibliography: p.
  Includes indexes.
  1. Psychology. I. Brothen, Thomas. II. Newell,
Jerry D. III. Gerow, Joshua R. Psychology. IV. Title.
BF121.G43 1988   150   88-29707
ISBN 0-673-38330-X

23456—VHJ—949392919089

Preface

Fundamentals of Psychology is based on the second edition of *Psychology: An Introduction* by Josh R. Gerow. *Fundamentals of Psychology* teaches what students must know about psychology without spending a great deal of time on issues less central to the field. It is designed for introductory psychology courses where time constraints make longer books difficult to use. As can be seen in the Table of Contents, it is divided into 12 chapters—each with numerous pedagogical aids that have proved highly effective and which are described in the section of the Preface called *Features of This Text*.

We received so much support and assistance preparing *Fundamentals of Psychology* that we fear once we start naming names, we'll leave someone out. We should begin by citing the help and understanding of our families. Textbook writing puts a strain on anyone's ability to lead a normal life; deadlines and other publishing requirements are unforgiving masters. Our colleagues have also been extremely cooperative as we worked on this project to the neglect of our other duties. They have been particularly helpful as they reacted to the manuscript and suggested improvements.

We were also fortunate to be able to count on the best professional assistance from the people at Scott, Foresman and Company. This project—in all its aspects, with all its ancillaries—has been from the start the project of Scott Hardy, editorial vice-president. Developmental editor Paula Fitzpatrick took on the major editorial tasks of dealing with our rough manuscript and coordinating all the input we received from our reviewers. Putting the pieces together fell to project editor, Jan Keller. Matthew Doherty created the attractive and functional design of the book, and Sandy Schneider selected the excellent pictures throughout. Iris Ganz kept thousands of pages of manuscript organized and directed to the right people at the right time. To all those at Scott, Foresman: Thank you.

Writing this text has significantly widened our acquaintances in the profession. We are all fortunate that there are so many bright, dedicated teachers of psychology. Users of this text are fortunate that so many of them took the time to contribute to its preparation. In particular, we would like to thank Ola Barnett, Pepperdine University; Thomas Bond, Thomas Nelson Community College; David Grilley, Cleveland State University; Charles Halcomb, Texas Tech University; James H. Korn, St. Louis University; Holly A. Pennock, Hudson Valley Community College; and William Reich, Nassau Community College. A special thanks goes to William Beneke and Robert Hancock of Lincoln University. Others who read and commented on at least portions of the manuscript are:

Michael Aamodt
Radford University

Robert Ahlering
Central Missouri State University

Roger Allen
North Central Michigan College

Lou Banderet
Northeastern University

Alan Benton
University of Illinois, Circle Campus

Linda Berg-Cross
Howard University

John Best
Eastern Illinois University

Elaine Blakemore
Indiana University—Purdue University at Fort Wayne

Tom Blakemore
Indiana University—Purdue University at Fort Wayne

Walter Bobkiewicz
Oakton Community College

Cynthia Brandau
Belleville Area Community College

Lynn Brokow
Portland Community College

Gary Brown
Kellogg Community College

William Calhoun
University of Tennessee, Knoxville

Edward Clemmer
Emerson College

Donald Cusumano
St. Louis Community College

William O. Dwyer
Memphis State University

Sandra Edwards
Auburn University

Barbara Engler
Union County College

Jody Esper
Valparaiso University

Terence Fetterman
West Valley College

Linda Flickinger
St. Clair County Community College

Cynthia Ford
Jackson State University

James Frost
Cuyahoga Community College

E. Scott Geller
Virginia Polytechnic Institute

David Griese
SUNY Farmingdale

Ernest Gurman
University of Southern Mississippi

Donald Hall
Radford University

Al Heldt
Grand Rapids Junior College

Sandra Holmes
University of Wisconsin, Stevens Point

Christine Jazwinski
St. Cloud State University

Carl Johnson
Central Michigan University

Linda Leal
Eastern Illinois University

Paulette Leonard
University of Central Arkansas

Ken LeSure
Cuyahoga Community College

Earl Magidson
Kennedy King College

Willie Manning
Clayton State College

Cynthia Marshall
Skyline College

Sue Martel
Cleveland State Community College, Cleveland, Tennessee

Terry Maul
San Bernardino Valley College

Karla Miley
Black Hawk College, Quad-Cities Campus

Hal Miller
Brigham Young University

James Nelson
Parkland College

Steve Nida
Franklin University

Radha Parker
University of Central Arkansas

Martin Pearlman
Middlesex County Community College

Donald Ragusa
Bowling Green State University

Joel Rivers
Indiana University—Purdue University at Fort Wayne

Steven Rosengarten
Middlesex County Community College

Michael Scoles
University of Central Arkansas

Fred Shaffer
Northeastern Missouri State University

W. S. Terry
University of North Carolina, Charlotte

Kathy Trabue
Ohio State University

Walter Vernon
Illinois State University

Paul Watson
University of Tennessee

Don Welti
Northern Kentucky University

Ursula White
El Paso Community College

Linda Wickstra
St. Louis Community College

Jeffrey Wilson
Indiana University—Purdue University at Fort Wayne

Mike Zeller
Mankato State University

Features of This Text

Before you get into the text, we would first like you to notice that included with each copy of *Fundamentals of Psychology* is *TIME—Psychology: 1923–1988*. Published in conjunction with TIME Magazine, this special edition of TIME offers a historical look at TIME's coverage of psychology since the magazine's first year of publication in 1923. There are articles reprinted in their entirety and many more that are excerpted for each decade from the '20s to the '80s. Each article is preceded by an annotation written by Josh R. Gerow.

Every student has her or his own favorite way of studying a textbook, and we won't suggest that anyone ought to radically change that approach. On the other hand, *Fundamentals of Psychology* does have some features built into it that have been expressly designed to help students get the most from the time they spend studying. These features are based on sound psychological research that tells us that learning and memory are enhanced if study sessions are brief, focused, and meaningful. We'll simply list here features of the text that we believe will help students.

1. *Chapter Outline.* Each of the chapters (and the Statistical Appendix) begins with a complete outline. This outline should be the first thing a student reads when beginning an assignment. It will provide an overview of what is to be covered and will show how that material is interrelated.

2. *Chapter Vignette.* Each chapter has a brief story or example which "sets the stage" for that chapter. It is designed to get students involved with some of the relevant issues in the chapter.

A sample chapter opener is shown above. Chapter outlines such as the one shown are helpful to students as they begin a new chapter or review material for an exam.

3. *Why We Care.* Following each opener is a unique section which attempts to tell the reader why psychologists care about the material covered in the chapter and, more importantly perhaps, why the reader should care. The *Why We Care* section also serves as a preview, letting the reader know in some detail precisely what will be covered.

Why We Care

4. *Marginal, Boldface Glossary.* In large measure, learning about psychology is a matter of developing the appropriate vocabulary for the subject. Important key words and concepts are printed in the

Boldface
important keywords and concepts
are printed in boldface type in the
text. Each term, along with its
definition, appears in the margin.

BEFORE YOU GO ON
**What are the two major
goals of psychology?**

text in **boldface** type. Each key term is defined in the text and the definition is repeated in the margin for ready reference. All definitions are also collected in a complete, page-referenced glossary at the end of the text.

5. *Before You Go On.* A series of questions labeled *Before You Go On* appears throughout the textbook. They occur after major content sections. *Before You Go On* questions can be easily answered if the reader has understood the previous material. They provide a quick and simple intermediate review. The student who cannot answer a *Before You Go On* question should go back and reread the previous material. (There's little point to continue reading if one doesn't understand what one has just read!)

6. *Chapter Summary.* As its name suggests, this section provides a review of all the important material presented within each chapter. Each *Chapter Summary* is comprised of *Before You Go On* questions—and answers. You realize, of course, that the brief answers to the *Before You Go On* questions provided in the *Chapter Summaries* are to be taken only as suggestions. The best, most complete answers are found in the text itself. A page number referring readers back to the appropriate section of the text follows each brief answer in the *Chapter Summaries*.

7. *Chapter Review Questions.* At the end of each chapter we have included eight multiple-choice questions that cover important concepts from that chapter. They are followed by an explanation of the question and each possible answer. Students should try to answer the questions before reading the explanations—that will give them quick feedback as to whether they understand the material.

To review for an examination, it should not be necessary to reread all of the assigned material. Students should only have to reexamine the *Chapter Outlines,* check all the marginal glossary terms, practice the *Review Questions,* and review the *Chapter Summaries* of answers to the *Before You Go On* questions.

Finally, for further study help there is a *Study Guide* to accompany *Fundamentals of Psychology.* Prepared by William Beneke and Rob Hancock of Lincoln University, it takes a "writing to learn" approach and provides students with an excellent way to organize their studying of psychology. If you want a copy of the workbook, and it is not available in your bookstore, contact either your professor or the publisher (Marketing Support Services, College Division/Scott, Foresman and Company/1900 East Lake Avenue/Glenview, IL 60025) for information on how to order a copy.

Your instructor will have additional advice for you on how to get the most out of your introductory psychology class. We hope and trust that you will find the experience pleasurable as well as informative. We wish you the very best and would like to hear from you to know how you liked this book and how we might make it a better one.

Contents

Introduction
The Nature of Psychology   1

Defining Psychology   4
  Psychology is a Science   4
  The Subject Matter of Psychology   5

The History of Psychology   7
  Psychology's Roots in Philosophy and
    Science   7
  Experimental Psychology Begins:
    Structuralism and Functionalism   9
  Gestalt Psychology   10
  Behaviorism   11

  Humanism and Cognitive Psychology   13
  A Focus on Application: Mental Measurement
    and Psychoanalysis   13

The Goals of Psychology   15

Research Methods in Psychology   16
  Observational Methods   16
  Experimental Methods   21

**Ethical Considerations in
  Psychological Research**   26

Chapter One
The Biological Bases Of Behavior   32

The Neuron   36
  Neural Structure   36
  Neural Function: The Impulse   39

**From One Cell to Another: The
  Synapse**   41

Nervous Systems: The Big Picture   43
The Spinal Cord   45
  Structure   45
  Function   46

"Lower" Brain Centers   48
  The Brain Stem   48
  The Cerebellum   50
  The Reticular Activating System   51
  The Limbic System   51
  The Hypothalamus   52
  The Thalamus   53

The Cerebral Cortex   53
  Lobes and Localization   54
  The Two Cerebral Hemispheres   57

Chapter Two
Sensation And Perception   64

The Stimulus For Vision: Light   68
    Wave Amplitude (Intensity)   68
    Wavelength   69
    Wave Purity   71

The Eye   73
    Structures that Focus Visual Images   73
    The Retina   75

Rods and Cones: A Theory of Vision   77
    What the Theory Claims   77
    Evidence to Support the Duplicity Theory   78

Color Vision   81

Hearing   84
    The Stimulus for Hearing: Sound   84
    The Ear   88

Other Senses   89
    The Chemical Senses   89
    The Skin (Cutaneous) Senses   92
    The Position Senses   93
    Pain: A Special Sense   94

Perceptual Selectivity: Paying
    Attention   96
    Gestalt Psychology and Figure-ground   97
    Stimulus Factors   97
    Personal Factors   100

Perceptual Organization   102
    Stimulus Factors   102
    Personal Factors   104

Chapter Three
Varieties Of Consciousness   110

The Nature of Consciousness   114

Sleep and Dreams   115
    Stages of Sleep   115
    REM and NREM Sleep   117
    The Function(s) of Sleep   120

Hypnosis   123

Meditation   125

Altering Consciousness with Drugs   127
    Stimulants   128
    Depressants   129
    Hallucinogens   131
    Marijuana—A Special Case   133

Chapter Four
Learning   138

A Definition of Learning   142
Classical Conditioning   143
  Pavlov and a Classic Demonstration   144
  Classical Conditioning Phenomena   146
  The Significance of Classical Conditioning:
    What About People?   149
  Recent Developments (and
    Complications)   152

The Basics of Operant Conditioning   155
  Defining Operant Conditioning   155
  The Procedures of Operant Conditioning   156
  The Course of Operant Conditioning   157

Reinforcement and Punishment   159
  A Definition of Reinforcer   160
  Positive Reinforcers   160

  Negative Reinforcers   161
  Primary and Secondary Reinforcers   163
  Scheduling of Reinforcement   164
  Punishment   165

Generalization and Discrimination   166
Can Any Response Be Operantly
  Conditioned?   167
Cognitive Approaches to Learning   169
  Edward Tolman and David Olton:
    Latent Learning and Cognitive Maps   169
  Albert Bandura: Social Learning and
    Modeling   172

Applying Conditioning and Cognitive
  Theories of Learning to Your Study of
  Psychology   175

Chapter Five
Memory and Cognition   182

Introduction: What Is Memory?   186
Sensory Memory   188
Short-term Memory (STM)   189
  The Duration of STM   190
  The Capacity of STM   192
  How Information Is Represented in STM   192

Long-term Memory (LTM)   193
  Encoding in LTM: A Matter of
    Repetition and Rehearsal   195
  Are There Different Types of Long-term
    Memories?   196

How Information Is Represented in
  Long-term Memory   198

Measuring Retrieval: Recall, Recognition,
  and Relearning   201
Encoding and Retrieval   203
  The Effects of Context   203
  Strategies That Guide Encoding   205
  Amount and Distribution of Encoding
    Practice   209

Inhibiting Retrieval: Interference   212
Higher Cognitive Processes   216
  The Concept of Concept   216
  Forming Concepts   222
  A Definition of Language   223
  The Structure in Language   226

Chapter Six
Developmental Psychology   236

Heredity and Environment; Nature
    and Nurture   240

Childhood   242
    Physical and Motor Development   242
    Sensory and Perceptual Development   245
    Cognitive and Social Development   246

Adolescence   256
    Physical Changes in Adolescence   258
    Cognitive and Social Development in
        Adolescence   261

Adulthood   265
    Early Adulthood   266
    Middle Adulthood   269
    Late Adulthood   271

Chapter Seven
Motivation, Sexuality, and Emotion   282

Approaches to Motivation   286
    Approaches Based on Instinct   287
    Approaches Based on Needs and Drives   287
    Approaches Based on Incentives   290
    Approaches Based on Balance or
        Equilibrium   292

Physiologically Based Motivation   294
    Temperature Regulation   294
    Thirst and Drinking Behavior   296
    Hunger and Eating Behavior   297

Sex Drives and Sexual Behavior   299
    Internal, Physiological Cues   300
    External, Psychological Cues   301

The Human Sexual Response   301
Homosexuality   304
Sexually Transmitted Diseases   306

Psychologically Based Motivation   309
    Achievement Motivation   309
    Power Motivation   311
    Affiliation Motivation   311
    Competency Motivation   311

Emotion   313
    The Nature of Emotion   313
    Outward Expressions of Emotion   316
    Physiological Aspects of Emotion   319

Chapter Eight
Individual Differences in Personality and Intelligence 328

Approaches to Personality 332
  Freud's Psychoanalytic Approach 333
  The Psychoanalytic Approach After Freud 337
  Evaluating the Psychoanalytic Approach 339
  The Behavioral/Learning Approach 339
  Evaluating the Behavioral/Learning
      Approach 342
  The Humanistic/Phenomenological
      Approach 342
  Evaluating the Humanistic/Phenomenological
      Approach 345
  The Trait Approach 345
  Evaluating the Trait Approach 349
The Nature of Psychological Tests 349
  A Working Definition 350
  Criteria for a Good Test 351

Personality Assessment 355
  Behavioral Observation 356
  Interviews 357
  Paper-and-Pencil Tests 358
  Projective Techniques 361
Intelligence 363
  Defining Intelligence 363
  Assessing Intelligence 364
  Variations in Intelligence 372
Nature-Nuture Revisited: The
  Influence of Heredity and the
  Environment on Intelligence 376
  Conceptual Problems 376
  A Tentative Answer 377
  What the Data Suggest: The Study of
      Twins 378

Chapter Nine
Abnormal Psychology 388

Definition and Classification 393
  Defining Abnormality 393
  The Classification of Abnormal Reactions 395
Anxiety-based Disorders 398
  Anxiety Disorders 398
  Somatoform Disorders 402
  Dissociative Disorders 404

Personality Disorders 406
Psychotic Disorders 407
  Organic Mental Disorders 409
  Mood Disorders 414
  Schizophrenia 418

Chapter Ten
Treatment and Therapy   430

A Historical Perspective   434

Biomedical Treatments of Psychological
  Disorders   438
  Psychosurgery   438
  Electroconvulsive Therapy   439
  Drug Therapy   441

Psychotherapy   444
  Psychoanalytic Techniques   444
  Humanistic Techniques   448
  Behavioral Techniques   449
  Cognitive Techniques   453
  Group Approaches   456
  Choosing a Therapist   457

Chapter Eleven
Social Psychology   466

The Social-Psychological Perspective   470

Attitudes   472
  The Structure of Attitudes   472
  The Usefulness of Attitudes   473
  Attitude Change and Persuasion   474

Attribution Theory   477

Interpersonal Attraction   480
  Theories of Interpersonal Attraction   480
  Factors Affecting Attraction   481

Social Influence   484
  Conformity   485
  Obedience to Authority   486
  Bystander Intervention   490

Other Examples of Social Influence   494
  Social Impact Theory and Social Loafing   494
  Social Facilitation   495
  Decision-making in Groups   496
  Television and Violent Behavior   498

Chapter Twelve
Applied Psychology 506

Industrial-organizational Psychology *510*
  Fitting the Person to the Job *510*
  Fitting the Job to the Person *521*

Psychology and Health *526*
  Personality and Physical Health *527*

Psychological Interventions and Physical
  Health *529*

Stress *530*
  Stressors: The Causes of Stress *531*
  Reactions to Stress *537*

Statistical Appendix 550

An Example to Work With *552*
Organizing Data *553*
  Frequency Distributions *553*
  Graphic Representations *554*

Descriptive Statistics *555*
  Measures of Central Tendency *555*
  Variability *557*

Inferential Statistics *560*
Some Normal Curve Statistics *562*

Glossary *G-1*

References *R-1*

Acknowledgments *A-1*

Name Index *I-1*

Subject Index *I-5*

Fundamentals of
Psychology

Introduction

The Nature of Psychology

Why We Care

Defining Psychology

Psychology is a Science
The Subject Matter of Psychology
Psychologists Study Behavior
Psychologists Study Mental Processes

The History of Psychology

Psychology's Roots in Philosophy and Science
Philosophy
Science
Experimental Psychology Begins: Structuralism and Functionalism
Gestalt Psychology
Behaviorism
Humanism and Cognitive Psychology
A Focus on Application: Mental Measurement and Psychoanalysis
Mental Measurement
Psychoanalysis

The Goals of Psychology

Research Methods in Psychology

Observational Methods
Naturalistic Observation
Surveys
Case Histories
Correlation
Experimental Methods
Exercising Control
Overcoming Bias

Ethical Considerations in Psychological Research

Let's suppose that you had a big biology mid-term exam this morning. You have been worried about this exam. For a number of reasons, you haven't been able to keep up with your studying as well as you would have liked. This mid-term will account for one-third of your final grade. Late in the afternoon, you stop by the biology department offices to see if grades have been posted. There they are. You quickly scan the list of identification numbers and locate your score: an A! Your score of 94 was the second highest in the class!

Once you recover from your initial excitement over having done so well, you stop to wonder why. Although you hadn't prepared as much as you could have, you recognize that you *did* put in a very good session of study and review last night. Everything seemed to come together and make sense. Why was last night's studying so much more effective than usual? Was there anything about your studying last night that was out of the ordinary? As you reflect on your efforts of the previous night, only one thing seems to have been different. It doesn't seem very significant at first, but last night you studied with classical music playing in the background. Everything else was basically the same as always. But usually you try to study in the quietest place you can find. Sometimes you have to study in noisy, crowded places;

sometimes you go to the library. You've never studied with classical music playing before—you don't even like classical music. Can classical background music improve the effectiveness of studying? This strikes you as a reasonable (and potentially important) psychological question. How might you go about answering it?

Can classical background music improve the effectiveness of studying? This strikes you as a reasonable (and potentially important) psychological question. How might you go about answering it?

You immediately recognize that your experience might simply reflect a unique coincidence. You realize that you cannot draw any general conclusions based on just one isolated incident. You need to find additional support for what has now become a hypothesis: Classical music is an aid to study. As is usually the case with such psychological questions, you will find that there are many ways you

could go about confirming or rejecting your hypothesis. You might ask other students about the conditions under which they study. You might examine the study habits of good students and poor students. You might observe students studying and note background conditions. You might keep careful, complete records of your own studying experiences. You will have to generate some operational definitions for the relevant aspects of your basic question. That is, how will you define "effective or ineffective studying"? What sorts of background conditions will you investigate?

Even if you were to discover that students who earn high grades *do* tend to listen to classical music more frequently than do those who earn low grades, will you be able to conclude that it was the music that *caused* the higher grades? If you *can* generalize your experience to others, you may have discovered that there is a relationship between effective study and classical music, but you won't be able to conclude that classical music causes better studying. To be able to draw that kind of conclusion, you'll need to do an experiment.

As a science, psychology uses a number of different techniques for answering questions about behavior and mental processes. We'll examine several of these techniques in this introduction.

Why We Care

Welcome to this year's class of psychology students! It may surprise you to know that you are now one of more than 1.5 million students who will be taking a general introductory psychology class this year in the United States and Canada. Why should psychology have such a broad appeal? Why do so many students want to learn about psychology? There are many different answers to such questions, of course, but let's explore two of the most common.

First, psychology is relevant. As we'll see, psychologists study many different kinds of reactions of many different kinds of organisms, but most importantly, psychology is concerned with people. As the weeks go by in this course, you'll learn even more about how psychology is related to your own life.

Second, psychology is dynamic; it is an active, still-emerging discipline. More than 3,000 people earn Ph.D.s in psychology each year (Pion, 1986). It's fair to say that most of what we know in psychology today we have learned in your lifetime. Psychologists are always devising new methods and techniques to study human behavior and mental activity and organizing their findings into new theories at a very rapid pace. There is excitement in psychology today, and that sense of excitement often attracts students.

In this text, we'll share some of the excitement of psychology. At the same time, we'll always be looking for ways in which the study of psychology can be applied to our everyday life experiences.

We begin our discussion by developing a definition, by looking at what psychology *is*. Some of the issues that psychologists study you already know about; some may surprise you.

To more fully appreciate what psychology is today, we will take a brief look at its history. Though that history has been short—just over 100 years—it has deep roots in both philosophy and science. Next, we'll consider the goals of psychology and a number of methods that psychologists use to study their subject matter. We will also introduce ethical considerations that psychologists face in their attempts to employ these methods. We care about these issues because they can help us understand the very nature of psychology, and because they provide a framework for all of the specific examples of psychology that follow.

DEFINING PSYCHOLOGY

psychology
the scientific study of behavior and mental processes

Psychology is the scientific study of behavior and mental processes. This is a rather standard definition of psychology, but it leaves something to be desired in terms of telling us precisely what it is that psychologists do, and it isn't quite as specific in terms of subject matter as we might like it to be. As a working definition, however, it makes a couple of important points about psychology: (1) It's a science, and (2) its subject matter is behavior and mental processes. Let's see just what these two points mean.

Psychology is a Science

science
an organized body of knowledge gained through application of scientific methods

If psychology claims scientific status for itself, we should know what qualifies a discipline to be a science. A **science** is an organized body of knowledge gained through application of scientific methods. So, for psychology to qualify as a science requires that we demonstrate two things: (1) an organized body of knowledge and (2) scientific methodology.

1. An organized body of knowledge. Psychologists have accumulated a great deal of information over the years. We are coming to understand how our thoughts, feelings, and behaviors affect our nervous systems, and vice versa. We are beginning to discover how we learn about the world in which we live. We can identify some of the major determinants of personal growth and development. We know how many of the processes of learning and memory work. We have isolated many of the factors that influence the adjustments people make to their environments and to each other. Throughout this book, we will be discussing what psychologists have learned.

To be sure, we can still ask many interesting (and important) questions for which we have no good answers as yet. Not having all the answers can be extremely frustrating at times, but that is also part of the excitement of psychology; there are still so many important issues to be resolved, so many questions to be answered. The truth is, nonetheless, that psychologists *have* learned a great deal about their subject matter. What we know is well-organized. You have in your hands one version of the organized collection of knowledge that is psychology. In terms of our first requirement, then, psychology does qualify as a science.

scientific methods
systematic procedures involving observation, description, control, and replication to gain knowledge

2. Gained through scientific methods. What we have learned in psychology, we have learned through the application of **scientific methods,** which are systematic procedures involving observation, description, control, and replication used to gain knowledge. The specific techniques or procedures that a psychologist may use to study some aspect of behavior or mental processes vary widely. We'll review some of psychology's more commonly employed methods later in this introduction. The one thing that all of psychology's methods have in common is that they are scientific.

Scientific methods rely upon careful observation, description, control, and replication. They do not rely solely on common sense. They do not even rely solely on logic. To explain something scientifically is often a matter of ruling out, or eliminating, alternative explanations.

The basic process goes something like this: The scientist (psychologist) makes observations about his or her subject matter (behavior and/or mental processes). On the basis of these observations, a **hypothesis** is developed. A hypothesis is a tentative explanation that can be tested and then confirmed or rejected. In a way, a hypothesis is an educated guess about one's subject matter.

After formulating a hypothesis, the scientist again observes and describes relevant events, which are then analyzed to see if the hypothesis is well-founded. Alternative hypotheses or explanations are also tested. In other words, the psychologist must explore whether there are any other ways in which the observed behaviors or mental processes can be explained. If alternative hypotheses can be eliminated, and if new observations continue to support the scientist's original hypothesis, a tentative conclusion is reached. This conclusion is then communicated to others who may also test it to see if it can be confirmed.

Hypotheses become conclusions ("guesses" become "facts") only if alternative explanations cannot be used to explain the same events. Observations, descriptions, and measurements must consistently reflect the same conclusion before they are accepted as part of the knowledge base of a science. Thus, through its reliance on scientific methods, psychology fulfills the second requirement for qualifying as a science.

hypothesis
a tentative proposition or explanation that can be tested and confirmed or rejected

What two points must we demonstrate in order to claim that psychology is a science?   **BEFORE YOU GO ON**

The Subject Matter of Psychology

Simply skimming through the chapters of this book should convince you that trying to list everything that psychologists study would be pointless. The list would be much too long to be useful. However, it would be fair to suggest, as our definition does, that psychologists study the behavior and mental processes of organisms.

Psychologists Study Behavior.   By **behavior** we mean what organisms *do:* how they act and react and how they respond. The behaviors that we study must be observable, and they should be measurable. If you are concerned with whether or not a rat presses a lever, you can directly observe the rat's behavior. If you wonder whether Susan can draw a circle, you can ask her to do so and observe her efforts. Such behaviors have an advantage as the subject matter of a science because they are **publicly verifiable.** That is, a number of observers (public) can agree on (verify) the behavior of the organ-

behavior
any action or reaction of an organism that can be observed and measured

publicly verifiable
the agreement (verifiability) of observers (public) that an event did or did not take place

ism being studied. We can all agree that the rat did or did not press the lever or that Susan drew a circle, not a triangle. Events and behaviors that cannot be publicly verified have little credibility in science.

Psychologists study what organisms do, but some of the reactions that organisms make are not so easily observed; however, they often can be measured in such a way as to make them verifiable. For example, your friend may not be able to tell just by looking at you whether or not you are anxious at this moment. He could, however, measure your blood pressure, rate of breathing, sweat gland activity, and a host of other internal physiological events. Then, by observing the gauges, meters, and dials of his instruments, he could note subtle changes that would not otherwise be obvious to him (or to you either for that matter). He still would not be observing anxiety directly, but he might be willing to propose that those reactions he *is* observing are consistent with those associated with anxiety.

In using this approach, we are providing an **operational definition** of anxiety. An operational definition defines a concept in terms of the operations used to measure or create it. In our example, we are defining anxiety in terms of the operations that we used to measure it—internal physiological changes. We might have chosen to operationally define anxiety in terms of responses that you might make to an "anxiety test" or a questionnaire. Similarly, we might wonder how our rat's lever pressing would be affected if it were hungry. How do we know when a rat is hungry? Simple: We operationally define a hungry rat as one that has been deprived of food for 24 hours (or, alternatively, as one that has lost 15 percent of its normal body weight). We may also want to operationally define what we mean by a lever press (that is, how far down will the rat have to press the lever to qualify as a full lever press?).

There are some limitations with operational definitions—they may tend to oversimplify complex concepts, for example—but they do allow us to specify the exact nature of the behaviors we are studying, and, as a result, they help us communicate accurately with others. These are both important aspects of a science. Operational definitions can also be used to avoid lengthy philosophical discussions. Rather than agonizing over the true nature of intelligence, we may operationally define intelligence as "that which an IQ test measures." Rather than considering all of the factors that affect the aging process, we may operationally define old age as "living for 65 years or more." We will see many examples of operational definitions at work throughout the rest of this text.

operational definition
a definition given in terms of the operations used to measure or create the concept being defined

BEFORE YOU GO ON   What is the subject matter of psychology?
What are operational definitions, and why do we use them?

mental processes
activities of consciousness not normally observable by others, including cognitions and affect

Psychologists Study Mental Processes.   When it first emerged as a separate discipline late in the eighteenth century; psychology was defined as the science of **mental processes.** Yet for nearly fifty years in this century, mental activities were virtually ignored by most psychologists. Instead, psychologists focused almost exclusively on studying observable behavior. No one had proposed that mental processes did not exist or that they were unimportant, but it was felt that the study of such processes should not be included in the science of psychology. The argument was that one's mental processes were too personal and private and, therefore, could not be publicly verified.

The study of mental processes is rapidly returning to the mainstream of psychology. We now see that we *can* use scientific methodology to study **cognitions**—the sensing, perceiving, knowing, judging, and problem-solving skills involved in the processing of information about the world in which we live—and **affect**—the feelings or mood associated with emotional responses.

Cognitions and affect are clearly mental events. They include our thoughts, ideas, beliefs, likes, dislikes, moods, and feelings. These are the stuff of mental life. Because such mental events are not directly observable, they are difficult to study scientifically, but modern psychology has developed techniques and procedures that allow us to once again seriously pursue the study of such processes.

Here we have a theme that will be repeated a number of times throughout this book: The **A, B, C**'s of psychology. The subject matter of psychology is **A**ffect, **B**ehavior, and **C**ognition. To truly understand you at any given time someone is going to have to understand what you are feeling, what you are doing, and what you are thinking—A, B, C.

cognitions
the mental processes of "knowing" —of thinking, attending, perceiving, remembering, and the like

affect
the feelings or mood that accompany an emotional reaction

THE HISTORY OF PSYCHOLOGY

In order to better appreciate the nature of psychology today, let's take a brief look at psychology's past. Even a brief examination of where we've been will help us understand where we are now and where we may be going.

Psychology's Roots in Philosophy and Science

Many of the basic concerns of psychology today have been with us for a long time. When we look at philosophy, we find that the ancient Greeks (roughly 450–300 B.C.) wrote at length about issues that are essentially psychological in nature. When we study the history of science, we see that many of the physicians, biologists, and physiologists of the eighteenth and nineteenth centuries were also interested in psychological processes, but from their own unique perspectives. Our roots may be ancient, but still we say that psychology is a twentieth-century science. Where did psychology come from, and with what issues did the early psychologists concern themselves?

Philosophy.   Although earlier philosophers made important contributions, there is good reason to begin our discussion of the history of psychology with the British empiricists, John Locke (1632–1704), George Berkeley (1685–1753), David Hume (1711–1776), and David Hartley (1705–1757).

British empiricism focused on the content of the mind and claimed that it is acquired through experience. John Locke and the other empiricists believed that we are each born into this world with our minds empty, essen-

British empiricism
the school of thought (associated with Locke, among others) that focuses on the source of mental processes, and claims they are learned through experience

John Locke

Gustav Fechner

Hermann von Helmholtz

tially like blank slates. (The mind as a blank slate, or *tabula rasa,* was not new with Locke; the term had been introduced as far back as Aristotle (384–322 B.C.) The question then became: "How does the mind come to be filled with all its ideas, thoughts, memories, and abilities?" To this question Locke answered, "In one word, from experience."

With Locke and those who followed in his intellectual footsteps, at least a segment of philosophy turned its attention to the content and the nature of the human mind, which is still a focus of psychology today. Mental life results from experience, from our perceptions of and interactions with the environment, the empiricists argued. Berkeley, in fact, equated knowledge with perception. What exists is what we perceive—knowing is perceiving.

Our perceptions, then, become real, at least in our minds. The content of our minds can be manipulated. Ideas can be associated, one with another, to form new and different ideas. The empiricists wondered about *how* ideas become associated and devised a number of laws of association. Although they never put their theories and ideas to experimental or scientific tests, their philosophy was becoming remarkably psychological in its concerns and its questions. All it lacked was the appropriate methodology to become "scientific" and a separate discipline.

Science.   During the nineteenth century, natural science was making tremendous progress on virtually every frontier. In 1860, a German physicist, Gustav Fechner (1801–1887), published a volume that was unique as a physics text. Fechner had chosen to apply his training in the methods of physics to an issue that involved the basic psychological process of sensation. He discovered (using precise scientific techniques) that there is a mathematical relationship between certain physical stimuli (such as light) and a person's experience of those stimuli. Fechner was able to apply science to a fundamentally psychological question about experience.

The mid-1800s also found physiology coming to a much fuller understanding of how the human body functions. By then it was known that nerves carry electrical messages to and from different parts of the body, and that the nerves that serve vision were different from those that serve hearing and the other senses. Hermann von Helmholtz (1821–1894) was a pioneer in areas of physiology that have a direct impact on psychology. Although a physician/surgeon by trade, von Helmholtz's true love was pure science, the laboratory, and research. In the physiology laboratory, from a point of view and with methods quite different from those of philosophy, von Helmholtz developed an interest in matters clearly psychological. Remember, however, that in the mid-1800s there was no psychology. However, von Helmholtz's interests and experiments on how our senses process information, how we experience color, and how the nervous system is involved in reflex behaviors were getting very close to mainstream concerns of psychology.

By the late nineteenth century, psychology's time had come. Philosophy had become intrigued with mental processes, the nature and source of ideas, and the perception of reality. Physiology and physics had begun to focus on the operation of the nervous system, sensation, and perception and were using scientific methods. All that was needed was someone to clearly unite these interests and methods and establish a separate discipline. Such a person was Wilhelm Wundt.

In what way did the philosophies of the British Empiricists prepare the way for psychology?
In what way did Fechner and von Helmholtz influence the emergence of psychology?

BEFORE YOU GO ON

Experimental Psychology Begins: Structuralism and Functionalism

It is generally claimed that psychology "began" in 1879 when Wilhelm Wundt (1832–1920) founded his laboratory at the University of Leipzig. Wundt was educated to enter medicine as a profession, and he studied physiology. In fact, at Heidelberg University he served as a laboratory assistant to von Helmholtz. He also held an academic position in philosophy. He was a scientist/philosopher with an interest in such psychological processes as sensation, perception, attention, word associations, and feelings.

For Wundt, psychology was the scientific study of the mind, of consciousness. He was a strict scientist who left nothing to chance; all of his ideas were to be tested and then retested in his laboratory, under carefully controlled conditions.

Wundt and his students were interested in the structure of the mind. This was very much in keeping with the science of the time. Astronomy was searching for the structure of the universe. Physics was trying to determine the basic structural units of nature. Chemistry was studying the structure of chemical compounds and elements. Biology was engrossed in the classification of living things based on their structure. How reasonable it was for Wundt to want to study the structure of the mind, the structure of consciousness. What, wondered Wundt, are the elements or atoms of the mind? Of what basic units are thoughts constructed? Can ideas be broken down into elements? How can ideas, once broken into elements, be reunited to form complex ideas? What are the essential structures of our emotions?

One of Wundt's most successful students was an Englishman, Edward B. Titchener (1867–1927). In 1892, Titchener went to Cornell University where he directed one of the first psychology laboratories and where he remained for 35 years. There, he championed Wundt's psychology and named it **structuralism.** Titchener is also credited with refining **introspection,** a method for studying consciousness first used in Wundt's laboratory. Introspection literally means to look within, and Titchener trained many students to do just that—to look into the workings of their own minds and report what they saw. We say "trained a great number of students" because neither Wundt nor Titchener believed that just anyone could introspect with accuracy and consistency—accuracy and consistency being two hallmarks of good science. Introspectors were to avoid using common words or labels for the objects they observed. Thus, a banana was not to be described simply as " a banana," but it was to be described as it was experienced, in the most basic of terms, such as "yellowness" and "smoothness," for example. The technique was used in many experiments where introspective descriptions of experiences were recorded over and over again under different conditions.

At about the same time that Wundt's and Titchener's laboratories were flourishing, an American philosopher at Harvard University, William James (1842–1910), began to take issue with the structuralists. James taught a

Wilhelm Wundt

Edward B. Titchener

structuralism
the school of psychology (associated with Wundt, among others) interested in the structure or elements of the mind or consciousness

introspection
a technique in which one examines one's own mental experiences and describes them in the most fundamental, basic way

William James

course called "Psychology," and in 1875 he opened a laboratory to be used in the class for demonstrations, four years before the founding of Wundt's lab. But James never did any experiments there and never founded a formal school of psychology. Although he had an enormous impact on psychology, James thought of himself as a philosopher, not a psychologist.

William James agreed that psychology should rightfully study the mind and consciousness. He defined psychology as the "science of mental life," a definition very similar to Wundt's. However, James argued that consciousness should not and could not be broken down into elements or particles or structures. Consciousness is dynamic, a stream of events, personal, changing, continuous, and active, and not a static "structure" that can withstand analysis into parts and subparts. Psychology should be concerned not with the structure of the mind, but with its function. The focus of study should be on the practical uses of the mind and mental life.

James' practical, pragmatic approach to psychology found favor in this country, and a new type of psychology emerged, largely at the University of Chicago. Under the guidance of John Dewey (1873–1954) and James Angell (1869–1949), this new school of psychology was called **functionalism,** and it was well established by the 1920s.

functionalism
the school of psychology that studies the function of the mind and consciousness as they help the organism to adapt to the environment

Functionalism focused on consciousness, on mental life, reflecting the influence of William James. Functionalists were also influenced by the theories of Charles Darwin (1809–1882). Among other things, Darwin's evolutionary theory emphasized survival through adjustment and adaptation to the environment. The functionalists, following Locke's tradition, believed that the content of the mind was learned through experience. Darwin's writings led the Chicago psychologists to stress the adaptive, utilitarian functions of the mind. What is thinking for? How can the mind adapt and change? How can the mind help the organism to adapt, change, and survive? How is mental life affected by the environment? Focusing on the functions of mental life, and always searching for useful applications of their psychology, the functionalists branched out rapidly into child psychology, educational psychology, and applications of psychological principles to business and industry.

Charles Darwin

As more and more bright young scientists were drawn to the study of psychology, academic departments and laboratories began to prosper. Scientific psychology was well under way. Whether from a structuralist or functionalist point of view, psychology was the scientific study of the mind, its structure and/or its function.

BEFORE YOU GO ON   Briefly compare and contrast structuralism and functionalism.

Gestalt Psychology

In the first quarter of this century, functionalism was well established in the United States and structuralism was holding its own in Germany. At about the same time, a new group of German psychologists was taking a different approach to psychology. Lead by Max Wertheimer (1880–1943), this school of thought became known as Gestalt psychology.

gestalt
whole, totality, configuration, or pattern; the whole (gestalt) is seen as more than the sum of its parts

Gestalt is one of those words that is very difficult to translate literally into English. It basically means "whole," or "configuration," or "totality." In

FIGURE I.1

Gestalt psychologists believe that the meaning of events reflects an appreciation of the context in which they appear. Is the bold figure a B or a 13?

A B C D E

11 12 13 14 15

general terms, if you can see the big picture, you may be said to have developed a gestalt. It was the big picture that intrigued the Gestalt psychologists.

Gestalt psychologists argued against trying to analyze perception, or awareness, or consciousness into discrete, separate entities. These psychologists took issue with the structuralists' attempts to analyze mental processes into elements. They argued that to do so is to destroy the very nature of what was being studied. "The whole is *more* than the sum of its parts," they said. When we look at a drawing of a cube, we do not see individual lines or surfaces. We combine these elements to form a whole, a gestalt, which we call a cube. When we look at a banana, what we see is a banana, not yellowness or smoothness. When we listen to someone speak, we do not hear individual speech sounds; rather, we form gestalts—words, phrases, sentences, ideas—and we attend to these larger units.

Focusing largely on perception, Gestalt psychologists also argued that all perceptions, and thus all knowledge, cannot be considered in isolation. Everything occurs in a context or frame of reference. It is often the context in which something occurs that gives it its meaning (see Figure I.1).

Unlike the functionalists who subscribed to Locke's view that experience or learning provides the content of the mind, Gestalt psychologists believed that some basic, set ways of perceiving the world are innate and unlearned. We see the world in three dimensions; we attend to contrasts between adjacent stimuli; stimuli in motion tend to grab our attention. Why? Gestalt psychologists would be willing to say, "because"—because that's the way we were born to see, and learning or experience have little or nothing to do with it.

Gestalt psychology, as a formal approach, lost its momentum in the 1930s as the Nazis came to power in Germany, and the leaders of Gestalt psychology emigrated to the United States. The influence of this school, however, is still very much with us and has been especially important in helping psychologists understand principles of perception (Chapter 2).

Max Wertheimer

What does "gestalt" mean? **BEFORE YOU GO ON**

What area of psychology is of major concern to Gestalt psychology?

Behaviorism

John B. Watson (1878–1958) was born on a farm in South Carolina. In his senior year at Furman University, his mother died, so he no longer felt compelled to enter the ministry, as she had wished. Instead, he enrolled as a

John B. Watson

graduate student in psychology at the University of Chicago. Originally, he was attracted to the functionalistic psychology of John Dewey. Dewey, and functional psychology in general, turned out to be major disappointments to Watson, however. He apparently had little flair for or sympathy with the study of mental activity. Nonetheless, he remained a psychology major, studying the behavior of animals, and of white rats in particular.

With his Ph.D. in hand, at the age of 29, Watson moved to Johns Hopkins University, where he had a spectacular, if brief, academic career. Within two years, he was chair of the department and editor of a prestigious psychology journal. Then Watson's career as a psychologist came to an abrupt halt. He became involved in a scandal. He fell in love with one of his graduate students. His wife discovered the affair and sued for a divorce. The local papers made the court proceedings front-page news. Watson was asked to leave Johns Hopkins in 1920. He then got divorced, married his graduate assistant, went to New York City, and began a successful career in advertising. Although his academic career was a brief one, few individuals have had as much influence on American psychology as did John Watson.

Watson argued that if psychology were to become a mature, productive scientific enterprise, it had to give up its preoccupation with the mind and mental activity. Psychology should concentrate on the observable and the measurable, such as *behavior;* hence the new name of a new school of psychology—**behaviorism.**

behaviorism
the school of psychology (associated with Watson and Skinner) that focuses on the observable, measurable behavior of organisms

Watson never claimed that people do not think, have ideas, or form mental images. He did argue that such mental processes were not the proper subjects of scientific investigation. Science must focus on those events that observers can measure and agree upon, and behaviors fit the bill. No one else, after all, can exactly share your thoughts, your ideas, or your images. We have no way of seeing what you see in your mind's eye. So Watson believed we should leave all these private, internal events to philosophy or religion and make psychology as rigorously scientific as possible. Watson once referred to behaviorism as "common sense grown articulate. Behaviorism is a study of what people *do*" (Watson, 1926, p. 714).

No one has epitomized the behavioristic approach to psychology more than B. F. Skinner (b. 1904). Skinner took Watson at his word and has spent his long and productive professional career in psychology attempting to demonstrate that we can predict (and even learn to control) the behavior of organisms by studying relationships between the overt, observable responses that organisms make and the consequences that follow those responses.

B. F. Skinner

Skinner has avoided any reference to the internal states of his subjects be they rats, pigeons, or people. What matters for Skinner is how organisms modify their behaviors through their interactions with their environments. Behaviorists would not address a question of "why" a rat turns left in a maze by talking about what the rat wanted or what it was thinking as it turned. Rather, they would try to specify the environmental conditions (the presence of food, perhaps) under which a rat is likely to make left turns. They claim that we should focus on observable events and leave the internal affairs of the organism out of our explanations. After more than 50 years of making this very claim, Skinner still finds it valid and continues to argue forcefully that psychology should be the science of behavior (Skinner, 1987).

Humanism and Cognitive Psychology

Behaviorism has remained popular in American psychology. This popularity is based largely on the fact that in many ways the approach is a logical one, and it works. The behavioristic approach has not gone unchallenged, however. We'll mention here just two of the challenges that we can find clearly reflected in psychology today.

A type of psychology we call humanism arose in many respects as a reaction against behaviorism. Its leaders were Carl Rogers (1902–1987) and Abraham Maslow (1908–1970). Humanistic psychologists believe that the individual or the self should be a central concern of psychology. It is their argument that we need to get the "person" back into psychology. A disregard for the organism that responds to stimuli is dehumanizing. Such matters as intention, will, caring, concern, love, and hate are real phenomena and worthy of scientific investigation. Any attempt to understand people without considering such processes will be doomed. Taking this approach led Maslow to develop a theory of human motivation (see Chapter 7) and Rogers to develop a system of psychotherapy (see Chapter 10).

Another shift away from behaviorism that has occurred in recent years is the emergence, in fact the reemergence, of **cognitive psychology.** Cognitive psychology deals with a myriad of topics: attention, memory, perception, consciousness, concept formation, language, problem solving, and thinking in general. You may recognize these as mental processes, largely of the sort that concerned experimental psychologists back at the turn of the century, and you're right. "Mental" issues are coming back into vogue, but very carefully and scientifically; those who support this view are trying to avoid the problems associated with the study of the mind that Watson pointed out nearly seventy years ago.

A number of reasons have been offered to explain why cognitive, or mental, issues are returning to psychology. Two important considerations are (1) the inherent interest in such topics, long ignored by behaviorists, and (2) our increased understanding of internal processes, which comes from our appreciation of computer science and the study of memory. The attempt to build machines that can "think" has forced us to look more closely at what thinking *is.*

Carl Rogers

humanism
the school of psychology (associated with Maslow and Rogers) that focuses on the person or the self as the central matter of concern

cognitive psychology
the subfield in psychology that studies the nature of cognitions and their formation

Abraham Maslow

BEFORE YOU GO ON

What is the major position of behaviorism?

Name two psychologists closely associated with behaviorism.

Identify two approaches to psychology that have challenged behaviorism.

A Focus on Application: Mental Measurement and Psychoanalysis

So far, our review of history has focused on formal, academic approaches to psychology. Paralleling these developments, others were taking a more applied approach to behavior and mental processes. These pioneers in psychology directed their attention to measuring individual differences and to treating mental disorders.

Sir Francis Galton

Mental Measurement.   Sir Francis Galton (1822–1911) was a first cousin of Charles Darwin and was greatly influenced by him. Galton was intrigued by the theory of evolution and by the possibilities for improving the human race. He reasoned that before one could improve the human condition, one first needed to measure and catalog the range of human abilities and aptitudes as they exist at the moment. He devised countless tests and measurements of individual differences. The tradition in psychology of recognizing individual differences and attempting to measure them accurately and reliably comes from his efforts. In many ways, it is quite fair to consider Galton the founder of psychological testing. Galton also devised many statistical procedures to help him deal with the vast amount of data (numbers) that his mental tests generated.

At the turn of the century, Alfred Binet (1857–1911) advanced Galton's work on testing. Binet was given a real, practical problem by the French Ministry of Education. Could he devise an instrument to assess the educational potential of young school children? Could "intelligence" be measured? Binet thought that it could, and by 1900 he had devised a number of tests to do just that. Aided by Théophile Simon, Binet published an individually administered intelligence test in 1905. The original Binet-Simon test has undergone a number of major revisions. One of the most notable revisions was published in 1916 by Lewis Terman at Stanford University. Naming the new test after his university, the now Americanized test became known as the Stanford-Binet Intelligence Scale. (We'll discuss this classic test in some detail in Chapter 8.)

Psychoanalysis.   We will have ample opportunity to discuss many of the specific theories of Sigmund Freud (1856–1939) in later chapters. We will find ourselves referring to Freud in topics on child psychology, memory, consciousness, personality theory, and therapy. Few individuals in history have had as great an impact on the way that we think about ourselves as this Viennese physician-psychiatrist.

Freud was not a laboratory scientist. He was a practitioner. Although his methods were not rigorously scientific, and some of his conclusions have turned out to be in error, his insights into the workings of the human mind are profound and influential. Through careful study of his patients, self-examination, beautifully written volumes of text, a unique force of will, and charisma, Freud began and sustained psychiatry through its early years. From Freud, his students, his intellectual followers, and his opponents has come the clinical tradition in psychology—the concern with the diagnosis and treatment of psychological disorders.

Sigmund Freud

BEFORE YOU GO ON   In what ways did Sir Francis Galton, Alfred Binet, and Sigmund Freud shape psychology in its early history?

As we have seen so far, psychology is the science of behavior and mental processes, which includes both cognitions and affect. In other words, psychologists use scientific methods to study affect, behavior, and cognitions. Psychology has deep historical roots in philosophy and science, but did not emerge as an independent discipline until late in the nineteenth century. Over the years, the subject matter focus of psychology has changed, from mental activity in its early years, to behavior throughout the mid-twentieth century, and now to both behavior and mental processes. We can operationally define psychology as "what psychologists do." In a sense, this book provides a definition of psychology. If you were to ask us what psychology is, we might answer, "Everything in this text—and more." What psychologists do—their goals and their methods—are issues to which we now turn.

THE GOALS OF PSYCHOLOGY

Generally speaking, we can say that psychology has two major, interrelated, goals. One goal is to discover the scientific laws of its subject matter—behavior and mental processes. The other is to apply those laws.

What, then, is a scientific law? To put it simply, a **scientific law** is a statement about one's subject matter that one believes, on the basis of evidence, to be true. For example, in physics, there is a law that states that "a gas when heated expands." This is a statement about their subject matter (gases) that physicists believe to be true. It describes the relationship between gases and heat. In biology, there is a scientific law that describes the relationship between the rate and depth of our breathing and the amount of carbon dioxide (not oxygen, curiously enough) that we inhale. In psychology, we have a law that tells us that when responses are rewarded, they are likely to be repeated. This law tells us about the relationship between rewards and the likelihood of responses.

Scientific laws, including those in psychology, have two important characteristics. (1) They describe *relationships.* How are carbon dioxide and breathing related? The greater the percentage of carbon dioxide in the air, the deeper and faster one's breathing will be. (2) They allow us to make *predictions* about our subject matter. What will happen to the gases in a balloon as the temperature rises? The balloon will get larger.

The second important goal of psychology is to apply what we have learned about mental processes and behavior in real-world settings. Most psychologists are, in fact, practitioners, which means that they put into practice existing psychological laws and principles. Of those psychologists who are practitioners, most are clinical or counseling psychologists. Their goal, put most simply, is to apply what we know to help people adjust to and deal with problems that affect their ability to cope and to adjust to the environment and to other people (see Chapter 10). Many have as their primary goal the application of psychological knowledge to human problems that occur in the workplace and are called industrial-organizational psychologists (see Chapter 10). Psychological practitioners can be found in a variety of settings, dealing with a variety of concerns. Some apply psychological principles in an attempt to improve the performance of athletes; some advise attorneys on how best to present legal arguments in the courtroom; some establish programs to increase the use of automobile safety belts; some help design prisons that attend to inmates' psychological needs; some help people to most effectively train their pets—and the list goes on.

Psychologists, then, have two goals—and they are not mutually exclusive. One is to discover psychological laws. The other is to apply those laws.

scientific law
a statement about one's subject matter thought to be true, based upon evidence

What are the two major goals of psychology? BEFORE YOU GO ON

RESEARCH METHODS IN PSYCHOLOGY

In this section, we will discuss some of the methods that psychologists use in their study of the relationships that exist among behaviors and mental processes. As you study the various content areas of psychology in the following chapters, you will appreciate that we are here describing research methods in very general terms. This section is in two major parts. The first deals with methods that rely on the careful, systematic observation of behaviors and mental processes. These include naturalistic observation, survey and case history methods, and correlation, a technique used to analyze data collected through observation. What these techniques have in common is the process of making observations of responses as organisms provide them. We may use instruments such as psychological tests and/or surveys to help us make our observations, but we make no attempt to manipulate the responses of the organisms we are studying. The second part of our discussion deals with methods that involve manipulating and/or controlling events in addition to observing them. These are called experimental methods.

Observational Methods

Observational methods in psychology are designed primarily to help us discover relationships between responses, be they behavioral or mental. These are called **R-R relationships.** Statements of R-R relationships tell us about how one set of **responses** is related to another set of responses. A response is an observable or measurable reaction of an organism. R-R relationships often sound something like this: "Whenever we have *these* responses, we also tend to find *those* responses," or "These two responses go together." Although they tell us nothing about cause and effect, such relationships can help us to make predictions about how someone may feel, what they may do, or what they may think (our A, B, C again).

R-R relationships
statements of correlation, telling us how and the extent to which two sets of responses are related to each other

responses
any observable or measurable actions or reactions of an organism

naturalistic observation
the method of observing and noting behaviors as they occur naturally

Naturalistic Observation.   As its name implies, the methodological approach called **naturalistic observation** involves carefully watching behaviors as they occur naturally—without any active involvement by the observer. There is a strong logical appeal to the argument that if you are trying to understand what organisms do in real life, you should simply watch them while they are doing it. Naturalistic observation is a method that often requires considerable patience on the part of the observer, who precisely notes the behaviors of the organisms being observed and the conditions under which different responses occur.

As straightforward and appealing as naturalistic observation may sound, it does present a few potential problems that we need to acknowledge. First, if we truly do want to observe people the way they naturally act, we must make sure that they do not realize that we are watching them. As you know from your own experience, people may act differently when they think they're being observed. You may do all sorts of things in the privacy of your own home that you would never do if you thought that someone was watching you.

observer bias
a problem in observational methods that occurs when an observer's motives and/or expectations interfere with objectivity

Second, we must be wary of **observer bias.** Observers should not let their own motives and expectations interfere with the objectivity of their observations. One solution to this problem may be to have observers note behaviors as they occur without full knowledge of the particular relationships they

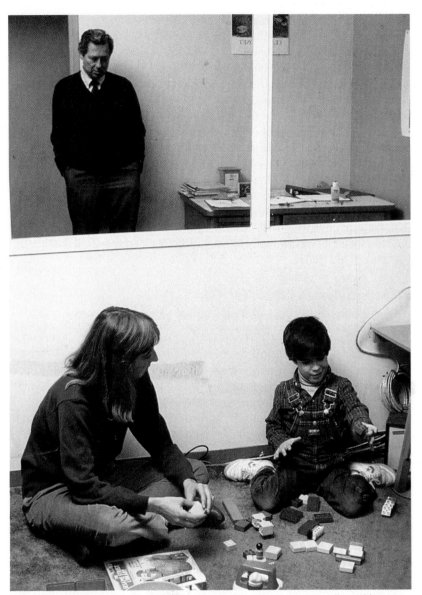

Naturalistic observation involves watching behaviors as they occur naturally—without any involvement by the observer. In this case, a doctor observes a child's behavior through a one-way mirror.

are looking for. Another protection against observer bias would be to check the reliability (dependability) of observations by using a number of observers and relying only on those observations that can be verified by a number of observers.

A third potential problem with naturalistic observation is more difficult to deal with. The behaviors that you want to observe may not always be there when you are. For example, if you are interested in conformity behaviors and want to observe people conform naturally, in the real world, just where do you go to watch conformity happen? To use naturalistic observation, you often have to be clever or lucky, and you will almost certainly have to be very patient.

Although it has its problems, there are occasions when naturalistic observation is the most suitable method available. For example, studying chimpanzees in zoos and laboratories will tell us little about how chimpanzees behave in the wild. Many psychologists have been frustrated trying to study the language development of very young children. By the time they are 3 or 4 years old, children demonstrate all sorts of interesting language behaviors. However, they may be too young to understand and properly follow the instructions that many experiments would require. They almost certainly will not be able to respond sensibly to questions about their language usage. Perhaps all we can do is carefully watch and listen to young children as they use their language and try to determine what is happening by observing them as they naturally interact with their environments. A psychologist who studies language development with her husband reports that they often spend their summers "looking quite foolish" following behind toddlers, "recording their every utterance in dime-store notebooks." (Gelman et al., 1987)

BEFORE YOU GO ON What is naturalistic observation?

What are three potential problems with the use of naturalistic observation?

survey
a means of collecting data (observations) from large numbers of subjects, either by interview or by questionnaire

sample
the portion of a larger population chosen for study

Surveys can show what large proportions of the population think and feel and can show what products or services they prefer.

Surveys. When we want to make observations about large numbers of subjects, we may use a **survey** method. Doing a survey amounts to asking a sample of respondents the same question or set of questions. The questions may be asked in a personal or telephone interview, or they may be asked in the form of a written questionnaire. Such studies yield data that would be very difficult to gather otherwise.

If we wanted to know, for example, if there was a relationship between income level and type of automobile one drives, or the television programs one watches regularly, we could survey large numbers of persons of different income levels. Surveys can also tell us what large proportions of the population think and feel about certain issues and can provide insights about preferences for products or services. Textbook publishers often survey psychology instructors to see what they like to have included in the books they use.

The survey method is also useful in providing us with information that we can use as a general data base. For example, the American Psychological Association regularly surveys its members to discover where they are employed and the area of psychology in which they are specializing. If the cafeteria on your campus really wanted to know what students wanted to eat, they could survey a portion (sample) of the student population.

A critical aspect of observations made from survey data is the size and representativeness of the **sample** that is surveyed. A sample is a subset or a portion of a larger population that is chosen to be studied. As is the case for most research in psychology, we would like to be able to extend or generalize our findings beyond those individuals we studied. The American Psychological Association does not question all of its members; rather, it samples those who are typical of the entire membership. Cafeteria staffs that only survey students who attend classes in the mornings may collect responses that do not generalize to other students on campus.

Case Histories. The **case history** provides yet a different sort of observational information. In the case history method, one person, or a small sample of persons, is studied in depth and detail, often over a long period of time. Using this method involves an intense and detailed examination of a wide range of variables. It is usually retrospective, which implies that we start with some given condition today and go back in time in order to see if there is any relationship between this condition and previous experiences. We may use interviews and/or psychological tests as means of making observations as we collect our data.

As an example, let's say we are interested in Mr. X, a known child abuser. Our suspicion is that some of Mr. X's own childhood experiences might be related to his present status as a child abuser. We talk to Mr. X at length and interview his family and friends—those people who knew him as a child—trying to form a (retrospective) picture of Mr. X's childhood. If we find some clues, we will then do the same with other known child abusers, looking to find commonalities in their experiences that might be related to the fact that they abuse children now that they are adults.

As we shall see, Sigmund Freud based most of his theories of personality on his intensive examination of the case histories of his patients and himself. The advantage of the case history method is that it provides us with a wealth of detailed information about individual cases. The disadvantage is that we may not be able to generalize our findings far beyond the individuals we have studied.

case history
an intensive, retrospective, and detailed investigation of certain aspects of one (or a few) individual(s)

How can surveys and case history studies be used to help us understand R-R relationships?

BEFORE YOU GO ON

Correlation. **Correlation** is a statistical procedure we can use to determine the nature and degree of R-R relationships. In fact, to say that observations are correlated is to claim that an R-R relationship exists, that the observed responses are co-related.

As an example, let's say that we are interested in whether or not there is a relationship—a correlation—between reading ability and performance in introductory psychology. We first need to decide how we will measure, or operationally define, the two responses in which we are interested. Once we have measured both responses for the same subjects, we will have two sets of numbers, and we can directly determine if a relationship exists between our two observed responses. Let's look at this procedure step by step.

First, we need to come up with operational definitions for the responses we want to measure. "Performance in introductory psychology" isn't difficult to deal with. We'll take that to mean the total number of points earned by a student on classroom exams over the course of the semester. "Reading ability" is a little more difficult. We might design our own test to measure what we mean by reading ability, but instead we'll use a readily available test published by someone else—the Nelson Denny Reading Test (Brown, 1973).

Now we're ready to collect some data (make some observations). We'll give a large group of students our reading test, and we'll have one set of numbers. At the end of the semester, we add up all exam points for the same group of students, and we'll have a second set of numbers. So for each student in our study, we have a pair numbers—one indicating reading abil-

correlation
a largely statistical technique used to determine the nature and degree of R-R relationships

correlation coefficient
a number (r) that indicates the nature (positive, negative) and the strength (zero to −1.00 or +1.00) of the relationship between measured responses

FIGURE I.2(A)
A graph depicting the reading test scores and semester point totals earned by 40 students. These data indicate a positive (+) correlation between the two measured responses. As reading test scores increase, so do semester point totals.

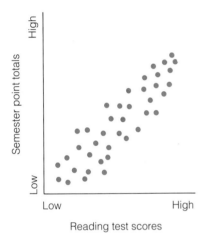

FIGURE I.2(B)
A graph depicting the body size and gymnastic ability of 40 students. These data indicate a negative (-) correlation between the two measured responses. As body size increases, gymnastic ability decreases.

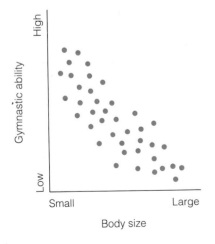

ity and one indicating performance in the introductory psychology course. We want to know if these responses are correlated. From here on out, our method is more statistical than psychological.

We enter our pairs of numbers into a calculator (or a computer if we have a large set of numbers). A series of arithmetic procedures is applied. Then, out comes a single number, called the **correlation coefficient.** The symbol for this number is "r," and it ranges in value from -1.00 to +1.00. What does this number mean? It takes some experience to be truly comfortable with this statistic, but we can make some general observations.

First, let's deal with the sign of the correlation coefficient, whether it is positive (+) or negative (−). A positive correlation would tell us that our two responses *are* related to each other, and that high scores on one response are associated with high scores on the other. It also tells us that low scores on one measure are associated with low scores on the other. Because our two responses are positively correlated, we can make predictions about one response if we know the other. If a student does well on the reading test, we can predict that she will probably do well in introductory psychology. If someone does poorly on the reading test, we might expect that student to have a hard time in the class. We can make these predictions only if the two responses are correlated, only if we have an R-R relationship. As it happens, there is ample evidence that the correlation would be positive for this example (Gerow & Murphy, 1980).

What if our calculations tell us that r is a negative (−) number? Here too we have a useful R-R relationship. We can still use scores on one response to predict scores on the other. The only difference is that the relationship is inverse, or upside down. Here, *high* scores on one response are associated with *low* scores on the other measured response. If we measured body size and looked to see if it were related to gymnastic ability, we would find a negative correlation: Large body size is associated with poor gymnastic ability, and small body size is associated with good gymnastic ability. We can still use body size to predict gymnastic ability, but now high scores on one measure are related to low scores on the other, and vice versa. There is also a negative relationship between the weight of clothing you are likely to be wearing and the outside temperature. As temperatures go down, the weight of clothing tends to go up, and we can use one measure to predict the other.

What happens if our correlation coefficient turns out to be zero, or nearly so? In this case, the relationship would be neither clearly positive nor clearly negative. A zero correlation coefficient indicates the absence of an R-R relationship. If r equals zero, then the two responses we have measured are not related in any useful way. Let's say you worked from the faulty notion that intelligence is a function of brain size, and that one's head size tells us how big a person's brain is. On this basis, you suggest that we can measure intelligence by measuring head size. No doubt if you were to measure the head size of a large number of students and also measure, say, grade point average for the same students, you would find a correlation coefficient very close to zero. As correlations approach zero, predictability decreases. Figure I.2 presents graphical representations of possible R-R relationships, indicating the form of a positive relationship (A), a negative relationship (B), and the lack of a relationship (C).

So much for the sign of the correlation coefficient, what about its actual numerical value? It takes a little practice to get used to working with numbers such as −.47, +.55, +.02. And there are statistical tests we can use to determine the significance of a calculated r value. Among other things, these tests can tell us the probability that our calculated correlation coefficient is or is not sufficiently different from zero. For now we can say that the closer we get to the extremes of +1.00 or −1.00, the better or stronger the relationship between the two responses that we have measured. This means that if our correlation coefficient approaches +1.00 or −1.00 (say, +.91 or −.87), we will have increased confidence in our ability to predict one response knowing the other. The closer our coefficient, r, gets to zero (such as, +.023 or −.017), the weaker the relationship and the less useful it is for making predictions. We should also mention that the confidence we place in the predictability of our correlations is in part determined by the number of observations used in calculating r. In general, the larger our sample—the more observations we have made—the greater the confidence we can put in our correlation coefficient.

As we go through this text, we'll encounter a number of studies that use a correlational analysis of measured observations. It is important, then, that you remember two important points about correlation and R-R relationships. (1) Even if two responses are correlated with each other, we cannot support the claim that one causes the other—they are simply related. (2) Even when two responses are correlated with each other, we can't make precise predictions for all individual cases. Reading ability and introductory psychology grades are positively correlated. We can use reading tests to predict grades, but we have to allow for exceptions; some poor readers do well, and some good readers do poorly in the course. Our correlation only holds in general.

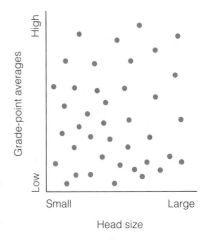

FIGURE I.2(C)
A graph depicting head size and grade point averages earned by 40 students. These data indicate a zero (0) correlation between the two measured responses. There is no relationship between head size and grade point averages.

Why do we use correlation?

What data are needed in order to calculate a correlation coefficient?

What is the meaning of a positive (+), negative (−), or zero (0) correlation coefficient?

BEFORE YOU GO ON

Experimental Methods

Most of what we know in psychology today we have learned from **experiments.** Experiments involve a set of operations used to investigate relationships between manipulated events and measured events, while other events are controlled. Like the other methods we have discussed, experiments involve making observations. What makes experiments different is that they also involve manipulating and controlling events. That may not make much sense to you at the moment, but it is important to understand what our definition means. After we define a few terms, we'll look at a couple of examples.

In order to see if a cause and effect relationship exists between two variables, an experimenter will manipulate one to see if it causes measurable changes in the other. Variables are simply things that can vary—measurable events that can take on different values. And now, with experimental methods, it is acceptable to use the term "cause," because these methods are designed to uncover cause and effect relationships, also known as **S-R relationships.** S-R relationships tell us what response, or responses, are likely to

experiment
a series of operations used to investigate relationships between manipulated events (independent variables) and measured events (dependent variables), while other events (extraneous variables) are controlled

S-R relationships
cause and effect statements relating stimuli to the responses they produce

Research Methods in Psychology **21**

stimulus
any event or energy that produces a response or reaction in an organism

independent variables
those events in an experiment manipulated by the experimenter that are hypothesized to produce changes in responses

dependent variables
those responses measured in an experiment whose values are hypothesized to depend upon manipulations of the independent variable

extraneous variables
those factors in an experiment that need to be controlled or eliminated so as not to affect the dependent variable

occur in the presence of a given **stimulus,** or stimuli. A stimulus is a condition or event that produces a reaction or a response. Because S-R relationships *do* tell us about cause and effect, they are often thought of as being more important than R-R relationships. They work something like this: "When this stimulus (S) is presented, this response (R) will tend to occur."

The conditions that the experimenter manipulates are called **independent variables.** Those the experimenter measures are **dependent variables**—their value should *depend* on what was manipulated. The hope is that manipulation of the independent variable will produce consistent, predictable changes in the dependent variable. Or, put another way, what one manipulates will cause changes in what one measures.

If there are systematic changes in what is measured, the experimenter would like to claim that these changes are due solely to the influence of the manipulated independent variable. In order to make such a claim, it must be demonstrated that all other variables that might have influenced what is being measured have been controlled or eliminated. Because these variables are not a part of the S-R relationship being studied, they are called **extraneous variables.** (Some psychologists refer to them as "control variables" because they are the very factors that need to be controlled.) So, to do an experiment, one manipulates independent variables, measures dependent variables, and controls extraneous variables. Again, that may sound a little confusing in the abstract. Let's look at an example.

Reflecting on your own experience as a student, it is your observation that audio-visual aids, such as movies, slides, and video tapes, have helped you learn the material presented in class. It is also your observation that such audio-visual (A-V) material was particularly helpful when you were younger. On the basis of these observations, you formulate a hypothesis (which, you recall, is a tentative proposition that can be tested). Your hypothesis is that A-V aids improve classroom learning. Now you want to put your hypothesis to an experimental test. An elementary school principal allows you access to two third-grade classes in her school, and you're ready to go.

You arrange (manipulate) things so that Class A gets every audio-visual aid you can get your hands on: movies, tapes, slides, overhead transparencies, graphs, and charts. Class B gets no A-V material at all. Because the amount of A-V aids is the variable you have manipulated, it is the independent variable of your experiment. A few months go by, and it is time to see if your manipulation has caused your hypothesized effect. You now have to measure your dependent variable, classroom learning. As is usually the case, there are a number of dependent variables for you to choose from (teacher's ratings or scores on a national achievement test for third graders, to name two). You decide to give your two classes your own exam as a measure of what they have learned. Let's now suppose that when you grade these exams, test scores confirm your hypothesis: Class A (which received the A-V material) earns an average test score of 93 percent correct, while the "deprived" Class B averages only 71 percent correct. It appears that your experiment has demonstrated an S-R relationship between audio-visual aids and the classroom performance of third graders.

Before we get too carried away, however, we had better consider the possible extraneous variables that might have been operating in this experiment. These, remember, are those factors that could have affected what was measured (classroom learning) over and above what was manipulated (audio-visual aids). Obviously, these factors should have been considered and controlled before you actually did your experiment. What extraneous variables might be operating in here?

Our basic concern in this experiment is that the two classes being used are treated as equally as possible in all respects except for the use or nonuse of audio-visual aids. Two questions come to mind immediately. Is there any evidence that the two teachers involved have the same abilities? A complete answer to this question may be difficult to deal with, but at least you would want to be able to counter the argument that Class B did so poorly on their final not because they were deprived of A-V aids, but because they had such a poor teacher. The second obvious question that arises concerns the abilities of the students in the two classes. What if someone claimed that the students in the two classes were not of equal ability and that Class A did well on your exam simply because it was comprised of brighter students? Discovering that bright students do better on classroom exams than less bright students is extraneous to your experiment. You would have to take some steps to insure that when the experiment began, before you introduced your manipulation of A-V aids, the two classes were not different in their exam performance. Even with these extraneous variables controlled, a number of questions remain, including which of the audio-visual aids were most useful. As you can imagine, in some experiments the list of potential extraneous variables that must be dealt with can be very long. In fact, it is the extent to which these extraneous variables are anticipated and sufficiently controlled that determines the quality of an experiment (see Figure I.3).

Let's take a quick look at another potential experimental question. Suppose you believe that a stimulating environment during early childhood improves intellectual functioning at adolescence. You propose to do an experiment to support your observation. You have two groups of newborn children, say 20 in each group. One group will be reared for three years in a very stimulating environment filled with toys and games, bright wallpaper and pictures in the nursery, and many adults around every day. The other group of children will be reared in isolation, in quiet, empty rooms, with only their basic biological needs attended to. Wait a minute! This sort of experimental manipulation is unethical and would be out of the question. You wouldn't isolate and deprive a group of children—particularly if your own hypothesis is that doing so will have negative consequences.

This problem provides a good example of an experiment that you might want to do with rats. Rats could be raised in cages that provide differing amounts of environmental stimulation. When the rats approach maturity, you could test their ability to negotiate mazes and/or learn a variety of responses. Early exposure to stimulation would be your independent variable, and your tests of learning ability would be your dependent variables.

One nice thing about using rats for your experiment is that extraneous variables would be relatively easy to control. You don't have to worry about previous experience, inherited differences, parental influence, and the like (all of your rats have a known genetic history and have been reared in very similar environments). You can exercise rather complete control over the rats you'll use in your experiment. The problem with using rats is obvious. Even if you demonstrate your point with rats, you will then have to argue

Using nonhuman subjects such as rats for experiments in psychology is commonplace. In this instance, food is available in only parts of the maze; rats will determine quickly which parts have food.

FIGURE I.3
The stages involved in our example experiment illustrating the different types of variables.

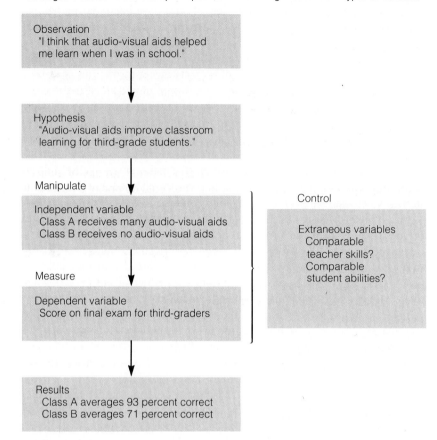

Observation
"I think that audio-visual aids helped me learn when I was in school."

Hypothesis
"Audio-visual aids improve classroom learning for third-grade students."

Manipulate

Independent variable
Class A receives many audio-visual aids
Class B receives no audio-visual aids

Measure

Dependent variable
Score on final exam for third-graders

Control

Extraneous variables
Comparable teacher skills?
Comparable student abilities?

Results
Class A averages 93 percent correct
Class B averages 71 percent correct

that the data you have collected for rats is, in some direct way, applicable to humans. As we shall see, in many cases such an argument is not too difficult to make, and the advantage of being able to easily exercise control over extraneous variables is one of the reasons why the use of nonhuman subjects is commonplace in psychology.

BEFORE YOU GO ON

What is the essence of doing an experiment?

Define independent, dependent, and extraneous variables in the context of an experiment.

Now that we have covered the essential procedures involved in doing experiments, let's examine in a little more detail a couple of the considerations that often determine the quality of an experimental method.

Exercising Control. As we have said, the value of an experimental finding is related to the researcher's ability to adequately control extraneous variables. The most difficult extraneous variables to deal with are often those that involve the past experience of the subjects. Such was the case in our example experiment involving the use of audio-visual aids. In a typical experiment, the independent variable is manipulated by presenting one group of subjects with some treatment (such as audio-visual aids) and withholding that treatment from another group of subjects. Subjects in both groups are then measured to see if the treatment produced any effect in the chosen dependent variable. By definition, those subjects who receive some treatment, or manipulation, are said to be **experimental group** subjects. An experiment may have a number of experimental groups. Our example on A-V aids used just one. If an additional class had been available, we might have presented them with only movies and slides and withheld all other A-V materials, for instance. Subjects who do not receive the experimental treatment are said to be in the **control group.** Experiments usually have just one control group of subjects; in our example this was the class that received no A-V aids.

To make sure that your control and experimental groups of subjects begin the experiment on an equal footing, you could do one of a number of things. You could try to match the subjects on your characteristics of interest. In our example, you might have done this by giving all the third graders a pretest at the beginning of the term and systematically assigning students to Class A and Class B in such a way that average pretest scores for the two groups were equal.

A more common technique would be to place subjects in groups through **random assignment,** which means that each participant in the study has an equal chance of being assigned to any one of the groups you are using in your experiment. If assignment is truly random, then those third graders of high ability would be equally likely to be in either of your two groups—those with or without A-V aids. And remember, this sort of consideration—matching or randomly assigning subjects—is something that must be considered before the experiment actually begins.

Another method to control extraneous variables that arise from the differing past experiences of subjects is called a **baseline design** experiment. Although there are a number of such designs, they each amount to arranging things so that each subject serves in both experimental and control group conditions. Imagine, for example, that you wished to see if a certain drug causes an increase in the running speed of white rats. Using a baseline design you would first measure the running speed of rats without administering the drug (a control, or baseline, measure). Then you would check the running speed of the same rats after they were given the drug. Changes in their behavior (your dependent variable again) could then be attributed to the drug (the independent variable). You then check the running speed of the rats again, after the drug's effects wear off, to see if their performance returns to its baseline rate.

Overcoming Bias. Human subjects in psychology experiments are usually very helpful and well-motivated to do whatever is asked of them. In their efforts to please, they may very well act in the experimental situation in ways they would never act otherwise. In other words, experimental subjects sometimes do what they think the experimenter wants them to do. If experimental subjects are reacting to their perception of the experimenter's wishes, they are not responding to the independent variables of the experiment. In order to overcome this difficulty, subjects are generally not told how the experimenter expects the subjects to respond. This is called a **single-blind technique** because the subjects are not aware of (are blind to) the purpose or hypothesis of the experiment.

experimental group
those participants in an experiment who receive some treatment or manipulation; there may be more than one such group in an experiment

control group
those participants in an experiment who do not receive any experimental treatment or manipulation

random assignment
the selection of members of a population in such a way that each has an equal opportunity to be assigned to any one group in an experiment

baseline design
a method in which subjects' performance with an experimental treatment is compared with performance without that treatment (the baseline)

single-blind technique
a protection against bias in which the subjects are not aware of the hypothesis of the experiment

For similar reasons, it is often helpful for the person measuring the dependent variable to be unaware of the goals or hypotheses of the experiment. It is very easy to misread a clock, misperceive a turn in a maze, misinterpret a subject's response, or give unintentional cues to the subject. Notice that we're not talking about downright dishonesty here; we're talking about the honest errors that can be made in analyzing data when one has a stake in the outcome of the analysis. To offset this possible source of bias, we use a **double-blind technique** in which neither the subject nor the person collecting the data knows what the hypothesis of the experiment is. (Obviously somebody has to know what is going on, but that somebody does not record or analyze the data.)

For example, in our study of the effects of audio-visual aids on learning, we would not tell the students about our hypothesis, nor would we tell the people scoring the final exams which of the two classes completed the exams that they were scoring. In our example of raising rats under different levels of stimulation, we would see to it that the experimenters rating the learning ability (dependent variable) of the rats did not know the conditions under which the rats were raised (independent variable).

double-blind technique
in an experiment, a protection against bias in which neither the subjects nor the experimenter collecting and/or analyzing the data is told the hypothesis of the experiment

BEFORE YOU GO ON

How do random assignment, baseline designs, and double-blind procedures help to control extraneous variables in experiments?

ETHICAL CONSIDERATIONS IN PSYCHOLOGICAL RESEARCH

Ethical and moral concerns can be found in all the sciences. In most sciences, ethical issues usually center on the application of knowledge. We know how to split an atom; should we build a bomb? We can manufacture effective insecticides; should we use them? We can devise means to render people infertile; should we? We can use machinery to keep a person alive indefinitely; should we? We can bury radioactive waste; where should we?

Psychology has something of a unique problem in that ethical issues often involve the accumulation of knowledge. After all, the objects of study in psychology are living organisms. Their physical and psychological welfare needs to be protected as we investigate their behaviors and mental processes. Psychologists have long been concerned with the ethical implications of their work. In 1973, again in 1981, and with regular revision, the American Psychological Association publishes guidelines for the ethical conduct of research with either animal or human subjects. Here we'll deal briefly with some of the issues that these guidelines address.

As one plans his or her research, the degree to which subjects in that research will be put at risk should be assessed. What are the potential dangers, physical or psychological, that might accompany participation? Even if potential risks are deemed to be slight, they should be considered and balanced in the light of what potential good might come from the proposed experiment. Seldom will one psychologist have to make the ultimate decisions about risk and/or potential benefits of a research program. Advisory committees of researchers, familiar with the techniques and problems of the proposed research, will have to approve it before the project begins.

What are some other ethical issues related to research in psychology? (1) The subject's confidentiality must be guaranteed. Often, the subject's name is not even used, replaced instead with an identification number. (2) Participation in research should be totally voluntary. No one should be coerced into being a subject in a psychology experiment. Volunteers should be allowed the option of dropping out of any research project, even after it has begun. Colleges cannot offer extra credit to students who participate in research unless all students are given an opportunity to participate and unless other options are also available for earning the same extra credit. (3) Subjects should participate in experiments only after they have given their advised consent. Within reason, subjects must know what is going to be expected of them when they participate in an experiment. They should be told the potential dangers, if any, why the project is being done, and what they will be expected to do. Obviously, some deception is sometimes required when doing experiments. Even so, the amount of deception needs to be balanced with the promise of outcome. (4) Particularly if subjects have been deceived about the nature of the experiment, and even if they haven't, all subjects should be debriefed after the research has been completed. That means, if nothing else, the true nature of the project and its basic intent should be explained to those who participated in it. Because they have something of a stake in it, subjects should be provided a copy of the results of the research when results become available.

Published ethical guidelines for the use of animals in research also are quite stringent. Only those who are trained and experienced in animal housing and care should be given responsibility for laboratory animals. Those experts, in turn, must train all others working with the animals in the proper, humane treatment of the animals under their care. Every effort must be taken to minimize discomfort, illness, and pain of animals. Subjecting animals to stress, or pain is acceptable *only* if no other procedure is available, and the goal is justified by its prospective scientific, educational, or applied value. As with human subjects, there are usually review committees that must approve the design of any research using nonhuman animals in research, where the major concern is the ethical protection of the subjects.

Cite some of the ethical issues that must be considered when doing psychological research.   **BEFORE YOU GO ON**

The aim of this introduction was to describe the nature of psychology in general terms, leaving many of the specifics to subsequent chapters. What have we learned? Psychology is a science that studies behavior and mental processes. It emerged as a separate discipline just over 100 years ago. Psychologists work in a variety of settings and specialize in a number of subfields within psychology. In general terms, though, psychology has just two broad goals: (1) to discover and understand the relationships that may exist among behaviors and/or mental processes and (2) to apply what is known about these relationships in real-world settings. In order to meet its first goal, psychologists use scientific methods that can be classified as methods of observation or experimentation. We will see throughout the following chapters how psychologists are meeting the second goal.

SUMMARY

What two points must we demonstrate in order to claim that psychology is a science?

To claim that a discipline qualifies as a science requires demonstrating (1) that it has an organized body of knowledge and (2) that it uses scientific methods. / 5

What is the subject matter of psychology?

What are operational definitions, and why do we use them?

Psychology is the scientific study of behavior and mental processes. An operational definition of concepts is one given in terms of the operations used to create or measure those concepts. We use them to increase specificity and communicability and to minimize philosophical discussions about definitions. / 6

Define the mental processes of cognition and affect.

Cognitions are intellectual mental activities, such as perceiving, remembering, and problem solving, while affect refers to those mental activities associated with mood and feelings. / 7

In what way did the philosophy of the British Empiricists prepare the way for psychology?

In what way did Fechner and von Helmholtz influence the emergence of psychology?

The British Empiricists directed the attention of philosophers to the mind—how it interacts with the body and how it comes to acquire information. Both Gustav Fechner (from physics) and Hermann von Helmholtz (from physiology) brought scientific and experimental methodology to answer basically psychological questions. / 9

Briefly compare and contrast structuralism and functionalism.

Both structuralism (Wundt and Titchener) and functionalism (James, Angell, and Dewey) defined psychology as the science of mental activity, but the former looked mostly for the structure or elemental units of the mind, while the latter focused on the adaptive usefulness or function of consciousness. / 10

What does ''gestalt'' mean?

What area of psychology is of major concern to Gestalt psychology?

''Gestalt'' means whole or configuration. Gestalt psychologists study many things, focusing on factors that affect the selection and organization of perceptions. / 11

What is the major position of behaviorism?

Name two psychologists closely associated with behaviorism.

Identify two approaches to psychology that have challenged behaviorism.

Behaviorism (associated with John B. Watson and B. F. Skinner) holds that the subject matter of the science of psychology should be measurable and observable—thus, behavior. Both humanistic psychology (Maslow and Rogers), which focuses on the self or the person, and cognitive psychology, which focuses on mental processes, have taken issue with behaviorists. / 13

In what ways did Sir Francis Galton, Alfred Binet, and Sigmund Freud shape psychology in its early history?

Galton, focusing on the importance of individual differences, may be called the founder of psychological testing. Binet authored the first truly successful test of general intelligence. Freud provided a foundation for psychologists who later devised theories of personality and engaged in the practice of trying to aid people with psychological disorders. / 14

What are the two major goals of psychology?

One goal of psychology is to discover and understand the scientific laws of behavior and mental processes. That is, psychologists aim to be able to make statements about their subject that they believe to be true on the basis of evidence. These statements tell us about the relationships that exist among behaviors and mental processes and allow us to make predictions. A second, related goal is to apply the knowledge about behavior and mental processes that has been accumulated. / 15

What is naturalistic observation?

What are three potential problems with the use of naturalistic observation?

Naturalistic observation involves the careful, reliable observation and notation of behaviors as they occur naturally. Use of this method requires that (1) the subjects are not aware of the fact that they are being observed, (2) the observer's biases do not influence observations, and (3) patience be exercised to observe events that occur infrequently. / 18

How can surveys and case history studies be used to help us understand R-R relationships?

Surveys provide responses (observations) from large samples of respondents, whereas case histories provide detailed information (observations) on just a few subjects. In either case, one may search for relationships among the responses gathered. / 19

Why do we use correlation?

What data are needed in order to calculate a correlation coefficient?

What is the meaning of a positive (+), negative (−), or zero (0) correlation coefficient?

Correlation is a statistical procedure that can tell us if observations are related to each other (co-related). In order to calculate a correlation coefficient (r), one needs to measure two responses from the same group of subjects, yielding a set of paired observations. Positive correlations indicate that high scores on one response are associated with high scores on another and that low scores on one response are associated with low scores on the other. Negative correlations tell us that high scores on one response are associated with low scores on the other, and vice versa. Zero correlations tell us that our measured responses are not related. / 21

What is the essence of doing an experiment?

Define independent, dependent, and extraneous variables in the context of an experiment.

An experiment involves manipulating independent variables, measuring dependent variables, and controlling extraneous variables. Independent variables are hypothesized to have an effect on some mental process or behavior. To see if such is the case, one looks for changes in some measured dependent variable that occur when the independent variable is manipulated. In order to claim a cause and effect relationship between the manipulated independent variable and the measured dependent variable, all oth-

er events that could affect the dependent variable must be controlled or eliminated. / 24

How do random assignment, baseline designs, and double-blind procedures help to control extraneous variables in experiments?

Random assignment of subjects to experimental or control conditions of an experiment insures that each subject has an equal opportunity to be in any treatment condition. Any pre-experimental differences among subjects should, thus, balance out over groups. With baseline designs, the same subjects serve in experimental and control group conditions, thus serving as their own controls. Single- and double-blind techniques protect against bias by not informing the subject (single-blind) or the experimenter *and* the subject (double-blind) about the hypothesis under investigation. / 26

Cite some of the ethical issues that must be considered when doing psychological research.

Whether one uses humans or animals in research, one must always be mindful of the balance between potential risk and harm to the subject on the one hand and potential benefit of the procedure on the other. A subject's confidentiality must be maintained. Subjects should provide advised consent before voluntarily participating in the research and should be debriefed about the project when it is over. / 27

REVIEW QUESTIONS

1. Which of the following is the best example of an operational definition?

a. Hypotheses are educated guesses about one's subject matter that can be confirmed or rejected.

b. Class participation is the number of times a student raises his or her hand in class in response to a question.

c. Cognitive processes include perception, memory, understanding, and problem solving.

d. Reading ability can be used to predict success or failure in introductory psychology classes.

Although each of these statements is essentially true, only the definition of class participation tells us how we can measure the concept being operationally defined. As is usually the case, there may be many ways to operationally define class participation, and this definition is just one example. / 6

2. To say that psychology studies affect is to say that part of the subject matter of psychology consists of one's:

a. thoughts, beliefs, and knowledge.

b. behavior, actions, and reactions.

c. underlying biological and physiological processes.

d. emotions, feelings, and moods.

This item assesses whether you know that affect refers to one's emotions, feelings, and moods. One's thoughts, beliefs, and knowledge are aspects of one's cognitions that are also part of the subject matter of psychology. / 7

3. Which of the following did philosopher John Locke share with psychologist Wilhelm Wundt?

a. A basic interest in the structure of consciousness and the contents of the mind.

b. A deep belief in the truth of Darwin's theories of evolution.

c. A reliance on the scientific method to support their claims.

d. All of the above.

In fact, neither Wundt nor Locke would have known about Darwin's theories, which were not published until well after both had made their mark on psychology. Although Wundt relied on scientific methods, these were of little concern to the philosopher, Locke. What they had in common was an interest in the structure of consciousness and the contents of the mind. / 8

4. About when in its history did psychology become known as the "science of behavior?"

a. When Wundt founded his laboratory at the University of Leipzig.

b. When Titchener came to direct the psychology laboratory at Cornell University.

c. When James was teaching psychology at Harvard University.

d. When Watson became head of the psychology department at John Hopkins University.

Psychology became the science of behavior when John B. Watson founded behaviorism while head of the psychology department at Johns Hopkins University. Both Wundt and Titchener were early structuralists. Along with James, who set the stage for functionalism, they defined psychology as the science of mental life, mental activity, or consciousness, not behavior. / 12

5. Of the following, who is most likely to say, "Psychology should focus on the person, the self in all its aspects as it interacts with the fabric of experience"?

a. A structuralist psychologist.

b. A behaviorist psychologist.

c. A humanistic psychologist.

d. A Gestalt psychologist.

Although no psychologist might violently disagree with such a statement, it is most likely to have been made by a humanistic psychologist whose focus is on the person or self. A structuralist would be more concerned with the elements of mental activity; a behaviorist with measurable behavior; and a Gestalt psychologist with the processes involved in perception. / 13

6. We know that Leslie earned a very high score on her college entrance exam, placing her in the top 5 percent of those taking the exam. What is our most reasonable prediction concerning her grade point average for her freshman year in college?

a. She will finish her freshman year well within the top 5 percent of her class.

b. She will probably earn good grades.

c. She is just as likely to finish with a D average as an A average.

d. Knowing her exam score tells us nothing that we can use to make predictions about her grade point average.

Correlations do not tell us about cause and effect relationships. They do allow for exceptions, but because we know that entrance exams are positively correlated with grade point averages, we can use this information to predict that Leslie is likely to earn good grades during her freshman year. / 19

7. A researcher interested in the relationship between college grades and the number of hours that students are employed each week records the hourly work schedules and the grade point averages of 1,500 college students. A correlation is computed, resulting in a correlation coefficient of +1.04. We may draw the following conclusion:

a. Working has a beneficial effect on college grades.

b. The more one works, the better one's grades are.

c. There is a weak relationship, at best, between grades and the number of hours a student is employed.

d. There is an error in the computation of the correlation coefficient.

This item—or one like it—has become a virtual classic. It should remind you not to get lost in details, but to reflect on what a question is asking. In this case, the basic issue is whether or not you remember that the correlation coefficient ranges in value between -1.00 and $+1.00$. Hence, a correlation of $+1.04$ is simply not possible (whether it's $+1.04$ or -1.04 does not matter), so *someone* made an error in the computation of the correlation coefficient. / 20

8. You conduct an experiment to see if Drug A affects students' ability to memorize. Subjects are randomly assigned to two groups. One group receives Drug A, while the other gets a sugar pill. Both groups are asked to memorize a list of unrelated words. In this experiment, what is the dependent variable?

a. How long on the average, it takes the subjects to learn the list.

b. The amount of Drug A given to the subjects in the two groups.

c. The age and learning abilities of the subjects in each group.

d. The difficulty of the words on the list.

In an experiment, the dependent variable is what you measure; in this case, how long it takes the subjects to learn the list. Drug dosage is what you have manipulated and is, therefore, the independent variable. Age and learning ability are potential extraneous variables, here controlled by randomly assigning subjects to your two groups. The difficulty of the words on the list is another potential extraneous variable, and here we may assume that both groups will be given the same list to memorize. / 22

Chapter One

The Biological Bases of Behavior

Why We Care

The Neuron
    Neural Structure
    Neural Function: The Impulse

From One Cell to Another: The Synapse

Nervous Systems: The Big Picture

The Spinal Cord
    Structure
    Function

"Lower" Brain Centers
    The Brain Stem
    The Cerebellum
    The Reticular Activating System
    The Limbic System
    The Hypothalamus
    The Thalamus

The Cerebral Cortex
    Lobes and Localization
        Sensory Areas
        Motor Areas
        Association Areas
    The Two Cerebral Hemispheres

Imagine the following scenario. You are wandering down the hall late at night in your bare feet. Suddenly, "Ouch!" You've stepped on a tack. You are now hopping around on one foot while you try to grab the other foot.

We will leave you there for now and ask, "What happens next?" What happens next goes something like this (with some questions interspersed that you probably wouldn't ask yourself at the time but which are an integral part of the experience you are having).

Your injured foot jerks up off the floor, and your arms flail out so you can maintain your balance. *(What stimulated the muscles of my leg to pull up my foot? How do my arms know what to do to keep me in balance?)* You realize that your foot hurts. *(Where does realization happen? In my brain?)* Perhaps we'd better be more specific. The point of the tack enters the sole of your foot and stimulates a nerve cell. *(How are nerve cells usually stimulated? What kind of nerve cell responds to tacks? For that matter, what's a nerve cell?)*

The cell that is stimulated by the tack sends a message to other nerve cells. *(Wait a minute! What do you mean by "message"? How do messages get from one cell to another?)* This message now races up your leg to the base of the spinal cord. *(How quickly does the message reach my spinal cord?*

Your injured foot jerks up off the floor, and your arms flail out so you can maintain your balance. (What stimulated the muscles of my leg to pull up my foot? How do my arms know what to do to keep me in balance?)

What does the spinal cord look like? What does it do?) From the spinal cord, messages go off in two directions: up toward the brain and back down the muscles in the leg. *(How do messages get to my brain? And how do they*

get back down to my leg?) Messages from the spinal cord to the leg stimulate muscles to quickly lift the leg off the floor. At the same time, messages to your brain are being interpreted. *(Do you mean to say that my leg lifts up off the floor without my even thinking about it? Doesn't my brain have to control the movement?)* Your brain will direct your eyes to focus on your foot. You'll identify the source of pain as a tack. Still hopping on one foot, you'll wonder who left a tack on the floor, and you may even get angry thinking about it. *(What part of the brain directs the movement of my eyes? To recognize the tack implies that I'm using memory. How are memories stored in the brain, and where? Are there separate parts of the brain that are involved in emotional responses like anger?)*

Even in a stimulus-response chain of events as simple as that involved in stepping on a tack, a remarkable series of biological, physiological, and biochemical reactions take place. Ultimately, all of our behaviors and mental processes—from the simple blink of an eye to profound and abstract thought—are no more (and no less) than the integrated reactions of our nervous systems.

Why We Care

Psychology is the study of behavior and mental processes. For us even to begin to understand how people behave, think, and feel as they do, we must understand at least the basic fundamentals of the biology and physiology of the organism. Our aim is not to become amateur biologists or physiologists. We needn't become experts in all areas of human anatomy. We need have little concern for bones, blood, or muscle tissues, or how the lungs pass oxygen into the bloodstream, or how the stomach digests food. We are primarily interested in the operation of the nervous system, and once we have laid the proper foundation, most of our attention will be focused on the brain. We choose to direct our attention there because it is the brain and the nerve cells leading to it and away from it that are most intimately involved in behavior and mental processes.

In this chapter, we'll first review some of what we know about the nervous system below the brain. We'll take a building block approach, first describing the single, individual nerve cell, then seeing how these cells communicate, or interact, with others. We'll discuss the billions of nerve cells that work together in the major nervous systems of the human body.

Then we'll try to describe the brain—a living structure so marvelously complex, so capable, so subtle, so dynamic that the task seems nearly impossible. Is the brain a vast computer? a great woven knot of nerve tissue? the seat of understanding? a warehouse of memories and past experiences? a reservoir of emotion? the source of motivation? Yes, it is all these, and more.

If we are to have any hope of understanding the intricacies of the brain, we have to focus on its small areas one at a time. We'll begin by discussing those "lower" areas of the brain that control very basic functions. Then we'll study the cerebral cortex, the area of the brain most fully developed in humans. When we fragment discussions of the brain in this way, we often lose sight of the fact that it is a unified organ in which all the various parts interact and work together. Some brain functions can be localized in particular areas or structures of the brain, but the adaptability of the brain and its integration of individual functions force us to consider it as a whole, as more than simply the sum of its various parts.

THE NEURON

neuron
a nerve cell that is the basic building block of the nervous system; transmits neural impulses

Our exploration of the nervous system begins at the level of the single nerve cell. Individual nerve cells are called **neurons.** They are unimaginably small—microscopically small—and were only recognized as separate entities at about the turn of the century. It is appropriate to think of neurons as the basic building blocks of the nervous system. They exist throughout our nervous system by the billions. Neurons are so tiny and complex that even estimating their number is clearly very difficult. For example, three sources give the number of nerve cells contained in the brain alone as "about 12 billion" (Bennett, 1982, p. 26), "50 billion or so" (Bloom et al., 1985, p.33), and "on the order of 100 billion" (Hubel, 1979, p. 45). The largest estimate is probably the most accurate.

Neural Structure

Nerve cells are like people in that no two are exactly alike. Though there is no such thing as a typical neuron, most *do* have many structures in common. Figure 1.1 illustrates these common structures, while Figure 1.2 shows what neurons really look like.

cell body
the largest mass of a neuron, containing the cell's nucleus, may receive neural impulses

One structure that all neurons have is a **cell body.** The cell body is the largest concentration of mass of the cell. It contains the nucleus of the cell, which, in turn, contains the genetic information that keeps the cell functioning and "doing its thing."

dendrite
a branchlike extension of a neuron's cell body, where most impulses are received by the neuron

Extending away from the cell body are a number of tentaclelike structures called **dendrites** and one particularly long structure called an **axon.** As you can see, our drawing is very much simplified, showing only a few dendrites. The dendrite extensions reach out to receive messages (called neural impulses) from other nearby neurons and send them toward the cell body. From the cell body, impulses are collected and then travel down the axon toward other neurons or to muscle fibers. Some axons can be quite long—as long as two or three feet in the spinal cord. It is generally true, then, that *within the neuron,* impulses travel from dendrite to cell body to axon.

axon
the long taillike extension of a neuron that carries an impulse away from the cell body toward the synapse

The neuron we have pictured in Figure 1-1 has a feature not found on all neurons. Here you can see that the axon is surrounded by a covering or

FIGURE 1.1
A schematic drawing of a typical neuron showing its major structures.

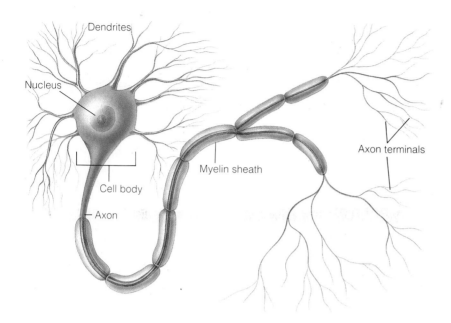

sheath of **myelin.** Myelin is a white, fatty substance that is found on about half the neurons in an adult's nervous system. It is the presence or absence of myelin that allows us to tell the difference between the gray matter (cell bodies and unmyelinated axons) and the white matter (myelinated axons) that we can see clearly in sections of nervous system tissue.

myelin
a white, fatty covering on some axons that protects and increases the speed of the neural impulse

FIGURE 1.2
A photograph of neurons taken through a powerful microscope.

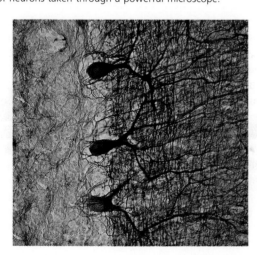

Myelin is a feature of neurons that is not fully developed at birth—it develops as the nervous system matures. Myelin serves to protect the long, delicate axon and helps speed neural impulses along their way. The differences in the rate of impulse transmission within a myelinated or an unmyellinated neuron are quite striking. Small unmyelinated axons may transmit impulses at about 0.5 meters per second, while large, myelinated axons may speed impulses along at a rate of 120 meters per second. We tend to find myelin sheaths on those neurons that transmit messages relatively long distances throughout the body. If you were to stub your toe, the first sensation you would have is that you bashed your toe against a solid object. The feeling of pain would come shortly after. This is because the nerve fibers that carry touch and pressure messages to your brain are highly myelinated, while pain-carrying fibers are made up of neurons with bare, unmyelinated axons. The distance between your toe and your brain is great enough for these differences in transmission rates to be noticed.

Axons end in a branching series of end points called **axon terminals.** It is at the axon terminals that each neuron connects with the dendrites, cell bodies, and (occasionally) axons of neighboring neurons to transmit impulses along to other neurons. The spreading axon terminals and the large number of dendrite extensions make it possible for one tiny neuron to interact with hundreds, even thousands, of other neurons.

One far-reaching observation about neurons is that we are born with as many neurons as we will ever have. As we grow and develop, our neurons may grow new dendrites and axon terminals, form new connections with other neurons, and develop myelin sheaths, but they do not increase in number. A related observation is that when our neurons die (or are killed by injury or drug use) new ones are not generated to take their place. This feature makes neurons unique. We are constantly producing new blood cells to replace lost ones. If we didn't, we could never donate a pint of blood. Skin cells are constantly being replaced by new ones. You rinse away skin cells by the hundreds each time you wash your hands. But neurons are different; once they are gone, they are gone forever. Because remaining neurons can develop new dendrites and axon terminals, the function previously performed by dead neurons can often be taken over by surviving neurons, particularly if only a few are lost at any one time.

Neurons are usually classified in terms of how and where they fit into general nervous system activity. Many neural impulses begin at our sense receptors (our eyes, ears, skin, and so on). There, individual receptor cells pick up energy from the world around us and change it into the energy of the nervous system. We'll discuss how these receptor cells function in Chapter 2. Once receptor cells have become activated, impulses are relayed by **sensory neurons** *toward the brain or spinal cord.* The neurons that carry impulses *away from the brain or spinal cord* toward our muscles and glands are called **motor neurons.** Those nerve cells that transmit impulses from one part of the brain or spinal cord to another (that is, *within* the brain or spinal cord) are called **interneurons.** So, it's *toward* the brain or spinal cord on sensory neurons, *within* on interneurons, and *away* on motor neurons.

Remember that a neuron is only a single cell. Neurons tend to work together, organized in nerves or nerve fibers that contain many individual nerve cells and axons.

axon terminals
the series of branching end points of an axon where one neuron communicates to the next in a series

sensory neurons
nerve cells carrying impulses from receptor cells toward the brain or spinal cord

motor neurons
nerve cells carrying impulses away from the brain or spinal cord toward the muscles and glands

interneurons
nerve cells within the brain or spinal cord

Describe the main structural features of a neuron.   BEFORE YOU GO ON
What is the role of myelin?
Classify neurons into three major types.

Neural Function: The Impulse

The function of a neuron is to transmit **neural impulses** from one place in the nervous system to another. The actual detailed story of how these impulses are generated and transmitted is a very complex one having to do with electrical and chemical changes that are extremely delicate and subtle. That the process is as well understood as it is is a wonder in itself. Here we'll describe it in very general terms.

Each neuron acts like a tiny battery, holding a small electrical charge, called a **resting potential.** When a neuron is stimulated to fire, or to produce an impulse of its own, the electrical charge of the resting potential is released. For a brief instant (about 1/1000 of a second) the electrical charge within the cell becomes more positive than the area outside the cell. The whole "charge" of the battery "releases" instantaneously. This charge is called the **action potential.** Then, for just a few thousandths of a second, there is a period (called the *refractory period*) during which the neuron cannot fire, because there is no tension present to release as an action potential. Very quickly, in just a few thousandths of a second, the neuron returns to its original state, and is ready to fire again.

To repeat, what happens is something like this. When at rest, there is a difference between the electrical charge inside and outside the neuron (the inside being overly negative). When the neuron is stimulated, this difference reverses, so that the outside becomes overly negative. This process is depicted in Figure 1.3.

When a neuron fires, when an impulse "travels along a neuron," nothing physically moves from one end of the neuron to the other. What moves along the neuron is *where* the action potential occurs. That is, where the action potential takes place moves down the neuron.

One aspect of neural activity is of particular interest to us because it relates directly to a psychological question. The question deals with how the nervous system reacts to differences in stimulus intensity. How do we react to the difference between a bright light and a dim one, a soft sound and a loud one, a tap and a slap on the back? An observation that is relevant to this question is this: A neuron either fires or it doesn't. The electrical charge of the resting potential is either released or it isn't. There is no in between, no degree of firing. This observation is called the **all-or-none principle.**

It is also true that neurons do not necessarily fire every time they are stimulated. Each neuron has a level of stimulation that must be surpassed in order to get it to transmit an impulse. The minimum level of stimulation required to get a neuron to fire is called the **neural threshold.** These two notions, that of threshold and the all-or-none principle, give us some insight as to how the nervous system processes differences in stimulus intensity. High-intensity stimuli (bright lights, loud sounds, and so on) don't get neurons to fire more vigorously, but may stimulate *more* neurons to fire and may get them to fire more *frequently*. High-intensity stimuli would be above

neural impulse
a sudden and reversible change in the electrical charges within and outside a neuron that travels from dendrite to axon when the neuron fires

resting potential
the difference in electric charge between the inside and outside of a neuron when it is at rest

action potential
the difference in electric charge between the inside and outside of a neuron when it fires

all-or-none principle
the observation that a neuron will either fire and generate a full impulse or it will not fire at all

neural threshold
the minimum amount of stimulation required to produce a neural impulse within a neuron

FIGURE 1.3
The transmission of a neural impulse in a section of an axon. While at rest, the inside of the neuron is full of negative ions (-), while positive ions (+) are outside the neuron. During the neural impulse, negative ions race outside the neuron while positive ions race inside. Then, the axon returns to a state of rest, with negative ions inside and positive ions outside. In this illustration, the impulse is traveling from left to right.

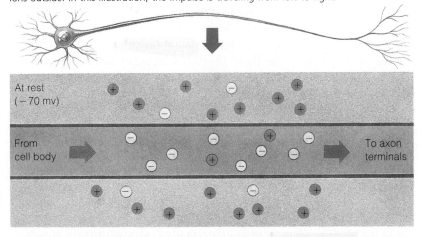

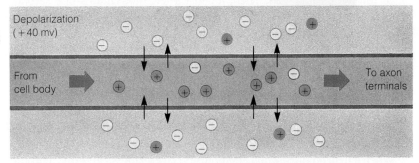

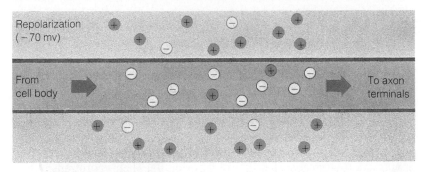

the necessary threshold for firing for a greater number of neurons than low-intensity stimuli. So, the difference in your experience of a flashbulb going off in front of your face and a candle viewed at a distance is largely a difference in the *number* of neurons involved and the *rate* at which they fire, not the *way* in which those neurons are responding.

BEFORE YOU GO ON   **Describe the basic process involved when a neuron fires. What is the all-or-none principle?**

FROM ONE CELL TO ANOTHER: THE SYNAPSE

We have seen that neurons are very active cells that transmit electrochemical impulses from dendrite to axon. Individual neurons do not accomplish much by themselves, however. Neural impulses must be transmitted from neuron to neuron. This transmission takes place at the **synapse.** The essential structures of a synapse are shown in Figure 1.4.

At the very end of each axon are a large number of axon terminals. These terminals contain small packets of chemical molecules. These packets are called **vesicles.** When a neural impulse reaches the axon terminal, some of these vesicles release the chemical molecules they are holding. These chemicals, called **neurotransmitters,** once released from their vesicles, flood out into the space between the axon of one neuron and the dendrite (or cell body or axon) of the next neuron. Notice that the two neurons involved do not touch; they are separated by a very small space, called the **synaptic cleft.** Once across the synaptic cleft, neurotransmitters may enter into specific places or sites on the receptor neuron's membrane. As you can see in the highly schematic Figure 1.4, not all neurotransmitters "fit" in the receptor cell sites.

At the synapse, then, neurotransmitters pass through the membrane of the axon *(presynaptic membrane)*, cross the synaptic cleft, and slip into spaces in the membrane of the next neuron *(postsynaptic membrane)*. Usually, this action stimulates the next neuron in the sequence to fire and thus begin a new neural impulse. That impulse then races down the second neuron, its vesicles are opened, transmitter substances are released, and the next neuron is stimulated to fire. It is indeed a remarkable chain of events. Now that we've covered some of the basics, let's add a few details.

In the last section, we mentioned that each neuron has a threshold of stimulation required to get it to fire and generate a new impulse. Now, perhaps, we can get a better picture of what that means. It may mean that the second neuron in a sequence (see Figure 1.4) has a threshold so high that if neurotransmitters from only one presynaptic axon terminal were to stimulate it, nothing would happen. More chemical may be needed to get it to fire than that one axon terminal can provide. It may not fire until the combined action of a number of axon terminals secrete large amounts of chemical into the synaptic cleft. Or the same axon may have to deliver its chemical a number of times in rapid succession to produce enough stimulation to be above threshold and to produce a new impulse.

We must also point out that some neurons hold an altogether different sort of chemical in their vesicles. These neurons do not stimulate new impulses at the synapse; they do just the opposite. Their neurotransmitters cross the synaptic cleft and inhibit, or decrease the likelihood of an impulse continuing to the next neuron.

Not long ago it was believed that neurons contained one of just two types of neurotransmitters. One was excitatory and stimulated new impulses, and the other was inhibitory and slowed or stopped impulse transmission. We now recognize that such a view is much too simplistic. There are now more than 60 known neurotransmitters, and it is virtually certain that there are more that we do not yet know about. Each neurotransmitter may have its own unique influence on what happens at the synapse, although we continue to group them together as being basically excitatory or inhibitory.

synapse
the location where an impulse is relayed from one neuron to another by chemical neurotransmitters

vesicles
the small containers, or packets of neurotransmitter substance found in axon terminals

neurotransmitters
chemical molecules released at the synapse that, in general, either excite or inhibit neural impulse transmission

synaptic cleft
the space between the presynaptic membrane of one neuron and the postsynaptic membrane of the next neuron

FIGURE 1.4
A synapse, in which transmission is from upper left to lower right. As an impulse enters the axon terminal, vesicles release neurotransmitter chemicals through the presynaptic membrane into the synaptic cleft. The neurotransmitter then stimulates the postsynaptic membrane of the next dendrite.

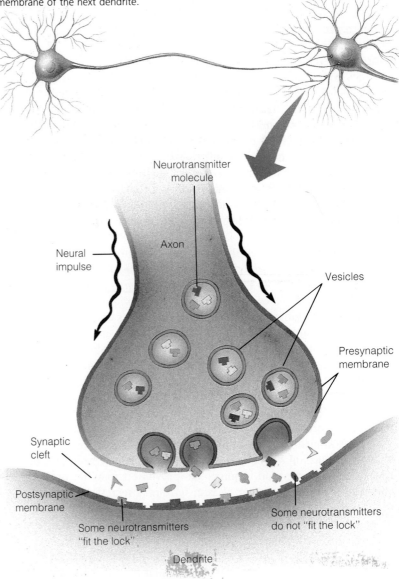

We will see repeated references to the role of neurotransmitters later on when we discuss the physiological changes that take place when we learn and remember, when we discuss the effects of drugs on behavior and mental processes, and when we discuss such disorders as schizophrenia and Alzheimer's disease. Neurotransmitters will also enter our discussions of emotion and health psychology.

Finally, so that our simplified description does not leave a false impression, let's make one point clear: Neural impulse transmission is seldom a matter of one neuron simply stimulating one other neuron that in turn stimulates but one more. Remember that any one neuron may have hundreds or thousands of axon terminals and synapses. Any one neuron, then, has the potential for exciting (or inhibiting) many others.

Summarize neural impulse transmission at the synapse. **BEFORE YOU GO ON**

NERVOUS SYSTEMS: THE BIG PICTURE

Now that we have a sense of how neurons work, individually and in combination, let's step back for a moment to consider the broader context in which they actually operate. We've already made the point that very little gets accomplished through the action of just a few individual neurons. Behavior and mental activity generally require large numbers of neurons working together in complex, organized systems. Figure 1.5 illustrates the overall organization of the nervous systems.

The first major division of the nervous system is determined largely on the basis of anatomy. The **central nervous system (CNS)** includes all the neurons and nerve fibers found in the spinal cord and the brain. In many ways, this system of nerves is the most complex and the most intimately involved in the control of our behaviors and mental processes.

The **peripheral nervous system (PNS)** is quite simply composed of all the other nerve fibers in our body—those in our arms, legs, face, fingers, intestines, and so forth. In general, neurons in the PNS carry impulses either

central nervous system (CNS)
those neurons in the brain and spinal cord

peripheral nervous system (PNS)
those neurons not located in the brain or spinal cord; that is, those in the periphery

FIGURE 1.5
The organization of the human nervous systems.

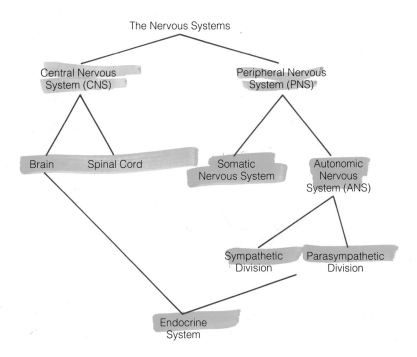

1 **somatic nervous system**
sensory and motor neurons outside
the CNS that serve the sense
receptors and skeletal muscles

2 **autonomic nervous system (ANS)**
those neurons that activate the
smooth muscles and the glands

2a **sympathetic division**
(of ANS) those neurons involved in
states of emotionality

2b **parasympathetic division**
(of ANS) those neurons involved in
the maintenance of states of calm
and relaxation

endocrine system
a series of glands that secrete
hormones directly into the
bloodstream

hormones
a variety of chemical compounds,
secreted by endocrine glands,
carried through the bloodstream

from the central nervous system to muscles and glands (with motor neurons) or *to* the CNS (with sensory neurons) from receptor cells.

The peripheral nervous system is divided into two parts, based largely on the part of the body being served. The **somatic nervous system** includes those neurons outside the CNS that serve the skeletal muscles and that pick up impulses from the major receptors—the eyes, ears, and so forth.

The other major component of the PNS is the **autonomic nervous system (ANS),** where "autonomic" means essentially the same thing as "automatic." This implies that the activity of the ANS is in large measure (but not totally) independent of voluntary CNS control. The fibers of the ANS are involved in activating smooth muscles (like those of the stomach and intestines) and glands. The ANS also provides feedback to the CNS about the activity of these internal processes.

Because the autonomic nervous system is so involved in emotional responding, we'll return to it again in that context. For now, we can note that the ANS is itself made up of two parts, the **sympathetic division** and the **parasympathetic division.** These two divisions of the ANS commonly work in opposition to each other, the former becoming active when we are in states of emotional excitement, and the latter becoming active when we are relaxed and quiet. An overview of the structures affected by the ANS and its two divisions is presented in Figure 1.6.

As you can see, there is one other system reflected in Figure 1.5—the **endocrine system.** Although the endocrine system is affected by the central nervous system and can, in turn, affect nervous system activity, it is not itself a system of nerves. It is an interconnected network of glands that affect behavior through the secretion of **hormones** into the bloodstream. The endocrine system's glands and hormones are controlled by both the brain and the autonomic nervous system, which is why we have pictured it as we have in Figure 1.5.

There is good reason to separate out all of these different organizations of neurons, fibers, and glands. It helps make a very complex system easier to deal with. But we have to keep in mind that the outline of Figure 1.5 is very simplified. All of the nerve fibers in each of these different systems have profound influences on each other. They are not as independent as our diagram might imply.

For example, let's trace some of the events that would occur if you were to step on a tack. Receptor cells in your foot would respond to the tack and send impulses up your leg (somatic division of the PNS) to your spinal cord (CNS). There, some impulses would be sent back down to your leg (PNS again) to get it to jerk up off the floor. Other impulses would be sent to your brain (CNS), where you would become aware of what had happened. At about the same time, you would become angry that someone left a tack on the floor. Hence, your autonomic nervous system would become active, particularly the sympathetic division. Perhaps, in your excitement of hopping about the kitchen, your endocrine system would be stimulated to provide extra doses of hormones. When you finally settled down, the parasympathetic division of your ANS would take over again.

It is almost always the case that even when we can classify a certain behavior as being largely determined by some part of the human nervous system, we need to recognize that no division of the nervous system operates without the others.

FIGURE 1.6

The division of the autonomic nervous system. The parasympathetic division becomes active when we are relaxed and quiet, while the sympathetic division is active when we are aroused or excited. (Adapted from Gardner, 1963.)

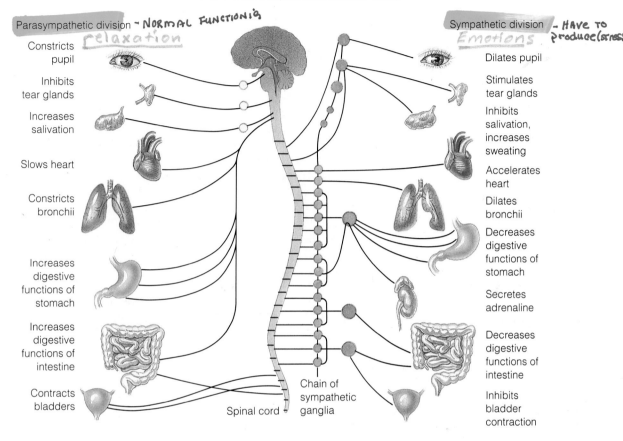

Parasympathetic division ~ NORMAL FUNCTIONIS relaxation

Sympathetic division - HAVE TO produce (stress) Emotions

Constricts pupil

Inhibits tear glands

Increases salivation

Slows heart

Constricts bronchii

Increases digestive functions of stomach

Increases digestive functions of intestine

Contracts bladders

Spinal cord

Chain of sympathetic ganglia

Dilates pupil

Stimulates tear glands

Inhibits salivation, increases sweating

Accelerates heart

Dilates bronchii

Decreases digestive functions of stomach

Secretes adrenaline

Decreases digestive functions of intestine

Inhibits bladder contraction

Reproduce the outline of the nervous systems without looking at it.   **BEFORE YOU GO ON**

THE SPINAL CORD

As we have just seen, the central nervous system consists of the brain and the spinal cord. Here we'll describe the structure and function of the spinal cord, reserving the next section for the brain alone. As we examine the spinal cord, we see for the first time the nervous system's involvement in behavior.

Structure

The **spinal cord** is a massive collection of neurons within the spine that looks rather like a section of rope or thick cord. It is surrounded and protected by the hard bone and cartilage of the vertebrae. It is sometimes difficult to remember that the spinal cord itself is made up of soft, delicate nerve fibers living inside our backbone.

spinal cord
a mass of interconnected neurons within the spine that conveys impulses to and from the brain and is involved in some reflex behaviors

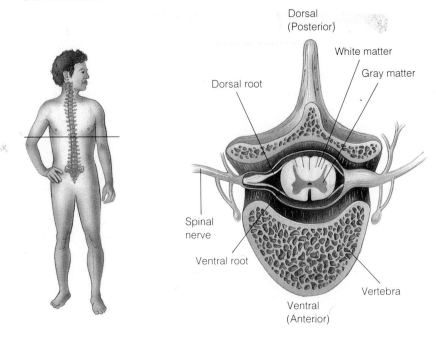

A cross-section view of the spinal cord is illustrated in Figure 1.7. There are a couple of structural details that we should point out. They will become relevant very shortly when we talk about the function of the spinal cord. First, note the orientation of the section of spinal cord we are viewing in this diagram. *Dorsal* means toward the back (it is a shark's dorsal fin that sometimes can be seen just above water level); *ventral* means toward the front. We can see, then, that nerve fibers *enter* the spinal cord from either side, but toward the back (dorsal roots), and *leave* toward the front (ventral roots).

Second, notice that the center area of the spinal cord is made up of dark gray matter—rather in the shape of a butterfly—while the outside area is light white matter. Remember that this means that the center portion is filled with cell bodies and unmyelinated axons, while the outer portion contains myelinated axons. Both of these observations about the structure of the spinal cord provide keys to understanding its function.

Function

The spinal cord has two major functions, one of which is to rapidly transmit neural impulses to and from the brain. Whenever sensory messages originate below the neck and go to the brain, they do so through the spinal cord. Whenever the brain transmits impulses to parts of the body below the neck, those impulses first travel down the spinal cord.

Impulses to and from different parts of our body leave and enter the spinal cord at different levels (impulses to and from the legs, for example, enter and leave at the base of the spinal cord). If the spinal cord, or the fibers leading in and out of it, is damaged or destroyed, the consequences can be disastrous, resulting in a loss of sensation or feeling from the part of the body served and in a loss of voluntary movement (paralysis) of the muscles in the region. Quite clearly, the higher in the spinal cord that such damage takes place, the greater will be the resulting losses.

Once inside the spinal cord, impulses race up and down the ascending and descending pathways found in the white matter areas of the spinal cord. Remember that this area appears white because of the myelin covering the axons found there. Remember, also, that one of the functions of myelin is to help speed impulses along their way—in this case over relatively long distances up and down the spinal cord.

The second major function of the spinal cord is its involvement in **spinal reflexes.** These are very simple automatic behaviors that occur without the conscious, voluntary action of the brain. To understand how these reflexes work look at Figure 1.8. Here we have another drawing of a section of the spinal cord, but we have added skin receptor cells, sensory neurons, interneurons, and motor neurons.

Let's again trace your reaction to stepping on a tack. The receptor cells would initiate neural impulses and transmit them to sensory neurons that enter through the dorsal root into the spinal cord. Then, two things would happen at almost the same time. Impulses would race up the ascending tracts (pathways) of the spinal cord's white matter to your brain. Impulses would also travel through interneurons and go right back out again through the ventral root on motor neurons back down to your leg where muscles would be stimulated to contract, and your foot would stay suspended in midair.

spinal reflex
an automatic, involuntary response to a stimulus that involves sensory neurons sending impulses to the spinal cord, (occasionally) interneurons within the spinal cord, and motor neurons

FIGURE 1.8
A spinal reflex. Stimulation of the receptor in turn stimulates sensory neurons, interneurons, and motor neurons. Impulses also ascend to the brain through tracts in the white matter.

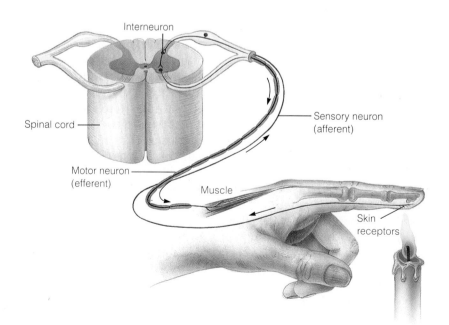

Here, then, we have a simple reflex. Impulses travel *in* on sensory neurons, *within* on interneurons, and *out* on motor neurons. We are now clearly involved with behavior. We have an environmental stimulus, activity of the central nervous system, and an observable response.

There are a couple of observations we must make about Figure 1.8 before we go on. First, the fact that impulses that enter the spinal cord also travel up to the brain is not indicated. It is also the case that some reflexes are even more simple than the one in Figure 1.8 in that no interneuron is involved. That is, it is quite possible for sensory neurons to synapse directly within the spinal cord with motor neurons. On the other hand, you should also realize the total complex pattern of behavior involved in stepping on a tack and hopping about on one foot will actually involve the stimulation of thousands of neurons.

BEFORE YOU GO ON **What are the major functions of the spinal cord?**
How does a spinal reflex work?

The workings of the human nervous systems are marvelous and complex. That living cells as tiny as neurons provide the bases for all our actions, mental or behavioral, is a notion that takes some time to get used to. But neurons do not act alone. The complexity of individual nerve cells multiplies geometrically with the activity of the neurotransmitters at synapses. We can clearly see the role of the nervous system in behavior when we examine spinal reflex activity. A spinal reflex involves impulses that travel toward the spinal cord on sensory neurons, within the spinal cord on interneurons, and away from the spinal cord on motor neurons to produce a behavioral reaction. The anatomy, physiology, and biochemistry of the brain is even more incredible and more directly involved with our everyday experiences, as we will see next.

"LOWER" BRAIN CENTERS

There are many different ways in which we could organize our discussion of the brain. Let's choose a very simple one and divide the brain into two parts: the cerebral cortex and everything else, which we'll refer to as lower brain centers. That may not strike you as fair, but for the human brain, where the cerebral cortex plays so many important roles, this is a reasonable division.

What we are in this section calling lower brain centers are "lower" in two ways. First, they are physically located below, or underneath, the cerebral cortex, and second, they are the brain structures first to develop, both in an evolutionary sense and within the developing human brain. They are the brain structures we most clearly share with other animals. In no way should you think of these lower centers as being less important. As you will soon see, our very survival depends on them. You can use Figure 1.9 as a guide to locate the different structures as we discuss them.

The Brain Stem

As you look at the spinal cord and brain, you really can't tell where the spinal cord ends and the brain begins. There is no abrupt line separating these two components of the central nervous system. Just above the spinal cord, at the

FIGURE 1.9

The major structures of the human brain. Note the orientation of the "lower" brain centers—the medulla, pons, cerebellum, and reticular activating system.

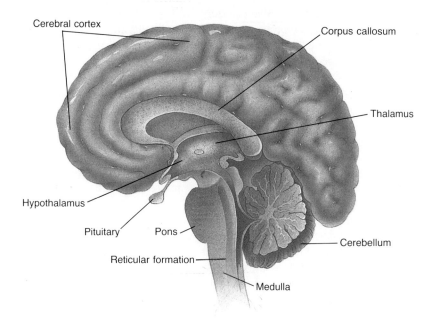

Cerebral cortex

Corpus callosum

Thalamus

Hypothalamus

Pituitary

Pons

Reticular formation

Cerebellum

Medulla

very base of the brain, there are two important structures that together form what we call the **brain stem.**

The very lowest structure is the **medulla** (or more formally, the medulla oblongata). In a sense, the medulla acts like the spinal cord in that its major functions involve involuntary reflexes. There are all sorts of important little structures called **nuclei** (actually, collections of neural cell bodies) within the medulla. These nuclei control such functions as reflexive eye movements and tongue movements; you don't, for example, have to think about blinking your eye as something rushes toward it; your medulla will control that blink reflexively.

The medulla also contains nuclei that control breathing reflexes and that monitor the muscles of the heart to see that it keeps beating rhythmically. We *can* exercise some voluntary control over the nuclei of the medulla, but only within limits. The medulla controls our level of respiration (breathing), but clearly we can override the medulla and hold our breath. We cannot, however, hold our breath until we die (as some children occasionally threaten). We can hold our breath until we lose consciousness, which is to say until we lose higher level, voluntary control, at which point the medulla picks up where it left off and breathing continues as usual.

It is at the level of the medulla that most nerve fibers to and from the brain cross over from left to right and vice versa. By and large, centers in the left side of the brain receive impulses from and send impulses to the right side of the body. Similarly, the left side of the body sends impulses to and receives messages from the right side of the brain (which explains why stimulating the correct portion of the *left* side of the brain may produce a movement in the *right* arm). This crossing over from one side to another takes place here in the brain stem.

brain stem
a portion of the brain just above the spinal cord comprised of the medulla and the pons

medulla
an area of the brain stem that monitors reflex functions such as respiration and heart rate and where cross-laterality begins

nuclei
nervous system structures made up of collections of cell bodies

pons
an area of the brain stem forming a bridge between the brain and spinal cord that plays a role in monitoring sleep-wake cycles

Just above the medulla is another area of widening, a structure called the **pons.** (The pons is one structure—there is no such thing as a "pon.") Primarily, the pons serves as a relay station, or bridge (which is what "pons" means), sorting out and relaying sensory messages from the spinal cord and the face up to higher brain centers and reversing the relay for motor impulses coming down from higher centers. The pons also plays an active role in regulating our cycle of sleep and wakefulness.

BEFORE YOU GO ON Name the two brain stem structures, and describe where they are and what they do.

The Cerebellum

cerebellum
a spherical structure at the lower rear of the brain that is involved in the coordination and smoothing of muscular activity

Athelets train their Cerebellum Also musicians "Phil Collins"

Your **cerebellum** is just about the size of your closed fist. It is more or less spherical in shape and sits right behind your pons, tucked up under the base of your skull. The cerebellum itself looks like a small brain. Its outer region is very convoluted, meaning that the tissue there is folded in upon itself, creating many deep crevices, lumps, and valleys.

The major role of the cerebellum is in smoothing and coordinating body movements. Most intentional, voluntary movements originate in higher brain centers and are only coordinated in the cerebellum, but some movements may actually originate there. Because body movement is so closely tied to vision, many eye movements also originate there.

Golfers working on their golf swings are really training their cerebellums.

Our ability to casually stoop, pick up a dime from the floor, and slip it into our pocket involves a series of movements made smooth and casual by our cerebellum. When athletes train a movement, like a golf swing or a gymnastic routine, we sometimes say that they are trying to get "into a groove" so that the trained movement can be made simply and smoothly. In a real sense, such athletes are training their cerebellum.

Few of our behaviors are as well coordinated or rapid as the movements required to make speech sounds. Next time you're talking to someone, pause to consider just how quickly and effortlessly your lips, mouth, and tongue are moving (thanks to your cerebellum) to form the sounds of your speech. Cerebellum damage disrupts fine coordinated movements. Speech becomes slurred; one staggers when walking; smoothly touching the end of the nose is difficult to do with closed eyes. In fact, a person with cerebellum damage may appear to be quite drunk. (On what region of the brain do you suppose that alcohol has a direct influence? The cerebellum, of course!)

Damage to the cerebellum may disrupt motor activity in other ways. If the outer region of the cerebellum is damaged, patients suffer jerky **tremors,** or involuntary trembling movements, when they try to move (called "intention tremors"). Damage to inner, or deeper, areas of the cerebellum leads to tremors at rest, where the limbs and/or head may shake or twitch even when the patient tries to remain still.

tremors
involuntary, trembling, jerky movements that are usually associated with damage in the cerebellum

Where is the cerebellum located, and what is its major function?   **BEFORE YOU GO ON**

The Reticular Activating System

The **reticular activating system,** or **RAS,** is a different sort of brain structure. In fact, it is hardly a brain structure at all. It is a complex network of nerve fibers that begins down in the brain stem and works its way up through and around other structures, all the way to the top portions of the brain (see Figure 1.9).

Just precisely what the reticular activating system does, and how it does it, remains something of a mystery. As its name implies, however, the RAS is very much involved in determining our level of activation or arousal. It no doubt influences whether we're awake and attentive, drowsy, asleep, or at some level in between. Electrical stimulation of the RAS can produce EEG patterns of brain activity associated with being awake and alert. Lesions or cuts in the RAS can cause a condition of constant sleep in laboratory animals (Lindsley et al., 1949; Moruzzi & Magoun, 1949). In a way, then, the RAS acts like a valve that either allows sensory messages to pass from lower centers up to higher centers of the brain or shuts them off, partially or totally. The mystery is how the RAS does its thing, and what prompts it to do what it does.

reticular activating system (RAS)
a network of nerve fibers extending from the brain stem to the cerebrum that is involved in one's level of arousal or activation

lesion
a cut or wound made on neural tissue to study the impact of the destruction of specific brain areas

The Limbic System

The **limbic system** is a collection of small structures rather than a single, unified one. It is of the utmost importance in controlling the behavior of nonhuman mammals, which do not have as large or well-developed a cerebral cortex as humans do. The limbic system controls many of the complex

limbic system
a collection of small structures, including the amygdala, septal area, and hippocampus, that are involved in emotional and motivational reactions as well as the transfer of memories to long-term storage

FIGURE 1.10
A number of small structures make up the limbic system, including the amygdala, septum, hypothalamus, thalamus, and hippocampus.

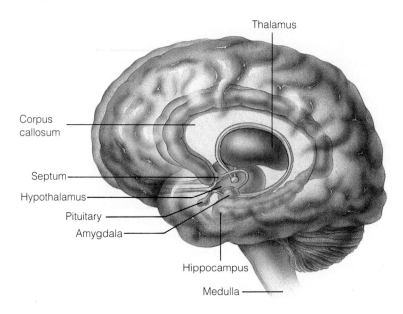

behavior patterns we usually think of as instinctive. You can see the limbic system most clearly in Figure 1.10.

Even within the human brain, parts of the limbic system are intimately involved in the display of emotional reactions. One center, the *amygdala,* produces reactions of rage and aggression when stimulated, while another area, the *septum,* seems to have the opposite effect, reducing the intensity of emotional responses when it is stimulated. The influence of the amygdala and the septum on emotional responding is quite direct in nonhumans. In humans, it is more subtle, being influenced by other brain centers as well.

Another part of the limbic system, called the *hippocampus,* seems to be less involved with emotion and more involved with the processing of memories. People with a damaged hippocampus are often unable to "move" experiences into permanent memory storage. They may remember events for short periods of time. They may also be able to remember events from the distant past, but only if those events happened before their hippocampus was damaged.

The Hypothalamus

The first thing to say about the **hypothalamus** is that it is often considered to be part of the limbic system. It is located near it, and it is also very much involved in our motivational and emotional behaviors. Among other things, it influences many functions of the endocrine system, which is involved in emotional responding.

The major responsibility of the hypothalamus seems to be to monitor critical internal bodily functions. It has centers (nuclei again) that control

hypothalamus
a small structure near the center of the brain involved in feeding, drinking, aggressive, and sexual behaviors; also involved in the regulation of the endocrine system

feeding behavior. It is sensitive to the amount of fluid in our body and indirectly gives rise to the feeling of being thirsty. The hypothalamus also acts something like a thermostat, triggering a number of reactions should we become too hot or too cold. This small structure is also very much involved in aggressive and sexual responding. It acts as a regulator of many hormones. To be sure, we'll discuss the hypothalamus again in more detail when we study motives, needs, and emotions in Chapter 7.

The Thalamus

The last structure to discuss as a lower brain center is the **thalamus.** It sits right below the covering of the cerebral cortex and is very involved with its functioning. It is a busy place. Like the pons, it acts as a relay station for impulses to and from the cerebral cortex.

Many impulses from the cerebral cortex going to lower brain structures, the spinal cord and eventually out to the peripheral nervous system first pass through the thalamus. Overcoming the normal function of the medulla (voluntarily holding our breath, for example) involves messages passing through the thalamus.

In handling incoming sensory impulses, the thalamus does more than simply pass those impulses on. It "integrates," or collects, organizes, and then directs, incoming sensory messages to the appropriate area of the cerebral cortex. Sensory messages from our lower body, our eyes, ears, and other senses (except for smell) pass through the thalamus. (Smell has its own special, direct route.) At the thalamus, nerve fibers, say from an eye, are spread out and projected onto the back of the cerebral cortex.

Because of its role in monitoring impulses to and from the cerebral cortex, the thalamus has long been suspected to be involved in the control of our sleep-wake cycle (Moruzzi, 1975). Although the issue is not yet settled, recent evidence (Lugaresi et al., 1986) suggests that nuclei in the thalamus have a role in integrating and expressing sleep and establishing the pattern of wakefulness and sleep.

thalamus
the final sensory relay station that projects sensory fibers to their proper location in the cerebrum and that may be involved in regulating sleep-wake cycles

Where are the following structures and what do they do: the RAS, the limbic system, the hypothalamus, and the thalamus?

BEFORE YOU GO ON

THE CEREBRAL CORTEX

The human brain is a homely organ. There's just nothing very pretty about it. When we look at a human brain, the first thing we are likely to notice is the large, lumpy, creviced outer covering of the **cerebral cortex** (in fact, "cortex" means outer bark or covering). The cerebral cortex (or cerebrum) of the human brain is much larger than any other brain structure. Indeed, it is the complex and intricate development of our cerebrum that makes us uniquely human. It is our center for the processing of information about the world in which we live. It is the starting place for all of our voluntary action.

cerebral cortex
3 names
(cerebrum) the large, convoluted outer covering of the brain that is the seat of cognitive functioning and voluntary action

Largest Part of Brain

Lobes and Localization

Figure 1.11 presents two views of the human brain, one a view of the top of the brain, the other a side view. You can see from these illustrations that the deep folds of tissue of the human cerebral cortex provide us with markers for dividing the cerebrum into major areas. The most noticeable division of the cortex can be seen in the top view. Here, we can clearly see the very deep fold or crevice that runs down the middle of the cerebrum from front to back, dividing it into the left and right cerebral **hemispheres.**

A side view of a hemisphere (Figure 1.11 shows us the left one) allows us to see the four major divisions of the cerebrum that are found in each hemisphere. These divisions are referred to as *lobes* of the brain. The **frontal lobe** is the largest and is defined by two large crevices, called the central fissure and the lateral fissure. The **occipital lobe** is defined somewhat more arbitrarily; it is the area at the back of the brain. The **parietal lobe** is wedged behind the frontal lobe, in front of the occipital lobe, and above the lateral fissure. Finally, the **temporal lobe** is located roughly at the temples, below the lateral fissure, and in front of the occipital lobe. Remember that the brain is divided into two symmetrical hemispheres, giving us a left and right frontal lobe, a left and right parietal lobe, and so on.

Psychologists and other researchers have learned a lot about what happens in different areas of the cerebral cortex. They have mapped out what normally goes on in most of the cerebrum. There are three major areas that have been mapped: *sensory areas,* where data from our sense receptors are sent, *motor areas,* where voluntary movements originate, and *association areas,* where sensory and motor functions are integrated and where higher mental processes are thought to occur.

hemispheres
the two halves of the cerebral cortex that are separated by a deep fissure running from front to back

frontal lobes
the largest of the cerebral lobes; in front of the central fissure and above the lateral fissure

occipital lobes
the lobes of the cerebrum at the back of the brain

parietal lobes
the lobes of the cerebrum behind the frontal lobes, in front of the occipital lobes, and above the lateral fissure

temporal lobes
the lobes of the cerebrum located at the temples

FIGURE 1.11
The human cerebrum is divided into the left and right hemispheres, which in turn are divided into four lobes that house various functional areas.

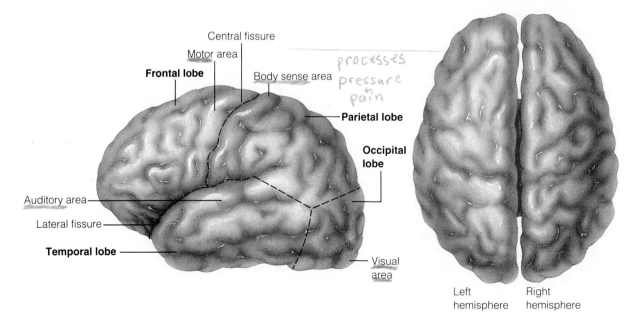

Sensory Areas.   Let's review for just a minute. Receptor cells in our senses respond to stimulus energy from the environment. These cells then pass neural impulses along sensory nerve fibers to the brain. Impulses from senses in our head usually pass through the pons in the brain stem, then up through the thalamus. Senses in our body below our neck first send impulses to the spinal cord. Then, it's up the spinal cord, through the brain stem and thalamus and beyond. After they leave the thalamus, impulses from our senses go to a variety of **sensory areas,** depending on the sense.

Reflecting their relative importance to us, two large areas of the cortex are involved with vision and hearing. Virtually the entire occipital lobe handles visual information, labeled "visual area" in Figure 1.11. Auditory (hearing) impulses end up in large centers in the temporal lobes.

Our body senses (touch, pressure, pain, and so on from different parts of our body) send impulses to a strip at the front of the parietal lobe (labeled "body sense area" in Figure 1.11). Within this area of the parietal lobe, we can map out specific regions of the body. When we do so, we find that some parts of the body—the face, lips, fingers, and so forth—reflecting their sensitivity, are overrepresented in the body sense area of the cerebrum. (In other words, these parts of the body are processed in larger brain areas.) See Figure 1.12 for a drawing of how the body senses are represented in the cerebral cortex.

This is a good place to reintroduce the important concept of **cross-laterality.** This is the term that describes the fact that sensory information from the left side of our body (usually) ends up in the right hemisphere of our cerebral cortex. Likewise, sensory impulses from the right side of our body end up in the left parietal lobe. When someone touches your right hand, that information ends up in the left parietal lobe of your cerebrum. Remember, also, that most crossing over of sensory fibers takes place well below the cerebrum in the brain stem (the medulla and the pons). We'll soon see how cross-laterality can help us to understand the different functions of the two cerebral hemispheres.

Motor Areas.   We have already seen that some of our behaviors—at least very simple and reflexive ones—originate in our central nervous system below the cerebral cortex. Conscious, voluntary cerebral control of muscle activity begins in a strip at the back of our frontal lobes. This **motor area** of the cerebrum is directly across the central fissure from the body sense area in the parietal lobe (see Figure 1.11). (The actual decision-making step of whether or not one should move is probably made toward the front of the frontal lobe.)

Modern research techniques such as electric stimulation (in which parts of the brain are stimulated with electrodes) have allowed us to map out locations in the motor area that control specific muscles or muscle groups. This mapping is also shown in Figure 1.12. As with the body sense mapping, note that different parts of the body, and the muscles serving them, are disproportionally represented in the cerebral cortex's motor area.

We also find cross-laterality with the motor area. It is your left hemisphere's motor area that controls the movements of the right side of your body, and vice versa. As you raise your right arm, impulses instigating that behavior are coming from your left cerebral cortex—from your left motor area.

sensory areas
those areas of the cerebral cortex that receive impulses from our sense receptors

cross-laterality
the principal that, in general, sensory and motor impulses to and from the brain cross from the left side of the body to the right side of the brain, and vice versa

motor area
that portion at the very back of the frontal lobe in which are found the centers that control voluntary movement

FIGURE 1.12
The primary motor and somatosensory areas of the cortex can be mapped out to indicate the specific regions responsible for controlling the various parts of the body.

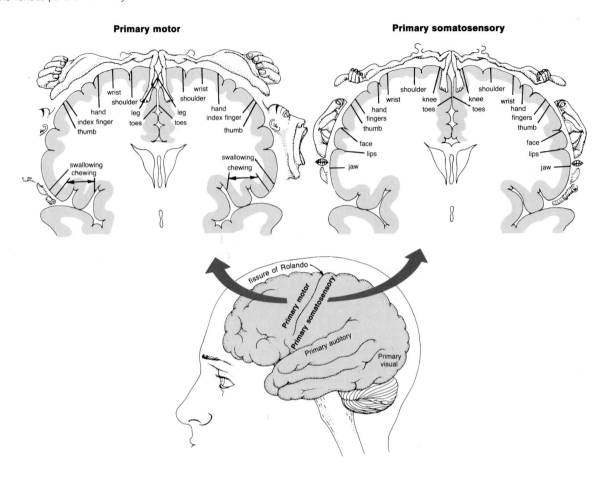

Association Areas.   Once we have located areas of the cerebral cortex that process sensory information and originate motor responses, we find that we've still got a lot of brain left over. The remaining areas of the cerebrum are called **association areas.** There are three of them: frontal, parietal, and temporal. The occipital lobe is so "filled" with vision, there is no room left over for an occipital association area.

Exactly what happens in our association areas is not well understood. We assume that it is here that incoming sensory information is associated with outgoing motor responses—which is why we call these association areas.

There is general support for the idea that it is in our association areas that so-called "higher" mental activities are processed. Frontal association areas (remember there are two of them, left and right) seem to be involved in a number of mental processes. Some language and speech behaviors are located in the left frontal association area. Damage to the frontal lobes seems to interrupt or destroy the ability to plan ahead, to think quickly, or to think things through.

association areas
those areas in the frontal, parietal, and temporal lobes that are neither sensory nor motor in function where cognitive activity is assumed to take place

In this context, we should remember not to get too carried away with cerebral localization of function. Let's not fall into the trap of believing that separate little parts of the cortex operate independently and have the sole responsibility for an important function. This is a point that neurologist Marcel Kinsbourne makes this way: "There are no discontinuities in the brain. No independent channels traverse it, nor is its territory divisible into areas that house autonomous processors" (1982, p. 412). This will be particularly important to remember as we now look at the division of the cerebral cortex into the right and left hemispheres.

BEFORE YOU GO ON

Given a side view of the brain, locate the four lobes of the cerebral cortex.

Locate the primary sensory, motor, and association areas of the cerebrum.

The Two Cerebral Hemispheres

Even the ancient Greeks knew that the cerebral cortex was divided into two major sections or hemispheres. That there should be a division of the cerebrum into two halves seems quite natural. After all, we have two eyes, arms, legs, lungs, kidneys, and so forth. Why not two major divisions of the brain? Within the last 20 years, interest in the division of the cerebral cortex has heightened as we have accumulated information that suggests that each half of the human cerebrum has primary responsibility for different functions.

In most humans, the left hemisphere is usually the larger of the two halves, contains a higher proportion of gray matter, and is thought to be the dominant hemisphere. We have already noted that language behaviors are usually processed in the left cerebral hemisphere. At least this is true for virtually all right-handed people. For some—but not all—left-handers, language may "live" in a dominant right hemisphere. Because humans are so language-oriented, not much attention was given to the lowly right hemisphere. Then, a remarkable surgical procedure, first performed in the 1960s, provided us with new insights about the two cerebral hemispheres (Sperry, 1968; Springer & Deutsch, 1981).

Normally, the two sides of the cerebral cortex are interconnected by a series of fibers called the **corpus callosum** (shown in Figures 1.9 and 1.10). Through the corpus callosum, one side of our cerebrum remains in constant contact with the other. Separating the functions of the two hemispheres is possible through a **split-brain procedure** that is neither as complicated nor as dangerous as it might sound. The procedure amounts to destroying the corpus callosum's connection between the two hemispheres. The procedure was first tried on humans in 1961 by Joseph Bogen in an attempt to lessen the severity of the symptoms of epilepsy. As a treatment of last resort, it was found to be very successful.

Most of what we know about the activities of the cerebral hemispheres we have learned from split-brain subjects—both human and animal. One thing that makes this procedure remarkable is that under normal circumstances, split-brain patients appear to behave quite normally. Only in the laboratory can we clearly see the results of having made the hemispheres of the cerebrum function independently (for example, Gazzaniga & LeDoux, 1978). To be sure, all the answers aren't in, but we can draw some tentative conclusions.

corpus callosum
the network of nerve fibers that sends impulses between the two hemispheres of the cerebrum

split-brain procedure
the surgical procedure of separating the functioning of the two cerebral hemispheres by destroying the corpus callosum

The use of speech and language is a major activity of the left brain.

Experiments with split-brain patients confirm very clearly that speech is a left cerebral hemisphere function in most people. Suppose you have your hands behind your back. If we place a house key in your left hand and ask you to tell us what it is, your left hand will feel the key. Impulses will travel up your left arm and cross over to your *right* cerebral hemisphere—remember cross-laterality. You can readily tell us that the object in your hand is a key because your brain is intact. Your right hemisphere tells your left hemisphere about the key, and your left hemisphere directs you to say "key." If your corpus callosum were cut (if you were a split-brain patient), you couldn't answer our question. Your right brain would know that the object in your left hand is a key, but it would have no way of communicating its knowledge to the speech centers in your left brain. You would be able to pick out the key from among other objects, under the direction of your right cerebral hemisphere; you just wouldn't be able to tell us about it.

So, a major activity of the left brain is the use of speech and language. Simple tasks of calculation are also left hemisphere functions. In addition,

The right cerebral hemisphere is the more creative side, involved with expression and visual imagery.

there is evidence that the left hemisphere is analytical, formalized, and almost rigid in the way it operates. The left hemisphere seems to process information sequentially, handling one thing at a time.

On the other hand, our right hemisphere seems better able to grasp the big picture, to see the overall view of an issue, and to be more creative. It is thought to be more visually and spatially oriented than the left hemisphere. Our right hemisphere is useful in solving spatial relations tasks such as jigsaw puzzles. Its activity involves more visual imagery than does the left hemisphere, and it is believed to be more musical, at least for nonmusicians. Some recent research also suggests that our right cerebral cortex is more involved than our left in our expression and interpretation of emotions.

BEFORE YOU GO ON

Briefly summarize the different functions of the left and right cerebral hemispheres of the human brain.

How is information shared between the left and right cerebral hemispheres?

Though we have learned a great deal about the human brain, its structures, and how it affects our thoughts, feelings, and behaviors, there remain many mysteries to be solved. The methods we have for studying the brain and its activities are becoming more refined and exact as medical technology improves. If nothing else, we have learned not to look for simple answers. We have learned that portions of the brain do not function independently in producing even the most basic of human reactions. Even apparently simple questions about how the brain works and affects us psychologically will require that we have an understanding of a number of interrelated brain structures. This observation will be reinforced in virtually every chapter that follows.

Chapter One
The Biological Bases of Behavior

SUMMARY

Describe the main structural features of a neuron.

What is the role of myelin?

Classify neurons into three major types.

Neurons are microscopically tiny, living cells made up of a cell body, which contains the cell's nucleus, a number of dendrites, and an axon that extends from the cell body. The axons of some neurons are covered with a white, fatty myelin sheath that serves to protect the delicate structure and to speed impulses along the axon. Sensory neurons carry impulses to the central nervous system; motor neurons carry impulses away from the CNS; and interneurons are those found within the CNS. / 39

Describe the basic process involved when a neuron fires.

What is the all-or-none principle?

When a neuron fires, electrical charges (resting potential) are quickly released (action potential). The neuron must then "rest" for awhile (refractory period). The all-or-none principle suggests that the process of a neuron firing either takes place totally, or not at all, that is, there is no such thing as a "partial" firing of a neuron. / 40

Summarize neural impulse transmission at the synapse.

At the synapse, an impulse triggers the release of a neurotransmitter from small vesicles (or containers) found in the axon terminal. These chemicals flood into the synaptic cleft, adhere to the postsynaptic membrane, and either stimulate a new impulse or inhibit impulse transmission. / 43

Reproduce the outline of the nervous systems without looking at it

See Figure 1.5.

What are the major functions of the spinal cord?

How does a spinal reflex work?

The spinal cord transmits neural impulses to and from the brain and is also involved in spinal reflexes. In a spinal reflex, impulses enter the spinal cord on sensory fibers, (may or may not) synapse with interneurons, and then exit the spinal cord on motor fibers to activate a muscle response. At the same time, impulses are sent to the brain on ascending tracts in the white matter. / 48

Name the two brain stem structures, and describe where they are and what they do.

The brain stem is made up of the *medulla*, which controls a number of important reflexes, monitors breathing and heart rate, and is where most cross-laterality occurs, and the *pons*, which acts like a bridge, passing impulses between the spinal cord and the brain. The pons has been found to play an active role in regulating the sleep-wake cycle. / 50

Where is the cerebellum located and what is its major function?

The cerebellum is located at the base of the brain and is most involved in the coordination of muscular responses. / 51

Where are the following structures and what do they do: the RAS, the limbic system, the hypothalamus, and the thalamus?

The RAS (or reticular activating system) extends from the brain stem to the cerebral cortex and is involved in maintaining one's level of arousal. The limbic system, just above the brain stem, is involved in emotional responses (the amygdala and septum, in particular) and the transfer of information to long-term memory storage (the hippocampus). The hypothalamus, which is near the limbic system, is involved in behaviors such as feeding, drinking, sex, aggression, and temperature regulation. The thalamus, which is located just below the cerebral cortex, is a final relay station for sensory messages that get projected to the cerebral cortex. Motor impulses from the cerebrum pass though the thalamus, which has also been implicated in the regulation of sleep and wakefulness. / 53

Given a side view of the brain, locate the four lobes of the cerebral cortex.

Locate the primary sensory, motor, and association areas of the cerebrum.

See Figures 1.11 and 1.12 to review the locations of the lobes of the cerebral cortex and of the primary sensory, motor, and association areas. / 57

Briefly summarize the different functions of the left and right cerebral hemispheres of the human brain.

How is information shared between the left and right cerebral hemispheres?

In most people, the left hemisphere of the cerebrum is primarily concerned with language, sequential thinking, and analytic thinking, while the right hemisphere seems to be more creative, more "global" in its approach to thinking, and more involved in tasks requiring spatial relations abilities. The right hemisphere may also be more involved than the left in emotional responding. The corpus callosum links the two hemispheres of the cerebrum, allowing them to share information. / 59

Chapter One
The Biological Bases of Behavior

REVIEW QUESTIONS

1. You observe a slice of unstained, human spinal cord and can clearly see that the outer portion appears white, compared to the grayer center of the section. What gives this tissue its white appearance?

a. tightly packed cell bodies.

b. concentrations of neurotransmitters.

c. dendrite terminals.

d. myelin-covered axons.

The outer portion of the spinal cord is largely devoted to the transmission of impulses to and from the brain. The coloration of this tissue is due to the white, fatty myelin that covers most axons found there. / 36

2. Which of the following is *true* concerning neural impulses?

a. Within neurons, they travel from cell body to axon to dendrite.

b. They force neurotransmitters into their appropriate vesicles.

c. They occur at different intensities depending on the intensity of the stimulus that produces them.

d. They involve a sudden, rapid change in the electrical charge of a neuron.

Within neurons, impulses typically travel from dendrite to cell body to axon, so (a) is false. Impulses may be said to cause the release of neurotransmitters into the synapse, so (b) is false also. Given the all-or-none principle, we know that (c) is false, which leaves us with (d), a statement that, although somewhat simplistic, is true. / 39

3. Which of the following may be referred to as parts, or divisions of the autonomic nervous system?

a. The brain and the spinal cord.

b. the sympathetic and parasympathetic systems.

c. the endocrine system and the somatic system.

d. the central and peripheral systems.

The autonomic nervous system, or ANS, activates smooth muscles and glands. ANS activity is often very related to endocrine system activity, but its major components are the sympathetic and parasympathetic systems. The brain and spinal cord comprise the central nervous system. If this item gives you trouble, check again with the figure in the text that diagrams all the human nervous systems. / 43

4. In a spinal reflex, the neurons that carry impulses to (or toward) the spinal cord are called:

a. sensory neurons.

b. interneurons.

c. ventral neurons.

d. motor neurons.

Here, the first alternative is the correct one. Impulses from sense receptors travel on sensory neurons to the spinal cord, form a synapse with interneurons within the spinal cord, and leave the spinal cord through the ventral root on motor neurons. / 47

5. As impulses travel up the spinal cord, the first brain structure they encounter is the:

a. pons.

b. cerebral cortex.

c. thalamus.

d. medulla.

This item involves pure anatomy. From the base of the brain upward, the ordering of these structures is medulla, pons, thalamus, and cerebral cortex. / 49

6. If an accident were to damage a person's cerebellum, which of the following symptoms would be most likely?

a. An inability to comprehend and produce language.

b. Major paralysis and a loss of feeling for all body parts below the neck.

c. Poor muscular coordination and/or jerky, tremor-like movements.

d. Partial to complete blindness, depending on the severity of the damage.

Language processing occurs in the cerebral cortex, so (a) is incorrect, although cerebellum damage might cause problems with speech (articulation). Damage to the pons would produce the symptoms described in alternative (b). Vision is processed in the occipital lobe of the cerebral cortex, so the correct answer is (c). Notice that the extensive inter-relatedness of the brain makes this item difficult. The main clue here is the phrase "most likely." / 50

7. Which of the following is *true* concerning the body sense area of the brain?

a. A touch on the left hand sends impulses to the body sense area in the left cerebral hemisphere.

b. It is positioned in the middle of both the left and right frontal lobes.

c. The largest portions of this area are connected to the most sensitive parts of the body.

d. Vision and hearing are represented with the most space in this area because of their importance.

Given the phenomenon of cross-laterality, alternative (a) is false—impulses from the left hand go to the right cerebral hemisphere. The body sense area is in the parietal lobes, not the frontal lobes, so (b) is also false. Vision is represented in the occipital lobe, and hearing is represented in the temporal lobe, not in the body sense area, so (d) is false. This leaves alternative (c) as the correct answer. / 55

8. A split-brain procedure separates the two hemispheres of the cerebral cortex at the corpus callosum, and as a result, a split-brain patient:

a. cannot tell you about an object placed in his or her left hand without looking at it.

b. will almost certainly have to remain institutionalized (that is, hospitalized) for the rest of his or her life.

c. can see spatial relationships, which are formed in the less dominant right hemisphere, more clearly.

d. will have to rely on lower brain centers for most thinking and problem-solving behaviors.

Information from one's left hand is first processed in the right hemisphere of the cerebral cortex. Since in a split-brain patient, that information cannot be transferred over to the left hemisphere, where language is processed (in almost all cases), alternative (a) is acceptable. What about the other choices? Each is essentially false. Split-brain patients are generally indistinguishable from persons who have not had the procedure. Although spatial relationships are generally processed in the right hemisphere, there's no reason to believe that a split-brain procedure would improve abilities in this area. Thinking and problem solving take place in the cerebral cortex, and lower brain centers cannot take over these higher functions. / 57

Chapter Two

Sensation and Perception

Why We Care

The Stimulus For Vision: Light
    Wave Amplitude (Intensity)
    Wavelength
    Wave Purity

The Eye
    Structures that Focus Visual Images
    The Retina

Rods and Cones: A Theory of Vision
    What the Theory Claims
    Evidence to Support the Duplicity Theory
        Dark Adaptation
        The Purkinje Shift

Color Vision

Hearing
    The Stimulus for Hearing: Sound
        Wave Amplitude (Intensity)
        Wave Frequency
        Wave Purity
    The Ear

Other Senses
    The Chemical Senses
        Taste (Gustation)
        Smell (Olfaction)
    The Skin (Cutaneous) Senses
    The Position Senses
    Pain: A Special Sense

Perceptual Selectivity: Paying Attention
    Gestalt Psychology and Figure-ground
    Stimulus Factors
        Contrast
        Repetition
    Personal Factors
        Motivation
        Expectation
        Past Experience

Perceptual Organization
    Stimulus Factors
        Proximity
        Similarity
        Continuity
        Closure
    Personal Factors

The classroom demonstration described below is something of a classic now, though it is potentially dangerous. When the senior author of this text (Gerow) was a graduate student, he had the opportunity to observe the demonstration. He tells the story:

I was able to find a seat in the back of the large introductory psychology class, unnoticed by the more than 600 students who had filed into the lecture hall. The instructor entered the room from a side door at the front and began his lecture on the basic principles of perception. After a few minutes, the class settled down to taking notes and listening to the professor lecture about the importance of attention in perception. The room was very quiet.

Suddenly, a screaming student burst through the large double doors at the rear of the lecture hall. I recognized this student as the professor's graduate student assistant, but no one else in the class knew who he was or what he was doing. I felt that he overacted a bit as he stomped down the center aisle of the lecture hall, yelling the foulest of obscenities at the professor, "Dr. XXXX, you failed me for the last time you *&*&@% so-and-so! You're going to pay for this you *&*&#@%!" Needless to say, the class was stunned. Everyone gasped as the crazed student raced down the

aisle and leaped over the lectern to grab the professor.

The student and the professor struggled briefly, and suddenly—in clear view of everyone—there was a bright silver, chrome-plated revolver! Down behind the lectern they fell. BANG! The sound of a

---

The student and the professor struggled briefly, and suddenly—in clear view of everyone—there was a bright silver, chrome-plated revolver! Down behind the lectern they fell. BANG! The sound of a loud, sharp gunshot filled the room.

---

loud, sharp gunshot filled the room. No one moved; the students were frozen in their seats. The graduate student raced out the same side door that the professor had entered just minutes before. (Here is one dangerous part of this demonstration—ensuring the safe escape of the "assailant.") The professor lay sprawled on the

floor, moaning loudly. (It was now *his* turn for some overacting.)

Still no one moved. Six hundred students sat stunned in their seats. At just the right dramatic moment, the professor slowly drew himself back up to the lectern, and in a quiet voice said, "Now I want everyone to take out a pencil and some paper and write down exactly what you saw." (Here, I suspect, is another dangerous part of the demonstration: Many of the students were quite upset and didn't appreciate having been put through such a trauma just for the sake of a classroom demonstration.)

I'm sure that I need not describe all of the results of this demonstration for you; you can guess what happened. I never did read all 600 descriptions of the events that had just taken place, but I did help summarize many of the responses. The graduate student was described as being from 5'4" to 6'3" tall and weighing between 155 and 235 pounds. Although there was some agreement, one would have a hard time coming up with a single physical description of the "suspect" in this "shooting."

The most remarkable misperception that took place had to do with the gun. As I watched the professor take his place at the front of the class before he began to lecture, I was sure that he had blown the entire demonstration. I clearly saw him remove the pistol from his suitcoat pocket and place it on top of his lecture notes. When the ''crazed student'' crashed into the classroom, the professor reached down, grabbed the gun and pointed it at the student as he came charging down the center aisle. The student *never* had the gun in his hand. The professor had it all along. The first move the student made was to grab the professor's wrist to point the gun toward the floor. The professor fired the shot that startled us all. Fewer than 20 students reported seeing these events the way they actually occurred! Virtually everyone placed the gun in the hand of the crazed student. The perceptions of the students in the psychology class that morning were influenced by a number of factors over and above what actually happened. As we shall note repeatedly in this chapter, seeing and believing are often two separate cognitive processes.

Why We Care

Our study of sensation and perception begins our discussion of how we find out about the world, make judgments about it, learn from it, and remember what we have learned. Sensation is the first of a number of stages involved in the processing of information about our environment. This information enters through our senses as physical energy from the world around us and takes many forms: light, sound, heat, pressure, and so on. We may then define **sensation** as a process that converts the physical energy of the environment into the neural energy of our nervous systems. Everything we know, all of the information we have stored in our memories, at some time or another entered through our senses. Therefore, it is important for us to understand how our senses work, how they take that first step in converting the physical world of our environment into the psychological world we have stored away in our minds.

We will begin our discussion of the various senses with vision because it provides us with so much of our information about the world in which we live. In our coverage of vision, we will first examine the nature of the relevant stimulus, in this case light, and then we'll discuss the relevant sense organ, the eye, and the specific receptors for vision, rods and cones.

After we consider vision, we'll briefly review several other senses, noting the relevant stimulus for each and indicating in general how each sense organ and its receptors work. We'll start with hearing and then move to the chemical senses of taste and smell, the skin senses of touch, pressure, and temperature, and those senses that help us maintain our balance and tell us where different parts of our bodies are positioned. Then we'll examine pain: a sense that is as mysterious as it is important.

sensation
the process of receiving information from the environment and changing that input into nervous system activity

Finally, we'll consider perception—a complex, active, often creative process which acts on stimulation received and recorded by the senses. **Perception** is defined as the selection, organization, and interpretation of stimuli. Thus, perception may be thought of as a more cognitive and central process than sensation.

We'll focus on two of the major issues involved in the psychology of perception. First, we'll deal with the fact that we cannot process fully, at any one time, all the stimuli that we are capable of sensing. Somehow we must select some stimuli while ignoring others and we'll consider some of the factors that determine which stimuli we pay attention to. Second, we'll discuss perceptual organization. Here the issue is how the bits and pieces of information relayed from our sense organs become organized and interpreted as meaningful events.

As we go through this chapter, it will become clear to you that sensation, perception, and memory are very much related. Perception is a process that helps us make sense of the multitude of various stimuli that bombards us every moment of every day. By giving sensory information meaning, perception readies information for storage in memory. In fact, perception may be thought of as bridging the gap between what our senses respond to and what we can later remember.

THE STIMULUS FOR VISION: LIGHT

We don't have to become physicists to understand how vision works, but it will be helpful to have some appreciation of the physical characteristics of light, the stimulus for vision. **Light** can be thought of as a *wave form of radiant energy*. What that means is that light *radiates* from its source in the form of *waves* (which we call light waves). Light waves have a number of physical characteristics that are related to psychological experiences. We will look at three: wave amplitude, wavelength, and wave purity.

Wave Amplitude (Intensity)

One of the ways in which light energy may vary is in its intensity. If we think about light as traveling in the form of waves of energy, differences in intensity correspond to differences in the **wave amplitude** of light. The amplitude of a wave is represented by its height. Refer to Figure 2.1 and assume that the two waves in the drawing represent two different light waves. One of the physical differences between light (A) and light (B) is in the height of the waves, or wave amplitude.

The amplitude of a light wave is the representation of a light's physical intensity. Our *psychological experience* of intensity is what we call **brightness.** The difference between a dim light and a bright light is due to the difference in wave amplitude. Of the two lights in Figure 2.1, (A) has the higher amplitude and thus would be seen as the brighter light. So when we

perception
the cognitive process of selecting, organizing, and interpreting stimuli

light
a radiant energy that can be represented in wave form with wavelengths between 380 and 760 nanometers

wave amplitude
a characteristic of wave forms (the height of the wave) that indicates intensity

brightness
the psychological experience associated with a light's intensity or wave amplitude

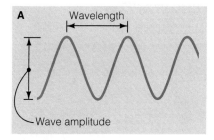

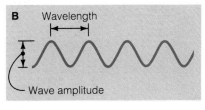

increase the amplitude of a light wave, we experience that as an increase in brightness. For example, dimmer switches that control the brightness of some light fixtures are in essence controlling the amplitude of light waves.

② Wavelength

A second characteristic of waves (such as light waves) is **wavelength,** which is the distance between any point in a wave and the corresponding point on the next cycle—the distance from peak to peak, for example. In Figure 2.1 one difference between waves (A) and (B) is their wavelength, where (A) has the longer wavelength. Although it is difficult to imagine distances so tiny, we *can* measure the length of a light wave. Our unit of measurement here is the **nanometer (nm),** which is equal to one billionth of a meter or one millionth of a millimeter!

As it happens, there are many types of radiant energy that we think of as traveling in waves. However, the human eye only responds to radiant energy in wave form that has a wavelength between (roughly) 380 and 760 nanometers. This is the range of light waves that makes up what we call the visible spectrum. Wave forms of energy with wavelengths shorter than 380nm (such as x-rays and ultraviolet rays) are so short that they do not stimulate the receptor cells in our eyes, and they go unnoticed. Wave forms of energy with wavelengths in excess of 760nm (microwaves and radar are two examples) do not stimulate the receptor cells in our eyes either.

We have seen that wave amplitude determines our experience of brightness. Wavelength is the attribute of light that determines the **hue,** or color we perceive. As light waves increase in length from the short 380nm wavelengths to the long 760nm lengths, our experience of them changes—from violet to blue to green to yellow-green to yellow to orange to red along the color spectrum (see Figure 2.2).

A source of radiant energy with a 700 nanometer wavelength will be seen as a red light. (A bright red light has a high amplitude, and a dim red light has a low amplitude, but both have 700nm wavelengths.) As we can see from Figure 2.2 if a light generated waves 550nm long, it would be seen as a yellow-green light, and so on. (Notice that yellow-green is a single hue

wavelength
a characteristic of wave forms that indicates the distance between any point on a wave and the corresponding point on the next cycle of the wave

nanometer (nm)
the unit of measurement for the wavelength of light, equal to one millionth of a millimeter

hue
the psychological experience associated with a light's wavelength

FIGURE 2.2
The visible spectrum, in which wavelengths of approximately 380–760 nanometers are visible to the human eye and are perceived as various hues. (Based on Lindsay & Norman, 1977.)

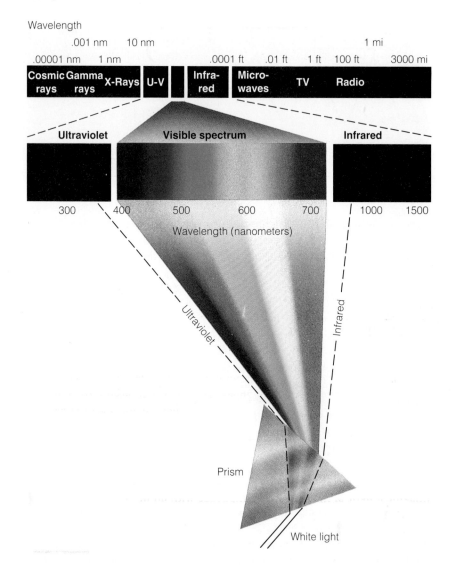

produced by a given wavelength of light. It is *not* some sort of combination of yellow and green. We simply have no other name for this hue, so we call it yellow-green.)

Given what we have so far, let me present you with an apparently simple problem: "I have two lights, one red (700nm) and the other yellow-green (550nm). I've adjusted the *amplitudes* of these two light sources so that they are exactly *equal.* They are of different hues because their wavelengths are different. What about their brightness? With both amplitudes equal, will the lights appear equally bright?"

As a matter of fact, they won't. The yellow-green light will appear much brighter than the red light. We seem to have a problem here with perceived

FIGURE 2.3
The apparent brightness of lights of different wavelength, assuming that all amplitudes are equal.

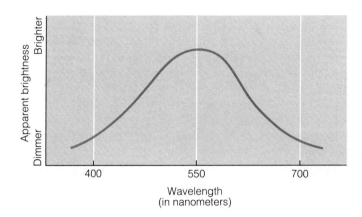

brightness. We say that wavelength and wave amplitude *interact* to produce apparent brightness. Wavelengths of light in the middle of the range of visible spectrum (such as yellow-green) appear brighter than do wavelengths of light from the extremes—*if* their amplitudes are equal.

I can get a red light to appear as bright as a yellow-green one, of course, but to do so I'll have to increase its amplitude (or physical intensity, if you prefer). What all this means is that, with *everything else being equal,* lights of different wavelengths may not appear equally bright, even if their amplitudes are equal. This relationship between wavelength and apparent brightness is shown in Figure 2.3.

③ Wave Purity

Imagine a light of medium wave amplitude with all its wavelengths exactly 700 nanometers long. The light would be of medium brightness. And because the wavelengths are all 700nm long, it would appear red. More than that, it would appear as a pure, rich red. We call such a light **monochromatic,** or pure, because it is made up of light waves all of one (mono) length or hue (chroma). In truth, we seldom see such lights outside the laboratory because producing a pure light is an expensive thing to do.

Even the reddest of red lights that we see in our everyday experience have other wavelengths of light mixed in along with the predominant 700nm red. (If the 700nm light wave did not predominate, the light wouldn't look red at all!) Even the red light on top of a police car has some violet and green and yellow wavelengths of light in it.

The physical purity of a light source determines the psychological characteristic that we call **saturation.** Pure, monochromatic lights are the most highly saturated; their hue is rich and obvious. As more and more different wavelengths get mixed into a light, it becomes lower and lower in saturation—and it starts to look pale and washed out.

monochromatic
literally *"one colored,"* a pure light made up of light waves all of the same wavelength

saturation
the psychological experience associated with the purity of a light wave, where the most saturated lights are monochromatic and the least saturated are white light

white light
a light of the lowest possible
saturation, containing a mixture of
all visible wavelengths

Here's a question: "What do we call a light that is of the lowest possible saturation; a light that contains a random mixture of *all* possible wavelengths of light?" By definition, that is what **white light** is. It is something of a curiosity that white light is in fact as *impure* a light as possible. A pure light has but one wavelength; a white light contains all the wavelengths.

True white light is as difficult (and as expensive) to produce as is a pure monochromatic light. Fluorescent light bulbs are reasonable approximations, but they still contain too many wavelengths from the short (or blue-violet) end of the spectrum. Regular incandescent light bulbs contain too many light waves from the orange and red end of the spectrum. A prism can take a beam of white light—sunlight is a reasonable approximation—and break it down into its various parts, giving us the experience of a rainbow of hues. Where did all those hues come from? They were there all along—mixed together to form the white light.

We have seen that three major characteristics of light influence the nature of our visual experience. Wave amplitude is the primary determinant of brightness, wavelength determines hue, and wave purity determines saturation. These relationships are summarized in Figure 2.4, and all three dimensions are represented in the color solid presented in Figure 2.5.

FIGURE 2.4
The physical characteristics of light waves influence our psychological experience of light.

Important

Physical characteristic	Psychological experience
Wave amplitude (intensity)	Brightness
Wave length	Hue
Wave purity	Saturation

These two interact

BEFORE YOU GO ON In what ways do the major physical characteristics of light waves of energy (amplitude, length, and purity) affect our psychological experience of light?

FIGURE 2.5
The color tree illustrates the psychological experiences of light: the circumference of the tree illustrates the experience of hue, the radius illustrates saturation, and the arrangement of "leaves" from top to bottom illustrates brightness.

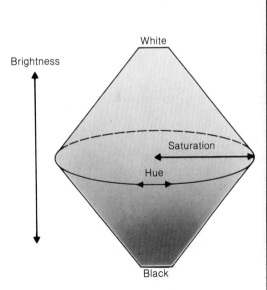

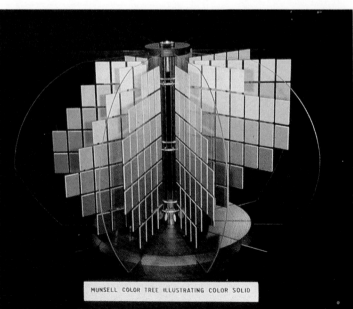

MUNSELL COLOR TREE ILLUSTRATING COLOR SOLID

THE EYE

Vision involves changing light wave energy into the neural energy of the nervous system. This transformation of energy takes place in the eye. Yet most of the structures of the eye have very little to do with the actual process of converting light energy into neural energy. Instead, they are there to ensure that the light waves that enter the eye are well focused by the time they get back to the layer of cells that directly responds to light waves.

Structures that Focus Visual Images

Using Figure 2.6 as a guide, let's trace the path of light as it passes through a number of structures, ultimately to produce a visual experience. Light first enters the eye through the **cornea.** The cornea is the tough, round, virtually transparent outer shell of the eye. Those of you who wear contact lenses float them on your corneas. The cornea has two major functions. One is to serve as a protector of the delicate structures behind it. The other is to start bending the entering light waves in order to focus an image on the back surface of the eye.

Having passed through the cornea, light then travels through the **pupil** which is an opening in the **iris.** The iris is that part of your eye which is pigmented, or colored. When we say that someone has blue, brown, or green eyes, we are really referring to the color of the iris. The iris contracts or expands, changing the size of the pupil. This is largely a reflexive reaction. It's not something you can control by conscious effort. Contractions of the

cornea
the outermost structure of the eye that protects the eye and begins to focus light waves

pupil
the opening in the iris that changes size in relation to the amount of light available and emotional factors

iris
the colored structure of the eye that reflexively opens or constricts the pupils

FIGURE 2.6
The major structures of the human eye.

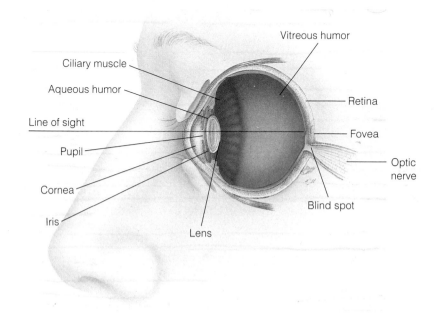

FIGURE 2.7
Sightedness. (A) Normal vision, where the inverted image is focused by the cornea and lens on the retina. (B) Nearsightedness, where the focused image falls short of the retina because the eyeball is too rounded. (C) Farsightedness, where the focused image falls beyond the retina because the eyeball is too short or the lens too flattened.

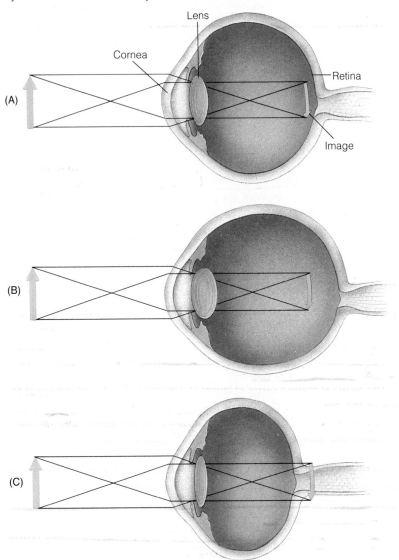

iris that change pupil size are most commonly made in response to the level of light present—opening the pupil wide when only small amounts of light are present and reducing its size (protectively) in response to high-intensity lights. Increasing pupil size is also one of the automatic responses that occurs with heightened levels of emotionality.

After the pupil, the next structure light encounters is the **lens.** As in a camera, the main function of the lens of the eye is to *focus* a visual image. The lens changes shape to bring an image into focus—becoming flatter when we try to focus on an object at a distance and becoming fatter, or rounder, when we try to view something up close. This too is largely a

lens
the structure behind the iris that changes shape to focus visual images in the eye

reflexive reaction. It is obvious that our lenses are not normally as hard as glass or they wouldn't be able to change shape. (Sometimes, with age, our lenses do tend to harden, making it difficult to focus and requiring that we use glasses to help out.)

Some very powerful little muscles control the shape of our lens. They are called **ciliary muscles,** and they push and pull the lens to change its shape. The process in which the ciliary muscles change the shape of the lens is called **accommodation.** It is often the case that an image does not focus as it should—either because of the shape of the lens or the eye itself or a failure of accommodation. The result is nearsightedness or farsightedness. Figure 2.7 shows examples of what happens in these cases.

There is a space between the cornea and the lens that is filled with a clear fluid called **aqueous humor.** This humor (which means "fluid") provides nourishment to the cornea and the other structures at the front of the eye. This aqueous humor is constantly being produced and supplied to the space behind the cornea, filtering out blood to keep the fluid clear.

There is another, larger space *behind* the lens that is also filled with a fluid or humor. This fluid is called **vitreous humor.** It is not nearly as watery as aqueous humor. It is thick and filled with tiny structures that give it substance. Its major function is to keep the eyeball rounded.

The Retina

So far we've mentioned a number of structures, each important in its own way, but none of them doing much more than allowing light waves back through the eye to other structures, perhaps in more focused form. It is at the **retina** of the eye that vision begins to take place. Here, light energy is changed into neural energy.

The retina is really a series of layers of very specialized cells located at the back of the eye. These cells are nerve cells, and in a true sense should be thought of as part of the brain. The location of the retina and its major landmarks are shown in Figure 2.6, while Figure 2.8 (on next page) shows the retina in more detail.

To describe the retina, let's change directions and move from back to front. The layer of cells at the very back of the retina are the light-sensitive cells, or **photoreceptors,** of the eye. It is here that lightwave energy is transformed into neural energy.

As it happens, there are two types of photoreceptor cells in this retinal layer: **rods** and **cones.** They are very aptly named, because that's just what they look like: small rods and cones. Their ends or tips respond to lightwave energy and begin a neural impulse. These impulses travel down the rods and cones and pass on to (technically, synapse with) a number of other cells, also arranged in layers.

At these layers of nerve cells there is considerable combination and integration of neural impulses. Each rod and each cone does not have a single direct pathway to the brain. Impulses from many rods and cones are combined right in the eye (by *bipolar cells* and *ganglion cells,* among others). Fibers from ganglion cells gather together to form the **optic nerve,** which leaves the eye and starts back toward other parts of the brain.

Notice again the arrow in Figure 2.8 that indicates the direction of the light entering the retina. It is correctly drawn. Yes, light waves first pass

ciliary muscles
small muscles attached to the lens that control its shape, and focusing capability

accommodation
the process in which the ciliary muscles change the shape of the lens in order to focus a visual image

aqueous humor
watery fluid found in the space between the cornea and the lens that nourishes the front of the eye

vitreous humor
the thick fluid behind the lens of the eye that helps keep the eyeball spherical

retina
layers of cells at the back of the eye that contain the photosensitive rod and cone cells

photoreceptors
light-sensitive cells (cones and rods) of the retina that convert light energy into neural energy

rods
photosensitive cells of the retina that are most active in low levels of illumination and do not respond differentially to different wavelengths of light

cones
photosensitive cells of the retina that operate best at high levels of illumination and are responsible for color perception

optic nerve
the fiber of many neurons that leaves the eye and carries impulses to the occipital lobe of the brain

FIGURE 2.8
The major features of the human retina.

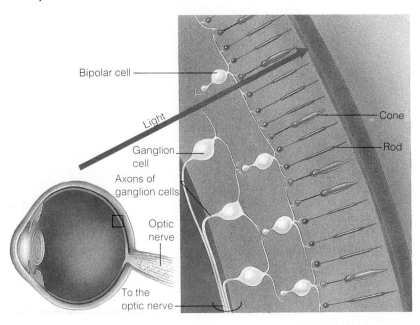

Bipolar cell

Light

Cone

Ganglion cell

Rod

Axons of ganglion cells

Optic nerve

To the optic nerve

through all those layers of cells to reach the tips of the rods and cones where they are transformed into neural impulses. The layering of cellular structures in the retina does seem to be somewhat inside-out. It would seem to make more sense to point the light-sensitive tips of the rods and cones out toward the incoming light, yet virtually all mammalian retinas are constructed in the manner shown in Figure 2.8.

The two main structures of the retina that are depicted in the overview of Figure 2.6 are the **fovea** and the **blindspot.** The fovea is a small area of the retina where there are very few layers of cells between the entering light and the cone cells that fill the area. There are no rods in the fovea, only cones. And the cones of the fovea are unusually tightly packed together. It is here at the fovea that our vision is best, that our *acuity,* or ability to discern detail, is best—at least in daylight or in reasonably high levels of illumination. If you were to try to thread a needle, you would want to focus the image of the needle and thread directly on the fovea.

The blindspot of the retina is where the nerve impulses from the rods and cones, having passed through all those other layers of cells, exit the eye. At the blindspot, there are no rods and cones—there's nothing there but the optic nerve threading its way back deeper into the brain. Because there are no rods or cones, there is no vision here, which is why we call this the blindspot. Every eye has to have a blindspot. Figure 2.9 provides you with a way to locate your own blindspot.

The eye is a marvelous organ. Most of its structures focus an image on the photosensitive rods and cones of the retinal layer at the back of the eye. If you think about all that light has to go through to get to the rods and cones, you have to wonder how it is that we can see *anything* clearly. The corneas of our eyes are seldom perfectly rounded, and they are often scratched or cov-

fovea
the region at the center of the retina, comprised solely of cones, where acuity is best in daylight

blindspot
the region of the retina, containing no photoreceptors, where the optic nerve leaves the eye

FIGURE 2.9
Finding your blindspot. (A) Close your right eye and stare at the cross. Hold the page about a foot from your eye. Move the page until the star falls on your blindspot and disappears. (B) Close your right eye and stare at the cross. Hold the page about a foot from your left eye and move the page until the break in the line falls on your blindspot. The line will look unbroken.

(A)

(B)

ered with dust and dirt. Aqueous humor is also filled with small particles of impurities. Light has to pass through a lens that is seldom perfectly shaped (most have flat spots and lumps that distort images). Then light has to go through a large volume of vitreous humor that contains all sorts of small structures and particles that can interfere with it. And finally, the light must pass through layer after layer of nerve cells (and the blood vessels that serve them) before reaching its destination at the rods and cones.

List the major structures of the eye and describe the function of each.

BEFORE YOU GO ON

RODS AND CONES: A THEORY OF VISION

It may have already struck you as odd that there are two separate photosensitive receptor cells in the retina of the eye: rods and cones. They are clearly different in their structure, as we have noted. Not only are there two different kinds of receptor cells in our retinas, but they are not there in equal numbers. In each eye, there are approximately 120 million rods, but only 6 million cones, which means that rods outnumber cones in a ratio of about 20 to 1.

Not only are rods and cones found in unequal numbers, but they are not evenly distributed throughout the retina. As we have already indicated, cones tend to be concentrated in the center of the retina, at the fovea. Rods are concentrated in a band surrounding the fovea, out toward the periphery of the retina, which is why this area is called the *peripheral retina*.

What the Theory Claims

These observations have led psychologists to wonder if the rods and cones of our eyes have different functions. They don't look alike. They're not found in equal numbers. They're not evenly distributed throughout the retina. Maybe they function differently. The theory that our rods and cones have different (duplicitous) functions is called the **duplicity theory of vision.**

duplicity theory of vision
the theory that rods and cones have different functions

The evidence supports the belief that cones function best in high levels of illumination (as in daylight) and are primarily responsible for our experience of color. On the other hand, our rods operate best under conditions of reduced illumination. This means that they are more sensitive to low-intensity lights. However, they do not discriminate among wavelengths of light, responding in essentially the same way to all visible wavelengths. This means that rods do not contribute to our appreciation of color.

Evidence to Support the Duplicity Theory

Some of the evidence supporting this point of view can be verified by our own experiences. Don't you find it difficult to distinguish among different colors at night or in the dark? The next time you are at the movies eating some pieces of candy that are of different colors, see if you can tell them apart without holding them up to the light of the projector. You probably won't be able to tell a green piece from a red one—something of a problem if you happen to have a favorite flavor. You can't discriminate colors well in a dark movie theater because you are seeing primarily with your rods, which are very good at seeing in the reduced light of the theater but which don't respond differentially to different wavelengths of light.

If you are looking for something small outside at night, you will probably not see it if you look directly at it. Say you're changing a tire along the road at night. You're replacing the wheel and can't find one of the lug nuts that you know is there someplace in the gravel. If you were to look directly at it, the image of the nut would fall on your fovea. Your fovea is made up almost entirely of cones. Cones do not operate well in relative darkness, and you'll not see the nut. To have the best chance of finding it, you have to get the image of the nut to fall on the periphery of your eye where your rods are concentrated (in that peripheral retina).

One of the reasons why nocturnal animals (such as many varieties of owls) get along so well at night is that they can see very well in the dark. They see so well because their retinas are packed with rods. Such animals necessarily have fewer cones and are demonstrably color-blind. Let's now examine two additional pieces of experimental evidence that support the view that our rods and cones have different functions.

Dark Adaptation.   One piece of evidence that supports the duplicity Theory of vision comes from the way that our eyes adapt to the dark. The phenomenon is a familiar one. You walk into a movie theater for a matinee on a sunny afternoon and at first cannot see much of anything. In a few minutes, you can make out some rough forms, so you may not trample anyone on the way to your seat. After about 20 or 30 minutes, you find that you are seeing rather well—about as well as you can in the darkened environment. Up to a point, the longer we stay in the dark, the more sensitive our eyes become to what light *is* available. (If the environment were entirely dark, with no light available, you would not see anything, no matter how long you waited. The stimulus for vision is light, remember.)

Figure 2.10 is a graphic representation of the dark adaptation process. With time spent in the dark, our sensitivity increases, or our *threshold* decreases. The term threshold refers to the least amount of light required to produce a visual experience. At first, we can only see very bright lights (say,

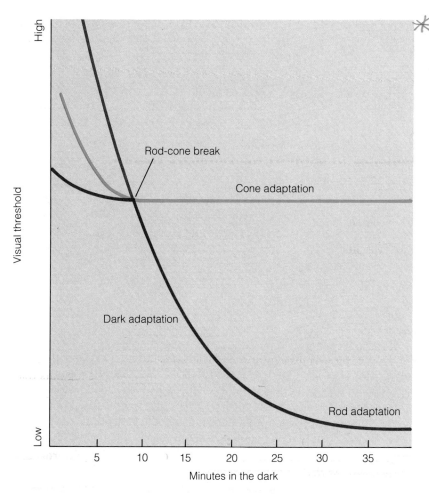

the light reflected from the movie screen), then dimmer lights (those reflected from people in the theatre), and then still dimmer ones (those reflected from your pieces of candy perhaps) are detected. As Figure 2.10 indicates, the whole process takes about 20 to 30 minutes.

But there is something strange going on. The dark adaptation curve is not a smooth, regular one. At about the 7-minute mark, there is a change in the shape of the curve. This break in the smoothness of the curve is called the *rod-cone break*. At first, and for 6 or 7 minutes, both rods *and* cones increase their sensitivity (represented by the first part of the curve). But our cones are basically daylight receptors. They're just not cut out for seeing in the dark, and after that first few minutes, they have become as sensitive as they are going to get. The rods, on the other hand, become more and more sensitive (represented by the second part of the curve).

The Purkinje Shift. Further evidence in support of the duplicity theory of vision comes from a phenomenon first described in 1825 by a Czech biologist, Johannes Purkinje. It is called the **Purkinje shift.** The Purkinje shift explains the change in the perceived brightness of lights as a function of overall light levels. That is, lights seem to change their apparent brightness as daylight changes to twilight. Let's explore this in a little more detail.

Purkinje shift
the phenomenon of perceived levels of relative brightness changing as a function of level of illumination

FIGURE 2.11

Perceived relative brightness is a function of wavelength for both daylight (cone) vision and twilight (rod) vision, illustrating the Purkinje shift.

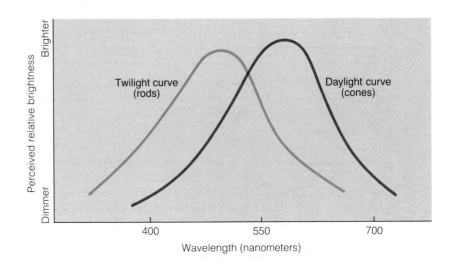

Because we know where the rods and cones of the human eye are located, we can stimulate each kind of receptor cell independently. We can test the sensitivity of rods and cones to lights of different intensity and wavelength. When this is done, it turns out that our rods, as we've been saying all along, are much more sensitive to low-intensity lights than are our cones, regardless of the wavelength of the light. What is curious is that the wavelength of light used to test sensitivity *does* make a difference, depending on which type of cell we are testing. Cones reach their maximum sensitivity when they are stimulated by wavelengths of light from the long end of the spectrum—toward the yellows and oranges. Rods, on the other hand, are most sensitive to wavelengths more toward the middle of the spectrum—toward the greens and blue-green.

Suppose that we have an apparatus (call it a rainbow generator) that produces all the wavelengths of light of the visible spectrum, from 380 to 760 nanometers. We adjust all of the wavelengths of light so that their intensities (amplitudes) are exactly equal and quite high. What will you see when we turn on the device? You'll see a rainbow of bright light from violet on the left to red on the right. It will look like a rainbow because of the gradual change in wavelengths from 380nm to 760nm, and it will appear bright because we have adjusted wave amplitudes to be high. And because all of the wave amplitudes are equal, they will not appear equally bright (we've already established that light wave amplitude and length interact to produce the impression of brightness). Now we lower the amplitudes of all the lights in the rainbow generator, and the relative brightness of the lights in the rainbow shift toward the left, toward the blue end of the spectrum (see Figure 2.11). This is the Purkinje shift.

Notice in Figure 2.11 that the shift toward the shorter wavelengths in reduced illumination is so large that the rods are shown as insensitive to the longer (red) wavelengths. Indeed, rods do not respond to red light. Among other things, that may lead you to wonder why we paint emergency vehicles like fire trucks and ambulances red. As a matter of fact, as you may have noticed, we don't anymore. More and more emergency vehicles are being painted a gaudy yellow-green. (And even police cars are now equipped with blue—not red—flashing lights.) The fact that red is more difficult to see than yellow-green, particularly at night, is not a new discovery. Why then did we ever paint fire trucks red? The answer is probably learning and experience: We have generations of people who have simply learned to associate red with danger. What we need to do now is train new generations to associate yellow-green and blue with danger.

To demonstrate the Purkinje shift, we don't need to use apparatus as fancy as a rainbow generator. You only need to look closely at a red flower and its green leaves on a bright, sunny day as sunset approaches. Note the relative brightness of the red and the green. Look at the same flower shortly after sunset and note the change in the relative brightness of the blossom and the leaves. Although the green leaves (to which the rods are sensitive) are still relatively bright, the red flower (to which the cones are sensitive) now appears quite dark, almost black. This is just the phenomenon which Purkinje noted back in 1825, except that he compared the relative brightnesses of red and blue-violet flowers.

In a literal sense then, we might claim that the rods and the cones of our retinas perform two different functions. Cones, concentrated in our foveas, work best in high levels of illumination and respond differentially to different wavelengths of light. Rods, concentrated in the peripheral retina, do not respond differentially to different wavelengths of light, but do respond to lower levels of illumination or light intensity.

What is the duplicity theory of vision, and what evidence can you cite to support it? **BEFORE YOU GO ON**

COLOR VISION

Explaining how the eye codes (responds to) different intensities of light is not too difficult. Coding is largely handled by the frequency of the firing of the receptor cells in the retina. High-intensity lights cause more rapid firings of neural impulses than do low-intensity lights. How the eye codes different wavelengths of light to produce different experiences of color, however, is another story. Here things are not simple at all. To be honest about it, we should say that we really don't know exactly how the process occurs. We do have two theories of color vision that have received research support, even though both theories were proposed many years ago. As is often the case with competing theories that try to explain the same phenomenon, both are probably partially correct.

The older of the two theories of color vision is called the *trichromatic theory.* It was first proposed by Thomas Young early in the nineteenth century and was then revised by Hermann von Helmholtz, the noted physiologist, about 50 years later. As its name suggests, the *tri*chromatic theory proposes that the eye contains *three* separate and distinct receptors for color. Although there is considerable overlap, each type of receptor responds best to one of three **primary colors** of light: red, green, and blue. These colors are primary because by the careful combination of these three wave-

(Von Helmholtz)

primary colors
red, green, and blue; those colors (of light) from which all others can be produced

FIGURE 2.12
The relative sensitivities of three different kinds of cones to light of different wavelengths. Note that although there is considerable overlap, each cell is maximally sensitive to different wavelengths (or colors).

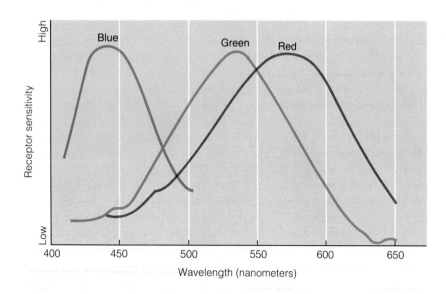

lengths of light, all other colors can be produced. Your television screen works on this principle. The picture on your TV screen is made up of a pattern of very small dots, each one being either red, green, or blue, of a given intensity. From these three wavelengths, all other colors are constructed, or integrated.

Because the sensitivity of the three types of receptors in our eyes overlaps, when our eyes are stimulated by a nonprimary color, such as orange, the orange-hued light will stimulate each receptor to varying degrees in such a way as to produce the sensation of orange. What gives this theory credibility is that there really *are* such receptor cells in the human retina. Obviously, they are cones (which are responsible for color vision). The relative sensitivity of these three cone systems is shown in Figure 2.12.

Ewald Hering thought that the Young-Helmholtz theory left a good bit to be desired, and in 1870 he proposed a theory of his own. This theory has come to be called the *opponent-process theory*. Hering's theory suggests that there are three *pairs* of visual mechanisms that respond to different light wave characteristics. One mechanism is a blue-yellow processor, one a red-green processor, and the third deals with black-white differences.

Each mechanism is capable of responding to *either* of the two characteristics that give it its name, but not to both. That is, the blue-yellow processor can respond to blue *or* to yellow, but can't handle both at the same time. The second mechanism responds to red *or* green, but not both. The third processor codes brightness. Thus, the members of each pair work to oppose each other, giving the theory its name. If blue is excited, then yellow is inhibited. If red is excited, then green is inhibited. A light may appear to be a mixture of red and yellow perhaps, but cannot be seen as a mixture of blue *and* yellow, because both blue and yellow cannot be excited at the same time. (It is rather difficult to imagine what a "reddish-green" or a "bluish-yellow"

FIGURE 2.13
To illustrate the experience of color fatigue, stare at the green figure for 30 seconds, and then shift your gaze to a completely white surface. You should see the same figure, but it will appear red because the green receptors are fatigued. Now try the same experiment with the blue figure. What color do you see when you shift your gaze?

(Herings)
Negative
Afterimages

would look like, isn't it? Can you picture a light that is bright and dim at the same time?)

Support for Hering's theory comes from our experiences with *negative afterimages*. If you stare at a bright green figure for a few minutes and then shift your gaze to a white surface, you will notice an image of a red figure. The explanation for the appearance of this image is as follows: While you were staring at the green figure, the green component of the red-green process became fatigued because of all the stimulation it was getting. When you stared at the white surface, both the red and green components of the process were equally stimulated, but because the green component was fatigued, the red predominated, producing the experience of seeing a red figure. (Figure 2.13 provides an example for you to try.)

Hering's theory also makes some observations about colorblindness sensible. Although some people are totally colorblind, much more commonly, people are blind to only certain wavelengths of light. Blindness to colors usually occurs in pairs: Some people are red-green colorblind, and some (fewer) are yellow-blue colorblind, suggesting a problem with one of the opponent-process mechanisms. (Two sample items that screen for colorblindness are presented in Figure 2.14.)

It is also the case that excitatory-inhibitory mechanisms such as Hering proposed for red-green, blue-yellow, and black-white have been found. As it happens, they are not at the level of rods and cones in the retina (as Hering had thought), but at the layer of the ganglion cells (see again, Figure 2.8) and also in a small portion of the thalamus called the *lateral geniculate body*.

Because cone cell systems have been found in the retina that respond differentially to red, blue, and green light, we cannot dismiss the trichromatic theory. Because there are cells that do operate the way the opponent-process theory predicts, we cannot dismiss this theory either. Well, which one is right? Probably they both are. Our experience of color probably depends upon the interaction of different cone cells *and* different ganglion cells in our retinas—a marvelous system indeed.

Briefly summarize the trichromatic and the opponent-process theories of color vision   **BEFORE YOU GO**

FIGURE 2.14
An illustration of the effect of red-green color-blindness. People with normal vision will be able to distinguish the images from the backgrounds, while people who are red-green color-blind will not.

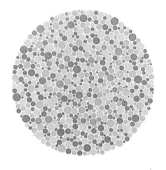 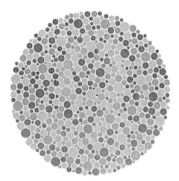

So far in this discussion of the process of sensation, we have summarized the physical characteristics of light, and examined how those characteristics affect our experience. We've seen how the minute and complex structures of our eyes pass a range of wave form energies in focused form to the photoreceptors of our retinas, where they are transformed into the visual representations of the world we live in. Next we'll go on to explore the other senses and see how they change various forms of physical energy into the energy of the nervous system.

HEARING

Hearing (or more formally, *audition*) provides us with nearly as much information about our environment as vision. One of its main roles is its involvement in our development of language and speech. Without hearing, these uniquely human skills are difficult to acquire.

The Stimulus for Hearing: Sound

The stimulus for vision is light; for hearing, the stimulus is sound. Sound is made up of a series of pressures of air (or some other medium, such as water) against our ear. We can represent these pressures as a sound wave. As a source of sound vibrates, it pushes molecules of air against our ears. Figure 2.15 shows how sound may be depicted as a wave form of energy.

As was the case for light waves, there are three major physical characteristics of sound waves—amplitude, frequency (the inverse of wavelength), and purity—and each of them is related to a different psychological experience. Let's briefly consider each in turn.

Wave Amplitude (Intensity). The amplitude of a sound wave depicts its intensity—the force with which the air strikes our ear. The physical intensity of a sound determines the psychological experience we call **loudness.** That is, the higher its amplitude, the louder we perceive the sound to be. Soft, quiet sounds have low amplitudes (see Figure 2.16).

FIGURE 2.15
Sound waves are produced as air pressure is spread by the tine of a tuning fork vibrating to the right (a) and left (b). The point of greatest pressure is the high point of the wave; least pressure is indicated by the low point of the wave.

(a) (b) (a) (b) (a) (b) (a) (b)

loudness
the psychological experience correlated with the intensity, or amplitude, of a sound wave

FIGURE 2.16
An illustration of how the physical characteristics of sound waves influence our psychological experiences of sound. (1) Though waves (A) and (B) have the same frequency, wave (A) has a higher amplitude and would be experienced as a louder sound. (2) Though waves (B) and (C) have the same amplitude, wave (C) would be experienced as having a higher pitch because of its greater frequency.

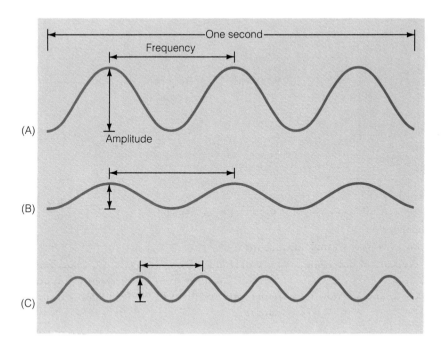

Measurements of the physical intensity of sound are given in units of force per unit area (which is really pressure, of course). Loudness is a psychological characteristic. It is measured by people, not by instruments. The **decibel scale** of sound intensity has been constructed so that it reflects perceived loudness in humans. Its zero point is the lowest intensity of sound that can be detected. Our ears are very sensitive receptors and respond to very low levels of sound intensity. (In fact, if our ears were much more sensitive, we could hear molecules of air bouncing off our eardrums.) Sounds that are louder than those produced by jet aircraft engines or fast moving subway trains (around 120 decibels) are experienced more as pain than as sound. Figure 2.17 lists decibel levels for some of the sounds we might find in our environment.

0–140

decibel scale
a scale of our experience of loudness in which 0 represents the absolute threshold and 140 is sensed as pain

Wave Frequency. When we discussed light, we noted that wavelength was responsible for our perception of hue. With sound, we use *wave frequency* rather than wavelength. Wave frequency is a measure of the number of times a wave repeats itself within a given period of time, usually one second. For sound, frequency is measured in terms of how many waves of pressure are exerted every second. The unit of sound frequency is the **Hertz,** abbreviated **Hz.** If a sound wave repeats itself 50 times in one second, it is a 50Hz sound; 500 repetitions is a 500Hz sound, and so on.

If you keep in mind where sounds come from, it is clear that a 50Hz sound, for example, is being produced by something that is vibrating back

20–20,000 Hz

hertz (Hz)
the standard measure of sound wave frequency that is the number of wave cycles per second

Hearing **85**

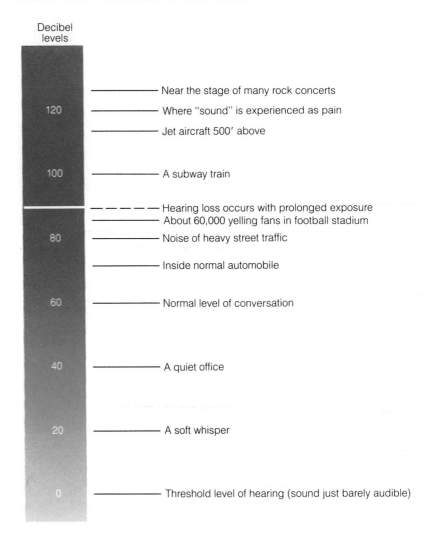

FIGURE 2.17
Loudness values in decibel units for various sounds.

Decibel
levels

120 — Near the stage of many rock concerts
— Where "sound" is experienced as pain
— Jet aircraft 500' above

100 — A subway train

- - - - — Hearing loss occurs with prolonged exposure
— About 60,000 yelling fans in football stadium
80 — Noise of heavy street traffic

— Inside normal automobile

60 — Normal level of conversation

40 — A quiet office

20 — A soft whisper

0 — Threshold level of hearing (sound just barely audible)

and forth, creating pressure changes in the air at the rate of 50 per second. Waves of different frequency are shown in Figure 2.16, where you can see the relationship between wavelength and frequency.

The psychological experience corresponding to sound wave frequency is **pitch.** Pitch is our experience of how high or low a tone is. The musical scale represents differences in pitch to the human ear. Low frequencies correspond to low, bass sounds, such as those produced by foghorns or tubas. High-frequency vibrations give rise to the experience of high-pitched sounds, such as the musical tones produced by flutes or the squeals of smoke detectors.

Just as the human eye cannot respond to all possible wavelengths of radiant energy, so the human ear cannot respond to all possible sound wave frequencies. The good, undamaged human ear responds to sound wave frequencies between 20 and 20,000Hz. If air strikes our ears at a rate less than

pitch
the psychological experience that corresponds to sound wave frequency and gives rise to high (treble) or low (bass) sounds

20 times per second, we'll not hear. Sound vibrations much faster than 20,000 cycles per second usually cannot be heard either—at least by the human ear. Many animals, including dogs, *can* hear sounds with frequencies above 20,000Hz, such as those produced by dog whistles.

You will recall that for light, wave amplitude and wavelength interact so that lights of different wavelengths do not appear to be equally bright, even if all their intensities are adjusted to be equal. We have the same sort of interaction when we deal with sound and sound waves. Sound wave intensities and frequencies interact to produce our sensation of loudness.

What this means is that all wave frequencies of sound do not sound equally loud (a psychological experience) even if all their intensities are equal (a physical reality). That is, sounds of very high and very low frequency do not seem as loud as sounds from the middle range of audible frequencies, everything else being equal. Put another way, to have a high frequency sound appear as loud as a medium frequency sound, we would have to raise the amplitude of the high-frequency sound. Fortunately, most of the sounds that are most relevant to us everyday—speech sounds, for example—are usually of mid-range frequency and thus are easily heard.

3 **Wave Purity.** A third characteristic of sound waves that we need to consider is wave purity (or its opposite, complexity). You'll recall that we seldom experience pure, monochromatic lights. Pure sounds are also uncommon in our experience. A pure sound would be one in which *all* of the waves from the sound source were vibrating at exactly the same frequency. Such sounds can be produced electronically, and tuning forks produce reasonable approximations, but most of the sounds we hear every day are complex sounds, composed of many different sound wave frequencies.

The psychological quality of a sound, reflecting its degree of purity, is called **timbre.** For example, each musical instrument produces a unique variety or mixture of overtones, so each type of musical instrument tends to sound a little differently from all others. If a trumpet, a violin, and a piano were each to play the same note, we could still tell the instruments apart because of our experience of timbre. (In fact, any one instrument may display different timbres, depending on how it is constructed and played.)

With light, we found that the opposite of a pure light was a white light, which is made up of all the wavelengths of the visible spectrum. Again, the parallel between vision and hearing holds. Suppose that we have a sound source that can produce all of the possible sound wave frequencies. We produce a random mixture of these frequencies from 20Hz to 20,000Hz. What would that sound like? Actually, it would sound rather like a buzzing noise. The best example would be the sound that one hears when a radio (and, as it happens, FM works better than AM) is tuned to a position in between stations. This soft, whispering, buzzing sound, containing a range of many audible sound frequencies, is useful in masking or covering other unwanted sounds. We call a random mixture of sound frequencies **white noise,** just as we called a random mixture of wavelengths of light *white light.*

The analogy between light and sound, between vision and hearing, is striking. Both types of stimulus energy can be represented as waves. In both cases, each of the *physical* characteristics of the waves (amplitude, length or

timbre
the psychological experience related to wave purity by which we differentiate the sharpness, clearness, or quality of a tone

white noise
a sound composed of a random assortment of all wave frequencies from the audible spectrum

FIGURE 2.18
The physical characteristics of light and sound waves affect our psychological experiences of vision and hearing as illustrated in this table.

Physical characteristic	Psychological experience for vision	Psychological experience for hearing
Wave amplitude	Brightness	Loudness
Wavelength or frequency	Hue	Pitch
Wave purity or mixture	Saturation	Timbre

frequency, and purity or complexity) is correlated with a *psychological* experience. These relationships are summarized in Figure 2.18.

BEFORE YOU GO ON   **What are the three major physical characteristics of sound, and which psychological experiences do they produce?**

The Ear

It is deep inside the ear that the energy of sound wave pressures is changed into neural impulses. As with the eye, most of the identifiable structures of the ear simply transfer energy from without to within. Figure 2.19 is a drawing of the major structures of the human ear, and we'll use it to follow the path of sound waves from the environment to the receptor cells for sound.

The outer ear is called the **pinna.** Its main function is to collect the sound waves from the air around it and funnel them (through the auditory canal) toward the **eardrum.** (Notice that when we are trying to hear soft sounds we sometimes cup our hand around our pinna to gather in as much sound as we can.) Air waves push against the membrane of the eardrum, setting it in motion, so that it vibrates at the same rate as the sound source. When the eardrum vibrates back and forth, the sound moves deeper inside the ear.

As you can see in Figure 2.19, there are three very small bones (collectively called *ossicles*) in the middle ear. These bones are, in order, the **malleus,** the **incus,** and the **stapes** (pronounced *stape-ese*). These bones pass the vibrations of the eardrum along to the *oval window,* another membrane like the eardrum, only smaller. As the ossicles pass the sound wave vibrations along to the oval window, they amplify them, increasing their force.

When sound is transmitted beyond the oval window, the vibrations are said to be in the inner ear. The main structure of the inner ear is the **cochlea,** a snaillike structure that contains the actual receptor cells for hearing. As the stapes vibrates against the oval window, it sets a fluid inside the cochlea in motion at the same rate.

There is yet another membrane in the ear, called the **basilar membrane,** that runs just about the full length of the cochlea, nearly in its center. As the fluid within the cochlea starts to move, the basilar membrane is bent up and down. Hearing takes place when very tiny **hair cells** are stimulated by the vibrations of the basilar membrane. Through a process not yet fully understood, the mechanical pressure of the basilar membrane on the hair cells

pinna
the outer ear that collects and funnels sound waves into the auditory canal toward the eardrum

eardrum
the outermost membrane of the ear that is set in motion by the vibrations of a sound; transmits vibrations to the ossicles

malleus, incus and stapes
(collectively, *ossicles*) three small bones that transmit and intensify sound vibrations from the eardrum to the oval window

cochlea
part of the inner ear where sound waves become neural impulses

basilar membrane
a structure within the cochlea that vibrates and thus stimulates the hair cells of the inner ear

hair cells
the receptor cells for hearing, located in the cochlea, stimulated by the vibrating basilar membrane, they send neural impulses to the temporal lobe of the brain

FIGURE 2.19
The major structures of the human ear.

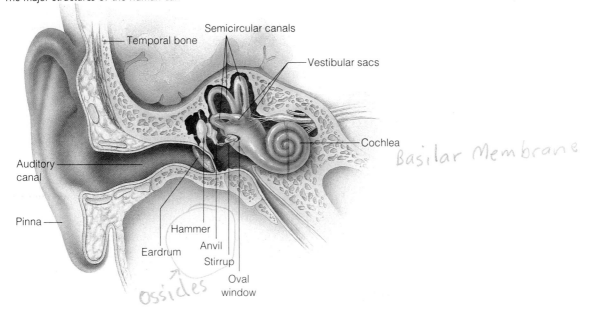

starts a neural impulse that leaves the ear on the auditory nerve and travels toward the temporal lobe.

So, the ear contains the sensory receptors for hearing, or audition. It is in the ear that the physical energy of sound is translated into a psychological experience. Most of the structures of the ear are responsible for focusing and directing waves of pressure to the hair cells in the cochlea where the neural impulse begins.

Summarize how sound wave pressures pass through the different structures of the ear.   BEFORE YOU GO ON

OTHER SENSES

Though vision and hearing are important senses, consider the quality of information that we do receive from our other, "lesser" senses. The aroma and taste of well-prepared barbecue, the touch and feel of textures and surfaces, the sense of where your body is and what it's doing, the feedback from your muscles as you move—all these experiences and more are through our "lesser" senses. In this section, we'll consider the chemical senses, the skin senses, the position senses, and pain.

The Chemical Senses

Taste and smell are referred to as chemical senses because the stimuli for both are molecules of chemical compounds. For taste, the chemical molecules are dissolved in liquid (usually the saliva in our mouths). For smell, the chemicals are dissolved in the air that reaches the smell receptors high inside our noses. The technical term for taste is *gustation;* for smell, it is *olfaction.*

Other Senses   **89**

FIGURE 2.20
This enlarged view of a taste bud shows how the sensation of taste travels from the gustatory receptor cells to the brain.

Enlarged view of taste bud

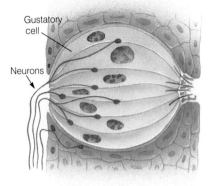

Gustatory cell

Neurons

10,000

taste buds
the receptors for taste located in the tongue

FIGURE 2.21
The four primary qualities of taste are experienced in specific areas of the tongue, as illustrated here.

Top view of tongue

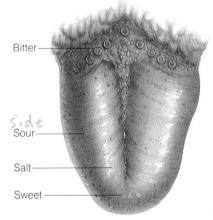

Bitter

side
Sour

Salt

Sweet

If you have ever eaten while suffering from a severe head cold that has blocked your nasal passages, you appreciate the extent to which our experiences of taste and smell are interrelated. Most foods seem to lose their taste when we cannot smell them—which is why we should differentiate between the *flavor* of foods (which includes such qualities as odor and texture) and the *taste* of foods. A simple test demonstrates this point very nicely. While blindfolded, eat a small piece of peeled apple and a small piece of peeled potato, and see if you can tell the difference between the two. You shouldn't have any trouble making this discrimination. Now hold your nose very tightly and try again. Without your sense of smell to help you, such discrimination—on the basis of taste alone—is very difficult.

Taste (Gustation).   Our experience of the flavors of foods depends so heavily on our sense of smell, texture, and temperature that we sometimes have to wonder if there is any sense of taste alone. Well, there is. Taste seems to have four basic psychological qualities—and many combinations of these four. The stimuli for taste, then, are chemical molecules that give rise to four primary qualities of taste: sweet, salty, sour, and bitter. You should be able to generate a list of foods that produce each of these basic sensations.

Some foods derive their special taste from their own unique combination of the four basic taste sensations. Have you noticed that it is more difficult to think of examples of sour and bitter tasting foods than it is to think of sweet and salty ones? This reflects the fact that we usually don't like bitter and sour tastes and have learned to avoid them.

The receptors for taste are located on (in might be more precise) the tongue, of course. The receptors for taste are called **taste buds.** We all have about 10,000 taste buds, and each one is made up of a number of separate parts. When parts of taste buds die (or are killed by foods that are too hot, for example) new segments are regenerated. Fortunately, we are always growing fresh new taste receptor cells. A diagram of a taste bud is shown in Figure 2.20.

Different taste buds respond primarily to chemicals that produce one of the four basic taste qualities. That is, some receptor cells respond mostly to salts, while others respond primarily to sweet-producing chemicals, like sugars. As it happens, these specialized cells are not evenly distributed on the surface of the tongue. Receptors for sweet are at the very tip of the tongue; receptors for salty tastes are toward the front; sour receptors are on the sides; and bitter receptors are at the back of the tongue. A sour vinegar solution dropped right at the tip of the tongue might very well go unnoticed until some of it gets washed over to the side of the tongue. To best savor a lollipop, children learned ages ago to lick it with the tip of the tongue. The locations of the receptors for the primary tastes are shown in Figure 2.21.

Smell (Olfaction).   Smell is a sense that is poorly understood. It is a sense that often gives us great pleasure—think of the aroma of bacon frying over a wood fire or of freshly picked flowers. It also produces considerable displeasure—consider the smell of old garbage or rotten eggs.

We do know that the sense of smell originates in cells located high in the nasal cavity, very close to the brain itself. We also know that the pathway

FIGURE 2.22
This illustration of the olfactory system shows its proximity to the brain and the relationship between the sensations of taste and smell.

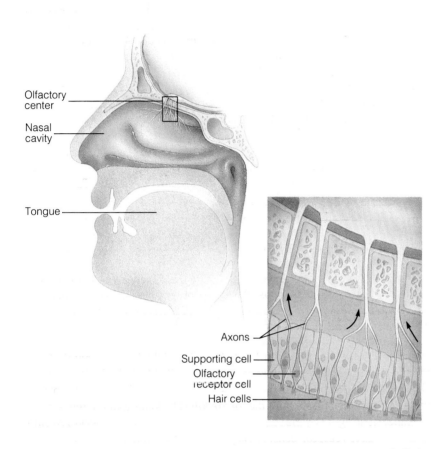

from these receptors to the brain is the most direct and shortest of all the senses (see Figure 2.22). What we don't understand well is just how molecules suspended in air (or some other gas) actually stimulate the small hair cells of the olfactory receptor to fire neural impulses.

We know that people can identify primary tastes. What about primary odors? A number of schemes have been proposed over the years, and each seemed reasonable in its day. One scheme suggests that there are four basic odors from which all others may be constructed: fragrant, acid, burnt, and of all things, goaty. Another scheme cites six primary odors. Yet another plan called the "stereochemical theory" (Amoore, 1970) names seven primary qualities of smell and further suggests that each primary quality is stimulated by a unique type or shape of chemical molecule. For the moment, it is difficult to be any more definite, since there seems to be evidence both for and against Amoore's theory.

Do taste and smell each have primary qualities?

Discuss the chemical senses of taste and smell, noting the stimulus and receptor for each.

Do taste and smell each have primary qualities?

BEFORE YOU GO ON

FIGURE 2.23
This illustration of a patch of hairy skin shows the different layers of the skin and the various nerves.

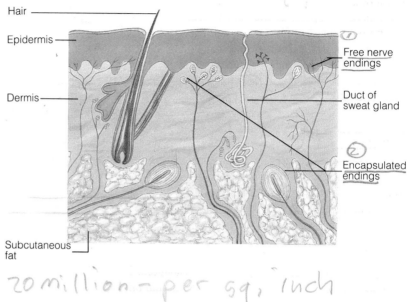

Hair

Epidermis

Dermis

Free nerve endings

Duct of sweat gland

Encapsulated endings

Subcutaneous fat

20 million - per sq. inch

The Skin (Cutaneous) Senses

Most of us take our skin for granted—at least we seldom think about it very much. We frequently abuse our skin by overexposing it to the sun's rays in summer and to excess cold in winter. We scratch it, cut it, scrape it, and wash away millions of its cells every time we shower or bathe.

Figure 2.23 is a diagram of some of the structures found in an area of skin from a hairy part of the human body. Each square inch of the layers that make up our skin contains nearly 20 million cells, including a large number of special sense receptors. Some of the skin receptors have *free nerve endings,* while others have some sort of small covering over them. We call these latter ones *encapsulated nerve endings,* and there are many different types. It is our skin that somehow gives rise to our psychological experience of touch or pressure and of warmth and cold. It would be convenient if each of the different types of receptor cells within the layers of our skin independently gave rise to a different type of psychological sensation, but such is not the case.

Indeed, one of the problems in studying the skin senses (or *cutaneous* senses) is trying to determine just which cells in the skin give rise to the different sensations of touch and temperature. We can discriminate clearly between a light touch and a strong jab in the arm and between vibrations, tickles, and itches. A simple proposal would be that there are different receptors in the skin that are responsible for each different sensation. Unfortunately, this proposal is not supported by the facts. Although *some* types of receptor cells are more sensitive to *some* types of stimuli, current thinking is that our ability to discriminate among different types of cutaneous sensation is due to the unique combination of responses that the many receptor cells have to different types of stimulation.

sensory adaptation
a condition in which there is a reduction in the level of sensation as a function of exposure to a constant stimulus

By carefully stimulating very small areas of the skin, we can locate areas that are particularly sensitive to temperature. We are convinced that warm and cold temperatures each stimulate different locations on the skin. Even so, there is no consistent pattern of receptor cells found at these locations, or temperature spots, as they are called. That is, we have not yet located specific receptor cells for cold or hot. As a matter of fact, our experience of hot seems to come from the simultaneous stimulation of both warm and cold spots. A rather ingenious demonstration shows how this works. Cold water is run through one metal tube and warm water is run through another tube. The two tubes are coiled together (see Figure 2.24). If you were to grasp the coiled tubes, your experience would be one of *heat*—the tubes would feel hot even if you knew that they weren't.

Perhaps no single sense better illustrates **sensory adaptation** than does our skin sense of temperature. Sensory adaptation is the name we give to the observation that there is a reduction in the level of sensation as a function of exposure to a stimulus. Adaptation underscores the idea that our senses respond best to *changes* in levels of stimulation rather than constant, stable levels. Once your hand is in hot water for a few minutes, the temperature of the water no longer feels hot, even if you maintain the high temperature of the water. The water does not get cooler in any physical way, it just seems to. We say that your sense of temperature has adapted. To make the water seem warm again, we would have to increase its actual physical temperature to a level higher than what it was when you first put your hand in it.

One of the oldest demonstrations of sensory adaptation (attributed to John Locke in the seventeenth century) is quite easy for you to do at home. You will need three large containers: one filled with very hot water, one filled with very cold water, and the third filled with lukewarm water. Place your left hand in the hot water and your right hand in the cold water. After a few minutes (of adaptation), place both hands in the lukewarm water. The experience ought to be immediate and very noticeable—the same lukewarm water now seems very cool to your left hand and very warm to your right. This demonstration also underscores the point that our perception of temperature depends in part on our own body temperature—which is why we can't feel our own forehead to see if we have a fever or why a parent with cold hands may think a child has a fever.

What are the cutaneous senses?

How can sensory adaptation be demonstrated with the sense of temperature?

BEFORE YOU GO ON

The Position Senses

Another sensory capacity we often take for granted is our ability to know how and where our bodies are positioned in space. Although we seldom worry about it, we can quickly become aware of how our bodies are positioned in regard to the pull of gravity. We also get sensory information about where different parts of our body are in relation to each other. We can tell if we are moving or standing still. And unless we are on a roller coaster, or racing across a field, we usually adapt to these sensory messages quickly and pay them little attention.

FIGURE 2.24
A demonstration that our sensation of hot may be constructed from the sensations of warm and cold. Even if you know the coiled tubes contain only warm and cold water, when you grasp the tubes they will feel hot.

Cold Water   Warm Water

vestibular sense
the position sense that tells us about balance, where we are in relation to gravity, acceleration, or deceleration

kinesthetic sense *located in our joints*
the position sense that tells us the position of different parts of our bodies and what our muscles and joints are doing

operates reflexively threw the spinal cord

Most of the information about where we are in space comes to us through our sense of vision. If we ever want to know just how we are oriented in space, all we have to do is look around. But notice that we can do the same sort of thing even with our eyes closed. We have two specific systems of the position sense over and above what vision can provide. One, the **vestibular sense,** tells us about balance, where we are in relation to gravity, and acceleration or deceleration. The other, the **kinesthetic sense,** tells us about the movement or position of our muscles and joints.

The receptors for the vestibular sense are located on either side of the head, near the inner ears. Five chambers are located there: three semicircular canals and two vestibular sacs. Their orientation is shown in Figure 2.19. Each of these chambers is filled with fluid. When our head moves in any direction, the fluid in the semicircular canals moves, drawn by gravity or the force of our head accelerating in space. The vestibular sacs contain very small solid particles that float around in the fluid within the sacs. When these particles are forced against one side of the sacs, as happens when we move, they stimulate different hair cells that start neural impulses. Overstimulation of the receptor cells in the vestibular sacs or semicircular canals can lead to feelings of dizziness or nausea, reasonably enough called *motion sickness.*

Receptors for our kinesthetic sense are located primarily in our joints, while some information also comes from muscles and tendons. These receptors sense the position and movements of parts of the body—again, information to which we seldom attend. Impulses from these receptors travel to our brain through pathways in our spinal cord. They provide excellent examples of reflex actions. As muscles in the front of your upper arm (your biceps) contract, the corresponding muscles in the back of your arm (triceps) must relax if you are to successfully bend your arm at the elbow. How fortunate it is that our kinesthetic receptors, operating reflexively through the spinal cord, take care of these details without our having to consciously manipulate all the appropriate muscular activity. In fact, about the only time we even realize that our kinesthetic system is functioning is when it *stops* working well, such as when our leg "falls asleep" and we have trouble walking.

BEFORE YOU GO ON   What are our position senses, and how do they operate?

Pain: A Special Sense

Our sense of pain is a very curious and troublesome one for psychologists who are interested in sensory processes. Pain, or certainly the fear of it, can be a very strong motivator; we'll do all sorts of things to avoid it. Also, our feelings of pain are particularly private sensations—they are psychological experiences that are difficult to communicate and share with others (Verillo, 1975).

Just what *is* pain? What causes the sensation of pain? What are its sensory receptors? At present, we really don't know, but we do appreciate that the very complexity of pain makes it a special sense.

Many stimuli can cause pain. Very intense stimulation of virtually any sense receptor can produce pain. Too much light, very strong pressures on the skin, excessive temperatures, very loud sounds, and even too many "hot"

The gate-control theory developed by Ronald Melzack (pictured here) and Patrick Wall proposes that pain centers in the brain are responsive to stimulation from a nerve fiber that "opens the gate" and allows for the sensation of pain.

spices can all result in our experiencing pain. But as we all know, the stimulus for pain need not be intense. Even a light pin prick can be very painful if it's in the right place.

Our skin seems to have many receptors for pain, but pain receptors can also be found deep inside our bodies—consider stomachaches, lower back pain, and headaches. About the only common focus in pain is discomfort and unpleasantness. On that point we are all agreed.

At one time it was believed that there was one particular type of receptor (probably some form of free nerve ending) that responded uniquely to pain-producing stimuli. We now know that such a theory is too simple. Free nerve endings in the skin often *do* respond whenever we sense pain, but there's got to be more to it. A theory that is still getting much attention (some of it supportive, some not) is that of Melzack and Wall (1965; Melzack, 1973). Their theory is called the **gate-control theory.** It suggests that our experience of pain is something that happens not so much at the level of the receptor (say, in the skin), but within the central nervous system. The theory proposes that pain centers in the brain are responsive to stimulation from a particular type of nerve fiber—one that "opens the gate" and allows for the sensation of pain. The theory further proposes that there are other nerve fibers that can offset the activity of the pain-carrying fibers and "close the gate."

There are a number of situations in which this notion of an opening and closing gate to pain seems reasonable. We know of many reports of people who, under certain circumstances, feel no pain, even when they should. The story of a football player who plays the entire second half of a game with a broken bone in his ankle comes to mind. We know that emotional excite-

gate-control theory
the theory of pain sensation that argues that there are brain centers that regulate the passage of pain messages from different parts of the body to the brain

endorphins
(painkillers)
located in the
Brain

ment and focusing of attention on other matters can alleviate the feelings of pain. When this happens (as in a number of natural childbirth methods), it is more likely that changes to alleviate the experience of pain have taken place within the brain rather than at the receptors. Perhaps our football player, focusing his attention on the game and filled with excitement, was able to "close the pain gate" in his brain. Neural impulses from the damaged tissue in his ankle no doubt raced up his leg and spinal cord to his brain, but his brain did not notice them—at least during the game (Sternbach, 1978).

Additional support for the idea that pain is sensed more in the brain than at the site of some specialized receptor cell was the discovery, in the mid-1970s, of *endorphins* (Hughes et al., 1975). Endorphins are complex chemicals found in the brain. They are neurotransmitters that act as natural painkillers, or analgesics. In fact, one's pain threshold, or sensitivity to pain (and there are very large individual differences here), is probably related to the level of endorphin production (Turkington, 1985). Unlike many manufactured analgesics (such as aspirin, morphine, or codeine), natural endorphins are nonaddictive, and they are very powerful. Attempts to reproduce endorphins artificially have so far met with little success.

BEFORE YOU GO ON   **What produces the sensation of pain?**

In this section, we have reviewed the structures and functions of a number of different human senses. We have seen that hearing, like vision, is stimulated by physical wave forms of energy and that the measurable characteristics of those waves (amplitude, frequency, and complexity) give rise to different psychological experiences of sounds (loudness, pitch, and timbre). We've seen how interrelated taste and smell are. We've reviewed a number of our different skin senses, as well as those senses (vestibular and kinesthetic) that inform us about our body's position in space. Finally, we introduced some of the current thinking about the sense of pain. It is clear that at any one time, our brains are receiving a remarkable amount of information from all of our sensory receptors. How we deal with all that information is the question we address next.

PERCEPTUAL SELECTIVITY: PAYING ATTENTION

Imagine that you are at a party, engaged in a dreadfully boring conversation with someone you've just met. From time to time, it occurs to you that wearing your new shoes was not a good idea—your feet hurt. You're munching on an assortment of appetizers that the hosts have provided. Music is blaring from a stereo system at the other end of the room. Aromas of foods, smoke, and perfumes fill the air. There must be at least 50 people at this party, and you don't know any of them. Your senses are being bombarded simultaneously by all sorts of information: sights, sounds, tastes, smells, even pain. Suddenly, you hear someone nearby mention your name. You redirect your attention, now totally disregarding the person talking right in front of you. What determines which of many competing stimuli attract and hold our attention? In fact, there are many factors. In this section, we'll discuss some of the more important ones.

Gestalt Psychology and Figure-ground

The study of factors that affect the selection of perceptions is not a new one in psychology. This issue was one of the major concerns of a group of psychologists we now refer to as Gestalt psychologists. The German founders of Gestalt psychology included Max Wertheimer (1880–1967), Kurt Koffka (1886–1941), and Wolfgang Kohler (1887–1967).

As you will recall from the introduction, *gestalt* is a German word that means something like "whole" or "configuration" or "totality." One forms a gestalt when one sees the overall scheme of things or can "see the forest for the trees." If you have a general idea of how something works or can appreciate the general nature of something without overattending to details, it can be said that you have formed a gestalt.

One of the basic principles of Gestalt psychology is that of the **figure-ground relationship.** Of all the stimuli in your environment at any one time, those you attend to are said to be *figures,* while the rest become the *ground.* As you focus your attention on the words on this page, they form figures against the ground (or background, if you prefer) formed by the rest of the page. When you hear your instructor's voice during a lecture, that voice is the figure against the ground of all the other sounds in the room that are entering your ear at the same time.

It was the Gestalt psychologists' belief that we can only attend to one figure at a time in any one sense or sense modality. That is, we can only hear one thing, or see one thing, or taste one thing clearly at a time. Furthermore, there are many examples of visual figure-ground patterns in which the figure and the ground can easily be reversed (these are usually called *reversible figures*). A classic example of this is presented in Figure 2.25.

In Gestalt psychology terms, the issue of perceptual selectivity, or attention, is one of determining which stimuli become figures and which remain part of the ground.

There are many factors that influence how we select and pay attention to stimuli, and they all usually operate at once. These many factors can be divided into two general types: stimulus factors and personal factors. By stimulus factors, we mean those characteristics of stimuli that make them more compelling (or attention-grabbing) than others, no matter who the perceiver is. By personal factors we mean those characteristics of the perceiver that influence which stimuli become figures.

Stimulus Factors   Physical Characteristics

Some stimuli are simply more compelling than others; they are more likely to get our attention and more likely to be selected for further processing and interpretation. They tend to operate regardless of who the perceiver is. Because individual differences seem to matter little here, we'll call these *stimulus factors* in determining attention. Contrast and repetition are the two main stimulus factors we'll discuss.

Contrast.   The most important and common stimulus factor in perceptual selectivity is **contrast,** which is the extent to which a given stimulus is in some (physical) way different from the other stimuli around it. One stimulus can contrast with other stimuli in many different ways. For example, we are

figure-ground relationship
the Gestalt psychology principle that stimuli are selected and perceived as figures against a ground or background

FIGURE 2.25
A classic reversible figure-ground pattern. What do you see here? A white vase or a birdbath? Or do you see two black profiles facing each other? Can you clearly see both figures at the same time?

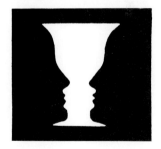

contrast
the extent to which a stimulus is in some physical way different from other surrounding stimuli

more likely to attend to a stimulus if its *intensity* is different from the intensities of other stimuli. Generally speaking, the more intense a stimulus, the more likely we are to select it for further processing. Simply put, a shout is more compelling than a whisper; a bright light is more attention-grabbing than a dim one; an extreme temperature is more likely to be noticed than a moderate one.

Notice that this isn't always the case, however. A shout may be more compelling than a whisper—unless, of course, everyone is shouting; then it may very well be the soft, quiet, reasoned tone that gets our attention. If we are faced with a barrage of bright lights, a dim one may, by contrast, be the one we process more fully.

The same argument holds for the stimulus characteristic of physical *size*. By and large, the bigger the stimulus, the more likely we are to attend to it. There is little point in building a small billboard to advertise your motel or restaurant. You'll want to construct the biggest billboard you can afford in hopes of attracting attention.

Again, when we are faced with many large stimuli, one that is smaller may be the one we attend to. If you have ever attended a professional football game, you may have experienced this very phenomenon. When the players first take the field, all dressed in similar uniforms and in full pads, they look huge (and most of them are). Almost immediately, your eyes fixate on one player who seems to stand out from the rest: the placekicker. The placekicker is generally much smaller than his teammates and seldom wears as much protective padding. By *contrast,* his size makes him the object of our attention.

A third physical dimension that often determines perceptual selectivity, and for which contrast is relevant, is *motion*. Motion is a powerful factor in determining visual attention. A bird in flight is much clearer to see (forms a much clearer figure) than a bird sitting in a bush. In the fall, walking through the woods, you may come close to stepping on a chipmunk before you notice it, so long as it stays still—an adaptive response of camouflage that chipmunks do well. But if that chipmunk makes a dash to escape, it is easily noticed scurrying across the leaves. Once again, the *contrast* created by sudden movement is important. As you enter a night club, your attention is immediately drawn to the dance floor by the bright lights and the moving throng dancing to the loud music. How easy it is to spot the one person, right in the middle of the dance floor, who, for whatever reason, is motionless, frozen against the back-ground of moving bodies, contrasting as an easily noticed figure.

Although intensity, size, and motion are three physical characteristics of stimuli that readily come to mind, there are many others. Indeed, any dimension in which two stimuli may be different (contrast) may be a dimension that determines which stimulus we attend to. (For example, even a small gray spot can easily grab one's attention if it's positioned in the middle of a solid yellow tie.) This is precisely why we have printed important terms in **boldface type** throughout this book.

The importance of stimulus contrast in determining attention has been nicely demonstrated in a number of classic experiments on selective listening tasks (Broadbent, 1958; Cherry, 1953). In these experiments, subjects wear stereo earphones that play a different message to each ear. Sometimes, subjects are required simply to follow the flow of a message in one ear while

Contrast is an important factor in perceptual selectivity. Generally, the bigger the stimulus, the more it attracts our attention.

disregarding the other. In some experiments, the subjects are asked to shadow, or immediately repeat, one of the messages that is being played into one of their ears. When both messages are produced by speakers whose voice qualities are very similar, the job is a difficult one. If one speaker is female, with a high-pitched voice, and the other speaker male, with a low-pitched tone, the task of attending separately to either of the two different messages is much easier. Here we have experimental support for an everyday observation: Stimuli that are physically different (that contrast) are easier to separate than are stimuli with similar physical characteristics.

Repetition. Another stimulus characteristic that often determines attention, and for which contrast is really not relevant, is repetition. The more often a stimulus is presented, the more likely it is that it will be attended to (everything else being equal, of course).

Instructors who want to get across an important point will seldom mention it just once, but rather will repeat it over and over. (Clever students recognize that there is a high correlation between the importance of a piece of information and the number of times it is mentioned in class.) This is why we have repeated the definitions of important terms in the text, in the margin, and again in the glossary at the end of the book.

Think again of the billboard you're going to erect to advertise your motel or restaurant. No matter how large or bright it is, and even if you have managed to build motion into it, you will be well-advised to construct as many billboards as your budget will allow if you want to get the attention of

Repetition is another stimulus characteristic that often determines attention. Instructors who want to get across an important point will repeat it over and over.

as many people as possible. The people who write and schedule television commercials want you to attend to their messages, and repetition is obviously one of their main techniques.

To summarize, there are many ways in which stimuli may differ—brightness, size, motion, color, pitch, and loudness, for example. The greater the contrast between any one stimulus and the others around it, the greater the likelihood that that stimulus will capture or draw our attention. And, everything else being equal, the more often a stimulus is presented, the greater the likelihood that it will be perceived and that it will be selected for further consideration and processing.

BEFORE YOU GO ON **What stimulus factors determine the selection of perceptions?**

Personal Factors

Sometimes, what we pay attention to is determined not so much by the physical characteristics of the stimuli present but by personal characteristics of the perceiver. For example, imagine two students are watching a basketball game on television. Both are being presented with identical stimulation from the same TV screen. One says, "Wow, did you see that rebound?" The other viewer responds, "No, I was watching the cheerleaders." The difference in perception here is hardly attributable to the nature of the stimuli since both students received the same sensory information from the same TV. The difference is due to characteristics of the perceivers, which we'll call *personal factors*. Although there may be many personal factors that ultimately determine the selection of our perceptions, we can categorize most of them as being a function of motivation, expectation, and/or past experience.

Motivation. Imagine that the two students watching the game on television are supporters of different teams. One is an avid fan of Team A; the other is a staunch backer of Team B. Our TV viewers may have a small wager on the outcome of this important game. We'll say that Team A wins the hard-fought contest with a last second shot at the buzzer. Both students watched exactly the same game on the same TV, but which of the two is likely to have perceived the officiating of the game as honest, fair, and above reproach? Which student is likely to have seen the game as "one of the poorest refereed games ever"? The perception of the quality of the officiating may depend on who won, who lost, and the motivation of the perceiver. In large measure, the viewers saw what they *wanted* to see.

One thing that most people are interested in is themselves, whether they like to admit it or not. Hence, when we are at a party, perhaps bored with the conversations going on around us, we are often drawn to a nearby discussion if we hear our own name. Similarly, many instructors have learned the old lesson that to capture the drifting attention of a class, he or she need only to say, "Now about your next exam. . . . ," or "With regard to sex. . . ." It's rather impressive to see so many heads turn at the slightest mention of these key motivating terms. Advertisers certainly know that one's motives can direct attention. Magazine and billboard advertisements are seldom populated by older, homely people. Rather, they tend to show young, attractive subjects, often scantily clad. Upon reflection, we may disapprove of such appeals to our sexual motives, but they do tend to get our attention.

Expectation. If it is true that we often perceive what we want to perceive, it is equally true that we often perceive what we *expect* to perceive, whether it's really there or not. When we are psychologically ready or prepared to perceive something, when we have developed an expectation, we say that we have formed a **mental set.**

Take just a second and quickly glance at the message in Figure 2.26. What did the message say? (If you've seen this demonstration before, you'll have to try it with someone who hasn't.) Many people claim that the message was "PARIS IN THE SPRING." In fact, there are two "the"s in the triangle— "PARIS IN THE THE SPRING." Most people familiar with the English language and with this particular phrase do not expect there to be *two* "the"s right next to each other. Following their mental set, they report seeing only one. Other people may develop a different mental set or expectation. Their line of reasoning may go something like this: "This is a psychology text, so there's probably a trick here someplace, and I'm going to find it." In this particular instance, such skeptics get reinforced. There is a trick, and if their mental set was to find one, they did so. We will see later (Chapter 5) that our inability to break out of a mentally set way of perceiving a problem may interfere with our finding a solution to that problem. Creative problem solving often involves perceiving aspects of a problem in new or unique ways. Thus, even as complex a cognitive process as problem solving often hinges on our perceptions.

Past Experience. Just as contrast is the most important of the stimulus factors that determine attention, so past experience is the most important of the personal factors in perceptual selectivity. One reason why past experience may be listed as the most important is that, in many ways, it

mental set
a predisposed (set) way to perceive something; an expectation

FIGURE 2.26
Our mental set affects our perception. How many "*the*"s did you see when you first glanced at this simple figure? Why?

memorize

FIGURE 2.27
Factors that can affect perceptual selectivity.

Stimulus Factors	Personal Factors
Contrast	Past experience
intensity	Expectation *Mental set*
size	Motivation
motion	
Repetition	

includes both motivation and mental set. Much of our motivation comes from our past experience. For example, why did those two viewers of the basketball game root for Team A or for Team B in the first place? Their allegiance was certainly not inborn, but was rather a reflection of their past experience. Similarly, our expectations develop largely from past experiences. We are likely to expect to perceive, or be set to perceive, what we have perceived in the past in similar circumstances.

Our selection of stimuli from our environment is usually automatic and accomplished without conscious effort. The process of selection is influenced by a number of factors. Some stimuli are compelling to us because they contrast with others or because they are frequently repeated. It is also the case that the determination of which stimuli become figures and which remain ground is influenced by the nature of the perceiver, whose motivation, mental set, and past experience may influence perceptual selectivity. Figure 2.27 summarizes the factors we have discussed.

BEFORE YOU GO ON   **What personal factors are involved in perceptual selectivity?**

PERCEPTUAL ORGANIZATION

As we have seen, one of our basic perceptual responses to the environment is to select certain stimuli from among all those that strike our receptors for further processing. Another related perceptual process involves organizing the bits and pieces of experience that are presented to our senses into meaningful, integrated, potentially useful, organized wholes, or gestalts. We do not really hear the individual sounds of speech; we organize them and perceive them as words and phrases and sentences. Our visual experience is not one of tiny bits of color and light and dark—as recorded at the retina—but of identifiable objects and events. We don't perceive a warm pat on the back as responses from thousands of individual receptors in our skin. As was the case for selection, there are many factors that influence how we organize and interpret our perceptual worlds. Again, we'll consider stimulus and personal factors separately.

FIGURE 2.28(A)
These Xs are organized as two groups, not four rows or columns, because of *proximity*.

These Xs are organized as two groups, not four rows or columns, because of *proximity*.

proximity
the Gestalt principle of organization that claims that stimuli will be perceived as belonging together if they occur together in space or time

Stimulus Factors   *Gestalt*

By stimulus factors, we are referring to characteristics of stimuli that promote our perception of them as being organized together in one figure or gestalt. Not surprisingly, it was the Gestalt psychologists who first investigated this issue and who first listed such factors. We'll consider four of the most influential: proximity, similarity, continuity, and closure.

Proximity.   Glance quickly at Figure 2.28(A). Without giving it much thought, what did you see there. A bunch of Xs yes, but more than that, there were two separately identifiable groups of Xs, weren't there? The group of eight Xs on the left seems somehow separate from the group on the right, while the Xs within each group seem to "go together." This illustration demonstrates **proximity**, or *contiguity*. What this means is that events that occur close together in space, or in time, are generally perceived as belong-

102   Chapter Two Sensation and Perception

ing together as part of the same figure. In Figure 2.28(A), it's rather difficult to see the Xs as falling into four rows or four columns. They just belong together as two groups of eight Xs each.

Proximity operates on more than just visual stimuli. For example, sounds that occur together (are *contiguous,* to use the technical term) in speech are perceived as going together to form words or phrases. Thunder and lightning are contiguous because they occur together in time. If two events consistently occur together, one always *following* the other, we often come to perceive contiguity as causality. What this means is that if B consistently follows right after A, we may come to perceive A as causing B. Indeed, many people believe that lightning causes thunder because it is always perceived just before the (slower moving) sound of the thunder. In fact, the two occur together, neither causing the other.

Similarity.   Now glance at Figure 2.28(B) and describe what you see there. We have a collection of Xs and Os that clearly are organized into a simple pattern. The usual way to organize these stimuli is to see them as two separate columns of Xs and two of Os. Seeing rows of alternating Xs and Os is very difficult. This figure demonstrates the principle of **similarity.** Stimulus events that are in some way alike, or have properties in common, tend to be grouped together in our perception—a "birds of a feather are perceived together" sort of thing. Perceived similarity and grouping are often the easy basis for the formation of stereotypes: "Oh, he's one of *those.*" Here the principle works in reverse. If someone is perceived as being a member of a given group, it is assumed (often incorrectly) that he or she will have characteristics in common with (similar to) others in the group.

Continuity.   The principle of **continuity** (or *good continuation*) suggests that we tend to see things as ending up consistent with the way they started off. Figure 2.28(C) illustrates this point with a simple line drawing. The clearest way to organize this drawing is as two separate but intersecting lines: one straight, the other curved. It's hard to imagine seeing this figure any other way. Very often our perceptions are guided by a logic that says, "Lines (for example) that start out straight, should continue as straight."

The related concept of *common fate* deals with stimuli in motion. When stimulus objects are viewed as moving in the same direction at the same speed, they are seen as belonging together. Remember that chipmunk sitting motionless on the leaves in the woods? So long as both the chipmunk and the leaves stay still, the chipmunk won't be noticed. Its coloration fits in and thus is organized with the ground. But when it moves, the moving parts of the chipmunk all move together (they have a common fate), are organized together, and we can see it scurrying away.

Closure.   A commonly encountered principle of organization is **closure.** This is our tendency to fill in gaps in our perceptual world. This concept is illustrated by Figure 2.28(D). At a glance, anyone would tell you that this figure is the letter R, but of course it is not. That's not the way you make an R. However, it may be the way we *see* an R due to closure.

Closure occurs commonly during our everyday conversations. Just for fun some day, tape record a casual conversation with a friend. Then write down *exactly* what was said during the conversation. A true and faithful

Here we see two columns of Os and two of Xs because of *similarity.*

FIGURE 2.28(C)
We tend to see this figure as two intersecting lines, one straight and one curved, because of *continuity.*

We tend to see this figure as two intersecting lines, one straight, one curved, because of *continuity.*

similarity
the Gestalt principle of organization that claims that stimuli will be perceived together if they share some common characteristic(s)

continuity
the Gestalt principle of organization that claims that a stimulus or a movement will be perceived as continuing in the same smooth direction as first established

closure
the Gestalt principle of organization that claims that we tend to perceive incomplete figures as whole and complete

This figure is perceived as the letter R — which it is not — because of *closure*.

FIGURE 2.29(A)
Is the highlighted letter an A or an H? In fact, it is neither and can be interpreted as one or the other only on the basis of context and our past experience with the English language.

THE CHT SHT
BY THE DOOR.

transcription will reveal that many words and sounds were left out. Even though they were not actually there as stimuli, they were not missed by the listener because he or she filled in the gaps (closure) and understood what was being said. In fact, because of closure, you will probably find it difficult to make a truly faithful transcription of your own conversation.

Personal Factors

We can cover the personal factors determining perceptual organization rather quickly because they are the same as those that influence selection: motivation, expectation, and past experience. We perceive things as belonging together because we want to, because we expect to, and/or because we have perceived them together in the past.

How we perceive—judge, interpret, organize—a stimulus is often flavored by how we perceive other stimuli presented at about the same time. In other words, a very important factor in how we organize our perceptions is the *context* in which they are perceived. We are seldom asked to make perceptual judgments in a vacuum. Figures are usually presented in a given ground, or context. Context often affects what we expect to perceive or think we have perceived. We might be startled when we turn on our car radio and hear what sounds like a loud, piercing scream. In a moment—given a context—we realize that we have just tuned in to a fine arts station and have heard two notes from a soprano's rendition of an operatic aria, not a scream after all.

Figure 2.29 provides two examples of the effect of context on visual perception. In Figure 2.29(A), is the highlighted stimulus the letter H or the letter A? In fact, by itself, it doesn't seem to be a very good example of either! But in the proper context—and given our past experience with the English language—that same stimulus may appear to be an A *or* an H.

Figure 2.29(B) presents Edwin Boring's (1930) classic *ambiguous figure*. After you study this drawing for a while, you may be able to see why it is called ambiguous. Looked at one way, it depicts a demure young lady, dressed in Victorian era clothing, a large feather in her hat, looking away from the viewer. Looked at another way, the same picture shows an old woman, chin tucked down into her collar, hair down to her eyes, with a rather large wart on her nose. Now, if we had shown you a series of pictures of young men and women dressed in Victorian costume, as if they were at a grand ball, and *then* presented Figure 2.29(B), you almost certainly would have seen the young lady. In the context of a series of pictures of old, poorly dressed men and women, you might have organized the very same line drawing to depict the old woman.

How we organize our experience of the world depends on a number of factors. Our perception that some stimuli in our environments "go together" with other stimuli is influenced by the proximity and similarity of the stimulus events, our interpretations of closure and continuity, and our own personal motives, expectations, and past experiences.

BEFORE YOU GO ON   **List stimulus and personal factors that determine how we organize stimuli in perception.**

FIGURE 2.29(B)
This perceptually ambiguous drawing can be interpreted in different ways depending on the context in which it is viewed. Do you see a young, Victorian woman or an old woman? (After Boring, 1930.)

Perception is a complex cognitive process that involves the selection and organization of stimuli received by our senses. Many factors help determine which of the stimuli we sense become figures, or are attended to. Some factors (such as contrast and repetition) involve characteristics of the stimuli themselves; others (such as mental set, motivation, and past experience) involve characteristics of the perceiver. The organization of the bits and pieces of sensory experience into meaningful units is also influenced by stimulus and personal factors. The world that we have stored in our memories is the world as our perceptions present it to us. As a psychological process we often take perception for granted, but without it, there would be no way we could interpret or give meaning to the world around us.

SUMMARY

In what ways do the major physical characteristics of light waves of energy (amplitude, length, and purity) affect our psychological experience of light?

We can think of light as a wave form of radiant energy having three major characteristics: wave amplitude, which determines our experience of the light's brightness; wavelength, which determines our experience of hue; and wave purity, which determines a light's degree of saturation, from the extremes of pure, monochromatic light to the lowest saturation white light. / 72

List the major structures of the eye and describe the function of each.

Before light reaches the retina, it passes through a number of structures whose major function is to focus an image on the retina. In order to reach the retina, light must pass through the cornea, pupil (or opening in the iris), aqueous humor, lens (whose shape is controlled by the ciliary muscles), and vitreous humor. Then, at the retina, after passing through layers of neural fibers that combine and integrate visual information (ganglion and bipolar cells, for example), light reaches the photosensitive rods and cones. Impulses that originate at the rods and cones travel to the optic nerve and then on to the occipital lobe at the back of the brain. / 77

What is the duplicity theory of vision, and what evidence can you cite to support it?

The duplicity theory asserts that rods and cones function differently. Cones respond to high levels of illumination and to color. While rods do not discriminate among colors, they do respond to relatively low levels of light. Evidence for this point of view comes from common experience, the examination of the retinas of nocturnal animals, and data on dark adaptation and the Purkinje shift. / 81

Briefly summarize the trichromatic and opponent-process theories of color vision.

These theories attempt to explain how cones code different wavelengths of light; a process that gives rise to our experience of color. The trichromatic theory (associated with Young and Helmholtz) claims there are three different kinds of cones, each maximally sensitive to just one of the three primary colors—red, green, or blue. According to the opponent-process theory (associated with Hering), there are three pairs of mechanisms involved in our experience of color: a blue-yellow processor, a red-green processor, and a black-white processor. Each of these can respond to either of the characteristics that give it its name, but not to both. There is anatomical/physiological evidence that supports both these theories. / 83

What are the three major physical characteristics of sound, and which psychological experiences do they produce?

Like light, sound may be represented as a wave form of energy with three major physical characteristics: wave amplitude, frequency, and purity (or complexity). These in turn give rise to the psychological experiences of loudness, pitch, and timbre. / 88

Summarize how sound wave pressures pass through the different structures of the ear.

Most of the structures of the ear (the pinna, auditory canal, eardrum, malleus, incus, stapes, and oval window) intensify and transmit sound wave pressures to the fluid in the cochlea, which then vibrates the basilar membrane, which in turn stimulates tiny hair cells to transmit neural impulses along the auditory nerve toward the temporal lobe of the brain. / 89

Discuss the chemical senses of taste and smell, noting the stimulus and receptor for each.

Do taste and smell each have primary qualities?

The senses of taste (gustation) and smell (olfaction) are highly interrelated. Together they are referred to as the chemical senses because each responds to chemical molecules in solution. The receptors for smell are hair cells that line the upper regions of the nasal cavity; for taste, the receptors are cells in the taste buds located in the tongue. Taste appears to have four primary qualities (sweet, sour, bitter, and salt), but for smell, primary qualities and how many there may be is less certain. / 91

What are the cutaneous senses?

How can sensory adaptation be demonstrated with the sense of temperature?

The cutaneous senses are our skin senses: touch, pressure, warm, and cold. Specific receptor cells for each identifiable skin sense have not yet been localized. The temperature sense readily demonstrates sensory adaptation: A hand that has been first in hot water for a few minutes, and then in lukewarm water, will sense the lukewarm water as cold, having adapted to the original hot water. / 93

What are our position senses, and how do they operate?

One of our position senses is the vestibular sense, which, by responding to the movement of small particles suspended in a solution within our vestibular sacs and semicircular canals, can inform us about our orientation with regard to gravity or accelerated motion. Our other position sense is kinesthesis, which, through receptors in our muscles and joints, informs us about the orientation of different parts of our body. / 94

What produces the sensation of pain?

There is a wide variety of environmental stimuli that can give rise to our experience of pain, from high levels of stimulus intensity, to light pin pricks, to internal stimuli of the sort that produce headaches. There seems to be no one receptor for the pain sense. The brain is clearly involved in our experience of pain, as the gate-control theory proposes and as the action of the neurotransmitters called endorphins supports. / 96

What stimulus factors determine the selection of perceptions?

Of all of the information that stimulates our receptors, only a small portion is attended to, or selected for further processing. One set of factors that affects which stimuli are noticed and which remain part of the background concerns the characteristics of the available stimuli. We are more likely to attend to a stimulus if it *contrasts* with others around it (where contrast may be in terms of intensity, size, motion, or any other physical characteristics). The simple *repetition* of a stimulus also increases the likelihood that it will be attended to. / 100

What personal factors are involved in perceptual selectivity?

The selection of stimuli is partly based on characteristics of the perceiver, such as motivation, expectation (or mental set), and past experience. / 102

List stimulus and personal factors that determine how we organize stimuli in perception.

The perceptual organization of stimuli depends in part on the characteristics of the available stimuli, such as proximity, similarity, continuity, and closure. The personal factors that affect perceptual organization include motivation, mental set or expectation, and past experience. / 104

Chapter Two
Sensation and Perception

REVIEW QUESTIONS

1. Our eyes are sensitive to light waves with lengths that range between 380 and 760 nanometers. As wavelengths vary from the short 380 to the long 760 nanometers, what is the major change in our visual experience?

a. The apparent color of the light changes from violets to blues to greens to yellows to reds.

b. The apparent purity or saturation of the light changes from monochromatic to a colorless white.

c. The apparent intensity of the light changes from white to black.

d. The apparent brightness of the light changes from very dim to very bright.

The wavelength of light is the primary determinant of our experience of color or hue. Saturation or purity is determined by whether a light source radiates a mixture of wavelengths or only one wavelength. Intensity is actually a physical characteristic of light energy (wave amplitude) that determines our experience of brightness. Therefore, of these choices, (a) is the best. / 68

2. Which of the following structures of the eye is most responsible for regulating the amount of light that strikes the retina?

a. the cornea.

b. the ciliary muscles.

c. the iris.

d. the aqueous and vitreous humors.

The cornea is the outermost structure of the eye and doesn't change its transparency. The ciliary muscles control the shape of the lens and the ability to focus images. The humors in the eye are fluids that serve to nourish the eye and to maintain its shape. It's the iris that moves, contracting and expanding, to change the size of the pupil, thereby regulating the amount of light that strikes the retina. / 73

3. Which of the following statements is *true* concerning the rods and the cones of the retina?

a. They are both found, tightly packed, in the fovea.

b. The rods are colorblind, while the cones respond differentially to different wavelengths of light.

c. The rods adapt to darkness first, taking about 5 minutes to do so, while the cones require an additional 15 to 20 minutes to adapt.

d. Nocturnal animals can see so well at night because their retinas are composed almost exclusively of cones. In fact, the fovea contains virtually no rods at all, only cones. Dark adaptation involves the increased sensitivity of the rods. The cones adapt very poorly, requiring only a few minutes to do so. The retinas of nocturnal animals are almost exclusively rods, not cones, which means that alternative (b) is correct—we perceive color with our cones, not with our colorblind rods. / 77

4. We can tell the difference between the voice of a soprano and a bass largely on the basis of ___pitch___, while we distinguish between the voices of two basses largely on the basis of ___Timbre___.

a. timbre; pitch.

b. amplitude; frequency.

c. loudness; amplitude.

d. pitch; timbre.

The idea here, of course, is to choose an alternative so that when the first term is placed in the first blank and the second term is placed in the second blank, we have a true statement. Again we're after the *best* choice. The difference between basses, tenors, altos, and sopranos is largely a matter of pitch. If we are dealing with two basses (or two sopranos, for that matter) pitch becomes less relevant, and we distinguish between the two based on voice or tonal quality, which is what we call timbre. / 84

5. The sense we call gustation is more commonly referred to as the sense of:

a. smell.

b. motion.

c. touch or pressure.

d. taste.

This is a simple, straightforward, vocabulary item. Smell is more technically called olfaction. Our sense of motion is due to many senses, largely the vestibular sense. Touch and pressure are cutaneous sense. Taste is referred to as gustation. / 90

6. Which of the following may be called the most important stimulus factor in directing our attention?

a. size.

b. contrast.

c. motivation.

d. motion.

We are directed to attend to those stimuli that most contrast in some way with other stimuli in our environments. Size and motion are thus potential dimensions of contrast. Although our motivation may affect our attention, it's a personal factor, not a stimulus factor. / 97

7. Over many years of taking multiple-choice tests, your experience tells you that "all of the above" is very commonly the correct answer when it appears as an alternative. In the context of factors that determine attention, which best explains your predisposition to see "all of the above" as the correct answer to a question you are not sure of?

a. contrast.

b. mental set.

c. motivation.

d. repetition.

Now this item requires a bit of thought. You might want to say that you are predisposed to choose *all of the above* simply because of past experience, but *past experience* is not one of your choices here. It's because of your past experience that you may develop a mental set (or be mentally predisposed) to choose *all of the above* when you are in doubt. / 101

8. Although each of the following may play a part, which is the one organizational factor of perception that best accounts for the formation of stereotypes or grouping people together?

a. proximity.

b. closure.

c. similarity.

d. continuity.

This item acknowledges that each of these organizational principles may contribute to the formation of stereotypes, but we generally group people together, overlooking individual differences, if they have some characteristic or characteristics in common. Therefore, similarity would be the best choice here. / 102

Chapter Three

Varieties of Consciousness

Why We Care

The Nature of Consciousness

Sleep and Dreams
>   Stages of Sleep
>   REM and NREM Sleep
>   The Function(s) of Sleep
>>   Deprivation Studies
>>   A Restorative Perspective
>>   An Evolutionary Perspective

Hypnosis

Meditation

Altering Consciousness with Drugs
>   Stimulants
>   Depressants
>   Hallucinogens
>   Marijuana—A Special Case

Fred looked at the calendar. It was March 15. He saw that he had a doctor's appointment that afternoon. Strange, his father had died of lung cancer two years before to the day. Fred's appointment was to check a bad cough that he couldn't seem to get rid of. He felt uneasy. He knew he should probably quit smoking, but although he had tried, he'd never been able to quit for more than a few weeks at a time.

After his appointment, Fred was relieved but puzzled. His doctor had told him that his cough was the result of a bronchial infection, but that his smoking was aggravating the problem. He really should quit, his doctor said. When Fred complained that he'd tried everything to quit but couldn't do it, the doctor referred him to a therapist who used hypnosis. A hypnotist?! Fred had heard that hypnosis could make people do crazy things, that hypnotized people lose control of themselves. He wasn't particularly excited about going. But then he had another coughing fit and thought again about his father. Maybe it wouldn't hurt to try!

At their first session, the therapist explained that hypnosis is an altered state of consciousness in which people can focus their attention on suggestions such as quitting smoking. But first the therapist needed to know if Fred was a suitable candidate for hypnosis because, he explained, not everyone is. Fred was a bit relieved to hear that being hypnotized wasn't an easy matter and that people couldn't be hypnotized against their will. Then the therapist gave Fred a test called the Barber Suggestibility Scale to determine Fred's suitability for hypnosis. The following is what happened.

Fred held his arm out straight. "Your arm is getting heavy and you can't hold it up any longer." No sooner had the therapist said this than Fred's arm fell to his side.

Fred was seated in a quiet room, and the therapist proceeded to ask him to do eight tasks.

"OK Fred. I want you to extend your arm."

Fred held his arm out straight.

"Your arm is getting heavy and you can't hold it up any longer."

No sooner had the therapist said this than Fred's arm fell to his side.

"OK," the therapist said, "Let's try another test. I want you to lock your hands in your lap. Make sure they're tight. In fact, they are permanently locked together."

For the next 15 seconds, Fred tried to pull his hands apart, finally succeeding.

"The next thing I want you to do is try to say your own name. It might not be so easy."

Again, it took Fred about 15 seconds before he could say his name correctly.

The therapist continued. "Now I want you to extend your arm horizontally and watch as it rises."

Out went Fred's arm, rising nearly four inches.

The therapist quickly informed Fred he was extremely thirsty. Fred licked his lips and later told the therapist that he had wanted to ask for a drink of water.

"Try to stand up now, Fred. Can you do it?"

After 15 seconds had elapsed, Fred finally got to his feet.

The therapist gave Fred half credit on the second, third, and sixth tasks since he performed them between 5 and 15 seconds after being told to.

"I'm going to make some clicking sounds now," the therapist said "and when you hear them, you will cough."

The therapist waited a few seconds and then clicked. Fred coughed. The therapist clicked. Fred coughed again.

"Fred, when I ask you about these tasks, you will not be able to remember what you did on the fourth task" (arm-raising).

Sure enough, when asked a little while later about the tasks, Fred remembered what he did on all but the fourth task.

Fred followed the suggestions for all eight tasks. People who perform at least six of the tasks are considered highly susceptible to hypnosis. The average person performs four or five of the tasks. Fred is an excellent candidate for hypnosis.

Can hypnotherapy really help Fred to quit smoking? Are there any particular traits that make some people more susceptible to hypnosis than others? Would you have performed as well as Fred on the eight tasks? Is hypnosis really an altered state of consciousness like sleep? What are the limitations of hypnosis?

We will explore some of these issues and answer questions about other varieties of consciousness in this chapter.

Why We Care

Consciousness is such an integral part of our lives that we might argue that to be alive is to be conscious. You may remember that the earliest psychologists (the structuralists, following Wilhelm Wundt, and the functionalists, following William James) actually defined psychology as the science of consciousness or mental activity. Dealing with consciousness scientifically has proven to be a very tricky business. After decades of struggling in their attempt to understand consciousness, psychologists were more than happy to abandon its study and turn their attention to observable behavior, as John Watson (and behaviorism) suggested they should. But consciousness would not go away, and over the past 20 years, its study has reemerged and resumed its place in mainstream psychology.

Why have we chosen to place our discussion of consciousness here, following a chapter on sensation and perception? Although we might have placed this chapter in a number of different places, we think it is sensible to consider the issues related to the psychology of consciousness here, right after our study of how we process information we receive from our environment. Consciousness refers to our awareness, our perception, of the environment and of our own mental processes. To be fully conscious is to be *awake, aware, alert,* and *attentive.* The extent to which we are conscious or aware of ourselves and our environment will necessarily influence the extent to which we can properly process information.

In this chapter, we will find two things helpful. Let us first consider some matters of definition to gain a better appreciation of just what consciousness *is.* We'll then look at a number of "altered" states of consciousness. Perhaps we can better understand "normal" consciousness if we examine those conditions in which our consciousness, or awareness, is altered, changed, or distorted. We'll look at what happens when our consciousness is affected by sleep, hypnosis, meditation, and drugs.

THE NATURE OF CONSCIOUSNESS

consciousness
our awareness or perception of the environment and of our own mental processes

We define **consciousness** as the awareness, or perception, of the environment and of one's own mental processes. Consciousness, then, is a state of the mind. It is a state of awareness. Normal, waking, or immediate consciousness is the awareness of those thoughts, ideas, feelings, and perceptions that are active in our minds. With this definition in mind, we might ask how best to characterize the nature of consciousness. What are its aspects or its dimensions?

When he addressed a group of psychology teachers at a national conference, Wilse Webb, a respected researcher in the field of sleep and dreaming, was faced with the task of defining consciousness. Webb (1981) claimed that we could do no better than to read what William James had to say about consciousness nearly 100 years ago. James (1890, 1892, 1904), it seems, had a great deal to say about consciousness.

For James, there were four basic realities that relate to what we are calling our normal, waking consciousness. We should keep these four observations in mind as we read through this chapter.

1. Consciousness is always *changing.* Consciousness doesn't hold still. "No state once gone can recur and be identical with what was before," James wrote (1892, p. 152).
2. Consciousness is a *personal* experience. Consciousness does not exist without an individual to have it, and each person's consciousness is separate and different.
3. Consciousness is *continuous.* Our awareness of our environment and of ourselves cannot be broken into pieces. We really can't tell where one thought begins and another leaves off. Here James' metaphor of the mind as a "stream of consciousness," sometimes flowing rapidly—ideas rushing through our minds—sometimes moving more slowly as we pause and reflect, is appropriate.
4. Consciousness is *selective.* Awareness is often a matter of making choices, of selectively attending to or focusing on some aspect of experience while ignoring others.

One way to gain a better understanding of normal states of consciousness is to examine consciousness when its nature has been altered. By definition, if we are in an altered state of consciousness, our perception, or awareness, of ourselves and the environment will be in some way changed, or altered. The nature of these changes and how they are produced is the focus of the remainder of this chapter. We will first discuss a change in the state of our consciousness that is quite normal and common: sleep. (Altered states of consciousness are not necessarily weird and bizarre.) Then we'll examine three means of altering one's consciousness that require some voluntary, deliberate action: hypnosis, meditation, and the use of drugs.

BEFORE YOU GO ON   **What is normal, waking consciousness, and what, according to William James, are its four basic characteristics?**

What is an altered state of consciousness?

SLEEP AND DREAMS

Sleep alters our consciousness by gradually reducing our alertness, awareness, and perception of events occurring around us. Sleep is a very normal process, yet it is one we do not understand well. We are not even aware or conscious of our own sleeping. Sleep can be considered a temporary (one hopes) loss of consciousness. We can know that we have been asleep. We can be certain that we will sleep again. Just as the level or degree of our conscious awareness varies during the day, so do we realize that our sleep varies in its level or quality from night to night and within the same night. But still we face the dilemma that we can't be conscious of our sleep while we're sleeping!

The study of sleeping and dreaming, as variants of normal consciousness, has intrigued psychologists for many years. Webb (1981) reports that the number of available sleep-related articles now exceeds 1,500 per year. In this section, we'll examine some of what we know about this state of consciousness we call sleep.

Stages of Sleep

How do we know when someone is asleep? Self-reports of sleeping are notoriously unreliable. A person who claims that he or she "didn't sleep a wink last night" may have slept soundly for many hours. It may be that some people who claim they have **insomnia** (the chronic inability to get to sleep and to get an adequate amount of sleep) actually dream that they are awake and then remember their dreams (Dement, 1974). Our best, most reliable indicators of sleep are physiological measurements, usually of brain activity and muscle tone. The **electroencephalogram (EEG)** is an instrument that measures and records (on an electroencephalo*graph*) the electrical activity of the brain. It does so through small electrodes that are pasted onto the scalp. The process may be slightly messy, but it is in no way painful. The **electromyogram (EMG)** similarly produces a record of a muscle's activity, tone, or state of relaxation.

When you are in a calm, relaxed state, with your eyes closed, but not yet asleep, your EEG pattern shows a rhythmic cycle of brain wave activity called **alpha activity.** In this presleep stage, we find slow, relatively smooth EEG waves cycling 8 to 12 times every second. If, as you sit or lie there, you start worrying about an event of the day, or start trying to solve a problem, the smooth alpha waves become disrupted and are replaced by a random pattern of heightened electrical activity typical of what we usually find in wakefulness.

As you drift from rest and relaxation into sleep, your brain waves change, as alpha waves give way to the stages of sleep. The EEG tracings of sleeping subjects reveal that sleep can be divided into four different stages. As we describe these four stages, you can refer to Figure 3.1, which shows the electroencephalograms of a subject in each of the stages of sleep. Remember that these tracings were chosen because they best illustrate each of the four stages. The interpretation of EEG patterns is not always this clear.

Stage 1. This is a very light sleep from which you can be easily aroused. The smooth, cyclical alpha pattern disappears, replaced by the slower **theta waves** (3 to 7 cycles per second). The amplitude (or magnitude) of the elec-

LOW

insomnia
the chronic inability to get to sleep and to get an adequate amount of sleep

electroencephalogram (EEG)
an instrument used to measure and record the electrical activity of the brain

electromyogram (EMG)
an instrument used to measure and record muscle tension/relaxation

alpha activity
an EEG pattern associated with quiet relaxation and characterized by slow wave cycles of 8 to 12 per second

theta waves
an EEG pattern characterized by slow wave cycles of 3 to 7 per second

FIGURE 3.1
The EEG records of sleeping subjects illustrate the brain wave activity associated with the different stages of sleep.

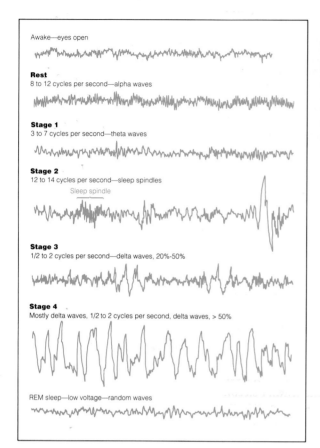

Awake—eyes open

Rest
8 to 12 cycles per second—alpha waves

Stage 1
3 to 7 cycles per second—theta waves

Stage 2
12 to 14 cycles per second—sleep spindles

Sleep spindle

Stage 3
1/2 to 2 cycles per second—delta waves, 20%-50%

Stage 4
Mostly delta waves, 1/2 to 2 cycles per second, delta waves, > 50%

REM sleep—low voltage—random waves

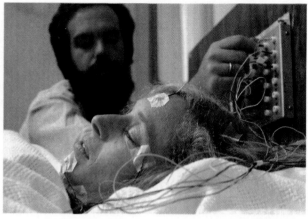

Subjects in sleep labs provide scientists with information about humans during sleep. By hooking the subjects to EEGs, scientists can study the activity of the brain during sleep.

trical activity lessens considerably. At the same time, your breathing is becoming more regular, and your heart rate is slowing and decreasing. This stage doesn't last very long—generally less than 10 minutes. Then, you start to slide into stage 2 sleep.

Stage 2. In this stage, the basic EEG pattern is similar to stage 1—low amplitude with no noticeable wavelike pattern. The difference is that we now see what are called **sleep spindles** in the EEG record. These are brief, high-amplitude bursts of electrical activity that occur with regularity (about every 15 seconds or so). You're really getting off to sleep now, but still can be easily awakened.

Stage 3. Now you're getting into deep sleep. There is a reduction in the brain's electrical activity. Now we can clearly make out **delta wave** activity in your EEG. Delta waves are high, but slow waves (from .5 to 3 cycles every second). In stage 3 of sleep, delta waves constitute between 20 and 50 percent of your EEG pattern. Your internal functions (temperature, heart rate, breathing) are lowering and slowing. It's going to be difficult to wake you now.

Stage 4. Now you're in deep sleep. Your EEG record is virtually filled with slow delta waves, recurring over and over again (as opposed to stage 3

sleep spindles
very brief, high-amplitude peaks in EEG pattern, found in stage 2 sleep

delta wave
an EEG wave pattern (.5 to 3 cycles per second) indicative of deepening levels (stages 3 and 4) of sleep

sleep, where delta waves comprised only a portion of your brain wave activity). At this point, readings from an electromyogram indicate that your muscles have become totally relaxed. About 15 percent of your night's sleep will be spent in this stage of deep sleep.

It usually takes about an hour to go from stage 1 to stage 4. How long it actually takes will, of course, depend somewhat on how tired you are and the physical conditions that surround you. We'll assume a nice, quiet, dark room, with a comfortable and familiar bed. After an hour's passage through these four stages, the sequence reverses itself. You go back through stage 3, then back to stage 2, but before going through the cycle again, something truly remarkable happens. Your eyes start to move rapidly under closed eyelids.

BEFORE YOU GO ON

What is the EEG and EMG?
Briefly describe the four stages of sleep.

REM and NREM Sleep

In the early 1950s, Nathaniel Kleitman and Eugene Aserinsky made quite a discovery. They noticed that as sleeping subjects began their second cycle into deeper levels of sleep, their eyes darted back and forth under their closed eyelids (Aserinsky & Kleitman, 1953). This period of **r**apid **e**ye **m**ovement is called **REM sleep.** The most noteworthy aspect of this discovery is that when sleeping subjects are awakened during REM sleep, they report that they are having vivid, storylike dreams. When awakened during sleep periods that are not accompanied by rapid eye movements (NREM sleep), reports of dreams are significantly fewer in number and much more fragmented (Kleitman, 1963). At first it was believed that eye movements during REM sleep were being made as the dreamer literally viewed, or scanned, images produced by the dream. It turns out that a dreamer's eye movements are unrelated to the content of his or her dream. Eye movements are produced instead by a cluster of cells in the brain stem that is very near other clusters of cells that have been implicated in moving us in and out of REM and NREM sleep cycles (Hobson, 1977; Kiester, 1980).

REM sleep patterns occur throughout the night, normally lasting from a few minutes to half-an-hour. About 90 to 120 minutes each night is spent "REMing." During these REM periods, we are probably dreaming. Dream time seems very well correlated with real time. That is, if subjects are awakened after five minutes of REM sleep, they report that they had been dreaming for about five minutes. If they are left to REM for 20 minutes, they report that they have had a longer dream (Dement & Kleitman, 1957). So much for the notion that all our dreaming is jammed into just the last few seconds before we wake!

Moreover, everyone REMs. Everyone dreams. Some of us may have difficulty remembering what we have dreamed when we awake in the morning, but we can be sure that in the course of a normal night's sleep, we have dreamed a number of times. (There's no great mystery involved in why we don't remember our dreams any better than we do. Most dreams are quite ordinary, boring, and forgettable, and unless we make some conscious effort

REM sleep
rapid eye movement sleep during which vivid dreaming occurs, as do heightened levels of physiological functioning

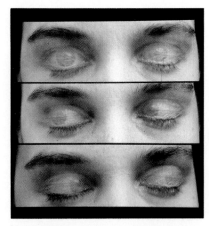

The rapid eye movements of REM sleep are captured in this double-exposure photograph.

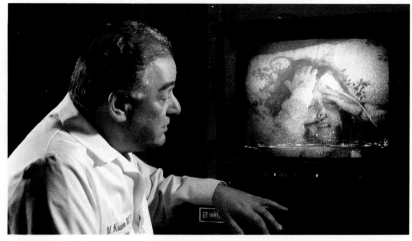

Dreams can be disruptive. Here, a five-year-old child suffering from nightmares followed by severe headaches is videotaped and studied by a psychiatrist.

to do so, we seldom try to store dream content in our memories so that they can be recalled later. That is, we are seldom motivated to remember our dreams.)

The normal pattern of REM occurrences is provided in Figure 3.2, from research by William Dement (1974). Notice in this figure that during the course of a night's sleep, one does not necessarily pass through all of the stages of sleep in an orderly fashion. That is, in some cycles, stage 3 may be passed over completely; in another cycle, stage 4 may be absent. Indeed, toward the end of our sleeping, we tend not to return to the deep sleep of stage 4 between REM cycles. If you refer back to Figure 3.1, you will find an EEG tracing typical of the sort found during REM sleep. Note that it looks very much like the tracing indicating wakefulness.

Although we're sure that everyone does dream, so far we have only theories to account for *why* everyone dreams. Some theories have their basis in the writings of Sigmund Freud (1900), who believed that dreaming allows us the opportunity to engage in fantasy and wish fulfillment of a sort that would cause us discomfort or embarrassment if we entertained such thoughts while we were awake. Freud saw dreams as a pathway (a *royal road,* as he called it) to the discovery of the content of our unconscious mind—content that might otherwise be kept (or repressed) from conscious awareness. He told his patients to remember their dreams so they could be examined for clues and insights into their present difficulties.

Freud was interested in the content of dreams at two levels. The first of these is the actual subject matter of the dream as it is recalled. This is called the **manifest content.** Ideas, thoughts, wishes, or desires might show up in dreams where they would not be expressed otherwise. More controversial is the Freudian notion of the **latent content** of dreams (many psychologists doubt that dreams have latent content). The latent content is the "true" meaning and significance of the dream for the dreamer. Understanding latent content often relies on interpreting the symbolism of dream content. That is, everything in the dream may not be as it appears; it may act as a symbol for something else.

Freud

manifest content
the literal content of a dream as it is recalled by the dreamer

latent content
the underlying meaning of a dream, thought to be symbolically representative

FIGURE 3.2

This illustration shows the typical sequence of sleep stages during a typical night of a young adult. Notice the recurring REM sleep throughout the night.

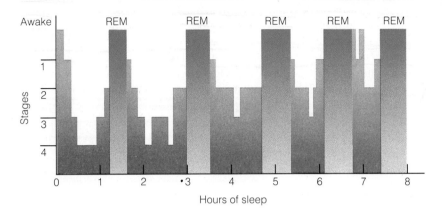

Freud's theory of personality (see Chapter 8) relies heavily on the role of sexual and aggressive motives. Therefore, most Freudian symbolism in dream content revolves around these themes. Dreaming about almost any long pointed object (such as pencils, telephone poles, rocket ships, rifles) is seen as symbolizing the male sex organ. Similarly, dreaming about caves, jars, closets, even coffee mugs can be taken as symbolizing female sex organs. Entering a tunnel, driving a sports car (particularly at high speeds), and riding a horse can symbolize sexual intercourse. Some psychoanalysts find this sort of symbolic interpretation useful in helping them understand their clients or patients. As a scientific theory of dreaming, however, a number of weaknesses arise, not the least of which is how to test the theory. Among other things, very few dreams (of subjects awakened in the laboratory during REM sleep) tend to be sexual at all, either in actual, manifest content or in symbolic, latent content.

More modern theories of the function of REM sleep and dreaming tend to emphasize the physiological activity that occurs during this phase of sleep. One hypothesis argues that REM sleep helps the brain consolidate memories of events that occurred during the day. In one study, for example, subjects were less able to recall stories they read before they went to bed if their REM sleep was interrupted during the night (Tilley & Empson, 1978). Another intriguing notion is that dreams (and/or our recall of them) represent convenient cognitive "explanations" for what may be simply the random activity of our brains. That is, if the area of the brain associated with the movement of our legs becomes active while we are asleep, our brain will "manufacture" a reasonable story—a dream—that involves our running, or kicking, or in some way using our leg muscles (Hobson & McCarley, 1977).

Dreaming isn't the only thing that happens during REM sleep. From the outside, a sleeper in REM sleep seems quiet and calm—except for those barely noticeable eye movements. On the inside, however, there is quite a different story. In many ways, the REM sleeper is very active, although oblivious to (or not conscious of) most external stimulation. One noticeable change is a type of muscular immobility—not because muscles become tensed, but because they become so totally relaxed. This relaxed state is occasionally interrupted by slight muscle "twitches" (which you may have observed if you've watched a sleeping dog that appears to be chasing some imaginary rabbit in its dreams). There is usually an excitement of the sex organs, males having a penile erection, females having a discharge of vaginal fluids (although this latter finding is not as common). Breathing usually becomes shallow and rapid. Blood pressure levels may skyrocket, and heart rates increase, all while the subject lies "peacefully" asleep. Because all this physiological activity is going on, REM sleep is sometimes referred to as "paradoxical sleep." There doesn't appear to be very much quiet and peaceful about it at all. These changes take place regardless of what the subject is dreaming about. It matters little whether one is dreaming about lying on the beach getting a tan or about hand-to-hand combat in World War II; physiologically the reactions are the same.

BEFORE YOU GO ON   **What is REM and NREM sleep?**
What occurs during REM sleep?

The Functions of Sleep

We know a lot about sleep. We can trace sleep through its various stages and cycles and note when dreams are likely to occur. We know that everyone sleeps, although for varying lengths of time. Among other things, how long we sleep is related to our age. We know that everyone REMs and dreams, although many people cannot remember many of their dreams. What we don't know yet is *why* we sleep. We have yet to agree on the *function* that sleep serves. "Perhaps sleep does not have a function. Perhaps, as some have argued, we should accept our failure to isolate a specific function of sleep as evidence for nonexistence of such a function" (Rechtschaffen, 1971, p. 87). But whereas we may not know why we sleep, we do have some hypotheses on the subject. Let's first examine what happens when we are deprived of sleep and then consider a couple of possible explanations for sleep's function.

Deprivation Studies.   In 1960, William Dement reported the results of a sleep deprivation experiment that he had just completed. His report had quite an impact. Dement had systematically deprived college student volunteers of the opportunity to engage in REM sleep. Whenever EEG records indicated that his subjects were falling into REM patterns of sleep, they were awakened. The number of REM deprivations increased as dawn approached; the experimenter had to awaken his subjects more and more frequently. After five nights of interrupted REM sleep, Dement's subjects showed a variety of strange behavioral reactions. They were irritable, somewhat paranoid, noticeably anxious, and lacked the ability to concentrate. Subjects who were awakened just as frequently, but during NREM sleep, showed no such deterioration. Here seemed to be a major breakthrough! We sleep because we need to REM; we need to dream.

The catch is that even Dement has been unable to replicate these findings in later studies (see, for example, Dement, 1974). In fact, most sleep deprivation studies (on animals as well as humans) show remarkably few adverse side-effects of deprivation of any kind of sleep. Even with lengthy deprivation, there are very few lasting changes in the subjects' reactions,

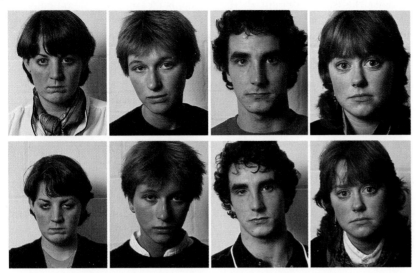

A study conducted at Loughborough University of Technology in England tested the effects of 72 hours of sleep deprivation on volunteers. Despite the weary looks of the four student volunteers in the "after" pictures, they did not experience any adverse side-effects, which supports the findings of previous studies.

particularly if the subject is in good physical and psychological health to begin with. If the task at hand is interesting enough, there is little impairment of intellectual functioning after prolonged sleep deprivation (Dement, 1974; Webb, 1975). Apparently, we can adapt to deprivation, perhaps by taking little "cat naps" while we're awake. Very short episodes of sleep, called *microsleeps,* can be found in the EEG records of waking subjects, both animal and human. Microsleeps increase in number when normal sleep is disrupted.

That's not to say that there aren't *any* effects that result from being deprived of sleep. Subjects deprived of REM sleep for a few nights and then left alone will spend long periods REMing, as if to catch up on lost REMs. But this *rebound effect* is generally only found for the first night after deprivation, and then patterns return to normal. There is some evidence that NREM sleep (particularly stage 4 deep sleep) also rebounds (Agnew, Webb, & Williams, 1964). When, in 1965, 17-year-old Randy Gardner set the Guinness world record by going without sleep for nearly 266 hours, he slept for 14 hours the first night after deprivation, but by the second night, returned to his normal 8 hours of sleep.

A Restorative Perspective.   One of the oldest and most intuitively appealing hypotheses of why we sleep suggests that during the restful course of a good night's sleep, the body has an opportunity to restore the energy it expended during wakefulness. If sleep restores energy or repairs bodily damage, there should be a clear correlation between amount of daily exercise and the extent and nature of nightly sleep. Unfortunately, such relationships are next to impossible to find. Nor is there any compelling evidence of significant changes taking place in blood chemistry as the result of sleeping (see, for example, Schneider & Tarshis, 1986, p. 395). And we clearly do have evidence that sleep, particularly REM sleep, is far from restful and quiet, at least at a physiological level. Recall that during REM sleep, many internal physiological processes (blood pressure, gastric secretions, and the like) are as active as during wakefulness, if not more so.

All of this is *not* to say, however, that significant physiological and biochemical events don't take place during sleep. Indeed, there are a number of significant changes that do take place when we sleep—at least some of the time. And at least some of the time we may sleep precisely so these changes can occur. For example, during sleep there *is* an increased production of growth hormone (GH) secretions. This hormone promotes the growth of bone tissue and increases the normal rate of cell division, two processes that are very important during childhood and adolescence (Oswald, 1980). Unfortunately, the relationship between sleep and increased GH production, although positive, is not very strong. Growth hormone production in infants and many older adults seems virtually unrelated to sleep. Recently, research has focused on changes that occur in brain chemistry (as opposed to blood chemistry) during sleep. Here results have been more positive. There is evidence, for example, that the brain (at least in cats) increases its production of certain complex chemicals called *proteins* during sleep, REM sleep in particular. It is further argued, as we noted earlier, that this process in turn aids in the consolidation of long-term memories of events experienced during the day (McCarley & Hoffman, 1981).

As we have seen before, and as we will see again, the issue is not a simple one. If there are processes of a physiological or biochemical sort that restore the brain or body and require that we sleep in order to do so, these processes are very subtle and complex.

An Evolutionary Perspective.   Sleeping does not seem to be a learned response. It just happens. That it happens is rooted in our biology. That it happens as it does is also rooted in our evolutionary history, according to sleep researcher Webb (1974, 1975). In this view, we sleep as an adaptation to our environment, not so much to restore energy, but to conserve it.

Sleeping is simply a part of being alive—a process we share with many organisms. Some animals, given the way that they have evolved, sleep for only a few minutes or hours each day. Examples include those animals whose only defense against predators is to be vigilant and quick to run away, such as rabbits, sheep, and antelope. Other animals (lions and tigers, for example) sleep even more than humans because they are relatively unthreatened by their environment and are able to find food and shelter easily. They can sleep when and where they please without fear. Humans are diurnal (daytime) animals, and we are guided largely by our visual sense, which works best during daylight hours. At night, we are free to rest and relax, conserving energy and preparing ourselves to face the new day in the morning. From this perspective, asking "Why do we sleep?" makes no more sense than asking "Why do we walk upright?"

BEFORE YOU GO ON   **What are the effects of depriving someone of sleep?**
Briefly summarize the restorative and evolutionary perspectives on the issue of the function of sleep?

HYPNOSIS

Hypnosis is an altered state of consciousness that one enters voluntarily. Hypnosis is characterized by (1) a marked increase in suggestibility, (2) a focusing of attention, (3) an exaggerated use of imagination, (4) an inability/unwillingness to act on one's own, and (5) an unquestioning acceptance of distortions of reality (Hilgard & Hilgard, 1975). There is little truth then, in the belief that being hypnotized is like going to sleep. In fact, few of the characteristics of sleep are found in the hypnotized subject. EEG patterns, for example, are significantly different.

Hypnosis has been used, with varying degrees of success, for a number of different purposes. As you know, it has been used as entertainment, as a show business routine where members of an audience are hypnotized to do usually silly things in public. It has long been viewed as a method for studying consciousness, particularly for gaining access to memories of events not in immediate awareness. Hypnosis has also been touted as a process of treatment for a wide range of psychological and physical disorders. In this section, we'll provide answers, as best we can, to some common questions about hypnosis.

1. *Can everyone be hypnotized?* No. The susceptibility to hypnosis varies rather widely from person to person. Some resist and cannot be hypnotized. Contrary to popular belief, you cannot be hypnotized against your will, which is why we say that one enters a hypnotic state voluntarily.

2. *What best predicts who can be easily hypnotized?* Although not everyone can be hypnotized, some people are excellent subjects, can readily be put into deep hypnotic states, and easily learn to hypnotize themselves (Hilgard, 1975; 1978). A number of traits are correlated with one's hypnotizability. The most important factor seems to be the ability to engage easily in fantasy and daydreaming, to be able to "set ordinary reality aside for awhile" (Wilkes, 1986, p. 25). Other positively related traits include suggestibility (but not gullibility) and a certain degree of passivity or willingness to cooperate, at least during the hypnotic session.

3. *Can I be made to do things under the influence of hypnosis that I would be embarrassed to do otherwise?* Next to being unknowingly hypnotized, this seems to be the greatest fear associated with hypnosis. Again, the answer is generally no. Under the influence of a skilled hypnotist, you may very well do some pretty silly things and do them publicly. But under the right circumstances, you might do those very same things without being hypnotized. It is unlikely that you would do under hypnosis anything that you would not do otherwise.

4. *Are hypnotized subjects simply more open to the suggestions of the hypnotist, or is their consciousness really changed?* This question does not get a yes or no answer. The issue is in dispute. Some believe that hypnosis is no more than a heightened level of suggestibility (Barber, 1972; Spanos & Barber, 1974). Others believe it to be a special state, separate from the compliance of a willing subject. When hypnotized subjects are left alone, they maintain the condition induced by their hypnosis. Subjects not hypnotized,

Regard Hyp [as] altered state of conscious. Viewpoint is that it is not because no altered brain pattern).

Hypnosis is an altered state of consciousness that one enters voluntarily. It has been used for a variety of purposes, including treatment of some psychological and physical disorders.

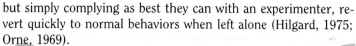

hallucinations
perceptual experiences without
sensory input; that is, perceiving
that which is not there or not
perceiving that which is there

Post Hypnotic Suggestion

*Answer is
unclear—
yes and no*

but simply complying as best they can with an experimenter, revert quickly to normal behaviors when left alone (Hilgard, 1975; Orne, 1969).

5. *Can hypnosis be used to alleviate pain—real, physical pain?* Yes. It won't (can't) cure it, but it can be used to control the feeling of pain. Hypnosis can be used to create **hallucinations** in the hypnotized subject. Hallucinations are perceptual experiences that occur without sensory input—that is, false experiences. Some hallucinations are termed "positive" because the subject is led to perceive something that is not there. Pain reduction can be accomplished through the use of negative hallucinations—that is, the failure to perceive something (pain in this case) that *is* there. **If** a subject is a good candidate for hypnosis in the first place, there is a good chance that at least a portion of perceived pain can be blocked from conscious awareness (Hilgard & Hilgard, 1975; Long, 1986).

6. *Is a person in an hypnotic state in any sense aware of what she or he is doing?* Yes, but in a very strange way. It seems that within the hypnotized subject is a "hidden observer" who may be quite aware of what is going on. In one study (Hilgard & Hilgard, 1975), a subject was hypnotized and told that he would feel no pain as his hand was held in a container of ice water (usually very painful indeed). When asked, the subject reported feeling very little pain, just as expected. The hypnotic suggestion was working. The Hilgards then asked the subject if "some part of him" was feeling any pain and to indicate the presence of such pain by using his free hand to press a lever (or even to write out a description of what he was feeling). Even though the subject continued to *verbally report* no feeling of pain, the free hand (on the behalf of the "hidden observer") indicated that it "knew" there was considerable pain in the immersed hand.

7. *Can I remember things under hypnosis that I couldn't remember otherwise?* Probably not, although this is the most hotly contested issue with regard to hypnosis. In the everyday sense of "Could someone hypnotize me to remember my psychology material better for the test next Friday?" the answer is "Almost certainly not." We might be able to convince you under hypnosis that you had better remember your psychology and that you *want* to remember your psychology, but there is no evidence that hypnotic suggestion can *directly* improve your ability to learn and remember new material. In the more restrictive sense of "I don't remember all the details of the accident and the trauma that followed. Can hypnosis help me remember those events more clearly?" the answer is less definite. When we get to our discussion of memory (Chapter 5) we'll see that distortions of memory in recollection can occur in normal states. In hypnotic states, the subject is suggestible and susceptible to distortions in recall furnished by the hypnotist (even assuming that the hypnotist has no reason to cause distortions). To the extent that hypnosis can reduce feelings of anxiety and tension, it may help in the recollection of anxiety-producing memories. The evidence is neither clear nor convincing on this issue in either direction.

Hypnosis alters one's consciousness, opens one to suggestions of the hypnotist, can be used to treat symptoms (if not their underlying causes), and can distort one's view of reality. However, we are learning that it is neither mystical nor magical; there are limits to what hypnosis can do.

BEFORE YOU GO ON

What is hypnosis?
What changes in consciousness does it produce?
Who can be hypnotized?

MEDITATION

Meditation is a self-induced state of altered consciousness characterized by an extreme focusing of attention and relaxation. Meditation is usually associated with ancient or Eastern cultures and has been practiced for many centuries. We tend to think of the practice of meditation in a religious context. Meditation became quite popular in this country in the 1960s. It was then that psychologists began to study the process seriously. In this section, we'll first review the process of meditation, and then we'll look at the claims that have been made about its potential benefits.

There are a number of different kinds of meditation, but specific techniques can be roughly divided into two types. In one type, an individual works at gradually ridding the mind of any content. The goal here is a literally open mind, devoid of its daily thoughts, feelings, and aggravations. The other, more popular, form of meditation requires a mental focusing, or concentration. *Transcendental meditation,* or TM, is a form of this second variety (Maharishi, 1963). In TM, one begins meditating by becoming calm, relaxed, and assuming a comfortable position. The meditator then directs attention toward one particular stimulus. This could be some simple bodily function, such as one's own breathing. Attention could be focused on some softly spoken or chanted word, or phrase, or **mantra,** such as "ummm," "one," or "calm." As attention becomes focused, other stimuli, either external or internal (like thoughts or feelings or bodily processes), are blocked from conscious consideration. Throughout, the attempt is to relax, to remain calm and peaceful. By definition, a state of meditation cannot be forced; it just happens, and its practitioners claim that to reach an altered state of awareness through meditation is not difficult (Benson, 1975).

Once in a meditative state, there *are* measureable physiological changes that take place that allow us to claim meditation to be an altered state of consciousness. The most noticeable is a predominance of alpha waves in the EEG record (remember, such waves characterize a relaxed state just *before* one enters into sleep). Breathing usually slows and becomes deeper. Oxygen intake is reduced, and heart rate may decrease (Wallace & Benson, 1972).

There is no doubt that many people can enter meditative states of consciousness. The doubts that have arisen concerning meditation center on the claims for the benefits that can be derived from doing so. One of the major claims for meditation is that it is a reasonably simple and very effective way to enter into a state of relaxation. The reduction of bodily (or "somatic") arousal is taken to be one of the main advantages of meditation. The claim is that by meditating, one can slow bodily processes and enter into a state of physical as well as psychological calm.

meditation
the focusing of awareness in order to arrive at an altered state of consciousness and relaxation

mantra
a soft word or sound chanted repeatedly to aid the meditation process

During meditation, breathing usually slows and deepens, oxygen intake is reduced, and heart rate may decrease.

Researcher David Holmes (1984, 1985) reviewed the evidence for somatic (bodily) relaxation through meditation. On a number of different measures of arousal and relaxation, including heart rate, respiration rate, muscle tension, and oxygen consumption, Holmes concluded that there were *no differences* between meditating subjects and subjects who were "simply" resting or relaxing. After reviewing the data of dozens of experiments, Holmes stated, ". . . there is not a measure of arousal on which the meditating subjects were consistently found to have reliably lower arousal than resting subjects. Indeed, the most consistent finding was that there were not reliable differences between meditating and resting subjects. Furthermore, there appear to be about as many instances in which the meditating subjects showed reliably higher arousal as there are instances in which they showed reliably lower arousal than their resting counterparts" (1984, p. 5).

Another claim that is often made for meditation is that people who practice meditation are better able to cope with stress, pressure, or threatening situations than are people who do not practice meditation. Once again, Holmes (1984, 1985) reports that he could find no evidence to support this claim. In fact, in four of the studies he reviewed, Holmes found that under mild threat, meditating subjects showed greater arousal than did non-meditating subjects.

We must add two important notes here: (1) A number of psychologists have taken issue with Holmes' methods and conclusions, arguing that meditation *does* offer advantages over simply resting, suggesting also that "resting" is a difficult concept to define (see, for example, Shapiro, 1985; Suler, 1985; West, 1985). (2) Notice that Holmes in no way argues that meditation isn't of any value. He just argues that with regard to somatic arousal, there is no evidence that it is any better than resting.

Some of the claims made for meditation techniques go beyond simple relaxation and somatic arousal reduction. Those claims that meditation can raise one to transcendental heights of new awareness and thus make you a better person are viewed with considerable skepticism in psychology. Some meditators claim that they have an enormous "openness" to ideas and feelings, that they have hallucinatory experiences, and that they can divorce themselves from their bodies and minds. Such experiences might, in some instances, be true. The idea that a meditator can exist apart from present experience and view life "as if from without" is not too far removed from Hilgard's notion of a "hidden observer" in hypnosis. Nonetheless, the majority of psychologists who have investigated meditation continue to question claims for a heightened state of well-being that is achieved through such little effort and that relies more on testimonials of personal experience than on hard scientific evidence (Webb, 1981).

BEFORE YOU GO ON

What is meditation?

Is meditation an effective means of relaxation and reduction of somatic activity?

ALTERING CONSCIOUSNESS WITH DRUGS

In this section, we will discuss some of those chemicals that alter our consciousness by inducing changes in our perception, mood, and/or behavior. Because of their effect on such basic psychological processes, these chemicals are referred to as **psychoactive drugs.**

Drugs have been used for centuries for the purpose of altering one's state of consciousness. No reasonable person would take a drug because he or she expected to have a bad, negative, unpleasant experience. Psychoactive drugs are taken—at least originally—in order to produce a state of consciousness that the user considers to be good, positive, pleasant, even euphoric. As we all know, however, the use of drugs that alter our mood, perceptions, and behaviors often have seriously negative outcomes. In this regard, there are a few terms that will be relevant throughout our discussion. Though there is not complete agreement on how these terms are used, for our purposes, we'll use the following definitions.

(1) **Dependence:** (a) when continued use of a drug is required to maintain bodily functioning (called physical dependence), or (b) when continued use of a drug is believed to be necessary to maintain psychological functioning at some level (called psychological dependence). *"I just can't face the day without my three cups of coffee in the morning."*

(2) **Tolerance:** a condition in which the use of a drug leads to a state where more and more of it is needed to produce the same effect. *"I used to get high with just one of these; now I need three."*

(3) **Withdrawal:** a (usually extreme) negative reaction, either physical or psychological, that results when one stops taking a drug.

(4) **Addiction:** an extreme dependency, physical or psychological, in which signs of tolerance and painful withdrawal are usually found. *"No way I'm gonna give it up no matter what. It feels too good, and the pain is too great without it."*

psychoactive drug
a chemical that has an effect on psychological processes and consciousness

dependence
a state in which drug use is either necessary or believed to be necessary to maintain functioning at some desired level

tolerance
in using a drug, a state where more and more of the drug is required to produce the same desired effect

withdrawal
a negative, painful reaction that may occur when one stops taking a drug

addiction
an extreme dependency, usually accompanied by symptoms of tolerance and painful withdrawal

Clearly, the use or abuse of drugs can and often does lead to a number of psychological or mental disorders. These we'll discuss in Chapter 9. The use of drugs as therapeutic agents in the treatment of psychological disorders will also be covered separately (see Chapter 10).

There are many psychoactive drugs. We'll focus on four different types: stimulants, depressants, hallucinogens, and (as a separate category) marijuana.

Stimulants

stimulants
those drugs (such as caffeine, cocaine, and amphetamines) that increase nervous system activity

Chemical **stimulants** do just that—they chemically stimulate, or activate, the nervous system. If nothing else, they produce a heightened sense of arousal. In general, they create not only an increase in activity, but also an elevation of mood.

Caffeine is one of the most widely used of all stimulants. It is found in a number of foods and drinks (most commonly coffee, tea, and chocolate) as well as in many varieties of over-the-counter and prescription painkillers. In moderate amounts, it seems to have no dangerous or life-threatening effects on the user. At some point, a mild dependence, at least of a psychological nature, may develop. Although it is not yet known precisely *how* caffeine does so, it temporarily increases cellular metabolism (the general process of converting food into energy), which then results in a burst of new-found energy. It also seems to block the effects of inhibitory neurotransmitters in the brain (Julien, 1985).

After excessive use, giving up sources of caffeine may result in the pain of withdrawal. There is usually a rebound sort of effect when caffeine intake is stopped. That is, you may drink many cups of coffee to help yourself stay awake and aroused enough to withstand an all-night study session, but within a few hours after you stop drinking the caffeine, you may rebound and experience a streak of real mental and physical fatigue—perhaps right at exam time!

Nicotine is another very popular stimulant. It is usually taken by smoking and is absorbed by the lungs. Nicotine is carried from the lungs to the brain very quickly—in a matter of seconds. There is no doubt that nicotine is a stimulant of central nervous system activity, but it does relax muscle tone slightly, which perhaps explains in part the rationalization of smokers who claim that they can relax by having a cup of coffee and a cigarette. Nicotine seems to have its stimulant effect by activating excitatory synapses in both the central and peripheral nervous systems (McKim, 1986).

Many individuals develop a tolerance to nicotine, requiring more and more of it to reach the desired state of stimulation. Indeed, beginning smokers generally cannot smoke more than one or two cigarettes without becoming ill. The drug often leads to dependency and, in many cases, addiction, where withdrawal can be accompanied by a wide range of unpleasant symptoms. How ultimately addictive nicotine (or perhaps any other drug) becomes may depend primarily on how quickly it enters the brain. That is, people who take many quick deep puffs when smoking may become addicted more easily to nicotine than will people who take slow, shallow puffs (Bennett, 1980).

Cocaine is a naturally occurring stimulant derived from leaves of the coca shrub (native to the Andes mountains in South America). Some time periods seem to have drugs of their own: alcohol in the 1920s and marijuana in the 1960s, for example. Cocaine and its derivative "crack" appear to be *the* drugs of the 1980s.

The allure of cocaine is the rush of pleasure and increased energy that it produces when it first enters the bloodstream, either through the mucous membranes when inhaled through the nose ("snorting") or directly through injection. A cocaine "high" doesn't last very long—15 to 20 minutes is standard. There are a number of reactions that result from taking cocaine. One is that the drug blocks the reuptake of two important neurotransmitters. That means that once these neurotransmitters have entered the synapse, cocaine will prohibit their being taken back up (reuptake) into the neuron from which they have been released. The end result is that, for some period of time at least, excessive amounts of these neurotransmitters are available in the nervous system. The neurotransmitters in question are *norepinephrine*, which acts in both the central and peripheral nervous systems to provide arousal and the sense of extra energy, and *dopamine*, which acts in the brain to produce feelings of pleasure and euphoria.

The rush of the psychological reactions to cocaine is short-lived, and these reactions are followed by a period of letdown approaching depression.

It seems that some of the physiological effects of cocaine use are very longlasting, if not permanent, even though the psychological effects last but a few minutes. Not only is the rush of the psychological reactions to cocaine short-lived, but these reactions are followed by a period of letdown approaching depression. As the user knows, one way to combat letdown and depression is to take more cocaine. Such a vicious cycle invariably leads to dependency and addition. Cocaine addiction tends to run in families to such an extent that current research is exploring the hypothesis that there is a genetic basis for cocaine addiction. Cocaine is a drug that no one can handle safely.

Amphetamines are synthetically manufactured chemical stimulants that usually come in the form of capsules or pills under many brand names and street names, such as bennies, uppers, wake-ups, cartwheels, dexies, or jellie babies. In addition to blocking reuptake, amphetamines actually cause the release of dopamine and norepinephrine. However, their action is considerably slower and somewhat less extensive than is that of cocaine. Once the amphetamine drug takes effect, users feel alert, awake, aroused, filled with energy, and ready to go. Unfortunately, such results are short-lived and deceptive. The drug does not create alertness so much as it is masks fatigue, which will ultimately overcome the user when the drug wears off. It now seems clear that these are not the only effects of amphetamine use; it has a direct effect on the heart and circulatory system, causing irregular heartbeat and increased blood pressure, for example (McKim, 1986). Once again, with the amphetamines, tolerance and dependency build quickly, and withdrawing from the use of amphetamines can be a long and painful process.

What are stimulant drugs, and what are their effects?

BEFORE YOU GO ON

Depressants

In terms of their effects on consciousness, **depressants** are the opposite of stimulants. They reduce one's awareness of external stimuli, slow normal bodily functioning, and decrease levels of overt behavior. Predictably, the reaction that one gets to depressants depends largely on how much is taken.

depressants
those drugs (such as alcohol, opiates, heroin, and barbiturates) that slow or reduce nervous system activity

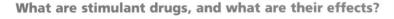

Cocaine and
Amphetamines
both block
"reuptake"

1) norepinephrine
   CNS - PNS
2) Dopamine
   Brain

Altering Consciousness with Drugs **129**

Despite the stimulated feeling some individuals claim to experience while drinking alcohol, it is important to remember that alcohol is a depressant that slows nervous system activity.

In small doses, they may produce relaxation, freedom from anxiety, and a loss of stifling inhibitions. In greater amounts, they may produce sedation, sleep, coma, or death.

Alcohol is doubtless the most commonly used of all the depressants. It has been in use for thousands of years. In many ways, alcohol is the most dangerous of all drugs, largely because of its popularity and widespread use. More than two-thirds of Americans drink alcohol on a regular basis, and more than $36 *billion* per year is spent on distilled spirits alone (Mayer, 1983). Alcohol is certainly the most deadly of drugs. Alcohol-related traffic fatalities alone are enough to qualify alcohol for this distinction.

Perhaps the first thing to remember about alcohol is that it is a depressant. Some individuals may feel that they are entertaining and stimulating when they drink alcohol, but their nervous system activity is actually being depressed and slowed. Alcohol increases urination, leading to overall loss of fluids. It affects vision by lowering visual sensitivity, making it more difficult to detect dim lights. There is virtually no doubt that alcohol affects mood, leading to feelings of friendly elation as levels rise and of anger, depression, and fatigue as alcohol levels drop (Babor et al., 1983).

The specific effects of alcohol on the drinker usually reflect a number of interacting factors, primarily *amount*. What matters most is the amount of alcohol that gets into the person's bloodstream, usually through the stomach. The amount of alcohol in one's bloodstream (blood alcohol level, or BAL) at any one time is affected by how much one drinks and by how fast the alcohol can get into the bloodstream, which in turn is affected by what else happens to be in the stomach at the time. Indeed, drinking on an empty stomach may be more dangerous than drinking while or after eating, because the alcohol will be more quickly absorbed. In most states, 1/10th of 1 percent alcohol in the bloodstream is considered legally drunk. At this level, brain activity is so affected that decision making becomes distorted and motor coordination is impaired (both are the sorts of skills usually required to drive safely).

The effect that alcohol has on a person may also be a function of the person's frame of mind. Sometimes a few drinks seem to produce little effect on a person. Sometimes a couple of beers can have that same person dancing around the room, lampshade on head, acting in a generally foolish way. At other times, the same two cans of beer may turn the same person into a crying, "sad drunk." That is, a person's reactions often reflect cognitive variables—one's frame of mind and one's perception of what is going on in the environment at the time.

Opiates, such as morphine and codeine, are also called "analgesics" because they can be used to reduce or eliminate sensations of pain. It was for this purpose that they were first commonly used. In small doses, they create feelings of well-being and ease, relaxation, and a trancelike state. Unlike alcohol, they seem to have little effect on motor behavior. The catch, again, is that they produce very strong dependence and addiction. Their removal results in extreme pain and depression.

Heroin is an opiate, originally (in the 1890s) derived from morphine, but thought not to be as addictive. That thought was soon proven wrong. Strong dependency and addiction grow rapidly as increased tolerance for the drug builds, leading to more and more chemical being required to produce the same effects that were once gained with small amounts. As with other drugs, we find that the addictive nature of heroin may be related to its very rapid entry into the brain. (Methadone, used in some treatment programs for long-term heroin users, is a drug with many of the chemical properties of heroin and many of the same psychological effects. A major difference is that methadone is very slow to reach the brain and as a result tends not to produce heroin's predictable "rush," which makes it somewhat less addictive.)

Those effects of heroin (above whatever pain-killing use it might have) seem to be most related to one's emotional state and mood. Unlike alcohol, or the opiates like morphine, there are seldom hallucinations or thought disturbances associated with heroin use. But as increased amounts of heroin are needed to produce the desired emotional states of pleasant euphoria, tolerance builds, and increased dosages of heroin can cause breathing to stop, often for long enough periods for death to result.

Barbiturates are synthetically produced sedatives. Like opiates, there are many types and varieties. All slow nervous system activity—in small amounts producing a sense of relaxed tranquility and in higher doses producing sleep or coma. They cause this effect either by blocking the receptor sites on the postsynaptic membrane of excitatory synapses and/or by enhancing the effects of inhibitory neurotransmitters. Some barbiturates are addictive, producing strong withdrawal symptoms when their use is discontinued. All will produce dependency if used with any regularity as users become habitual users. As is generally the case, once addiction develops, getting off these drugs is very hard to do.

What are depressant drugs, and what are their effects?   BEFORE YOU GO ON

Hallucinogens

Those chemicals we call **hallucinogens** have the most unpredictable effects on consciousness. One of the main reactions to these drugs is the formation of hallucinations, usually visual. That is, users often report seeing things when there is nothing there to see, or they tend to see things in ways that others do not. Hallucinations of hearing, smell, touch, and taste are possible, but much less common.

LSD, or lysergic acid diethylamide, is a potent and popular hallucinogen. Psychologically, LSD raises levels of emotionality and causes profound changes in perception, often producing vivid visual hallucinations. Only quite recently have scientists discovered exactly how LSD works (Jacobs & Trulson, 1979; Jacobs, 1987). One of the first steps toward discovery was finding that levels of a particular neurotransmitter, called serotonin, increased when LSD was given to animals. This was not too surprising, because LSD (and similar hallucinogens, such as mescaline) has a chemical composition much like that of serotonin. Serotonin has its effects, both excitatory and inhibitory, on many areas of the brain. To quote neuroscientist Barry Jacobs, "Once a drug acts upon the brain serotonin system, it sets in motion a cascade of events involving much of the enormous complexity of the brain and many of its constituent neurochemical systems. Thus, the brain serotonin system acts as a trigger for a multitude of changes whose

hallucinogens
those drugs (such as LSD) whose major effect is the alteration of perceptual experience and mood

serotonin

Hallucinogens bring about very unpredictable effects on consciousness. Visual hallucinations are one of the main effects. This painting was done by a Huichol Indian under the influence of the drug peyote. It shows a deer's heads rotating around the god of fire.

elaboration generates the hallucinatory experience"(1987, p. 387). We now know that levels of serotonin increase with LSD use because the LSD acts on serotonin receptor sites, acting just like it was a neurotransmitter. And very small doses (measured in only millionths of a gram) can produce major behavioral effects.

The changes in mood that take place under LSD may simply be extreme exaggerations of one's present mood. From the start, this has been viewed as one of the dangers of LSD. Many individuals are drawn to drugs like LSD because things are not going well for them, and they are simply in a bad mood. They hope that LSD will help cheer them up. In fact, it will probably make their moods worse, resulting in a "bad trip," by exaggerating the feelings they had when they took the drug.

The hallucinations that occur under the influence of LSD usually involve an exaggeration of some actual perception. That is, colors seem much more vivid, stationary objects appear to move, dimly lit stimuli take on a glow, and otherwise unnoticed details become very apparent. On some occasions, LSD gives rise to an experience of **synesthesia.** In this condition, a stimulus of one modality is perceived in a different modality, a crossing-over of sensory processing. For example, the individual may "hear" colored lights, "see" sounds, "feel" odors, and so forth. Whether people really experience synesthesia is hard to tell for sure. What matters is that the subjects themselves believe they can.

synesthesia
a condition of cross-sensory experience—seeing sounds, hearing colors, tasting odors, and the like—associated with hallucinogen use LSD

BEFORE YOU GO ON   **What are hallucinogenic drugs, and what are their effects?**

Marijuana—A Special Case

Marijuana is a consciousness-altering drug that we'll consider as a special case because it doesn't fit neatly into any of the other three categories. In some ways, marijuana acts as a depressant. In small dosages, its effects are very similar to those of alcohol: decreased nervous system activity and depression of thought and action. In higher doses, however, marijuana acts very much as if it were an hallucinogen, producing hallucinations and alterations in mood.

Marijuana is produced from the cannabis plant, which often grows wild as a weed (given strong profit motives, the plant is also illegally cultivated and harvested as a cash crop). The active ingredient in marijuana is the chemical compound THC (tetrahydrocannabinol). THC is also the active ingredient in hashish (a similar, but more potent drug also made from the cannabis plant). Although marijuana has been found to increase overall levels of some neurotransmitters, it is not known just how it produces this effect. There don't seem to be any specific receptor sites at neural synapses for THC, or at least none have been found yet.

Marijuana is one of the most difficult drugs for society to deal with. It is currently illegal to sell, possess, or use the drug. In many ways, the drug seems no worse than alcohol. There is a little evidence that marijuana tolerance develops, but virtually none that it is addictive. Is marijuana dangerous? Certainly, if for no other reason than it is usually smoked, and smoking is clearly a danger to one's health. It is also dangerous in the sense that alcohol is dangerous. Excessive use leads to impaired judgment, impaired reflexes, unrealistic moods, and poor physical coordination (Bennett, 1982; Weil et al., 1968).

The most debatable aspect of marijuana use involves the results of moderate to heavy long-term use. People are tired of hearing this response (users in particular), but the evidence just isn't in yet. The data are more suggestive than definitive. Marijuana use seems to cause bronchitis and other lung ailments (usually associated with smoking, but with marijuana, even more so). It may have genetic implications (it seems to produce chromosomal abnormalities in nonhumans at least). It may adversely affect the body's immune system and white blood cells. Its use often impairs memory function, affecting memories of recent events in particular. It seems to have predictably negative effects when taken during pregnancy, resulting in smaller babies, increased numbers of miscarriages, and so on. (Grinspoon, 1977; Julien, 1985).

Though there is little evidence that smoking marijuana is addictive, it is harmful to the lungs and can cause impaired judgment, slower reflexes, and poor coordination.

What is the active ingredient in marijuana, and what effects does it produce?   BEFORE YOU GO ON

To be conscious is to be aware of one's mental processes and one's environment. Our conscious perception is personal, ever changing, continuous, and selective. Our states of consciousness change subtly as we move from alert wakefulness through the stages of sleep and dreaming. We can voluntarily induce changes in the state of consciousness by meditating, undergoing hypnosis, or using any one of a wide variety of psychoactive drugs.

Chapter Three
Varieties of Consciousness

SUMMARY

What is normal, waking consciousness, and what, according to William James, are its four basic characteristics?

What is an altered state of consciousness?

We define consciousness as the perception or awareness of our environment and our own mental processes. According to William James, consciousness can be defined as always (1) changing, (2) personal, (3) continuous, and (4) selective. By definition, we experience an altered state of consciousness whenever the nature of our awareness or perceptions is changed or altered. / 114

What is the EEG and the EMG?

Briefly describe the four stages of sleep.

The EEG (electroencephalogram) is an instrument that measures the general pattern of the electrical activity of the brain, the most common indicator of sleep stages. The EMG (electromyogram) measures muscle tone or tension, another indicator of sleep. In addition to a state of relaxed wakefulness, characterized by EEG alpha waves, we say there are four stages, or levels, of sleep: (1) light sleep with

low amplitude, slow theta waves; (2) low amplitude EEG waves with sleep spindles present, (3) delta waves enter the EEG pattern; and (4) deep sleep, with more than 50 percent delta wave activity. / 117

What is REM and NREM sleep?

What occurs during REM sleep?

REM sleep is rapid eye movement sleep, and it occurs 4 to 7 times per night. A number of events occur during REM sleep, most noticeably vivid, story like dreams. During REM sleep, we also find loss of muscle tone, excitement of sexual organs, shallow, rapid breathing, and increased heart rate and blood pressure. During NREM sleep, one progresses through the four stages of sleep, accompanied by little dream activity. / 120

What are the effects of depriving someone of sleep?

Briefly summarize the restorative and evolutionary perspectives on the issue of the function of sleep.

People who have been deprived of sleep show a rebound effect by making up for lost sleep at the earliest possible time, usually in just one

night. This is true for REM sleep more than for NREM sleep. In most cases, we show remarkably few adverse effects of sleep deprivation. The restorative view of sleep suggests that it is a time needed by the body to restore energy and repair damage. Little evidence supports this view directly. Alternative versions suggest that sleep promotes physical growth, the formation of memories, and restoration of chemical depletion in the brain. The evolutionary perspective claims that sleep is an evolved, adaptive response that promotes conservation of energy at night when humans (being diurnal) don't function well anyway. / 122

What is hypnosis?

What changes in consciousness does it produce?

Who can be hypnotized?

Hypnosis is an altered state of consciousness into which one enters voluntarily and is characterized by an increase in suggestibility, a strict focusing of attention, an exaggeration of imagination, a reduction of spontaneous activity, and an unquestioning acceptance of distortions in reality. Not everyone can be hypnotized. Those that can most readily be hypnotized are persons who easily engage in fantasy and daydreaming and who show signs of suggestibility and a willingness to cooperate with the hypnotist. / 125

What is meditation?

Is meditation an effective means of relaxation and reduction of somatic activity?

Meditation is an altered state of consciousness characterized by an extreme focusing of attention and a distortion of perceptions. It is usually self-induced. There are many claims for the benefits of meditation. It does seem to be an effective means of relaxing and reducing overall levels of somatic activity, but there is considerable evidence that it is not significantly more effective in these regards than a number of other techniques. / 127

What are stimulant drugs, and what are their effects?

Stimulants are psychoactive drugs such as caffeine, nicotine, cocaine, and amphetamines. Their basic effect is to increase the level of nervous system activity and to elevate mood, al-most always by affecting the activity of the neural synapse, increasing levels of the neurotransmitters norepinephrine and dopamine. With heavy use, tolerance may develop, as may dependence and addiction. / 129

What are depressant drugs, and what are their effects?

The depressants include such drugs as alcohol, the opiates (for example, morphine, codeine), heroin, and a variety of synthetic barbiturates. All depressants slow nervous system activity, reduce one's awareness of external stimuli, and, in small doses, may alleviate feelings of nervousness and anxiety. In large doses, however, they produce sedation, sleep, or coma. Tolerance, dependency, and addiction may result from the use of these drugs. / 131

What are the hallucinogenic drugs, and what are their effects?

Hallucinogens are drugs that alter mood and perceptions. LSD is an example. They get their name from their ability to induce hallucinations, where a user may have an experience unrelated to what is going on in the user's environment. Synesthesia, an halluci-natory experience that crosses sensory modalities ("hearing" lights, for example), may occur under the influence of LSD. / 132

What is the active ingredient in marijuana, and what effects does it produce?

The active ingredient in marijuana is the chemical compound THC. Listing its short- and long-term effects is difficult because of contradictory evidence. However, it does seem that in small doses, there is nothing particularly dangerous about the drug, at least in terms of its psychological effects. It is at least as dangerous as cigarette smoking, and it is illegal. Of more concern is long-term, heavy use. Here many of the negative side affects that we associate with long-term alcohol use seem present: impaired judgment and reflexes, unrealistic mood, and poor coordination. In addition, marijuana may have adverse effects on the body's immune system and has been implicated in producing a range of negative consequences when taken during pregnancy. / 133

Chapter Three
Varieties of Consciousness

REVIEW QUESTIONS

1. William James characterized consciousness as having four major aspects or components. Of the following characteristics, which was *not* listed by James as typical of consciousness?

a. It is selective.

b. It is continuous.

c. It is automatic.

d. It is personal.

James argued that one's consciousness is intensely personal. Each person has her or his own consciousness which cannot be directly shared with others. Using the phrase "stream of consciousness," James claimed that consciousness is continuous and cannot be broken into fragments or pieces. He also said that consciousness is selective, a matter of making choices, and shifting focus. Although some conscious processes may be automatic, we certainly can exert voluntary control over our consciousness, making (c) the correct choice for this item. / 114

2. Which of the following levels or stages of sleep/wakefulness is characterized by smooth, regular EEG waves (alpha activity) that cycle about 8 to 12 times per second?

a. the calm, relaxed state that precedes sleep.

b. REM sleep.

c. deep sleep, when it is difficult to awaken the sleeper.

d. an awake state with eyes open.

EEG alpha activity is associated with the calm, relaxed state of consciousness that precedes sleep. In REM sleep, EEGs are typified by small, random waves. Deep sleep patterns are of much greater amplitude and reflect delta activity. Being awake with eyes open, produces a pattern of EEG activity much like REM sleep—low amplitude with essentially random activity. / 115

3. Which of the following statements concerning sleep and dreaming is *not* true?

a. Everyone dreams.

b. Depriving a person of REM sleep produces the same effects as depriving someone of NREM sleep.

c. During REM sleep there is a noticeable lack of muscular movement, except for eye movement.

d. Physiological activity during dreams seems to be unrelated to the content of one's dreams.

Everyone dreams, although we all do not necessarily remember our dreams. Assuming a normal night's sleep, everyone dreams for about an hour and a half to two hours each night. During REM sleep, our skeletal muscles become immobile, and the content of our dreams seems to have no effect on internal, physiological reactions. The effects of depriving someone of NREM sleep are different (and often hardly noticeable) from the effects of depriving someone of REM sleep, making (b) the correct choice. / 117

4. Which theoretical explanation for why we sleep and dream is best associated with Sigmund Freud?

a. Sleeping and dreaming give the body an opportunity to restore and replenish its resources.

b. Dreaming provides the unconscious mind time to express itself free from conscious control.

c. We have evolved as organisms that are awake and alert during the day and sleep at night.

d. Sleep and dreaming allow the brain to consolidate and store in long-term memory its experience of the previous day.

Although each of these present theoretically possible positions, Freud's view of dreaming is that it allows the unconscious mind to express itself free from conscious control. Remember that Freud called dreams the royal road to the unconscious mind. / 118

5. A true state of hypnosis is characterized by all of the following *except*:

a. an exaggerated use of imagination.

b. an uncritical acceptance of distortions of reality.

c. a significant increase in physical strength.

d. an inability or unwillingness to act on one's own.

Hypnosis is an altered state of consciousness into which one enters voluntarily. In addition to the descriptions given in alternatives (a), (b), and (d), hypnosis is also characterized by an increase in suggestibility and a focusing of attention. Hypnosis, thus, has a number of defining characteristics, but being able to demonstrate a significant increase in physical strength (c) is not one of them. / 123

6. Which of the following best predicts a subject's tendency to be easily hypnotized?

a. sex (whether the subject is male or female).

b. ability to think independently.

c. ability to easily engage in daydreaming.

d. ability to solve complex problems.

Not everyone can be hypnotized. Even willing subjects are not equally susceptible. Since hypnosis is an altered state of consciousness, we should not be surprised to learn that an ability to suspend reality, to engage in fantasy and daydreaming, provides a good indication of the likelihood that someone can be hypnotized. The other alternatives listed in this item have virtually no effect. / 123

7. What do we call the condition in which the use of a psychoactive drug leads to a state where more and more of the drug is needed to produce the same effect?

a. tolerance.

b. physical dependence.

c. addiction.

d. withdrawal.

By definition, this condition is known as tolerance. A physical dependence occurs when the continued use of a drug is required to maintain bodily functioning at some level (no increase in dosage is required). Addiction is an extreme dependency which may provide evidence of both tolerance and withdrawal, the negative reaction that occurs when one stops taking a drug. / 127

8. Which of the following drugs is classified as a stimulant?

a. alcohol.

b. heroin.

c. LSD.

d. nicotine.

This is a straightforward item. You should be able to classify each of the psychoactive drugs mentioned in the text as a stimulant, depressant, or hallucinogen. Of the drugs listed in this item, both alcohol and heroin are depressants, LSD is a hallucinogen, and nicotine is the stimulant. / 128

Chapter Four

Learning

Why We Care

A Definition of Learning

Classical Conditioning
Pavlov and a Classic Demonstration
Classical Conditioning Phenomena
Acquisition
Extinction and Spontaneous Recovery
Generalization and Discrimination
The Significance of Classical Conditioning: What About People?
A Demonstration
Conditioned Emotional Responses
Recent Developments (and Complications).
Can Any Stimulus Serve as a CS?
Must the Time Interval Between the CS and the UCS Be Brief?
Can Classical Conditioning be Used to Explain Drug Addiction?

The Basics of Operant Conditioning
Defining Operant Conditioning
The Procedures of Operant Conditioning
The Course of Operant Conditioning
Shaping
Acquisition
Extinction
Spontaneous Recovery

Reinforcement and Punishment
A Definition of Reinforcer
Positive Reinforcers
Negative Reinforcers
Escape Conditioning
Avoidance Conditioning
Primary and Secondary Reinforcers
Scheduling of Reinforcement
Punishment

Generalization and Discrimination

Can Any Response Be Operantly Conditioned?

Cognitive Approaches to Learning
Edward Tolman and David Olton: Latent Learning and Cognitive Maps
Albert Bandura: Social Learning and Modeling

Applying Conditioning and Cognitive Theories of Learning to Your Study of Psychology

There were approximately 25 students enrolled in the Psychology of Learning class that met every Monday, Wednesday, and Friday morning from 9:00 to 9:50. The instructor was a dynamic lecturer. The topic for the week was operant conditioning. After describing the procedures of operant conditioning and stressing its importance in everyday life, the instructor suggested that the class try to use operant conditioning principles to change the behaviors of one of its professors.

The idea seemed like a good one, and the choice was easy to make. Following the learning class, most of the students moved across the hall for a class in child psychology. It was a larger class, with as many as 75 to 80 students in attendance on a good day. The professor in the child psychology class had a very boring lecture style: He simply read his notes to the class. Every day he would go through the same ritual. He would find his place in his notes, check the time on his pocket watch, and then read to the class for 50 minutes. He wasn't a poor reader, and what he was reading was no doubt quality psychology. But the students thought his classroom style left much to be desired. They decided to condition his behavior.

The class decided to reward the professor for doing what they wanted him to do by smiling, looking attentive, and appearing to take many notes. When he did

what the students did not want him to do, they would look away, appear bored, and stop taking notes.

The project began on a Wednesday. When the students assembled after class that day, they realized that they weren't very well organized. They hadn't specifically defined exactly *what* it was they wanted to reward. They only thought that they wanted

---

In just five days these students lifted their professor from his chair and placed him in the corner!

---

their professor to stop reading to them. The students thought that after that first day the professor *was* looking up from his notes a bit more than usual, but they weren't even sure of that.

After their first "failure" on Wednesday, the students did get some results on Friday. By the end of class, the professor was looking up from his notes more than usual and he was moving around in his chair. Monday's class brought a major breakthrough: The professor rose from the chair! From time to time he would sit

down again (only to be ignored), and he would not give up physical contact with his notes. He was still reading, but occasionally he would stand to do so.

On the first Wednesday: nothing. The following Friday: some movement. The next Monday: standing. By the following Friday, about halfway through the class period, the professor was standing in the corner; notes still on his desk, he was talking to the class about child psychology. Think about that. In just five days these students lifted their professor from his chair and placed him in the corner! The students had no doubt that within 10 minutes they could have moved their professor from one corner to another. All this was done simply by rewarding some behaviors with attention and ignoring others—and in fewer than five classes. The class was impressed.

This is a true story, but the end is not a happy one. As you might imagine, when the instructor got to the corner, the class could no longer control itself. When the students started laughing, the instructor demanded to know what was going on. When he was told, he did not take kindly to having been the subject of the classes' experiment and went back to reading his notes. If you try this exercise, choose the subject of your experiment and the behaviors you want to condition with care.

Why We Care

Who we are as individuals is ultimately a reflection of the unique combination of our inherited characteristics (our nature) and our experiences with our environment (our nurture). Our nature is largely established at the moment of conception. There isn't much we can do about the genes we have inherited from our parents. At least there is some hope that we can influence who we are—what we know, what we feel, what we do—by attending to how we learn, how we change our behaviors as a function of our experience.

How we change and learn and adapt to our environment is clearly a major issue in psychology. In this chapter we'll begin by defining learning. Then we'll concentrate on a deceptively simple form of learning: classical conditioning. Whether they realize it or not, most people are familiar with the basic work of Ivan Pavlov on classical conditioning, and for the sake of simplicity, most of our descriptions of classical conditioning will be based on Pavlov's work with salivating dogs. Once we have the basic procedures in hand, we'll consider why classical conditioning is so important in our daily lives. We'll also cover some of the more recent research that is being done on this variety of learning.

Next we'll turn our attention to operant conditioning. In operant conditioning, what matters most are the consequences of an organism's behavior. The basic premise is that our behaviors are controlled by the consequences they produce. Learning is a matter of increasing the rate of those responses that produce positive consequences and decreasing the rate of responses that produce negative consequences. We shall see that a great deal of human behavior can be explained by operant conditioning. We'll define some basic terminology and spend a good deal of time examining some principles of reinforcement—and punishment.

Finally, we'll examine a sample of the views of psychologists who argue that we should consider more than a simple conditioning approach to learning. We'll begin by considering Edward Tolman and David Olton's notion that we (and rats) learn without even trying. Then we'll examine Albert Bandura's evidence that learning can result from the simple observation of others.

A DEFINITION OF LEARNING

learning
demonstrated by a relatively permanent change in behavior that occurs as the result of practice or experience

Let's begin this topic with a definition. We shall say that **learning** is demonstrated by a relatively permanent change in behavior that occurs as the result of practice or experience. This is a rather standard definition, and it raises some important points that we should explore for a moment.

For one thing, we say that learning is *demonstrated by* changes in behavior. The major issue here is that learning is a process (like many others in psychology) that cannot be observed directly. In a literal sense, there is no way that your instructors can directly observe, or measure, what you have learned. All they can measure directly is your performance or your behavior. To determine if you have learned something, someone must ask you to perform and then make inferences about your learning on the basis of your performance. Sometimes they may be wrong.

For example, you may learn everything there is to know about the psychology of learning for your next exam. But just before your exam, someone you care about becomes seriously ill. As a result, you don't get much sleep. Then you develop a sinus headache and catch the flu. When you come in to take your exam, you have a high fever and feel miserable, and you fail the exam. Your instructor may infer (incorrectly in this case) that you haven't learned very much psychology. On the other hand, there may be someone else in class who has not studied at all and has actually learned very little. But the exam is of the multiple-choice type, and she correctly guesses the answers to 95 percent of the questions. Here your instructor might assume (incorrectly again) that this student has learned a great deal.

One way to express this issue is to say that what is learned is some *potential,* or predisposition, to respond. Because what is learned is simply potential, we will not recognize that learning has taken place until that potential is realized in behavior. (This issue will reemerge in our discussion of memory. What gets graded on most exams, after all, is not so much what you have learned, as what you appear to have remembered.)

We also say that the changes that take place in learning must be *relatively permanent.* They are not fleeting or cyclical changes, such as those due to fatigue or temporary shifts in motivation. Imagine, for example, that you want to study the behavior of a skilled typist. You are going to observe Sharon, a secretary who reportedly types 95 words per minute without error, where typing 60 to 65 words per minute is considered to be a good rate.

Early Monday morning you go watch Sharon type. You find her typing only 54 words per minute and making an error every other line. Disappointed, you seek out another typist, but are told that there is no one better than Sharon. Two hours later, after pausing for breakfast, you return to Sharon's desk and now find her typing away at 91 words per minute without error!

No matter how conscientious and attentive a student may be in class, the teacher cannot observe directly what he or she has learned. The closest measurement is an exam which only measures performance.

Surely you wouldn't want to claim that between 8:15 and 10:15 on that Monday morning Sharon "learned" how to type. There's a better explanation for the change in behavior that you have observed. It's called *warm-up*. Sharon will probably go through this short-lived, cyclical change in her behavior every Monday morning and to a lesser degree on every other morning of the week. And *fatigue*, not forgetting, would best account for her decreased typing skills if you were to watch her again at the end of the day. These are important changes in behavior, but they are not due to learning. Learned changes are relatively permanent.

We have another phrase in our definition to remind us that there are other changes in our behavior—and important ones—that are not considered to result from learning. We say, by definition, that learned changes in behavior result from *practice* or *experience*. For one thing, this phrase reminds us that some changes may be due to maturation (that is, heredity). The fact that birds fly, that salamanders swim, or that humans walk probably has more to do with genes and physical development than with learning and experience. This phrase also serves to remind us that those changes in our behaviors due to automatic physiological reactions, such as sensory adaptation, are not learned. When we enter a darkened theater, we don't really "learn" to see in the dark. Our vision improves and our behaviors change as our eyes adapt to the lighting in the theater. Consider your own behavior when you sit in a tub of hot water. Your behavior changes as you settle down and relax, as you adapt to ("get used to") the hot water—more of a physiological change than a learned one.

One final point about the nature of learning is worth mentioning. As students and parents and teachers, we often fall into the habit of thinking that learning is necessarily a good thing. Clearly, it isn't always so. We can learn bad, ineffective habits as readily as we learn good, adaptive ones. For example, smokers rarely ever honestly claim to have enjoyed the first cigarette that they smoked. Yet many people have learned the habit, which is hardly an adaptive one.

If we put these ideas together, we come up with our definition of learning: Learning is demonstrated by (or inferred from) a relatively permanent change in behavior that occurs as the result of practice or experience. In this chapter we will discuss two forms or varieties of learning that we call **conditioning**. Conditioning and learning are synonymous terms and can be used interchangeably. We simply agree to call the most basic, fundamental types of learning *conditioning*.

In learning to ride a bicycle, a relatively permanent change has occurred. Seldom does someone "forget" the skill.

*fixed action
patterns = instinct*

conditioning
demonstrated by a relatively permanent change in behavior that occurs as the result of practice or experience

How do we define learning?
How do we define conditioning?

BEFORE YOU GO ON

CLASSICAL CONDITIONING

When we think about learning, we generally think about such activities as memorizing the Bill of Rights, studying for an exam, or learning to *do* something like ice skate. But our study of the psychology of learning begins in the laboratory of a Russian physiologist who taught dogs to salivate in response to tones. How salivating dogs could possibly be relevant to college students is difficult to imagine at first, but the relevance will become apparent soon.

Pavlov and a Classic Demonstration

Psychology was just beginning to emerge as a science late in the nineteenth century. At this time, Ivan Pavlov was using his skills as a physiologist to try to understand the basic processes of digestion—work for which he was awarded the Nobel Prize in 1904. Focusing on the salivation reflex in dogs, Pavlov knew that he could produce salivation in his subjects by blowing food powder into their mouths. A **reflex** is defined as an unlearned, automatic response that occurs in the presence of a specific stimulus. Every time Pavlov presented the food powder, his dogs salivated.

Pavlov's fame in psychology stems from the fact that he pursued something not so simple as reflex responses. Occasionally, his dogs would salivate *before* the food was put in their mouths. They would salivate at the very sight of the food or even at the sight of the laboratory assistant who delivered the food. With this observation, Pavlov went off on a tangent that he pursued for the rest of his life (Pavlov, 1927; 1928). We now call the phenomenon he studied **classical conditioning**—a type of learning in which an originally neutral stimulus comes to evoke a new response after having been paired with another stimulus that reflexively evokes that same response. In his honor, we sometimes refer to this type of learning as Pavlovian conditioning.

To demonstrate classical conditioning, we first need a stimulus that reliably (that is, consistently) produces a predictable response. The relationship between this stimulus and the response it evokes is usually a natural, unlearned, reflexive one. Given this stimulus, the same response always follows. Here is where Pavlov's food powder comes in. If we present the stimulus food powder, the salivation response reliably follows. There is no learning in this reflexive association, so we call the stimulus an **unconditioned stimulus (UCS)** and the response that it evokes an **unconditioned response (UCR).** So now we have a UCS (food powder) producing a UCR (salivation).

To get classical conditioning under way, we need a second, neutral stimulus that, when presented, produces a minimal response or a response of no particular interest. For this stimulus, called the **conditioned stimulus (CS),** Pavlov chose a tone.* At first, when a tone is sounded a dog *will* respond. It will, among other things, perk up its ears and try to orient toward the source of the sound. As a result, we call this response an *orienting reflex*. After awhile, however, the dog will get used to the tone and will essentially ignore it. Technically, we call this process *habituation* and say that the dog "habituates" to the tone; habituation is itself a simple variety of learning.

Now we are ready to go. We have two stimuli—a tone (CS) that produces a minimal response of no particular interest and food powder (UCS) that reliably produces salivation (UCR).

Once we get our stimuli and responses straight, the rest is easy. The two stimuli are paired. That is, they are presented at about the same time—first, the tone, then the food powder, CS then UCS. The salivation response occurs

---

reflex
an unlearned, automatic response that occurs in the presence of specific stimuli

classical conditioning
learning in which an originally neutral stimulus comes to evoke a new response after having been paired with a stimulus that reflexively evokes that same response

unconditioned stimulus (UCS)
in classical conditioning, a stimulus (for example, food powder) that reflexively and reliably evokes a response (the UCR)

unconditioned response (UCR)
in classical conditioning, a response (for example, salivation) reliably and reflexively evoked by a stimulus (the UCS)

conditioned stimulus (CS)
in classical conditioning, an originally neutral stimulus (for example, a tone) that, when paired with a UCS, comes to evoke a new response (a CR)

---

*Literally, a "condition*ed*" stimulus would be one that has been already learned, which hardly seems reasonable, because we haven't even started yet! We prefer to call this stimulus a "to-be-conditioned stimulus." Pavlov originally used the term "condition*al*" for this stimulus, but he was mistranslated. Convention and common usage dictate that we use the term *conditioned stimulus,* or *CS.*

Here, the effects of classical conditioning on Pavlov's famous dog are studied.

automatically in response to the food powder. So we have CS, then UCS, which is followed by UCR, or tone-food-salivation. Each pairing of the CS and the UCS may be considered a conditioning *trial*. If we repeat this procedure a number of times—have a number of trials—conditioning (learning) takes place. We produce a relatively permanent change in behavior as a result of this experience. After a number of trials, when we present the tone by itself, the dog salivates, something it did not do before. Now the dog salivates not just in response to the food powder, but also in response to the tone, or the CS. To keep *this* response separate from the salivation we get in response to the food powder, we call it a **conditioned response (CR),** indicating that it has been learned or conditioned.

Let's review this one more time, referring to Figure 4.1 which presents the procedure in a schematic diagram. (1) We start with two stimuli—the CS, which originally evokes no response, and the UCS, which evokes the UCR. (2) We repeatedly present the two stimuli together. (3) We find that when we present the CS alone, it now produces a CR.

If you have a pet at home, you've no doubt seen this very process in action. If you keep your pet's food in the same cabinet all the time, you may

conditioned response (CR)
in classical conditioning, the learned response (for example, salivation) evoked by the CS after conditioning

---

FIGURE 4.1
Pavlovian classical conditioning. See text for explanation.

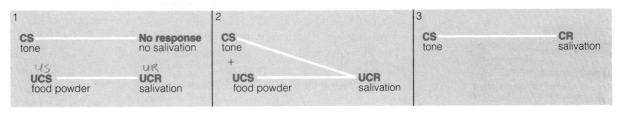

1		2		3	
CS tone	**No response** no salivation	**CS** tone +		**CS** tone	**CR** salivation
UCS food powder	**UCR** salivation	**UCS** food powder	**UCR** salivation		

Classical Conditioning **145**

note a full range of excited, anticipatory behaviors by your pet every time you open that cabinet door. The open cabinet door (CS) has been repeatedly paired with the food within it (UCS), now producing the same sort of reaction (CR) that was originally reserved only for the food (UCS).

Before we examine some phenomena associated with classical conditioning, there are two technical points to make. First, the CR seldom reaches the strength of the UCR no matter how many times the CS and the UCS are paired. For example, in Pavlov's demonstration, we never get as much salivation in response to the tone (CR) as we originally got in response to the food powder (UCR). Second, *how* the CS and the UCS are paired does matter. If you think about it, you'll realize that there are many ways in which two stimuli can be presented at about the same time (that is, simultaneously, or UCS then CS, or CS then UCS, with varying time intervals in between). One method consistently seems to work best: the CS comes first, followed shortly (within a second) by the UCS, or tone-food-salivation again.

BEFORE YOU GO ON   **Summarize the essential procedures of Pavlovian classical conditioning.**

Classical Conditioning Phenomena

Now that we have the basics of classical conditioning in mind, we can consider some of the details that go along with it—some of the insights developed in Pavlov's laboratory. We'll first see how a classical conditioning experiment actually proceeds. Just to keep our terminology firmly in mind, we'll continue to refer to the original Pavlovian example of salivating dogs.

Acquisition.   The stage of classical conditioning during which the strength of the CR increases—where a dog acquires the response of salivating to a tone—is called **acquisition.** When conditioning begins, the conditioned stimulus (CS) does not produce a conditioned response (CR). After a few pairings of the CS and UCS together (conditioning trials), we can demonstrate the presence of a CR. There will be some saliva produced in response to the tone presented alone. The more trials, or presentations of the CS and UCS together, the more the dog will salivate in response to the tone when it is presented alone. Over repeated trials, the increase in CR strength (here, the amount of saliva in response to the tone) is rather rapid at first, but soon starts to slow and eventually levels off. Figure 4.2 illustrates this acquisition phase of a classical conditioning demonstration.

Extinction and Spontaneous Recovery.   Assume that we now have a dog that produces a good deal of saliva at the sound of a tone. Continuing to present the CS + UCS pair adds little to the amount of saliva we get when we present the tone alone. Now suppose that we go through a series of trials during which the CS (the tone) is presented, but is *not* paired with the UCS (no more food powder). The result of this procedure is that the CR will weaken. If we keep it up, the dog will eventually stop salivating to the tone. This process is called **extinction,** and we say that the CR has extinguished.

It would appear that we're right back where we started. Because the CR has extinguished, when we present the tone, our dog does nothing—at least

acquisition
the process in classical conditioning in which the strength of the CR increases with repeated pairings of the CS and UCS

extinction
the process in classical conditioning in which the strength of the CR decreases with repeated presentations of the CS alone (without the UCS)

FIGURE 4.2
The stages of conditioning. (1) Acquisition is produced by repeated pairings of the CS and the UCS. The strength of the CR increases rapidly at first and then more slowly. (2) Extinction is produced by presenting the CS without the UCS. The strength of the CR decreases. (3) After a rest, spontaneous recovery produces a partial return of the CR.

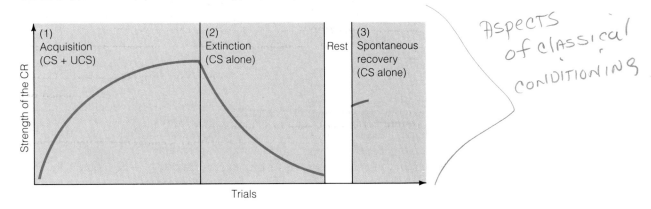

Aspects of classical conditioning

it no longer salivates. Let's give our dog a rest and return it to the kennel. When the dog is returned to the laboratory later and the tone is sounded, the dog salivates again! Not a lot, perhaps, but the CR salivation does return, or recover. Since it recovers automatically, or spontaneously, we call this phenomenon **spontaneous recovery.** Both extinction and spontaneous recovery are illustrated in Figure 4.2.

Spontaneous recovery typically takes place after extinction and following a rest interval, which indicates two things. First, one series of extinction trials may not be sufficient to eliminate a conditioned response. To get our dog to stop salivating altogether, we may have to run a series of extinction trials, many of which may be followed by a small spurt of spontaneous recovery. Second, what is happening during extinction is not literally "forgetting"—at least not in the usual sense. It seems that the response is not forgotten so much as it is *suppressed.* That is, the salivation response is still there, but it is not showing up in performance during extinction, which is why it can (and does) return later, in spontaneous recovery.

spontaneous recovery
the phenomenon in classical conditioning in which a previously extinguished CR returns after a rest interval

In classical conditioning, what are acquisition, extinction, and spontaneous recovery?

BEFORE YOU GO ON

Generalization and Discrimination.   During the usual course of conditioning, let us consistently use a tone of a given pitch as the conditioned stimulus. After repeated pairings of this tone with food powder, a dog salivates when the tone is presented alone.

What will happen if we present a different tone, one that the dog has not heard before? Typically, the dog will salivate in response to it also. This response may not be as strong as the original CR (again, there may not be as much saliva). How strong it is, or how much saliva is produced, depends primarily on how similar the new tone is to the original CS. The closer it is to the original, the more saliva will be produced. This process is called **generalization,** and we say that the conditioned response will generalize to other new, yet similar stimuli.

generalization
the phenomenon in classical conditioning in which a CR is evoked by stimuli different from, but similar to, the CS

Classical Conditioning   **147**

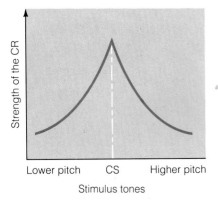

Lower pitch   CS   Higher pitch

Stimulus tones

discrimination
the phenomenon in classical conditioning in which an organism learns to make a CR in response to only one CS, but not to other stimuli

experimental neurosis
a condition of anxiety and agitation evidenced by subjects that are required to make too fine a discrimination in a classical conditioning task

This is a powerful phenomenon. It means that an unconditioned stimulus need not be paired with all possible conditioned stimuli. If you choose an average, or midrange CS, the conditioned response will automatically generalize to many other similar stimuli. Conditioning trials do not have to be applied over and over again for separate stimuli. A graph of the generalization process is presented in Figure 4.3.

So if a dog is conditioned to salivate to a tone of middle pitch, it will also salivate to higher and lower tones through generalization. What if we do not want it to? What if we want our dog to salivate to the CS alone and *not* to other tones? We would use **discrimination** training. In a sense, discrimination is the opposite of generalization. In discrimination training, we would present the dog with many tones, but would pair the UCS food powder with only one of them—the CS we want the dog to salivate to. We might, for example, pair the food powder with a tone of middle C. A lower tone, say A, would also be presented to the dog, but would not be followed by food powder. At first, there might be some saliva produced in response to the A tone (through generalization). Eventually, however, our subject would learn to discriminate and would no longer respond by salivating to the A tone.

Some discriminations may be too difficult to make. One of Pavlov's students conditioned a dog to salivate to a stimulus circle. The circle was paired with food powder, and after awhile the dog learned to salivate when the CS circle was presented. When the dog was then presented with a stimulus in the shape of an ellipse, salivation followed—generalization again. The circle and the ellipse were then presented many times. Now the circle was always followed by food powder; the ellipse never was. Eventually, the dog learned to discriminate, salivating only to the circle and never to the ellipse. This procedure was repeated, gradually changing the shape of the oval to make it rounder and more similar to the conditioned stimulus circle. The circle was always followed by food powder; the ellipses were not.

At one point, the dog could no longer discriminate between the two stimuli. The oval now looked too much like the circle. Because it was unable to discriminate between the two stimuli, we might predict that the dog would simply salivate to both of them. However, the behavior of the animal in this situation changed markedly. It stopped salivating altogether. It began to bark and whimper and tried to escape.

To Pavlov, the dog appeared to be very nervous and anxious. The dog was being asked to make a discrimination that it could not make. It was in conflict. Pavlov referred to the dog's reactions as **experimental neurosis,** adding that ". . . in short, it presented all the symptoms of acute neurosis" (Pavlov, 1927, p. 291). Whether or not the reaction of this laboratory animal provides us with insight about neuroses in humans is open to debate. Do anxiety and nervousness originate simply from an inability to make proper discriminations among stimuli? Probably not, but as Barry Schwartz (1984, p. 128) says, it is tempting to think of neurosis in such terms, and, if nothing else, "What Pavlov's demonstration showed is that a very specific, isolated conditioning experience can transform the general behavior of an animal. It is not implausible that some human neuroses might stem from particular conditioning experiences of this sort."

BEFORE YOU GO ON   In classical conditioning, what are generalization and discrimination?

The Significance Of Classical Conditioning: What About People?

It is time to leave our discussion of dogs and salivation and Pavlov's laboratory. We now need to turn our attention to the practical application of all of this. In fact, we can find examples of classically conditioned human behaviors all around us.

A Demonstration.   Of one thing we can be sure: We can bring the procedures of classical conditioning directly into the human learning laboratory. Here is a laboratory demonstration that you can do with a friend. Have your subject seated at a desk, relaxed and staring straight ahead. Position a drinking straw just off to the side of your subject's face so that it cannot be seen. (Getting your subject to relax and stare ahead under these conditions is the only difficult part of this procedure.)

Your UCS (unconditioned stimulus) will be a strong puff of air through the straw into your subject's eye. The obvious UCR (unconditioned response) will be an involuntary, sudden blink of the eye. For a CS (conditioned stimulus), just tap on the desk. After a brief habituation period, your subject will not respond to your tap, and you'll be ready to go. Remember the best sequence: CS-UCS-UCR, or tap-puff-blink. Repeat this procedure a dozen times or so and then present the CS alone. Tap on the desk and your subject will (should) respond with the CR (conditioned response) by blinking to the tap on the desk.

This does qualify as conditioning. There will be a relatively permanent change in your subject's behavior as a result of the experience of pairing together a tap and a puff of air to the eye. As it happens, this is not a particularly useful or significant sort of learning—the response here is rather trivial—but it is learning.

Conditioned Emotional Responses.   One of the most significant aspects of classical conditioning is its role in affecting our emotional responses to stimuli in our environment. There are very few stimuli that naturally, or instinctively, produce a specific emotional response. Yet think of all those things that *do* directly influence how we feel.

For example, very young children seldom seem afraid of spiders, airplane rides, or snakes. (Some children actually seem to enjoy each of these.) Now consider how many people you know who *are* afraid of these things. There are many stimuli in our environments that cause us to be afraid. Many of our fears are quite rational and realistic. When we claim that many emotional responses are learned through classical conditioning, we are not just referring to intense, irrational, phobic fears.

What scares you? What makes you feel at ease, calm, and comfortable? Why? Might you not feel particularly upset or distressed in a certain store because you once had an unpleasant experience there? Might you fondly anticipate a vacation at the beach because of a very enjoyable vacation you had there as a child? Do you shudder at the sight of a police car? Do you smile at the thought of a payroll envelope? Does walking into the classroom on the day of an exam cause you some anxiety? In each of these cases, we're talking about classical conditioning. (To be fair, we must say that not all of our learned emotional reactions are acquired through classical conditioning alone. As we shall see later in this chapter there are other possibilities.)

For many children, flying is an enjoyable experience that they anticipate with great excitement. For others, the thought of flying instills fear that they are likely to carry through adulthood.

Classical Conditioning **149**

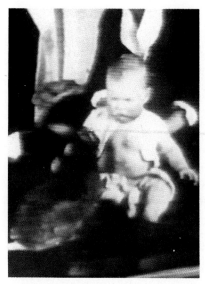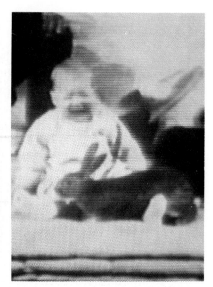

In 1920, Little Albert's conditioned fear of a white rat generalized to other similar stimuli, including a rabbit as pictured here.

Let's take a detailed look at a famous example of the conditioning of an emotional response. In 1920, John B. Watson (the founder of behaviorism) and his student assistant Rosalie Raynor published a summary article on a series of experiments they performed with "Little Albert." Little Albert's experiences have become quite well known, and even though Watson and Raynor's summary of their own work tended to oversimplify matters somewhat (Samuelson, 1980), the story of Little Albert still provides a good model for the classical conditioning of emotional responses.

Eleven-month-old Albert was given many toys to play with. Among other things, he was allowed to play with a live white rat. Albert seemed to enjoy the rat—he certainly showed no signs of fearing it. Then conditioning began. One day, just as Albert reached for the rat, one of the experimenters (Raynor) made a sudden loud noise by striking a metal bar with a hammer. The loud noise was frightening—that much Watson and Raynor had established two months earlier during initial observations of Albert in the laboratory. At least Albert made responses that Watson and Raynor felt indicated fear.

After repeated pairings of the rat and the noise, Albert's reaction to the rat underwent a relatively permanent change. Now when presented with the rat, Albert would at first start to reach out toward the rat, then he would recoil and cry, often trying to bury his head in his blanket. He was clearly making emotional responses to a stimulus that did not evoke those responses before it was paired with sudden loud noises. This sounds like classical conditioning: The rat is the CS and the loud sudden noise is the UCS that evokes the UCR of an emotional fear response. After repeated pairings of the rat and the noise (the CS and UCS), the rat evokes the same sort of fear response (or CR).

Watson and Raynor then went on to demonstrate that Albert's fear of the white rat *generalized* to all sorts of other stimuli: a dog, a ball of cotton, and even a mask with a beard and mustache. Albert's emotional reaction surely did generalize to other similar stimuli. In a number of instances, however, Watson and Raynor did not test for generalization in a straightforward way. They occasionally paired the loud noise (UCS) with new stimuli (S) before testing to see what the reaction might be (Harris, 1979).

As it happens, there are a number of issues that have been raised concerning the Watson and Raynor demonstration of learned fear—not the least of which is the unethical treatment of poor Albert. Watson had previously argued (1919) that emotional experiences of early childhood could affect an individual for a lifetime, yet here he was purposely frightening a young child (without the advised consent of his mother). In fact, Albert's mother removed him from the hospital before Watson and Raynor had a chance to undo the conditioning. They were convinced that they could uncondition Little Albert, but as fate would have it, they never got the chance. It should also be mentioned that a number of researchers who tried to replicate Watson and Raynor's experiment (despite ethical considerations), were not totally successful (Harris, 1979).

Even with all these technical disclaimers, it is easy to see how the Little Albert demonstration can be used as a model for describing how fear and other emotional responses can develop. When they began their project, Albert didn't respond fearfully to a rat, cotton, or a furry mask. After a few trials of pairing a neutral stimulus (the rat) with an emotion-producing stimulus (the loud noise), Albert appeared afraid of a number of white, furry, fuzzy objects.

As a final example, assume that you have before you two small boys, each 3 years old. You ask them to say quickly, out loud, everything they think of when you say a word. You say "dog." Boy #1 responds, "oh, doggie; my doggie; Spot; my friend; good dog; go fetch; friend; my dog; Spot." Boy #2

Words mean different things to different people. For example, young children who have pleasant experiences with dogs will probably have pleasant thoughts and feelings about dogs as they grow older.

responds, "Oooo dog; bite; teeth; blood; bad dog; hurts me; bad dog." Now both of these boys know what a dog *is*. How they feel about dogs is another matter and is quite obviously a function of their experience with dogs—a classically conditioned emotional reaction.

BEFORE YOU GO ON   **What sorts of responses are most readily influenced by classical conditioning?**

Briefly summarize the Little Albert experimental demonstration.

Recent Developments (and Complications)

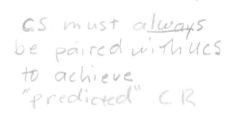

LIMITATIONS TO STIMULUS

You may get the impression from this discussion of classical conditioning that what we are describing here is only of historical interest. After all, most of our discussion has dealt with procedures and phenomena that we associate with Pavlov's laboratory soon after the turn of the century. Psychologists' interest in classical conditioning did not begin and end with Pavlov's lab, however. In fact, Pavlovian conditioning has lately become a very active area of research in experimental psychology (Domjan, 1987; Rescorla 1987).

Psychologists today are interested in understanding precisely what happens when conditioned responses are formed during classical conditioning. They are also interested in understanding the factors that affect the effectiveness or efficiency of the basic procedure. In this section, we'll mention just three recent lines of research in classical conditioning. This section is intended to fill you in on some current thinking about conditioning and to remind you that things are seldom as simple as they may first appear.

CS must always be paired with UCS to achieve "predicted" CR

Can Any Stimulus Serve as a CS?   Pavlov believed—and so did generations of psychologists who followed him—that *any* stimulus paired with an unconditioned stimulus could effectively serve as a conditioned stimulus. It is easy to see how Pavlov and others could have come to their conclusion. Indeed, we can pair any one of a wide variety of stimuli with the presentation of food powder and demonstrate a classically conditioned CR of salivation. However, there are some circumstances in which a stimulus will not serve as a CS, even when it is repeatedly paired with an effective UCS. Let's briefly consider two such circumstances.

A rat can be conditioned to fear the sound of a tone by presenting the rat with the tone and following it with a strong shock. It doesn't take many of the tone-shock, CS-UCS pairings for the CR (fear of tone) to develop. This is true even if shocks don't always follow tones. What does matter is that whenever a shock occurs, it is always preceded by a tone. What if another rat is presented with the same number of tone-shock pairings, but this rat will occasionally be shocked without the preceding tone. For the first rat, the tone reliably "predicted" the onset of a shock. Every time the tone sounded, a shock followed. For the second rat, tone-shock pairings were just as frequent, but the tone did not reliably "predict" the shock. Sometimes, the shock would occur without the preceding tone. The first rat will be classically conditioned to fear the tone; the second will show no acquisition of CR fear of the tone (Rescorla, 1968; 1987).

In another set of experiments (Kamin, 1968; 1969) rats were shocked (UCS) at the same time a noise was presented (CS). Classically conditioned fear of the noise was readily established. The rats were then presented with a number of trials in which the noise *and* a light (a new CS) were paired with the UCS of a shock. Even though the light was paired with the shock a number of times, no conditioned fear of the light could be found.

In both these cases (and others), it seems that what matters most in determining whether or not a stimulus will act as a CS is the extent to which that stimulus provides useful information to the organism or predicts the occurrence of another stimulus. In the basic Pavlovian demonstration, the tone was highly informative: Every time it was presented, food powder followed, and in this case the tone served as an effective CS. In Rescorla's experiments, we see that if a tone does not predict the onset of shock (if some shocks occur without a "warning" tone), then that tone will not serve as a CS no matter how many times it is paired with the UCS. And in Kamin's experiments, we see that because the rats had already learned that the noise predicted the onset of shocks, adding the light as a potential CS provided no additional useful information and hence was ineffective. Barry Schwartz has provided a human example of what we're talking about here (1984, pp. 91–92). As experienced drivers, we react to a number of road signs as conditioned stimuli. If we see a sign that says "bridge out—road closed," we turn around and try another route. We have learned this response (a complicated CR) because our experience has told us that such signs predict actual occurrences. If we began to discover that such road signs did not accurately predict road conditions, we would begin to ignore them. Signs serve effectively as CSs only to the extent that they predict the occurrence of a UCS.

Under what circumstances are stimuli likely to serve effectively as CSs?   BEFORE YOU GO ON

Must the Time Interval Between the CS and the UCS Be Brief?   Pavlov recognized that the time interval between the CS and the UCS was a critical variable in classical conditioning. For nearly 50 years, it was generally assumed that the best interval between the CS and UCS was a very brief one (about 2 seconds for salivary conditioning, about 0.5 second for eyeblink conditioning, for examples (Beecroft, 1966)). The claim found in most textbooks on learning was that the shorter the interval between the CS and UCS, the faster conditioning would be. It now appears that there is at least one excellent example of classical conditioning in which the CS-UCS interval may be much longer than just a few seconds—even hours long. This example also reinforces the point that some stimuli make more effective conditioned stimuli than others. The example is found in the research on the formation of aversions (very strong dislikes) to certain tastes.

Many studies have confirmed that rats, and people, can be classically conditioned to avoid particular foods (Garcia, et al., 1966; Gemberling & Domjan, 1982; Revusky & Garcia, 1970). In the rat experiments, subjects eat (or drink) a food that has been given a distinctive taste. The rats are also poisoned, or treated with X-rays, so that they will develop nausea. However, the feelings of nausea do not occur *until hours after the food has been eaten.*

(In a few days, the rats are perfectly normal and healthy again.) Even though there has been a long delay between the flavored food (CS) and the feelings of nausea (UCS), the rats learn to avoid the food, often in just one trial. Similarly, children undergoing treatment for cancer typically experience nausea as an unpleasant side effect of chemotherapy. Such children will often show a strong taste aversion for whatever they ate hours before their treatment—even if that food was ice cream (Bernstein, 1978).

The time delay between the CS and the UCS here is obviously at odds with the standard belief that, to be effective, CS and UCS need to be paired together in time. Another difficulty centers on why the *taste* of previously eaten food should so commonly serve as the CS for nausea that occurs hours later. That is, why is the nausea associated with the taste of food instead of some other stimulus event that could be paired with the nausea? Think of this experience happening to you. You go to a restaurant and order a piece of pumpkin pie and a cup of coffee. Hours later, you suffer severe stomach cramps and nausea. Why should you associate these with the pie and/or coffee and not the type of chair you sat on, or the color of the car you drove to the restaurant, or the person you happened to eat with? As it happens, we may have a predisposition or bias, perhaps rooted in our biology, toward associating some things with others, particularly if they have a functional basis. Food followed by nausea is an excellent example of just such a predisposed association.

BEFORE YOU GO ON   **What do taste aversion studies tell us about the CS-UCS interval?**

Can Classical Conditioning be Used to Explain Drug Addiction?   There is some evidence to suggest that a person's increased tolerance for a drug, and ultimate addiction to that drug may be due at least in part to learning. The type of learning most frequently implicated is classical conditioning, but we are dealing here more with intriguing and substantial hypotheses than with proven facts. Here's the way the hypothesis goes according to one theorist (Siegel, 1979; 1983, 1986).

In using a drug (say, heroin as an example), the drug acts as UCS, naturally producing physiological and psychological reactions, which we may call the UCR. When drugs are used, there are usually a number of predictable stimuli present also, such as a hypodermic needle, a particular set of friends, or a given location. Any one of these or a combination may serve as the CS, paired with the UCS of the drug. The strange thing that happens next is that with conditioning, with repeated experiences of, say, the hypodermic needle (CS) and the heroin (UCS), the conditioned response (CR) is actually quite the *opposite of* the original UCR! That is, the needle becomes conditioned to signal or "warn" the body that heroin is on the way, and the body reacts, or braces itself, to prepare for the injection of the drug. Having been alerted by the sight of the needle that heroin is on the way, the user experiences a momentary "low" as the body compensates for the anticipated drug. Now that classically conditioned "low" state needs to be overcome to produce the desired "high." The more and more that the needle and the drug are paired, the stronger the protective, preparatory response (the CR) and the more drug will be needed to overcome the body's CR to produce the desired "high."

How might classical conditioning be used to account for drug addiction?

BEFORE YOU GO ON

Learning is a process that cannot be observed directly. It is inferred from our observation of relatively permanent changes in behavior (or performance) that occur as the result of practice or experience. So far, we have reviewed the procedures of classical, or Pavlovian, conditioning, noting that some of these procedures have recently come into question. We have seen that one of the major applications of Pavlovian conditioning is its role in emotional behavior. Many of the stimuli to which we respond emotionally do not evoke that response naturally or reflexively; rather, they do so through classical conditioning. In other words, many of the stimuli in our environments that give rise to pleasant and unpleasant feelings do so because they have been previously paired with more inherently pleasant or unpleasant experiences or situations. We have also looked at other ways in which classical conditioning can have an impact on our daily lives. Now we move on to consider other types of learning.

THE BASICS OF OPERANT CONDITIONING

Most of the early research on operant conditioning was done by B. F. Skinner, and for that reason we may call this form of learning *Skinnerian conditioning.* Although we correctly associate operant conditioning with Skinner, he did not discover it in any literal sense. The techniques of operant conditioning had been applied for hundreds of years before Skinner was born. What Skinner did was to bring that earlier work, most of it casual, some of it scientific, into the psychology laboratory. There, he studied the procedures of operant conditioning with a unique vigor and helped the rest of us realize the significance of the process.

Response → Reward

Defining Operant Conditioning

Skinner uses the term **operant** to refer to a behavior (or a group of behaviors) that an organism may use to *operate* on its environment. Operants are said to be controlled by their consequences—they will maintain or increase their rate if they are reinforced; they will decrease their rate if they are not reinforced or if they are punished. Thus, **operant conditioning** changes the probability or rate of responses on the basis of the consequences that result from those responses. Responses followed by reinforcers tend to increase in rate; those not followed by reinforcers tend to decrease in rate. (Some psychologists call this sort of learning *instrumental conditioning* in the sense that a response (or group of responses) is *instrumental* in producing reinforcement. For the sake of simplicity, we'll use the term *operant conditioning*.)

operant
behavior(s) that operate on the environment to produce reinforcement or punishment

operant conditioning
changing the rate of a response on the basis of the consequences that result from that response

E. L. Thorndike

As it happens, our description of the essential nature of operant conditioning comes not from Skinner, but from E. L. Thorndike. Thorndike observed (in his "law of effect") that responses are learned when they are followed by a "satisfying state of affairs" (1911, p. 245). If an organism makes a response and then experiences a satisfying state of affairs (is reinforced), the organism will tend to make that response again. On the other hand, if a response is *not* followed by a satisfying state of affairs (is not reinforced), then the organism will tend *not* to make that response again. Thorndike seemed to be saying something like, "We tend to do, and continue to do, whatever makes us feel good." This seemingly simple observation is also a profound one because it is true. Our behaviors *are* shaped by their consequences.

Examples of operant conditioning are all around us. One hardly needs special apparatus or a laboratory to observe the principle at work. Imagine a mother rushing through the supermarket with her toddler seated in the shopping cart. The youngster is screaming at the top of his lungs for a candy bar—over and over, echoing throughout the store, "I wanna candy bar I wanna candy bar!" Mother is doing a good (and appropriate) job of ignoring this monstrous behavior until she spies a neighbor coming down the next aisle. The neighbor has her three children with her, and all three are acting like perfect, quiet angels. What's a mother to do? She races by the checkout lanes, grabs a chocolate bar, and gives it to her child. Does one have to be an expert in child psychology (or operant conditioning) to predict what will happen on the next visit to the store? Screaming "worked" this time so it will be tried again. Reinforced behaviors tend to recur.

As we did with classical conditioning, we'll use examples from the laboratory to summarize the procedures and phenomena of operant conditioning. You should have little difficulty finding examples from your own experience that make the same points.

The Procedures of Operant Conditioning

To demonstrate operant conditioning in the controlled environment of the laboratory, Skinner built a special piece of apparatus. He called it an operant chamber. Although Skinner never uses the term and says he doesn't like it (Skinner, 1984), we often call this device a Skinner box. There's not much to it. Figure 4.4 shows a standard operant chamber. The chamber pictured here is designed for rats. The box is empty except for a small bar or lever that protrudes from one wall and a small cup to hold a piece of rat food. Pellets of food are automatically dispensed from a pellet holder through a tube into the food cup. Pellets are released one at a time when a switch is closed, and depressing the bar or lever all the way down is one way to close the switch and release a pellet.

Now that we have our chamber, we need a subject. If we place a hungry rat (operationally defined as one deprived of food for a certain period of time) into the chamber and do nothing else, the rat will occasionally press the bar. There is very little else for it to do in there. The rate at which the rat emits such a response is called its *base rate* (or baseline rate) of responding. Over the course of an hour, a typical rat may press the lever 8 to 10 times.

FIGURE 4.4
A drawing of an operant chamber, or Skinner box.

Lever

Pellet dispenser

Dispenser tube

Food cup

After a reasonable period of observation, we activate the food dispenser so that a pellet of food is delivered every time the bar is pressed. In accord with Thorndike's law of effect, the rate of the bar pressing response increases. Having been reinforced for doing so, the rat increases its rate of lever pressing. The rat may reach the point of pressing the lever not 8 to 10 times per hour, but at a rate of as many as 500 to 600 times per hour. Learning has taken place. There has been a relatively permanent change in behavior as a result of experience.

Here is a little subtlety: Has the rat learned to press the bar? In any sense can we say that we have taught the rat a bar-pressing response? No. The rat knew how to press the bar and did so long before we introduced the food pellets as a reward for its behavior. What it did learn—the change in behavior that took place—was a change in the *rate* of response, not in response per se.

What is the essence of operant conditioning? BEFORE YOU GO ON

The Course of Operant Conditioning

Now that we have the basic idea of operant conditioning in mind, let's explore just how one goes about using the procedure.

Shaping. One reality of operant conditioning is that before you can reinforce a response, you have to get that response to occur in the first place. If your rat never pressed the bar, it would never get a pellet. What if you

place your rat in an operant chamber and discover that after grooming itself and wandering about, it stops, stares off into space, and settles down, facing away from the lever and the food cup? Your apparatus is prepared to deliver a food pellet as soon as your rat presses the bar, but it appears that you may have a long wait. You want to get going now.

In such a circumstance, you could use the procedure called **shaping.** Shaping involves reinforcing *successive approximations* of the response that you ultimately want to condition. We say that you can shape the bar-pressing response.

You have a button that delivers a pellet to the food cup even though the bar is not pressed. When your rat turns to face the lever you deliver a pellet, reinforcing that behavior. It's not exactly the response you want, but at least the rat is now facing in the right direction. You don't give your rat another pellet until it moves toward the bar. It gets another pellet for moving even closer to the bar. The next pellet doesn't come until the rat touches the bar.

A reinforcement is delivered each time your rat successively approximates the bar-press response you are looking for. Eventually the rat will press the bar far enough to close the switch and deliver a pellet by itself. Shaping is over, and the rat is on its own. In practice, this procedure is not as easy as it may sound. You have to be quick with your button, and you must make sure that each reinforced response is really closer to the one you ultimately want. Remember that your rat will continue to do whatever it was doing just before it got reinforced. If you're not careful, your rat may be reinforced for just running to the lever, or bobbing its head up and down, or turning in circles, instead of pressing the lever. This point is especially important: To be effective at increasing the rate of a response, reinforcers need to be delivered immediately after the desired response takes place. As a rule of thumb: The greater the delay of reinforcement, the less effective the conditioning.

Acquisition. Once an organism begins to emit the responses you wish to reinforce, the procedures of operant conditioning are simple. Immediately following a desired response, a reinforcer is provided to the organism. As responses produce reinforcers, those responses become more and more likely to occur. The increase in response rate that follows reinforcement will generally be slow at first, then become more rapid, and eventually will level off. We call this phase or stage of operant conditioning **acquisition.** Figure 4.5 is a curve depicting the stages of operant conditioning, including acquisition. It is very important to note that the Y-axis in this curve is a measure of rate of response, not response strength. That is, what increases in acquisition for operant conditioning is the rate of a response.

Extinction. Once an organism is responding at a high rate of response, what happens if reinforcement is withheld? Let's say that because we have reinforced its bar pressing, a rat is pressing a bar at a rate of 550 presses per hour. From now on, however, it will receive no more pellets of food for its efforts—no more reinforcers. What happens is predictable: The rat's rate of bar pressing response decreases gradually until it returns to the low baseline

FIGURE 4.5

The stages of operant conditioning. (1) During acquisition, response rates increase when responses are reinforced. (2) In extinction, reinforcers are withheld and the response rate returns to the baseline operant rate. (3) During spontaneous recovery, an increase in response rate is noted following a rest interval after extinction. The stages here are the same as those found in classical conditioning.

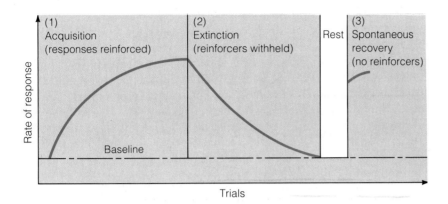

rate at which it began. That is, eventually the conditioned response (bar pressing) has extinguished, and we can say that **extinction** has taken place.

(4) Spontaneous Recovery. After extinction has occurred, we remove the rat from the operant chamber and return it to its cage for a few days. When we again deprive it of food and return it to the chamber, what will it do? It will go right over to the bar and begin to press it again—and at a high rate. Even though it has gone through extinction training—even though the last time we saw this rat in the operant chamber it was not pressing the bar—it will again press the bar after a rest interval. Remember, this return of an extinguished response following a rest interval is called **spontaneous recovery.** As was the case in classical conditioning, the significance of spontaneous recovery is that once acquired, a conditioned response can seldom be eliminated in just one series of extinction trials. Figure 4.5 also shows extinction and spontaneous recovery for operant conditioning.

extinction
the process in operant conditioning in which the rate of a response decreases as reinforcers are withheld

spontaneous recovery
the phenomenon in operant conditioning in which a previously extinguished response returns after a rest interval

Why do we need shaping, and how does it work?

Describe acquisition, extinction, and spontaneous recovery as they occur in operant conditioning.

BEFORE YOU GO ON

REINFORCEMENT AND PUNISHMENT

From what we have said so far, it is obvious that reinforcement is an important concept in operant conditioning. Reinforcement is the process of administering, or delivering, a reinforcer. In this section, we'll examine different types of reinforcers: positive reinforcers, negative reinforcers, primary reinforcers, and secondary reinforcers. We'll also see that we can schedule the administration of reinforcers in a variety of ways. We'll end this section by considering the nature of punishment and its effects on behavior.

A Definition of Reinforcer

What qualifies as a good reinforcer? What creates the satisfying state of affairs that Thorndike claimed is necessary to increase response rate? For hungry rats in operant chambers, the answer seems to be deceptively simple. Here we can ensure that a rat is hungry, and we can confidently predict that the delivery of food will be reinforcing. For people, or for rats who are no longer hungry, the answer may not be so obvious.

Skinner and his students argue that we should define reinforcers operationally. That is, we should define reinforcers only in terms of their effect on behavior. Reinforcers are stimuli. Stimuli that increase the rate or the probability of the responses that they follow are **reinforcers.**

At first reading, that logic may appear somewhat backward. A reinforcer is something that increases the rate of those responses it follows. This line of reasoning suggests that nothing is *necessarily* going to be a reinforcer. Reinforcers are defined only after we have noted their effect on behavior. Thus, we don't know ahead of time what will or will not produce an increased rate of response—or a satisfying state of affairs. We may have some strong suspicions, based on what has worked in the past, but we will not know for sure until we try.

For example, for many people money is a very powerful reinforcer. Your instructor might decide to offer you $10 for every test item you answer correctly this term. Such a reinforcement scheme might drastically increase the rate of students' studying behavior. But (hard as this may be to believe) some students might not be interested in such reinforcement. For them, the monetary award would not be at all reinforcing. In that case, it would not lead to an increase in their studying behaviors. Farfetched, perhaps, but the point is that we cannot always tell whether or not a given stimulus will be reinforcing until we try it. It is reinforcing *only* if it increases the rate or the likelihood of the response that it follows (Kimble, 1981).

BEFORE YOU GO ON   **Provide an operational definition of reinforcer.**

Positive Reinforcers

positive reinforcer
a stimulus that increases the rate of a response when that stimulus is presented to an organism after the response is made

Now that we have a general idea of what a reinforcer is, we can begin to get a little more specific. A **positive reinforcer** is a stimulus presented to an organism that increases (or maintains above baseline) the rate of a response that precedes it. The term does appear to be somewhat redundant: If something is positive, it certainly ought to be reinforcing. Positive reinforcers are sometimes like rewards. Examples include such stimuli as food for hungry organisms, water for thirsty ones, high letter grades for well-motivated students, and money, praise, and attention for most of us.

reinforcer
a stimulus that increases the rate of the response that it follows

We need to be a little careful when we attempt to equate positive reinforcers with rewards, however. We usually think of rewards as being pleasant, but positive reinforcers do not always appear to be pleasant. For instance: A mother fusses at her daughter for not cleaning her room. She soon discovers that "the more I yell and scream at her, *the worse she gets!*" If her daughter's messiness gets worse, it is because the messy behavior is being strengthened. The yelling and screaming are acting as positive reinforcers, increasing the rate of the behavior that they follow. Now yelling and screaming do not appear to be very pleasant, yet here they are, acting as positive reinforcers. Perhaps the daughter doesn't get very much parental attention and any kind of attention—even being yelled at—in her case acts as a reinforcer.

What is a positive reinforcer?   **BEFORE YOU GO ON**

Negative Reinforcers

A **negative reinforcer** is a stimulus that increases the rate of a response that precedes *its removal.* "Negative reinforcer" is a strange term. There is something contradictory about the very sound of it. If something is negative, how can it be a reinforcer? The secret is to remember that the key word here is *reinforcer* and that reinforcers increase the rate of responses. In terms of Thorndike's law of effect, negative reinforcement must produce some sort of satisfying state of affairs. That it does. The reinforcement comes not from the delivery or presentation of negative reinforcers, but with their removal. (Another secret is to remember that reinforce*ment* is a process. It is something that happens in response to stimuli called reinfor*cers.* If you'd like, you may think of negative reinforcers as being generally unpleasant stimuli, while negative reinforcement is a pleasant process.)

So, negative reinforcers are stimuli that increase the probability of a response when they are removed or withheld. They may include such stimuli as shocks, enforced isolation, and low letter grades. They are exactly the sorts of things that an organism would work (respond) to avoid or escape. They are the very stimuli that could be used to punish an organism if they were presented following an undesired response. A child who cleans her room to get her mother to *stop* nagging is responding to a negative reinforcer.

Escape Conditioning.   One clear demonstration of negative reinforcement can be found in a type of operant conditioning called **escape conditioning.** In this procedure, an organism learns to escape from a painful, noxious, or aversive situation. If an appropriate response is made and the escape is successful, the organism is reinforced and will tend to make the same response again in the future. Notice that the reinforcement comes not from giving the organism a positive reinforcer, but from its escaping (getting away from) a negative reinforcer.

Do people ever respond to escape conditioning? All the time. For example, bully Ken has little Wayne's arm twisted up behind his back, demanding

negative reinforcer
a stimulus that increases the rate of a response when that stimulus is removed after the response is made

escape conditioning
a form of operant conditioning in which an organism learns to escape, thus earning negative reinforcement

FIGURE 4.6
A shuttle box apparatus of the sort used to demonstrate avoidance conditioning.

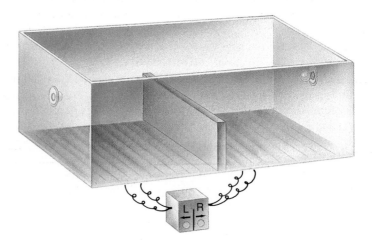

that Wayne say "uncle." The longer Wayne resists, the harder Ken twists. Finally, Wayne mutters "uncle," and Ken releases his grasp. Wayne has probably learned how to escape from Ken's bullying in just one trial: submit to his demands. The next time Ken grabs Wayne's arm, Wayne is likely to say or do whatever Ken asks. (Note that if all Ken wanted was for Wayne to say "uncle," he could have used positive reinforcement, offering Wayne a quarter for saying "uncle." The behavioral result would have been the same. But Ken has probably chosen *this* approach because he has been reinforced for doing so in the past; that is, he has found that being a bully works.)

Avoidance Conditioning. Another example of negative reinforcement in action is **avoidance conditioning.** In avoidance conditioning, an organism learns to *avoid* an unpleasant, painful, or aversive situation *before* it occurs. The major difference between avoidance conditioning and escape conditioning is the addition of a cue or signal that precedes the negative reinforcer. Responding appropriately to the signal allows the organism to prevent the painful, unpleasant situation before it occurs.

Let's look at a laboratory example of avoidance conditioning that uses a *shuttle box apparatus*—a long, narrow empty box, separated into two compartments by a divider, or hurdle (see Figure 4.6). The divider is high enough to present some obstacle, yet low enough so that it can be jumped over with some effort. There is a signal light in each compartment of the box. In addition, the metal flooring of each side of the shuttle box is wired to a device that can deliver a painful shock to the feet of an animal in the box.

A dog is placed in the left compartment of a shuttle box. A light (signal) comes on. Five seconds later, a strong, painful shock is delivered to the floor of the left compartment. The dog hops around, squeals, barks, and eventually jumps the hurdle into the right compartment where there is no shock. Thus, the dog is negatively reinforced for jumping. After the dog settles

avoidance conditioning
a form of operant conditioning in which an organism learns to respond to a cue or signal in order to avoid a stimulus situation, thus earning negative reinforcement

down, a light comes on-in the right compartment, followed five seconds later by a shock to the floor. The dog now jumps quickly back to the left. One more trial: light, five second delay, shock, jump. Now the dog is once again in the right compartment of the box. The next time the signal light comes on, the dog jumps into the left side of the box within five seconds, thus *avoiding* the shock. On each subsequent trial, the dog jumps the hurdle when the light comes on. It has learned to avoid the shock.

This example is impressive in a number of ways. Here, a painful, aversive stimulus (a shock) is used to bring about a relatively permanent change in behavior. In just a few trials, after only a few shocks, we have trained a dog to jump from one side of a box to the other when a light is turned on. One of the most noteworthy aspects of avoidance conditioning is that responses acquired in this way are highly resistant to extinction. After all, once the jump is made in response to the signal light, the shock is no longer required. Our dog will continue to jump from side to side for a long time.

The important thing to remember in this demonstration is that we are using the shock as a negative reinforcer, not as a punisher. We are not shocking the dog for doing something that it has already learned how to do. We are not punishing any particular response. Indeed, when the appropriate response is made, the shock is avoided, and the dog is reinforced. Notice also that in both escape and avoidance conditioning, we make no special effort to introduce any motivational state into this procedure other than the escape or avoidance of the shock. These are not hungry or thirsty dogs, for example. The dog is motivated solely to escape or avoid the shock, the negative reinforcer.

It is also important to note that a response for avoiding the shock is readily available to the subject. There is something the dog *can* do to avoid getting shocked. All it has to do is jump to the other side of the box. When dogs, for example, are shocked at random intervals in a situation in which there is no way to escape or avoid the shock, an unusual thing happens. The dogs eventually reach a state where they appear to give up. They just lie down and passively take administered shock. This pattern of behavior is called **learned helplessness.** One curiosity of this phenomenon is that once learned helplessness is acquired, it is difficult to overcome. That is, if dogs are then placed in a situation in which escape from shock is possible, it is very difficult for them to learn to escape, and some dogs never learn it at all (Maier & Seligman, 1976; Seligman, 1975).

learned helplessness
a condition in which a subject does not attempt to escape from a painful or noxious situation after learning in a previous, similar situation that escape is not possible

BEFORE YOU GO ON

What is a negative reinforcer?
How are negative reinforcers used in escape and avoidance conditioning?

Primary and Secondary Reinforcers

Reinforcers are defined in terms of their effects on behavior. We have seen that both positive and negative reinforcers increase response rate. Now we need to make a distinction between primary and secondary reinforcers.

The distinction between primary and secondary reinforcers is subtle. What is at issue here is the extent to which reinforcers are natural and

primary reinforcers
stimuli (usually biologically or physiologically based) that increase the rate of a response with no previous experience required

secondary reinforcers
stimuli that increase the rate of a response because of their being associated with other reinforcers; also called conditioned, or learned, reinforcers

unlearned or acquire their reinforcing capability through learning and experience. **Primary reinforcers** are those that do not require any previous experience to be effective. They are, in some way, related to the organism's survival. They are usually biological or physiological in nature. Food for a hungry organism or water for a thirsty one are common examples. Some believe that attention, at least for children, may qualify as an unlearned, primary reinforcer.

Secondary reinforcers are often referred to as learned or conditioned reinforcers. There is nothing about them that suggests that they are inherently reinforcing or satisfying in any biological sense, yet they operate to strengthen responses.

Most of the reinforcers that we all work for are of this sort. Money, praise, high letter grades, and promotions are good examples. For example, money, in and of itself, is not worth much. But our previous learning experiences have convinced most of us of the reinforcing nature of money, and it can serve to increase the rate of a wide variety of responses. Among other things, we have learned that money can provide us with access to many other powerful reinforcers.

Secondary reinforcement can be nicely demonstrated even with rats. Most food pellet dispensers in operant chambers are noisy affairs, buzzing rather loudly before they release a food pellet reinforcer into the chamber's food cup. Imagine a rat that has been operantly conditioned to press a bar to receive a pellet of food from a dispenser. You now begin extinction by removing all the pellets from the dispenser so that when the rat presses the bar, the dispenser whirs and buzzes, but delivers no pellet. You will probably discover that your rat will maintain its bar-pressing response for quite some time, reinforced only by the buzzing sound of the now empty pellet dispenser. If you remove the entire dispenser apparatus from the operant chamber, extinction occurs much more rapidly.

Notice that this distinction between primary and secondary reinforcement is equally appropriate for negative reinforcers. Some negative reinforcers are primary: shock, pain-producing stimuli, intense stimulation. We will learn to escape or avoid these naturally aversive events (and in doing so, will provide ourselves with negative reinforcement). Some negative reinforcers are useful only because of our previous learning experiences. Examples of learning through negative reinforcement might include traffic tickets, letter grades of "D" or "F," or demotions.

BEFORE YOU GO ON **What is the difference between primary and secondary reinforcers?**

Scheduling of Reinforcement

In all of our discussions and examples so far, we have implied that operant conditioning requires that we provide a reinforcer after every desired response. In fact, particularly at the start, it probably *is* best to reinforce each response as it occurs. But once response rate begins to increase, there may be good reason for doing otherwise—for reinforcing responses intermittently.

The procedure of reinforcing each and every response after it occurs is called a **continuous reinforcement (CRF) schedule.** One problem with CRF schedules is that earning a reinforcer after each response may soon reduce the reinforcing nature of that reinforcer. For example, once a rat has eaten its fill (is satiated), it will have to be removed from the operant chamber until it becomes hungry again (Skinner, 1956).

The alternative to reinforcing every response is called an **intermittent** (or partial) **reinforcement schedule.** Quite simply, this is a strategy for reinforcing a desired behavior less frequently than each and every time it occurs. As it happens, there are any number of ways in which one might systematically go about reinforcing responses according to an intermittent schedule. The main point to remember is that operant conditioning does not require that each and every response be reinforced. There are advantages to an intermittent reinforcement schedule, one of the most important being its resistance to extinction. A rat, a dog, or a person who is never sure just when the next response might be reinforced is likely to keep responding longer than one used to the idea that every response is reinforced.

continuous reinforcement schedule (CRF)
a reinforcement schedule in which each and every response is followed by a reinforcer

intermittent reinforcement schedules
reinforcement in which responses are not reinforced every time they occur

more imune to distinction

What is intermittent reinforcement, and what is the advantage of using it? BEFORE YOU GO ON

Punishment

We've talked at length about reinforcement, positive and negative, primary and secondary, and whether reinforcers should be continuous or intermittent. Let's now consider punishment. **Punishment** occurs when a stimulus delivered to an organism *decreases* the rate or the probability of occurrence of the response that preceded it. In common usage, punishment is usually in some way painful—either physically (a spanking) or psychologically (ridicule). It is a painful, unpleasant, aversive stimulus that is presented to an organism after some response is made. If the rate, or probability, of the organism's response then drops, or decreases, we may say that the response has been punished.

Determining ahead of time what stimulus will be punishing is often as difficult to do as determining ahead of time what will serve as a reinforcer. We only know for sure that something is a punisher in terms of its effect on behavior. For example, we may *think* that we are punishing Richard by sending him to his room because he has begun to throw a temper tantrum. It may be that "in his room" is exactly where Richard would like to be. We may have reinforced Richard's temper tantrum behaviors simply by attending to them. Once again, the only way to know for certain is to note the effect on behavior. If stimuli decrease the rate of the behaviors they follow, those stimuli may be called punishers. So if Richard's tantrum-throwing behaviors become less frequent as a consequence of our actions, sending him to his room may indeed be a punishing thing to do.

punishment
the administration of a punisher, which is a stimulus that decreases the rate or probability of a response that precedes it

decrease rate of response

What is a punisher? BEFORE YOU GO ON

GENERALIZATION AND DISCRIMINATION

In classical conditioning, we saw that a response conditioned to one particular stimulus could be evoked by other, similar stimuli. We have the same phenomenon occurring in operant conditioning, and again we call it **generalization**—reinforced responses that have been conditioned to a specific stimulus may appear in response to other, similar stimuli.

For example, Priscilla may be reinforced for saying "doggie" as a neighbor's poodle wanders across the front yard. "Oh yes, Priscilla, good girl. That's a doggie." Having learned that calling the neighbor's poodle a "doggie" earns parental approval, the response is tried again, this time with a German shepherd from down the street. That is, Priscilla's operantly conditioned response of "doggie" in the presence of a poodle generalizes to the German shepherd. When it does, it will no doubt also be reinforced. The problem is, of course, that Priscilla may overgeneralize to virtually any small, furry four-legged animal and start calling cats and raccoons "doggie" also. When a child turns to a total stranger and utters "dada," generalization can (usually) be blamed for the embarrassing mislabeling.

The process of generalization can be countered with the reverse process of **discrimination** conditioning. Discrimination learning is basically a matter of differential reinforcement. What that means is that responses made to appropriate stimuli will be reinforced, while (differential) responses made to inappropriate stimuli will be ignored or extinguished (by withholding reinforcers, *not* by punishing the response).

To demonstrate how discrimination training works, let's consider a strange question: Are pigeons color-blind? Disregarding for the moment why anyone would care, how might you go about testing the color vision of a pigeon? The standard tests we use for people certainly wouldn't work. What we do is take advantage of something pigeons can do.

Pigeons *can* be trained to press levers in operant chambers, but they are better at pecking at things, so we usually use a pecking response when we operantly condition pigeons. A pigeon can be readily trained to peck at a single lighted disk in order to earn a food reward. A pigeon in an operant chamber pecks at a lighted disk, and a grain of food is delivered. Soon the pigeon pecks the disk at a high rate.

Now let's present the pigeon with *two* lighted disks. One disk is red and one is green. Otherwise, they are identical: the same shape, size, brightness, and so on. Our basic question is whether or not the pigeon can tell the difference between red and green. We decide that we'll make the green disk the (positive) discriminative stimulus (abbreviated S^D). Responses to the red disk (the S^Δ) will be extinguished. This means that every peck at the green disk will be followed by a piece of grain, and that pecks at the red disk will not be reinforced. The position of the two colored disks are randomly altered, so we aren't simply demonstrating that the pigeon can tell left from right.

The results of this sort of manipulation are depicted in Figure 4.7. At first, the red and green lighted disks are responded to at an approximately equal rate. But in short order, the pigeon is ignoring the red disk and pecking only at the green one, for which it receives its reinforcer.

In order to maintain such behavior, the pigeon must be able to discriminate between the two colored disks. We still do not know what green and red look like to a pigeon, but we may conclude that pigeons can tell the differ-

A pigeon in an operant chamber with a red disk and a green disk is able to distinguish one from the other.

FIGURE 4.7

Discrimination training. Response rates of a pigeon pecking at a green disk and a red disk presented together. Pecks at the green disk are reinforced; those to the red disk are not.

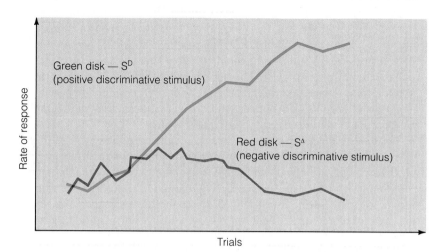

ence between the two. This is sensible and predictable because in many ways the eyes of pigeons are like those of humans. They contain many cones in their retinas, and as you'll recall, cones are the receptors for color vision. Some varieties of owls are virtually without cone receptor cells in their retinas and are color-blind. They cannot make the discrimination between red and green, for example, and appear very frustrated in a discrimination learning task based on color.

BEFORE YOU GO ON

In the context of operant conditioning, what are generalization and discrimination?

CAN ANY RESPONSE BE OPERANTLY CONDITIONED?

Animals can be trained to make unusual responses. Rats *can* be operantly conditioned to press lighted disks on the side of an operant chamber. Pigeons *can* be trained to press levers in a Skinner box. Yet, typically, we demonstrate conditioning with these organisms by having rats press levers and pigeons peck at disks. Somehow these responses seem more natural for the animals we're using. Even so, it was believed for a long time that if we could find the right reinforcer, we could train almost any animal to do almost anything.

Keller and Marion Breland, psychologists who had worked with B.F. Skinner, were convinced of the power of operant conditioning as a means of modifying behavior. They applied their expertise in psychology to the practical matter of animal training, and many of their trained animals became quite popular and famous. Along with their many successes at training animals to do a number of very involved things, the Brelands experienced noteworthy failures. Some of their animals just seemed totally contrary and unable to learn apparently simple routines. They described their frustrations in a 1961 article titled "The Misbehavior of Organisms," a take-off on Skinner's classic operant conditioning book, *The Behavior of Organisms* (1938).

As an example of the sort of difficulty the Brelands encountered, consider their efforts to teach a raccoon and a pig to deposit large coins in a bank. Both the raccoon and the pig had previously demonstrated that they were capable of responding to operant conditioning. They were not in any way unintelligent animals. But the raccoon never quite learned to drop coins into the bank. He would grab the coins, rub them together, begin to enter them into the bank's slot, and then withdraw them at the last moment, rubbing them together again. The pig never got that close. The pig would drop the coins from its mouth and then push them around the floor with its nose. When the coins were put back into the pig's mouth, they were promptly dropped again and pushed around the ground.

What was happening here, the Brelands concluded, was that their animals were simply acting naturally. They were acting toward the coins the way they would instinctively act toward food—the raccoon manipulating the coin (food) with its hands, the pig rooting it around the ground. No training or reinforcement seemed sufficient to overcome this instinctive predisposition. Yes, reinforcement might get an animal to perform some task a few times, but even then it would eventually drift back to more natural, or instinctive patterns of behavior. The Brelands labeled this phenomenon **instinctive drift.** It suggests that there *are* indeed limits on the types of responses an organism can learn, and many of these limits are established by the organism's genetic history.

instinctive drift
the tendency of behaviors that have been conditioned to eventually revert to more natural, instinctive behaviors

BEFORE YOU GO ON   **What is instinctive drift, and what does it tell us about the limits of conditioning?**

In their studies of operant conditioning, Keller and Marion Breland found that even though they could get a raccoon and other animals to perform certain tasks, they were unable to get them to do others, such as dropping a coin into a bank. The Brelands concluded that animals tend to return to more instinctive, natural behaviors.

COGNITIVE APPROACHES TO LEARNING

There is no doubt that classical and operant conditioning can and do account for many of our learning experiences. Each of these procedures is, in its own way, a matter of forming associations. We associate pleasant or unpleasant feelings with certain situations. We associate some responses with reinforcers and others with punishers. In either case, we make relatively permanent changes in our behaviors on the basis of our experiences. Both classical and operant conditioning are behavioristic in their orientation. They focus on observable events (stimuli) in the environment and on observable behaviors (responses) of the learner. That these two procedures have been the focus of our attention in the psychology of learning for so long is an indication of the influence of behaviorism on American psychology.

But now it is time to look beyond conditioning. The data from a number of experiments, and from our own experiences, suggest that there is more to learning than just the simple formation of associations between stimuli and between stimuli and responses. There seem to be a number of situations in which an organism's behaviors are changed that stretch the credibility of explanations given only in terms of observable stimuli and responses.

To understand some types of learning, we may have to consider the nature of the learner (organism) in addition to considering the nature of stimuli and responses. Such approaches go by a number of different labels, but we may refer to them all as being basically cognitive. That is, these approaches emphasize the mental processes or mental activity (cognitions) of the organism involved in the learning task. They argue that learning often involves the acquisition of information and knowledge. In this section, we will briefly review the work of the following three theorists who have stressed cognitive approaches to learning: Edward Tolman, David Olton, and Albert Bandura.

Edward Tolman and David Olton: Latent Learning and Cognitive Maps

Do rats have brains? Of course they do. Their brains aren't very large (and the cerebral cortex of a rat's brain is small indeed). A more intriguing question about rats is whether or not they have minds. Can they figure things out? Can they understand? Can they manipulate cognitions? Surely they can form simple associations. They can learn to associate a light with a shock. They can associate a bar-press response with a reinforcer. They can modify their behaviors on the basis of these associations. Can they do more?

Consider a now-classic experiment performed nearly 60 years ago by Tolman and Honzik (1930). Even at that time, it was well established that a rat could learn to run through a complicated maze of alley-ways and dead-ends to get to a goal box where it would receive a food reward. Tolman and Honzik wanted to understand just *what* the rats were learning when they learned to negotiate such a maze. They used three different groups of rats with the same maze.

Edward Tolman

One group of hungry rats was given a series of exposures to the maze (trials). Each time they ran from the starting point to the goal box, they were given a food reward for their efforts. Over the course of 16 days, the rats in this group showed a steady and predictable improvement in their maze-running. Their rate of errors dropped from approximately nine per trial to just two. Getting quickly and errorlessly from the start box to the goal box was just what they had been reinforced for doing.

A second group of rats was also given an opportunity to explore the same maze for 16 days of test trials. They were never given a food reward for making it to the end of the maze. When they got to the goal box, they were removed from the maze. The average number of errors made by the rats in this group also dropped over the course of the experiment (from about nine errors per trial down to about six). That the rats in this group *did* improve their maze-running skills suggested that simply being removed from the maze provided some measure of reinforcement. Even so, after 16 days of experience, this group was having much more difficulty in their maze-running than was the group being given a food reinforcer.

Now for the critical group of rats. A third group of rats was allowed to explore the maze on their own for 10 days. They were *not* given a food reward upon reaching the goal box. Beginning on day 11, a food reward was introduced when they reached the end of the maze. The food was then provided as a reinforcer on days 11 through 16. The introduction of the food reward had a very significant effect on the rats' behaviors. Over the course of the first 10 days in the maze—without the food—their performance showed only a slight improvement. Soon after the food was introduced, their maze running improved markedly. In fact, on days 13 through 16, they made even fewer errors than did the rats reinforced with food all along. A graph showing the relative performance of these three groups of rats is shown in Figure 4.8.

What do you make of this experiment? Why did that third group of rats perform so much better after the food reward was introduced? Might they have learned something about the pattern of that maze *before* they were explicitly reinforced for getting to the goal box? Might they have figured out the maze early on, but failed to rush to the goal box until there was some good reason to do so?

Tolman thought that they had. Tolman argued that the food only rewarded a change in the rats' performance, and that the actual learning had taken place earlier. This sort of learning is called **latent learning** because it is, in a sense, hidden and not shown in behavior at the time it occurs.

During those first 10 days in the maze, the rats developed what Tolman called a **cognitive map** of the maze; that is, they formed a mental picture, or representation, of what the maze was like. The rats "knew" about the maze, but until food was provided at the goal box, there was no reason, or purpose, for getting there in any big hurry. This sort of logic led Tolman to refer to his approach as "purposive behaviorism" (Tolman, 1932).

Here then was Tolman, arguing that even rats form a mental representation, or cognitive map, of their environment at the very time that behaviorism was dominating American psychology. Interest in cognitive maps died out for awhile, but has recently been making a comeback, thanks to a series of well-controlled experiments by David Olton (1976, 1978, 1979). Let's briefly review just one.

latent learning
hidden learning that is not demonstrated in performance until that performance is reinforced

cognitive map
a mental representation of the learning situation or physical environment

FIGURE 4.8

The performance of rats in a maze that (A) were never rewarded, (B) were rewarded on every trial, or (C) were rewarded only on trials 11–16. (After Tolman & Honzik, 1930.)

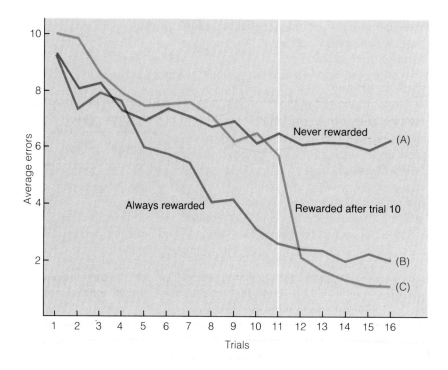

Handwritten note:
Learning to Learn —
By Learning one task
easier to learn similar

Motor programs —
mental scan of
skilled movement

The maze pictured in Figure 4.9 was used in one of Olton's experiments. A piece of food was placed at the end of each of the eight arms, or runways, that extend from the center of the maze. In order to solve this maze, a rat placed at the center has to learn to run to the end of each arm, eat the food there, and move on to other runways where food could still be found. Going back to a runway arm already visited constitutes an error—there is no food there.

As it happens, rats perform beautifully in this maze. Within 20 trials, they race from arm to arm without ever retracing their path down an "old" runway. What's more, on each trial, the rats run around the maze in a different pattern. Their behavior doesn't seem rigidly compulsive. They don't start with one arm and then move around the maze in one direction. Their pattern of visits seems almost random. But they don't go down the same arm twice on any one trip around the maze!

The rats' performance is not disrupted even if odor cues are removed by splashing a strong-smelling after-shave lotion on the maze. (That is, the rats don't smell—or see for that matter—where the food is and isn't. And they don't smell where they have and have not been before. The lotion masks all these odors.) On the other hand, if the maze is rotated after a trial has begun, the rats *do* make errors and go down runways they have traveled before, even though food is not present there. They may be "old" runways, but after the maze is rotated, they are in new positions. Olton and his colleagues argue

FIGURE 4.9

An eight-arm maze of the sort used by Olton to demonstrate the formation of cognitive maps in rats. (After Olton, 1976.)

that they have demonstrated that their rats have learned a mental representation of the maze (a cognitive map) and have learned where they have and have not been to get food.

This may all make sense for rats, but what about people? For one thing, there is the argument that if we can demonstrate that cognitive restructuring takes place when *rats* learn, it seems rather clear that such processes can also occur in humans.

You should be able to find examples from your own experiences that very closely approximate the latent learning and cognitive maps of Tolman. You may take the same route between home and campus every day. If one day an accident blocks your path, won't you be able to use your knowledge of other routes (a cognitive map) to get where you are going?

Another setting in which we may find an application of Tolman's purposive behaviorism is in athletics. Before the "big game," the coaching staff may devise a perfect game plan—basically a set of ideas or cognitions dealing with what the team should do. The team members may learn the coaches' defensive strategy and may understand a number of offensive formations and plays. In theory, they know (latent learning) what they are supposed to do to win. But what will ultimately decide the contest is not their understanding, but their performance. In sports, this is usually called execution. Knowing what to do, and doing it, are often two different things.

BEFORE YOU GO ON   What is learned when one forms a cognitive map?
What is latent learning?

Albert Bandura: Social Learning and Modeling

Albert Bandura's approach to learning is also cognitive in nature, but it adds a decidedly social flavor to the process and for that reason is often referred to as **social learning theory** (Bandura, 1977). The central idea of this theory is that learning often takes place through the observation and the imitation of models. What makes social learning theory *social* is the notion that we often learn from others. What makes it *cognitive* is that what is learned through observation or modeling usually involves changes in cognitions that may never be expressed as behavior nor be directly reinforced.

The classic demonstration of observational learning was reported in 1963 by Bandura, Ross, and Ross. For this demonstration, 96 preschool children were randomly assigned to one of four experimental conditions. One group observed an adult model act aggressively toward an inflated plastic "Bobo" doll toy. The adult model vigorously attacked the doll. Children in the second group watched the same aggressive behaviors directed toward the "Bobo" doll, but now in a movie, not live and in person. The third group watched a cartoon version of the same behaviors, this time performed by a cartoon cat. Children in the fourth group comprised the control group and did not watch anyone interact with "Bobo" dolls, either live or on film.

Then the test began. Each child (tested individually) was given a variety of new and interesting toys to play with, but only for a brief time. The child was then led to another room that contained fewer, older, and less interesting toys—including a small version of the inflated "Bobo" doll. Each child

social learning theory
the theory that learning takes place through observation and imitation of models

Albert Bandura

was left alone in the room while researchers watched the child's behavior. The children did not know they were being observed.

There was no doubt that the children who had seen the aggressive behaviors of the model—whether live, on film, or in cartoon form—were themselves more aggressive in their play than were the children who did not have the observational experience. Children who were in the first three experimental conditions attacked the "Bobo" doll (see Figure 4.10). What's more, they attacked it in the same vigorous, stereotyped sort of way the model had!

According to social learning theory, the children in the first three groups learned simply by observing. Once again, as we saw with latent learning, the learning was separated from performance. The children had no opportunity to imitate (to perform) what they had learned until they had a "Bobo" doll of their own. The learning that took place during observation was symbolic, or cognitive. As Bandura puts it, "Observational learning is primarily concerned with processes whereby observers organize response elements into new patterns of behavior at a symbolic level on the basis of information conveyed by modeling stimuli" (Bandura, 1976, p. 395).

Later studies on observational learning have shown that reinforcement and punishment can play a part. For example, a new twist was added to an experiment that basically replicated the one just described. The difference was that after attacking the "Bobo" doll, adult models were either rewarded or punished for their behavior by another adult. As you might guess, children who saw the model being punished for attacking the doll engaged in very little aggressive behavior toward their own "Bobo" dolls. Those who saw the model being reinforced for attacking the doll acted very aggressively, again imitating the model's behaviors in considerable detail (Bandura, 1965).

FIGURE 4.10

In Albert Bandura's classic study, children who watched adults behave aggressively toward the "Bobo" doll displayed the same sort of behavior themselves. The children learned aggressive behavior through observation.

The application of this sort of data is very straightforward. For example, most of Bandura's research suggests that children can and do learn all sorts of potential behaviors by watching TV. Our real concern, however, should be reserved for those occasions where behaviors deemed inappropriate are left unpunished. So long as children are exposed to the consequences of inappropriate behaviors, they will be less likely to imitate them. This logic suggests that it would be most unfortunate for one of a child's TV heroes to get away with murder, much less be reinforced for doing so. Also, reinforced behaviors of valued models are more likely to be imitated than punished behaviors of less valued models (for example, Bandura, 1965).

Learning about the consequences of one's behaviors by observing the consequences of someone else's behavior is called **vicarious reinforcement** or **vicarious punishment.** Our own experiences speak to the usefulness of these concepts. You are much more likely to imitate (as best you can) the behaviors of a person who is rewarded for his or her efforts than you are to imitate the behaviors of someone who gets punished. A child, for example, does not have to burn her fingers in a fire to learn to avoid the fireplace. Just watching someone else getting burned (or pretending to get burned) will usually suffice (Domjan, 1987).

In fact, learning through observation and imitation is a common form of human learning. Your television on any Saturday will provide many examples, particularly if you choose to watch a PBS station. All day long there are people (role models) trying to teach us how to paint landscapes, build solar energy devices, do aerobic exercises, improve our golf game, remodel a basement, replace a carburetor, or prepare a low-calorie meal. The basic message is "here, you watch me, see how I do it, then try it yourself."

vicarious reinforcement (or punishment)
increasing the rate (reinforcement) or decreasing the rate (punishment) of responses due to observing the consequences of someone else's behaviors

BEFORE YOU GO ON   Summarize the basic concepts of social learning theory and modeling.

Learning through observation and imitation is a common form of human learning. Children often imitate the behavior of their parents and, therefore, learn by doing.

APPLYING CONDITIONING AND COGNITIVE THEORIES OF LEARNING TO YOUR STUDY OF PSYCHOLOGY

Every so often, it is a good idea to pause and reflect on the psychology you have been reading to see if you can find a practical application for what you have been learning. As we come to the end of this chapter, now might be just such a time.

One thing that many "how to study" books recommend is that students find one special place to do most of their studying. This place may be at home or somewhere on campus, but the suggestion is usually given that some location be reserved *only* for studying. What is behind this idea is the logic of classical conditioning.

Recommending that students find a special place for studying is based on the observation that even common locations in our environment can act as conditioned stimuli and can come to evoke conditioned responses. For example, it wouldn't be a good idea to recommend studying in bed. Being in bed has been associated with anything but studying—being sick perhaps, or just sleeping. Studying at the kitchen or dining room table is seldom a good idea either for the same sort of reason: Those places have been conditioned to a different set of responses (eating) that are not compatible with effective studying.

You should condition yourself to study in the same place or, at most, two or three places. Try to do nothing there but study. For this purpose, college libraries serve very well. It makes excellent sense to slip into an unused classroom during the day to study. There is an advantage to studying and learning in the same physical environment in which you will be tested later. (We'll return to this point in Chapter 5, "Memory and Cognition.")

In educational settings, we tend to think of the faculty as being the dispensers of reinforcers and punishers. Now it is true that your instructor will ultimately dispense letter grades (secondary reinforcers) based on the behavior of you and your classmates this term. Effective studying and learning will (should) be reinforced, and ineffective studying and learning will (should) not be reinforced.

It is also clear that as a student, you need not wait for your instructor to dispense reinforcers. You can do that yourself. You can reinforce yourself. In terms of study, plan to work very hard for, say, one hour. *If* at the end of that hour you feel that you have indeed studied very hard, go ahead and reinforce your effort. How can you do that? Well, that's up to you. You know best what might work as a reinforcer for you—extra TV time, a candy bar, something to drink, and so on—something that will create for you a satisfying state of affairs. Now we all hope that you will find effective studying inherently reinforcing, and you will feel reinforced simply for having done a good job, but it won't hurt to provide yourself some extra bonus for a job well-done. After a few weeks, you should be able to tell if your reinforcement plan is working: Has your rate of effective study increased? If it has, you have chosen an appropriate reinforcer.

How might you apply cognitive learning theories to your studying? Most of what you will be asked to learn this term is conceptual or cognitive in nature. Do you *understand* vicarious reinforcement? Do you *know* what a cognitive map is? Much of your learning may be latent: You may never be asked about some of what you learn.

Here is a practical application. Choose an appropriate model to imitate. Is there someone in your class who is doing very well, perhaps better than you are? What is she or he doing that you are not? Ask them. How are they studying for exams? By imitating an appropriate model, you may develop some of the same effective behaviors.

BEFORE YOU GO ON   **How can conditioning and cognitive approaches to learning be used to improve your study skills?**

In this chapter we have seen how complex learning is. We found that classical conditioning affects us in many varied ways. We also found that operant conditioning is a procedure by which the rate of one's response is changed by the manipulation of the consequences of that response. Responses that are followed by reinforcers, be they positive or negative, primary or secondary, and regardless of how they are scheduled will increase in rate from some baseline. Responses that are not reinforced, or that are punished, will decrease in rate. We have also seen, in a number of cases, that learning may not be overtly evidenced in behavior. What is learned in such circumstances are new cognitions, ideas, beliefs, or mental representations. This observation serves to remind us why we originally defined learning as being *demonstrated* by relatively permanent changes in behavior that occur as the result of practice or experience.

SUMMARY

How do we define learning?

How do we define conditioning?

Learning and conditioning have the same definition. Both are demonstrated by a relatively permanent change in behavior that occurs as a result of practice or experience. / 143

Summarize the essential procedures of Pavlovian classical conditioning.

In classical, or Pavlovian, conditioning, a stimulus that originally does not evoke a response of interest (a conditioned stimulus, CS) is paired with a stimulus (an unconditioned stimulus, UCS) that reflexively and reliably produces a response (an unconditioned response, UCR). As a result of this pairing, the CS comes to evoke a response (a conditioned response, CR) that is the same kind of response as the original UCR. / 146

In classical conditioning, what are acquisition, extinction, and spontaneous recovery?

In classical conditioning, acquisition is an increase in the strength of the CR that occurs after repeated pairings of the CS and the UCS. Extinction is a noticeable decrease in the strength of the CR and occurs when the CS is repeatedly presented without being paired with the UCS. Spontaneous recovery is the return of the CR after extinction and a rest interval. / 147

In classical conditioning, what are generalization and discrimination?

In generalization, we find that a response (CR) conditioned to a specific stimulus (CS) will also be evoked by other, similar stimuli. The more similar the new stimui are to the original CS, the greater the CR. In many ways, discrimination is the opposite of generalization. It is a matter of learning to make a CR in response to a specific CS and learning not to make a CR in response to other stimuli. / 148

What sorts of responses are most readily influenced by classical conditioning?

Briefly summarize the Little Albert experimental demonstration.

Classical conditioning has its most noticeable effect on emotion and mood, or affect. This effect was clear in the Watson and Raynor "Little Albert" demonstration which involved pairing a sudden loud noise (the UCS) with the neutral stimulus of a white rat (the CS). As a result of presenting these two stimuli together, Albert came to display a learned fear response (a CR) to the originally neutral rat. It was also claimed that the conditioned fear generalized to other similar stimuli. This demonstration has been used to explain learned emotional reactions to events in our environments. / 152

Under what circumstances are stimuli likely to serve effectively as CSs?

Pavlov, and many others, believed that any stimulus could serve effectively as a conditioned stimulus (CS) if it were repeatedly paired with an unconditioned stimulus (UCS). We now believe that this is an oversimplification. Those stimuli that are most effective as CSs are those that best or most reliably predict or signal the UCS. / 153

What do taste aversion studies tell us about the CS-UCS interval?

Taste aversion studies, in which subjects develop a strong dislike and avoidance of a particular taste, tell us that the time interval between the CS and UCS may be very long, even hours long. This result is in conflict with early conclusions that classical conditioning progressed most rapidly with very short CS-UCS intervals (seconds or fractions of a second). / 154

SUMMARY continued

How might classical conditioning be used to account for drug addiction?

The drug acts as a UCS, naturally evoking a UCR of pleasure, or a "high." Usually, the drug is consistently paired with some other stimulus, perhaps a hypodermic needle, which acts like a CS. Once the CS-UCS (needle-drug) association develops, the CS evokes a CR that is the *opposite* of the UCR. That is, the needle produces displeasure or a "low." Now, to overcome the compensatory, preparatory conditioned response (CR), more and more drug is needed to produce the desired result of pleasure and a high. This condition is known as drug tolerance and is often followed by addiction. / 155

What is the essence of operant conditioning?

Operant conditioning is that type of learning in which the probability or rate of a response is changed as a result of its consequences. That is, reinforced responses increase in rate while nonreinforced responses stay the same or decrease in rate. / 157

Why do we need shaping, and how does it work?

Describe acquisition, extinction, and spontaneous recovery as they occur in operant conditioning.

Shaping is a procedure used in operant conditioning to establish a response that can then be reinforced—that is, to get the response that we want to occur in the first place. We shape a desired response by reinforcing successive approximations to that response.

In operant conditioning, acquisition is produced by reinforcing a desired response so that its rate will increase. Extinction is the phenomenon of decreasing the rate of a response (to return to baseline levels) by withholding reinforcement. After a rest interval, a previously extinguished response will return to a rate above baseline; that is, in the same situation, it will spontaneously return or recover. / 159

Provide an operational definition of reinforcer.

A reinforcer is a stimulus that increases the rate or probability of a response that precedes its administration. / 160

What is a positive reinforcer?

A positive reinforcer is a stimulus that increases the rate or probability of a response when it is presented following that response. / 161

What is a negative reinforcer?

How are negative reinforcers used in escape and avoidance conditioning?

A negative reinforcer is a stimulus that increases the rate of a response that precedes its removal. In escape conditioning, an organism is reinforced by escaping from a negative reinforcer, while in avoidance conditioning, an organism is reinforced for avoiding a negative reinforcer before it occurs by reacting to a cue or signal. / 163

What is the difference between primary and secondary reinforcers?

Primary reinforcers are stimuli (reinforcers) that are in some way biologically important or related to an organism's survival (for example, food for a hungry organism), whereas secondary reinforcers act to increase the rate of a response because of the organism's previous learning or conditioning experience. That is, secondary reinforcers are learned reinforcers (for example, money or praise). / 164

What is intermittent reinforcement, and what is the advantage of using it?

Intermittent reinforcement is a strategy that provides a reinforcer for less than each and every response. A major advantage is that, when it is used, conditioned responses are resistant to extinction. / 165

What is a punisher?

A punisher is a stimulus that decreases the rate or probability of a response that precedes it. / 165

In the context of operant conditioning, what are generalization and discrimination?

In operant conditioning, generalization occurs when a response reinforced in the presence of one stimulus also occurs in the presence of other, similar stimuli. Discrimination, on the other hand, is a matter of differential reinforcement: reinforcing responses to appropriate stimuli while extinguishing responses to inappropriate stimuli. / 167

What is instinctive drift, and what does it tell us about the limits of conditioning?

Instinctive drift is the term used by the Brelands to note that some behaviors are more difficult to condition than others. That is, in spite of conditioning efforts, over time, an organism will "drift" toward doing what comes naturally, or instinctively. / 168

What is learned when one forms a cognitive map?

What is latent learning?

According to Tolman, when one acquires a cognitive map, one develops a mental representation (or picture) of one's surroundings—an appreciation of general location and where objects are located. The forming of cognitive maps can be viewed as a type of latent learning. That is, latent learning is the acquisition of information (a cognitive process) that may not be demonstrated in performance until later, if at all. / 172

Summarize the basic concepts of social learning theory and modeling.

Bandura's social learning theory emphasizes the role of observation of others and imitation in the acquisition of cognitions and behaviors. We often learn by imitating models through vicarious reinforcement and punishment. / 174

How can conditioning and cognitive approaches to learning be used to improve your study skills?

Designate a special place as a study area. Responses conducive to good study should then become associated with that area. Effective studying should be reinforced and ineffective studying should not be. Students may modify their own studying behaviors by also supplying reinforcers at appropriate times. Cognitive theories suggest that one should imitate successful models. / 176

REVIEW QUESTIONS

1. With regard to our definition of learning, which of the following statements is *not* true?

a. Learned changes are relatively permanent.

b. Learning involves changes in observed behaviors.

c. Learning results from practice or experience.

d. None of the above; that is, they are all true.

This is a deceptively tricky item. It is basically asking you about the distinction between learning and performance. Learned changes are said to be relatively permanent and must demonstrably result from practice or experience. Learning does not have to involve changes in observed behaviors. We say that learning is *demonstrated* by behavioral changes. Some say that learning is *inferred from* changes in observed behavior. / 142

2. Every time you open the door to the cupboard in which your dog's food is stored, your dog turns in circles, hops about, yelps, and begins to salivate and drool. This is true even if you open the cupboard door simply to retrieve a bowl that is stored there. If this is the case, then the behavior

that your dog exhibits when the cupboard door is opened may be called a(n):

a. orienting reflex.

b. unconditioned response.

c. conditioned stimulus.

d. conditioned response.

First recognize that the dog's behavior constitutes a response, not a stimulus, so alternative (c) is incorrect. The described behavior is almost certainly not reflexive, nor is it natural, or unlearned. The dog has learned to respond this way which makes it a learned or conditioned response. The dog has previously paired the response with the food in the cupboard, and now opening the cupboard door serves to signal or predict the likelihood of food. / 144

3. The dog referred to in the previous item is also found to hop about, yelp, drool, and turn circles when a nearby cupboard door is opened. This cupboard does not, and never did, contain dog food. The dog is here demonstrating:

a. spontaneous recovery.

b. extinction.

c. generalization.

d. habituation.

When conditioned responses occur in the presence of stimuli that are similar to the conditioned stimulus, we say that generalization has taken place, which seems to be the situation here. The definitions of the other alternatives, although relevant to conditioning, do not apply to this item. You should check these definitions in the text. / 147

4. In operant conditioning, we use a method of reinforcing responses that successively approximates some ultimately desired response in a process called:

a. discrimination.

b. spontaneous recovery.

c. establishing a baseline.

d. shaping.

To demonstrate discrimination learning in operant conditioning, one reinforces responses made in the presence of one stimulus but not in the presence of others. Spontaneous recovery refers to the reappearance of a conditioned response following extinction and after a subsequent rest interval. An organism's baseline is the rate at which a to-be-conditioned response occurs before conditioning begins. So the best alternative here correctly identifies shaping as the reinforcement of successive approximations of some desired behavior. / 158

5. By definition, a positive reinforcer is something that:

a. is evaluatively positive or pleasant.

b. is directly related to an organism's physiology.

c. makes the organism "feel good" when it is removed.

d. increases the rate of those responses that it allows.

We often think of positive reinforcers as being pleasant or evaluatively positive, but they need not be so. Positive reinforcers tend to increase (or, to be more accurate, maintain) the rate of responses they follow. Reinforcers that are tied to an organism's physiology (for example, food, or a painful shock) are called primary reinforcers. Alternative (c) is a rather sloppy way of defining a negative reinforcer. / 160

6. The major advantage of using intermittent (rather than continuous) schedules of reinforcement is that:

a. they are generally more resistant to extinction.

b. more reinforcers will be delivered, or used, in the same period of time.

c. acquisition almost always occurs more rapidly.

d. the organism has a better understanding of when reinforcers will occur.

The first alternative for this item is true. What about the others? In fact, intermittent schedules, because responses are reinforced only intermittently, will use fewer reinforcers. The most rapid acquisition generally occurs with continuous reinforcement. There is no reason why an organism should have a better understanding of what is happening under any particular schedule of reinforcement, and there is little to lead us to believe that understanding just what is going on makes any difference in operant conditioning anyway. / 165

7. The tendency of an organism to resist operant conditioning procedures and revert to more natural, unlearned behavioral reactions is called:

a. counter conditioning.

b. extinction.

c. ontological confabulation.

d. instinctive drift.

Counter conditioning implies a direct intervention to replace a conditioned response with another. Extinction is simply the reduction in response rate that occurs in operant conditioning when reinforcers are withheld. Ontological confabulation is the name of no particular process at all that we know of—it's just a nonsense term.

The term that does describe this phenomenon, introduced by the Brelands, is instinctive drift—a drifting back to what comes naturally, or instinctively. / 168

8. Paul has cheated on his exams before, and plans to do so again. Paul wants badly to cheat on his next exam but changes his plans when he sees that another student caught cheating in his class is given a grade of F on the exam and is put on academic probation. Assuming that Paul no longer engages in cheating, we may credit _____ as an explanation of his change in behavior.

a. latent learning.

b. experimental neurosis.

c. trial and error.

d. vicarious punishment.

None of the first three alternatives explain or describe Paul's learned change in behavior. The best alternative here is the term from Bandura's theory of social learning, vicarious punishment. / 174

Chapter Five

Memory and Cognition

Why We Care

Introduction: What is Memory?

Sensory Memory

Short-term Memory (STM)
The Duration of STM
The Capacity of STM
How Information Is Represented in STM

Long-term Memory (LTM)
Encoding in LTM: A Matter of Repetition
and Rehearsal
Are There Different Types of Long-term
Memories?
Procedural Memory
Semantic Memory
Episodic Memory
Metamemory
How Information Is Represented in Long-term
Memory
Category Clustering
Subjective Organization
A Hierarchical Network Model

**Measuring Retrieval: Recall, Recognition, and
Relearning**

Encoding and Retrieval
The Effects of Context
Strategies That Guide Encoding
Meaningfulness
Mnemonic Devices
Amount and Distribution of Encoding Practice
Overlearning
Scheduling Practice

Inhibiting Retrieval: Interference

Higher Cognitive Processes
The Concept of Concept
Concepts in the Laboratory
Concepts in the Real World
Forming Concepts
A Definition of Language
The Structure in Language
Speech Sounds and Structure
Meaning and Structure
Sentences and Structure

We would like you to take a short vocabulary test. This test is a little different from most because we'll provide you with the definitions, and ask you to come up with the word described by each definition. These are not easy words, but perhaps you have heard them before. See if you can notice what you are doing as you search for answers.

What words fit the following definitions:

—"A small flat-bottomed boat or skiff used along rivers and coastal regions of China and Japan."
—"A navigational instrument used in measuring angular distances, especially the altitude of the sun, moon and stars."
—"Favoritism, especially in governmental patronage, based on family relationships rather than merit."

Did you get any of those? Were you able to find in your memory the words for which these definitions are appropriate? These words, and others, were used in a 1966 experiment by Roger Brown and David McNeill to demonstrate what they labeled a "tip-of-the-tongue" phenomenon, or TOT. This same sort of procedure was used to create a condition we're all familiar with: the sense of *knowing* that you know something, being unable to fully recall it when it is wanted, but feeling that it is right at the tip of your tongue. What Brown and McNeill discovered was that many of their college student subjects didn't have the faintest idea what one calls a "small flat-bottomed boat or skiff used along rivers and coastal regions of China and Japan." A number of their subjects did know immediately what the correct response was. But many subjects experienced a TOT—a condition that these

---

Tip-of-the-tongue phenomena provide evidence . . . that we often have information stored in our memories that we cannot get out when we want to . . .

---

researchers likened to "mild torment, something like the brink of a sneeze," (p. 326) as they fought to pull the word out of their memories.

When asked about the word for which they were searching, Brown and McNeill's subjects could often correctly report the letter with which the word began, the number of syllables it contained, and which syllable is stressed when the word is pronounced. For example, in response to the first question, subjects often responded with words that sounded like the correct response—for example, "Saipan," "Siam," "Cheyenne," "sarong," "sanching," and "sympoon." Subjects recognized that these weren't correct responses, but felt that they were close. Other subjects responded with words that were semantically similar, but also recognized that the words were incorrect—for example, "barge," "houseboat," and "junk." When the correct response was provided (in this case, "sampan"), the reaction was common: "Oh yes! That's right!" Correct words were easily recognized by subjects who had experienced a TOT. Did you have a TOT for any of the three words for which you were searching? By the way, the other two words that are defined as indicated above are "sextant" and "nepotism." Did either of these provide a tip-of-the-tongue experience for you?

Obviously, TOT states can be found in many retrieval tasks, not just those requiring a search for words. Tip-of-the-tongue phenomena provide evidence, both in the laboratory and real life, that we often have information stored in our memories that we cannot get out when we want to; there are some things we simply cannot seem to remember.

Why We Care

It's nearly impossible to imagine what life would be like without memory, isn't it? For one thing, this sentence in your textbook would make no sense whatsoever. Without your memory, you would have no idea of what a textbook is or why you had it open in front of you. The black patterns of print that you recognize as words would appear to be no more than random marks. In fact, without memory, we would have no idea of who we are. All those things that define us as individuals—our feelings, beliefs, experiences, behaviors, moods, and attitudes—are stored away somehow in our memories. There are few psychological processes that are as central to our sense of self and to our perception of the world as memory.

Of the many changes that have taken place in psychology over the past 30 years, few have been as striking as the changes in the way we view memory. One of these changes involves the belief that memory may not be one unified structure or process at all; rather, there may be a number of types or levels of memory. This view suggests that all the information stored in memory does not necessarily get processed in the same way or stored in the same place. There may very well be two or three (or more) memory processes or storehouses. This basic idea provides the centerpiece for our discussion in this chapter.

A second significant change in our way of thinking about memory reflects the idea that memory is not simply a passive receptacle of information. We now view memory as an *active*, creative process, whereby information is actively processed into memory, stored there, and then actively retrieved.

We care about retrieval because when our memory does fail us, it seems that our problem is most commonly a retrieval failure. We also care about retrieval because we believe that there are a number of factors that influence the effectiveness and efficiency with which we retrieve information from our memory systems.

It turns out that our ability to get information out of our memory depends—perhaps more than anything else—on how (or if) we got it into memory in the first place. We'll examine two factors that work to inhibit successful retrieval of memories. As we have done before, we'll review some of the research data on these issues and try to point out how you can apply what we know about memory retrieval to your everyday life.

Next, we'll consider the complex cognitive tasks of concept formation and use of language. Because these cognitive tasks rely heavily on our perceptual, learning, and memory experiences, we can refer to them as "higher" cognitive processes.

We will generate a working definition of what a concept *is.* We'll see that there are a number of types of concepts: some found only in psychology laboratories, others found in nature and our everyday life experiences. Then, having defined concepts, we will turn our attention to how they are acquired or learned. Most psychologists agree that concepts *are* learned. *How* they are learned is the debatable issue.

The second higher cognitive process we'll examine in this chapter is language. Our use of language reflects a remarkable set of mental processes. Again, our first step will be to define what language is. Then we'll review some research and theory that deal with our ability to rapidly and effortlessly produce and comprehend language.

INTRODUCTION: WHAT IS MEMORY?

memory
the cognitive ability to encode, store, and retrieve information

encoding
the active process of putting information into memory

storage
the process of holding encoded information in memory until the time of retrieval

retrieval
the process of locating, removing, and using information that is stored in memory

Using **memory** is a cognitive activity. It involves three interrelated processes or stages. First, we speak of putting information *into* memory, a process we call **encoding.** Once information is in memory, we must keep it there. This process we call **storage.** And, of course, to use the stored information, we need to be able to get it out again. This process is **retrieval.** Memory, then, involves the cognitive processes of encoding, storing, and retrieving information.

For a very long time in psychology, the study of memory was quite simple and very straightforward. Memory was viewed as a static, passive storehouse or receptacle for information. Things somehow got stored away in memory and there they stayed until we wanted to get them out. Psychology textbooks illustrated memory as a large file cabinet, crammed with papers and folders, or as bookshelves in a crowded library. There was thought to be just one kind of memory and one kind of storage that either worked when we wanted it to or failed.

In this way, memory was seen as being essentially automatic. Psychology, following the tradition of the ancient Greeks, saw memory as being like a block of wax. Although no psychologist in the twentieth century really believed we have wax in our heads, the metaphor seemed workable. Experience makes impressions, or imprints, in the wax. Sometimes the wax is soft and malleable, and the impression (memory) is a good, clear one. Sometimes the wax is hard, and our memories are only faint, imperfect impressions of our experiences. The Greeks also recognized individual differences in memory abilities and argued that some people were born with larger and softer blocks of wax than others (Adams, 1980).

Now we think of memory as being the last step in a series of psychological activities that deal with information processing. We come into this world knowing very little about it. By the time we are adults, we know an incredible number of things about ourselves and the world. Much of that information may be trivial and irrelevant, but much of it is essential for survival. How do our minds come to be filled with so much information? As we pointed out in Chapter 2, the processing of information begins with sensation when our sensory receptors are stimulated. Then, through the process we call perception, information from our senses is selected and organized. Through learning, some experiences bring about relatively permanent changes in our behaviors. With memory, we form a record of the information we have processed.

As we have said, modern views see memory as being more than one, simple unified process. That is, not all of the information that gets stored in memory necessarily gets stored in the same way or in the same place. Some psychologists (for example, Atkinson & Shiffrin, 1968; Tulving, 1985; Waugh & Norman, 1965) argue that there are actually different types of memory and that each type has different characteristics and different mechanisms for processing information. Psychologists who talk about separate, distinct memories, or memory stores, support what is called a **multistore model of memory.** Others (for example, Cermak & Craik, 1979; Craik, 1970; Craik & Lockhart, 1972) argue that there is but one memory, and within that memory there are different levels or depths to which information gets processed. Their argument is that some information simply gets more (deep) or less (shallow) processing within the same memory. This view is called the **levels of processing model of memory.**

In this chapter, we will examine the basic idea of and supporting research evidence for three stores or levels of memory: a sensory memory, a short-term memory (STM), and a long-term memory (LTM). Sometimes we'll refer to sensory, short-term, and long-term memories as if they were *stores or structures* (or something you put information in). Sometimes we'll refer to processing information at different *levels,* as if the levels referred to activities (what you do with information to remember it), not places. This mixing of viewpoints is intentional, because at the moment we can't declare with any certainty which model of memory is "the right one." In either case, we will have a number of questions to ask about each memory structure or level. For example, what is its capacity, or how much information can it deal with? What is its duration, or how long will information be held there without further processing? How does information get into this memory, or how does it get processed to this depth? In what form is it stored?

② Theories Of Memory

multistore model of memory
the view that there are three separate and distinct types (or stores) of memory, each with its own manner of processing information

levels of processing model of memory
the view that there is but one memory, but that information can be processed within that memory at different degrees, levels, or depths

How do we define memory?
What are the basic ideas of the multistore and levels of
processing models of memory?

SENSORY MEMORY

sensory memory
the type of memory that holds large
amounts of information registered at
the senses for very brief periods of
time

STM is Automatic

Sensory memory involves the storage of large amounts of sensory information for very short periods of time (a few seconds or less). This idea of a very
brief, sensory memory is a controversial one in cognitive psychology.

A sensory memory does fit into the overall picture of information processing. All of the information that ultimately gets stored in our memories
must first have entered through our senses. Simply put, to be able to
remember what a lecturer says, you first must be in class to hear the lecture.
To remember a drawing from this book, the image of the drawing first must
enter your visual system. You can't remember the aroma of fried onions if
you've never smelled them in the first place.

The basic idea here is that information does not pass directly through
our sensory systems; instead, it is held in our sensory memory for a brief
period of time. Even after a stimulus has left our environment and is no
longer physically present, it has left its imprint, having formed a sensory
memory.

The *capacity* of sensory memory seems, at least in theory, to be very
large indeed. At one time it was believed that we could keep as much in our
sensory memory as our sense receptors could respond to at any one time.
Everything to which our senses reacted got stored in our sensory memory.
Such claims give sensory memory more credit than it is due. Our sensory
memory can hold much more information than we can attend to, but there
are limits on its capacity.

The practical problem with sensory memory lies in its *duration.* We may
be able to get vast amounts of information into our sensory memory (encoding), but we aren't able to keep it there (storage) very long. What *is* the
duration of sensory memory? It's difficult to say exactly, but memories
remain in sensory memory very briefly—about 0.5 seconds for visually presented materials (Sperling, 1960, 1963), perhaps for as long as 3–4 seconds
for orally presented information (Darwin et al., 1972; Massaro, 1975). It
certainly won't be of much help for your next psychology exam if you can
process information to this store or level and no further.

0.5 Vision
3-4 sec. Oral

Sensory memory is typically viewed as being a rather physical or
mechanical type of storage. The information stored there cannot be acted
upon. You can't *do* anything with it. You simply have to take the information
in your sensory memory pretty much as your receptors deliver it to you. It's
as if stimuli from the environment make an impression on our sensory
systems and then rapidly fade or are replaced by new stimuli. A very good
word to describe the action of the sensory memory is *reverberate,* which
means to continue like a series of echoes. That is, our senses hold on to
information as it reverberates or echoes within our nervous system, even
after the physical stimulus is gone.

reverberate

Here are two examples that demonstrate our sensory memory in action.
In a reasonably dark area, stand about 20 feet away from a friend who is

pointing a flashlight at you. Have your friend swing the flashlight around in a small circle, making about one revolution per second. What do you see? You see a circle of light, and you do so because of your sensory memory. At any one instant, not only are you seeing where the light *is,* but you are also experiencing where the light *has just been.* If your friend moves the flashlight slowly, you may see a "tail" of light following it, but you won't see a circle any more because the image of the light's position will have decayed from memory.

Example of sensory memory involving vision

Have you ever had this experience? Someone asks you a simple question to which your reply is something like "Huh? What did you say?" Then, before the person even gets a chance to repeat her question, you go ahead and answer it. (Which may in turn provoke a response such as "Why didn't you answer me in the first place?") Perhaps you didn't clearly hear all of the question you were asked, but while it was still reverberating (echoing) in your sensory memory, you listened to it again and formed your answer.

Example involving hearing

As we said, this notion of a sensory memory as the very brief storage of large amounts of minimally processed information is a controversial one. However, there is considerable evidence that sensory memory is a real phenomenon, at least for vision and audition. It may not be particularly useful in any practical sort of way, but perhaps that extra fraction of a second or two of storage in sensory memory provides us with the time we need to fully attend to information so that we can then move that information along into our memory systems. Notice, too, that a sensory memory is in keeping with the levels of processing model of memory. What we are here referring to as a separate, sensory memory may just be the first, simplest, or shallowest level of processing information. Processing at this level requires very little effort, but information processed only to this level decays very quickly and is thus difficult to retrieve.

What is sensory memory?
What is its capacity and duration?

BEFORE YOU GO ON

SHORT-TERM MEMORY (STM) (WORKING memory)

We have seen that a good deal of information can easily get into our sensory memory. Once information gets to sensory memory, where does it go next? As we have noted, most of it rapidly fades or is quickly replaced with new stimuli. With a little effort, however, we can process material in our sensory memory more fully by moving it on to **short-term memory (STM).** Short-term memory has a limited capacity and, without the benefit of rehearsal, a brief duration. To encode information into STM requires that we pay attention to it. Short-term memory is frequently referred to as *working memory.* It is viewed as something like a workbench or desk top where we can use and manipulate the information to which we pay attention. Information can get into STM directly from our sensory memory, or it can be retrieved from our long-term memory for use at the moment. Because of its limited duration and capacity, STM acts like a bottleneck in the processing of information from our senses into long-term storage. Let's see just how limited our short-term memories are.

working — Rehearsal

short-term memory (STM)
a type of memory with limited capacity (7 ± 2 bits of information) and limited duration (15 to 20 seconds)

STM capacity - 7 bits of info can keep in shrt Term Memory

FIGURE 5.1

Recall of letters as a function of retention interval where maintenance rehearsal is minimized.
(Adapted from Peterson & Peterson, 1959.)

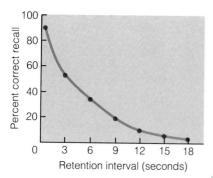

Peterson's experiment

The Duration of STM

Interest in short-term memory processing can be traced to two similar experiments reported independently in the late 1950s (Brown, 1958; Peterson & Peterson, 1959). We'll review the Petersons' experiment.

On a typical trial, a subject is shown three consonants, such as KRW, for 3 seconds. Presenting the letters for 3 seconds assures that they are attended to and, hence, encoded into STM. The subject is then asked to recall the three letters after retention intervals ranging from 0 to 18 seconds. This doesn't sound like a very difficult task, and it isn't. Almost anyone can remember three letters for as long as 18 seconds. However, in this experiment, subjects are prohibited from rehearsing the three letters during the retention interval. They are given another task to perform right after they see the letters. They are asked to count backward, by threes, from a three-digit number supplied by the experimenter.

For example, if you were a subject, you would be shown a letter sequence, say KRW, and then you would have to count backward from, say, 397 by threes, or 397, 394, 391, 388, and so forth. You'd be instructed to do your counting out loud and as rapidly as possible. The idea is that the counting task interferes with your rehearsal of the three letters you were just shown.

Under these conditions, your ability to recall the letters correctly *depends on the length of the retention interval*. If you are asked to recall the letters after just a few seconds of counting, you won't do too badly. If you have to count for as long as 15 to 20 seconds, your ability to recall the letters drops to almost zero (see Figure 5.1). Because you are unable to rehearse them and are distracted by the counting task, the letters are soon unavailable to you.

This experimental example is not as abstract as it may first appear. Consider this scenario. Having studied psychology for 3 hours, you decide to reinforce yourself and have a pizza. You decide to splurge and have your pizza delivered. (You heard this afternoon that Pizza City now offers free delivery.) Never having called Pizza City before, you turn to the yellow pages to find the number: 555-5897. You repeat the number to yourself as you think about your choice of pizza toppings—555-5897. You close the phone book and return it to the desk drawer. You dial the number without error. Buzzz-buzzz-buzzz-buzzz. Darn, the number's busy! Well, you'll call back in a minute.

Just as you hang up the phone, the doorbell rings. It's the paper boy. You owe him $11.60 for the past 2 weeks' deliveries. Discovering that you don't have enough cash on hand to pay for the paper *and* a pizza, you write a personal check. "Let's see, today's date? What *is* today's date? Oh yes, 10-15-88. How much did you say I owed you? Oh yes, $11.60, plus a dollar tip, comes to $12.60. This is check number 1079; I'd better write that down—#1079. There you go. Thanks a lot."

The paper boy leaves, and you return to your studying. Then you remember that you were going to order a pizza. Only 5 or 6 minutes have passed since you got a busy signal from Pizza City. As you go to dial the phone, however, you cannot for the life of you remember their phone number. Back to the yellow pages. A number once attended to became active in your working short-term memory long enough for you to use it. When you were kept

Maintenance rehearsal enables a caller to keep a phone number in short-term memory long enough to recall it and dial it.

When they are learning math, children often count on their fingers. As they become more familiar with math fundamentals, their short-term memories can help them solve simple problems in their heads.

from rehearsing it—and when other numbers entered STM as potentially interfering information—that number was soon inaccessible.

One way in which we can increase or stretch the duration of short-term memory is to rehearse the information stored there. The type of rehearsal we use simply to keep material active in our short-term, working memory is called **maintenance rehearsal,** or rote rehearsal, which amounts to little more than simple repetition of the information already in our STM. Remember, to get material into STM (encoding), we have to attend to it. By repeating that information over and over (as we might if we wanted to remember a telephone number until we could dial it), we are essentially reattending to it with each repetition.

So one reason why our STM is a bottleneck in our memory system is that it does not store information for very long. By attending to information, we *do* keep it available well beyond the limits of sensory memory. As a rule of thumb, we can say that, if left unrehearsed, material will stay in STM for about 15 to 20 seconds. That's better than sensory memory, but it still won't help much when it comes to taking an exam next week.

At least the duration of STM is long enough to allow us to use it occasionally in everyday activities. Again, our telephone number example is relevant. Usually all we want to do with a telephone number is remember it long enough to dial it. It's not often that we feel the need to make a permanent record of a telephone number. Using STM in mathematical computations is another good example, particularly when we do those computations "in our head." And, as you read one of our longer sentences, it is useful to have a short-term storage place to keep the beginning of the sentence that you are reading in mind until you finally get to the end of the sentence, so that you can figure out the basic idea of the sentence. Now let's deal with the capacity of STM. Just how much information can we hold in STM for that 15 to 20 seconds?

maintenance rehearsal
a process of rote repetition, (attending again) to keep information in STM

(handwritten margin note, top right) ACUSTIC is RELIED upon more in SHT termemory

(handwritten margin note, right) Chunk is when you TAKE INTO A more meaningful MANNer You CAN INcrease The amouNT oF bits.

How long is information stored in STM?
What is required to get material into STM and then keep it there?

BEFORE YOU GO ON

Chunking information together while listening to a lecture is an effective way to store it for later study.

The Capacity of STM

In 1956, George Miller wrote a charming paper on "the magical number seven, plus or minus two." In it, he argued that the capacity of our working memories is very small—limited to just 5 to 9 (or 7 ± 2) bits or chunks of information.

As we all know, we can readily store a telephone number in our short-term memories. Adding an area code makes the task somewhat harder because the 10 digits now come fairly close to the upper limit of our STM capacity. Notice, though, how we tend to cluster, or chunk, the digits of a phone number into a pattern. The digit series 2194935661 is more difficult to deal with as a simple string than when it is seen as a telephone number: (219) 493-5661 (Bower & Springston, 1970).

By chunking bits and pieces of information together, we can add meaningfulness to what we are attending to and storing in our memories. Can you hold this number in your STM: 49162536496481? The 14 digits here are beyond the capacity of most people's STM. But if you recognize these as a series of numbers, each being the *square* of the digits 2 through 9 (4/9/16/25/36/49/64/81), the task is an easy one because you have chunked the material in a meaningful way. Using a similar system of chunking digits into meaningful clusters, one student demonstrated an ability to recall more than 80 randomly presented digits (Ericsson & Chase, 1982).

You should notice that adding the notion of chunking to our discussion of the capacity of STM significantly affects our ability to specify the capacity of STM with any precision. Although we can say that the capacity of STM is 7 ± 2 chunks of information, there are enormous differences in how information may be chunked. In other words, "chunk" is a very imprecise measure of capacity (Anderson, 1980).

In any event, short-term memory acts like a bottleneck, working something like a leaky bucket. From the vast storehouse of information available in our sensory memory, we scoop up some (and not much at that) by paying attention to it and hold it for a while until we either use it, maintain it with rehearsal, move it on to long-term storage, or lose it.

BEFORE YOU GO ON How much information can be held in STM?
How can chunking affect the capacity of STM?

How Information Is Represented in STM

We noted that the material or information that is stored in our sensory memory is encoded there in virtually the same form in which it was presented. Visual stimuli form visual memories or impressions, auditory stimuli form auditory memories, and so on.

We recognize that getting information into STM is not necessarily an automatic process. First we have to attend to the material to encode it into short-term memory. How, then, is information stored or represented in STM?

Conrad (1963, 1964) was one of the first to argue that information is stored in STM with an acoustic code. What that means is that material tends to be processed in terms of what it *sounds* like. Conrad's conclusion was based on his interpretation of the errors that subjects make in short-term memory tasks.

For example, he would present subjects with a series of letters to remember. The letters were presented *visually,* one at a time, and then subjects were asked to recall the letters they had just seen. It was not surprising that many errors were made over the course of the experiment. What *was* surprising was that when subjects responded with an incorrect letter, it was very frequently with a letter that *sounded* like the correct one. For example, if subjects were supposed to recall the letter E and failed to do so, they would commonly recall in error V, G, or T, or a letter that sounded like the E they were supposed to recall. They rarely responded F, which certainly looks more like the E they had just seen than does V, G, or T.

Experiments by Baddeley (1966) made the same point, but with a different technique. In these experiments, subjects were asked to recall short lists of common words. Some lists were made up of words that all sounded alike (for example, man, ban, fan, can). Other lists contained words that had similar meanings; that is, they were semantically alike (for example, large, huge, giant, big). A third type of list contained a random assortment of words. Lists were only five words long and, hence, were well within the capacity of short-term memory. The lists that were hardest to recall were those that contained acoustically similar items (that is, the "man, ban, fan" list). Baddeley's argument is that the acoustic similarity caused confusion within STM, whereas semantic similarity did not.

It seems then that using short-term memory is a matter of talking to ourselves. No matter how it is presented, we tend to encode and process information acoustically, the way it sounds. At least that's what most of the early evidence seemed to suggest. Subsequent research has not changed the view that acoustic coding is the most important method of coding for STM. However, it has presented the possibility that some material may be encoded in STM in other ways—such as being represented visually or semantically (Cooper & Shepard, 1973; Martindale, 1981; Wickens, 1973). Presently, perhaps the most we can say is that there is a tendency to rely heavily on the acoustic coding of information in short-term memory, but other codes may be used also.

What evidence do we have that information tends to be encoded acoustically in STM? **BEFORE YOU GO ON**

LONG-TERM MEMORY (LTM)

Long-term memory (LTM) is memory as people usually think of it—memory for large amounts of information held for long periods of time. As we did for sensory and short-term memory, we'll begin by considering two basic issues: capacity and duration.

Our own experiences tell us that the capacity of our long-term memories is huge, virtually limitless. At times we may even impress ourselves with the amount of material we have stashed away in LTM (for instance; when we play games such as Trivial Pursuit). Just how much can be stored in human memory may never be measured, but we can rest assured that there is no way we will ever learn so much that there won't be room for more.

For an example of memory's huge capacity, consider an experiment by Standing, Conezio, and Haber (1970). Over the course of five days, they presented subjects with 2500 different pictures and asked them to try to

long-term memory (LTM)
a type of memory with virtually unlimited capacity and very long, if not permanent, duration

The capacity of our long-term memories seems almost limitless, which is especially apparent when we use LTM to play games such as Trivial Pursuit.

remember them all. Even a day or so later, subjects correctly identified, in a new collection of pictures, 90 percent of the ones they had seen before. Standing (1973) increased the number of pictures that subjects viewed to 10,000. As you can imagine, it took quite awhile simply to view 10,000 pictures! Again, subjects later correctly recognized more than 90 percent of them.

There seems to be no practical limit to the amount of information we can process (or encode) into this long-term store of memory. (Getting information out again when we want it is another matter, which we'll get to later in the chapter.) How long will information stay in LTM once it is there? Assuming that you remain free from disease or injury, you are likely never to forget information such as your own name, your parents' names, or the words to "Twinkle, Twinkle Little Star."

At the moment, it is impossible to even imagine an experiment that could tell us with any certainty how long our memories remain stored in LTM. One thing we know for a fact is that we often cannot remember things we know we once knew. We do tend to forget things. The issue is *why*. Do we forget because the information is no longer *available* to us in our long-term memories, simply not there any more? Or do we forget because we are unable to get the information out of LTM, which implies that the information is still available, but now somehow not accessible?

For a very long time in psychology we believed that once information was processed into LTM, it stayed there until we died. (In fact, in a survey published in 1980, 84 percent of the psychologists who were asked agreed with the statement that "everything we learn is permanently stored in the mind, although sometimes particular details are not accessible" (Loftus & Loftus, 1980, p. 410).) In this view, forgetting is a failure of *retrieval* of stored information. Have you ever handed in an exam paper, walked out the classroom door, turned down the hall, and suddenly realized very clearly the answer to an exam question you could not think of minutes before while you were taking the exam? This sort of experience reinforces the notion that memories may always be available, but not always accessible. How pleasant it is to think that everything we ever knew, everything that ever happened to us, is still there someplace, ultimately retrievable if we only knew how to get it out.

As comforting as this view may be, there is reason to believe that it is not totally accurate. A review article by Loftus and Loftus (1980) has raised again the issue of the relative permanence of long-term memories. The Loftuses reviewed the data supporting the argument for permanence and found that "the evidence in no way confirms the view that all memories are permanent and thus potentially recoverable" (p. 409). They claim that the bulk of such evidence is neither experimental nor reliable. They further claim that when we think we are recalling specific memories of the long-distant past, we are often reconstructing a reasonable facsimile of the original information from bits and pieces of our past. That is, when we remember something that happened to us a long time ago, we don't recall the events as they happened (as if our memories work like perfect video recorders). Rather, we recall a specific detail or two and then actively reconstruct what are basically new memories. (Of course, even if we *do* reconstruct new recollections of past experiences, that would not necessarily mean that our original memory was no longer available. It might only suggest that we can maintain a number of versions of the same event in long-term memory (McCloskey & Zaragoza, 1985).)

There are a number of implications of this line of research that have practical importance. One of the most obvious is in the area of eyewitness testimony. If it is in fact true that long-term memories are not permanent and that they can be distorted or replaced by information processed later, we may be forced to reconsider the weight that is given to eyewitness testimony in courts of law (for example, Buckhout, 1975; Clifford & Lloyd-Bostock, 1983; Loftus, 1984).

WE RECONSTRUCT The INFO.

Inaccurate eyewitness testimony indicates that our longterm memories are not perfect and are subject to distortion. On the basis of eyewitness testimony, the man on the bottom was imprisoned for 5 years for a crime committed by the man on the top.

Are long-term memories necessarily permanent? **BEFORE YOU GO ON**

Encoding in LTM: A Matter of Repetition and Rehearsal

We have already seen how simple, rote repetition (maintenance rehearsal) can be used to keep material active in short-term memory. There is reason to believe that this simple sort of rehearsal is also one way to move information from STM to LTM. The basic idea is that the more one repeats a bit of information, the more likely it will be remembered—even beyond the limits of short-term memory. Although there *are* circumstances when this is true, the simple repetition of material is seldom sufficient to process it into LTM.

Doesn't work very well

Repetition can be helpful, but getting information into long-term memory usually requires more. We need to do more than simply repeat information over and over. We need to think about it, reorganize it perhaps, form images of it, make it meaningful, or relate it to something already in our long-term memories. In other words, to get information into LTM we need to "elaborate" on it, to use the term proposed by Craik and Lockhart (1972). We need to process it more fully, using **elaborative rehearsal.**

elaborative rehearsal
a mechanism for processing information into LTM that involves the meaningful manipulation of the information to be remembered

Do you see how the distinction between maintenance and elaborative rehearsal fits a model of memory that deals with levels of processing? For sensory memory, we need do very little to process information; stimuli are stored automatically at this level. To get to the next level requires deeper processing; at the very least, attention is required for STM. Long-term memory, then, represents the deepest level of processing. Items must be elaborated, expanded, and made meaningful to reach this level. And indeed, the model claims that the more we can relate to new material, the more meaningful we can make it, and the more we can elaborate on it (the deeper we can process it), the easier it will be to remember (Cermak & Craik, 1979; Craik & Tulving, 1975).

BEFORE YOU GO ON Contrast elaborative rehearsal with maintenance rehearsal as a means of encoding information into long-term memory.

Are There Different Types of Long-term Memories?

Our own experiences tell us that the information we have stored away in LTM can be retrieved in many different forms. We can remember the definitions of words. We can picture or visualize people and events from the past. We can remember the melodies of songs. We can recall how our bodies moved when we first tried to ski or roller skate. It may be that information in our long-term memories is processed by different systems or types of LTM. Different kinds of information may be stored in different places by different processes. This notion of different LTM systems is a relatively new one in psychology, and as you might expect, there is no general agreement on just what all of the systems within LTM might be (Johnson & Hasher, 1987). Here, we'll briefly review four possible LTM systems.

Procedural Memory.   Endel Tulving (1972, 1985, 1986) has suggested that the information we have stored in LTM is of three different types. Although the three can and do interact with each other, he sees them as being basically different. One type of long-term memory is called **procedural memory.** This is the lowest level of the three proposed by Tulving. Procedural memory enables "organisms to retain learned connections between stimuli and responses, including those involving complex stimulus patterns and response chains, and to respond adaptively to the environment" (Tulving, 1985, p. 387). In this memory, we have stored our recollections of learned responses, or chains of responses, to particular stimuli. Classically and operantly conditioned responses are stored here. Those automatic, pleasant feelings that we recall when we see pictures of a favorite vacation spot come from procedural memory. Also stored here is our collection of patterned responses that we have learned well, such as how to balance and ride a bicycle, how to type, or how to swing a golf club.

procedural memory
in LTM, where learned S-R associations and skilled patterns of responses, are stored

Semantic Memory.   A more complex type of memory is what Tulving calls **semantic memory.** In it we have stored all our vocabulary, simple concepts, and rules (including the rules that govern our use of language). Here we have stored our knowledge of ourselves and the world in which we

semantic memory
in LTM, where vocabulary, facts, simple concepts, rules, and the like are stored

Our semantic memories store vocabulary, simple concepts, and rules, including the rules of spelling.

live. In a way, our semantic memories are crammed with facts, both important and trivial, such as:

> Who opened the first psychology laboratory in Leipzig in 1879?
> How many stripes are there on the American flag?
> Is "Colorless green ideas sleep furiously" a well-formed, grammatical sentence?

If we can answer these questions, we have found those answers in our long-term semantic memories.

Episodic Memory.   The third type or system of memory proposed by Tulving is called **episodic memory.** It is here that we store our life events and experiences. It is a "time-related memory", and, in a sense, it is autobiographical. For example:

episodic memory
in LTM, where life events and experiences are stored

> What were you doing the day the Challenger space shuttle exploded?
> When and where did you first learn how to ride a bike?
> What did you have for lunch yesterday?

The answers to these sorts of questions are stored in our episodic memories.

Metamemory.   A fourth possibility for a long-term memory system is what John Flavell calls **metamemory** (1971; Flavell & Wellman, 1977; Maki & Swett, 1987). Metamemory refers to our knowledge of how our own memory systems and subsystems work. If we were to ask you your mother's maiden name, your metamemory might direct your memory search to your semantic memory, looking somewhere there among your knowledge of names and family relationships for your mother's maiden name. If you couldn't find that name quickly, your metamemory might direct your search to your episodic memory, where you might be directed to recall last spring's

metamemory
in LTM, our stored knowledge of how our own memory systems work; directs LTM searches

Our episodic memories store our life events and experiences. Being in a flood is an experience that few people would ever forget.

family reunion to see if those memories might help you recall the name you're searching for. (Notice how this example underscores the interrelationship among memory systems.) Now if we were to ask you to recall the maiden names of our mothers you probably wouldn't even begin to search your memory anyplace for that information. You just know that you don't know, and such is the function of one's metamemory.

BEFORE YOU GO ON **Name and briefly describe four possible systems or types of LTM.**

How Information Is Represented in Long-term Memory *Organized*

The capacity of our short-term memory is so small that if we wanted to retrieve an item from it, we could easily scan all of the information stored there to find the item we were looking for. On the other hand, our long-term memory has such a huge capacity that to engage in an exhaustive search of all the information we have stored there would be a very inefficient strategy for locating any particular piece. Fortunately, the facts in our long-term memory tend to be stored in an organized fashion. On this point we are agreed. What is much less certain is *how* the information is organized. Although we cannot review all the possibilities here, we'll take a look at some of the data and hypotheses that have emerged concerning how we store information in our long-term memory.

category clustering
at recall, grouping words together into categories even if they are presented in a random order

Category Clustering.   Just to give you an idea of what we mean when we talk about the organization of long-term memory, consider a classic experiment by W. A. Bousfield (1953). Bousfield showed that in recall, we tend to group words together in conceptual categories, even if they were presented in a random order. He called this phenomenon **category clustering.** For example, subjects are presented with a list of words to learn: *How-*

ard, spinach, zebra, plumber, Bernard, dentist, carrot, weasel, and so on. There are 60 words on the list. After hearing the list, subjects are asked to write down, in any order, as many of the words from the list as they can recall. Subjects are told nothing about the nature of the list of words, but it is in fact made up of 15 words from each of four different conceptual categories: animals, men's names, professions, and vegetables (which you may have noticed as you read the sample list above).

When subjects recall such a list, they almost always do a rather strange thing. They do not write down their recall in a random order or in the order in which the words were presented, but they group them together into categories. For example, they might write down a number of men's names, then some animals, then a couple of professions, followed by a few vegetables. Then, at the end of their recall, they may just add a word or two from any category. So one way in which words (nouns in particular) may be stored in long-term memory is by conceptual category. When we can sort and store information in categories, we do so.

Subjective Organization.   What about words that do not fit so neatly into categories? How might they be organized? Research by Tulving shows just how powerful our tendency to organize verbal material is. He called the type of clustering that he studied **subjective organization.**

Tulving (1962) presented subjects with a list of 16 random and apparently unrelated words to be learned and later recalled. He presented the same list to subjects over and over, each time in a different order until the list was learned. Because there was no organization in the list itself, any consistency at recall must reflect an organization imposed by the subject recalling the list. Tulving found a strong tendency for subjects to recall many words together, in the same sequence, on successive recall trials. Each subject tended to organize his or her own recall in his or her own way, consistently grouping together clusters of two or three words in the same order on different recall attempts, even though the items were always presented in a different order.

A Hierarchical Network Model.   Collins and Quillian (1969) suggest that our semantic memories are organized in hierarchies of information. Approaches like that of Collins and Quillian are called **network models** of memory. To see what that means, refer to Figure 5.2 which presents a very small segment of a possible network, or hierarchy, for a few of the words that we all have in our semantic memories. At the top of this flow chart of semantic organization is the term *animal.* Associated with it are some of its defining characteristics: "has skin," "can breathe," "moves around." Below *animal* are found (among others) two concepts, *bird* and *fish,* each with their defining characteristics. Below this level we find even more specific examples, including *canary, robin, shark,* and *salmon,* each with its defining characteristics. It is possible, of course, to go even further. That is, if you once had a canary named Pete, your semantic memory might include a level below *canary,* separating Pete and his (or her) characteristics from all other canaries. Or you might have a level above *animal* called *living things.*

This system looks quite complicated as presented in Figure 5.2, and in this figure we've left out many of the things that we know about animals, fish, birds, and canaries just to make it reasonably simple. Is there any

subjective organization
the tendency for subjects to impose some order on their recall of randomly presented events or items.

network models
organizational schemes that describe the relationships among meaningful units stored in semantic memory

FIGURE 5.2
An illustration of how information is organized in semantic memory. Members of a category are organized in a hierarchy. The information to be retrieved must be located within the hierarchy to be recalled.
(Adapted from Collins & Quillian, 1969.)

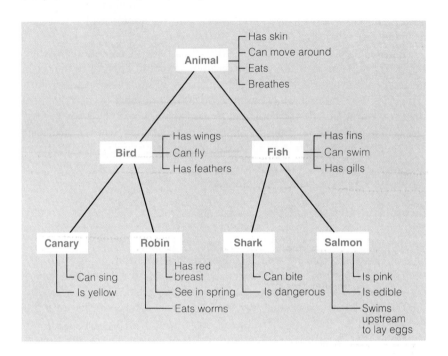

evidence that memories are stored in this fashion? Yes, there is. Suppose we ask you the following three questions about canaries and ask that you respond "yes" or "no."

1. Can canaries sing?
2. Do canaries have feathers?
3. Do canaries have skin?

We suspect that none of these questions gave you a hard time. But if we were to have measured how long it took you to answer each question, we might have found what Collins and Quillian found. The first was answered most quickly, the second took longer, and the third, longer yet. Each question required that you search a higher and higher level of memory to find the answer (singing is associated directly with canaries, feathers with birds in general, and skin with animals in general). An assumption of this model is that concepts can be clearly and neatly defined and then organized. Such is not always the case, as we shall see later. The exercise we just went through for *canary* might yield different results if our example hadn't been such an obvious example of a bird (Rosch, 1973). How might you answer the same three questions if they dealt with an ostrich or a penguin?

It would be altogether improper to leave the impression that psychologists know how words, concepts, and facts are organized in our memories. We are quite sure that there *is* organization, but we have conflicting ideas about what that organization is. It may be categorical or hierarchical; it may reflect a series of interrelated networks of information, or it may reflect some combination of these models; or our memories may be organized in ways not yet imagined.

Briefly summarize ways in which information may be represented in long-term memory.

We have covered a lot of ground so far, much of it very technical. We have tried to show that memory is not a simple receptacle for information that passively enters our bodies and gets dumped someplace where we can get it out whenever we wish. The multistore model of memory claims that to encode and store information requires a series of processes to move it through three distinct memory stores: from sensory memory to short-term storage, and from short-term to long-term memory. A levels-of-processing model claims that there is one memory where information is processed at different levels: information is moved easily into sensory memory; into short-term memory only by attending to it; and into long-term memory only when it is elaboratively rehearsed. We also have seen that information stored in LTM is clearly organized, although we may not yet fully appreciate the complex patterns of organization that characterize our memory systems. In any event, what ultimately matters for most of us, day in and day out, is whether or not we can get material out of our memory systems when we want to. We consider this process of retrieval next.

HARder Than

MEASURING RETRIEVAL: RECALL, RECOGNITION, AND RELEARNING

One factor that affects our ability to retrieve information from our long-term memories is how we are asked to go about retrieval. This is a factor over which any of us seldom have much control. For instance, unless you have a very democratic instructor, you will not be allowed to vote on what kind of exams will be given in class. Students are generally asked to retrieve information in one of a number of standard exam formats chosen by their instructor.

Let's design a laboratory example to work with for a while. Imagine that we have subjects come to the laboratory on a given Tuesday to learn a list of 15 randomly chosen words. Some subjects take longer than others, but eventually all come to demonstrate that they have learned the list. All subjects report back to the laboratory two weeks later when our basic question is: "How many of the words you learned two weeks ago do you still remember?" How could we find out?

One thing we might do is ask for simple **recall** of the list of words. To do so, we need only provide the subjects with a blank sheet of paper and ask them to write down, in any order, as many of the words from the previously learned list as they can. This is a very difficult type of retrieval task. For recall, we provide the fewest possible cues to aid their retrieval. We merely specify the information we want and essentially say, "There, now go into your long-term memories, locate that information, get it out, and write it down." Let's assume that one subject correctly recalls six words. So, for our example, we have a subject who can remember six words.

recall
a measure of retrieval in which an individual is provided with the fewest possible cues to aid retrieval

FIGURE 5.3
Two curves demonstrating retention for nonsense syllables over a 2-day period. In one case, retention is measured with a test for recognition, while the other tests for recall. (From Luh, 1922.)

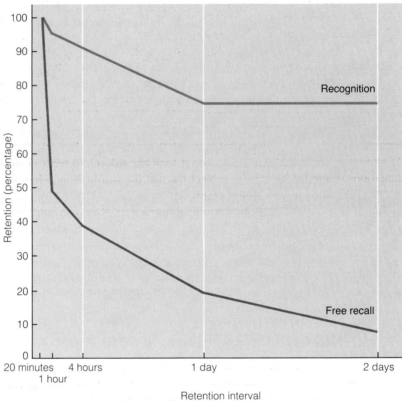

recognition
a measure of retrieval in which an individual is required to identify as familiar, material previously learned as being familiar

What if we furnished our subject with a list of 50 words, including those on the previously learned list? Now our instructions are to "circle the words on this list that you *recognize* from the list you learned two weeks ago." In this case, we would not be asking for recall, but for **recognition,** a retrieval task requiring a subject to simply identify material learned previously. Isn't it likely that our subject will do better on this task? She recalled 6 words of the original 15, so let's say she recognizes 11 words. Now, in a way, we have a small dilemma: Should we say that our subject remembered 6 words or 11 words? The answer is, "Both or either." How many words our subject remembered depends on how we asked her to go about remembering.

In virtually all cases, retrieval by recognition will be superior to retrieval by recall. Figure 5.3 provides some clearcut data to support what we have been saying. It shows that over a two-day period, tests of retrieval by recognition are superior to tests of retrieval by recall. With recall, we provide minimal retrieval cues; with recognition, we provide maximum cues and ask the subject to identify a stimulus as being one that she or he has seen before (Mandler, 1980). Or, as Benton Underwood, a psychologist who has studied memory processes for many years puts it, in recall we ask "What is the item?" and in a recognition task we ask "Is this the item?" (cited in Houston, 1986, p. 280).

Most students we know would much rather take a multiple-choice exam, in which they only have to recognize the correct response from a small number of alternatives, than a fill-in-the-blank test (or an essay test) that requires recall. Multiple-choice tests are easier than fill-in-the-blank tests. But, consistent with an argument we will be developing below, there are situations in which just the opposite is true. If, for example, students *expect* a fill-in-the-blank test and study for such a test, they may very well do better on it than they would on a multiple-choice test, even though the latter measures retrieval through recognition (Leonard & Whitten, 1983).

What if one of the subjects in our hypothetical example came back to the laboratory two weeks after memorizing a list of words and could neither recall nor recognize any of the items? We'd be a bit surprised, but we might be wrong if we assumed that our subject retained nothing from the learning experience two weeks earlier. What if we ask this subject to relearn the list of 15 words? We note that two weeks ago it took the subject 10 trials or presentations of the list before the subject learned the words. Now, when relearning the same list, we find it takes only seven trials. This is a common finding in memory research. **Relearning** almost always takes less effort than did original learning, and the difference is attributed to the advantage provided by one's memory of the original learning.

relearning
a measure of memory in which one notes the improvement in performance when learning material for a second time

How do recall, recognition, and relearning measures affect our assessment of retrieval?

BEFORE YOU GO ON

ENCODING AND RETRIEVAL

At the beginning of this chapter, we said that, by definition, memory involves the related processes of encoding, storage, and retrieval. In this section, we'll explore the important relationship that exists between retrieval and encoding. The issue here is quite simple: If you do not encode information (get it into memory) appropriately, you will have difficulty retrieving it. For example, you could not recall our middle names because you've never known them in the first place. You have never heard these names before, but you *have* had countless encounters with pennies. Can you draw a picture of a penny, properly locating each of its features? Can you recognize from a series of drawings which one accurately depicts a penny (see Figure 5.4)? In fact, few of us can correctly recognize a drawing of a penny, and even fewer can recall all of its essential features, nearly 90 percent forgetting that the word "LIBERTY" appears right behind Lincoln's shoulder (Nickerson & Adams, 1979). These retrieval failures do not result from a lack of experience, but from a lack of proper encoding. There are three general encoding issues that we'll discuss here: context effects, encoding strategies, and the amount and spacing of encoding practice.

The Effects of Context

Retrieval tends to be best when the situation, or context, in which retrieval takes place matches the context that was present at encoding. This observation has been called the **encoding specificity principle,** which asserts that we can only retrieve what has been stored, and how we retrieve information

encoding specificity principle
the hypothesis that we can only retrieve what we have stored and that how we retrieve information depends on how we encoded it

FIGURE 5.4
Fifteen drawings of the top side of a penny, testing encoding and retrieval.
(Nickerson & Anderson, 1979.)

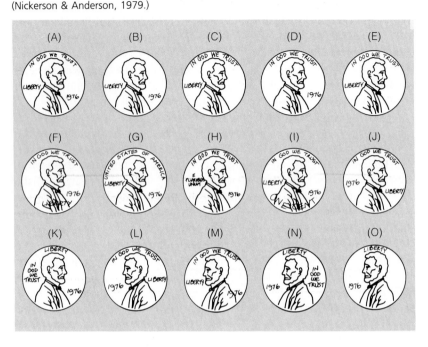

depends on how it was encoded (Flexser & Tulving, 1982; Newby, 1987; Tulving & Thompson, 1973). Part of this principle suggests that not only do we encode and store particular items of information, but we also note and store the context in which those items occur.

Don't study at a kitchen Table

Here's a hypothetical experiment (based on one by Thompson & Tulving, 1970) that demonstrates encoding specificity. Subjects are asked to learn a list of 24 common words. Half of the subjects are also given cue words to help them remember each item on the list. For the stimulus word "wood," the cue word is "tree," for "cheese," the cue word is "green," and so on for each of the 24 words. The other half of the subjects receive no such cue during their memorization (that is, while encoding). Later, subjects are asked to recall as many words from the list as they can. What we discover at recall is that the cue helps those subjects who had seen it during learning, but it actually decreases the recall for those subjects who had not seen it during learning. If learning takes place without a cue, recall will be better without it.

We suggested back in Chapter 4 that you should find one special place for studying and that your kitchen table, for example, would not be a good choice because that setting is already associated with eating experiences. In other words, the context of a kitchen is not a good one for encoding information unless you expect to be tested for retrieval in that same context—which seems highly unlikely. This advice was reaffirmed by a series of experiments by Steven Smith (1979). In one case, he had subjects learn some material in one room, and then he tested their recall for that material in either the same room or a different one. When a different room—a different context—was used for recall, performance dropped substantially. Simply instructing students to try to remember and think about the room in which learning took place helped recall considerably.

These context effects are clearly related to what has been called **state-dependent memory.** The idea here is that, to some degree, retrieval depends on the extent to which a person's state of mind at retrieval matches the person's state of mind at encoding (Leahey & Harris, 1985, p. 146). If learning takes place while a subject is under the influence of a drug, for example, being similarly under the influence of that drug at the time of retrieval has beneficial effects (for example, Eich et al., 1975; Parker et al., 1976). Some intriguing research by Gordon Bower (Bower et al., 1978; Bower, 1981) and others suggests that our mood state may predict our ability to remember certain events. Using moods (sad or happy) induced by posthypnotic suggestion, Bower found that retrieval was best when mood at retrieval matched mood at learning—regardless of whether that mood was happy or sad.

There is also evidence that our memories for emotionally arousing experiences are likely to be easier to recall than emotionally neutral events (Thompson, 1982). This may be because emotional arousal increases the levels of certain hormones (adrenaline in particular) that in turn (perhaps by increasing glucose levels) help to form vivid memories associated with the emotional arousal (Gold, 1987; McGaugh, 1983). That emotional arousal may help to form particularly vivid memories helps us to understand what Brown and Kulik (1977) call **flashbulb memories.** These are memories of (usually important) events that are unusually clear, detailed, and vivid. You probably have flashbulb memories of a number of events: your high school graduation; the funeral of a close friend; or what you were doing on January 28, 1986, when the space shuttle Challenger exploded, killing all on board.

In this section, we have seen that our ability to retrieve information from our memories depends in large measure on the context provided by events that occur at the time of encoding. Retrieval is enhanced to the extent that the situation, or one's state of mind, is the same at retrieval as it was at encoding. Emotional arousal at encoding seems to provide a strengthening of encoded information.

state-dependent memory
the hypothesis that retrieval can be affected by the extent to which one's state of mind at retrieval matches one's state of mind at encoding

flashbulb memories
particularly clear, detailed, vivid, and easily retrieved memories from one's episodic memory

How does the situation in which one encodes information affect the retrieval of that information? **BEFORE YOU GO ON**

Strategies That Guide Encoding

Once again using the term of Craik and Tulving (1975), we may say that to practice material in such a way as to maximize the chances of being able to retrieve it when we want it, we need to use *elaborative rehearsal.* In other words, we need to develop strategies that will meaningfully encode information into our long-term memories in such a way that we can easily get it out again. In this section, we'll examine some of the ways in which we can elaborate information to improve our chances of retrieval. We'll begin by considering meaningfulness in general, and then we'll briefly review some specific strategies we can use to improve memory retrieval. These strategies are often referred to as mnemonic devices (after the Greek goddess of memory, Mnemosyne). They involve using existing memories to make new information more meaningful.

In order to learn new material, students should do whatever they can to make what they are studying meaningful. Asking questions about a new subject and relating it to things that are already familiar add more meaning to the material.

meaningfulness
the extent to which information to be retrieved evokes associations with material already in one's memory

Meaningfulness. We have a hypothesis. We believe that we can determine the learning ability of students by noting where they sit in a classroom. The good, bright students tend to choose seats farthest from the door. The poor, dull students sit by the door, apparently interested in easily getting in and out of the room. (Although there may be some truth to this, we're not serious.) To make our point, we propose an experiment. Students seated away from the door are asked to learn a list of words that an experimenter reads aloud only once. We need a second list of words for those students seated by the door because they've already heard the first list.

The list that the "smart students" hear is made up of words such as *cat, dog, mother, father, black, white,* and so forth. As we predicted, they have no problem recalling this list after just one presentation. The students huddled by the door get our second list: *insidious, tachistoscope, sophistry, flotsam, episcotister,* and so forth. Needless to say, the hypothesis will be confirmed.

This is obviously not a very fair experiment. Those students sitting by the door will yell foul. The second list of words is clearly more difficult to learn and recall than the first. The words on the first list are shorter, more familiar, and easier to pronounce. However, the major difference between these two lists is in the **meaningfulness** of the items—the extent to which they evoke existing associations in one's memory. The *cat, dog* list is easy to remember because each word in it is meaningful. Each word makes us think of many other things, or produces many associations. That is, these items are easy to elaborate. Words like *tachistoscope* are more difficult because they evoke few, if any, associations.

An important point to keep in mind is that meaningfulness is not a characteristic built into materials to be learned. Meaningfulness resides in the memory of the learner. *Tachistoscope* may be a meaningless collection of letters for many people, but for others, it may be a word rich in associations. What is meaningful and what is not is a function of our individual experiences.

It then follows that one of your tasks as a learner is to do whatever you can to make the material you are learning meaningful. You need to seek out and establish associations between what you are learning and what you already know. You need to elaboratively rehearse what you are encoding so that you can retrieve it later. You need to be prepared to ask yourself a series of questions about what you are studying. What does this mean? What does it make me think of? Does this remind me of something I already know? Can I make this material more meaningful? If you cannot, there is little point in going on to more confusing material. Perhaps you now see a major reason for our including "Before you go on" questions within each chapter.

BEFORE YOU GO ON **What is meaningfulness?**
How does meaningfulness relate to retrieval?

mnemonic devices
strategies for improving retrieval that take advantage of existing memories in order to make new material more meaningful

Mnemonic Devices. Retrieval is enhanced if we can actively elaborate the material we are learning, if we can make it meaningful and organize it in some way during the encoding process. Often this is simply a matter of reflecting on what we are learning and actively forming associations with previously stored memories. Now let's examine some specific encoding techniques, called **mnemonic devices,** that we can use to aid our retrieval.

An experiment by Bower and Clark (1969) shows us that we can improve the retrieval of otherwise unorganized materials if we can weave that material into a meaningful story. This technique is called **narrative chaining.** One group of college students was asked to learn a list of 10 simple nouns in order. It's not a difficult task, and subjects had little trouble with it. Then they were given another list of 10 nouns to learn, and then another—12 lists in all. These subjects were given no instructions other than to remember each list of words in order.

A second group of subjects was given the same 12 lists of 10 nouns each to learn. It was suggested to them that they make up little stories that used each of the words on the list in turn. Right after each list was presented, both groups were asked to recall the list of words they had just heard. There was virtually no difference in the recall scores for the two groups. Then came a surprise. After all 12 lists had been presented and recalled, subjects were told that they were going to be tested again on their recall for each list. The experimenters provided one word from one of the 12 lists, and the subjects were to recall the other nine words from that list. The difference in recall between the two groups of subjects in this instance was striking (see Figure 5.5). Those who used a narrative chaining technique (made up stories) recalled 93 percent of the words (on the average), whereas those who did not so organize the random words recalled only 13 percent of them.

The message seems clear and consistent with what we have said so far. A technique that adds organization and sense to otherwise meaningless material is a means of elaborative rehearsal that will improve retrieval.

Organizing unrelated words into meaningful stories helps us remember them. Forming **mental images,** or pictures in our minds, can also be very helpful (Marschark et al., 1987). Assume, for example, that you have to memorize a large number of Spanish words and what they mean. You could use simple rote memorization, but this technique is tedious at best and not very efficient.

Atkinson (1975) suggests that to help your memory of foreign language vocabulary, it is useful to imagine some connection visually tying the two words together. (He calls this the *key word* method of study.)

For example, the Spanish word for "horse" is "caballo," which is pronounced "cab-eye-yo." To remember this association, you might choose "eye" as the key word and picture a horse actually kicking someone in the eye. Or, if you're not prepared to be that gruesome, you might imagine a horse with a very large eye. The Spanish word for "duck" is "pato." Here your key word might be "pot," and you could picture a duck wearing a pot on its head (see Figure 5.6) or sitting in a large pot on the stove. We realize that this sounds strange, but research data suggests that it works (Pressley et al., 1982).

The same basic technique works whenever you need to remember any paired sort of information. It needn't be restricted to foreign language vocabulary building. Gordon Bower (1972), for example, asked students to learn lists of pairs of English words. Some subjects were instructed to form a mental image that showed some interaction between the two words. One pair, for instance, was *piano-cigar*. There are many ways to form an image of a piano and a cigar: The cigar could be balanced on the edge of the piano, for one. Recall for word pairs was much better for those subjects who formed mental images than it was for those who did not. It is also the case that more

FIGURE 5.5
Percent correct recall for words from 12 lists learned under two conditions. In the narrative condition, subjects made up short stories to aid recall, while in the control condition, rote memorization—no mnemonic device—was used. (After Bower & Clark, 1969.)

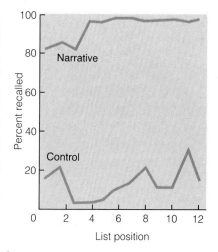

narrative chaining
the mnemonic device of relating words together in a story, thus making them more meaningful

mental images
pictures or visual representations in one's mind

FIGURE 5.6
An illustration of how the key word method can help foreign vocabulary retention. (After Atkinson, 1975.)

PATO — POT — DUCK

FIGURE 5.7
The key word method can also be used to help remember pairs of English words. (After Wollen, Weber, & Lowry, 1972.)

Piano   Cigar

peg word method
the mnemonic device of forming interactive visual images of materials to be learned and items previously associated with numbers

method of loci
the mnemonic device that mentally places information to be retrieved at a series of familiar locations (loci)

commonplace interactive images are more useful than strange and bizarre ones (Bower, 1970; Wollen et al., 1972). That is, to remember the *piano-cigar* pair, it would be better to picture a cigar balanced on a piano than it would be to picture a piano actually smoking a cigar (see Figure 5.7). If you wanted to remember that it was Bower and Clark who did the study on narrative chaining, try to picture two *storytellers chained* together, each holding a *Clark Bar* in their hands as they take a *bow* on a theater stage. Again, it sounds silly, but it works.

One of the better-known mnemonic devices that involves imagery is called the **peg word method** by its originators Miller, Galanter, and Pribram (1960). This strategy is most useful when we have to remember a series of items in order. Using this device is a two-step process. The first step is to associate common nouns (peg words) that rhyme with the numbers from 1 to 10 (and beyond 10 if you're up to it). Figure 5.8 is the scheme of associations that Miller and his colleagues suggested. Now, if you have a list of words to memorize, the second step is to form an interactive image of the word you're memorizing and the appropriate peg word.

To see how this might work, suppose that you have to remember the following words in order: *textbook, glass, ring, nose.* Having already memorized your peg word scheme, you make an image association between each word on the list and its peg word, perhaps: (1) a *textbook* in the middle of a hamburger *bun,* (2) a *shoe* in a *glass,* (3) a wedding *ring* around the trunk of a *tree,* (4) someone's *nose* stuck in a *door,* and so on. At retrieval, you first recall the peg words in order (*bun, shoe, tree,* and *door*), and then recall the word from the list that you've associated with each peg word. This may sound like a lot of extra work to go through, but once you've mastered your peg word scheme, the rest is remarkably easy.

The last imagery-related mnemonic device we'll mention may be the oldest in recorded history. It is attributed to the Greek poet Simonides and is called the **method of loci** (Yates, 1966). The idea here is to get in your mind a well-known location (*loci* are locations), say the floor plan of your house or apartment. Visually place the material you are trying to recall in different places throughout your house in some sensible order. When the time comes for you to retrieve the material, visually walk through your chosen location, recalling (or retrieving) the information you have stored at different places.

In this section, we've reviewed a number of specific techniques that we can use to improve the retrieval of information from memory. In each case,

FIGURE 5.8
The peg-word mnemonic scheme proposed by Miller, Galanter, and Pribam (1960).

One is a Bun
Two is a Shoe
Three is a Tree
Four is a Door
Five is a Hive
Six are Sticks
Seven is Heaven
Eight is a Gate
Nine is a Line
Ten is a Hen

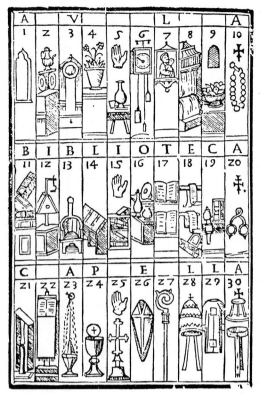

The method of loci is an ancient mnemonic device. This illustration was done by a Dominican monk in the sixteenth century. On the left are the abbey and the surrounding buildings through which the speaker will mentally walk, picking up the ideas (illustrated on the right) that he or she needs to recall.

the basic idea is to organize otherwise unrelated material in a meaningful way.

BEFORE YOU GO ON

Describe narrative chaining, mental imagery, the peg word method, and the method of loci as mnemonic devices.

Amount and Distribution of Encoding Practice

The point that we have made over and over again about our ability to retrieve information is that no matter how we choose to measure it, retrieval depends largely on how we go about encoding or practicing that information. We'll end this section with the observation that retrieval is also a function of the extent or the amount of practice we engage in and how we distribute or space that practice. One of the reasons why some students do not do as well on classroom exams as they would like is that they simply do not have (or make) enough time to study or practice the material covered on the exams. A related reason is that some students do not schedule wisely what time they have.

Overlearning.   What we all often do once we decide to learn something that we want to remember is read, practice, and study the material until we know it. We practice until we are satisfied that we have encoded and stored

FIGURE 5.9

Idealized data showing the effect of overlearning on retrieval. Note the "diminishing returns" with additional overlearning.
(Based on Krueger, 1929.)

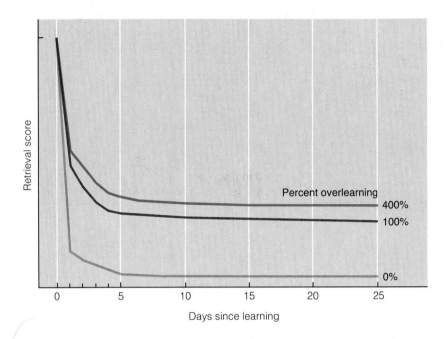

overlearning
the practice or rehearsal of material over and above what is needed to just barely learn it

the required information in our memories, and then we quit. Another way of expressing this is to say that we often fail to engage in **overlearning,** which is the process of practicing or rehearsing material over and above what is needed to just barely learn it. Consider this fictitious laboratory example, and see if you can extend this evidence to your study habits.

A subject comes to the laboratory to learn a list of nonsense syllables, verbal items such as: *dax, wuj, pib, zuw,* and so on. There are 15 items on the list, and the material has to be presented repeatedly before our subject can recall all of the items correctly. Having correctly recalled the items once, our subject is dismissed with instructions to return two weeks later for a test of his recall of the nonsense syllables. Not surprisingly, our subject doesn't fare too well on the retrieval task.

What would have happened to that subject's recall if we had continued to present him with the list of syllables over and over at the time of learning, well beyond the point where he first learned them? Say the list was learned in 12 trials. We have the subject practice the list for six more presentations (50 percent overlearning, or practice that is 50 percent over and above that required for learning). Or let's require an additional 12 trials of practice (100 percent overlearning). What if we required an additional 48 trials of practice (400 percent overlearning)?

The effects of such overlearning practice are well-documented and very predictable. The recall data for this imaginary experiment might look like the data presented in Figure 5.9. Notice three things about these data: (1) If we measure retrieval at different times after learning, forgetting is rather impressive and quite sudden. (2) Overlearning improves retrieval, having its greatest effects with longer retention intervals. (3) There is a "diminishing returns" phenomenon; that is, 50 percent overlearning is much more useful than no overlearning; 100 percent overlearning is somewhat better than 50 percent, and 400 percent is better than 100 percent, but not by very much. For any task or individual, there is probably an optimum amount of overlearning. In summary, with everything else being equal, the more we practice what we are learning, the easier it will be to retrieve it. How one *schedules* one's practice or learning time is also an important factor in determining the likelihood of retrieval, and it is to this issue that we turn next.

Scheduling Practice.   Some of the oldest data in psychology supports the notion that retrieval can be improved if practice (encoding) is spread out over time with rest intervals spaced in between. The data provided in Figure 5.10 are fairly standard. In fact, this 1946 experiment provides such reliable results that it is commonly used in psychology laboratory classes. The task is to write the letters of the alphabet, but upside down and from right to left. (If you think that sounds easy, you should give it a try.)

FIGURE 5.10
Improvement in performance as a function of distribution of practice time. The task was the printing of inverted capital letters with twenty 1-minute trials separated by rest intervals of varying lengths.
(After Kientzle, 1946.)

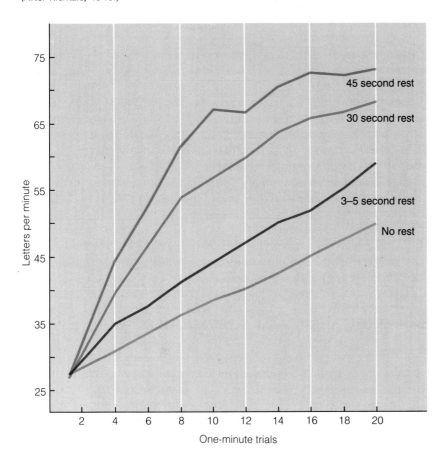

massed practice
rehearsal in which there is no break in one's practice

distributed practice
rehearsal in which practice is done in segments with rest intervals interspersed *Best Results with this Method, 1 exception to rule doing Math Problem*

Subjects are given the opportunity to practice this task under four different conditions. The **massed practice** group works on the task without a break between trials. The three **distributed practice** groups receive the same amount of actual practice, but get rest intervals interspersed between each 1-minute practice trial. One group gets a 3- to 5-second break between trials, a second group receives a 30-second rest, and a third group gets a 45-second break between practice trials.

As we can see clearly in Figure 5.10, subjects in all four groups begin at about the same (poor) level of performance. After 20 minutes of practice, the performance of all the groups shows improvement. By far, however, the massed practice (no rest) group does the poorest, and the 45-second rest group does the best.

The conclusion to be drawn from years of research like this is that, almost without exception, distributed practice is superior to massed practice. There are exceptions, however. There are some tasks that suffer from interspersing rest intervals within practice time. In general, whenever you must keep track of many things at the same time, you should mass your practice until you have finished whatever it is you are working on. If, for example, you are working on a complex math problem, you should work through the problem to a solution, whether it's time for a break or not. And, of course, you should not break up your practice in such a way as to disrupt the meaningfulness of the material you are studying.

Quite clearly, what we're talking about here is the scheduling of study time. Discussions of study schedules make up the major part of any how-to-study book. The message is always the same: Many short (yet meaningful) study periods with rest periods interspersed are more efficient than a few study periods massed together. There may be occasions when cramming is better than not studying at all, but as a general strategy, cramming is inefficient.

Now let's assume that you're going to follow this advice and use a 45-minute break between classes to study. Unless you are an outstanding student, it is unlikely that you can usefully study an entire chapter of any college-level textbook in that time frame. There is simply too much information to deal with in a standard textbook chapter. So you should distribute your practice. Break it down into smaller chunks. Study just one section at a time. (To help you do just that is one of the reasons that we have divided chapters into sections marked by "Before you go on" questions.)

BEFORE YOU GO ON

What is overlearning, and how does it affect retrieval?

Compare and contrast massed and distributed practice, noting their effects on retrieval

INHIBITING RETRIEVAL: INTERFERENCE

Think back to when you were 15 years old. Can you remember all the gifts you got for your birthday that year? Can you remember *any* of them? Because most people have experience with teenagers' birthday parties, we suspect that they can guess what they might have gotten for birthday presents that year and generate a fairly reasonable list. But there seems to be no way that most people can directly retrieve that information from long-term memory with any certainty. Now one possibility is that that information is no longer there. It may in some literal sense be lost forever. Perhaps people who can't remember never encoded that information in a way that would allow them to retrieve it effectively. Another possibility is that that information is in fact available in memory, but inaccessible at the moment because they have had so many birthdays since their fifteenth one and so much has happened and entered their memories since then, that the material is covered up and being *interfered with* by information that entered later.

If IT IS NOT Properly
encoded CANT have
Recall

How about your most recent birthday? Can you recall the gifts you received for your last birthday? That's a little easier, but remembering with confidence is still not that easy. Here again, our basic retrieval problem may be one of interference. Assuming that what we are searching for is still there (and that *is* an assumption), we may not be able to retrieve it because so many *previous* experiences (presents received earlier) are getting in the way, interfering with retrieval.

The basic idea that interference accounts for retrieval failure is an old one in psychology. Some early experiments, for example, demonstrated that subjects who were active for a period after learning remembered what they had learned less well than subjects who used the intervening period for sleep. The graphs in Figure 5.11 show apparently comparable data from two experiments—one with college students who had learned a list of nonsense syllables, the other with cockroaches(!) that had learned to avoid an area of their cage. In either case, subjects who engaged in normal waking activity did worse on tests of retrieval over different retention intervals.

FIGURE 5.11

These graphs illustrate how activity following learning can interfere with the retrieval of the learned material. In both cases, normal waking activity caused more interference with retrieval than did forced inactivity (for cockroaches) or sleeping (for students). (Based on Minami & Dallenbach, 1946.)

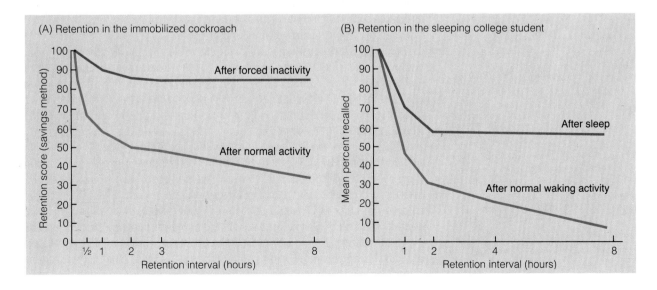

FIGURE 5.12

Designs of experiments to demonstrate retroactive and proactive interference.

(A) Retroactive Interference

Experimental Group	Control Group
Learn Task A	*Learn* Task A
Learn Task B	*Learn* Nothing
Test Retrieval of Task A	*Test* Retrieval of Task A

(B) Proactive Interference

Experimental Group	Control Group
Learn Task A	*Learn* Nothing
Learn Task B	*Learn* Task B
Test Retrieval of Task B	*Test* Retrieval of Task B

Note: If interference is operating, the control group will demonstrate better retrieval than will the experimental group.

retroactive interference
the inhibition of retrieval of previously learned material caused by material learned later

When interfering activities come *after* the learning of material to be remembered, we are dealing with **retroactive interference.** Let's first go to the laboratory. We'll need two groups of subjects randomly assigned to either an experimental group or a control group. The subjects in both groups are asked to learn something (almost anything will do; we'll assume a list of nonsense syllables). Having learned their lists, the groups are then treated differently. Subjects in the experimental group are now asked to learn something else, perhaps another list of nonsense syllables. At the same time, the control group subjects are asked to do nothing (which is impossible, of course, in a literal sense). These subjects might be asked to rest quietly or engage in some simple game.

Now for the test. Both groups of subjects are asked to retrieve the material presented in the *first* learning task. In almost every instance, the control group subjects will show a higher retrieval score than the experimental group subjects. For the latter group, the second set of learned material interferes with the retrieval of the material learned first. Figure 5.12(A) summarizes this experimental design.

Most of us are familiar with examples of retroactive interference from our own educational experiences. A student who studied French in high school takes a few courses in Spanish at college and now can't remember much French at all. The Spanish keeps getting in the way. Let's consider two students who are scheduled to take a psychology exam tomorrow morning at 9:00. Both are equally able and equally well motivated. One is taking only one class—psychology. She studies psychology for two hours, watches TV for two hours, and goes to bed. She comes in the next morning to take the exam. The other student also studies psychology for two hours, but then must read a chapter and a half from her sociology text, just in case she is called on in class. After reading sociology, she goes to bed, comes to class, and takes the exam. Everything else being equal, this second student will be at a disadvantage. The sociology that she has studied will retroactively interfere with her retrieval of the psychology she has learned. What is this student to do? She *has* to study her psychology, and she knows she had better read her sociology. If the psychology exam is an important one to her, we might suggest that she set herself up for proactive interference, rather than retroactive interference. She should read her sociology assignment and then study for her psychology exam. Even then, she'll be at a disadvantage, but generally, the effects of proactive interference are not as powerful as those of retroactive interference.

Proactive interference occurs when *previously* learned material interferes with the retrieval of material learned later. Follow along in Figure 5.12(B). Again we have two groups of subjects, experimental and control. The experimental group again starts off by learning something—that same list of syllables perhaps. This time the control group subjects begin by doing nothing, by resting quietly while the experimental group goes through the learning task. Both groups then learn some new material, say a second list of syllables. We now test for retrieval, but this time we test for the retrieval of the more recently learned material. Once again, the control group subjects will be at an advantage. They have none of that first list in their memories to interfere with the retrieval task. But the advantage is not as great as it was in the case of retroactive interference. As we said, proactive interference is generally not as detrimental as retroactive interference.

One simple way to demonstrate proactive interference is to ask subjects to learn a series of word lists. As subjects go through learning, trying to remember more and more lists, their recall tends to get worse. As subjects try to recall the items from list 5, for example, the words from lists 1 through 4 interfere with retrieval. By the time subjects are trying to recall words from list 10, they have nine other lists causing interference (Underwood, 1957).

Although both retroactive and proactive interference effects are well-documented, there are many factors that influence the *extent* of such interference. For example, it seems that meaningful, well-organized material is less susceptible to interference than is less meaningful material, such as nonsense syllables. It should also strike you as reasonable that *the nature of the interfering task* matters a great deal. As a general rule of thumb, the more similar the interfering material is to the material being retrieved, the greater will be the interference. Think back to the student who had to study for her psychology exam *and* read a sociology assignment. She will experience more interference (retro- *or* pro-) than will a student who has to study for the psychology exam and work on calculus problems. In this context, we might even suggest that working on calculus is rather like doing nothing in that there is little about the calculus that is going to get in the way, or interfere, with the psychology lesson. Hence the advice that suggests that if you're going to take more than one course at a time, those courses should be as different from each other as possible to minimize possible interference effects.

proactive interference
the inhibition of retrieval of recently learned material caused by material learned earlier

Briefly describe retroactive and proactive interference. Which of these two generally has the greater impact on retrieval?   BEFORE YOU GO ON

So far, we have reviewed quite a bit of data and have summarized a number of laboratory experiments dealing with factors that affect our ability to retrieve information from our memories.

Our ability to retrieve information from memory often depends on how retrieval is measured and the quality of retrieval cues that are available to us. We have seen that the quality and quantity of one's learning, or encoding, have a definite influence on memory. We need to spend time with the material we are learning. We need to try to encode that material in a meaningful and well organized way, whenever possible matching cues available at retrieval with those present at encoding and we need to avoid interference effects. Later, in chapter 9, we will discuss repression—forgetting because we don't really *want* to remember. We now must add one final point to our discussion. Something else that we can do to improve our ability to retrieve information from memory is to *practice retrieval* itself.

Perhaps you'll recall from our discussion about learning that we cannot assess or measure learning directly. We can only measure performance and, on that basis, make inferences about what someone may have learned. We say that classroom exams are designed to measure what you have learned in a given course. But they do so indirectly by measuring what you can remember or retrieve at the time of the test. Why don't we spend more time, then, practicing what is really going to matter—getting learned material out of our memories? In short: Retrieval is a skill that can be practiced. The more you practice it, the better you will be at it. Try to anticipate test questions and work example problems at the end of textbook chapters or in accompanying study guides, if they are available. Ask yourself questions about the material you are studying. The time spent doing so will pay off.

HIGHER COGNITIVE PROCESSES

Our next area of concern is higher cognitive processes. We already discussed a number of them as we dealt with the selective and organizing nature of *perception* in Chapter 3, the relatively permanent changes in mental processes that take place with *learning* in Chapter 4, and the encoding, storing, and retrieving of information in *memory* in the first part of this chapter.

Perception, learning, and memory provide the foundation for our more complex thinking activities. Psychologists refer to this general area of concern as cognition. As we discussed in the Introduction, *cognitions* include one's ideas, beliefs, thoughts, and images so that when we know, understand, or remember something, we use cognitions to do so. **Cognitive processes,** then, are mental activities that involve forming, manipulating, and using cognitions. We can gain an understanding of cognitive processes through the study of concepts, how they are formed, and how they are used to communicate through language.

cognitive processes
the mental activities that involve forming and using cognitions

BEFORE YOU GO ON **What are cognitive processes, and why may concept formation and the use of language be called higher cognitive processes?**

The Concept of Concept

Think about chairs. Really. Take a minute or two to think about chairs. As you do this, try to notice what is happening.

Images come to mind. You can "see" a large variety of chairs in different contexts. You may have thought about high chairs, armchairs, dining-room chairs, rocking chairs, chairs in a classroom, easy chairs, chairs with smooth leather seats, overstuffed chairs upholstered with flowery fabric, broken chairs, kitchen chairs, and so on. We all know what a chair is. We have all formed a category or concept that we've agreed to label *chair*.

As you thought about chairs, did any one particular chair—a standard, definitional chair—come to mind? As you contemplated chairs, were there any features or attributes that all (or most) had in common? Are there defining characteristics of chairs? Most have four legs, although bean-bag chairs have no legs at all. Most chairs are used primarily for sitting, although we often stand on a chair to reach high places. Many are used in association with tables and some with desks. Most chairs have a back. However, if the back gets too low, you have a stool, not a chair. Chairs have limited widths: they can usually accommodate only one person. If they are wider, they become love seats or sofas. Chairs are usually seen as pieces of furniture.

Now try a different task. Consider the following statements:

A *rogaritz* is usually white.
A *rogaritz* is hard and dry.
Rogaritzen (the plural of *rogaritz*) can be of any color.
Rogaritzen can be used to write on a blackboard.
A piece of *rogaritz* will fit comfortably in one hand.
You shouldn't put a *rogaritz* in your mouth.
Using *rogaritzen* usually creates messy dust.

Have you figured out what a *rogaritz* is? Have you ever used *rogaritzen*? Would you recognize one if you saw it? How many uses for *rogaritzen* can you think of? If you can answer these questions—if you know what a *rogaritz* is—you have acquired a new concept—the concept of *rogaritz* (after Werner & Kaplan, 1950). You recognize it as basically the same thing we call chalk. Because we already have a perfectly good word with which to label this concept, there's no compelling reason to try to remember the new concept label *rogaritz*.

We've asked you to go through these mental gymnastics so that you can better appreciate our definition of concept. A **concept** is a *mental* event used to represent a category or class of events or objects. Note that concepts represent categories, classes, or groups of things, not just single individual cases.

A world without concepts would be unimaginable. If we had no way to organize or classify our experiences, our impressions of our environments (and of ourselves) would be chaotic. Because we have a *concept* of chair, for example, we do not have to treat each and every encounter with a chair as a new experience. We do not have to make up a new and different label or word for every single chair we see. We only have to recognize an object as having the characteristics appropriate for this category and refer to it as a chair. This is an important reason why concepts are so valuable to us.

We can define a concept, then, in terms of a set of attributes or features that are related according to some rule or rules. This *attribute-rule* approach works fairly well for a concept like chair. We've listed above some of the *attributes* associated with the category of events called chair. Perhaps you've thought of others. The *rule* that relates these features states that chairs share many (if not all) of these attributes at the same time. According to this view, learning a new concept is a matter of learning the attributes that characterize it and the rule that relates those attributes (Bourne et al.,

concept
a mental event used to represent a category or class of events or objects

A concept is a mental event that represents a category or class of objects. Vegetables are one such category. Tomatoes, often classified as vegetables when they are really fruits, become an exception to the attribute-rule approach.

1979). As we will soon see, there are some concepts for which this attribute-rule approach does not seem to apply. Let's first consider concepts in a formal sense, as they are studied in the psychology laboratory. Then we'll look at concepts as they are used in the world outside the laboratory.

Concepts in the Laboratory. Defining concepts in the psychology laboratory is fairly easy. We can take the attribute-rule approach to concepts and apply it quite literally. First we decide which attributes we'd like to deal with—perhaps color, shape, and size. Then we provide a limited number of values for each of our attributes. *Color:* Our possible values of this attribute may be red, green, or blue. *Shape:* The possible values may be round, square, or triangular. *Size:* The values may be small, medium, or large. So, we have chosen three attributes, each of which may have one of three values. All we need to do is decide what rules we'll use to relate these values to form concepts.

Let's say that we want to define a new concept: the concept of *wug.* To do so, we now need a rule that tells us the relationships among the values of our attributes. Let's say a *wug* is square, blue, and small. We have thus assigned *wug* a value on each of the three attributes. Moreover, we have specified that to qualify as a *wug,* an event must have all three values. Simply put, *wugs* are small, blue squares. We might use these same attributes to define *luks* as large, red triangles, and so on. Take a look at Figure 5.13. Given these items, can you find the *wugs* and the *luks?* Doing so demonstrates that you've learned a couple of new formal concepts. **Formal concepts** are those in which the attribute values are relatively few in number, clearly defined, and clearly related by a rule.

There are a number of ways in which the values of attributes can be related by rules to define formal concepts. Let's briefly mention just four attribute-rule combinations.

First, rules specifying that concepts must have each one of a number of values define **conjunctive concepts.** Thus, *wug* is a conjunctive concept

formal concepts (4) types
concepts with relatively few, well-defined attribute values and clearly defined rules to relate them

conjunctive concepts (1)
concepts that are defined by "and" rules; that is, having all attributes of the concept

because *wugs* must be small *and* blue *and* square. Blueness, or squareness, or smallness alone does not define a *wug*. One value of each of our three attributes must be present for us to have a *wug*. Another example might be the concept of short-term memory, which we discussed at the beginning of the chapter. The defining characteristic of this memory is that it has a limited capacity *and* a limited duration.

In the second combination, membership in a concept is defined by an "either/or" rule regarding attributes. Such concepts are called **disjunctive concepts.** For example, a *dax* is defined as being *either* red *or* large. Can you find a *dax* in Figure 5.13? There are many more *daxs* than *wugs*—18 in all. In baseball, the concept of a strike provides us with a reasonable example of a disjunctive concept. One may define a strike as being either a "pitch that crosses home plate in a prescribed area," *or* "a ball batted into foul territory," *or* "a pitch swung at and missed."

Affirmation rules represent a third attribute-rule combination. They simply specify membership in a concept by stating or affirming just one attribute value. They define **affirmative concepts**—for instance, *all green objects.* In this case, size and shape do not matter at all. An item is a member of an affirmative concepts category if it has the affirmed value of one given attribute.

disjunctive concepts
concepts defined by "either/or" rules; that is, either having some attributes or others

affirmative concepts
concepts defined by the presence of one particular attribute

FIGURE 5.13
Stimuli of the sort used in studies of formal concepts.

relational concepts
concepts defined in terms of their comparative relation to other concepts

A fourth attribute-rule combination involves a formal concept with which you are familiar—the **relational concept.** These concepts are defined in terms of comparisons of values on some dimension or attribute. The concepts of *larger than, nearer than,* and *smarter than* are relational concepts. When we identify a concept as being bigger than a bread basket or faster than a speeding bullet, we are using a relational rule (bigg*er*, fast*er*) to tell us about attributes (size and speed) that are relevant for that concept.

Formal concepts such as these we've just listed are very useful in the psychology laboratory where we can carefully exercise control over the various features that define particular concepts. We'll see shortly that most of the research on concept formation, for example, has involved formal concepts. But there is another, more informal, approach to concepts that psychologists have found useful.

BEFORE YOU GO ON **How can we use attributes and rules to define concepts?**

more informal

natural concepts
the "fuzzy" sorts of concepts that occur in real life, with ill-defined attributes and/or rules

(prototypes)

Concepts in the Real World.   Talking about attributes with values and the rules that combine them may be reasonable for the sorts of concepts we study in psychology laboratories, but what about concepts as they occur in real life (so-called **natural concepts**)? Is it always possible to define concepts in terms of attributes and rules? Remember the problems we had when we tried this with *chair?* Real or natural concepts are often not easily defined and may be referred to as "fuzzy" concepts (Labov, 1973; Oden, 1987; Zadeh, 1965).

FIGURE 5.14
Series of cuplike objects for classification.

How would you characterize the difference between a cup and a bowl? Somehow we know what a cup is, and we know what a bowl is, but because each is a fuzzy concept, there is no clear distinction between the two (Labov, 1973). If you think this distinction is clear, consider the drawings of cups in Figure 5.14. Do *any* of them look at least a little like a bowl? This is why we often find ourselves saying things like, "Technically speaking, a tomato is a fruit, not a vegetable." Or, "In a way, a bat is rather like a bird." Or, "Actually, a spider is not an insect." We didn't have this problem with formal concepts, such as *wugs* and *daxs,* but we encounter it regularly when we use natural concepts.

One way to deal with this complication is to follow the lead of Eleanor Rosch (1973, 1975, 1978). She has proposed that we think about naturally occurring concepts or categories in terms of **prototypes.** A prototype is a member of a category that best typifies or represents the category to which it belongs.

prototype
the member of a concept or category that best typifies or represents that concept or category

What Rosch is suggesting is that within our concept of chair, there are some instances that are more typical and better examples—more "chairish" than others. A robin may be a prototypic bird. Crows are less prototypic. Vultures are even less typical, and the fact that a penguin even *is* a bird is occasionally hard to remember. (Although here we may quote Oden, (1987, p. 215): "Penguins, of course, really are birds biologically speaking, although it is not clear why we should be willing to give biologists the last word on the matter.")

Figure 5.15 lists the elements in the furniture category (Rosch, 1978). You can see which are the *best* examples of the concept of furniture. Within this category, *lamp* turns out to be a poor example, and of the 60 items rated, *ashtray, fan,* and *telephone* ranked at the bottom of the list, just barely qualifying as furniture at all. Automobile manufacturers created something of a concept-definition problem when they introduced a vehicle now gener-

Using prototypes is one way to help us better define natural concepts. In this way, a robin may be a more likely prototype for the concept of bird than is a penguin.

FIGURE 5.15
Goodness of example rankings for the furniture category. (From Rosch, 1975.)

Member	Goodness of example rank	Member	Goodness of example rank	Member	Goodness of example rank
chair	1.5	vanity	21	mirror	41
sofa	1.5	bookcase	22	television	42
couch	3.5	lounge	23	bar	43
table	3.5	chaise lounge	24	shelf	44
easy chair	5	ottoman	25	rug	45
dresser	6.5	footstool	26	pillow	46
rocking chair	6.5	cabinet	27	wastebasket	47
coffee table	8	china closet	28	radio	48
rocker	9	bench	29	sewing machine	49
love seat	10	buffet	30	stove	50
chest of drawers	11	lamp	31	counter	51
desk	12	stool	32	clock	52
bed	13	hassock	33	drapes	53
bureau	14	drawers	34	refrigerator	54
davenport	15.5	piano	35	picture	55
end table	15.5	cushion	36	closet	56
divan	17	magazine rack	37	vase	57
night table	18	hi-fi	38	ashtray	58
chest	19	cupboard	39	fan	59
cedar chest	20	stereo	40	telephone	60

ally called a mini-van. Mini-vans are not real vans, but they aren't cars either, nor are they station wagons. Hence, a new label for a new concept was devised: mini-van.

In Rosch's view, then, some categories are rather poorly delineated and may very well spill over into others. This view argues that there is structure *within* concepts—some instances providing good examples, others providing poorer examples. Excellent examples (prototypes) share the largest number of attributes common to members of the category *and* have few attributes that cause them to be confused with others. Notice, then, that concepts defined in terms of prototypical examples may also include rules; rules that allow us to determine if new experiences fit a given concept (Lasky & Kallio, 1978).

BEFORE YOU GO ON How does the concept of prototype help our understanding of what a concept is?

Forming Concepts

By the time we get to be college students, our minds are crammed with a huge variety of formal and natural concepts. How were those concepts acquired? Where did they come from? As the philosopher John Locke asked, "How comes it [the mind] to be furnished?" To his own question, Locke had a ready answer, ". . . I answer in one word, from experience." Few psychologists today would argue with Locke's conclusion that concepts are learned. Concepts are formed through experience. Psychologists have found that the basic process of concept formation can be studied in the laboratory and that people develop predictable strategies (systematic plans) for acquiring concepts.

Subjects in concept-learning studies often go about forming concepts in systematic ways. To be sure, some people just guess at random whether or not a presented item belongs in a given category. Most, however, develop some strategy to guide their responding (Bruner, et al., 1956; Johnson, 1978). In this context, a strategy is a systematic plan or procedure for identifying members of a particular category or concept.

One way to think about concept formation is to say that subjects go through a process of *hypothesis testing*. That is, they develop a hypothesis, or reasonable guess, about what is going on, and then they test that hypothesis when presented with new stimuli. Saying to yourself, "I think that all members of this concept are green," is a hypothesis. You test it by finding another green stimulus and seeing if it fits within the category too.

Notice that this approach to concept formation works whether we are dealing with formal concepts in terms of rules and/or natural concepts in terms of prototypes. In the former case, hypotheses about specific attributes and rules are formed and tested. In the latter case, new stimuli are tested or judged in terms of their similarity to a prototype (Posner & Keele, 1968, 1970). For example, "I think that a spider looks a lot like my notion of what an insect is. It may not be the best example of an insect, but it sure looks like one to me." When you test that hypothesis (perhaps in a biology class), you discover that you're wrong, because as much as a spider may appear similar to your prototypic insect, it belongs in a different category (*arachnid*).

Notice also that forming new concepts requires the active involvement of memory. When presented with a brand new stimulus, we retrieve from memory other, similar stimuli and make judgments concerning whether or not we can match the new stimulus with any example from an already existing category or concept. If the newly presented stimulus matches the prototypic example of a concept (stored in memory), then we will have very little difficulty adding it to our preexisting concept. If the new stimulus does *not* match a prototype, then we have to decide if we're faced with a poor example of a known concept or if we should devise a whole new category to include the new stimulus (Stern, 1985).

In 1946, Edna Heidbreder did a classic study which demonstrated that concept formation tasks could be brought into the laboratory and studied systematically. What many experiments since Heidbreder's in 1946 have demonstrated is that subjects form concepts in a very systematic way, developing strategies and testing hypotheses. But even as Heidbreder's own study suggested, people are not always aware of the particular strategies they may be using. For example, even young children (ages 6 to 8) have a very reasonable notion of the concept of *family*, but even much older children (ages 12 to 13) can seldom tell you the rule or the attributes or the prototype that defines "family" for them (Watson & Amgott-Kwan, 1984).

BEFORE YOU GO ON Briefly review what we know about the process of concept formation.

A Definition of Language

Because we form concepts, we can bring order and economy to our understanding of events in the world. Because we use language, we can communicate that understanding to others. In this sense, the use of language is clearly a social process. But it is a social process that reflects a marvelously complex cognitive activity. The philosopher Suzanne Langer put it this way: "Language is, without a doubt, the most momentous and at the same time the most mysterious product of the human mind. Between the clearest animal call of love or warning or anger, and a man's least, trivial *word,* there lies a whole day of Creation—or in modern phrase, a whole chapter of evolution" (1951, p. 94).

In this section, we'll review some of the concerns of **psycholinguistics.** Psycholinguistics is a hybrid discipline of scientists trained in psychology *and* linguistics. Psycholinguists "are interested in the underlying knowledge and abilities which people must have in order to use language and to learn language in childhood" (Slobin, 1979, p. 2). First, let's formally define the concept of language.

How shall we characterize this mysterious product of the human mind called language? The following definition is somewhat complex, but it makes a number of psychologically important points. That is, it lists a number of the attributes that we associate with the abstract concept *language.* It is a paraphrase of a definition proposed by Charles Morris (1946). **Language** is a large collection of arbitrary symbols that have significance for a language-using community and that follow certain rules of combination. Now let's pull this definition apart and examine some of the points that is raises.

First, language is made up of a large number of *symbols.* The symbols that make up language are commonly referred to as words. In many cases, words are labels that we have assigned to concepts. When we use the word *chair* as a symbol, we don't use it to label one specific instance of a chair. We use the word as a symbol to represent our concept, our mental idea, of chair. Notice that as symbols, words do not have to stand for real things in the real world. We have words to describe a number of objects or events that cannot be perceived directly, such as *ghost* or, for that matter, *mind.* With language, we can talk about owls and pussycats in teacups, four-dimensional, time-warped hyperspace, and a beagle that flies his doghouse into battle against the Red Baron. Words stand for our cognitions and concepts, and we have a great number of them. They allow us to communicate what we know. Hence, language involves a large collection of symbols.

psycholinguistics
the science that studies the cognitive processes involved in the use and acquisition of language

goes BACK 40 yrs

language
a large collection of arbitrary symbols that have significance for a language-using community and that follow certain rules of combination

Language is the vehicle for communicating our understanding of events to others.

Although we say the symbols of language are arbitrary, a number of people need to agree on what the symbols are and how they will be used.

للباصات السياحية فقط

אוטובוסים לתירים בלבד

TOURIST BUSES ONLY

It is important that we define the symbols of language as being *arbitrary*. By that we mean that there is no necessary reason for representing anything with the particular symbol we do. You call what you are reading a book (or a textbook, to use a more specific symbol for a more specific concept). We have all agreed (in English) that *book* is the appropriate symbol for what you are reading. But we don't have to. We could all agree to call it a *fard,* if we'd like. Or a *relm*. The symbols of a language are arbitrary. They are not wired into our biology somehow, nor are they genetically determined. They can be whatever we like.

To be part of a language, however, our symbols need to *have significance for a language-using community*. That is, a number of people need to agree on the symbols that are used in a language and need to agree on what those symbols mean. This is another way of saying that language use is a social enterprise. For example, there is a language-using community for which the utterance, "Kedinin üstünde halt var" makes sense or has significance. We're not part of that community, but many people are. To them, the statement reads roughly, "The cat is on the mat" (from Slobin, 1979, p. 4). We might decide to call what you are now reading a *fard,* but then we would be in a terribly small language-using community. We're better off going along with the majority here and using the word *book*.

The final part of our definition—*that follow certain rules of combination*—is a crucial one. What this means is that language is made up of much more than just a large collection of arbitrary symbols or words. Language is structured. Language is rule-governed. For one thing, there are rules about how we can and cannot string symbols together in any language. In English, we can say "The small boy slept late." We cannot say "Slept boy late small the." Well, we can say it, but no one will know what we mean by it, and everyone will recognize that the utterance has violated the combinatorial rules of the English language. When the rules of language are violated, utterances lose their meaning, and the value of language as a means of communication is lost. We'll have more to say about the structure of language in the next section.

Even with this lengthy definition of language, there are a few points we've left out. For one, using language is a remarkably creative, generative process. What that means is that very few of the utterances we make are utterances we've ever made before or even encountered before. It's unlikely, for example, that you have ever read a sentence just like this one. Virtually every time we use the language, we use it in a new and creative way, which emphasizes the importance of the underlying rules of structure of language.

One final point: Language and speech are not synonymous terms. Speech is but one common way in which language is expressed as behavior. There are others, including writing, coding (as in Morse code), or signing (as in American Sign Language).

BEFORE YOU GO ON   **What are some of the defining characteristics of language?**

The Structure in Language

When psycholinguists analyze a language, they usually do so at three levels. At all three levels, we can see rules and structure at work. The first level involves the system of sounds that are used when we express the language as speech. The second level deals with the meaning of words and sentences, while the third concerns the rules for combining words and phrases to generate sentences. Let's briefly consider each of these levels of analysis.

phoneme
the smallest unit of sound in the spoken form of a language

Speech Sounds and Structure.   The individual speech sounds of a language are called **phonemes.** These are the sounds we use when we talk to each other. Phonemes themselves have no meaning, but when they are put together in the proper order, the result is a meaningful utterance. The word *cat,* for example, is made up of three phonemes; the initial consonant sound (actually a "k" sound here), the vowel sound of "a" in the middle, and yet another consonant sound, "t." How phonemes are combined to produce words and phrases is rule-governed, as we have said. If we were to reverse the two consonant sounds in *cat,* we'd have an altogether different utterance, with an altogether different meaning: *tack.* There are approximately 45 different phonemes in English. (And because the correspondence between those 45 sounds and the 26 letters of our alphabet is often muddled at best, it is no wonder many of us have problems spelling.)

To use a language requires that we know which speech sounds (phonemes) are part of that language and how they may be combined to form larger language units. For example, the difference between *time, climb, rhyme,* and *grime* is the initial phoneme of each utterance. We recognize each of these as acceptable words in English. We also recognize that *blime* and *frime* are not English words, although we also know that they could be. The "bl" and "fr" sound combinations of *blime* and *frime* are acceptable in

English: They follow the rules. Even if you could manage to pronounce them, you'd recognize that *gzlime* or *wbime* are clearly not words. They violate the English rules for combining sounds into words.

Meaning and Structure.   Having analyzed a language's phonemes, noting which sounds are relevant for that language and which combinations are possible, the next level of analysis involves *meaning*. The study of the meaning of words and sentences is called **semantics.**

A **morpheme** is the smallest unit of meaning in a spoken language. It is a collection of phonemes that means something. In many cases, *morpheme* and *word* are synonymous terms, although there are more morphemes in any language than there are words. For one thing, morphemes include all of the prefixes and suffixes of a language. For example, the utterance *write* is a morpheme and a word; it has meaning, and it is not possible to subdivide it into smaller, meaningful units. The utterance *rewrite* is also a word and has meaning, but it is composed of *two* morphemes, *write* and *re*, which in this context does have meaning—roughly, "write it again." *Tablecloth* is another word that is composed of two morphemes, *table* and *cloth.* When we change a noun from singular to plural, *boy* to *boys,* or *ox* to *oxen,* for example, we are adding a morpheme to the noun—a morpheme that indicates plurality—which changes our meaning.

Notice that how we generate morphemes is governed by rules. For example, we cannot go around making nouns plural any old way. The plural of ox is oxen, not oxes. The plural of mouse is mice, not mouses, or mousen, or meese. If I want you to write something over again, I have to ask you to *rewrite* it, not *write-re* it. We all know what a *tablecloth* is, but the collection of phonemes in *clothtable* is without meaning. Notice too, how morphemes are verbal labels for acquired concepts (mental representations). Telling you to rewrite something would make no sense if we did not share a concept of "writing" and a concept of "doing things over again."

In English, meaning is related to word ordering. How words and morphemes are strung together to form longer utterances, such as phrases and sentences, has important implications for the meaning being expressed. There is all the difference in the world between "The girl hit John" and "John hit the girl." The rules that govern the ordering of elements to form phrases and sentences get us to our next level of analysis.

semantics
the study of the meaning of words and sentences

morpheme
the smallest unit of meaning in a language

What are phonemes and in what way are they rule-governed?

What is sematics?

What are morphemes?

BEFORE YOU GO ON

Sentences and Structure.   The aspect of our language that most obviously uses rules is reflected in our ability to generate sentences—to string words (or morphemes) together to create meaningful utterances. "Communication surely does not consist of an unordered pile of morphemes. How can morphemes be combined into sensible utterances in a certain language?" (Hörmann, 1986, p. 57). The rules that govern the way sentences are formed (or structured) in a language are referred to as the **syntax** of a language.

syntax
the rules that govern how the morphemes of a language may be combined to form meaningful utterances

Higher Cognitive Processes   **227**

To know the syntax, or syntactic rules, of one's language involves a peculiar sort of knowledge or cognitive ability. We all know what the rules of English are in the sense that we can and do use them, but few of us know what the rules are in the sense that we can tell anyone else what they are. We say that language users have developed a *competence*—a cognitive ability that governs their language behavior. That ability allows us to judge the extent to which an utterance is a meaningful, well-formed sentence. Our competence with the syntactic rules of English can be demonstrated with a few examples of what are called *linguistic intuitions* (Howard, 1983; Slobin, 1979).

For example, we know that "The small boy slept late" fits the rules of English and that "Slept boy late small the" does not. The first utterance is a sentence. It means something. The second does not. At the same time, we recognize that the utterance, "Colorless green ideas sleep furiously" fits the rules of English even though it doesn't make any sense (Chomsky, 1957). It may be a silly thing to say, but we realize intuitively that it is an acceptable thing to say.

We are also able to recognize that the following two utterances communicate the same message, even though they look (and sound) quite different.

The student read the textbook.
The textbook was read by the student.

Not only do we recognize that these are acceptable sentences in English, we also recognize that they express the same basic idea. In either case, we know who is doing what. However, putting this basic idea in either of two forms does change the psychological focus of what is being said. In the first, we find out what the student did, and in the second, we focus on the notion that it was the textbook that was read. Again, we see that how elements are structured in language affects the meaning of what is being communicated. Semantics and syntax cannot be separated.

Another way in which we demonstrate our cognitive competence with the rules of our language is in our ability to detect ambiguity. Consider these two sentences:

They are cooking apples.
They are cooking apples.

Now there's no doubt that they appear to be identical, but we can also see that they may be communicating very different (ambiguous) ideas. In one case, we may be talking about what some people are cooking (apples as opposed to spaghetti). In the other, we may be identifying a variety of apple (cooking apples as opposed to eating apples).

In part, this sentence about apples is ambiguous only when we are not aware of the context in which it was used. Is the sentence in response to a question about what some people are doing or in response to a question about different sorts of apples? This is not an isolated example. There are many, such as, "The shooting of the policemen was terrible," or "Flying airplanes can be dangerous."

pragmatics
the study of how context affects the meaning of linguistic events

Pragmatics is the study of how the meaning of linguistic events is affected by the context in which they occur. Our understanding of ambiguity and sarcasm (as in, "It certainly is a beautiful day!" when in fact it is rainy, cold, and miserable), or simile (as in, "Life is like a sewer..."), or metaphor (as in, "that slam dunk certainly delivered the knockout blow"), or cliché (as in, "It

Writing sentences demonstrates the idea of rules in our language.

rained cats and dogs") depends on our appreciating the context of the utterance and the intention of the speaker.

Psycholinguistics has some very high goals. To understand the underlying knowledge and cognitive abilities that people must have in order to use language requires understanding how we use the sounds (phonemes) of spoken language, how we assign meaning to morphemes, and how we combine morphemes to form sentences. We hope we have made it clear to you that the study of the psychology of language involves us with the most complex of cognitive tasks.

What is syntax?   BEFORE YOU GO ON
What are linguistic intuitions?
What is pragmatics?

Cognition is the mental process through which we come to know about ourselves and the world in which we live. Cognitive processes include perception, learning, and memory. They also include concept formation and the use of language.

Concepts are our mental representations of our experiences. They represent classes, or categories, of objects and events and, in so doing, help us to bring order and meaningfulness to our observations. Most of our concepts are symbolized by words—the meaningful, arbitrary units of our languages. Language provides an excellent example of structured, rule-governed behavior. All language users demonstrate a knowledge—a competence—of the rules of their language, whether or not they can explicitly state the nature of those rules.

Chapter Five
Memory and Cognition

SUMMARY

How do we define memory?

What are the basic ideas of the multistore and levels of processing models of memory?

Memory is the cognitive process of putting information into memory (encoding), keeping it there (storage), and later bringing it out again (retrieval). There are two current theoretical views of memory. One view, the multistore model, suggests that there are three different, distinct memories, or stores of information, each with its own mechanism for processing information. The so-called levels of processing model contends that there is but one memory, but three different levels, or depths, to which information is processed into that memory. / 187

What is sensory memory?

What is its capacity and duration?

Sensory memory involves the very brief storage or shallow processing of large amounts of information. We can't manipulate information in this memory, which is assumed to be stored in the form in which it is received by our sense receptors. Visually presented material lasts in sensory memory for but a fraction of a second, auditorially processed material may last for 3 or 4 seconds. / 189

How long is information stored in STM?

What is required to get material into STM and then keep it there?

Information can be held in short-term memory for approximately 15 to 20 seconds before fading or being replaced by new information. Processing information to this memory or to this depth requires that we attend to it. We can keep material in STM by reattending to it, a process called "maintenance rehearsal." / 191

How much information can be held in STM?

How can chunking affect the capacity of STM?

It is reasonable to say that the capacity of STM is limited to approximately 7 ± 2 bits of information. This assumes that the information is unrelated and meaningless. By "chunking" bits and pieces of information together into meaningful clusters, more can be processed at the level of STM. / 192

What evidence do we have that information tends to be encoded acoustically in STM?

Information in our short-term memories may be processed there in any number of forms, but acoustic coding seems most likely. When errors in short-term memory are made, those items recalled in error are most likely to *sound* like the items that were to be recalled. Words that sound alike are more likely to cause STM confusion than are words that mean the same thing. / 193

Are long-term memories necessarily permanent?

Although LTM may hold information for a very long time, it should not necessarily be thought of as a literally permanent memory. Information in LTM may be subject to distortion or replacement. / 195

Contrast elaborative rehearsal with maintenance rehearsal as a means of encoding information into long-term memory.

Although the simple repetition of information (maintenance rehearsal) may sometimes be sufficient to encode material from STM into LTM,

Chapt 4+5
STEPS AND process
classical
differences?
classical
aberant
ass-
Reinforcement
before
response
of
Behavo

there seems little doubt that the best mechanism for placing information into LTM is elaborative rehearsal—that is, to think about the material and form associations or images of the material, relating it to something already stored in LTM. The "deeper" the elaboration, the better retrieval will be. / 196

Name and briefly describe four possible systems or types of LTM.

Information may be stored in different ways in a variety of LTM systems. One of the most basic is our procedural memory, in which we retain learning connections between stimuli and responses. Within our LTM, episodic memories are those that record and store our life experiences and events. They are somewhat autobiographical and time-ordered. On the other hand, semantic memories are those that store our facts, knowledge, and vocabularies. Metamemory is the name for the LTM system that refers to our knowledge of how our own memory systems work and that directs memory searches for information. / 198

Briefly summarize ways in which information may be represented in long-term memory.

We believe that we store semantic, or meaningful, units in LTM, and we further assume that these units are well-organized and structured, perhaps in a number of interrelated ways. For example, there is ample evidence that we access words in LTM as if they were stored in conceptual categories (known as category clustering). In fact, even when structure is not imposed on a list of ways to be memorized, subjects generally impose their own "subjective organization" onto the list. Recently, attention has focused on complex systems, called network models, that show us the hierarchical structure that relates concepts to the propositions that we have stored in LTM. / 201

How do recall, recognition, and relearning measures affect our assessment of retrieval?

One's ability to retrieve material from memory is often a function of how we ask for or assess retrieval. When we ask for retrieval by recall, we provide an individual with the fewest possible retrieval cues. With recogni-

tion, we provide the information to be retrieved and ask that it be identified as familiar. Retrieval by recognition is generally superior to retrieval by recall. Relearning methods note the improvement in performance (in time or trials) when one relearns material that may not be retrievable by recall and/or recognition. / 203

How does the situation in which one encodes information affect the retrieval of that information?

The greater the extent to which the cues or context available at encoding match the cues or context available at retrieval, the better retrieval will be. The "encoding specificity hypothesis" asserts that how we retrieve information depends on how it was encoded. We have found that even matching the individual's state of mind at encoding and retrieval improves retrieval. Heightened emotionality at encoding generally produces memories that are easier to retrieve. / 205

SUMMARY continued

What is meaningfulness?

How does meaningfulness relate to retrieval?

Meaningfulness is the extent to which material can be related to, or associated with, information already stored in memory. In general, meaningful material (or material that can be made meaningful) is easier to retrieve than meaningless material. / 206

Describe narrative chaining, mental imagery, the peg word method, and the method of loci as mnemonic devices.

In general, mnemonic devices are strategies used at encoding to help organize and add meaningfulness to material that will be retrieved later. Narrative chaining involves making up a story that weaves together, in meaningful fashion, a list of otherwise unrelated words that need to be remembered in order. A number of mnemonic devices suggest forming visual images involving the material to be learned. The peg word method requires first learning a word associated with the number 1 to 10 (if there are 10 items to be learned) and then forming an interactive image of these words and items that need to be recalled in order. The method of loci, another technique involving mental imagery, involves mentally placing terms to be retrieved in a sequence of familiar locations. / 209

What is overlearning, and how does it affect retrieval?

Compare and contrast massed and distributed practice, noting their effects on retrieval.

Overlearning involves the rehearsal of information (encoding) above and beyond that needed for immediate recall. Within limits, the more one overlearns, the greater the likelihood of accurate retrieval. In massed practice, study or rehearsal occurs without intervening rest intervals. Distributed practice uses shorter segments of rehearsal interspersed with rest intervals. In almost all cases, distributed practice leads to better retrieval than does massed practice. / 212

Briefly describe retroactive and proactive interference.

Which of these two generally has the greater impact on retrieval?

Retroactive interference occurs when previously learned material cannot be retrieved because it is inhibited or blocked by material or information learned *later*. Proactive interference occurs when information cannot be retrieved because it is inhibited or blocked by material learned *earlier*. Retroactive interference is generally more detrimental to retrieval than is proactive interference. / 215

What are cognitive processes, and why may concept formation and the use of language be called higher cognitive processes?

Cognitive processes are the mental activities involved in knowing and understanding ourselves and the world around us. They involve forming, manipulating, and using cognitions, which include ideas, beliefs, thoughts, and images. Concept formation and the use of language may be referred to as higher cognitive processes because they rely on the more basic processes of perception, learning, and memory. / 216

How can we use attributes and rules to define concepts?

Concepts are mental representations of categories or classes of objects and events. They are often defined in terms of certain attributes of objects or events that are related to each other by a rule. Formal concepts are those in which the number of attributes is relatively small, the values of attributes are well known, and the rules that relate them are clear. Concepts may be defined by conjunctive rules, disjunctive rules, affirmation rules, or relational rules. / 220

How does the concept of prototype help our understanding of what a concept is?

A prototype is the best example or most typical member of a category or concept. It is the member of a concept class that has most of the attributes that define that concept and few attributes that cause it to be confused with other concepts. The notions of prototype and best fit allow us to deal with the fuzzy concepts that we often encounter in nature. / 222

Briefly review what we know about the process of concept formation.

Concepts are learned, usually by developing a systematic plan or strategy for discovering the essential attributes of a concept and the rule that unites those attributes. In large measure, concept formation strategies involve generating and then testing hypotheses about potential membership in a class or concept. Forming and testing hypotheses about concept membership applies to natural as well as formal concepts. / 223

What are some of the defining characteristics of language?

Language is a complex and creative cognitive skill used for communication. A language is made up of a large number of arbitrary symbols, usually words that "stand for" our conceptualization of objects and events, that have meaning for users of that language, and that are combined in accordance with certain rules. The use of language is a generative process. / 226

What are phonemes, and in what way are they rule-governed?

What is semantics?

What are morphemes?

A phoneme is the smallest unit of sound in the spoken form for a language—that is, a speech sound. Phonemes are rule-governed in the sense that each language is comprised of only a portion of all possible phonemes, and how they may be combined within a given language follows strict rules. Semantics is the name we give to the study of the meaning of words and sentences. Morphemes are the smallest units or elements of meaning in a language. Morphemes include words, prefixes, and suffixes. In many ways, morphemes provide labels that allow us to communicate about concepts. How morphemes are ordered, or structured, in language generally affects their meaning. / 227

What is syntax?

What are linguistic intuitions?

What is pragmatics?

Syntax refers to the rules that govern the way that morphemes in a language are structured to produce sentences. Language users demonstrate a competence with these rules even though they may not be able to state them explicitly. Our knowledge of syntax is reflected in linguistic intuitions, judgments that language users can make about the structure of utterances. For example, we can determine intuitively when utterances are syntactically correct and when they are not. We can tell when two sentences that take different forms are communicating the same idea or message. We can identify ambiguous sentences and can often remove that ambiguity only when we are aware of a larger context in which the utterance occurred. A concern with how context affects meaning is called pragmatics. / 229

Chapter Five
Memory and Cognition

REVIEW QUESTIONS

1. Whether one supports a multistore or levels of processing model of memory, one would agree that there are three stores or levels into which information can be processed. These are, in order:

a. shallow, medium, and deep.

b. episodic, process, and semantic.

c. storage, encoding, and retrieval.

d. sensory, short-term, and long-term.

Regardless of the model one supports, a common view of memory divides it into sensory, short-term, and long-term processes. Encoding, storage, and retrieval are (in this order) the processes by which information is passed into, kept, and passed out of memory. Episodic, process, and semantic memories are three components of long-term memory. / 187

2. Which of the following processes will move information into short-term memory?

a. paying attention to it.

b. rehearsing it.

c. saying it silently to ourselves.

d. all of these.

Information enters short-term memory from either long-term or sensory memory when we pay attention to that information. To correctly answer this question, one must recognize that rehearsing information or saying it to ourselves involves paying attention to that information. Therefore, all of these alternatives are true. / 189, 192

3. The phenomena of category clustering and subjective organization both demonstrate the following:

a. Meaningful information is easier to retrieve from long-term memory than is meaningless information.

b. Whenever possible, we tend to impose stucture and order on the way we store and retrieve information.

c. The capacity of short-term memory can be increased to the extent that we can chunk information together.

d. All of the above.

This is an item that requires some careful consideration. In fact, alternatives (a), (b), and (c) are all true. *But* neither (a) nor (c) really have anything to do with subjective organization or category clustering, and therefore, do not answer this item. Only alternative (b) completes this statement in a sensible way. / 198

4. An instructor who is interested in measuring her student's abilities to recall information would be advised to give what type of exam?

a. true-false (assessing if a given statement is true or false).

b. matching (associating items in one list with items on a second list).

c. multiple-choice (choosing an alternative that best answers a question or completes a statement).

d. fill-in-the-blank (providing a term or phrase that is omitted from a statement).

With true-false, matching, or multiple-choice exams, test takers are provided with correct answers and must recognize them as such. They are provided with many retrieval cues. Fill-in-the-blank exams provide more cues than do most essay exams but still require that one recall information from long-term memory. / 201

5. The encoding specificity principle implies that the best place for you to study for an important exam is:

a. in the library.

b. in the room in which the exam will be given.

c. wherever you can be in the best, anxiety-free mood.

d. in a familiar location at home, listening to the sort of music you like the best.

The encoding specificity principle asserts that retrieval is improved when the context in which retrieval occurs most closely matches the context in which encoding occurred. So, although it may not be terribly practical, studying in the exam room would be your best strategy. Given these alternatives, the library would probably be the second best choice. / 203

6. Which of the following mnemonic devices is useful when we are required to remember new material in a specific order?

a. the peg word method.

b. narrative chaining.

c. the method of loci.

d. all of the above.

Here's another *all of the above* item. The peg word method was specifically designed to aid the recall of items in order, first requiring that we match peg words with numbers (one is a bun, two is a shoe, and so on). Putting items together in a story

(narrative chaining) makes them more meaningful and easier to recall. If the story is recalled correctly, the items to be remembered will be recalled in order. The method of loci can also be used to remember material in a specified order as the material is associated with an ordered set of locations (loci) that one mentally travels through at retrieval. / 206

7. There are many reasons why you may not be able to recall all of the presents you received for your birthday when you were ten years old. Of the following, which is the most reasonable?

a. retroactive interference.

b. distributed practice.

c. failure to encode in LTM.

d. lack of meaningfulness.

The presents you received on your tenth birthday were (and still are) meaningful to you, no doubt. The information about those gifts was almost certainly encoded into LTM (you were able to recall those presents a few days after you received them). Distributed practice simply has nothing to do with this item. If anything, distributed practice enhances retrieval. You probably

cannot remember what you got for your tenth birthday because you've had so many birthdays and received so many presents since then. These later experiences are interfering with recall, which is precisely what retroactive interference is. / 213

8. The study of how the meaning of language behaviors is affected by the context in which those language behaviors occur is called:

a. syntax.

b. pragmatics.

c. linguistic intuitions.

d. morpheme analysis.

Syntax refers to the linguistic rules that must be followed in order to combine units into meaningful sentences. Linguistic intuitions are those cognitive abilities language users possess that allow them to make judgments about the meaning and the appropriateness of language behaviors. Morphemes are simply the smallest units of meaning in the spoken form of a language. The stem of this item provides a reasonable definition of the subfield of psycholinguistics called pragmatics. / 228

Chapter Six

Developmental Psychology

Why We Care

Heredity and Environment; Nature and Nurture

Childhood
- Physical and Motor Development
  - The Neonate
  - The Motor Development of Children
- Sensory and Perceptual Development
- Cognitive and Social Development
  - The Cognitive Abilities of the Neonate
  - Piaget's Theory of Cognitive Development
  - Reactions to Piaget
  - Erikson's Theory of Psychosocial Development
  - Kohlberg's Theory of Moral Development

Adolescence
- Physical Changes in Adolescence
- Cognitive and Social Development in Adolescence
  - Identity Formation
  - Adolescent Egocentrism
  - The Influence of the Family
  - Teenage Suicide

Adulthood
- Early Adulthood
  - Marriage and Family
  - Career Choice
- Middle Adulthood
- Late Adulthood

Let's consider Emily for a moment. Emily is 10 years old and a third-grade student in public school. She is a slightly above-average student, reporting that spelling and recess are her two favorite subjects in school. In most regards, she seems to be a normal 10 year old but Emily *is* different. It is apparent to everyone who knows her that Emily is a very talented young girl.

Emily is very musical. She can play the piano exceptionally well, even without sheet music to guide her. She has given a number of recitals and has recently been invited to be a guest artist with the local symphony orchestra for next year's concert season. Emily has always enjoyed listening to music. When she was only 3 years old, she entertained her relatives by singing along with the radio or television. It was when she was 3 that she began taking piano lessons. Our question is: Why is Emily such an unusual 10 year old? Many 10-year-old girls (and boys) take lessons and play the piano, but why is Emily so much better than most? This sort of question has been at the core of a controversy in psychology that continues unresolved even today—a controversy over the relative importance or impact of one's inheritance (one's nature) and one's experiences and interactions with the environment (one's nurture).

It is very easy and convenient . . . to talk about inheriting musical talent, or aggressiveness, or intelligence, or artistic ability, or a host of other traits and characteristics. But we'd better be careful.

Emily's father never showed much talent for music. He never learned to play an instrument. He can barely carry a tune when he tries to sing, which mercifully, isn't very often. Emily's mother, on the other hand, is an accomplished musician. When she was a teenager, she earned money by playing the piano in a band. She studied music in college. It seems clear to everyone that Emily inherited her musical abilities from her mother's side of the family. Even her maternal grandmother was known to be quite a musician.

It is very easy and convenient in situations such as these to talk about inheriting musical talent, or aggressiveness, or intelligence, or artistic ability, or a host of other traits and characteristics. But we'd better be careful. Just what does it mean to say that Emily inherited her musical ability from her mother? If Emily had a sister, would *she* necessarily be as talented as Emily? Might Emily have turned out to be so musically inclined if she had been reared by foster parents who had neither the interest nor the ability of her biological parents? In such cases, we have to answer, "maybe, maybe not." The issue here is not a simple one. But it is an issue that permeates all of psychology and is of special interest in this chapter: What are the roles of nature and nurture in development?

Why We Care

From conception to death, all of us as human beings share certain developmental events that unite us as one species. As we have already mentioned a number of times, it is also true that each of us is unique and, in our own way, different from everyone else. Developmental psychologists are interested in the common patterns and the ways in which we differ as we grow and develop throughout our lives.

Our normal sequence of development usually appears to be continuous, slow, and gradual. You probably don't believe that you are much different today than you were yesterday. You probably won't feel significantly changed by tomorrow or the next day either. Though development may appear to be very slow and gradual to us now, it is not necessarily so throughout our life span. Young children often seem to grow and change on a day-to-day basis. Physically and psychologically, we experience spurts of growth, periods of leveling off, and times of decline. Rates of development change throughout the life cycle—sometimes fast, sometimes slow. What we will be searching for in this chapter is orderliness—for the patterns and sequences of development common to us all which influence our development across the lifespan.

We'll begin with a discussion of an interaction alluded to in the description of Emily—the interaction between the forces of nature and nurture. Throughout this chapter, this interaction will be apparent. Then we'll look at the development of children from birth to puberty, focusing on three areas or domains of child development: physical-motor, sensory-perceptual, and cognitive-social. Growth and development do not come to a halt when one is no longer a child. We continue to develop, in fact, through adolescence and adulthood until the day we die. Many of the changes that reflect our development as adults and adolescents are often more gradual and subtle than those that occur in childhood. They may be more difficult to observe, but they are no less significant.

We'll define adolescence and review the physical changes that usually occur during this development period. Then we'll discuss the mental and social development of adolescents. We'll sample just some of the issues that are of concern to developmental psychologists who study adolescents: identity formation, egocentrism, family influences, and suicide among teenagers. Finally, we'll discuss the psychology of adult development—an area of research and theory of comparatively recent origin. As more and more of us enter the age group we classify as late adulthood, interest in this segment of our population has increased. We'll arbitrarily divide adulthood into three segments: early adulthood, middle adulthood, and late adulthood and we'll examine some of the psychologically important milestones of each of these periods.

HEREDITY AND ENVIRONMENT; NATURE AND NURTURE

genes (Nature)
the basic structures of heredity that determine, in part, one's development

nature-nurture controversy
a long-standing discussion in psychology over the relative importance of one's heredity and one's environment as shapers of development

epigenetic model
the point of view that developmental processes emerge based on genetic programming *interacting with* experiences with the environment

(Nature and Nurture)
very popular

There you sit—billions upon billions of individual living cells. It is very difficult to imagine that this mass of interconnected cells that is you was ever just one single cell. But it was. Much of who we are was determined well before we were born, when we were each but one cell. In other words, a major influence on our development has been, and continues to be, our heredity, our nature, or our **genes.** That the authors of this book are male was determined at conception by the genes we inherited from our parents. As for our vocational choices we might more easily attribute the fact that we are psychologists to the influences of our environment, our nurture, and our experiences rather than to genes. What about our temperaments, intelligence, aggressiveness, abilities, and aptitudes (or lack thereof)? Are these inherited or do they reflect our learning experiences? This so-called **nature-nurture controversy** has been with psychology from its very beginning.

What determines a particular behavior, our nature or our nurture? How much of a given behavior is due to heredity and how much can be attributed to the environment? Which is more important, our genes or our experiences? Developmental psychologists now recognize that these are often the wrong questions to be asking. *Both* heredity and the environment shape the course of development; *neither* is sufficient alone.

Today, most psychologists ascribe to what is called the **epigenetic model** of development (Gottlieb, 1970; Lerner, 1978). This point of view is an *interactionist* position, claiming that development *emerges* based on one's genetic programming *and* one's experiences in the environment. In this model, development is influenced by the forces of both nature and nurture, "experienced in an inseparable tangle" (McGraw, 1987, p. 103).

For example, the fact that someone might happen to be 6'4" tall and not 4'6" tall reflects the fact that his parents and grandparents happen to have

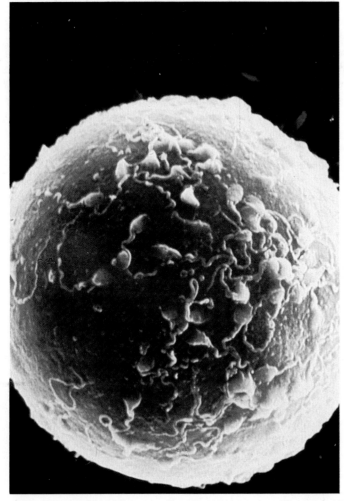

At conception, as pictured here, the egg cell unites with the sperm cell. During this time, the zygote receives all of its inherited characteristics.

[Handwritten margin note: Genes: Every cell contain exact same heridity component.]

[Handwritten margin note: genetic components maybe more than environment]

been taller than average *and* that he has been well fed and cared for. Our genes may provide the foundation—the framework—for development, but we must recognize the extent to which the environment can produce variation within that framework. Developing organisms demonstrate a capacity to be molded and shaped by the environment, nurture, and experience. This capacity is called **plasticity,** and we now recognize that developing organisms are enormously plastic in this sense of being capable of expressing genetic predispositions in a variety of ways (Hall & Oppenheim, 1987). The extent of plasticity may vary at different stages or periods of development and also may vary from species to species, with humans showing the greatest plasticity in development (Gallagher & Ramey, 1987).

So, as we cover the processes of development in this chapter, you should be ever mindful of the interaction of nature and nurture.

plasticity ✳
a term describing the variability involved in expressing genetic predispositions

[Handwritten note: (Nurture)]

What is the epigenetic model, and what does it say about the nature-nurture controversy?　　**BEFORE YOU GO ON**

CHILDHOOD

To their parents, children are a source of great joy and considerable aggravation. They are quiet, peaceful angels one minute and noisy screamers demanding attention the next. Children are a source of joy and aggravation to psychologists as well. They are living laboratories, changing from week to week and even from day to day. Sometimes children seem to change by the hour. The psychology of child development is particularly important when we realize how many traits, ideas, attitudes, and habits are formed in this period that remain with us well into adulthood.

In this section, we'll consider some of the major landmarks in the development of children, from birth to adolescence. We'll summarize physical-motor, sensory-perceptual, and cognitive-social development. In each case, we'll focus attention first on the capabilities of the newborn child before tracing further development through childhood. Even though we'll be looking at these three areas of development separately, it is important to remember that the divisions are really very artificial—each area of development is continually interacting with and influencing the others.

③ Areas of Development

Physical and Motor Development

In this section, we focus on the physical growth of children and note the orderly sequence of the development of their motor responses—their abilities to do things with their bodies. We'll begin by considering some of the abilities of the newborn infant, or the neonate.

The Neonate.   As recently as 20 years ago, textbooks on child psychology seldom devoted more than a few paragraphs to the behaviors of the **neonate**—the newborn through the first 2 weeks of life. It seemed as if the neonate did not do much worth writing about. Today, most child psychology

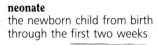

neonate
the newborn child from birth
through the first two weeks

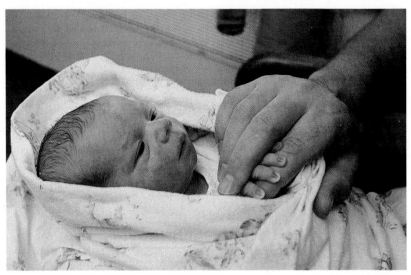

Psychologists have discovered that while some of a neonate's behaviors may not serve a definite purpose to him or her, they do reveal a lot about the newborn's development.

FIGURE 6.1
Reflexes of the Neonate

Name	Stimulus	Response	Age When Disappears
Moro	Loud sound, or sudden loss of support	Arms and legs thrown outward; fingers spread; then, with fists clenched, arms and legs pulled back	4–6 months
Rooting	Light stroke on cheek	Head turns toward stimulus; mouth opens; sucking begins	3–4 months
Sucking	Object (e.g. nipple) inserted in mouth 3–4 cm.	Rhythmic sucking and mouth movements	variable
Grasping	Rod pressed in palm	Close fist and grasp firmly	3–5 months
Walking/Stepping	With feet just touching surface, baby moved forward	Coordinated rhythmic stepping movements	2–4 months
Babinski	Stroke sole of foot from heel to toes	Small toes spread; big toe raised	9–12 months
Tonic Neck	With baby on its back, turn head to one side	Arm and leg on that side thrust outward, while other arm and leg drawn in to body	3–4 months
Swimming	Place infant in water	Rhythmic swimming movements	4–6 months

texts devote substantially more space to discussing the abilities of newborns. It is unlikely that over the past 20 years neonates have gotten smarter or more able. Rather, psychologists have. They have devised new and clever ways of assessing the abilities of neonates.

When a baby is first born, it looks like it just can't do a thing. Oh, it can cry, and it can dirty a diaper, but mostly it just sleeps. In fact, most newborns *do* sleep a lot, about 15–17 hours each day. As parents are quick to discover, however, that sleep tends to occur in a series of short naps, seldom lasting for more than a few hours at a time.

A careful examination of babies reveals that they are capable of a wide range of behaviors. Almost all of these behaviors are reflexive—simple, unlearned, involuntary reactions to specific stimuli. Many of the neonate's reflexive responses serve a useful purpose; they help to respond to a basic need. Some do not seem to have any particular survival value, but even these are very important to know about because they can be used as diagnostic indicators of the quality of the neonate's development. In all, there are more than a dozen reflexes that can be observed and measured (for strength and duration, for example) in the newborn child. Figure 6.1 provides a summary of some of the major neonatal reflexes.

What are some of the reflexes that can be observed in neonates?

Why do we care about neonatal reflexes?

BEFORE YOU GO ON

The Motor Development of Children. Parents trying to keep their young children in properly fitting clothes know how quickly children can grow. In their first 3 years, children will increase in height and weight at a rate never again equaled. Although changes in size and motor skills are rapid, they tend to be orderly and well sequenced, following a prescribed pattern. It is with that pattern that we are concerned here.

As we have said repeatedly, one of psychology's most reliable observations is that individuals differ. No two children are alike. No two children can

interaction between Nervous & muscular system.

Developmental stages

be expected to grow at exactly the same rate or to develop control over their bodies at the same time. Joanne may walk unaided at the age of 10 months. Bill may not venture forth on his own until he's 13 months old. The differences between children are often as great as their similarities. And those children who happen to develop more slowly might benefit from having others appreciate the notion of individual differences in developmental rates.

Regardless of the *rate* of one's motor development, there are regularities in the *sequence* of one's development. No matter when Joanne does walk, she will first sit, then crawl. It's an old adage, and it's true: We have to stand before we walk and walk before we run.

A summary of the development of common motor skills is presented in Figure 6.2. There are two important things for you to notice about this figure. First, the sequence of events is very regular, and second, *when* each stage develops includes a wide range of ages that should be considered normal. It is also true that the sequence and timing of the events listed in this figure hold equally for boys and girls. That is, in these basic motor skills, there are no significant sex differences. Figure 6.3 shows some of the motor skills that can be found among school-aged children and notes sex differences when they are present.

Whether a child begins to walk at 10 months or 12 months, he or she will still follow the same sequence of sitting, crawling, and then walking.

BEFORE YOU GO ON   **Briefly summarize some of the landmarks of early motor development.**

FIGURE 6.2
The increasing mobility of a child is illustrated in this time-sequencing chart. As the child increases in age, so does he or she increase in strength and mobility. Though merely able to hold its head up at 2 months, the child can usually walk by 12 months.

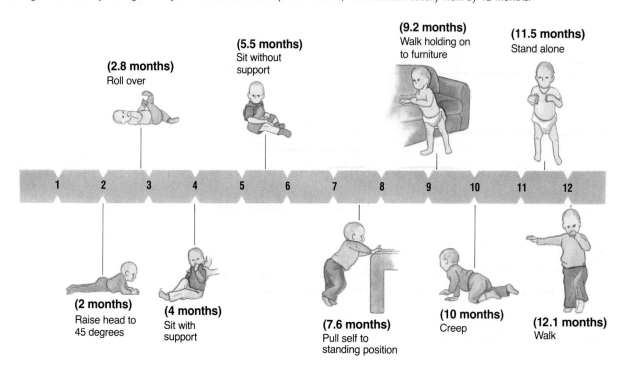

FIGURE 6.3

Typical behaviors found in school children. Note the orderly progression, but now some gender differences are apparent. (Based on Cratty, 1970.)

Age	Selected Behaviors
6 years	Girls superior in movement accuracy; boys superior in forceful, less complex acts. Skipping acquired. Throwing with proper weight shift and step.
7 years	One-footed balancing without vision becomes possible. Can walk 2 in. balance beams. Can hop and jump accurately into small squares. Can execute accurate jumping-jack exercise.
8 years	12 lb. pressure on grip strength by both sexes. The number of games participated in by both sexes is greatest at this age. Can engage in alternate rhythmical hopping in 2–2, 2–3, 3–3 pattern.
9 years	Girls can throw a small ball 40 ft. Girls can vertical jump 8½ in. and boys 10 in. over their standing height-plus-reach. Boys can run 16½ ft. per second.
10 years	Boys can throw a small ball 70 ft. Can judge and intercept pathways of small balls thrown from a distance. Girls can run 17 ft. per second.
11 years	Standing broad jump of 5 ft. possible for boys, 6 in. less for girls.
12 years	Standing high jump of 3 ft. possible.

Sensory and Perceptual Development

One of the reasons psychologists used to think that newborn children couldn't do much was that it was commonly believed that newborns could not sense or perceive very much. We now understand that neonates can and do respond to a wide range of stimuli in their environments. In fact, all of a human's sensory modalities are functioning at birth, having developed in order: touch, body position, balance, taste, smell, hearing, and finally vision (Gibson, 1987; 1988; Hall & Oppenheim, 1987).

The neonate's ability to sense even subtle changes is quite remarkable. However, there *are* limitations. The ability of the eyes to focus on an object, for example, does not develop fully until the child is about 4 months old. Neonates can focus well on objects held at about their arms' length, but everything nearer or farther appears blurred or out of focus.

For their first few weeks, babies have difficulty coordinating the movements of their eyes, although within hours after birth they can follow (track) a stimulus object that is swung slowly back and forth in front of them. Newborns can detect differences in brightness and some develop the ability to detect surfaces, edges, or borders and to differentiate among colors (Cohen et al., 1978; Termine et al., 1987).

An issue that has been of considerable interest to psychologists is just when the perception of depth and distance develops. Apparently, even newborns have some simple reflexive reactions to depth. They will close their eyes and squirm away if you rush some object, such as your hand, toward their face. Like so many other reflexes, however, this one too seems to disappear in a few months.

FIGURE 6.4

The visual cliff was designed to determine if depth perception is innate or learned. By the time they can move about, most infants will avoid the "deep" side of the apparatus. There does seem to be an innate ability to sense depth, but the ability to react to it apparently needs to be learned.

In the late 1950s, two Cornell University psychologists, Eleanor Gibson and Richard Walk (1960), constructed an apparatus to test the depth perception of very young children. The *visual cliff,* as it is called, is a deep box covered by a sheet of thick, clear plexiglass. It is divided into two sides, one shallow, one deep. The deep and shallow sides are separated by a center board (see Figure 6.4).

Gibson and Walk discovered that 6-month-old children would not leave the center board to venture out over the deep side of the box, even to get to their mothers. By crawling age, then, the child seems able to perceive depth *and* judge it to be dangerous.

When neonates, who obviously can't crawl, are placed on the plexiglass over the deep side of the visual cliff, their heart rates decrease, indicating that at least they notice the change in visual stimulation (Campos et al., 1970). When 9-month-old infants are placed over the deep side of the visual cliff, their heart rates *increase.* This increase in heart rate is believed to indicate fear, a response that develops after the ability to discriminate depth (Campos, 1976). So it seems that in some rudimentary form, even a neonate may sense depth, but knowing how to react appropriately to depth may require experience and learning that come later.

What about the other senses: hearing, smell, taste, and so on? Newborn infants can hear very well. They can certainly direct their attention to the source of a sound—even a faint sound. Sounds probably don't *mean* much to neonates, but they can respond differently to sounds of different pitch and loudness. Even 3-day-old newborns are able to discriminate the sound of their mother's voice from other sounds (DeCasper & Fifer, 1980; Kolata, 1987; Martin & Clark, 1982).

Newborns can also respond to differences in taste and smell. They clearly discriminate among the four basic taste qualities of salt, sweet, bitter, and sour. They display a distinct preference for sweet-tasting liquids. Although they are unable to use it then, the sense of smell seems to be established before birth. Right after birth, neonates respond predictably—drawing away and wrinkling their noses—to a variety of strong odors.

In summary, a wide range of sensory and perceptual capabilities appears to be available to the newborn child. The neonate may require some time to learn what to do with the sensory information that it acquires from its environment, but many of its senses are operational. What the newborn makes of the sensations it receives will depend upon the development of its mental or cognitive abilities. This is the subject that we turn to now.

BEFORE YOU GO ON   Summarize the basic sensory capacities of the neonate.

Cognitive and Social Development

In preceding chapters, we have had occasion to refer to cognitive skills and abilities many times. Cognitive processes are those that enable us to know and understand ourselves and the world around us. In this section, we'll look at how these skills develop throughout childhood, beginning with a summary of the cognitive capacities of the newborn infant. Our major focus will be on the theories of Jean Piaget. Then, we'll consider development from a more social perspective, considering the psychosocial theory of Erik Erikson and Lawrence Kohlberg's theory of moral development.

The Cognitive Abilities of the Neonate.   As we have seen, reflex reactions can help neonates survive. For long-term survival, however, the neonates must learn to adapt to their environments and profit from their experience. Neonates will have to begin forming memories of their experiences and learn to make discriminations among the many stimuli with which they are presented. Are any of these cognitive processes possible in a baby just a couple of weeks old? In a number of specific ways, the answer seems to be yes.

Friedman (1972) reported a demonstration of what we might call memory in neonates only 1 to 4 *days* old. Babies were shown a picture of a simple figure, say a checkerboard pattern, for 60 seconds. Experimenters recorded how long the baby looked at the stimulus pattern. After the same pattern was shown over and over again, the baby appeared to be bored and gave it less attention. When a different stimulus pattern was introduced, the baby stared at it for almost the full 60 seconds of its exposure.

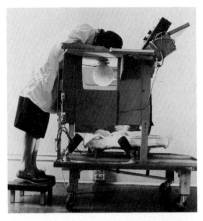

When presented with two visual stimuli, babies usually chose the more complex of the two. Pictured here is the equipment originally designed by Fantz for this study.

So what does this have to do with memory? The argument is that for the young neonate to stare at the new stimulus, it must have formed some memory of the old one. Otherwise, how would it recognize the new pattern as being new or different? In fact, if the new stimulus pattern was very similar to the old one, the baby would not give it as much attention as it would if it were totally different. It is as if a judgment were being made about the distinctiveness of the new stimulus and the old (remembered) ones.

In talking about recognizing visual patterns, we should mention the research of Robert Fantz (1961, 1963). Fantz presented newborn children with pairs of visual stimuli. In most pairs, one stimulus was more complex than the other. As the babies lay on their backs, looking up at the stimuli, the experimenters could note which one of the two stimuli received the most attention from the child. In almost every case, a preference was shown for the more complex stimulus pattern.

This in itself is interesting—and difficult to explain. The major finding of these studies is that the babies could at least discriminate between the two

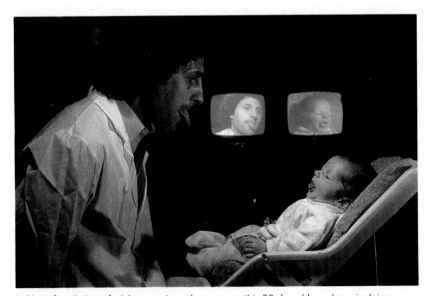

Babies often imitate facial expressions they see, as this 23-day-old newborn is doing.

stimuli. That attention equals preference is more of an assumption than a research finding. Fantz also discovered something curious when he found that even newborn infants show a distinct preference for (choose to attend to) drawings of a human face. They choose the face pattern as the focus of their attention no matter what it is paired with.

One more step takes us to the research of Meltzoff and Moore (1977) who discovered something in the controlled setting of a laboratory that many parents have discovered by accident. Not only do newborns look at a human face, but they often try to imitate facial expressions. When experimenters stick out their tongues at babies, the babies stick out their tongues. Infants open their mouths to imitate the same facial expression of the experimenter. These attempts at imitation—a cognitive skill indicating an appreciation of the environment—are clearly present by the age of 2 weeks and are often found in neonates only 1 hour old!

BEFORE YOU GO ON **Cite an example that demonstrates more than a simple reflexive reaction by a neonate.**

Piaget's Theory of Cognitive Development.   The physical growth and development of a child is remarkable. Even more impressive are the increases in cognitive and intellectual abilities that occur during childhood. By the time the human organism reaches adolescence, it has acquired an enormous stockpile of information. More than just learning facts, the child comes to appreciate how to learn. Strategies for survival and/or success begin to develop in childhood (Siegler, 1983).

Accounting for how children's intellectual capacities and abilities change is a difficult business. The theory that has attracted the most attention in this regard is that of the Swiss psychologist Jean Piaget (1896–1980). Though there *are* others, Piaget's theory of cognitive development (Piaget, 1948, 1954, 1967) has been so influential that it will be the focus of our discussion.

In Piaget's theory, cognitive development amounts to acquiring **schemas,** which are organized mental representations of the world. Organizing the world into an interrelated network of schemas is, for Piaget, a process that can be found in all children. Children develop a schema for "daddy," for "mommy," for "eating breakfast," and for "bedtime," for example. The function of schemas is to aid the child in adapting to the demands and pressures of the environment. Schemas are formed by experience.

Organizing and forming mental representations of the environment involve two basic processes, assimilation and accommodation. **Assimilation** involves taking new information and fitting it into an existing schema. Children develop a rather complex schema for mealtime. When, for the first time, they are taken to "eat out" at a fast-food restaurant, new information will have to be assimilated into the mealtime schema. Having developed a schema for "dogs," a child may incorrectly assimilate the neighbor's cat into the same schema, simply enlarging it.

Accommodation involves changing and revising existing schemas in the face of new experiences or new information. As children are shifted away from the bottle to strained foods, to chunkier foods, to regular food, they must accommodate their schemas for efficient feeding—what used to work in the past doesn't work any longer. Once the child gets to go out to the

schemas
in Piaget's theory, one's organized mental representations of the world

assimilation
in Piaget's theory, taking in new information and fitting it into existing schemas

accommodation
in Piaget's theory, the changing or revising of existing schemas in response to new experiences

fast-food restaurant, not only will new information have to be assimilated, but old ideas about how and where one eats will have to be accommodated. Learning that mommy and daddy won't *always* come running when one cries may require an accommodation.

Piaget proposed that as children assimilate new ideas into existing schemas and modify or accommodate old ones, they progress through four identifiable stages of development: the sensorimotor stage, the preoperational stage, the concrete operations stage, and the formal operations stage. Determining precisely when each stage begins or ends is not always possible, since two adjacent stages may overlap and blend for awhile. Even so, each stage is characterized by its own schemas, cognitive methods, insights, and abilities. The four stages are summarized in Figure 6.5 and are described more fully below.

Jean Piaget

1. Sensorimotor Stage. (Ages 0 to 24 months.) For children under age 2, language isn't terribly relevant. Such children are unable to discover much about their world by asking questions about it or by trying to understand long-winded explanations. Trying to explain to a 10-month-old baby *why* it shouldn't chew on an electrical extension cord is likely to be an unrewarding piece of parental behavior. In this **sensorimotor stage,** children discover by *sensing* (sensori-) and by *doing* (motor). A child may come to appreciate, for example, that a quick pull on a dog's tail (a motor activity) reliably produces a loud yelp (a sensory experience), perhaps followed in turn by parental attention.

   One of the most useful schemas to develop in the sensorimotor stage is that of *causality*. Infants gradually come to the realization that events sometimes have knowable causes and that some behaviors cause predictable reactions. Pushing a bowl of oatmeal off the

sensorimotor stage
in Piaget's theory, the stage (ages 0–24 months) in which the child comes to know about the world by sensing and doing

---

FIGURE 6.5
A summary of Piaget's stages of cognitive development

1. Sensorimotor stage (birth to age 2 years)
"knows" through active interaction with environment
becomes aware of cause-effect relationships
learns that objects exist even when not in view
imitates crudely the actions of others

[handwritten: Develop senses & motor]

2. Preoperational stage (ages 2 to 6 years)
begins by being very egocentric
language and mental representations develop
objects are classified on just one characteristic at a time

[handwritten: Center of universe]

3. Concrete operations stage (ages 7 to 12 years)
develops conservation of volume, length, mass, etc.
organizes objects into ordered categories
understands relational terms (e.g., bigger than, above)
begins using simple logic

[handwritten: develop concepts but thinks does not think abstractly]

4. Formal operations stage (ages over 12)
thinking becomes abstract and symbolic
reasoning skills develop
a sense of hypothetical concepts develops

*[handwritten: ** Read Memorize]*

high chair causes a mess and gets mommy's attention: If A, then B—a very practical insight.

Another important discovery that occurs during this stage of development is that objects may exist even when they are not immediately in view. Early in this stage, an object that is out of sight is more than out of mind. The object ceases to exist for the child. By the end of the sensorimotor period, children have learned that objects can exist even if they are not physically present, and children can anticipate their reappearance. This awareness is called **object permanence** (see Figure 6.6).

One of the skills that best characterizes the sensorimotor period of development is that of imitation. So long as it is within the baby's range of abilities, a baby will imitate almost any behavior it sees. A cognitive strategy has developed, one that will be used for a lifetime: trying to imitate the behaviors of a model.

object permanence
the realization that objects that are not physically present and are not gone forever and may still reappear

BEFORE YOU GO ON   **Briefly summarize some of the cognitive skills that develop during the sensorimotor stage.**

preoperational stage
in Piaget's theory, the stage (ages 2–6 years) of cognitive development characterized by symbol formation, but without rules, and egocentric thinking

egocentric
seeing everything from one's own point of view, unable to appreciate someone else's perspective

2. Preoperational Stage. (Ages 2 to 6 years.) By the end of the sensorimotor stage, a child has recognized that he or she is a separate, independent person in the world. Throughout most of the **preoperational stage,** a child's thinking is self-centered, or **egocentric.** According to Piaget, the child has difficulty understanding life from someone else's perspective. In this stage, the world is very much *me, mine,* and *I* oriented.

Perhaps you have seen two preschool children at play. They are right next to each other, one playing with a truck, the other coloring in a coloring book. They are jabbering at each other, taking turns, but each is quite oblivious to what the other is saying:

Jill: "This sure is a neat truck!"
Leslie: "I think I'll paint the sky a kinda purple."

Jill: "I'm gonna be a truck driver some day."
Leslie: "But if I make the sky a kinda purple, what'll I make the trees?"
Jill: "Maybe I'll drive a milk truck. Broooom!"
Leslie: "I know, blue."

Such exchanges, called *collective monologues,* demonstrate the egocentrism of children's thinking in this stage.

In the preoperational stage, children begin to develop and use symbols—usually in the form of words to represent concepts. But, at this stage, children do not appreciate how to manipulate those symbols, which is why it is referred to as *pre*operational. It's not until the end of this period that they find riddles about rabbits throwing clocks out of windows to "see time fly" as at all funny.

In Piaget's theory, what is meant by egocentrism?

BEFORE YOU GO ON

3. Concrete Operations Stage. (Ages 7 to 12 years.) In the **concrete operations stage,** children begin to develop many concepts *and* show that they can manipulate those concepts. For example, they can organize objects into classes or categories of things. That is to say, they can classify things: balls over here, blocks over there, plastic soldiers in a pile by the door, and so on. Each of these items is recognized as a toy, ultimately to be put away in the toy box and not stored in the closet, which is where clothes are supposed to go. Thus, it is in this period that we may say that rule-governed behavior begins. The concrete, observable objects of the child's world can be classified, ranked, ordered, or separated into more than one category.

A sign of the beginning of the concrete operations stage is an ability to solve conservation problems. **Conservation** involves the cognitive awareness that changing the form or the appearance of something does not necessarily change what it really is. Many experiments convinced Piaget that the ability to demonstrate conservation marked the end of the preoperational stage of development. Figure 6.7 shows a demonstration of a test for conservation of volume. We can show the conservation of size by giving two, equal-sized balls of clay to a 4 year old. One is then rolled into a long cigar shape, and the child will now assert that it has more clay in it than the ball does. A 7 year old will seldom hesitate to tell you that each form contains the same amount of clay. The 7 year old has moved on to the next stage of cognitive development.

During this stage, youngsters enjoy simple games, if the rules are easy. Moving pieces around a board to squares that match the color indicated by a spinner is easy; so is moving pieces along a board the same number of spaces as indicated on a pair of dice. Problems arise when choices need to be made that force decisions beyond the (concrete) here and now: "Should I buy this piece of property now or build a house on Boardwalk?" "If I move my piece there, I'll get jumped, but then I can jump two of his pieces." "Should I save 7s or go for a run of clubs?"

concrete operations stage
in Piaget's theory, the stage (ages 7–12 years) characterized by the formation of concepts, rules, and ability to solve conservation problems

conservation
the understanding that changing something's form does not change its essential character

During the concrete operations stage, children enjoy simple games. They can follow simple rules and can move pieces around a board by specified numbers of spaces.

FIGURE 6.7
A test of conservation of volume. In (A), the child acknowledges that there is an equal amount of liquid in both beakers. In (B), the child watches the liquid being poured from one short beaker into a taller one. In (C), the child in the preoperational stage will report that there is more liquid in the taller beaker.

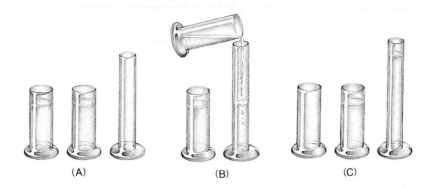

(A)   (B)   (C)

As its name suggests, in the concrete operations stage, children begin to operate on (use and manipulate) concepts and ideas. However, their manipulations are still very concrete, very much tied to real objects in the here and now. For example, an 8 year old can easily be expected to find her way to and from school, even if she throws in a side trip or two along the way. What she will have a hard time doing is *telling* you with any precision just how she gets from one place to another. Drawing a sensible map is very difficult for her. If she actually stands on the corner of Maple Street and Oak Avenue, she knows where to go next to get home. Dealing with such knowledge later, in abstract terms, is what is difficult.

BEFORE YOU GO ON **What cognitive skills might we expect from a child in the concrete operations stage of development?**

4. Formal Operations Stage. (Ages over 12 years.) The logical manipulation of abstract, symbolic concepts does not appear until the last of Piaget's stages—**formal operations.** The key to this stage, usually begun at adolescence, is abstract, symbolic reasoning. By the age of 12, most children can develop and then mentally test hypotheses—to work through problems in their minds.

It is only at the stage of formal operations that youngsters are able to reason through hypothetical problems: "What if you were the only person in the world who liked rock music?" "If nobody had to go to school, what would happen?" Similarly, children are now able to deal with questions that are literally contrary to fact: "What if Walter Mondale had been elected president in 1984 instead of Ronald Reagan?"

formal operations stage
in Piaget's theory, the stage (ages over 12 years) characterized by abstract, symbolic reasoning

BEFORE YOU GO ON **What cognitive ability characterizes the stage of formal operations?**

Reactions to Piaget.   There can be no doubt of Piaget's influence on the study of the cognitive abilities of children. His observations, insights, and theories about intellectual development spanned decades. On the other hand, there has been a sizable quantity of research that has brought into question some of Piaget's basic ideas. The two major criticisms of Piaget's theory are that (1) the borderlines between his proposed stages are much less clearcut than his theory suggests, and (2) Piaget significantly underestimated the cognitive talents of preschool children (Flavell, 1982, 1985; Gelman, 1978).

For example, the egocentrism said to characterize the preoperational preschool child may not be as flagrant as Piaget would have us believe. In one study (Lempers et al., 1977), children were shown a picture that was pasted inside a box. They were asked to show the picture to someone else. Not only did they do so, but in showing the picture, they turned it so that it would be right-side up to the viewer. Every child over 2 years of age indicated such an appreciation of someone else's point of view. Similarly, there is considerable evidence that object permanence may be neither universal nor consistently found in any one child—it depends on how you test for it (Harris, 1983).

Even Piaget's well-researched notion of conservation may not be such an obvious indicator of cognitive development as was once thought. When experimenters pour liquid from a short beaker into a tall one, a 5 year old will probably say that the taller beaker now holds more liquid—evidence of a failure to conserve in the preoperational stage. If the *child* actually does the pouring from one beaker to the other, as opposed to just watching, even 5 year olds show definite signs of conservation and recognize that the amount of liquid is the same in both containers (Rose & Blank, 1974).

A further criticism is that Piaget's theory, focusing from the start on a stage approach, gives little attention to the impact of language development. Piaget had little to say about the smooth and gradual increase in the capacity of a child's memory. Indeed, some children may appear to fail at a task designed to measure a cognitive skill simply because they lack the words to describe what they know or because the task puts too great a strain on their abilities to remember (Pines, 1983). Just because a child of whatever age *can* demonstrate some cognitive skill is no guarantee that the child normally *does* use that skill in her or his daily activities.

Cite two criticisms of Piaget's theory of cognitive development.   **BEFORE YOU GO ON**

Erikson's Theory of Psychosocial Development.

Erik Erikson (1963, 1968) is a psychologist who, like Piaget, proposed a stage theory of human development. Unlike Piaget, his theory focuses on much more than cognitive development, although these aspects are clearly included. Piaget based most of his theory on the observation of young children—and not many of them at that. Erikson's theory is based on his observations of a wide range of different sorts of people of different ages. He did not just study children. As we'll see, his theory extends through adolescence into adulthood. Many of his observations had more of a crosscultural basis than did Piaget's. Erikson was born in Germany, studied with Sigmund Freud in Vienna, and came to the United States to do this research. Erikson's views of

Erik Erikson

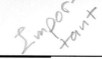

FIGURE 6.8
Erikson's eight stages of development. (Based on Erikson, 1963.)

Approximate age	Crisis	Adequate resolution	Inadequate resolution
0–1½	Trust vs. mistrust	Basic sense of safety	Insecurity, anxiety
1½–3	Autonomy vs. self-doubt	Perception of self as agent capable of controlling own body and making things happen	Feelings of inadequacy to control events
3–6	Initiative vs. guilt	Confidence in oneself as initiator, creator	Feeling of lack of self-worth
6–puberty	Competence vs. inferiority	Adequacy in basic social and intellectual skills	Lack of self-confidence, feelings of failure
Adolescent	Identity vs. role confusion	Comfortable sense of self as a person	Sense of self as fragmented; shifting, unclear sense of self
Early adult	Intimacy vs. isolation	Capacity for closeness and commitment to another	Feeling of aloneness, separation; denial of need for closeness
Middle adult	Generativity vs. stagnation	Focus on concern beyond oneself to family, society, future generations.	Self-indulgent concerns; lack of future orientation
Later adult	Ego-integrity vs. despair	Sense of wholeness, basic satisfaction with life	Feelings of futility, disappointment

developmental processes were influenced more by Freud than by Piaget. Unlike Freud, however, Erikson chose to emphasize the *social* environment, which is why his theory is referred to as "psychosocial."

Erikson's theory lists eight stages of development through which an individual passes. These stages are not so much periods of time as they are a series of conflicts, or crises that need to be resolved. Each of the eight stages can be referenced by a pair of terms that indicates the nature of the conflict that needs to be resolved in this period of development.

As a stage theory, Erikson's implies that we naturally go through the resolution of each conflict or crisis in order and that facing any one type of crisis usually occurs at about the same age for all of us. Figure 6.8 provides a summary of each of the eight stages of development according to Erikson. Also included are very brief descriptions of how each crisis might be resolved.

As you can see, only the first four stages or crises are relevant for children. In fact, one of the major strengths of Erikson's view of development is that it covers the entire life span. While Piaget (and, as we shall see, Freud) focused only on the stages of development of children, Erikson extended his views to late adulthood. For now, we'll leave Erikson's theory as summarized in Figure 6.8, but we will return to it later.

BEFORE YOU GO ON According to Erikson, what are the four crisis stages of development that develop in childhood?

Kohlberg's Theory of Moral Development. How children acquire the capacity to judge right and wrong is a process of cognitive development that has received a great deal of interest in psychology. Piaget included the study of moral development in his theory, arguing that morality is closely related to one's cognitive awareness (Piaget, 1932). A child's notion of right and wrong depends on the development of basic concepts, rule learning, and understanding the bases for rules. These cognitive abilities develop only as the child progresses through developmental stages, argued Piaget.

Lawrence Kohlberg has offered a theory of moral development (1963, 1969, 1981, 1985). Like Piaget's theory of cognitive development, Kohlberg's is a theory of stages; of progressing from one stage to another in an orderly fashion. Kohlberg's original data base comes from responses made by young boys who were asked a number of questions about stories that involve some moral dilemma. The most commonly cited example of such a story concerns whether or not a man should steal a drug in order to save his wife's life after the pharmacist who invented the drug refuses to sell it. Should the man steal the drug; why or why not?

This method led Kohlberg to propose three major levels of moral development, with two stages (or "orientations") at each level. The result is the six stages of moral development briefly summarized in Figure 6.9. A child who says, for example, that the man should not steal the drug to save his wife's life because, "He'll get caught and be put in jail," would be classified as being at the first, preconventional level of moral reasoning. A child who says that the man should steal the drug because "it'll make his wife happy, and probably most people would do it anyway," is reflecting a type of reasoning we can classify at the second level. Predictably, it is more difficult to give clear examples of moral reasoning at the third level. The argument that, "no, he shouldn't steal the drug for a basically selfish reason, which in the long run would just promote more stealing in the society in general," would qualify.

Research suggests that the basic thrust of Kohlberg's theory has merit (Rest, 1983) and that is has crosscultural application, at least at the lower stages (Edwards, 1977; Snarey, 1987). Problems with the theory also exist, however. For one thing, there is very little evidence that many people (including adults) operate at the higher stages of moral reasoning that Kohlberg describes (Colby & Kohlberg, 1984).

FIGURE 6.9
Kohlberg's stages of moral development.

Level 1	Preconventional Morality **1. Obedience and Punishment Orientation** **2. Naive Egotism and Instrumental Orientation**	—Rules are obeyed simply to avoid punishment; "If I take the cookies, I'll get spanked." —Rules are obeyed simply to earn rewards; "If I wash my hands, will you let me have two desserts?"
Level 2	Conventional (conforming) Morality **3. Good Boy/Girl Orientation** **4. Authority-maintaining Orientation**	—Rules are conformed in order to avoid disapproval and gain approval; "I'm a good boy 'cause I cleaned my room, aren't I?" —Social conventions blindly accepted to avoid criticism from those in authority; "You shouldn't steal because it's against the law, and you'll go to jail if the police catch you."
Level 3	Postconventional Morality **5. Contractual-legalistic Orientation** **6. Universal Ethical Principle Orientation**	—Morality based on agreement with others to serve the common good and protect the rights of individuals; "I don't like stopping at stop signs, but if we didn't all obey traffic signals, it would be difficult to get anywhere." —Morality is a reflection of internalized standards; "I don't care what anybody says, what's right is right."

A rather strong argument has been raised concerning Kohlberg's theory as it applies to women (Ford & Lowery, 1986; Gilligan, 1982). All of Kohlberg's original data came from the responses of young boys, remember. Later, when young girls were tested, some studies seemed to suggest that girls showed slower, more retarded moral development when compared to boys. Carol Gilligan's argument is that the moral reasoning of females is neither slower nor faster so much as it is *different* from the reasoning of males. Males, concerned with rules, justice, and an individual's rights, simply approach moral dilemma problems differently than do females, who are characteristically more concerned with caring, personal responsibility, and interpersonal relationships (Gilligan, 1982). Gilligan's book has brought a new slant to research on morality and value development in general. The issue is not a judgmental one in the sense of trying to determine if men are more or less moral in their thinking than women. The question is whether or not women and men develop different styles of moral reasoning and/or different types of moral behaviors.

BEFORE YOU GO ON **Briefly summarize the stages of Kohlberg's theory of moral development.**

With birth, the neonatal period begins. As we have seen, this period is one of great development and growth. Although a number of useful reflexes and sensory capacities are available to the newborn, interaction with the environment shapes and modifies the developmental process. A number of theories concerning the patterning of cognitive and social development have stimulated research in child psychology. So far, we have reviewed Piaget's theory of cognitive development, Erikson's theory of psychosocial development, and Kohlberg's theory of moral development. We now turn our attention to adolescence—a time of intense growth and learning.

ADOLESCENCE

adolescence
the developmental period between childhood and adulthood, often begun at puberty and ending with full physical growth—generally between the ages of 12 and 20

The period of development that we call **adolescence** is an exciting one. It is filled with discovery, turmoil, growth toward independence, and the beginning of lifelong commitments. It is clearly a period of transition—from the dependence of childhood to the independence of adulthood. It is very difficult, however, to specify exactly when adolescence begins or when it ends.

We may choose to define adolescence in biological terms. In that case, adolescence begins with the onset of puberty (with sexual maturity and a readiness to reproduce) and ends with the end of physical growth. An individual's developing sexuality and physical growth certainly have psychological implications that need to be addressed, but there are other ways of defining adolescence.

A more psychological perspective to this period emphasizes the development of the cognitions, feelings, and behaviors that characterize adolescence. This approach views adolescence "as a psychological process occurring within the individual" (Forisha-Kovach, 1983, p. 8). Psychological

Adolescent boys often seem gangly, awkward, and clumsy as different parts of their bodies grow at different rates and at different times.

approaches emphasize the development of problem-solving skills, and an increased reliance on the use of symbols, logic, and abstract thinking. Such approaches also stress the importance of identity formation, and a developing appreciation of self and self-worth.

It is also possible to think about adolescence from a social perspective by examining the role of adolescents in society (Kett, 1977). Such views generally define adolescence in terms of being in between—not yet an adult, but no longer a child. In this context, the period usually lasts from the early teen years through one's highest level of education, when the individual is thought to enter the adult world. In this case, we can see that the limits of adolescence may presently be changing as more and more youngsters opt to go on to college right after high school, still maintaining contact with and dependence on family and other support groups developed during the teen years.

Actually, whether we accept a biological, psychological, or social approach to defining adolescence, we usually are talking about people between the ages of approximately 12 and 20. Some psychologists consider this period in terms of growth and positive change, others view adolescence as a period of great turmoil, stress, rebellion, and negativism (Conger & Peterson, 1984). Adolescence may very well be fraught with conflict, storm, and stress, but it is a period of adjustment that most of us manage to survive quite well. In fact, the picture of the troubled, rebellious, difficult, uncooperative adolescent is probably more of a social stereotype than a reality (Garbarino, 1985; Manning, 1983; Offer & Offer, 1975).

How might adolescence be defined from a physical, social, and psychological point of view?   **BEFORE YOU GO ON**

Physical Changes in Adolescence

The onset of adolescence is generally marked by two biological or physical changes. First, there is a marked increase in height and weight, known as a **growth spurt,** and second, there is sexual maturation.

The growth spurt of early adolescence usually occurs in girls at an earlier age than it does in boys. Girls begin their growth spurt as early as 9 or 10 years of age and then slow down at about age 15. Boys generally show their increased rate of growth between the ages of 12 and 17 years. Indeed, males usually don't reach their adult height until their early 20s, whereas girls generally attain their maximum height by their late teens (Roche & Davila, 1972; Tanner, 1981). Figure 6.10 illustrates one way to represent the adolescent growth spurt in graphic form.

At least some of the potential psychological turmoil of early adolescence may be a direct result of the growth spurt. It is not uncommon to find increases in weight and height occurring so rapidly that they are accompanied by real, physical growing pains, particularly in the arms and legs. Unfortunately, the spurt of adolescent growth seldom affects all parts of the body uniformly—especially in boys. Thirteen- and 14-year-old boys often appear to be incredibly clumsy and awkward as they try to coordinate their large hands and feet with the rest of their body. One of the most noticeable areas of growth in boys is that of the larynx and vocal cords. As the vocal cords grow and lengthen, the pitch of the voice is lowered. Much to the embarrassment of many a teenaged boy, this transition is seldom a smooth one, and he may suffer through weeks or months of a squeaking, crackling change of pitch right in the middle of a serious conversation (Adams, 1977; Adams & Gullotta, 1983, pp. 103–107).

With the onset of **puberty,** there is a noticeable increase in the production of the sex hormones, primarily the androgens in males and the estrogens in females. In fact, all of us have both androgens *and* estrogens in our bodies. Males simply have more androgens, and females have more estrogens. Boys seldom know when puberty begins for them. For some time they have been experiencing penile erections and nocturnal emissions of seminal fluid. Biologically, we say that puberty in males begins with the appearance of live sperm in the testes and ejaculate of males, and most males have no idea when *that* happens—such determinations require a laboratory test.

With females, puberty is quite noticeable. It is indicated by the first menstrual period, called **menarche.** With puberty, both boys and girls are ready, in a biological sense, to reproduce. However, coming to deal with that readiness and making the adjustments that we associate with psychological maturity do not come automatically with sexual maturity.

By now you should realize that the ages we indicate for the beginning and ending of major developmental periods vary considerably from person to person. Such is also the case for puberty. Many boys and girls reach puberty before or after most of their peers, or age mates, and are referred to as early or late bloomers. Reaching puberty well before or after others of one's age does have some psychological effects, although few are long-lasting. Let's first get an idea of what early and late puberty means. Figure 6.11 depicts the age ranges during which the major developments associated with puberty may be expected to occur. In some cases, the age range is quite large.

growth spurt
a marked increase in both height and weight that marks the onset of adolescence

puberty
the stage of physical development at which one becomes capable of sexual reproduction

menarche
a female's first menstrual period, often taken as a sign of the beginning of adolescence

FIGURE 6.10
Females begin their main growth spurt at around age 10, while the growth spurt in males does not begin until about age 12. In general, males will grow faster and for a longer period of time than females.
(After Tanner, Whitehouse, & Takaishi, 1966.)

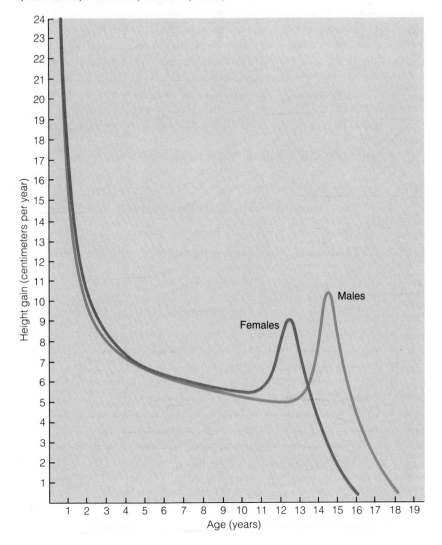

What are the advantages and disadvantages of early maturation? An early blooming girl will probably be taller, stronger, faster, and more athletic than other girls (and many of the boys) in her class at school. She is more likely to be approached for dates, to have more early sexual encounters, and to marry at a younger age than her peers. She may have problems with her self-image, particularly if she puts on extra weight and shows marked breast development (Conger & Peterson, 1984). She is likely to be rated as below average in prestige, popularity, leadership skills, and poise (Jones, 1971), although there seems to be no advantage or disadvantage with regard to objective measures of intellectual functioning (Duke et al., 1982).

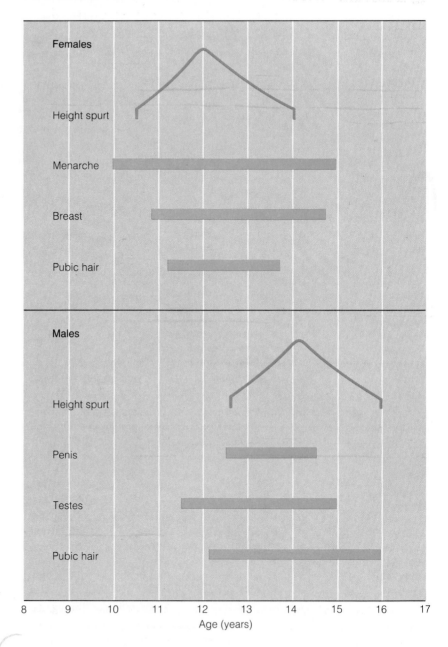

FIGURE 6.11
These graphs illustrate the ages at which certain physical changes occur in the average male and female during puberty.
(After Tanner, 1973.)

Because of the premium put on physical activity in boys, the early maturing boy is at a greater advantage than the early maturing girl. He will have more dating and sexual experiences than his age mates, which will raise his status among his peers.

For young teenagers of both sexes, being a late bloomer is more negative in its impact than being an early bloomer (Gross & Duke, 1980). There is some evidence (for example, Jones, 1957) that late-maturing boys carry a sense of inadequacy and poor self-esteem into adulthood. Late maturity for girls seems to have little long-term negative consequence. Some feel—at least in retrospect—that being a late bloomer was an advantage because it offered them an opportunity to develop other, broadening interests, rather than becoming "boy-crazy" like so many of their peers in early adolescence (Tobin-Richards et al., 1984). Summary generalizations are often dangerous, but we may suggest that (1) early maturity is more advantageous than late maturity, at least at the time of one's adolescence, and (2) boys profit from early maturity more than do girls, but they may also suffer more from late maturity.

With all of the physical and physiological changes that occur in early adolescence, it is easy to see why G. Stanley Hall, in the first textbook written about adolescence, was moved to describe the period as one of "second birth" (Hall, 1905).

Briefly describe the physical changes that accompany the beginnings of adolescence.   BEFORE YOU GO ON

Cognitive and Social Development in Adolescence

Adolescence is a developmental period that is marked by the stage of formal operations in Piaget's theory of cognitive development and by the stage of identity formation in Erikson's theory of psychosocial development. According to Piaget, in adolescence one is now able to think abstractly and to imagine, to think about what *is,* and to ponder what *might be.* This new, higher level of mental operations often gets turned toward self-analysis, toward a contemplation of one's self in a social context (Keating, 1980). In this section, we'll examine four issues related to cognitive and social processes in adolescent development: identity formation, adolescent egocentrism, the influence of family, and teenage suicide.

Identity Formation.   Adolescents give the impression of being great experimenters. They experiment with hair styles, music, religions, drugs, sexual outlets, fad diets, part-time jobs, part-time relationships, and part-time philosophies of life. In fact, it often seems that teenagers' commitments are made on a part-time basis. They are busily trying things out, doing things their way, off on a grand search for Truth.

This perception of adolescents as experimenters is not without foundation. It is consistent with the view that one of the major tasks of adolescence is the resolution of an **identity crisis**—the struggle to define and integrate the sense of who one is, what one is to do in life, and what one's attitudes, beliefs, and values should be. During adolescence, we come to grips with many questions: "Who am I?" "What am I going to do with my life?" "What is the point of it all?" Needless to say, these are not trivial questions. A person's search for his or her identity may lead to conflicts. Some of these conflicts may be resolved very easily, some continue into adulthood.

As we saw earlier, the concept of identity formation is associated with the personality theorist Erik Erikson (1963). For Erikson, the search for identity

identity crisis
the struggle to define and integrate one's sense of self, and what one's attitudes, beliefs, and values should be

Attending a life management class as these 8th graders are doing is one way to at least discuss and maybe resolve some of the issues they face as adolescents.

is the fifth of eight stages of psychosocial development (see Figure 6.8). It is the stage that occurs during the adolescent years. For many youngsters, adolescence brings very little confusion or conflict at all in terms of attitudes, beliefs, or values. Many teenagers are quite able and willing to accept without question the values and sense of self that they began to develop in childhood.

For many teenagers, however, the conflict of identity is quite real. They have a sense of giving up the values of parents and teachers in favor of new ones—their own. On the other hand, physical growth, physiological changes, an increased sexuality, and perceived societal pressures to decide what they want to be when they "grow up" may lead to what Erikson calls *role confusion.* Wanting to be independent, to be one's own self, often does not fit in with the values of the past, of childhood. Hence, the teenager tries to experiment with different possibilities in an attempt to see what works out best, occasionally to the dissatisfaction of bewildered parents.

BEFORE YOU GO ON **Summarize the adolescent's search for identity as described by Erikson.**

Adolescent Egocentrism. Egocentrism—a focusing on one's self and an inability to take the point of view of others—was used by Piaget to describe part of the cognitive functioning of young children (between the ages of 2 and 6) during the stage of preoperational thought. David Elkind (1967, 1981, 1984) uses the term egocentrism in a slightly different way. In **adolescent egocentrism,** not only do individuals engage in self-centered thinking, but they also come to believe that virtually everyone else is thinking about them too. Because they can now think abstractly, adolescents begin to think about the thoughts of others and have a tendency to believe that they are usually the focus of the attention. Needless to say, adolescent egocentrism often leads to a heightened sense of self-consciousness.

adolescent egocentrism
self-centered cognitions, plus the belief that one is the center of others' attention

Elkind proposes two particular manifestations of adolescent egocentrism. For one thing, teenagers often feel that they are constantly "on stage," performing. They become quite convinced that when they enter a room, everyone is watching them and making judgments about everything—from what they are wearing to how their hair is styled. Now, in truth, it may be that no one is watching, but the youngster believes that they are. Elkind calls this the construction of an *imaginary audience.* Coming to think that everyone is watching and analyzing you is explanation enough for the extreme self-consciousness of many young teens, argues Elkind (Elkind & Bowen, 1979).

Adolescents often tend to overemphasize their own importance. They are, after all, the focus of their own attention, and given their imaginary audience, they feel they're the focus of everyone else's attention as well. As a result, they tend to develop some rather unrealistic cognitions about themselves, which Elkind calls *personal fables.* These are essentially stories about themselves that teenagers generate, often on the basis of irrational beliefs. They come to believe (egocentrically) that no harm can come to *them. They* won't become addicted after trying a drug at a party. *Their* driving won't be affected by alcohol consumption. *They* won't get pregnant. Those sorts of things happen to others. These sorts of beliefs (cognitions) can be dangerous, of course, and they can be the source of considerable parental aggravation. Let's now briefly consider some parental influences on the developing adolescent.

The Influence of the Family.   No matter what label we give it, one of the major processes involved in adolescence is separating in some real way from one's family. With the emergence of one's own identity comes independence and autonomy. The resulting conflict for teenagers is often very real. On the one hand, they want to become autonomous and strike out on their own. At the same time, they sense a sadness, and even fear over giving up the security of home and family.

How adolescents resolve conflicts they have with their parents often hinges significantly on what is termed *parental style*. Psychologists have identified three major approaches used by parents in dealing with their adolescent children. (We should point out quickly that few parents adopt and use one and only one style.) The *authoritarian style* of parenting decrees that, "you should do so, because I said so!" As often as not, the adolescent isn't even allowed to express his or her beliefs. The teenager is seen as a member of low standing in family affairs. Not surprisingly, this style of parenting behavior often leads to rebellion, alienation, and more conflict. On the other hand, the authoritarian style can lead to submissiveness and conformity, which, for the emerging teenager, is maladaptive. The style of parenting called *permissive* is in many ways at the other extreme from the authoritarian style. Here, the teenager has an almost free rein. Parents are supportive, but set few limits. The style most recommended is usually called *democratic.* Here, parents act as experts, give advice, and do set limits, but they also consult with the teenager, allow some independence of choice, and involve the teenager in decision making.

Most teenagers feel that their parents use a democratic type, and they

A democratic parental style involves more interaction between parents and teenagers. Parents give advice and consult with teenagers, who are able to participate in decision-making.

value that style (Kelly & Goodwin, 1983). Reports of family difficulties with adolescents can often be traced to either an overly authoritarian or overly permissive style (Baumrind, 1978; Collins, 1982).

We next turn to an outcome of adolescent development of importance to all of us: suicide.

BEFORE YOU GO ON   How may parenting style affect adolescent development?

Teenage Suicide.   The death of any young person is a tragic and sad occurrence. When that death is the result of suicide, our emotional reaction is often magnified. As a final solution to perceived problems, suicide is certainly final, but it solves little. Rates of successful and failed suicide attempts among the young are definitely on the increase (for example, Curran, 1987). Holinger (1978) estimates a 131 percent increase in successful suicide attempts between 1961 and 1975. Colt (1983) claims a 300 percent increase since 1960. Peck (1982) suggests that more than one million adolescents harbor serious thoughts of suicide each year. After accidents and murder, suicide is the third leading killer of teenagers.

In an effort to determine why so many young people turn to suicide, Bem Allen recently surveyed the research literature and came up with a number of helpful insights (Allen, 1987). Allen suggests that there are many general *determinants* of suicide. These are broad, predisposing factors. In addition, there are a number of *predictors* of suicide, which usually are found through

---

FIGURE 6.12
Some of the general determinants of suicide among adolescents. (List modified from Allen, 1987.)

Predisposing Factors (general background variables)

1. **Family:** Family problems such as divorce, poor communication, imposition of many restrictions, and alcoholism rank high; alcohol use in the family may be more important than alcohol use by the youngster
2. **Peers:** Isolation or peer relations in conflict
3. **Birth trauma:** (Surprisingly) difficulty at or soon after birth may predispose for later problems
4. **Personal factors:** Low self-esteem; drug/alcohol use; loss of girl/boyfriend; poor academic performance; loss or lack of a confidant; depression (which is NOT necessary, but the best single predictor); SEX (most attempts are by females, most successes by males)
5. **Technological advance:** Technology provides an ever-increasing number of choices, but not necessarily the means to best choose, leading to helplessness, perhaps despair
6. **Acceptance of suicide:** Exposure may lead to desensitization, making it an acceptable alternative
7. **Mobility and rootlessness:** Fosters a lack of long-term relationships that could be used for support

---

Predictors (diagnoses from psychological tests)

1. **Depression:** Many measures of depression are related to suicide, but thinking about suicide need not be premised on depression
2. **Locus of control:** A reliance on the belief that one's life is under the control of others, including fate and chance
3. **Hopelessness:** May be more important than depression, perhaps even being the cause of depression

---

Precipitating Events (factors that lead directly to suicide attempts)

1. **Clustering:** Implies that suicide is virtually "contagious," seems to be of recent vintage; perhaps conveys notion that suicide is acceptable, or the "thing to do;" why suicides sometimes occur in clusters remains a mystery
2. **Independent traumatic events:** Things beyond the control of the individual, such as: death of a close friend or relative, parental divorce, loss of confidant through no fault of the individual, sudden economic setback
3. **Nonindependent events:** Events initiated by the suicidal individual, such as: drug or alcohol consumption, acquisition of a lethal weapon, pregnancy out of wedlock, "accidents" resulting from deliberately dangerous behaviors, and the disruption of close relationships

---

some sort of psychological testing or assessment. And finally, there are *precipitating events* that may lead directly to an attempt at suicide. These determinants, predictors, and precipitating events are summarized in Figure 6.12.

What can be done even to begin to stem the tide of teenage suicide? Allen (1987) suggests a number of things can be done, and most revolve around *education.* First, we all most realize that suicide among teenagers *is* a real and present problem, and we must bring discussions of suicide out into the open. In addition, we must all learn the signs and symptoms of impending suicide. Peers must be educated to be good and open listeners and to suggest therapy and professional help for friends and acquaintances who may be contemplating suicide. When one considers the cost in terms of grief, as well as in terms of lost human resources, there is ample reason for our commitment to efforts to mount a national campaign against suicide.

List some of the factors that indicate the potential for suicide among teenagers.   **BEFORE YOU GO ON**

ADULTHOOD

Growth and development are life-long processes. The changes that occur during our adult years may not seem as striking or dramatic as those that typify our childhood and adolescence, but they are no less real. Many of the adjustments that we make as adults may go unnoticed by others as we accommodate physical changes and psychological pressures. As adults, the status of one's health may become a real concern for the first time. Psychological and social adjustments need to be made to marriage, parenthood, job and career, the death of friends and family, retirement, and, ultimately, one's own death.

Our adult lives end with our deaths. Just when adulthood begins is difficult to say. In a legal sense, adult status is often granted by governments—at age 18 for some activities or at age 21 for others. Psychologically speaking, adulthood is marked by two possibilities that at first seem almost contradictory: (1) *independence,* in the sense of taking on responsibility for one's actions and no longer being tied to parents, and (2) *interdependence,* in the sense of building new commitments and intimacies in interpersonal relationships.

Following the lead of Erikson (1968) and Levinson (1974, 1986), we'll consider adulthood to be comprised of three overlapping periods, eras, or seasons: early adulthood (roughly ages 18 to 45), middle adulthood (approximately 45 to 65), and late adulthood (over 65). Conceptualizing adult development in this way may mislead us, so we must be careful. Although there is support for the notion of developmental stages in adulthood, these stages may be better defined by the individual adult than by the developmental psychologist (Datan, et al., 1987). In fact, a number of psychologists find little evidence for orderly transitions in the life of adults at all (Costa & McCrea, 1980; McCrea & Costa, 1984), while others find that there are significant sex differences in what determines the stage or status of one's adult life (Reinke et al., 1985).

Early Adulthood

If anything marks the transition from adolescence to adulthood it is choice and commitments independently made. The sense of identity fashioned during adolescence now needs to be put into action. In fact, the achievement of a strong sense of self by early adulthood is an important predictor of the success of intimate relationships later in adulthood (Kahn et al., 1985). With the attainment of adult status, there are new and often difficult choices to be made. Advice may be sought from elders, parents, teachers, or friends, but as adults, individuals make their own choices. Should I get married? Should I stay single? Perhaps I should live with someone. Should I get a job? Which one? To what sort of career shall I devote my life? Do I need more education? What sort of education? Where? How? Should we have children? How many? When? Now, while we're young, or should we wait until we're more experienced and have our careers established? Many of these issues are first addressed in adolescence, during identity formation. But, for the adult, these questions are no longer abstract. They are very real questions that demand some sort of response.

Levinson (1986) calls early adulthood the "era of greatest energy and abundance and of greatest contradiction and stress" (p. 5). In terms of physical development, we are at something of a peak during our 20s and 30s, and we're apparently willing to work hard to maintain that physical conditioning (McCann & Holmes, 1984; Shaffer, 1982). On the one hand, young adulthood is a season for finding our niche, for working through the aspirations of our youth, for raising a family. On the other hand, it is a period of stress, taking on parenthood, finding and maintaining the "right" job, and keeping a balance among self, family, job, and society at large. Let's take a brief look at two important decision-making processes of young adulthood, the choice of mate and family life and the choice of job or career.

Marriage and Family.   It is Erikson's claim (1963) that early adulthood revolves around the basic choice of *intimacy versus isolation.* A failure to establish close, loving, or intimate relationships is said to result in loneliness and long periods of social isolation. Marriage is certainly not the only source of interpersonal intimacy, but it is still the first choice for most Americans. More young adults than ever before are postponing marriage plans, but fully 95 percent of us do marry (at least once). In fact, we are more likely to claim that happiness in adult life depends more on a successful marriage than any other factor, including friendship, community activities, or hobbies (Glenn & Weaver, 1981).

Individuals reach the point of being ready to marry at different ages. Some may decide to marry simply because they perceive that it is the thing to do. Others choose marriage as an expression of an intimacy that has already developed (Stinnett, 1984). In addition to the choices of *when* (and *how*) to marry, of no small consequence is the choice of *who* to marry. If we have learned nothing else about the choice of marriage partners over the last 30 years, it is that mate selection is a complex process.

There are at least three factors that influence the choice of a marriage partner (Newman & Newman, 1984). The first deals with availability. Before we can develop an intimate relationship with someone, there needs to be the opportunity to develop the relationship in the first place. Availability is one

Although more young adults than ever before are postponing marriage plans, about 95 percent of us do marry at least once.

FIGURE 6.13
Characteristics sought in mates (From Buss & Barnes, 1986.)

Rank (most important)	Male choices	Female choices
1	kindness and understanding	kindness and understanding
2	intelligence	intelligence
3	physical attractiveness	exciting personality
4	exciting personality	good health
5	good health	adaptability
6	adaptability	physical attractiveness
7	creativity	creativity
8	desire for children	good earning capacity
9	college graduate	college graduate
10	good heredity	desire for children
11	good earning capacity	good heredity
12	good housekeeper	good housekeeper
13	religious orientation	religious orientation

thing, eligibility may be another. Here, matters of age, religion, politics, and background come into play. Available and eligible, yes; now how about attractive? To a degree, attractiveness here means physical attractiveness, but as we all know, judgments of physical beauty often depend on who's doing the judging. In many ways, "attractiveness" also involves judgments about psychological characteristics such as understanding, emotional supportiveness, similarity in values and goals, and so on.

Psychologist David Buss has reviewed the available evidence on mate selection with a particular focus on the question of whether or not opposites attract (Buss, 1985). He concluded that, at least in marriage, they do not. He found that "we are likely to marry someone who is similar to us in almost every variable" (Buss, 1985, p. 47). Most important are matters of age, education, race, religion, and ethnic background (in order), followed by attitudes and opinions, mental abilities, socioeconomic status, height, weight, and even eye color. More than that, he found that men and women are in nearly complete agreement on those characteristics they commonly seek in a mate (Buss, 1985; Buss & Barnes, 1986). Figure 6.13 presents 13 such characteristics ranked by men and women. There is a significant *difference* in ranking for only two: good earning potential and physical attractiveness.

You should not conclude from this discussion that choosing a marriage partner is always a matter of making a sound, rational decision. Clearly it isn't. The truth is that many factors, including romantic love, affect such decisions. The fact that approximately 40 percent of all first marriages end in divorce and that, in the United States, 9.4 years is the average life-span of a marriage are unsettling reminders that the choices people make are not always the best. Just as men and women agree on what matters in choosing a mate, so do they agree on what matters in maintaining a marriage, listing first such matters as liking one's spouse as a friend, agreeing on goals, and a mutual concern for making the marriage work (Lauer & Lauer, 1985).

Beyond establishing an intimate relationship, becoming a parent is generally taken as a sure sign of adulthood. For many young couples, parenthood has become more a matter of choice than ever before because of more

Having a baby around requires new parents to make adjustments to their daily lives. As a result, they find themselves staying at home more often.

available means of contraception and new treatments for infertility. Having one's own family helps foster the process of *generativity* that Erikson associates with middle adulthood. This process reflects a growing concern for family and for one's impact on future generations (Chilman, 1980). Although such concerns may not become central until one is over 40, parenthood usually begins much sooner.

There is no doubt that having a baby around the house significantly changes established routines, often leading to negative consequences (Miller & Sollie, 1980). The freedom for spontaneous trips, intimate outings, and privacy is in large measure given up in trade for the joys of parenthood. As parents, men and women take on the responsibilities of new social roles— that of father and mother. These new roles of adulthood add to the already established roles of being a male or a female, a son or a daughter, a husband or a wife, and so on. There seems to be little doubt that choosing to have children (or at least choosing to have a large number of children) is becoming less and less popular (Schaie & Willis, 1986). Although many people still regard the decision not to have children as basically selfish, irresponsible, and immoral (Skolnick, 1978), there is little evidence that such a decision leads to a decline in well-being or life satisfaction later in life (Beckman & Houser, 1982; Keith, 1983).

Career Choice. By the time a person has become a young adult, it is generally assumed that he or she has chosen a vocation or life's work. With so many possibilities to choose from, this decision is often a difficult one to make. Selection of a career is driven by many factors; family influence and the potential for earning money are just two. In truth, most young adults are dissatisfied with their initial choice(s) (Rhodes, 1983; Shertzer, 1985).

Jeffrey Turner and Donald Helms (1987) suggest that choosing a career path involves seven identifiable stages. Let's review their list (which is based on Tiedeman & O'Hara, 1963):

1. *Exploration:* Here there is a general concern that something needs to be done, a choice needs to be made, but alternatives are poorly defined, and plans for making a choice are not yet developed. This period is what Daniel Levinson (1978) calls formulating a dream.
2. *Crystallization:* Now some actual alternatives are being weighed, plusses and minuses are associated with each possibility, and although some are eliminated, a choice is not made.
3. *Choice:* For better or worse, a decision is made. Now there is a sense of relief that at least one knows what one wants, and an optimistic feeling that everything will work out develops.
4. *Career clarification:* In this phase the individual's self image and career choice are meshed together. Adjustments and accommodations are made. Details are worked out. This is largely a matter of fine tuning one's initial choice, as in, "I know I want to be a teacher; now what do I want to teach, and to whom?"
5. *Induction:* The career decision is implemented. This presents a series of scary challenges to one's own values and goals.
6. *Reformation:* Here one finds that changes need to be made if one is to fit in with fellow workers and do the job as one is expected to do it.

7. *Integrative:* The job and one's work become part of one's self, and one gives up part of self to the job. This is a period of considerable satisfaction.

Occasionally, a person may make the wrong decision or a poor choice. This is most likely to happen, of course, in the third stage of choosing a career path, but probably won't be recognized until the fourth or fifth stage. In such cases, there is little to do but begin again and work through the process, seeking the self-satisfaction that comes at the final stage.

What developments may be said to characterize early adulthood?   **BEFORE YOU GO ON**

Middle Adulthood

As the middle years of adulthood approach, many aspects of life become settled. By the time most people reach the age of 40, their place in the framework of society is fairly well set. They have chosen their lifestyle and have grown accustomed to it. They have a family (or have decided not to).

They have chosen what is to be their major life work or career. "Most of us during our 40s and 50s become 'senior members' in our own particular worlds, however grand or modest they may be." (Levinson, 1986, p. 6.)

The movement to middle adulthood involves a transition filled with reexamination—at least for men (Levinson et al., 1974). During the middle years, one is forced to contemplate one's own mortality. The so-called middle-age spread, loss of muscle tone, facial wrinkles, and graying hair are evident each day in the mirror. At about the age of 40, sensory capacities and abilities begin to slowly diminish. Most people in this stage now notice obituaries in the newspaper where more and more people of the same age (or even younger) are listed every day.

For some people, perhaps for men more than women, the realization that time is running out produces something of a crisis, even approaching panic. For most, however, middle age is a time of great satisfaction and true opportunity (Rossi, 1980). In most cases, children are grown. Careers are in full bloom. Time is available as never before for leisure and commitment to community, perhaps in the form of volunteer work.

Robert Havighurst (1972) says there are seven major tasks that one must face in the middle years:

1. *Accepting and adjusting to the physiological changes of middle age:* Although there certainly are many physical activities that middle-aged persons can engage in, they sometimes must be selective or must modify the vigor with which they attack such activities.
2. *Reaching and maintaining satisfactory performance in one's occupation:* If career satisfaction is not attained, one may attempt a mid-career job change. And, of course, changing jobs in middle age is often more a matter of necessity than choice. In either case, the potential for further growth and development or for crisis and conflict exist.

By middle adulthood, most people have chosen careers and lifestyles and have more time for leisure activities.

3. *Adjusting to aging parents:* This can be a major concern, particularly for "women in the middle" (Brody, 1981) who are caring for their own children and parents at the same time. In spite of widespread opinions to the contrary, individual concern and responsibility for the care of the elderly has not deteriorated in recent years (Brody, 1985).

4. *Assisting teenage children to become happy and responsible adults:* During the middle years of adulthood, parents see their children mature into and through adolescence. Helping to prepare them for adulthood and independence (leaving the nest) becomes a task viewed with ambivalence.

5. *Achieving adult social and civic responsibility:* This task is very much like what Erikson calls the crisis of *generativity vs. stagnation.* People often shift from thinking about all that they have done with their life to considering what they will do with what time is left for them and how they can leave a mark on future generations (Erikson, 1963; Harris, 1983).

6. *Relating to one's spouse as a person:,* and

7. *Developing leisure-time activities:* Although all seven of these tasks are clearly related and interdependent, this is particularly true of these last two. As children leave home and financial concerns diminish, there is more time for one's spouse and for leisure. Taking advantage of these changes in meaningful ways provides a unique challenge for some adults whose whole lives have been previously devoted to children and career.

BEFORE YOU GO ON **What are some of the issues typically faced during the middle years of adulthood?**

Late Adulthood

The transition to what we are here calling late adulthood generally occurs in our early to mid-60s. Perhaps the first thing we need to realize is that persons over the age of 65 comprise a sizable proportion of the population in the United States. More than 25.5 million Americans are in this age bracket, and the numbers are increasing by an average of 1,400 per day (Kermis, 1984; Storandt, 1983). Given the fact that people are living longer, coupled with the declining birth rates in this country, it is no surprise that the U.S. population now includes a greater percentage of people over the age of 65 than ever before. In 1940, fewer than 4,000 Americans were more than 100 years old, but by 1986, nearly 40,000 reached that milestone. And this trend should continue for some time. By the year 2020, Americans over 65 will make up nearly 20 percent of the population (Eisdorfer, 1983).

Ageism is the name given to the discrimination or negative stereotypes that are formed on the basis of age. Ageism is particularly acute in our attitudes about the elderly. One misconception about the aged is that they live in misery. Yes, there are often some miseries that have to be attended to. Sensory capacities are not what they used to be. But, as Skinner (1983) suggests, "If you cannot read, listen to book recordings. If you do not hear well, turn up the volume of your phonograph (and wear headphones to

ageism
discrimination or negative stereotypes about someone formed solely on the basis of age

Many people who reach late adulthood use the time very productively. They look forward to visits with their grandchildren and continue to be active in organizations, such as a senior legislature.

protect your neighbors)." Many cognitive abilities suffer with age, but others are developed to compensate for most losses. Apparent memory loss may reflect more a choice of what one chooses to remember rather than an actual loss. There is no doubt that mental speed is lost, but the accumulated experience of years of living can, and often does, far outweigh any advantages of speed (Meer, 1986). Perhaps you will recognize this as yet another example of plasticity, a concept we first introduced in our discussion of early childhood development.

Yes, death becomes a reality. As many as 50 percent of the women in this country over 65 are widows. But many elderly people (3,000 in 1978) choose this time of their lives to marry for the *first time* (Kalish, 1982).

Yes, children have long since "left the nest," but they are still in touch, and now there are grandchildren with whom to interact. Moreover, the children of the elderly have themselves now reached adulthood and are more able and likely to provide support for aging parents. In fact, only about 5 percent of Americans over the age of 65 live in nursing homes, and fewer than 20 percent are unable to get around, to come and go as they please (Harris, 1975, 1983).

Yes, many individuals dread retirement, but most welcome it as an opportunity to do those things they have planned on for years (Haynes et al., 1978). Many people over 65 become *more* physically active after retiring from a job where they were tied to a desk all day long.

Although we often assume that old age necessarily brings with it the curse of poor health, a 1981 Harris survey tells us that only 21 percent of the respondents over age 65 claimed poor health to be a serious problem. That compares to 8 percent in the 18 to 54 age range and 18 percent in the 55 to 65 age range. So although health problems are more common, they are not nearly as widespread or devastating as we might think. (It should also be noted that poor health among the elderly is very much related to income and educational levels. For example, 31 percent of those with incomes below $5000 reported serious health problems.)

One of the findings of a 1975 Harris poll dispelled another myth of ageism: that old people are lonely. Eight percent claimed that they had no close person to talk to, but 5 percent of those surveyed who were younger than 65 agreed to the same statement. In short, old age is not as bad as we sometimes let ourselves believe; that is, it is not necessarily so.

To return one last time to Erikson, we find that his final stage of psychosocial development is reserved for this period beyond the age of 65. According to Erikson, it is at this stage that it is common for individuals to pause and reflect on their lives, what they have accomplished, the mark they have left, and what they might do with the time remaining. If all goes well with this self-examination, the individual develops a sense of *ego identity*—a sense of wholeness, an acceptance that all is well and can only get better. If self-examination results in regret, if life seems unfulfilled, with choices badly made, then one may face despair and turn only to death.

The concept of "successful aging" has been with us for some time. It is, however, a concept that seldom gets much attention, either in public policy or in psychological research. A recent article by John Rowe and Robert Kahn (1987) would have us do no less than change the entire focus of our study of human aging, particularly aging late in life. Most research, they argue, has focused on *average* age-related losses and deficits. Further, they claim that, "the role of aging per se in these losses has often been overstated and that a major component of many age-associated declines can be explained in terms of life style, habits, diet, and an array of psychosocial factors extrinsic to the aging process" (p. 143). What goes unnoticed is the variability in adjustments made by older persons. Rowe and Kahn's argument simply put is that the declines, deficits, and losses of the elderly are not the result of advanced age, but of factors over which we all can exercise some degree of control. The major contributors to decline in old age are nutrition, smoking, alcohol consumption, inadequate calcium intake, not maintaining a sense of autonomy and control over one's life circumstances, and lack of social support (so long as the support does not erode self control). Attention to these factors may not significantly lengthen the life span, but should extend what the authors call the "health span, the maintenance of full function as nearly as possible to the end of life" (p. 149).

Of the two sure things in life, death and taxes, the former is the surer. There are no loopholes. Dealing with the reality of our own deaths is the last major conflict or crisis that we face in life. As it happens, many people never have to deal with their own death in psychological terms. These are the people who die young or suddenly from natural or accidental causes. But many individuals do have the time to contemplate their own death and this usually takes place in late adulthood.

Much attention was focused on the confrontation with death in the popular book *On Death and Dying* by Elisabeth Kübler-Ross (1969, 1981). Her description of the stages that one goes through when facing death was based upon hundreds of interviews with terminally ill patients who were aware that they were dying. Kübler-Ross suggests that the process takes place in five stages: (1) *Denial*—a firm, simple avoidance of the evidence; a sort of, "No, this can't be happening to me" reaction. (2) *Anger*—often accompanied by resentment and envy of others, along with a realization of what is truly happening; a sort of "Why me? Why not someone else" reaction. (3) *Bargaining*—a matter of dealing, of barter, usually with God; a search for more time; a sort of "If you'll just grant me a few more weeks or months, I'll go to church every week; no, every day" reaction. (4) *Depression*—a sense of hopelessness that bargaining won't work, that a great loss is imminent; a period of grief and sorrow both over past mistakes and what will be missed in the future. (5) *Acceptance*—a rather quiet facing of the reality of death, with no great joy or sadness; simply a realization that the time has come

It turns out that the Kübler-Ross description is an idealized one—perhaps even too much so. Many dying patients do not seem to fit this pattern at all (Butler & Lewis, 1981). Some may show behaviors consistent with one or two of the stages, but seldom all five (Schultz & Alderman, 1974). There is some concern that this pattern of approaching death may be viewed as the "best" or the "right" way to go about it. The concern here is that caretakers may try to force dying people into and through these stages, instead of letting each face the inevitability of death in his or her own way (Kalish, 1976, 1985).

Although elderly people may have to deal with dying and death, they are generally less morbid about it than are adolescents (Lanetto, 1980). In one study (Kalish & Reynolds, 1976), adults over 60 did more frequently think about and talk about death than did the younger adults surveyed. However, of all the adults in the study, the oldest group expressed the least fear of death, some even saying they were eager for it.

BEFORE YOU GO ON   Summarize some of what we know about the elderly in this country.

After reading this chapter, you might now be quite impressed with how orderly and predictable human development can be. Neonates are born with a range of adaptive reflexes and sensory capabilities. Motor development progresses through identifiable stages. Cognitive development appears to progress through five stages, psychosocial development passes through eight stages, and moral development through six. Many of the conflicts of adolescence are predictable. Adulthood moves from choice to commitment to preparation for death.

As easy as it is to be impressed with the orderliness of human development, we must always remember not to take all of this too literally. Orderly sequences of development emerge from examining averages and progressions *in general.* Developmental trends and stages are like so many other things: If one looks hard enough, they can be found. But the individual differences that we see around us constantly remind us that for any one individual—child, adolescent, or adult—many of our observations may not hold true. The orderliness of development may very well exist only in the eyes of the observer. It is important to keep in mind that the picture we have drawn in this chapter is one of general conclusions to which there will always be exceptions.

SUMMARY

What is the epigenetic model, and what does it say about the nature-nurture controversy?

The epigenetic model is an interactionist position that suggests that psychological characteristics are the result of neither heredity nor the environment working alone. Rather, organisms develop through the interaction of one's genetic programming *and* one's experiences in the environment. At most, our nature sets limits on what our nurture may provide through development. / 241

What are some of the reflexes that can be observed in neonates?

Why do we care about neonatal reflexes?

Some reflexes have obvious survival value for the neonate; for example, the rooting reflex, in which the newborn turns toward a slight pressure on its cheek, the sucking reflex, or even the grasping reflex. Other reflexes, such as the Moro reflex (thrusting arms to the sides and then quickly bringing them back to the chest in reaction to a sudden noise or loss of support), or the walking reflex, seem to serve no particular function for the neonate but may be used to diagnose developmental delays or confirm normal physical development. / 243

Briefly summarize some of the landmarks of early motor development.

Although the particular age at which motor abilities develop does show considerable variability from child to child, the sequence is quite regular and predictable. In order, and with approximate ages, a child can hold his or her chin up at 2 months; reach for an object at 3 months; sit with support at 4 months; sit alone at 5.5 months; stand with help at 7.6 months; crawl at 10 months; walk if led at 9.2 months; stand alone at 11.5 months; walk alone at 12.1 months. / 244

Summarize the basic sensory capacities of the neonate.

The neonate's senses function quite well right from birth. The eyes can focus well at arm's length, although they will require a few months to focus over a range of object distances. Rudimentary depth perception seems to be present even in the neonate. Hearing and auditory discrimination are quite good, as are the senses of taste, smell, and touch. / 246

Cite an example that demonstrates more than a simple reflexive reaction by a neonate.

We have recently come to appreciate that neonates can demonstrate memory. They will attend to a new and different visual pattern after coming to ignore a familiar one, showing an appreciation of the difference between familiar and new. They show definite preferences for complex visual patterns over simple ones and seem most to prefer (attend to) visual representations of the human face. Even babies only one hour old make attempts to imitate the facial expressions of someone in their field of view. / 248

Briefly summarize some of the cognitive skills that develop during the sensorimotor stage.

During Piaget's sensorimotor stage of cognitive development, the child learns to develop schemas through an active interaction with the environment, by sensing and doing. The baby appreciates some cause and effect relationships, imitates the actions of others, and by the end of the period, develops a sense of object permanence. / 250

In Piaget's theory, what is meant by egocentrism?

Egocentrism is one of the most notable cognitive reactions during the preoperational stage of cognitive development. The child becomes very *me* and *I* oriented, unable to appreciate the world from anyone else's perspective or point of view. / 251

What cognitive skills might we expect from a child in the concrete operations stage of development?

In the concrete operations stage of cognitive development, the child organizes concepts into classes or categories and begins to use simple logic and to understand relational terms. The cognitive skills of conservation are not acquired until the end of the preoperational stage and mark the beginning of the concrete operations stage. Conservation involves understanding that changing something's form (rolling out a ball of clay, pouring liquid from one type container to another) does not change its essential nature. / 252

What cognitive ability characterizes the stage of formal operations?

The essential nature of the formal operations stage of cognitive development is the display of the ability to think and reason and solve problems symbolically or in abstract rather than concrete, tangible form. / 252

Cite two criticisms of Piaget's theory of cognitive development.

As influential as Piaget's theory of cognitive development has been, it has not escaped criticism. Two of the major criticisms of the theory are that (1) there is little actual evidence that cognitive abilities develop in a series of well-defined, sequential stages, (that is, the borders between stages are very poorly defined), and (2) preschool children in particular seem, in fact, to have more cognitive strengths and abilities than Piaget's methods seem to credit them with. / 253

According to Erikson, what are the four crisis stages of development that develop in childhood?

Of Erikson's eight stages, or crises, of development, four occur during childhood; (1) trust vs. mistrust, dealing with whether the child develops a sense of security or anxiety, (2) autonomy vs. shame and doubt, which deals with whether the child will develop a sense of self and competence or shame and doubt, (3) initiative vs. guilt, which deals with whether the child will gain confidence in his or her own ability or develop a sense of guilt and inadequacy, and (4) industry vs. inferiority, which deals with whether the child develops a sense of confidence in intellectual and social skills or develops a sense of failure and lack of confidence. / 254

Briefly summarize the stages of Kohlberg's theory of moral development.

Kohlberg proposes that one's sense of morality develops through three levels and six stages. First, one decides right from wrong on the basis of avoiding punishment and gaining rewards (preconventional morality), then on the basis of conforming to authority or accepting social convention (conventional morality), and finally on the basis of one's understanding of the common good, individual rights, and the internalization of standards (postconventional morality). Although much of the theory has been supported by research, there is little evidence that many individuals reach the higher levels of moral reasoning, and there may be serious deficiencies in applying the theory equally to both sexes. / 256

SUMMARY continued

How might adolescence be defined from a physical, social, and psychological point of view?

Adolescence may be defined in a number of ways. Physically, it is said to begin with puberty (attainment of sexual maturity) and last until the end of one's physical growth. Psychologically, it is defined in terms of the cognitions and feelings that characterize the period, searching for identity and abstract thinking. Socially, it is a marginal period, coming between childhood and adulthood, and is defined in terms of how others view the adolescent. / 257

Briefly describe the physical changes that accompany the beginnings of adolescence.

Two significant physical developments mark adolescence: a spurt of growth (seen at an earlier age in girls (9–15) than in boys (12–17)) and the beginnings of sexual maturity, a period called puberty. That is, as adolescents, individuals are for the first time physically prepared for sexual reproduction and begin to develop a number of secondary sex characteristics. / 261

Summarize the adolescent's search for identity as described by Erikson.

The search for one's identity—a sense of who one is and what one is to do with one's life—is, for Erikson, the major crisis of adolescence. Most teenagers do develop such a sense of identity, while some enter adulthood in a state of role confusion. / 262

What is adolescent egocentrism and how is it manifested?

When youngsters engage in adolescent egocentrism they think mostly about themselves and come to believe that everyone else is thinking about them also. It is demonstrated by the creation of an *imaginary audience* when the adolescent comes to feel that everyone is watching and that they are "on stage," performing for and being noticed by others. This form of egocentrism also leads to the creation of *personal fables* when the individual develops unrealistic, story-like cognitions in which harm comes only to others. / 263

How may parenting style affect adolescent development?

An adolescent's ability to deal with conflict and succeed at identity formation often reflects the predominant style of his or her parents. Psychologists have identified three such styles, authoritarian, permissive, and democratic. There is little doubt that the democratic parenting style best facilitates adolescent development. / 264

List some factors that indicate the potential for suicide among teenagers.

Suicide among adolescents has become a serious problem of national concern, as rates of suicide attempts continue to increase rapidly. There are many determinants, predictors, and predisposing events that may lead us to suspect suicide as a real possibility. Some of these include: family problems such as alcohol abuse or divorce, isolation from or conflict with peers, birth trauma, low self-esteem, loss of a confidant, poor academic performance, drug and/or alcohol use, lack of long-term relationships, depression, a belief that one's fate is out of one's control, a sense of helplessness, other suicides among teenagers, death of a close friend or relative, sudden economic setbacks, acquisition of a lethal weapon, and pregnancy out of wedlock. / 265

What developments may be said to characterize early adulthood?

Early adulthood (roughly ages 18 to 45) is a period characterized by commitments and choices independently made. One assumes new responsibilities, and is faced with a series of difficult decisions concerning career, marriage, and family. For Erikson, the period is marked by the conflict between intimacy and social relationships on the one hand and social isolation on the other. / 269

What are some of the issues typically faced during the middle years of adulthood?

In many ways, middle adulthood (roughly ages 45 to 65) defines a period first of reexamination and then of settling down to one's life goals. Entering into the period may be troublesome for some, but most find middle age a period of great satisfaction and opportunity. The individual comes to accept his or her own mortality in a number of ways. The tasks or issues of middle age involve one's changing physiology, one's occupation, one's aging parents and growing children, one's social and civic responsibilities, and one's spouse and leisure time. / 271

Summarize some of what we know about the elderly in this country.

There are now more than 25 million Americans over the age of 65, and the number of elderly is growing daily. Although there are often sensory, physical, and cognitive limits forced by old age, only 21 percent of elderly people rate health problems as a major concern (and one's economic status is a major predictor of problems in this area). Although some elderly persons are isolated and lonely, fewer than 5 percent live in nursing homes and only 8 percent consider themselves lonely. Older people are naturally concerned about death, but they are neither consumed nor morbid about it. It may be that with appropriate nutrition and diet, with the development of a healthy lifestyle, with proper social support, and with the maintenance of some degree of autonomy and control over one's life, "successful aging" can become more common than it is today. / 274

Chapter Six
Developmental Psychology

REVIEW QUESTIONS

1. To say that one ascribes to an epigenetic view of development implies that she or he:

a) will emphasize prenatal, genetic influences in development, not postnatal, environmental influences.

b) takes an interactionist position, claiming that development emerges, influenced by both the environment and genetics.

c) believes that embryonic development usually takes place within one year after birth.

d) holds that biological or genetic factors play virtually no role in the development of psychological traits.

This wordy item tests whether you recognize what is meant by the epigenetic model of development. This popular, interactionist position claims that both the environment and genetics are important determinants of development. It would not claim that either determinant predominates, and surely would not claim that the prenatal embryonic stage of development occurs at any time *after* birth. / 240

2. What may we conclude from experiments using the visual cliff apparatus?

a) Newborns are afraid of heights.

b) The sense of touch is last to develop in humans.

c) Although they cannot understand what is being said, even 3-day-old newborns can recognize their mother's voices.

d) The ability to perceive depth is established by the time a child is old enough to crawl.

The visual cliff is an apparatus used to test depth perception in the young. We suspect that very young children detect depth. They surely can by the time they are old enough to crawl. Alternative (c) is a true, but irrelevant statement. Alternative (b) is irrelevant and is also false—in fact touch is one of the first senses to develop. / 245

3. Robbie doesn't know what to make of the dry dog food he has just found in the kitchen closet. It doesn't smell or taste very good, and breaks apart when thrown or stepped on. Robbie's difficulty with the assimilation of dry dog food indicates that he is probably in Piaget's _____ stage of cognitive development.

a) formal operations.

b) sensorimotor.

c) preoperational.

d) concrete operations.

It is in the first of Piaget's stages, or the sensorimotor stage of cognitive development, that children find out about their world (assimilating dry dog food, for example), by sensing (smelling and tasting) and by doing (throwing and stepping on). The other stages then follow in order: preoperational, concrete operations, and formal operations. / 248

4. Which of the following has *not* been mentioned as a criticism of Piaget's theories of child development?

a) He overestimated the cognitive abilities of preschool children.

b) He underestimated the importance of language as a cognitive skill.

c) He overestimated the regularity with which children move from one stage of development to another.

d) He underestimated the abilities of 4 and 5 year olds to solve conservation problems.

As influential as Piaget's theories have been, they have not escaped criticism. Indeed, each of the statements made in this item have been cited as criticisms of Piaget's work except for the comment concerning the cognitive abilities of preschool children. In fact, Piaget *under*estimated these abilities by a wide margin. There are many negatives in this item; it needs to be read very carefully. Basically it asks: Which of the following is not true? / 253

5. Gilligan's major criticism of Kohlberg's developmental theory is that:

a) it is so closely tied to physical or biological development.

b) his conclusions were based only on Europeans.

c) it ignores the stages through which children and adolescents pass.

d) it is based on data collected only from boys and therefore incorrectly and unfairly draws conclusions concerning the orientations of girls.

Kohlberg's theory concerns moral development, and is not tied to physical or biological development at all. It is a theory that proposes that moral development passes through a series of identifiable stages. So alternatives (a) and (c) are clearly not correct. In fact, Kohlberg's theories of moral development are based on the reactions of a large number of subjects. Gilligan's major complaint, however, is that most of Kohlberg's theory is based on data collected only from boys. Girls, Gilligan argues, have a different system of developing morality. / 255

6. According to Erikson, one of the major struggles of adolescent development is identity formation. Failure to develop what Erikson calls a "comfortable sense of self as a person," leads to what he calls:

a) basic mistrust.

b) ego-integrity.

c) generativity.

d) role confusion.

The crisis of settling between basic trust and mistrust is associated with the very young, and is usually resolved by the age of 2 years. Ego-integrity vs. despair is a conflict found in late adulthood. Generativity (as opposed to stagnation) involves a focus beyond oneself to family and society and is associated with middle adulthood. If one does not develop an adequate sense of self in identity formation, the alternative is role confusion. / 262

7. With regard to selecting a marriage partner, which of the following is most *true*?

a) Opposites attract.

b) Wealthy people make better mates.

c) Men and women each look for very different characteristics in potential mates.

d) We tend to be most attracted to those who are most like us.

The answer here is the last alternative, which makes the first alternative quite wrong indeed. Although money, per se, is not an impediment to a successful marriage, it seems not to be a very important consideration for both men and women, who, by and large, tend to look for the same characteristics in potential mates. / 266

8. Among those Americans over the age of 65, poor health:

a) is reported to be a serious problem by more than 50 percent of those in this age group.

b) is directly related to socioeconomic and educational levels.

c) accounts for the fact that nearly 35 percent of those in this age group live in nursing homes.

d) evokes reactions of denial, anger, bargaining, depression, and acceptance.

Let's take these alternatives one at a time. A Harris poll tells us that 21 percent of those over the age of 65 report poor health as a serious problem, but 18 percent between the ages of 55 and 64 also report the same thing, so (a) is false. Alternative (b) is true—31 percent of those over the age of 65 with incomes below $5,000 report serious problems with poor health. Actually only about 5 percent of Americans over the age of 65 are in nursing homes, so (c) is false, and the reactions listed in (d) are those (proposed by Kübler-Ross) that persons go through when facing death, although poor health may evoke similar reactions. / 273

Chapter Seven

Motivation, Sexuality, and Emotion

Why We Care
Approaches to Motivation
    Approaches Based on Instincts
    Approaches Based on Needs and Drives
        Hull's Drive-reduction
        Maslow's Hierarchy
    Approaches Based on Incentives
    Approaches Based on Balance or Equilibrium
        Homeostasis
        Arousal
Physiologically Based Motivation
    Temperature Regulation
    Thirst and Drinking Behavior
        Internal, Physiological Cues
        External, Psychological Cues
    Hunger and Eating Behavior
        Internal, Physiological Cues
        External, Psychological Cues
Sex Drives and Sexual Behavior
    Internal, Physiological Cues
    External, Psychological Cues
    The Human Sexual Response
        Phase 1. Excitement
        Phase 2. Plateau
        Phase 3. Orgasm
        Phase 4. Resolution
    Homosexuality
    Sexually Transmitted Diseases
Psychologically Based Motivation
    Achievement Motivation
    Power Motivation
    Affiliation Motivation
    Competency Motivation
Emotion
    The Nature of Emotion
        Studying Emotion
        Defining Emotion
        Classifying Emotion
    Outward Expressions of Emotion
    Physiological Aspects of Emotion
        The Role of the Autonomic Nervous System
        The Role of the Brain

Try to remember what it was like to start grade school. Can you remember the excitement, the anticipation, the scary feeling of leaving home to go to school? It's unlikely that you had any specific educational or career goals in mind as you began your school years. After a few years in grade school, however, a definite goal begins to take shape for many youngsters: to get out of grade school and go to junior high.

"In junior high, they have different teachers and change classes and have athletics instead of recess and everything." Upon entering junior high school, you probably felt quite pleased with yourself; you had reached your goal. But soon, a new goal became clear in your mind: You wanted "to get out of junior high school and go to senior high school, with all the big kids."

As your final spring term approached in high school, you may have suffered from a common ailment: "senioritis." More than anything else, you wanted high school to be over with. You were motivated to finish to get out. What mattered then was a new goal: to go to college.

Well, here you are. You're in college. You're taking an introductory psychology course and have probably just recently begun your college career. If you're like many other students, a new goal may have entered your life: You want to get on with it; you want to get out of college so you can get a job. The goals have changed yet remained very much

---

In a way, to be a motivated organism is to be in a cycle.

---

the same: You want to finish the job at hand so that a new one can be attempted.

There are three points that can be made about this scenario, and they will be relevant throughout this chapter. (1) The chain of events we've described here certainly does not apply to everyone. It may not apply to you. There are any number of people who never had much desire to get out of junior high school and go

to high school. Many more have no desire or motivation to go to college. Getting out of high school, one way or another, was good enough for them; going to college was unthinkable. And not all college students enter college and immediately start dreaming about graduation—although that goal is clear in the minds of some. The point is that different people, even in the same situation, are often motivated by different needs and goals.

(2) A second point that this example makes about motivation is that it draws our attention to the *cyclical nature* of motivation. In a way, to be a motivated organism is to be in a cycle. Soon after one goal is reached (getting out of grade school, for instance), another often comes to take its place (getting out of junior high), and then another and another. Think of this motivational cycle in terms of something very basic, such as hunger and eating. If you are hungry, you are motivated to eat; getting something to eat is your goal. No matter how much you eat, however, you will not eat so much that you won't be hungry again. Soon the need for food and the goal of eating will reappear.

(3) A third point about this discussion is that motivational cycles imply no value judgment, no right or wrong, good or bad. Some students see the cyclical nature of motivation as downright depressing. "What's the point," they argue, "if everytime I finally reach a goal, there's just going to be another one there to take its place; I'll never be happy."

Such arguments miss an important point. In order for new goals to become established, old ones often need to be satisfied first. It may be true that many of us do not spend enough time reflecting on past goals achieved. Instead of focusing on how long it's going to take to graduate from college, reflect on the fact that you *have* graduated from high school. It is a good idea to remember how badly you wanted to do that and get into college.

Why We Care

In this chapter we will address some important practical issues. We are going to deal with questions concerning **motivation,** the process that arouses, directs, and maintains behavior. For the first time, our concern is with questions that begin with the word *why.* "Why did she *do* that (as opposed to doing nothing)?" "Why did she do *that* (as opposed to something else)?" "Why does she *keep* doing that (as opposed to stopping)?" Thus, the study of motivation deals with the origin of behaviors, the choice or direction of behaviors, the maintenance of behaviors, and, of course, the cessation of behaviors.

You certainly don't need a psychologist to convince you that motivation is an important concept in your daily life. We have already seen that motivation affects virtually everything we do. Motivation influences our ability to learn, affects our memory, and even has an impact on so basic a process as perception.

We'll get our discussion underway by considering some different ways in which psychologists have approached the study of motivation, and we'll define some basic terms. We will then review what we know about two different sorts of motives. First, we'll examine those that are related to our survival and are clearly rooted in our biology or physiology. Second, we'll examine those motives that are not rooted in biology, but that are more clearly learned and/or social in nature. In between, we'll consider the nature of sex drives, sexual behaviors, and human sexuality in general. We've placed our discussion of sexuality here to emphasize the observation that although sex drives surely have their bases in biology and physiology, the expression of those drives— at least in humans—is significantly affected by many learned, social, and psychological factors.

---

motivation
the process of arousing and directing behavior

Motivation deals with the issue of why we do things, and humans like to think of themselves as reasonable, rational, logical, intellectual organisms. We'd all like to think that our cognitive abilities—perceiving, learning, remembering, and problem solving cause us to do what we do. But if we were totally honest, we probably would admit that it is our *emotions* that affect us the most. We enjoy reflecting on our pleasant emotions and are concerned with finding ways to minimize our unpleasant emotions.

Some emotional reactions *are* quite unpleasant—fear, rage, jealousy, shame, and so on. Just the same, we would not want to give up our ability to experience emotions. To do so would be to surrender love, joy, satisfaction, and ecstasy. What causes us to become emotional and how we deal with our emotional reactions are important aspects of our identity, our personality.

We'll begin our discussion of emotion by examining how one might go about studying emotions scientifically, and we'll see that even defining and classifying emotional reactions have proven to be difficult tasks. Having laid a basic foundation for the topic, we'll then go on to summarize some of what we know about two active areas of research on emotions: how deep, inner feelings are outwardly expressed, and the nature of the physiological bases of emotionality.

APPROACHES TO MOTIVATION — Behavior

arousal
one's level of activation or excitement; indicative of a motivational state

An assumption that we make about motivation is that it is comprised of two subprocesses. First, we see motivation as involving **arousal,** or the activation of behavior and/or mental processes. Here we are using the term motivation in the sense of a force that initiates behaviors, that gets an organism to do something. The second process is that of providing *direction* or focus to one's behaviors. Here we are using the term motivation in the sense of answering the question, "Why did he or she do *that?*" In this sense, a motivated organism's behavior is viewed as being goal-directed and in some way purposeful.

From its earliest days, psychology has attempted to find a systematic approach, or theory, that could summarize and organize what different motives or motivational states have in common. In this section, we'll review some of these approaches in a somewhat chronological order. Don't be concerned about the fact that we occasionally refer to these approaches as "theories." All we mean to imply by doing so is that this matter is far from settled in psychology. There is no one approach to motivation that answers all our questions in such a way as to satisfy everyone. Even though each of the approaches summarized below may have its drawbacks, we should focus our attention on how each makes a contribution to our understanding of behavior and mental processes. Let us also draw your attention to Chapter 12, which includes a unit on different approaches to motivation, specifically those related to work motivation.

Approaches Based on Instincts ①

INSTINCT Theory

In the early days of psychology, behaviors were often explained in terms of innate **instincts.** Instincts are unlearned, complex patterns of behavior that occur in the presence of certain stimuli. They are inherited, or innate. Why do birds build nests? A nest-building instinct. Why do salmon swim upstream to mate? Instinct.

That may explain some of the behavior of birds and salmon, but what about people? William James (1890) reasoned that humans, being more complex organisms, had many more instincts than did "lower" animals.

No one expressed the instinctual explanation of human behaviors more forcefully than William McDougall (1908). He suggested that human behaviors were motivated by 11 basic instincts (repulsion, curiosity, flight, parental, reproductive, gregarious, acquisitive, constructive, self-abasement, pugnacity, and self-assertion). Soon he extended his list to include 18 instincts. As new and different behaviors required explanation, new and different instincts were devised to explain them.

As lists of human instincts got longer and longer, the basic problem with this approach became obvious. Particularly for humans, *explaining* behavior patterns by alluding to instinct simply renamed or relabeled them and didn't explain anything at all. But, lest we simply dispense with this approach totally, the psychologists who argued for instincts did introduce and draw attention to an idea that is still very much with us today—that we may engage in some behaviors for reasons that are basically physiological and more inherited than learned.

instincts
unlearned, complex patterns of behavior that occur in the presence of particular stimuli

Nest-building is an instinct present in birds. It is an unlearned, innate complex pattern of behavior.

Approaches Based on Needs and Drives ②

An approach that provided an alternative to explaining behavior in terms of instincts was one that attempted to explain the "whys" of behavior in terms of needs and drives. This approach, dominant in the 1940s and 1950s, is best associated with the psychologist Clark Hull (for example, Hull, 1943). We'll also take a brief look at the approach of Abraham Maslow, who also spoke of needs, but in a somewhat different way.

NEED AND DRIVE THEORY

Hull's Drive-reduction. In Hull's system, a **need** is a shortage or lack of some biological essential required for survival. Needs arise from deprivation. When an organism is kept from food, it develops a need for food. If deprived of water, a need develops. A need then gives rise to a drive. A **drive** is a state of tension, arousal, or activation. When an organism is in a *drive state,* it is motivated. It is aroused and directed to do something to reduce the drive by satisfying or eliminating the underlying need. The implication is that drives produce tensions that the organism then seeks to reduce, hence this approach is referred to in terms of (drive-reduction.)

This approach *is* less circular than a direct appeal to instincts. For example, having gone without food for some time, a need develops. The need for food may give rise to a hunger drive. Then what? Here is where learning and experience can come into play. Whereas instincts are directly tied to a specific pattern of behavior, needs and drives are not. They are concepts that can be used to explain why we do what we do, while still allowing for the influence of experience and the environment.

need
a lack or shortage of some biological essential resulting from deprivation

drive
a state of tension resulting from a need that arouses and directs an organism's behavior

need and drive are connected

There are a number of complications that arise with a drive-reduction theory of motivation. One complication concerns the relationship between the strength of a need and the strength of the drive that results from it. In general, as needs increase in strength, so do drives. But the relationship between needs and the drives that result from them is often complex. If you have ever been on a strict diet for a reasonable length of time, you may appreciate this point. When you first begin a diet, depriving yourself of food, a need develops, and so does a resulting hunger drive, which causes you to feel very hungry indeed. After a week or so on your diet, you may notice that you no longer feel quite as hungry as you did during those first few days. Your need for food may now be even greater than it was at first, but the drive is no longer quite as strong.

A second complication of a need-drive approach centers on the biological nature of needs. To claim that drives arise only from needs that arise from biological deprivations seems unduly restrictive.

It seems that not all of the drives that activate a person's behavior are based on biological needs. Humans often engage in behaviors to satisfy *learned* drives. Drives based on one's learning experiences are called *secondary drives,* as opposed to *primary drives,* which are based on unlearned, physiological needs. In fact, most of the drives that arouse and direct our behaviors have little to do with our physiology at all.

You may feel that you need a new car this year. Your friend may convince himself that he needs a new set of golf clubs, and you'll both work very hard to save the money to buy what you need. Although you both may say that you are "driven" to work for money, it is difficult to imagine how your car or your friend's golf clubs could be satisfying a biological need. A good bit of advertising is directed at trying to convince us that we "need" many products and services that will have very little impact on our survival.

Yet another related complication arises when we consider behaviors that organisms engage in even after all their biological needs are met. Skydivers jump out airplanes; mountain climbers risk life and limb to scale sheer cliffs of stone; monkeys play with mechanical puzzles even when solving the puzzles leads to no specific reward; children explore the pots and pans stored in kitchen cabinets even when repeatedly told not to. We might suggest, as some psychologists have, that these organisms are attempting to satisfy exploration drives, or manipulation drives, or curiosity drives. But when we do so, we run the risk of trying to explain why people behave as they do by generating an ever-increasing list of drives, which is the same sort of problem we have when we try to explain behavior in terms of instincts.

So what do all these complications mean? It does seem that people often behave to reduce drives and thus satisfy needs. Sometimes, drives are produced by biological, tissue needs, and we call these primary drives. At other times, the drives that arouse and direct our behaviors are learned or acquired, and we call these secondary drives. How drives are satisfied, or reduced, will reflect the learning history of the organism. Thus, the concepts of need and drive are useful ones and are still very much with us in psychology, but they cannot be taken as providing a complete explanation for motivated behaviors. Let's now turn to an approach to motivation that relies on the concepts of drives and needs and places them in a hierarchy of importance.

Activities ranging from mountain climbing to exploring around the house suggest that people often try to reduce a primary (biological) or secondary (learned) drive in order to satisfy certain needs.

Humanistic Approach

Maslow's Hierarchy.   Abraham Maslow's is one of the names we associate with the humanism movement in psychology (see the Introduction). Humanistic psychologists emphasize the person and his or her psychological growth. Maslow combined his concern for the person with Hull's drive-reduction theory and proposed that human behavior does in fact respond to needs. Not all of those needs are physiological, tissue needs, however. It was Maslow's belief that the needs that ultimately motivate human action are limited in number and hierarchically arranged (Maslow, 1943, 1970). Figure 7.1 summarizes this hierarchy of needs in pictorial form.

FIGURE 7.1
Maslow's hierarchy of needs.

Refers to becoming the best you can be.

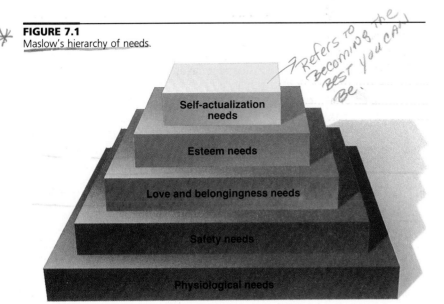

By participating in organized competitions, such as the International Games for the Disabled, disabled athletes are fulfilling what Maslow calls their self-actualization needs.

What this means is that Maslow's approach is essentially a stage theory. It proposes that the first things that motivate us are *physiological needs.* These include the basic needs that are related to survival—for example, the need for food, water, shelter, and so on. Until these needs are met, there is little reason to suspect that an individual will be concerned with anything else. But once physiological needs are under control, a person is still motivated, now by *safety needs*—the need to feel secure and protected from dangers that might arise in the future. We are thus motivated to see to it that the cupboard has food for later, that we won't freeze this winter, and that there's enough money saved to protect against sudden calamity. Notice here the hierarchical nature of this scheme. We're surely not going to worry about what we'll be eating tomorrow if there's not enough to eat today; but if today's needs *are* taken care of, we can then focus on the future and safety. And so the list goes on. One moves higher in the hierarchy only when lower needs are met. Ultimately, we may get to the highest level of needs in Maslow's hierarchy: *self-actualization needs.* These are the most difficult to achieve. We are self-actualizing when we become the best that we can be, when we are taking the fullest advantage of our potential as human beings. We are self-actualizing when we strive to be as creative and/or productive as possible.

In many ways, Maslow's arrangement of needs in a hierarchical fashion conforms to common sense. We can hardly expect someone to be motivated to grow and achieve "success" when they are concerned about their very survival on a day-to-day basis. When a person's needs for safety, belongingness, and esteem are reasonably fulfilled, they don't just stop behaving, unmotivated to do anything else.

However, as a comprehensive theory of human motivation, Maslow's hierarchy has some serious difficulties. Perhaps the biggest stumbling block is the idea that one can assign ranks to needs and put them in a neat order—regardless of what that order may be. It is quite clear that some persons are motivated in ways that violate the stage approach of this theory. Many individuals will, for example, freely give up satisfying basic survival needs for the sake of "higher" principles (as in hunger strikes). For the sake of love and belongingness, people may very well abandon their own needs for safety and security. It remains the case, however, that Maslow's hierarchical approach to human needs has found considerable favor both within and outside of psychology.

Approaches Based on Incentives

One alternative to a drive-reduction approach to motivation focuses not on what starts behavior, but on the *end state,* or goal, of behavior. According to this approach, external stimuli serve as motivating agents, goals, or **incentives** for our behavior. Incentives are external events that act to *pull* our behavior, as opposed to drives, which are internal events that *push* our behavior. Incentive theory frees us from relying on biological or physiological concepts to explain the "whys" of one's behaviors.

When a mountain climber says that he or she climbs a mountain "because it is there," the climber is indicating a type of motivation through incentive. After a very large meal, we may order a piece of cherry cheesecake, not because we need it in any physiological sense, but because it's there on

incentives
external stimuli that an organism may be motivated to approach or avoid

the dessert cart and looks so good. You may read this chapter because reading it will help you reach your goal of a good grade on the next exam. This is a good place to mention that some of our motivated behavior may occur not so much to enable us to reach positive goals as to escape or avoid negative goals. That is, some students may be motivated to read this chapter not to earn an "A" on their next exam, but to avoid getting an "F." The behaviors may be the same, but the incentives involved are clearly different.

Some parents want to know how to motivate their child to clean up his or her room. We can interpret this case in terms of establishing goals or incentives. What those parents *really* want to know is how they can get their child to value, work for, and be reinforced by a clean room. They don't necessarily want to motivate anyone. What they want is a clean room, and they would like to have the child clean it. If they want the child to be motivated to clean his or her room, the child needs to learn the value or incentive of having a clean room. You can imagine the child's response: "Why should I?" "Because I told you to" becomes the almost reflexive response. Now, *how* to teach a child that a clean room is a thing to be valued is, in fact, another story, probably involving other incentives that the child does value. For now, let's simply acknowledge that establishing a clean room as a valued goal is the major task at hand. Having a clean room is obviously not an innate, inborn need. The parents have learned to value clean rooms, and there is hope that their child can also learn to be similarly "motivated."

If this discussion of incentives sounds something like our discussion of operant conditioning (Chapter 4), you're right. Remember that the basic principle of operant conditioning is that one's behaviors are controlled by their consequences. We tend to do (are motivated to do) whatever leads to reinforcement (positive incentives), and we tend not to do whatever leads to punishment or failure of reinforcement (negative incentives).

Washing the dinner dishes is one of many chores that parents may assign to their children. The challenge is not only to motivate the child to wash the dishes but also to instill in him or her the value of the task.

How have the concepts of instinct, drive, and incentive been used to explain motivated behaviors?

Approaches Based on Balance or Equilibrium

A concept that has proved to be very useful in discussions of motivated behaviors is that of balance, or equilibrium. The basic idea here is that we are motivated or driven to maintain a state of balance. Sometimes balance involves physiological processes that need to be maintained at some level (or restricted range) of activity. Sometimes balance involves our overall level of arousal or excitement. Sometimes balance is required among our thoughts or cognitions; sometimes among our affective or emotional reactions. In this section, we'll briefly review two approaches to motivation that emphasize a basic, general drive or motive (in this context these two terms are synonymous) to maintain a state of equilibrium, or optimum level of functioning.

Homeostasis. One of the first references to a need to maintain a balanced state is found in the work of Walter Cannon (1932). Cannon was concerned with our internal physiological reactions, and the term he used to describe a state of balance or equilibrium within those reactions is **homeostasis**. The idea here is that each of our physiological processes has a normal, balanced, **set point** of operation. Whenever anything happens to upset this balance, we become motivated. We are driven to do whatever we can to return to our set, optimum, homeostatic level. If we drift only slightly from our set point, our own physiological mechanisms may act to return us to homeostasis without our intention or our awareness. If these automatic involuntary processes are unsuccessful, then we may take action, motivated by the basic drive to maintain homeostasis.

For example, everyone has a normal, set level of body temperature, blood pressure, basal metabolism (the rate at which energy is consumed in normal bodily functions), heart rate, and so on. When any of these are caused to deviate from their normal, homeostatic level, we become motivated to do something that will return us to our state of balance. Cannon's concept of homeostasis was devised to explain physiological processes. As we shall see in Chapter 11, however, the basic ideas of balance and optimum level of operation have been applied to social psychological processes as well.

Arousal. We have already defined arousal in terms of one's overall level of activation or excitement. A person's level of arousal may change from day to day and within the same day. After a good night's sleep and cold morning shower, your level of arousal may be quite high. (Your level of arousal may also be quite high as your instructor moves through your class handing out exams.) Late at night, after a busy day at school, your level of arousal may be quite low. Your arousal level is probably at its lowest when you are in the deepest stages of sleep.

Arousal theories of motivation (for example, Berlyne, 1960, 1971; Duffy, 1962; Hebb, 1955) claim that there is an optimal level of arousal (an arousal set point) that organisms are motivated to maintain. Drive reduction approaches, remember, argue that we are motivated to reduce the tension or arousal of drives by satisfying the needs that give rise to them. Arousal

homeostasis
a state of balance or equilibrium among internal, physiological conditions

set point
a normal, optimum level (or value) of equilibrium or balance among physiological or psychological reactions

In order to maintain a certain arousal level, we may seek out arousing, tension-producing activities such as a roller coaster ride.

FIGURE 7.2
For each task we attempt there is an optimal level of arousal. What that level is will depend on the task. In other words, it is possible to be *too* aroused (motivated) just as it is possible to be under aroused.
(After Hebb, 1955.)

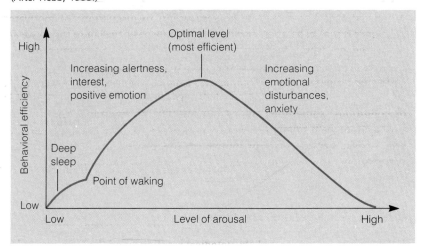

theories argue that sometimes we actually seek out arousing, tension-pro-ducing activities, motivated to maintain our optimal arousal level. If we find ourselves in a rut, bored, and tired, the idea of going to an action-adventure movie may seem like a good idea. On the other hand, if we've had a very busy and hectic day, just staying at home doing nothing may sound appealing. This approach is, of course, much like Cannon's idea of homeostasis, but in more general terms than specific physiological processes.

This point of view suggests that for any activity or situation, there is a "best," most efficient level of arousal. To do well on an exam, for example, requires that a student have a certain level of overall arousal. If a student is tired, bored, or just doesn't care one way or the other about the exam, we can expect a poor performance. If, on the other hand, a student is *so* worried, nervous, and anxious that she or he can barely function, we'll also predict a poor exam score. The relationship between arousal and efficiency is depicted in Figure 7.2.

Arousal theory also takes into account the difficulty or complexity of the task or the activity in which a person is engaged. That is, for very easy, simple tasks, a high level of arousal may be optimal, while that same high level of arousal would be disastrous for very difficult, complex tasks. This observation that optimum levels of arousal vary with the nature (difficulty) of a task can be traced back to an article published in 1908 by Yerkes and Dodson, even though the concept of arousal in the context of motivation did not appear in psychology until several decades later (Winton, 1987).

An interesting twist on the theory that we are motivated to maintain a set, optimal level of arousal is the observation that, for some as yet unknown reason, optimum levels of arousal may vary considerably from individual to individual. Some people seem to need and seek particularly high levels of arousal and excitement in their lives. They are what Marvin Zuckerman (1976, 1980) calls "sensation seekers." They enjoy skydiving or mountain climbing and may look forward to the challenge of driving in heavy city traffic. Others may actively avoid such situations, preferring instead quiet, more restful, low-excitement pursuits.

PHYSIOLOGICALLY BASED MOTIVATION

Now that we have reviewed some theoretical approaches to the motives that activate and direct our behaviors, we can turn our attention to a few specific examples. As you can imagine, this discussion could be organized in a number of different ways. We'll use a system that suggests that there are two major types of motivators: those that have a biological basis, which we will call *physiologically based*, and those that are more clearly learned or social in nature, which we'll call *psychologically based*. Although sex drives are clearly physiologically based, many human sexual behaviors are strongly influenced by social and psychological factors. For this reason, we treat sexuality as a separate topic.

There are two points for you to keep in mind as we go through this discussion. For one thing, remember that we are treating the terms *drive* and *motive* as synonyms. However, we will follow convention here and use the term *drive* for those activators of behavior that have a known physiological basis (for example, a hunger drive) and the term *motive* for those that do not (for example, a power motive). Second, you should note that even drives that are rooted in an organism's physiology can be affected by psychological processes. Hunger, for example, is clearly a physiologically-based drive, but what we eat, when we eat, and how much we eat are often influenced by psychological and social factors.

Temperature Regulation

Most of us seldom give our own body temperature much thought. We all have a fuzzy notion that 98.6°F is our normal, homeostatic body temperature. That body temperature has anything to do with motivation becomes sensible only in the context of homeostasis. Whenever anything happens to elevate or depress our body temperature above or below its homeostatic level, we become motivated. We become motivated to return our body temperature to its normal, balanced 98.6°.

Let's say you are outside on a very cold day, and you are improperly dressed for the low temperature and high wind. Soon your body temperature starts to drop. Automatically, your body starts to respond to do what it can to elevate your temperature back to its normal level: blood vessels in the hands and feet constrict, forcing blood back to the center of the body to conserve heat (as a result, your lips turn blue); you start to shiver, and the involuntary movements of your muscles create small amounts of heat energy.

As another example, imagine that you are walking across a desert, fully dressed, at noon on a day in August. Your temperature begins to rise. Automatically, blood is forced toward the body's surface. You begin to perspire, and the moisture on the surface of the skin evaporates, cooling the skin—all in an attempt to return your body's temperature to its very precise homeostatic level.

There are two centers in your brain that together act as a thermostat and instigate these attempts at temperature regulation. Both are located in the

When our body temperature is above or below its normal level, we are motivated to return our temperature to its normal 98.6°. Feeling cold may motivate you to put on more clothes before starting the long trek to the bus stop. Feeling hot may motivate you to douse yourself with water after running a long race.

hypothalamus deep inside the brain (see Figure 7.3). One center is particularly sensitive to elevated body temperatures, the other to lowered temperatures. Together they act to mobilize the internal environment when normal balance is upset.

If these automatic reactions are not successful, you may be motivated to take some voluntary action on your own. You may have to get inside, out of

hypothalamus
a small structure at the base of the brain involved in many drives, including thirst, hunger, sex, and temperature regulation

---

FIGURE 7.3
A number of small structures make up the limbic system, including the amygdala, septum hypothalamus, thalamus, and hippocampus.

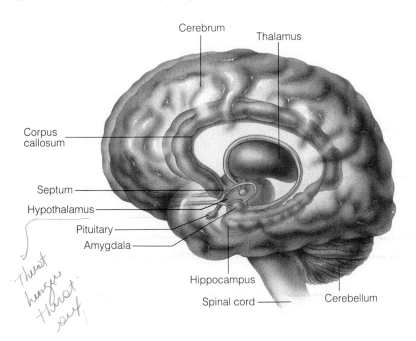

the cold or heat. You may need to turn on the furnace or the air conditioner. In fact, you may very well *anticipate* the lowering or raising of your body temperature and act accordingly—by putting on your coat before going outside on a blustery day, for example. Over and above what your body can do automatically, you may have to engage in (learned) voluntary behaviors in order to maintain homeostasis.

BEFORE YOU GO ON Given the concept of homeostasis, how might temperature regulation be thought of as a physiologically-based drive?

Thirst and Drinking Behavior

We need water for survival. If we don't drink, we die. As the need for water increases, it gives rise to a thirst drive. The intriguing issue is not so much that we need to drink, but how we *know* that we're thirsty. What actually causes us to seek liquid and drink it?

Internal, Physiological Cues.   For a very long time, we thought that we knew the simple answer to the question of why we drink: to relieve the discomfort caused by the dryness of our mouths and throats. No doubt, the unpleasantness of a dry mouth and throat *does* cause us to drink. But there must be more to drinking behavior than this.

Animals with no salivary glands, whose mouths and throats are constantly dry, drink no more than normal animals (more frequently, yes, but no more in terms of quantity). Normal bodily processes (urination, perspiration, exhaling, and so on cause us to lose about 2 1/2 liters of water a day (Levinthal, 1983). That water needs to be replaced, but how do we know when to do so?

About two-thirds of the fluid in our bodies is contained *within* our body's cells (intracellular), and about one-third is held in the spaces *between* cells

We drink because we need to, because we are driven by thirst to satisfy our needs for liquids.

(extracellular). There seem to be two separate mechanisms sensitive to losses of fluid, one associated with each of these areas. Intercellular loss of fluid is monitored by regions of the hypothalamus. One small center seems to "turn on" the thirst drive when fluid levels are low, and another center "turns off" thirst when fluid levels are adequate. Thirst that stems from extracellular fluid loss is monitored (in a complex chain of events) by the kidneys, which stimulate the production of a hormone that leads to a thirst drive.

Hypothalamus + Kidney

External, Psychological Cues.   Often our drinking is motivated by a physiological drive that arises from our physiological need for water. Sometimes, however, our drinking behavior may be influenced by external factors, or incentives. The implication here, as we have mentioned earlier, is that we may become motivated to drink, not in response to internal needs, but in response to external stimulation. For example, the aroma of freshly brewed coffee may stimulate us to order a second (unneeded) cup. A frosty glass of iced tea may look too good to refuse. We may drink a cold beer or a soda simply because it tastes so good, whether we *need* the fluid they contain or not.

Notice also that once motivated (in terms of being aroused), *what* we drink may be strongly influenced by our previous learning experiences. Some people prefer Coke, some prefer Pepsi, while others would choose a different brand. Some people do not like cola drinks at all. Choices and preferences for what we drink are shaped by availability (people from New England do not regularly drink coconut milk) and past experience.

"we not only have physiological we have external cues also"

List some of the factors that influence drinking behavior.   **BEFORE YOU GO ON**

Hunger and Eating Behavior

Our need for food is as obvious as our need for water. If we don't eat, we die. Again, the interesting question is what gives rise to the hunger drive? As it happens, there are many factors that motivate a person to eat. Some of them are physiological in nature. Some are more psychological and reflect learning experiences. Some involve social pressures. Let's briefly summarize some of the evidence.

Internal, Physiological Cues.   People and animals whose stomachs have been surgically removed still feel hungry periodically and eat amounts of food not unlike those eaten by people with stomachs intact. Cues from our stomachs, then, don't seem to be important in producing a hunger drive. The two structures that seem most involved in the hunger drive are the hypothalamus (again) and the liver.

Theories of hunger that focus on the role of the hypothalamus are referred to as *dual-center* theories. This label is used because such views suggest that there are *two* regions in the hypothalamus that regulate food intake. One is an "eat" center that gives rise to feelings of hunger, while the other is a "no eat" center that lets us know when we've had enough.

There are two centers (called *nuclei*) in the hypothalamus that have predictable effects on eating behavior when they are electrically stimulated

Hypothalamus + Liver

or when they are destroyed. Removing the "eat center," for example, leads to starvation, while removing the "no eat center" leads to extreme overeating (Friedman & Stricker, 1976; Keesey & Powley, 1975).

Although the hypothalamus may be involved in eating behaviors, normal eating patterns are not under the influence of artificial laboratory procedures. What activates the brain's food-regulating centers in a normal organism? Here, we are still at the level of hypothesis, not fact.

A long-accepted view was that the body responds to levels of blood sugar, or glucose, in our blood that can be metabolized, or converted into energy for the body's use. When glucose metabolism levels are low—which they are when we haven't eaten for a while—we are stimulated to eat. When blood sugar levels are adequate, we are stimulated to stop eating. And, it may be that the *liver* is the organ that most closely monitors such blood chemistry for us.

Another view holds that we respond (through a complex chain of events) to levels of fat stored in our bodies. When fat stores are adequately filled, we feel no hunger. When fat supplies are depleted, a hunger drive arises.

Another view that emphasizes the role of internal, physiological cues also relies heavily on the concept of set-point, or homeostasis. The logic here is that the critical factor is one's body weight, which like blood pressure or temperature is physiologically regulated (Nisbett, 1972). "Being so regulated, weight is normally maintained at a particular level or set-point, not only by the control of food intake, as is often assumed, but also by complimentary adjustments in energy utilization and expenditure" (Keesey & Powley, 1986). The implication, of course, is that as body weight decreases significantly, either through dieting, or exercise, or both, the organism becomes motivated to return to the set-point level. The result may be either abandoning the diet, cutting down on exercise, or both. Conversely, if one eats too much—more than is necessary to maintain one's homeostatic level of energy consumption and storage—one will become motivated to expend energy to return to set-point. What is yet to be determined are the mechanisms involved in establishing one's set-point body weight and energy utilization levels to begin with. There is some evidence that these are influenced by both genetic factors (Nisbett, 1972) and feeding behaviors during infancy (Knittle, 1975).

We no doubt receive a number of internal cues that simultaneously inform us of our physiological need for food (Friedman & Stricker, 1976). Many of the cues may be subtle and effective in the long term (for example, sensitivity to stored fat levels or energy utilization), while others may be more immediate. Eating behaviors may also be influenced by factors over and above those from our physiology.

External, Psychological Cues.   We often respond to external cues that stimulate us to engage in eating behavior. Here we'll list a few of the nonphysiological influences that may motivate us to eat.

Sometimes, just the *stimulus properties* of foods—their aroma, taste, or appearance—may be enough to get us to eat. You may not want any dessert after a large meal until the waitress shows you a piece of creamy cheesecake with cherry topping. Ordering and eating that cheesecake has nothing to do with your internal physiological conditions.

Sometimes people eat more from *habit* than from need. "It's twelve o'clock. It's lunch time; so let's eat." We may fall into habits of eating at certain times, tied more to the clock than to internal cues from our bodies. Some people are virtually unable to watch television without poking salty foods in their mouths—a behavioral pattern motivated more by learning than by physiology.

Occasionally, we find that we eat simply because others around us are eating. Such "socially facilitated" eating has been noted in a number of species (for example, Harlow, 1932; Tolman, 1969). For example, if a caged chicken is allowed to eat its fill of grain, it eventually stops eating. When other hungry chickens are placed in the cage and begin to eat, the "full" chicken starts right in eating again, its behaviors not noticeably different from those just added to the cage.

Ours is a weight-conscious society. Being overweight has negative health consequences and surely is not the model that most of us try to follow. It may very well be the case that overweight people tend to be less sensitive to internal hunger cues from their bodies and more sensitive to external eating cues from the environment (Schachter, 1971), although there is also research evidence that this logical analysis is not always true (Rodin, 1981). On the other hand, some persons may have a body weight set-point that is genetically, or physiologically, higher than average. Persons who are significantly overweight generally have larger *and* greater numbers of fat cells (Nisbett, 1972). For those people who are overweight, it would be nice to know that there is some simple, foolproof way to lose weight. Given that there are so many factors that influence eating, such a hope is not likely to be fulfilled in the near future. It seems that no one physiological mechanism has the sole control of our hunger drive (Thompson, 1980). And it seems that no one personality trait leads to obesity (Leon & Roth, 1977).

Habit is another external cue that can motivate us to eat. For many people, watching television and consuming salty snacks go hand in hand.

List those internal and external factors that influence our drive to eat.   **BEFORE YOU GO ON**

SEX DRIVES AND SEXUAL BEHAVIOR   *Seperate Topic*   physiological and Psychological and Social

As a physiologically based drive, the sex drive is unique in a number of ways. First, the survival of the individual does not depend on its satisfaction. If we don't drink, we die; if we don't regulate our temperature, we die; if we don't eat, we die. If we don't have sex—well, we don't die. The survival of the *species* requires that an adequate number of its members successfully respond to a sex drive, but an individual member can get along without doing so.

Second, most physiologically based drives, including hunger, thirst, and temperature regulation, provide mechanisms to replenish and/or maintain the body's energy. When satisfied, the sex drive depletes bodily energy. In fact, the sex drive actually motivates the organism to seek tension, as opposed to drives that seek to reduce tension to return to homeostasis.

A third point about the sex drive that makes it different from the rest is that it is not present—at least in the usual sense—at birth, but requires a certain level of maturation (puberty) before it is apparent. The other drives are present, and even most critical, early in life.

The sex drive is a physiologically-based drive. It satisfies both physical and emotional needs. Unlike the eating, drinking, and temperature regulation drives, the sex drive is not present at birth, but requires a certain level of maturation.

androgen
the male sex hormones produced by the testes

estrogen
the female sex hormones, produced by the ovaries

A fourth unique quality of the sex drive is the extent to which internal and external influences have different degrees of impact depending on the species involved. The importance of internal, physiological states is much greater in "lower" species than it is in primates and humans. At the level of human sexual behaviors, sex hormones may be necessary, but they are seldom sufficient for the maintenance of sexual responding, and for an experienced human, they may not even be necessary. We'll see this complication as we consider the internal and external cues for the sex drive, as we have done for the other physiologically based drives. Then we'll go on to review some of the research that deals with *human* sexuality, focusing on the work of Masters and Johnson, what we know about homosexuality, and sexually transmitted diseases.

Internal, Physiological Cues

With rats, the matter of sex is quite simple and straightforward. In the male rat, if adequate **androgen** (the male sex hormone) is present, and if there is the opportunity, the rat will respond to the hormone-induced sex drive and will engage in sexual behaviors. In the female rat, if adequate **estrogen** (the female sex hormone) is present, and if the opportunity is available, the female rat will also engage in appropriate sexual behaviors. For rats at least, learning and past experience seem to have little to do with sexual behaviors—they are tied closely to physiology, to hormonal levels. It is very difficult to tell the difference between the mating behaviors of sexually experienced rats, rats that have mated only once or twice, and virgin rats.

If the sex hormones of a female rat are removed (by surgically removing the ovaries), there will be a complete and immediate loss of sexual receptivity. If these sex hormones are then replaced by injection, sexual behaviors return to normal (Davidson et al., 1968). Removing the sex hormones from male rats produces a slightly different story. Sexual behaviors do diminish and may eventually disappear, but they take longer to do so. Again, injections of sex hormones quickly return the male rat to normal sexual functioning.

Removal of the sex hormones from male dogs or cats ("higher" species than rats) also produces a reduction in sexual behaviors, but much more gradually than for rats. An experienced male primate ("higher" still) may persist in sexual behaviors for the rest of his life, even after his sex hormones have been removed. (The same also seems true of human males, although the data here are sketchy.)

Even in primate females, removal of the sex hormones (by removing the ovaries) results in a rather sudden loss of sex drive and a cessation of sexual behaviors. In female primates (and in dogs, cats, rats, and so on), sexual responsiveness is well predicted by the hormone-driven fertility cycle. The period during which ovulation (the release of the eggs or ova from the ovary) occurs is the time of greatest sexual drive and activity. In the human female, we find a different situation. The human female's receptiveness to sexual activity appears not to be related to the fertility, or estrous, cycle (Bennett, 1982). And menopause, the period after which the ovaries no longer produce ova and sex hormones, does *not* bring about an end to sexual interest or sexual behavior for the human female.

So what we find is that the sex drive in "lower" species is tied to its physiological, hormonal base. As the complexity of the organism increases, from rats, to dogs, to primates, to humans, the role of internal cues becomes less certain and less noticeable.

External, Psychological Cues

No one would get far arguing that sex is not an important human drive. However, it is easy to lose sight of the fact that it is basically a *biological* drive. Particularly in societies like ours, where so much learning is involved, one could easily come to believe that sexual drives are learned through experience and practice alone. (Considerable unlearning may also be involved here: Satisfying the sex drive may involve unlearning many prohibitions acquired in childhood and adolescence.) Hormones may provide humans with an arousing force to do something, but *what* to do, *how* to do it, and *when* to do it often seem to require training and practice.

Sex manuals of a "how to" nature sell well, and sex therapy has become a standard practice for many clinical psychologists trying to help people cope with the pressures that external factors put on their "natural" sexual motivation.

In addition to the internal forces produced by the sex hormones, sex drives can be stimulated by a wide range of environmental stimuli. Some people engage in sexual behaviors simply to reproduce; others do so for the physical pleasure they experience; others because they feel it demonstrates a romantic "love" for another; yet others want to display their femininity or masculinity.

Sexual drives in humans are seldom satisfied with "just anybody." Many social and cognitive (external) constraints are often placed on the choice of a sexual partner. What "turns someone on" sexually varies considerably from person to person. Virtually any of the senses—touch, smell (particularly important in lower mammals and primates), sight, and sound—can stimulate sexual arousal.

In what ways is the sex drive a unique physiologically based drive? **BEFORE YOU GO ON**

The Human Sexual Response

Much of what we know about human sexuality we have learned through survey research. In 1966, William Masters and Virginia Johnson published *Human Sexual Response,* a landmark book that demonstrated the value of the direct observation of sexual behaviors in a controlled laboratory setting. Masters began making his observations of sexual behaviors in 1954, choosing female prostitutes as his subjects. His belief at the time was that he would be unable to get a sufficient number of volunteers to act as subjects. After all, he wanted people to engage in a wide range of sexual behaviors while being observed by others and while hooked up to a variety of instruments designed to measure their physiological reactions as they engaged in those sexual behaviors.

For a number of reasons, Masters' sample of prostitutes did not provide him with the quality of data he was looking for. Fortunately, he was quite

William Masters and Virginia Johnson

wrong about the willingness of people to volunteer for his studies of sexual responses. As word spread throughout the Washington University (St. Louis) community that subjects were needed for sex research, more than 1,273 persons volunteered. From these, 382 women and 312 men were chosen for the studies reported in *Human Sexual Response*. These studies allow us to fashion an accurate picture of the physiological reactions that occur during sexual behaviors. To be sure, the Masters and Johnson sample was not a random one, but there is no evidence, as yet, that the results from their sample differ in any significant way from those that would have been found with a different sample. The Masters and Johnson model of the human sexual response is not the only one available (for example, Kaplan, 1979; Zilbergeld & Evans, 1980); but it is by far the most widely known and accepted. In this section, we'll review the four stages of the Masters and Johnson model of the human sexual response.

Phase 1. Excitement. The excitement stage of the sexual response is a reaction of arousal, often in anticipation of an actual sexual experience. In both sexes there is increased muscle tension and increased blood flow in the genital area. The most noticeable effects include an erection of the penis and an elevation of the scrotum in males and a lubrication of the vagina and an erection of the nipples in females. In both males and females, there is an increase in heart rate and blood pressure, and a "flush" or blotchy redding (or darkening) of the skin, usually on the abdomen and chest.

The excitement phase may last from a few minutes to several hours, depending on the individual and the situation. What initiates this stage; what stimulates sexual arousal? There are no simple answers to these questions, but we do have evidence that arousal may result from a number of interacting factors. There is an undeniable logic that the sex hormones (androgens in males and estrogens in females) ought to be related to sexual arousal. The logic may be sound, but the evidence is far from clearcut. There is more support for the notion that androgen levels affect interest and sexual arousal in males than there is for the interaction of estrogen and female arousal (Crooks & Baur, 1987, pp. 161–164). (There is even some evidence that androgen levels affect female arousal as well as male arousal.)

Sexual arousal normally occurs through some variety or combination of sensory experiences. Sensory experiences that are sexually arousing often vary considerably from person to person, supporting the position that learning and past experience are very relevant. What one person finds exciting and arousing, someone else may find boring and even repulsive. Of all the senses, touch is the most commonly associated with sexual arousal. Individuals do indeed have a number of **erogenous zones,** or areas of their bodies which, when they are stroked or touched, lead to sexual arousal. These areas usually include the genitals, the breasts (in both sexes, but more commonly in women), the inner surface of the thighs, the ears (particularly the lobes), and the mouth region. It is important for sex partners to know which of these areas—or some other—are erogenous and lead to sexual excitement.

Arousal may be instigated visually by the viewing of erotic materials—or even at the sight of a nude sex partner. It used to be thought that sexual arousal brought about by viewing sexual or erotic materials was much more common in men than in women (for example, Kinsey et al., 1948, 1953). In

erogenous zones
areas of the body which, when they are stroked, lead to sexual arousal

fact, sexual arousal brought about in this way is just as common in women as in men, although women are less likely to verbally report (admit to) being sexually aroused by looking at erotic stimuli (Kelley, 1985).

The sense of smell—through the detection of odors which attract the opposite sex—is very important in stimulating the sexual responsiveness of nonhumans. There is evidence that humans produce such odors also, although their relationship to sexual arousal is still not firmly established. Before we leave our discussion of sexual arousal to consider the next stage in the human sexual response, we should note that there is no evidence for the existence of a human **aphrodisiac**. An aphrodisiac is any substance that, when drunk or eaten, increases one's sexual arousal. For generations, people of many different cultures have believed in the power of certain concoctions (from alcohol to "Spanish fly," to amphetamines and marijuana, to oysters and a powder made from rhinoceros tusks) to stimulate sexual responsiveness. In fact, none of these work as intended, and most have precisely the opposite effect.

aphrodisiac
a substance that, when drunk or eaten, increases sexual arousal; none are known to exist

Phase 2. Plateau.   It's rather difficult to determine just when the plateau phase begins. The reactions involved carry the processes begun in the excitement phase to the brink of orgasm. In the male, the erection of the penis becomes fully complete; the testes enlarge and rise up very close to the body; the penis reddens. In the female, the opening to the vagina reddens in color; the outer third of the vagina, gorged with blood, enlarges; the clitoris elevates and shortens. In both men and women, blood pressure and heart rate increase, breathing becomes more shallow and rapid, and skin flushing becomes more pronounced. This stage seldom lasts very long, generally a few minutes, although with practice this stage can be extended. Tension has now built to its maximum, ready for the release of the next stage.

Phase 3. Orgasm.   The orgasm stage of sexual behavior is by far the shortest, lasting only a matter of seconds. Once a male has reached the plateau stage, orgasm is almost sure to follow. In the male, orgasm is comprised of two separate substages, "coming"—in which one senses, through a series of contractions, that ejaculation is about to happen—and ejaculation itself, in which semen is forced out through the penis. Orgasm in the female, which need not necessarily follow from the plateau stage, also involves a series of short, intense contractions in the genital area.

The experience of orgasm is apparently very much the same (and highly pleasurable) for both men and women, although women don't experience any real parallel to male ejaculation. Describing the experience of orgasm, however, seems to be quite difficult for most women. We should also mention that Masters and Johnson have found female orgasms to be of only one type. There is a common belief (which derives directly from the writings of Freud) that women experience either "clitoral" or "vaginal" orgasms, depending on which of these two structures is most stimulated. Although there is no physiological difference between these orgasms, some women do express a definite preference for one or the other.

Phase 4. Resolution.   As its name suggests, in the resolution phase of sexual behavior, the body returns to its unaroused state. If orgasm has been reached, this stage begins immediately. If orgasm has not been reached,

refractory period
during the process of the human sexual response, that period following orgasm during which arousal in the male is not possible

stimulation may repeat the entire process. In the resolution phase, we can see a major difference between males and females. Once a male has experienced orgasm he enters a **refractory period** during which arousal, erection, and another orgasm are impossible. This period may last for a few minutes, hours, or even days, depending on the person. The length of one's refractory period generally increases with age. Women, on the other hand, do not experience a refractory period and thus may experience multiple orgasms if appropriately stimulated.

The different physiological changes that develop during sexual activity take varying amounts to time to resolve, and return to normal. In both males and females, heart rate and blood pressure return to normal very quickly. The coloration of the genital area and skin flushing are usually gone in minutes. The oversupply of blood to the genital region takes a bit longer to resolve.

Masters and Johnson found these four phases of sexual response in their subjects with such frequency and consistency that they were willing to claim them to be "standard" reactions during sexual behavior. Psychologists are always pleased to find such regularities in behavior of any kind. Years of research on the human sexual response have convinced Masters and Johnson that there are enormous individual differences in the intensity to which each or any of these four phases is felt or experienced. They acknowledge that what best stimulates the excitement phase and thus begins the chain of events we call the human sexual response also varies considerably from one individual to another. But what is most impressive is that, in spite of these individual differences the basic pattern of human sexual resposiveness is always the same.

BEFORE YOU GO ON   Briefly describe the changes that occur during the excitement, plateau, orgasm, and resolution phases of the human sexual response.

Homosexuality

homosexuals
those persons who are sexually attracted to and aroused by members of their own sex

The complexities of human sexual responsiveness are no more apparent than when we consider those persons who are **homosexuals.** Homosexuals are individuals who are sexually attracted to and aroused by members of their own sex, as opposed to heterosexuals who seek outlets for their sexual drives among members of the opposite sex. Psychologists argue that homosexuality should be referred to as an orientation (or a status) and *not* as a matter of sexual preference. *"Sexual preference* is a moral and political term. Conceptually it implies voluntary choice. . . . The concept of voluntary choice is as much in error here as in its application to handedness or to native language. You do not choose your native language, even though you are born without it" (Money, 1987, p. 385).

Psychologists agree that homosexuality and heterosexuality are not mutually exclusive categories, but rather end points of sexual orientation and that many combinations are possible. Alfred Kinsey and his colleagues (1948, 1953) first brought the prevalence of homosexuality to the attention of the general public. Kinsey devised a seven-point scale (0 to 6) of sexual orientation with those who are exclusively heterosexual at one end point and persons who are exclusively homosexual at the other extreme (see Figure

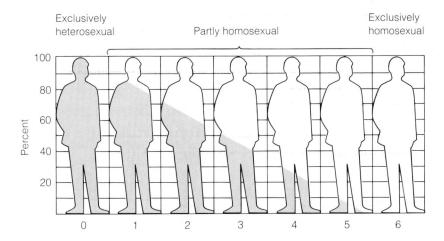

7.4). Kinsey found that about half of the males who responded to his surveys fell somewhere *between* these two end points. Even though homosexuality is now more openly discussed than it was in the 1940s and 1950s (more "out of the closet"), it is still difficult to get accurate estimates of the numbers of persons who are exclusively or predominantly homosexual. Conservative estimates suggest that about 2 percent of American males are exclusively homosexual in their sexual preferences and that 8 to 10 percent have had more than just an occasional homosexual encounter. Comparable figures for females indicate that female homosexuality, or lesbianism, is approximately half as prevalent as male homosexuality. These figures surely are much higher in some situations, such as in prisons, leading to what has been called "deprivational homosexuality." In these cases, homosexuals almost always return to heterosexuality when the deprivation situation changes.

In most ways, there is very little difference between homosexuals and heterosexuals, including the pattern of their sexual responsiveness. Most gays and lesbians have experienced heterosexual sex. They simply find same-sex relationships more satisfying and pleasurable. In fact, gay and lesbian couples are often more at ease and comfortable with their sexual relationship than most heterosexual couples (Masters & Johnson, 1979). Contrary to popular opinion, most gays and lesbians are indistinguishable from heterosexuals in their appearance and mannerisms.

As yet, we have no generally accepted theory of the causes of homosexuality. (Some homosexuals argue that we have no acceptable theory to explain heterosexuality either.) What we do know is that the matter is not a simple one and probably involves some interaction of genetic, hormonal, and environmental factors (Money, 1987). There are now a number of hypotheses along each of these lines. For example, there is some evidence that homosexuality tends to "run in families," but the evidence for a direct genetic cause of homosexuality is very weak (Diamond & Karlen, 1980).

Likewise, there is scant evidence of any significant differences in hormone levels of heterosexuals and homosexuals at adulthood. Some differences have been reported (and sexual preferences of rats can be influenced by

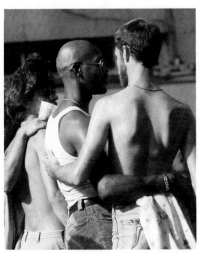

Though homosexuality is becoming more prevalent and homosexuals are able to be more open about their sexual preferences, homosexuality is still a controversial issue.

the manipulation of hormone levels). But simply providing gays and lesbians with extra amounts of sex hormones may increase overall sex drive and the incidence of sexual behaviors, but seems to have virtually no effect on sexual orientation. A hypothesis with more research support suggests that prenatal hormonal imbalances may affect one's sexual orientation in adulthood (Money, 1987). The claim of this hypothesis is that embryos (genetically male or female) exposed to above average concentrations of female hormones will develop into adults attracted to persons having masculine characteristics, and vice versa (Ellis & Ames, 1987).

Psychologists remain unwilling to disregard hypotheses that emphasize the importance of environmental influences. It is clear, however, that sexual orientation cannot be attributed to any one simple early childhood experience. Most gays and lesbians themselves claim that their parents had little influence on their adult sexual orientation (Bell et al., 1981). On the other hand, one's sexual orientation does seem to be established before adolescence (Bell et al., 1981), and the early family life of homosexuals, when compared to that of heterosexuals, is sometimes found to be more "troubled" (more one-parent families (Wolfe, 1971), more domination of opposite-sex parent (Saghir & Robins, 1973), more marital problems (Hoffman, 1977), and so on). Although we may not yet be able to discount such factors totally, environmental causes of sexual orientation seem to be mostly of theoretical interest, with scant research evidence to support them. One major problem with much of our current data on the early experiences of gays and lesbians is that it most often comes from homosexuals who are in therapy, distressed with their sexual orientation. We have much less data about those homosexuals (the clear majority) who are comfortable with their sexuality. A reasonable position would be to hypothesize that genetic and hormonal predispositions MAY interact with subtle environmental influences in complex ways to form one's adult sexual orientation.

BEFORE YOU GO ON   **What is homosexuality?**

Sexually Transmitted Diseases

sexually transmitted diseases (STDs)
contagious diseases that are usually transmitted through sexual contact

Sexually Transmitted Diseases (STD) are those contagious diseases that are usually (although not exclusively) transmitted through sexual contact. *Sexually transmitted diseases* is a label that has all but replaced the term venereal disease, or VD. In this section, we'll briefly describe a few of the most common STDs. Even though STDs are mainly a medical problem, we've chosen to include this section here for two reasons: (1) Sexually transmitted diseases, and the fear of them, often have a profound influence on sexual behaviors, and (2) persons with STDs often suffer as many psychological consequences as medical ones. STDs affect millions of individuals each year. This year alone, more than 1.8 million cases of gonorrhea; more than 85,000 new cases of syphilis, more than 500,000 new cases of genital herpes, and more than 35,000 new cases of AIDS will be reported. For each person we know of with a STD, there may be two to five others with the disease, but in a stage that is nonsymptomatic, so the disease is not yet diagnosed.

gonorrhea
an STD caused by a bacterial infection of moist tissues in the genital area

Gonorrhea is both the oldest and the most common of all the sexually transmitted diseases. It is largely a disease of the young and the sexually active; most cases are diagnosed in men between the ages of 20 and 24.

Gonorrhea is a bacteria infection that affects the moist tissue areas around the genitals (or any other opening to the body that is used sexually). The bacteria that produce the symptoms of gonorrhea can live for only a few seconds outside of the human body, so the likelihood of contracting the disease from toilet seats, eating utensils, towels, or drinking fountains is very slim.

In many cases, one may be infected with the gonorrhea bacteria and not even know it. This is particularly true for women, most of whom remain relatively free of symptoms. When symptoms do develop, they include frequent, painful urination, vaginal discharges, and a reddening of the genital area. In men, there is a thin milky discharge from the penis and painful, frequent urination. Left untreated, complications can develop in both males and females. Fortunately, treatment for gonorrhea—penicillin, or tetracyline for those allergic to penicillin—is simple and successful.

Syphilis is another STD with a very long and ignoble history. Syphilis is a disease caused by a little bacterium called a "spirochete." If left untreated, the disease may run its course through four known stages, from a relatively simple and painless sore, all the way to the infection of other, nonsexual organs, which may lead even to death. Although as many as 25 percent of those infected by the spirochete bacterium may ultimately die as a result, there is some comfort in the knowledge that the incidence of this disease is on the decrease. Treatment is relatively simple, once diagnosis has been confirmed. Penicillin (or tetracyline) is used, and the prognosis is related to length of infection—as is the case for so many diseases, the sooner treatment begins, the better the prognosis.

Genital herpes is a skin disease that affects the genital area, producing small sores and blisters. It is not caused by bacteria, but by a virus. Herpes Type I is a very common viral infection of the skin that almost always occurs above the waist—in the form of cold sores or fever blisters for example. It is the Herpes II virus that infects the genital area and is the true STD. This Herpes II virus was virtually unknown until the mid 1960s. Now, genital herpes is *the* most common STD. Some estimates place incidence rates as high as 40 million Americans. Herpes is a disease that has no cure, although some recently developed medications can reduce the occasionally painful symptoms of genital herpes. A person with genital herpes is most infectious when the sores and blisters are active and erupting. There may be long periods during which an infected person remains symptom free, only to have sores and reddening reoccur. Although there are no known life-threatening complications of this disease in males, genital herpes in females does increase the risk of contracting cervical cancer. Another complication may occur when pregnant women contract genital herpes. The herpes virus may be passed along during childbirth, which may cause considerable damage to the newborn, even death.

No STD has attracted so much public attention and debate as has **acquired immune deficiency syndrome**, or **AIDS**. This disease was virtually unknown in the United States before 1981. Since then, nearly 70,000 cases of AIDS in the United States (and 40,000 deaths) have been reported by the Centers for Disease Control. Good estimates of incidence rates for the future are frankly hard to come by. Conservative estimates generally place the number of AIDS cases expected by the year 2000 at more than one million. Just what is AIDS?

syphilis
an STD caused by a bacterial infection, which may pass through four stages, ultimately resulting in death

genital herpes (Herpes Type II)
the most common STD; a skin infection in the form of a rash or blisters in the genital area

virus

acquired immune deficiency syndrome (AIDS)
a deadly STD caused by a virus (the HIV) that destroys the body's natural immune system

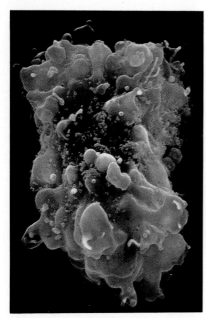

Here, under the microscope, the AIDS virus (blue) attacks a helper T cell.
© Boehringer Ingelheim International GmbH. Photo: Lennart Nilsson.

AIDS is caused by a virus called the *human immunodeficiency virus,* or HIV (of which a new strain, the HIV-B, was discovered in early 1988). The HIV almost always enters the body through sexual contact or through the use of contaminated needles in intravenous (IV) drug use. In infected individuals, concentrations of the AIDS virus are highest in the blood and semen. Once infected, a person may experience very few symptoms other than those usually associated with a common cold. Then the person enters what is called a "carrier state." He or she is infected with the virus and may pass it on to others, but remains free of any noticeable symptoms. What is not clear is just how many persons infected with the HIV will develop the full-blown symptoms of AIDS. Of those with a diagnosis of AIDS (not just the presence of the HIV), virtually all will die within four years.

The HIV directly attacks the body's immune system—the system that naturally fights off infections. With a weakened or nonfunctioning immune system, a person with AIDS does not have the resources to defend against other infections that normally would not be life-threatening. In other words, AIDS patients don't die from AIDS directly, but from other diseases (often pneumonia) that the body cannot defend itself against because of AIDS.

Acquired immune deficiency syndrome is *not* a highly contagious STD (certainly not when compared to diseases such as herpes or gonorrhea). It cannot be transmitted by casual contact—there has to be an interchange of bodily fluids, blood or semen. Early in the 1980s, it was believed that AIDS was a disease restricted to the gay male population and to intravenous drug users. This is now clearly not the case. That the disease first appeared and spread through the homosexual population is, as much as anything else, an accident of history. Intercourse, anal intercourse in particular, commonly leads to the transmission of the HIV, and whether or not both sex partners are male seems to matter little.

Whereas other sexually transmitted diseases may cause discomfort and/or pain, AIDS can be fatal. There is no vaccine to prevent it. There is no cure for AIDS, and none is on the horizon. There is no effective treatment for AIDS, but here there is more hope. At the moment, the only reasonable way to protect against AIDS is through the monitoring of behavior. Not using IV drugs would help. Totally abstaining from sexual activity certainly would. On the assumption that many adolescents and adults won't abstain from sex altogether, many experts counsel "safe" sex. After that, there is disagreement on just what safe sex *is*. Advice is, for the most part, reasonably sensible. The fewer sexual contacts one has, the less the probability of encountering someone infected with the AIDS virus. The more selective one is in choosing a partner (has your partner been tested for the HIV?), the less the risk. Using condoms during intercourse significantly reduces (but does not eliminate) the likelihood of infection. Engaging in sex behaviors in which there is no exchange of bodily fluids at all (such as mutual masturbation, for example) also constitutes safe sex (Masters et al., 1987).

AIDS is a physical disease. A biological organism (a virus) attacks a physiological system (the immune system), which then increases the possibility of further infection, which may ultimately result in death. But AIDS is a physical disease with unprecedented psychological complications. AIDS researcher Tom Coates recently put it this way, "AIDS, as I see it, is primarily a psychological problem. What we're dealing with is a disease that gets in the way of people relating in intimate ways. And it becomes a psychological problem to figure out how we, as people who know something about motivation and know something about behavior, can help people not do something that's natural" (quoted in Landers, 1987, p. 28). Because AIDS is such a frightening disease, AIDS patients are often shunned—by loved ones and even by health care professionals. (In late 1987, the American Medical Association felt it had to issue a statement that it is unethical for a physician to refuse treatment to an AIDS patient.) Because AIDS began in the homosexual community (and is still largely concentrated there), gays and lesbians are concerned that they will become the focus of even greater discrimination than they have suffered in the past. The alienation, fear, and stress experienced by AIDS patients (and often their friends and family) are in many ways as painful as the disease itself and require psychological treatment.

Name and briefly describe four sexually transmitted diseases   BEFORE YOU GO ON

Human sexuality is primarily a physiologically based motive. But, as we have seen, in addition to its having numerous psychological consequences, it is greatly affected by psychological factors. We'll now turn to motives that are more clearly psychological in nature.

PSYCHOLOGICALLY BASED MOTIVATION

From time to time, you may be able to analyze your own behavior in terms of physiologically based needs and drives. For example, you woke up this morning for reasons largely biological. The fact that you had breakfast might be explained in terms of a hunger drive. That you got dressed might have been your attempt to do what you could to control your body temperature, which may also have influenced your choice of clothes. Perhaps some sexual motivation affected what you chose to wear today.

Many of our behaviors seem to be aroused and directed (that is, motivated) by forces that are more subtle and less clearly biological in origin. In this section, we'll review some of the motivators that clearly reflect a learned or social influence. Remember that we are going to refer to these psychologically based drives as *motives*. Although there are potentially a large number of such motives, we'll review four that have received considerable attention as mechanisms for "explaining" human behavior: achievement, power, affiliation, and competency motivation.

Achievement Motivation

The hypothesis that people are motivated to varying degrees by a **need to achieve**—or **nAch**—was introduced to the literature of psychology in 1938 by Henry Murray. Measuring nAch and determining its sources and its implications has been a major contribution of David McClelland and his associates (for example, McClelland et al., 1953; McClelland, 1975, 1985). Achievement motivation is determined by one's need to attempt and succeed at tasks in such a way as to meet or exceed some standard of success or excellence.

Although there are short, paper-and-pencil tests for the same purpose, achievement motivation is usually assessed by means of the **thematic apperception test,** or **TAT**. This test is a *projective test* (see Chapter 8). Subjects

need to achieve (nAch)
the (learned) need to meet or exceed some standard of excellence in performance

thematic apperception test (TAT)
a projective personality test requiring a subject to tell a series of short stories about a set of ambiguous pictures

FIGURE 7.5
A TAT example.

are asked to tell short stories about a series of rather ambiguous pictures that depict people in various settings (see Figure 7.5). Subjects' stories are then interpreted and scored according to a series of objective criteria that note references to trying difficult tasks, succeeding, being rewarded for one's efforts, setting short-term and long-term goals, and so on. Because there are no right or wrong responses to the pictures of the TAT, judgments can be made about the references to achievement that a subject "projects" into the picture and his or her story describing it.

One of the first things that McClelland and his coworkers found was that there *were* consistent differences in measured levels of nAch among the male subjects they tested. One of the most reliable findings concerning people with high needs for achievement involves the nature of tasks they choose to attempt. When given a choice, they generally try to do tasks in which success is not guaranteed (otherwise, there is no challenge), but in which there still is a reasonable chance of success. Both young children (McClelland, 1958) and college students (Atkinson & Litwin, 1960) who were high in nAch were observed playing a ring-toss game, where the object was to score points by tossing a small ring over a peg from a distance. The farther from the peg one stood, the more points could be earned with success. High nAch subjects in both studies chose to stand at a moderate distance from the peg. They didn't stand so close as to guarantee success, but they didn't choose to stand so far away that they would almost certainly fail. Subjects with low nAch scores tended to go to either extreme—very close, earning few points for their successes, or so far away they hardly ever succeeded.

McClelland would argue that you are reading this text at this moment because you are motivated by a need to achieve. You want to do well on your next exam. You want to get a good grade in this course, and you have decided that to do so, you need to study the assigned text material. Some students read text assignments not because they are motivated by a need to achieve, but because they are motivated by a *fear of failure* (Atkinson & Feather, 1966). In this case, the incentive that is relevant is a negative one (wanting to avoid an "F"), which is a different matter than working toward a positive incentive (wanting to earn an "A"). Individuals motivated by a fear of failure tend to take very few risks. They either choose to attempt tasks that they are bound to do well or to attempt tasks that are virtually impossible (if the task is impossible, they can't blame themselves for their failures).

It seems that the need to achieve is learned, usually in early childhood. Children who show high levels of achievement motivation are generally those who have been encouraged in a positive way to excel ("Billy, that grade of 'B' is very good; do you think you could make an 'A' next time?" as opposed to, "What! only a 'B' "). High nAch children are generally encouraged to work things out for themselves, independently, with parental support and encouragement ("Here, Billy, you see if you can do this" as opposed to, "Here, dummy, let me do it; you'll never get it right!"). McClelland is convinced that achievement motivation can be specifically taught and acquired by almost anyone of any age, and he has developed training programs designed to increase achievement motivation levels (for example, McClelland & Winter, 1969).

BEFORE YOU GO ON   **What is achievement motivation, and how is it usually measured?**

Power Motivation

Some people are motivated not only to excel, but also to be in control, to be in charge—of the situation and of others. In such cases, we may speak of a **need for power** (McClelland, 1982; Winter & Stewart, 1978). Power needs are generally measured in the same way as achievement needs, through the interpretations of stories generated with the Thematic Apperception Test.

People with high power needs like to be admired. They prefer situations in which they can control the fate of others, usually by manipulating access to information. They present an attitude of, "If you want to get this job done, you'll have to come to me to find out how to do it." Individuals with low power needs tend to avoid situations in which others would have to depend on them. They tend to be rather submissive in interpersonal relationships.

need for power
the (learned) need to be in control of events or persons, usually at another's expense

Affiliation Motivation

Another psychologically based motivator that has been found to be very helpful in explaining the behaviors of some people is the **need for affiliation.** This motive involves a need to be with others, to work together with others toward some end, and to form friendships and associations.

One interesting implication of having a high need for affiliation is that it is often at odds with a need for power. As you might imagine, if you are simultaneously motivated to be in control *and* to be with others (in a supportive way), conflicts may arise. It is more difficult to exercise power over people whose friendship you value than it is to exercise power and control over people whose friendship is of little concern to you. It is also the case that affiliation and achievement motives are somewhat independent. Achievement and success can be earned either with others (high affiliation) or on one's own (low affiliation).

Although we might be quite confident that achievement and power motives are learned, we are less confident about the sources of affiliation motivation. There is a reasonable argument that the need to affiliate and be with others is at least partly biologically based. We are basically social animals for whom complete social isolation is quite difficult (particularly when we are young). On the other hand, it seems clear that the extent to which we value affiliation relationships can be attributed to our learning experiences.

need for affiliation
the need to be with others and to form relationships and associations

Many behaviors can be explained on the basis of a need for affiliation. We all feel the need to be with others, to work toward a common goal, and to form associations and partnerships.

Competency Motivation

Robert White (1959, 1974) has proposed that all people are motivated by a **need for competence.** To be competent doesn't imply excellence, nor does it suggest success at the expense of others. It simply means managing to cope effectively, on one's own, with the challenges of everyday living.

More general than either the needs for achievement, power, or affiliation, the need for competence has been used to account for a wide range of behaviors. Some people develop competence with musical instruments, others in their jobs, others at some hobby or sport. The point is that we are all motivated to find something we can do well—some way to show that we are effective in dealing with our environments.

need for competence
the need to meet the challenges (large and small) provided by one's environment

Our behaviors are often motivated by a need for competence. We are all motivated to find something we can do well—perhaps some artistic or creative hobby that we can enjoy and master.

When you try to help a child who is attempting to do something that you judge it cannot do, the child may respond, "I can do it myself!" The child is trying to maintain (or develop) a sense of competence, which you may have challenged simply by offering to help.

As with other types of human motivation, we can see individual differences in the degree of a need for competency. Some people are satisfied with being able to handle a small number of everyday tasks. Others seek to find new and different ways to express their competency or mastery over the environment (Harter, 1978).

The motivational concepts we have briefly introduced in this section might be useful in trying to understand why students decide to attend college. Although there may be many reasons, all operating at once, some people become college students to satisfy achievement needs. Some see a college as a means of gaining power. Some students see attending college as providing opportunities for meeting new people and establishing relationships. Others try college just because they want to see if they can do it—they appreciate the challenge.

Before we leave this section we should point out that the very nature of the motives we have been discussing has been challenged for some time. The issue involved is the extent to which these motives are under the control of intrinsic or extrinsic factors. By **intrinsic control** we are referring to internal personal processes that motivate our behaviors. By **extrinsic control** we mean external, environmental processes. For example, no one doubts that some people are "motivated" to achieve, while others seek power, affiliation, or effective control over their lives. The question is whether or not (or the extent to which) one's behaviors reflect intrinsic, internalized motives or one's learning history through the identification of those responses that consistently lead to reinforcement and those that do not.

intrinsic control
internal, personal processes that control and/or motivate our behaviors

extrinsic control
external, environmental processes that exercise control over our behaviors or that motivate us

Let's say we see someone clearly taking advantage of others. Should we attempt to explain that behavior by saying that the person has high power needs (intrinsic control)? Or should we say that taking advantage of others is a response that has been rewarded before and, hence, is being repeated (extrinsic control)? As is so often the case when questions are posed in terms of either/or, the answer seems to be that there is value in maintaining *both* perspectives. Both intrinsic motives and extrinsic reward systems exercise control over our behaviors. Of particular interest in psychology now is when and how control over our behaviors shifts from internal to external processes and back again (Pittman & Heller, 1987).

BEFORE YOU GO ON Define the needs for power, affiliation, and competence. What is meant by intrinsic and extrinsic control of motivated behavior?

So far, we have examined some of the issues related to the psychology of motivation. The study of motivation is directed at trying to explain what arouses and directs an organism's behaviors and/or mental processes. As we have seen, psychologists have generated a number of concepts in their attempt to explain why organisms do what they do: instinct, need, drive, homeostasis, and arousal to name just a few. The approaches that these terms represent have each added to our understanding of motivation. We have also seen, by looking at a few examples, how these concepts can help us explain some common behaviors.

EMOTION

Now we turn to a topic that belies the picture of humans as totally rational creatures—emotion. We'll begin by reviewing some of the things that psychologists do know about emotion. We'll tackle the matter of definition, see how emotions tend to be expressed in behavior, and finally, we'll examine the aspect of emotionality we probably know most about: the physiological reactions that accompany emotions.

The Nature of Emotion

Psychology has been interested in emotional reactions since its very earliest days in the late 1800s. Many people find the psychology of emotions somewhat disappointing. Our expectations are too high, perhaps. We want psychology to tell us precisely what emotions are. We want to know where they come from. And we want to know what we can do to increase the "good" ones and eliminate the "bad" ones. It is in regard to our emotional reactions that we most want simple, easy, and direct answers. These are the very reactions about which we tend to get emotional.

In the last 100 years, psychologists *have* learned a great deal about what emotions are and where they come from. There are good reasons, however, why psychology may not be able to provide direct and simple answers to all our questions about emotions.

Studying Emotion.   In a way, one of our problems with the study of emotion involves limits on our methodology. In the Introduction to this book we made the case that psychology's best, most useful method is the experiment. We noted that most of what we know in psychology today we have learned through doing experiments. One of the problems we have when studying emotion is that we often find our best method difficult or impossible to use—at least with humans.

For example, we might want to measure the physiological changes that occur in subjects who are very afraid, very angry, and very happy. There's no doubt that we have at our disposal many instruments and techniques for monitoring physiological changes. But ethical considerations (and common sense) prohibit us from wiring subjects to measuring devices and then scaring them out of their wits, making them very angry, and then making them very happy just because we want to measure physiological changes! Even if we were not concerned with ethics, how could we ever be sure that our subjects' reactions of fear, anger, and joy were in any way equal in magnitude or strength? For that matter, how could we precisely manipulate these emotional reactions in the laboratory in the first place?

Doing experiments is not psychology's only method, however. Why not use naturalistic observation? Why not observe emotional behaviors as they occur naturally, outside the laboratory? The problem here, at least with humans, and particularly for adults, is that it is often very difficult to accurately assess someone's emotional state on the basis of observable behaviors and reactions.

Growing up, becoming a mature adult, often involves learning to control or hide one's true feelings and emotions. No matter how sad they may be, children may learn that "big boys don't cry." We learn that, in some circumstances at least, it is inappropriate to display our happiness outwardly in the presence of others. We are taught that when we are angry, we should count to ten and try to control our expressions of anger. As a result, it is often very difficult to make accurate observations about a person's emotional state by simple observation.

BEFORE YOU GO ON   Why are emotional responses particularly difficult to study scientifically?

Defining Emotion.   For the moment, try to recall the last time you experienced an emotional reaction of some significance—perhaps the fear of going to the dentist, the joy of receiving an "A" on a classroom exam, the sadness at the death of a friend, or the anger at being unable to register for a class you really wanted to take. A careful analysis suggests that there are four components to your emotional reaction, whatever it may be. You will experience a *feeling*, or *affect*—which you may label fear, joy, sadness, or anger. You will have a *cognitive* reaction—you will recognize, or "know," what has just happened to you. You will have an internal, *physiological* reaction. This reaction will be largely visceral, involving your glands, hormones, and internal organs. And you will engage in an observable, *behavioral* reaction. You may tremble as you approach the dentist's office. You may run down the hallway, a broad smile on your face, waving your exam paper over your head. You may cry over the death of your friend. You may shake your fist and yell at the registrar when you cannot enroll in the class of your choice.

Emotions have four components: subjective feelings, cognitive interpretations, bodily reactions, and behavioral responses. Viewing the Vietnam Veterans War Memorial in Washington D.C. is an emotional experience that causes sadness for many visitors. Graduation brings on a variety of emotions; while being a sad time of leaving friends and favorite school activities, it is also one of the most joyful times.

In these examples, we can see four (interacting) dimensions of emotion: subjective feelings or affect, cognitive interpretations, bodily or physiological reactions, and overt expression or behavioral response. Many psychologists have theorized about how the four major aspects of emotional reactions interact and which are more or less important. (This very issue was addressed at length in William James' psychology text back in 1890.) Final resolution is not likely to occur in the very near future. For now, we're going to have to settle on a working definition of **emotion** as a reaction that includes the subjective experience of a *feeling* or *affect*, a *cognitive* interpretation, an internal *physiological* reaction, and some *behavioral* expression. That may seem a little too intellectual and devoid of emotion, but that's the best we can do.

emotion
a reaction involving subjective feelings, physiological response, cognitive interpretation, and behavioral expression

An emotional state can be said to involve which four possible reactions?

BEFORE YOU GO ON

Classifying Emotion. Although one's cognitions, physiology, and overt behavior are usually involved in an emotional reaction, there does seem to be little doubt that the most important aspect is the subjective feeling component. Perhaps it would help if we could devise a scheme or plan to describe and classify different, specific emotional reactions in a systematic way.

In fact, there are a number of ways to classify emotional responses, and each has its own supporters. Wilhelm Wundt, in that first psychology laboratory in Leipzig, was concerned with emotional reactions. He organized emotions on three intersecting dimensions: pleasantness/unpleasantness, relaxation/tension, and calm/excitement.

Emotion 315

FIGURE 7.6

Plutchik's eight primary emotions and how they relate to adaptive behaviors

Emotion, or feeling	Common stimulus	Typical behavior
1. Anger	blocking of goal-directed behavior	destruction of obstacle
2. Fear	a threat or danger	protection
3. Sadness	loss of something valued	search for help and comfort
4. Disgust	something gruesome or loathsome	rejection; pushing away
5. Surprise	a sudden, novel stimulus	orientation; turning toward
6. Curiosity	a new place or environment	explore and search
7. Acceptance	a member of own group; something of value	sharing; taking in; incorporating
8. Joy	potential mate	reproduction; courting; mating

FIGURE 7.7
Plutchik's emotion solid.

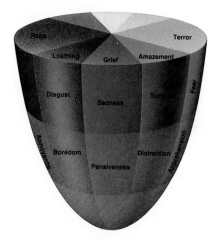

Carroll Izard (1972) has proposed a classification scheme that calls for nine primary emotions. From these nine, all others can be constructed. Izard's nine primary emotions are fear, anger, shame, contempt, disgust, distress, interest, surprise, and joy. These emotions are primary because they cannot be dissected into simpler, more basic emotions. Any other known emotion is thought to be a combination of any two or more of these nine.

Robert Plutchik (1980a), on the other hand, argues for eight basic emotions. What makes these emotions primary is that each can be directly tied to some adaptive pattern of behavior; they are emotions that can be related to survival. Plutchik's eight primary emotions, and their adaptive significance, are listed in Figure 7.6.

Plutchik also believes that emotions in addition to these eight can be seen as variants or combinations of the primary emotions. While rage, for example, may be an extreme emotion, it is viewed as being essentially the same as anger. Anger in a weaker form becomes annoyance (Plutchik, 1980b) (see Figure 7.7).

Whether there are eight or nine primary emotions (or more or fewer) and how they might be combined to form different emotions will depend on one's theoretical perspective. There isn't even complete agreement on how to distinguish between positive and negative emotions. Fear, for example, seems like a reasonable candidate for a list of negative emotions. Yet it is clear that fear can be useful and can act in many ways to protect and guide one's behavior in adaptive ways. So on what basis shall we make our judgments of positive and negative?

BEFORE YOU GO ON   Can emotions be classified?

Outward Expressions of Emotion

It is very useful for one organism to be able to let another know how it is feeling. As one wild animal approaches a second, the second had better have a good idea about the emotional state of the first. "Is it angry?" "Does it come in peace?" "Is it just curious, or is it looking for dinner?" "Is it sad, looking for comfort, or is it sexually aroused, looking for a mating partner?" An inability to make such determinations quickly can be disastrous. Animals need to know the emotional state of other animals if they are to survive for long.

Charles Darwin (1872) was among the first to recognize the importance of the ability to display one's emotions accurately to others. Nonhuman animals have many ritualistic, complex, and instinctive patterns of behavior to communicate aggressiveness, interest in courtship, submission, and many other emotional states (see Figure 7.8).

Humans can also express their emotional state in a variety of ways, including verbal report. Surely, if I am happy, sad, angry, or jealous, I can try to *tell* you how I feel. In fact, the human ability to communicate with language often puts us at a great advantage.

Even without verbal language, there is a school of thought that suggests that the human animal, like the nonhuman, uses a *body language* to communicate its emotional condition (for example, Birdwhistell, 1952; Fast, 1970). Someone sitting quietly, slumped slightly forward with head down, may be viewed as feeling sad, even from a distance. We may similarly interpret postural cues and gestures as being associated with fear, anger, happiness, and so on. But, as we have already noted, such expressions are often the result of learning or may be modified by cultural influences.

Darwin recognized facial expression as a common cue to emotion in animals, especially mammals. Might facial expression provide a key to underlying emotions in humans, too? Might there be a set of facial expressions of emotional states that is universal among the human species, just as there appears to be among nonhumans (Andrews, 1963)? A growing body of evidence supports the idea that facial expressions of one's emotional state may be an innate response, only slightly sensitive to cultural influence.

Paul Ekman has conducted a number of studies to see if there is a reliable relationship between emotional state and facial expression and if such rela-

FIGURE 7.8
Animals have many complex and instinctual patterns of behavior that communicate emotion. To display aggression and threat, mandrills bare their teeth and grimace, while Australian frilled lizards unfurl flaps of skin on their necks in order to appear larger than they really are.

FIGURE 7.9
Photos with these types of facial expressions were shown to subjects from the United States, Brazil, Chile, Argentina, and Japan. The subjects were asked to identify the emotion being displayed. The percentage of subjects who identified the photographs with the emotions listed is indicated.

    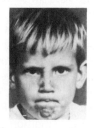 

	Happiness	Disgust	Surprise	Sadness	Anger	Fear
United States (N = 99)	97%	92%	95%	84%	67%	85%
Brazil (N = 40)	95%	97%	87%	59%	90%	67%
Chile (N = 119)	95%	92%	93%	88%	94%	68%
Argentina (N = 168)	98%	92%	95%	78%	90%	54%
Japan (N = 29)	100%	90%	100%	62%	90%	66%

relationship between emotional state and facial expression and if such relationships can be found in a number of different cultures (Ekman et al., 1987). In one large, crosscultural study, Ekman and his associates (1973) showed college students six pictures of people's faces. In each picture, a different primary emotion was being displayed—happiness, disgust, surprise, sadness, anger, and fear. When students from the United States, Argentina, Japan, Brazil, and Chile were asked to identify the emotion experienced by the people in the photographs, their agreement was remarkable (see Figure 7.9).

A problem with this study is that all of the subjects did have many shared experiences, even though they were from basically different cultures. They were, after all, college students and had many experiences in common (they had seen the same movies, watched the same TV shows, and so on). So even though Ekman's subjects came from different countries, perhaps their agreement as raters could be explained in terms of the similarities of their experiences, rather than some innate tendency to express emotions through facial expression.

An argument against this line of reasoning can be found in another project by Ekman (1972). Here, natives of a remote New Guinea tribe were asked to make faces depicting different emotional reactions (For example, "A friend has come and you are happy"). No one in our culture (or any other) would have much difficulty deciding what emotion the subjects (who were videotaped) were trying to display (see Figure 7.10).

A follow-up study (Ekman et al., 1983) has shown that simply moving one's facial muscles into the positions that are associated with emotional expression can actually cause distinctive physiological changes associated

FIGURE 7.10

Paul Ekman went to New Guinea to study the relationship between facial expression and emotional state. The first man was told that he was happy because a friend was coming. The second man was told that his child had died. The third man was told he was angry and about to fight. And the fourth man was told he had just seen a dead pig that had been lying in one place for a long time. People from any culture would not have any trouble identifying their facial expressions as indicating happiness, grief, anger, and disgust, respectively.

with an emotional state. As bizarre as that sounds, the idea is that if you raise your eyebrows, open your eyes widely, and raise the corners of your mouth, you will produce an internal physiological change not unlike that which occurs when you are happy, and you will smile as a result!

Is there any evidence that the facial expression of emotion may be innately determined? BEFORE YOU GO ON

Physiological Aspects of Emotion

Let's generate a somewhat unusual, although useful, example to work with in this section. You are on a camping trip with some friends. Having just eaten a large meal, you decide to take a short, solitary stroll down a nearby path through the woods. Totally relaxed, you are about 200 yards from your friends, who are sitting around the campfire. Suddenly, you hear a strange sound. Just as you have decided to head back a large, growling black bear appears suddenly, without warning, from behind a dense thicket. It takes one look at you, bares its teeth, and roars! To say that your reaction would be an emotional one seems an understatement. You will experience affect (call it fear if not panic). You will have a cognitive reaction (realizing that you've just encountered a bear and that you would rather you hadn't). You will engage in some overt behavior (either freezing in your tracks or racing back to the campfire). You will probably agree that a significant part of your reaction in this situation (or one like it) would be internal, physiological, and "gut-level." Responding to a bear is not something that most people would do in a purely cognitive, intellectual sort of way. When we are emotional, we respond with our insides; our visceral organs respond.

Our biological reaction to emotional situations takes place at a number of different levels. Of primary interest is the activity of our autonomic nervous system, or ANS (see Chapter 1). The brain has a role to play in emotion, but first we'll consider the autonomic response.

autonomic nervous system (ANS)
the system of nerves that serves the smooth muscles, glands, and internal, visceral organs

parasympathetic division
division of the ANS that functions to maintain a calm, relaxed state of the organism

sympathetic division
division of the ANS that becomes involved during emotional states

epinephrine
(ADRENALIN) a hormone produced by the adrenal glands that is involved in emotional activity, mostly affecting heart activity

norepinephrine
a hormone secreted by the adrenal glands; involved in emotional arousal

adrenal glands
located on the kidneys, part of the ANS especially involved in emotional reactions

The Role of the Autonomic Nervous System. As you will recall, the **autonomic nervous system,** or **ANS,** is made up of two parts, or *divisions,* that serve many of the same organs, but that have quite the opposite effect on those organs. The **parasympathetic division** is actively involved in maintaining a relaxed, calm, and unemotional state. As you first strolled down the path into the woods, the parasympathetic division of your ANS actively directed your digestive processes to do the best they could with the meal you'd just eaten. Blood was diverted from the extremities to the stomach and intestines. Saliva flowed freely. With your stomach full, and with blood diverted to it, you tended to feel somewhat sleepy as you brain began to respond to the lower levels of blood supply. Your breathing was slow, deep, and steady, as was your heart rate. All of these internal acitivities were under the control of the parasympathetic division of your autonomic nervous system.

Suddenly, there's that bear! Now the **sympathetic division** of your autonomic nervous system takes over. Automatically, all sorts of physiological changes take place. And these changes are usually quite adaptive.

A number of things happen under the direction of your sympathetic system. (1) The pupils of your eyes dilate, letting in as much of what light there is available, increasing your visual sensitivity. (2) Your heart rate and blood pressure are elevated—you've got a bear here, and energy needs to be mobilized as fast as possible. (3) Blood is diverted away from the digestive tract toward the limbs and brain, and digestion stops; again, you've got a bear to deal with; dinner can wait until later. Let's get the blood supply out there to the arms and legs where it can do some good (with what is called the "fight or flight" response).

(4) Even without your doing anything, respiration increases, becoming deeper and more rapid—you'll need all the oxygen you can get. (5) Moisture is brought to the surface of the skin in the form of perspiration—as it evaporates, the body is cooled, conserving energy. (6) Blood sugar levels increase, making more energy readily available. (7) You may lose control of your bladder and bowels—messy, perhaps, but there are more important things to worry about now. (8) Blood will tend to clot more readily than usual—again for obvious, but hopefully unnecessary reasons.

The sympathetic system makes some of these changes rather directly (stopping salivation and stimulating the cardiac muscle, for example). The rest are made indirectly through the secretion of hormones into the bloodstream, mostly **epinephrine** and **norepinephrine** from the **adrenal glands** of the endocrine system.

Because part of the physiological component of emotion *is* hormonal, under the control of the endocrine system, it *does* take a few seconds for the hormones to have their felt effect. As a result, we sometimes sense a delayed reaction of an emotional response. If you were, in fact, confronted by a bear in the woods, you probably would not have the presence of mind to notice, but the physiological reactions of sweaty palms, gasping breaths, and "butterflies in your stomach" take a few seconds to develop.

Is the autonomic and endocrine system reaction exactly the same for each and every emotion that we experience? That is a very difficult question. There is some evidence that there may be some differences. There appears to be a small difference in the hormones produced during rage and fear reactions. Consistent differences in physiological reactions for different emotional states are, at best, very small indeed. This issue has been very controversial in psychology for many years and is likely to remain so (Levinthal, 1983; Selye, 1976).

Summarize the activities of the sympathetic division of the autonomic nervous system during states of emotionality.

BEFORE YOU GO ON

The Role of the Brain.   When we become emotional, our sympathetic nervous system does not spring into action on its own. Autonomic nervous system activity is closely related to, and coordinated by, central nervous system activity.

The two brain structures most intimately involved in emotionality are the **limbic system**, deep in the brain, and the hypothalamus, that small structure at the base of the brain so involved with physiological needs and drives. The limbic system is a "lower" center in the brain made up of a number of small structures (of which the amygdala may be the most important center for emotionality). These centers are "lower" in the sense of being well below the cerebral cortex and also in the sense of being present in the brains of "lower" animals, such as rats and cats.

The limbic system (refer back to Figure 1.10) seems most involved in those emotional responses that call for defensive or attacking responses—those emotions stimulated by threat. Electrical stimulation and/or surgical destruction of portions of the limbic system reliably produce a variety of intense emotional reactions.

It is almost to be expected that the hypothalamus would have a role to play in emotionality. It is very involved in many motivational states. Strong emotional reactions can be produced by hypothalamic stimulation—including reactions that lead to attacking and killing any nearby prey (Flynn et al., 1970).

Precisely how these lower brain centers of the limbic system and hypothalamus are involved in the normal experience and expression of emotion is not yet fully understood. However, there is little doubt that they are involved.

The role of the cerebral cortex in emotionality is also poorly understood. Its role seems to be largely inhibitory. That is, the limbic system and hypothalamus seem to act as the sources for extreme and poorly directed emotional reactions. The cortex interprets impulses from these lower centers and other information available to it and then modifies and directs the emotional reaction accordingly.

Perhaps the clearest involvement of the cerebral cortex in emotionality is in the *cognitive* aspect of an emotional response. It is clearly the cerebral cortex that is involved in the interpretation and memory of emotional events. When you get back to the campfire, having just been frightened by a black bear, you will use your cortex to tell all the emotional details of your story. There is also some evidence that emotional reactions tend to be processed more in the right hemisphere of the human brain and that the left hemisphere is usually rather unemotional (Sperry, 1982; Tucker, 1981).

limbic system
a set of small structures located low in the brain, involved in motivational and emotional states

To review, the limbic system and the hypothalamus, two lower brain structures, appear to be centers of emotional reaction. These centers are coordinated and often controlled by higher centers in the cerebral cortex, which, among other things, provides the cognitive interpretation of emotional responses.

BEFORE YOU GO ON   **What brain centers are involved in emotionality?**

In this section, we have summarized some of what we know about the psychology of emotion. Have you noticed that we have used the ABC model we introduced back in the introduction? When we discuss emotions, there is little doubt that our primary focus is on the subjective experience of feeling or *a*ffect. But we've also seen that emotionality implies *b*ehavior, in terms of both overt action and physiological reaction. Although its precise role in emotionality may be questioned, being emotional also involves *c*ognitive reactions, perception, knowing, and thinking. We've seen how difficult it is to study emotion, and to classify emotional reactions. We've seen a consistency in how emotion may be displayed in facial expressions, and have reviewed the physiological bases of those reactions we call emotional.

Chapter Seven
Motivation, Sexuality, and Emotion

SUMMARY

How have the concepts of instinct, drive, and incentive been used to explain motivated behaviors?

In trying to explain why organisms do what they do, three concepts have proven useful. *Instincts* are complex patterns of behavior that occur in the presence of certain stimuli. Instinct approaches take the position that complex behavioral patterns are un-learned (innate). The concept of in-stinct has not proved to be a satisfac-tory explanation of human behavior. *Needs* are shortages of some biologi-cal necessity. Deprivation leads to a need, which leads to a drive, which arouses and directs the organism's be-havior. The relationship between de-privation, need, drive, and behavior is often not very straightforward; and many drives are more learned than bi-ologically based. Maslow has pro-posed that human needs can be placed in an ordered hierarchy, begin-ning with basic survival needs and ending with a need to achieve. Focus-ing on *incentives* explains behaviors more in terms of their goals and out-comes than on their internal driving forces. We may say that incentives "pull" behavior, whereas drives "push" behavior. In this sense, we are motivated to reach some desired end-state. These three approaches are not mutually exclusive, and each may be used to explain some types of moti-vated behavior. / 292

How can the concept of balance or equilibrium be used to help us understand motivated behaviors?

The basic idea here is that organisms are motivated to reach and maintain a state of balance. With *homeostasis*, we have a general drive to maintain a state of equilibrium among internal physiological conditions such as blood pressure, metabolism, and heart rate. Others argue for a general drive to maintain a balanced state of *arousal*, with different optimal levels of arousal being best suited for different tasks or situations. / 294

Given the concept of homeostasis, how might temperature regulation be thought of as a physiologically based drive?

Temperature regulation can be viewed as a physiological drive because we clearly have a need, (and are driven) to maintain our body temperatures within certain strict (homeostatic) lev-els. Doing so often involves voluntary as well as involuntary responding. / 296

List some of the factors that may influence drinking behavior.

We are motivated to drink for a num-ber of reasons: to relieve dryness in our mouths and throats and to main-tain a homeostatic level of fluid within our bodies (monitored by the hypo-thalamus). We also engage in drinking behavior in response to external cues (stimulus values), such as taste, aro-ma, or appearance. What we drink is often influenced by our learning expe-riences. / 297

List those internal and external factors that influence our drive to eat.

There are a number of factors that lead to eating behaviors, some inter-nal, some external. Internal cues for eating include cues mediated by the hypothalamus, which may be re-sponding to fat store levels, blood sugar levels, or some other indicator that our normal, homeostatic balance has been disrupted. Associated with this view is the position that body weight is maintained at a given set point both by food intake and exer-cise levels. The stimulus properties of foods may motivate eating, as may habit patterns and social pressures. / 299

In what ways is the sex drive a unique physiologically based drive?

The sex drive is an unusual physiolog-ical drive for four reasons. (1) Indi-vidual survival does not depend on its satisfaction. (2) The drive involves seeking tension rather than seeking relief from tension. (3) It is not fully present at birth, but matures later. (4) The extent to which it is influenced by learned or external influences varies from species to species. / 301

SUMMARY continued

Briefly describe the changes that occur during the excitement, plateau, orgasm, and resolution phases of the human sexual response.

Masters and Johnson have identified four standard phases of human sexual responsiveness. In the *excitement phase,* both males and females becomes sexually aroused; there is increased tension in the genital area. Males attain an erection, and the female's vagina becomes lubricated. There are many stimuli that may evoke this phase. The *plateau phase* carries arousal to the brink of orgasm. Blood pressure levels and heart rates increase for both males and females. The penis becomes fully erect. The vagina enlarges and the clitoris elevates into the body. The *orgasm phase* is the shortest of the four. In the male, there is a series of pelvic contractions followed by ejaculation. Females also experience a series of short, intense contractions. The *resolution phase* returns the body to its more relaxed, nonaroused state. After orgasm, males experience a refractory period during which they cannot be stimulated to repeat the cycle phases just described. Females have no refractory period and, hence, may experience multiple orgasms if properly stimulated. / 304

What is homosexuality?

Homosexuals are those who are attracted to and sexually aroused by members of their own sex. There is thought to be a continuum, or gradual dimension that extends from exclusively homosexual on the one extreme to exclusively heterosexual on the other. / 306

Name and briefly describe four sexually transmitted diseases.

Sexually transmitted diseases (STDs) are very common. Among the most troublesome are: (1) *Gonorrhea,* a bacterial infection of the moist tissues around the genitals. It is transmitted only by sexual activity. Its symptoms increase in severity when the disease is left untreated. Penicillin is an effective treatment. (2) *Syphilis* is another bacterial infection. It passes through four stages as symptoms increase in severity. Left untreated, it may result in death. Penicillin, again, is an effective treatment. (3) *Genital herpes* is a viral infection that affects the skin in the genital area. It is the most common STD and has no cure. A person with herpes may go for prolonged periods without any noticeable symptoms. (4) *Acquired immune deficiency syndrome (AIDS),* is perhaps the most frightening of all STDs. It is a viral (HIV) infection that can only be transmitted through the exchange of bodily fluids, as in sexual activity. Once in-

fected, a person remains symptom-free (but capable of infecting others) in a "carrier state" until full-blown symptoms of AIDS develop. Virtually all persons with AIDS symptoms will die within four years. There is, at the moment, no effective vaccine or treatment for AIDS. Preventing HIV infection through behavioral (sexual practice) change is recommended. / 309

What is achievement motivation, and how is it usually measured?

Achievement motivation (nAch) is defined as one's need to attempt and succeed at tasks in such a way as to meet or exceed some standard of excellence. Achievement motivation is usually assessed through the interpretation of short stories generated in response to the Thematic Apperception Test, in which one looks for themes of striving and achievement. / 310

Define the needs for power, affiliation, and competence.

What is meant by intrinsic and extrinsic control of motivated behavior?

The need for power is defined as the need to be in charge, to be in control of a situation or of others and usually at the expense of others. Affiliation needs involve being motivated to be with others, to form friendships and interpersonal relationships. A need for competence implies a need to demonstrate the ability to do something, to cope on one's own with the challenges of daily living. A matter as yet unresolved is the extent to which (or when) behaviors are manifestations of these internal needs and drives (intrinsic control) or are reflecting one's learning experiences in terms of behaviors that have resulted in rewards in the past (extrinsic control). / 313

Why are emotional responses particularly difficult to study scientifically?

It is difficult to study emotions in humans because (1) ethical considerations make it impossible to do many experiments, and (2) adults usually have learned to hide their emotions from public view, making the use of naturalistic observation questionable. / 314

An emotional state can be said to involve which four possible reactions?

There are four possible components of an emotional reaction: the experience of a subjective feeling, or *affec-* tive component; a *cognitive* appraisal or interpretation; an internal, visceral, *physiological* reaction; and an overt *behavioral* response. / 315

Can emotions be classified?

There have been a number of attempts to sort or categorize emotional reactions, dating back to Wundt in the late 1800s. Carroll Izard has one scheme that calls for nine primary emotions: fear, anger, shame, contempt, disgust, distress, interest, surprise, and joy. (Izard adds guilt when considering prime emotions of infants.) Robert Plutchik argues that there are eight basic emotions and many combinations and degrees of these eight. Thus, there appears to be some sense in attempting to classify basic emotions, although there is no agreement on which scheme is best. / 316

Is there any evidence that the facial expression of emotion may be innately determined?

It is a common observation that facial expressions can indicate the internal, emotional state of an individual. What leads us to believe that facial expression of emotion is unlearned (and, hence, innate) is that there is such universal reliability in the interpretation of facial expressions, even across widely different cultures. / 319

Summarize the activities of the sympathetic division of the autonomic nervous system during states of emotionality.

Among the many changes that take place when we become emotional are those produced by the sympathetic division of the autonomic nervous system. Occurring to varying degrees and dependent on the situation, these reactions include dilation of the pupils, increased heart rate and blood pressure, cessation of digestive processes, deeper and more rapid breathing, increased perspiration, and elevated blood sugar levels. / 321

What brain centers are involved in emotionality?

The cerebral cortex is involved in the cognitive interpretation of emotional events and also acts as an inhibitory mechanism, controlling and coordinating the activity of lower brain centers for emotionality (largely the limbic system and the hypothalamus). Basically, the brain coordinates the physiological aspect of emotionality. / 322

REVIEW QUESTIONS

1. The two aspects, or subprocesses, that characterize all of the approaches that psychologists have taken toward motivation are:

a. drives and their underlying needs.

b. arousing and directing forces.

c. instincts and incentives.

d. positive and negative goals.

All of the terms mentioned in these alternatives are in some way related to various theories or approaches to motivation. The only two that are by definition common to all approaches reflect the observation that motivation arouses and directs the behaviors of organisms. All the other terms are specifically related to just one or another of the various approaches describing just what it is that does arouse and direct behaviors. / 286

2. As originally proposed by Cannon in 1932, the concept of homeostasis refers to:

a. a state of balance among internal, physiological processes.

b. the learned need to offset negative goals with positive goals.

c. the driving force to find sufficient stimulation from the environment.

d. the fact that what motivates us involves both physiological and psychological factors.

Cannon's basic concern was with internal, physiological processes. He argued that all of our physiological functions have a set point, or a narrow range, of operation that can be considered normal, optimal, balanced, or homeostatic. Whenever events cause an imbalance among these physiological conditions, we are motivated to return them to their set point, homeostatic level. / 292

3. The physiological basis for most human physiological drives seems to be centered in:

a. hormonal regulation.

b. the hypothalamus.

c. the reticular activating system.

d. instinctive responses.

For virtually all of our physiological drives, we can identify some region and some function of the hypothalamus as important. Hormonal regulation is surely important in the sex drive, and the reticular activating system helps to control our level of arousal, but the hypothalamus plays some role in all our physiological drives. Reference to instinct as an explanatory concept in human motivation has not proven very helpful. / 295

4. According to Masters and Johnson, which of the following is the greatest difference between male and female sexual response?

a. Women have erogenous zones. Men do not.

b. Men experience orgasm and find it pleasurable. Women do not.

c. Women are affected by aphrodisiacs. Men are not.

d. Men have a refractory period following resolution. Women do not.

The first three of these alternatives are simply not true. Both men and women have erogenous zones or areas which, when stimulated, produce sexual arousal, and both experience orgasms. Neither men nor women are affected by any known aphrodisiac. Following the fourth stage of the human sexual response, resolution, men experience a refractory period during which arousal, an erection, and another orgasm are not possible. There is no evidence of a comparable period in the sexual responsiveness of women. / 304

5. Which of the following statements concerning AIDS is best supported by research evidence?

a. AIDS is the most common of the sexually transmitted diseases.

b. AIDS is caused by a bacterial infection of the genitals which spreads to the immune system.

c. Individuals who develop the full-blown symptoms of the AIDS disease will almost surely die.

d. It is easier to contact AIDS than either herpes or gonorrhea.

AIDS is a devastating, untreatable, life-threatening disease, but it is much less common than syphilis, herpes, or gonorrhea. Contracting AIDS requires the interchange of bodily fluids, blood or semen, which makes it more difficult to contract than either herpes or gonorrhea. It is caused by a virus (HIV), not a bacterial infection. Because it remains untreatable, those who develop the full-blown symptoms of AIDS will die, generally within four years of the initial diagnosis. / 306

6. Which task would a person with a high nAch tend to choose?

a. one in which success is possible, but not guaranteed.

b. one in which success is simply not possible.

c. one in which success is guaranteed.

d. none of the above.

A person with a high need to achieve (nAch) has a need to attempt and succeed at tasks in such a way as to meet or exceed some standard of success or excellence. Such a person would not attempt a task in which there was no chance of success, nor would she or he choose to bother with a task where success was guaranteed. They value tasks that offer some challenge but where success may be earned through effort and hard work, which is what is implied in alternative (a). / 310

7. Someone with many friends and acquaintances, who often volunteers to join community and social groups, is displaying a high:

a. need for power.

b. need for achievement.

c. need for affiliation.

d. need for competence.

Although the person referred to in this item may have needs for achievement, power, and competence, someone with a desire to be with others, to work together toward some end, and to form friendships, is displaying a high need for affiliation. / 311

8. Which of the following is *least* involved in emotional reaction?

a. the parasympathetic division of the ANS.

b. the limbic system.

c. the adrenal glands.

d. the hypothalamus.

The hypothalamus and structures of the limbic system are brain centers (along with the cerebral cortex) that are implicated in emotionality. It is the sympathetic division of the ANS, either directly or through action of the adrenal glands, that is responsible for many emotional reactions. On the other hand, the parasympathetic division of the ANS is actively involved in maintaining a relaxed, calm, and unemotional state. / 319

Chapter Eight

Individual Differences in Personality and Intelligence

Why We Care

Approaches to Personality

    Freud's Psychoanalytic Approach

        Levels of Consciousness   The "Structure" of Personality

        Basic Instincts   The Development of Personality

    The Psychoanalytic Approach After Freud

        Alfred Adler   Karen Horney

        Carl Jung

    Evaluating the Psychoanalytic Approach

    The Behavioral/Learning Approach

        John B. Watson   B. F. Skinner

        John Dollard   Albert Bandura

          and Neal Miller   Julian Rotter

    Evaluating the Behavioral/Learning Approach

    The Humanistic/Phenomenological Approach

        Carl Rogers   Abraham Maslow

    Evaluating the Humanistic/Phenomenological Approach

    The Trait Approach

        Gordon Allport   Hans Eysenck

        Raymond B. Cattell

    Evaluating the Trait Approach

The Nature of Psychological Tests

    A Working Definition

    Criteria for a Good Test

        Reliability   Norms

        Validity

Personality Assessment

    Behavioral Observation

    Interviews

    Paper-and-Pencil Tests

    Projective Techniques

Intelligence

    Defining Intelligence

    Assessing Intelligence

        The Stanford-Binet Intelligence Scale

        The Wechsler Tests of Intelligence

        Group Differences in Intelligence

    Variations in Intelligence

        The Distribution of Intelligence   The Mentally Retarded

        The Mentally Gifted

Nature-Nurture Revisited: The Influence of Heredity and the Environment on Intelligence

    Conceptual Problems

    A Tentative Answer

    What the Data Suggest: The Study of Twins

Here's a test for you to try. It's an adaptation of a personality test recently found in a national magazine. After you've taken the test, we'll let you know what it's about. In the meantime, try to guess what this test is supposed to be testing.

1. Suppose a shopping center was under construction in your neighborhood. Would you protest against it?
   (A) No.
   (B) Maybe. It would depend on which stores were in it.
   (C) Yes, I definitely would.

2. Do you feel that today's teenagers have looser morals than the teenagers of the 1960s?
   (A) Yes, definitely.
   (B) Some do and some don't.
   (C) No, I don't feel that things have changed that much.

3. How do you feel about modern art, compared to the art of the "great masters"?
   (A) I prefer it. It's fascinating.
   (B) It's ugly.
   (C) I don't like art of any sort.

4. Would you enjoy having your picture taken in the nude?
   (A) No, I would not under any circumstances.
   (B) Yes, I'd enjoy that.
   (C) Only if I were paid a lot of money.

5. When you visit a zoo, which animals do you most enjoy watching?
   (A) The monkeys. They're fun to watch.
   (B) The penguins.
   (C) The big cats—lions, tigers, and leopards.

Do you think a divorced father should be given custody of his children?
(A) Yes, more often than not.
(B) Occasionally.
(C) No, never.

---

6. How do you feel about young couples who choose to live together rather than marry?
   (A) It's a very good idea for most couples.
   (B) It's okay for a few, under certain circumstances.
   (C) It's wrong and a bad idea for any couple.

7. Should a person feel embarrassed or uncomfortable about getting their hair cut by a person of the opposite sex?
   (A) No, of course not. It's perfectly normal.
   (B) Yes, I think it would be embarrassing.
   (C) Maybe. It would depend on the people involved.

8. What do you think about women who never wear make-up?
   (A) It's their right, and it's perfectly okay with me.
   (B) They are crude and only trying to attract attention.
   (C) They are simply lazy.

9. Do you envy the good looks of television actors and actresses?
   (A) Yes, I wish I looked that good.
   (B) No, good looks are only skin deep.
   (C) Usually not, but there are definite exceptions.

10. Do you think a divorced father should be given custody of his children?
    (A) Yes, more often than not.
    (B) Occasionally.
    (C) No, never.

Now that you've taken this quiz, do you have any idea what

it might be about? A test very much like this one was discovered in a magazine at the checkout stand of a supermarket. The test in the magazine claimed that it could indicate whether or not one was naturally sexy. According to the text that accompanies the quiz, being sexy is largely a state of mind, and "This test will help you find out just how much of this magical quality you are fortunate enough to possess." This "test" can serve as an example (and there are many such examples) throughout this chapter. It *is* a psychological test. Whether or not it is a *good* psychological test remains to be seen. (If you're curious about how you scored, how "naturally sexy" you are, we suggest that you can score your responses on *this* quiz however you'd like. We suspect that your grading scheme would be as useful as ours.)

Why We Care

Most of us think that we understand ourselves fairly well. We feel that we have a pretty good sense of who we are, how we tend to think and feel, and what we are likely to do in almost any situation. To a somewhat lesser extent, we also feel that we understand a few other people such as very close friends and family members because we have gathered—over the years—some insight into their personalities. We've come to believe that knowing someone's personality is required if we are to truly understand that person. We have also come to appreciate that knowing someone's personality is not easily done—that somehow or other, what makes up someone's personality are internal, private experiences, often very difficult to determine from the outside.

Over the years, a number of theories have emerged in psychology that have sought to describe the nature of personality. In this chapter, we will examine a number of those theories and then examine the techniques by which personality is assessed.

There is good logic behind the claim that a science is only as good as its measurement. Making accurate predictions hinges on the degree to which one can accurately measure one's subject matter. Much of the measuring that is done in psychology involves psychological tests, and psychological testing is a major focus of this chapter. If experience counts for anything, you are already something of an expert on psychological tests. At least you are an expert on *taking* tests. To have simply survived to this point in your education means that you have taken hundreds of tests—most of them designed to assess some cognitive ability or skill. Surely you will be faced with more of them in the future.

Psychological testing is an integral part of our lives. Psychological tests are used for a number of different reasons in our society. As you know from your own experience, there is a wide range of instruments that we can label as tests. In this chapter, we will do a number of things. We will examine the nature and the definition of psychological tests in general, and discuss criteria by which tests and other assessment techniques can be judged and compared.

We will also consider the often emotional issue of intelligence and how to measure it. Throughout this text we have repeatedly made the point that no two people are exactly alike, that each of us is different from everyone else. One of the most important ways in which people differ is in their intellectual capabilities. We will define intelligence, explore how people differ in intelligence, and see how intelligence is tested.

We will also try to give tentative answers to questions about why people differ in intelligence and where intelligence comes from. Providing answers to these sorts of questions honestly, scientifically, and completely is not really possible at the present time. There are a number of reasons why we can't offer definitive answers to such questions. For one thing, there is less than perfect agreement on just what intelligence *is*. There may be many different ways in which intelligence can be expressed (for example, Gardner, 1983). There are also serious questions about the precision, and the fairness, of even our best instruments for measuring intelligence.

So what we'll do in this chapter is raise some interesting questions about differences in intelligence, provide the best answers we can at the moment, and continually caution against overinterpretation of incomplete data. We'll finish with a general discussion of the roles of heredity and the environment in determining intellectual functioning. We've addressed this "nature-nurture" issue earlier (in Chapter 6 on development) but nowhere is the issue more focused and more controversial than in the context of intelligence.

theory
a collection of related assumptions that are used to explain some phenomenon and that lead, through logical reasoning, to testable hypotheses

personality
relatively enduring and unique traits (including affects, behaviors, and cognitions) that can be used to characterize an individual in different situations

APPROACHES TO PERSONALITY

Before we examine how psychologists assess personality, we must consider just what personality is. By this point in your study of psychology you might imagine that there are several different approaches to understanding personality. In fact, there are, and we will begin our study of personality with a brief survey of personality theories. We'll organize specific theories into four basic types, or approaches. Before we do, let's see what we mean by **theory** and what we mean by **personality** in this context.

A theory is a series of assumptions; in our particular case, these are assumptions about people and their personalities. The ideas or assumptions that comprise a theory are reasonably and logically related to each other. Further, the ideas of a theory can lead (through reason) to specific, testable hypotheses. In short, a theory is an organized collection of ultimately testable ideas used to explain a particular subject matter.

Now then, what is personality? Few terms have been as difficult to define as personality. In many ways, each of the theoretical approaches we will study in this section generates its own definition of personality. What we are looking at with personality are the *affect* (feeling, mood, or emotion), *behaviors,* and *cognitions* (thoughts, beliefs, ideas, and so on), of people that can characterize them in a number of situations over time. We assume that these affects, behaviors, and cognitions help them to adapt to their environments. Personality also includes those dimensions we can use to judge people to be different from one another. So basically we are looking for ways to describe individuals that let us recognize all those differences we know exist among people. And when we refer to personality, the descriptors we use are psychological (*a*ffect, *b*ehavior, and *c*ognition) instead of physical. Psychologist David Buss (1984) puts it this way, "The field of personality psychology is centrally concerned with the traits that characterize our species as well as the major ways in which individuals characteristically differ" (p. 1143).

Wait a minute. Just what are these personality theories *for?* How are we going to *use* them? Theories of personality can help us explain and predict a person's behaviors and/or mental processes. Now that's a large order, but that's precisely what personality theories are for. If we want to predict what you will do in a certain situation, let's say, we'll need to know about the situation (which will influence your reactions) and we'll need to know about you (your private experiences, which will also influence your reactions). What theories of personality do is direct our attention to those traits, characteristics, or processes that the theorist believes will best help us to explain and/or predict a person's reactions—be they behavioral or mental—in a wide variety of situations. In this regard, you can judge the worth of the theories we describe here as well as can anyone else.

What is a theory of personality?   **BEFORE YOU GO ON**

Freud's Psychoanalytic Approach

We will begin our study of personality theories by considering the **psychoanalytic** approach. This is the approach associated with Sigmund Freud and his students. We begin with Freud because he was the first to present a truly unified theory of personality.

Freud's theory of personality has been one of the most influential and, at the same time, most controversial in all of science. Although there are many facets to Freud's theory (and the theories of the neo-Freudians), two basic premises characterize the psychoanalytic approach: (1) a reliance on innate, inborn instincts as explanatory concepts for human behavior, and (2) an acceptance of the power and influence of unconscious forces to mold and shape our behavior.

Sigmund Freud was born in Moravia (now a part of Czechoslovakia) in 1856. After a brief stay in Leipzig, his family moved to Vienna when Freud was 4 years old. Freud lived in Vienna until the Nazi invasion in 1938. He then moved to England and died in London on September 23, 1939.

psychoanalytic
the approach to personality associated with Freud and his followers that relies on instincts and the unconscious as explanatory concepts

The son of a Jewish wool merchant, Freud graduated from the University of Vienna Medical School in 1881. He didn't want to enter the private practice of medicine, favoring instead scientific research and study. However, economics (and a growing family) forced him into practice at the General Hospital of Vienna, where he became interested in what were then called "nervous disorders." He was struck with how little was known about the cause or treatment of such disorders, and he chose to specialize in psychiatry. His theories about the nature of personality arose largely from observations of his patients and intense self-examination. This context provided Freud with the experience he needed to propose a general theory of personality and to develop a technique of therapy called *psychoanalysis*. A discussion of psychoanalysis appears in Chapter 10. For now, let's review some of Freud's basic ideas about the structure and dynamics of the human personality.

Levels of Consciousness.   It was Freud's view that only a small portion of one's mental life was readily available to a person's awareness at any one time. Ideas, memories, motives, and desires of which we are actively aware are said to be *conscious*.

Aspects of our mind that are not conscious at any one moment, but that can be easily brought to awareness, are stored or housed at a *preconscious* level. For example, right now you may not be thinking about what you had for dinner last night or what you might do for dinner tonight. But with very little effort, the matter of tonight's and last night's dinner can be brought into your conscious awareness.

Cognitions, feelings, and motives that are not available to the conscious mind are said to be at the *unconscious* level. At this level, we have stored a number of ideas, memories, and desires of which we are not and cannot easily become aware. This is a strange notion—that there are ideas, thoughts, and feelings stored away in our minds of which we are completely unaware. However, the contents of the unconscious mind do influence us. Unconscious content passing through the preconscious may show itself in slips of the tongue, humor, neurotic symptoms, and, of course, dreams. There was no doubt in Freud's mind that unconscious forces could be used to explain much of one's behavior that otherwise seemed irrational and beyond description.

As we shall see, a good deal of Freudian psychoanalysis as a psychotherapeutic technique is aimed at helping a patient get in touch with the contents of the unconscious level of the mind. A husband, for instance, who constantly forgets his wedding anniversary and occasionally cannot remember his wife's name when he tries to introduce her may be experiencing some unconscious conflict or doubts about being married in the first place. (There *are*, of course, other possibilities.)

BEFORE YOU GO ON   **What are the three levels of consciousness proposed by Freud?**

Basic Instincts.   According to Freudian theory, our behaviors, thoughts, and feelings are governed largely by the operation of a number of instincts. These are inborn impulses or drives, forces that rule our personalities. There may be many individual instincts, but they can be grouped into two categories.

On the one hand are **life instincts (eros),** which are impulses for survival, in particular those that motivate sex, hunger, and thirst. Each instinct has its own energy that compels us into action. Freud called the energy through which the sexual instincts operate **libido.** Opposed to the life instincts are **death instincts (thanatos).** These are impulses toward destruction. Directed inward, they give rise to feelings of depression or suicide; directed outward, they result in aggression toward other people or their property. In large measure, life (according to Freud) is an attempt to resolve conflicts between these two natural and diametrically opposed instincts.

The "Structure" of Personality.   Freud proposed that the human mind or personality is composed of three separate, though interacting, structures or subsystems: the id, ego, and superego. Each of these subsystems has its own job to do, its own principles to follow.

The **id** is the totally inborn or inherited portion of personality. It is through and in the id that one's basic instincts develop. The driving force of the id is libido, or sexual energy, although it may be more fair to Freud to say "sensual" than "sexual."

The id constantly seeks satisfaction for instinctual impulses, regardless of the consequences. It operates on what Freud labeled the **pleasure principle,** indicating that the major function of the id is to find satisfaction of pleasurable impulses. Although two other divisions of personality develop later, our id remains with us always and constantly provides a major force in our lives.

The **ego** is that part of the personality that develops through our experience with reality. In many ways, it is our self, the rational, reasoning part of our personality. The ego operates on the **reality principle.** One of the ego's main jobs is to try to find satisfaction for the id, but in ways that are reasonable. The ego may have to delay gratification of some libidinal impulse or may need to find an acceptable outlet for some desire. When the ego cannot find acceptable ways to satisfy the drives of the id, conflict and anxiety result. Then ways must be found to deal with the resulting anxiety.

The last of the three structures to develop is the **superego,** which we can liken to one's sense of morality or conscience. The superego operates on an **idealistic principle.** One problem we have with the superego is that it— like the id—has no contact with reality, and, therefore, often places unrealistic demands on the individual. The superego demands that we do what it deems to be right and proper, no matter what the circumstances. Failure to do so may lead to guilt and shame. Again, the ego tries to maintain a realistic balance between the conscience of the superego and the libido of the id.

Now this isn't as complicated as it may sound. Let's suppose a bank teller discovers an extra $20 in her cash drawer at the end of the day. She certainly could use an extra $20. "Go ahead. Nobody will miss it. The bank can afford a few dollars here and there. Think of the fun you can have with an extra $20," is the basic message from her id. "The odds are that you'll get caught if you take this money. You may get away with it, but if you *are* caught, you may lose your job, then you'll have to find another one," reasons her ego. "But you shouldn't even consider taking that money. Shame on you! It's not yours. It belongs to someone else and should be returned," the superego protests. Clearly, the interaction of the three components of one's personality is not always this simple and straightforward, but this example illustrates the general idea.

life instincts (eros)
those inborn impulses proposed by Freud that compel one toward survival, including hunger, thirst, and sex

libido
the energy that activates the life (sexual) instincts (largely of the id)

death instincts (thanatos)
those inborn impulses proposed by Freud that compel one toward destruction, including aggression

id
that instinctive aspect of personality that seeks immediate gratification of impulses; operates on the pleasure principle

pleasure principle
the impulse of the id to seek immediate gratification to reduce tensions

ego
that aspect of personality that encompasses the sense of "self;" in contact with the real world, operates on the reality principle

reality principle
governs the ego; arbitrating between the demands of the id, the superego, and the real world

superego
that aspect of personality that refers to ethical or moral considerations; operates on the idealistic principle

idealistic principle
governs the superego; opposed to the id, seeks adherence to standards of ethics and morality

During the oral stage, babies find pleasure and satisfaction in oral activities, such as feeding, sucking, and making noises.

The Development of Personality.   Freud obviously put a lot of stock in the biological basis of personality, relying as he did on concepts like instinct. This same orientation flavored his view of how one's personality develops. According to Freud, the personality develops naturally in a series of overlapping stages. The events that occur in early stages have the potential to profoundly influence later development.

One of Freud's most controversial assumptions was that even infants and young children are under the influence of the sexual strivings of the id and its libidinal energy. The outlet for the sexual (again, *sensual* may be a better term) impulses of young children is not the reproductive sex act. But Freud claimed that much of the pleasure derived by children is often essentially sexual in nature, hence we refer to Freud's stages of development as *psychosexual*. Freud claimed that there are five such stages:

(1) *Oral stage* (birth to 1 year). Pleasure and satisfaction come from oral activities: feeding, sucking, and making noises. The mouth continues to be a source of pleasure for many people long into adulthood, as demonstrated by overeating, fingernail biting, smoking, or talkativeness.

(2) *Anal stage* (ages 1 to 3 years). Sometime in their second year, children develop the ability to control their bowel and bladder habits. At this time, the anus becomes the focus of pleasure. Satisfaction is gained through bowel control. Aggressiveness (the id again) can be displayed (particularly against parents) by either having bowel movements at inappropriate times or by refusing "to go" when placed on the "potty chair." Here we can clearly see the thoughtful, reasoning ego emerging and exercising control. After all, the parents can't *make* their child do what they want it to. The child is in control, and that control leads to great satisfaction.

(3) *Phallic stage* (ages 3 to 5 years). Here there is an awareness of one's sexuality. The genitals replace the mouth and anus as the source of pleasure, and masturbation or fondling of the genitals may become a common practice. It is during this stage of development that children form close (sexually based) attachments to the parent of the opposite sex, and feelings of jealousy and/or fear of the same-sex parent may arise. This pattern of reaction is called the _Oedipus complex_ in boys and the _Electra complex_ in girls. It is in the phallic stage that the superego begins to develop.

(4) *Latency stage* (ages 6 years until puberty). At this point in one's life, sexual development gets put on hold. Now the ego is developing very rapidly. There is much to be learned about the world and how it operates. Sexual development can wait. Sexuality is suppressed. Friends tend to be of the same sex. You have no doubt heard the protestations of a 9-year-old boy, "Oh yuck, kiss a girl! Never! Yuck!" And you counsel, "Just wait, soon girls won't seem so 'yucky.'"

During the phallic stage, children sometimes develop an Electra (for girls) or Oedipus (for boys) complex in which they form close, sexually based relationships with their opposite-sex parent and exhibit jealousy and/or fear of their same-sex parent.

During the latency stage, sexuality is suppressed and children focus on same-sex friendships.

(5) *Genital stage* (From puberty on). With puberty, there is a renewal of the sexual impulse, a reawakening of desire, and an interest in matters sexual, sensual, and erotic.

Briefly review Freud's five psychosexual stages of development.

BEFORE YOU GO ON

The Psychoanalytic Approach After Freud

Sigmund Freud was a persuasive communicator. In person, he was a powerful speaker. In his writings, he was without peer. His ideas were new and different, and they attracted many students. Freud founded a psychoanalytic society in Vienna. He had many friends and colleagues who shared his ideas and his theories, but some of his colleagues did not entirely agree with his theory. Among other things, they were bothered by the focus on biological instincts and libido and the lack of concern for social influences. Some of these psychoanalysts left Freud and proposed theories of their own; they became known as **neo-Freudians.** Because they had their own ideas, they had to part from Freud; he apparently would not tolerate disagreement with the basic ideas of his theory. One had to accept all of psychoanalysis—including psychoanalysis as a treatment for mental disorders—or one had to leave Freud's inner circle of associates.

Remembering that a theory consists of a series of logically interrelated, testable assumptions, it is obvious that we cannot do justice to someone's theory of personality in a short paragraph or two. However, we can sketch the basic idea behind the theories of a few selected neo-Freudians.

neo-Freudians
those theorists of the psychoanalytic school who have taken issue with some parts of Freudian theory, including Adler, Jung, and Horney

Alfred Adler (1870–1937). At first, as the psychoanalytic movement was beginning to take shape, Adler was one of Freud's closest friends and associates. However, Adler left Freud and, in 1911, founded his own version of a psychoanalytic approach to personality. Two things seemed

Alfred Adler

develope inferikty complex *social orientared*

Approaches to Personality **337**

most to offend Adler: the negativity of Freud's views (the death instinct, for example) and the idea of sexual libido as a prime impulse in life.

Adler proposed that we are very much a product of the social influences on our personality. We are motivated not so much by causes, such as instincts, but by goals and incentives (pulled rather than pushed, as we noted in Chapter 7 when we discussed motivation). The future and what it holds for us is more important than our past. For Adler, our major goal is the achievement of success or superiority. This goal is fashioned in childhood when, because we are then weak and vulnerable, we develop an **inferiority complex.** Though we may seem inferior as children, with the help of social influences and our own creativity, we can overcome and succeed. Thus, Adler's view of people is much more upbeat and positive than Freud's.

inferiority complex
the Adlerian notion that as children we develop a sense of inferiority in dealing with our environment; needs to be overcome to reach maturity

Carl Jung (1875–1961). Adler left Freud's inner circle in 1911. Two years later, another student, Carl Jung, left. Jung was more mystical in his approach to personality and (like Adler) was certainly more positive about one's ability to control one's own destiny. He believed that our major goal in life was to bring together in unity all of the aspects of our personality, conscious and unconscious, introverted (inwardly directed) and extroverted (outwardly directed).

Carl Jung

Jung accepted the idea of an unconscious mind, but expanded it, claiming that there are *two* types of unconscious: the *personal unconscious,* which is very much like Freud's view of the unconscious, and the *collective unconscious,* which contains very basic ideas and notions that go beyond an individual's own personal experiences. These ideas and notions are common to all of humanity and are inherited from all past generations.

Karen Horney (1885–1952). Trained as a psychoanalyst in Germany, Horney came to the United States in 1934. She preserved some Freudian concepts, but changed most of them significantly. Horney believed that levels of consciousness make sense, as do anxiety and repression. But she theorized that the prime impulses that motivate behavior are not biological and inborn or sexual and aggressive. A major concept for Horney was *basic anxiety,* which grows out of childhood when the child feels isolated and alone in a hostile environment. If proper parental nurturance is forthcoming, this basic anxiety can be overcome. If, however, parents are inconsistent, indifferent, or overly punishing, children may also develop *basic hostility* and may feel very hostile and aggressive toward their parents. Little children, however, cannot express hostility toward their parents, so the hostility gets repressed (into the unconscious) and even more anxiety builds.

Karen Horney

So, like Freud, Horney placed great emphasis on early childhood experiences, but more from a perspective of social interaction and personal growth. Horney claimed that there are three distinct ways in which people tend to interact with each other. In some cases, people *move away from* others, seeking independence and self-sufficiency. The idea here is something like, "If I am on my own and uninvolved, you won't be able to hurt me." On the other hand, some may *move toward* others, tending to be compliant and dependent. This style of interaction protects one against anxiety in the sense of, "So long as I always do what you want me to do, you won't be upset with me." The third interpersonal style involves *moving against* others, where the effort is to be in control, to gain power and dominate; "If I am in control, you'll have to do what I want you to do." Now the ideal, of course, is to maintain a balance among these three styles of interpersonal relationship, but Horney argued that many people tend to have one of these three predominate in their interactions with others.

Horney also disagreed with Freud's position regarding the biological necessity of differences between men and women. Freud's theories have been taken to task a number of times for their male chauvinist bias (Fisher & Greenberg, 1977). Horney was one of the first to do so. *called Freud theories male chauvinist Bias*

Briefly summarize the contributions of Adler, Jung, and **BEFORE YOU GO ON**
Horney to the psychoanalytic approach to personality.

Evaluating the Psychoanalytic Approach

There is a common misconception that when Freud died in 1939, psychoanalytic theory died with him. Psychoanalytic theory is still alive and well. It has changed and evolved (some would say matured) over the years, but it is very much with us (Silverman, 1976). Current psychoanalytic theory tends to emphasize the role of the ego more than the role of the id and superego (Kohut, 1977; Rappaport, 1951).

Two major criticisms of Freudian psychoanalytic theory are that it is largely derived from the observations of disordered patients and that many of its assumptions are untestable. Freud thought of himself as a scientist, but he tested none of his theories experimentally. Some of them seem to be beyond testing. What, after all, *is* libidinal energy? How can it be measured? How would we recognize it if we saw it? It does seem that the heavy reliance on instincts as explanatory concepts—especially instincts with sexual and aggressive overtones—goes beyond where many psychologists are willing to venture.

focused on early childhood
Very importANT.
a sexual impulses

On the other hand, Freud must be credited (along with other psychoanalytically oriented theorists) for focusing our attention on the importance of the early childhood years and for suggesting that some (even biologically determined) impulses affect our behaviors even though they are beyond our awareness. And although Freud may have overstated the matter, drawing attention to the impact of sexuality and sexual impulses as influences on behavior and personality was a major contribution to psychology.

The Behavioral/Learning Approach

Many American psychologists in the early twentieth century did not think much of the psychoanalytic approach, regardless of its form or who happened to propose it. From its very beginnings, American psychology was oriented toward the laboratory and theories of learning. Explaining personality in terms of learning and focusing on observable behaviors seemed the reasonable course of action. In this section, we'll briefly review some of the approaches to personality that are behavioral and rely on learning theory to explain personality.

John B. Watson. John B. Watson (1878–1958) and his followers in behaviorism argued that psychology should turn away from the study of the mind and consciousness because they are unverifiable and ultimately unsci-

Behaviorism
Learning

The behaviorists believe that who we are is determined by our early learning experiences. For example, concern for the well-being of others would be attributed to our childhood experiences, like playing doctor, rather than to any innate tendencies.

entific. Behaviorists argue that psychologists should study observable behavior. Yet psychoanalysis argued for *un*conscious and *pre*conscious forces as determiners of behavior. "Nonsense," the behaviorist would say. "We don't even know what we mean by consciousness, and you want to talk about levels of unconscious influence!"

Among other things, Watson and his followers believed in the importance of the environment in shaping one's responses. They could not accept the Freudian notion of inborn traits or impulses, whether called id or libido or anything else. What mattered was *learning*. A personality theory was not needed. A theory of learning would include all the details about so-called personality that one would ever need to know.

Who we are is determined by our learning experiences, and early experiences do count heavily—on that one point Watson and Freud might have agreed. Even our fears are conditioned (remember Watson's Little Albert study). So convinced was Watson that instincts and innate impulses had little to do with the development of behavior that he had no qualms about writing, "Give me a dozen healthy infants, well-formed, and my own specified world to bring them up in and I'll guarantee to take any one at random and train him to become any type of specialist I might select—doctor, lawyer, artist, merchant, chief, and yes, even beggarman and thief, regardless of his talents, penchants, tendencies, abilities, vocations, and race of his ancestors" (1925).

John Dollard and Neal Miller.   John Dollard (1900–1980) and Neal Miller (b.1909), as behaviorists and learning theorists, tried to see if they could use the basic principles of learning theory to explain personality and how it developed. What matters for one's personality, Dollard and Miller argued, was the system of habits one developed in response to various cues in the environment. Behavior was motivated by primary drives, upon whose satisfaction survival depended, and learned drives, which developed through experience. Motivated by drives, those habits that get reinforced are those that tend to be repeated and eventually become part of the stable collection of habits that make up one's personality. For example, repression into the unconscious is a matter of learned forgetfulness—forgetting about some anxiety-producing experience is reinforcing and, consequently, tends to be repeated. It was Miller (1944) who proposed that conflict is explainable in terms of tendencies (habits) to approach or to avoid goals and has little to do with the id, ego, and superego or with unconscious impulses of any sort.

Neal Miller

Primary Drives
Learned Drives

B. F. Skinner.   In this context, we should again mention B. F. Skinner, although he claims to have proposed no particular theory of learning, much less of personality. In many ways, Skinner's is a radical sort of behaviorism, because he consistently refuses to refer to any sort of internal or "organism" variables to explain behavior—which is, essentially, what personality is taken to mean. Look only at observable stimuli, observable responses, and for relationships among these; do not go meddling about in the mind of the organism, Skinnerians argue.

Refuses to Recognize any inner organism to explain behavior

Behavior is shaped by its consequences. Some behaviors result in reinforcement and tend to be repeated. Some behaviors result in punishment and tend not to be repeated. Consistency in one's behavior reflects the consistency of one's reinforcement history. The question is, how shall external conditions be manipulated to produce the consequences we want?

Albert Bandura.   Albert Bandura (b. 1925) is one learning theorist who is more than willing to consider the internal, cognitive processes of the learner. Bandura claims that many aspects of our behavior, of our personality, *are* learned, but they are often learned through observation and social influence. For Bandura, learning involves more than simple connections between stimuli and responses or between responses and resulting reinforcers; it involves a cognitive rearrangement and representation. In simpler terms, this approach argues that you may very well learn to behave honestly, for example, through the observation of others. If you view your parents as being honest and see them and others being reinforced for their honest behaviors (vicarious reinforcement), you may acquire similar responses.

Learning psychology & observation

Bandura's approach to learning has a decidedly social flavor. We learn by observing others. When we see others being reinforced, we experience some vicarious reinforcement ourselves. The theory also suggests that we can influence our environments and the people in them just as our environments can influence us.

Julian Rotter.   Like Bandura, Julian Rotter (b. 1916) has proposed a learning theory of personality that is characterized as a social learning theory. It is more cognitive than the approaches of either Dollard and Miller or Skinner. Rotter claims that events themselves have much less of an effect on behavior than do a person's perceptions of those events. An important component of Rotter's views about personality is one's perception of **locus of control.**

persons perception of events

locus of control
a general belief that what happens is either under our control (internal locus) or a matter of chance and environmental factors (external locus)

Julian Rotter

Rotter (1982) believes that some people develop attitudes or expectancies that reinforcement is controlled either by internal or external forces. This is mostly a matter of learning the extent to which one's behaviors, and the consequences of one's behaviors, are under one's own control (internal) or under the control of others and the environment (external). People with an *internal locus of control* tend to blame themselves for failures and congratulate themselves for successes. If they fail at something, it is because of lack of hard work on their part, and steps are taken to do better. People with an *external locus of control* tend to see failure *and* success as a result of chance, luck, or the intervention of others. If they fail at something, they do not view their failure as their fault, nor do they take much credit should they succeed. Rotter believes that neither extreme is better than the other, and that most of us would fall between the extreme externalizers and internalizers when we seek to find attribution for our successes and failures.

BEFORE YOU GO ON   **Specify a contribution to the notion of personality contributed by Watson, Skinner, Dollard and Miller, Bandura, and Rotter.**

Evaluating the Behavioral/Learning Approach

In a number of ways, the major strengths of a behavioral/learning approach to personality also constitute its major weaknesses. It is somewhat simplistic. It tends to focus only on the observable and measurable. A number of psychologists argue that Dollard and Miller and Skinner totally dehumanize personality and that even the social learning approaches of Bandura and Rotter tend to be too deterministic. That is, virtually everything a person may do, think, or feel is in some way directly determined by his or her environment through learning or conditioning. This leaves virtually nothing for the person, for personality.

Behavioral/learning approaches to personality are often not theories at all—at least not comprehensive theories. They tend to be very specific and focused (again, a mixed blessing). They tend to avoid any mention of biologically determined characteristics. They demand that terms be carefully defined and that assumptions be experimentally verified.

The Humanistic/Phenomenological Approach

The humanistic/phenomenological approach to personality contrasts sharply with both the psychoanalytic and behavioral approaches. For one thing, it is not deterministic. It claims that people have an ability to shape their own destiny, to chart and follow their own course of action, and that any biological, instinctive, or environmental influences can be overcome. What matters most is *how people view themselves and others,* how they think, and, more importantly, how they feel, which is essentially what **phenomenological** means.

phenomenological
an approach that emphasizes one's perception and awareness of events as being more important than the events themselves

In many ways, the humanistic view is more positive and optimistic than either the Freudian view (with its death instincts and negative impulses of aggression) or the learning view (with its emphasis on control exerted by forces of the environment). It also tends to focus much more on the here and now than on early childhood experiences as important molders of personality. This point of view tends to emphasize the wholeness or completeness of personality, rather than focusing on its structural parts.

Carl Rogers.   Carl Rogers' (1902–1986) view of personality is referred to as a person-centered or self theory. Like Freud, Rogers developed his views of human nature through the observation of clients in a clinical setting. (Rogers preferred the term "client" to "patient" and even preferred the term "person-centered" rather than "client-centered" to describe his approach.) Unlike Freud, Rogers finds very little negative about basic human drives. For Rogers, the most overwhelming of human drives is the drive to become fully functioning.

To be fully functioning implies that the person has become all that he or she can be. But it means more than that. When we are children, some of what we do brings reward and reinforcement, but some of what we do does not. How we are regarded by those we care about is conditional on how we behave. We tend to receive only conditional positive regard. *If* we do what is expected or desired, *then* we get reinforced. As a result, we try to act in ways that bring positive rewards, in ways that satisfy others rather than ourselves. Our feelings of self and self-worth are thus dependent on the actions of others who either reward us or don't reward us.

So long as we are acting only to please others, we are not fully functioning. To be fully functioning involves an openness to one's self and one's own feelings and desires, an accurate awareness of one's inner self, and a positive self-regard. Helping children to become fully functioning requires that we offer them more of what Rogers calls unconditional positive regard and that we separate the child's behaviors from the child's self. What that means is that we may punish a child for doing a bad thing, but never for being a bad child (e.g., "I love you very much, but what you have done is inappropriate

[handwritten margin notes: MOST INFLUENTIAL / PERSON centered / self Theory / NON DIRECTIVE / TheRAPY / Important]

According to Carl Rogers, unconditional positive regard involves separating a child's behaviors from the child's self. When punishing a child for doing something wrong, the parent should be sure they are doing only that and not punishing the child for being a bad person.

and, therefore, will be punished"; or more simply, "You're a good girl, but you've done a bad thing"). Helping people to achieve positive self-regard is one of the major goals of Rogers' form of psychotherapy.

Notice that what matters here is often not so much what *is,* but what is *felt* or *perceived.* One's true self (whatever that may be) is less important than one's *image* of one's self. How the world is experienced is what matters—a clearly phenomenological point of view. You may, in fact, be an excellent piano player (better, perhaps, than 98.8 percent of all of us), but if you feel that you are a rotten piano player, that perception of self-regard is what most matters.

Abraham Maslow.   Abraham Maslow's (1908–1970) basic criticism of the psychology he had studied was that it was altogether too pessimistic and negative. The individual was seen as being battered about by either a hostile environment or by depraved instincts, many of which propelled the person on a course of self-destruction.

There must be more to living than this, thought Maslow. Someone should attend to the positive side of human nature. Maslow felt that people's needs are not base or evil, but are positive or, at worst, neutral (Maslow, 1954). Our major goal in life is to actualize (realize and put into practice) those positive needs, to *self-actualize.*

Let's look, Maslow argued, at the very best among us. Let's focus our attention on the characteristics of those who have realized their fullest positive potential and have become self-actualized (see Figure 8.1). In his search for such individuals, Maslow couldn't find many. Most were historical figures, such as Thomas Jefferson and Eleanor Roosevelt (and the scientific status of Maslow's search for self-actualizers has been questioned by many psychologists).

As we have seen (Chapter 7), one of Maslow's major concerns was the hierarchical arrangements of motives that activate our behaviors. At lower

To illustrate his theory of self-actualization, Maslow cites Thomas Jefferson and Eleanor Roosevelt as individuals who have reached their fullest potentials or have become self-actualized.

FIGURE 8.1
Some of the characteristics or attributes of self-actualizers.
(Adapted from Maslow, 1954.)

1. They tend to be realistic in their orientation.
2. They accept themselves, others, and the world for what they are, not for what they should be.
3. They have a great deal of spontaneity.
4. They tend to be problem-centered rather than self-centered.
5. They have a need for privacy and a sense of detachment.
6. They are autonomous, independent, and self-sufficient.
7. Their appreciation of others (and of things of the world) is fresh, free, and not stereotyped.
8. Many have spiritual or mystical (although not necessarily religious) experiences.
9 They can identify with mankind as a whole and share a concern for humanity.
10. They have a number of interpersonal relationships, some of them very deep and profound.
11. They tend to have democratic views in the sense that all are created equal and should be treated equally.
12. They have a sense of humor that tends more to the philosophical than the hostile.
13. They tend to be creative in their approach.
14. They are hard working.
15. They resist pressures to conform to society.

levels, and to be satisfied first, were basic survival needs (he called them *deficiency needs*). Some deficiency needs are physiological (need for water, sleep, and so on), while others are psychological (need for security, self-esteem, and so on). Once the lower needs have been tended to, one can turn to higher needs, called *metaneeds* or *growth needs*. These needs include some rather abstract ideas, such as the need for justice, order, truth, and beauty.

Hierarchy *meta needs* *Deficiency Needs*

Briefly summarize the humanistic/phenomenological approach to personality as epitomized by Rogers and Maslow.

BEFORE YOU GO ON

Evaluating the Humanistic/Phenomenological Approach

The humanistic/phenomenological approach has a number of strengths. For one thing, it does remind us of the wholeness of personality and of the danger in analyzing something complex in artificial segments. That the approach is positive and upbeat in its flavor also serves as a useful reminder that at least such views are possible. And, as we shall see in Chapter 10 on therapy, this humanistic/phenomonological approach has had a considerable impact on many therapists and counselors.

The basic problem with the approach is not unlike the basic problem with Freudian theory. It may make sense, but how does one go about scientifically testing any of its basic assumptions? As with Freudian theory, many of the key terms are defined in very general, fuzzy ways. What really is self-image? How would we recognize a self-actualizer if we saw one? How can one test the effects of delivering unconditional positive regard? In many ways, what we have here is more philosophical than psychological theory.

The Trait Approach #4

Trait theories of personality have a markedly different flavor from any of the theories we have looked at so far. Trait theories tend to be more concerned with the adequate *description* of personality than with the *explanation* of personality. With this approach, the argument is that an individual's personality can be adequately described on the basis of a reasonable number of **traits.** We may define a trait as "any distinguishable, relatively enduring way in which one individual differs from others" (Guilford, 1959, p. 5). This approach comes close to our everyday usage of the term *personality*. When someone says something like, "Jim has a good personality," what he is saying is that he recognizes in Jim certain traits, and that the traits he recognizes are those he tends to value.

Traits are descriptive *dimensions*. That is, any trait (such as friendliness) is not a simple either/or proposition. Friendliness falls along a continuum, ranging from extremely unfriendly to extremely friendly, with many possibilities in between. To be useful, traits need to be measurable, and our measurements should yield numerical scores so we can assess the extent to which two people may differ on those traits.

Over the years, the issue for psychologists who have taken this approach has been which traits are the important ones. Which traits can best characterize a person and how she or he is different from everyone else? Is there

TRAIT Theories *DesCRIpTive* *NOT explanitory*

traits
distinguishable, relatively enduring ways in which individuals may differ

"HE WON'T LET ME ON. HE SAYS I SHOW ALL THE HIJACKER'S PERSONALITY TRAITS."

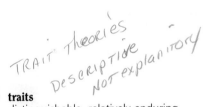

any way in which our personality traits can be organized? The different answers to these (and related) questions have given rise to a number of trait theories. Let's briefly look at three: Allport's, Cattell's, and Eysenck's.

Gordon Allport

Gordon Allport. Gordon Allport (1897–1967) and his colleagues systematically examined an unabridged dictionary looking for words that could be used to describe people (Allport & Odbert, 1936). They found nearly 18,000 terms! Allport's logic was that if he could describe any person in terms of all 18,000 of the words he had found, he would have a complete description of that person—at least he would have as complete a description as his language would allow. The problem, of course, is that nobody wants to deal with thousands of descriptive terms. In some sensible, reasonable way, Allport's 18,000 words had to be reduced to a manageable number that would serve the same basic purpose of description. The result became Allport's notion of traits and a scheme by which to organize them.

For Allport, a personality trait was a real force that existed within an individual and could be used to explain the consistency in a person's behaviors. In different situations, for example, a trait of friendliness might produce a range of different specific responses, but those responses would be, in their essence, very much alike.

Allport's theory proposes that personality traits are of two types: *common traits* and *personal traits* (or personal dispositions). By common traits, Allport means those traits or dimensions of personality that are shared by almost everyone (to greater or lesser degrees perhaps, but shared in common with everyone else). Aggressiveness is a good example of a common trait, and so is intelligence. These are traits that can be readily used to make comparisons between people. Personal dispositions, on the other hand, are those traits that are unique to just some persons. How one displays a sense of humor (sharp wit, cutting sarcasm, dirty jokes, philosophical puns, and so on) is usually thought of as being a unique disposition.

Personal dispositions or traits can be analyzed into one of three types. A *cardinal trait* is one trait that is so powerful, so overwhelming that it influences virtually everything that the person does. Very few people's personalities are ruled by cardinal traits. Even Allport could only imagine a few examples (Don Quixote, the Marquis de Sade, and Don Juan among them). No, what predominates in influencing behavior are not likely to be cardinal traits, but *central traits* or dispositions. These traits can generally be described in just one word, and are the 5 to 10 traits that best characterize any person (for example, honest, friendly, outgoing, fair, kind, and so on).

Finally, each of us is occasionally influenced by *secondary dispositions.* These are characteristics that seldom govern many of our reactions and may be applied only in specific circumstances. Someone, for example, may be very calm and easygoing, even when threatened (a collection of central traits). However, when threatened in their own home (by intruders, let's say), they can be very aggressive and not calm at all.

Dressing and acting as a clown is one way to display a sense of humor or personal trait.

Raymond B. Cattell. Raymond Cattell's (b. 1905) approach to personality is an empirical one, relying on the results of psychological tests, questionnaires, and surveys. Talking about personality traits without talking about how they are measured would make little sense to Cattell.

measured Traits

Using a statistical technique called *factor analysis,* Cattell has looked at measurements of personality traits that give basically redundant information. (If you know that someone is outgoing, you really don't need to test them to see if they are sociable or extroverted.)

Cattell argues that there are two types of personality traits. *Surface traits* are the clusters of behaviors that go together, like those that make up curiosity, trustworthiness, or kindliness. These traits are easily observed and can be found in a number of different settings. More important than these traits that can be seen on the surface are the fewer number of traits from which surface traits develop. These are called *source traits.* It is one's pattern of underlying source traits that determines which surface traits will get expressed in behavior. Obviously, source traits are not as easily measured because they are not directly observable. Cattell's list of source traits is presented in Figure 8.2.

FIGURE 8.2
Sixteen source traits as identified by Cattell (remember that each trait is a dimension). (From Cattell, 1973, 1979.)

Reserved ⟷ **Outgoing**
(detached, aloof) (participating)

Less intelligent ⟷ **More intelligent**
(dull) (bright)

Affected by feelings ⟷ **Emotionally stable**
(easily upset) (calm)

Submissive ⟷ **Dominant**
(obedient, easily led) (assertive)

Serious ⟷ **Happy-go-lucky**
(sober, taciturn) (enthusiastic)

Expedient ⟷ **Conscientious**
(disregards rules) (moralistic, staid)

Timid ⟷ **Venturesome**
(shy, restrained) (socially bold)

Tough-minded ⟷ **Sensitive**
(rejects illusions) (tender-minded)

Trusting ⟷ **Suspicious**
(accepting) (circumspect)

Practical ⟷ **Imaginative**
(down-to-earth) (absent-minded)

Forthright ⟷ **Shrewd**
(unpretentious) (astute, worldly)

Self-assured ⟷ **Apprehensive**
(secure, complacent) (insecure, troubled)

Conservative ⟷ **Experimenting**
(disinclined to change) (experimenting)

Group-dependent ⟷ **Self-sufficient**
(a joiner) (resourceful)

Uncontrolled ⟷ **Controlled**
(follows own urges) (shows will power)

Relaxed ⟷ **Tense**
(tranquil, composed) (frustrated, driven)

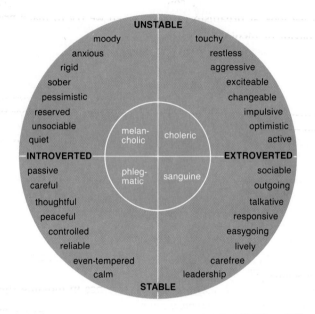

FIGURE 8.3
The interaction of Eysenck's extroversion-introversion and stability-instability dimensions and the traits they produce.
(From Eysenck, 1973.)

Hans Eysenck. The theory of Hans Eysenck (b. 1916) claims that personality can be divided into just two main *types*. Each type is defined by a dimension. One is the *extroversion-introversion* dimension. People who are high on extroversion seek stimulation; they are active and sociable. Introverts, on the other hand, are reserved, cautious, and withdrawn. (Few people are pure extroverts or introverts—most of us fall somewhere in between.)

Eysenck's other major dimension is one of *stability-instability* (often called neuroticism). People high on stability tend to be calm and easygoing, while people at the other extreme tend to be moody, anxious, and temperamental. The interaction of these two types (dimensions) gives rise to a number of different, specific traits (see Figure 8.3).

More recently (1976), Eysenck proposed a third major type of personality, a *psychoticism* dimension that interacts with the first two. This dimension is essentially a measure of the degree to which a person takes a realistic view of life and of the world or is in some way out of touch with reality. Although the specific traits that develop through the interaction of these three personality types may be molded by learning and experience, Eysenck claims that one's position on his three main dimensions is largely inherited or instinctive.

BEFORE YOU GO ON What is a personality trait?

What are the major traits that influence personality, according to Allport, Cattell, and Eysenck?

Evaluating the Trait Approach

Trait theories have some obvious advantages. They provide us not only with descriptive terms, but with the means of measuring or assessing those characteristics so that we can make comparisons among individuals. They suggest that we look at organism variables when we try to make predictions about behavior or mental processes.

On the other hand, as theories, they offer little more than description. To say that someone acted in a certain way "because they are introverted" doesn't really *explain* their reaction, it just labels it. And, obviously, there is less than perfect agreement about which traits are the most important. How a person may be rated on any dimension may depend on who does the rating and which types of measuring devices are used. Also, these theories suppose a consistency of reaction over time and in different situations that may be more fictional than real.

In this section, we have briefly outlined a number of different approaches to human personality and have examined a sample of specific theories. Which of these various approaches or theories is the right one? Which is best? These are clearly unanswerable questions. Each approach is qualitatively different from the others, emphasizing different aspects of personality. The psychoanalytic approach emphasizes inborn impulses and the power of the unconscious. The behavioral/learning approach emphasizes the influence of the environment, learning, and experience in molding the person. The humanistic/phenomenological approach emphasizes the power of the self, of conscious choices and personal growth. The trait approach emphasizes the measurement and organization of consistent patterns of behavior of individuals.

In their own separate ways, each approach has a contribution to make; each is "right" and the "best one." To be eclectic is to choose or select from the best of all possible sources. That might be—for the time being—our wisest course of action: to pick and choose those aspects of each of these approaches that best serve whatever problem or aspect of human nature we may be dealing with at the moment.

Our task now is to examine how psychologists measure or assess personality. Our concern will be with how we measure the characteristics and differences between people stated in the theories just reviewed. We begin by discussing the nature of psychological tests in general.

THE NATURE OF PSYCHOLOGICAL TESTS

Psychological tests are designed to measure human characteristics. In a strict sense, **measurement** is the assignment of numbers to some characteristic of interest according to rules or according to some agreed upon system. The rules for physical measurement are simple and well established. You are 5'10" tall because from top to bottom, your height equals 70 inches, where an inch is defined as a standard measure of length, and you have 70 of them. The rules for psychological measurement are seldom as clear cut. Are you extroverted and outgoing, or are you shy and introverted? Just how extroverted are you? How do we know? Are you of average intelligence? Compared to whom, and measured how? What is the standard, the rule, or the system against which we can compare you and your behavior?

> **measurement**
> the assignment of numbers to some characteristic of interest according to rules or some agreed upon system

personality assessment
the measurement of affect, or personality characteristics, i.e. one's "typical behaviors"

intellectual assessment
the measurement of intelligence, ability, or aptitude, i.e. one's "best performance"

psychological test
an objective, standardized measure of a sample of behavior

In this chapter, we'll consider psychological tests in two broad categories. **Personality assessment** will include those techniques designed to measure aspects of your personality and/or your emotional state (your affect, or how you feel). **Intellectual assessment** will include those tests designed to measure cognitive abilities and aptitudes. In other words, personality assessment is taken to be a measure of one's "typical behavior," while intellectual assessment measures one's "maximum performance" (Cronbach, 1984, p. 26). With the former type of assessment, we want to know about how you *usually* behave and feel, and with the latter, we want to know the *best* you can do. Before we get to specific examples, let's first define what a psychological test *is*. Then we'll see what makes the difference between a "good" test and a "poor" one.

A Working Definition

A leading expert in the field of psychological testing defines a **psychological test** as "an objective, standardized measure of a sample of behavior" (Anastasi, 1982). Let's look at the important terms within this definition.

A psychological test measures *behavior*. It measures behavior because that is all we *can* measure directly. We simply cannot measure those mental concepts that we call feelings, aptitudes, or abilities. All we can measure directly is overt observable behavior. On the basis of our assessment of behavior, we may be willing to make inferences and assumptions about any number of underlying, internal processes. But behavior is all we can measure directly. (We've encountered this situation before, most notably when we considered the difference between learning and performance.)

It should be clear that any one psychological test can measure only a *sample* of behavior. Let's say that we want to know about your tendency to be aggressive. We cannot very well ask you everything about you that relates to aggression in your life. ("List *all* of the situations in which you have acted aggressively," for instance.) What we have to do instead is sample (systematically draw a portion of) the behaviors in which we are truly interested. We then assume that responses to our sample of items can be used to predict responses to questions we have not asked. Even a classroom exam only asks you about a sample of the information you have learned in preparation for that exam.

Notice that psychological tests are twice removed from what we often think we are doing when we test someone. For instance, let's say that we are interested in how you feel about psychology. Maybe we want to compare your feelings with those of someone who has never taken a psychology course. First, there is no way that we can get inside the two of you and assess your feelings directly. We have to assume that your responses (behaviors) to our test items accurately reflect your feelings (and that you're not just trying to be nice and make us feel good, for example). Second, because time prohibits us from asking everything that we might wish to ask, we have to assume that our questions and your answers provide an adequate sample of what we are interested in. So, instead of assessing your feelings directly, we end up making *inferences* based on a *sample* of behavior.

There are two other definitional points to consider. If a psychological test is to have any value, its administration must be *standardized* and its scoring should be *objective*. Here is where your experience as a test-taker may be

Personality assessment involves measuring an individual's usual behavior, while intellectual assessment involves measuring maximum performance.

relevant. Imagine taking a college placement test that will be used to determine which courses in English composition you will be required to take. You are given 45 minutes to answer 50 multiple-choice items *and* write a short essay on a prescribed topic. Later you discover that some other students were given the same examination; but with instructions to "take as long as you'd like to finish the test." You also discover that these students could write their essay on any one of three suggested topics. You would be justified in complaining that something is wrong with the testing system. What it lacks is standardization. As much as possible, everyone taking a test—any kind of test—should take it under the same standard conditions, follow the same instructions, have the same time limits, and so on. What we want to know about are differences between individuals, not differences between testing situations.

A psychological test should also be objective. In this context, objectivity refers to the evaluation of the responses that exam takers make to test items—scoring the test, in other words. Different examiners (at least those of the same level of expertise) should be expected to give the same interpretation and evaluation to a test answer response. If the same responses to a psychological test lead one psychologist to declare a person perfectly normal, a second psychologist to consider the person a mass of inner conflict and overridden with anxiety, while a third wonders why this person is not now in a psychiatric institution, we have a problem. Assuming that the problem is with the test and not the three psychologists, the problem is one of objectivity. Although strict, literal objectivity is a goal seldom reached by psychological tests (particularly those designed for personality assessment), it is a worthy goal.

So it looks like all we need for a psychological test is a series of items or questions for subjects to respond to that are administered in a standard fashion and scored objectively. That doesn't sound very hard to do. It isn't. The world is full of "tests" that meet these minimal criteria. Weekly newspapers at supermarket checkout lanes, scores of magazines, newspapers, and even television programs regularly include psychological tests. Remember the test that was meant to determine how sexy one was, that you took at the beginning of the chapter? As a consumer of such tests as well as a student of psychology, you should be able to assess the value of measuring devices that we call psychological tests. It is to this matter that we turn next.

BEFORE YOU GO ON

Define measurement.

What is a psychological test?

What is the difference between personality assessment and intellectual assessment?

Criteria for a Good Test ②characteristics

As easy as it may be to write a test, it is very difficult to write a good one. To qualify as a good psychological test or assessment tool, a technique needs to have three characteristics: reliability, validity, and adequate norms. To ensure that a test has these important characteristics takes time and effort (and money). It is for this reason that many of the tests found in the popular press tend not to be good tests. In this section, we'll define and give examples of these three criteria for a good test.

①

reliability
consistency or dependability; in testing, <u>consistency</u> of test scores

Reliability.   In the context of psychological testing, **reliability** means the same thing that it means in other contexts: consistency or dependability. Suppose that someone gives you an objective, standardized measure of a sample of your behavior and, on the basis of your responses, suggests that you have an IQ that is slightly below average—86, let's say. Two weeks later, you take the same test and are told that your IQ is now 127—nearly in the top 3 percent of the entire population! Something is terribly wrong. We have not yet discussed IQ scores, but surely we recognize that one's intelligence as indicated by a psychological test should not change by 40 points within two weeks.

<u>A test is said to be reliable if it measures something (anything) consistently.</u> Let's say that we have developed a short multiple-choice test that supposedly measures the extent of one's extroversion or introversion. We give the test to a group of 200 college freshmen. If we administered the same test one month later to the same subjects, we would be surprised if everyone earned exactly the same score. We'd expect *some* fluctuation in scores, but changes on a retest a month later should be small if we have a good, reliable instrument. If a test does not measure whatever it measures with some consistency, it will not be very useful. If a month ago your test scores indicated that you were a very extroverted person and today's test indicates tendencies toward introversion, which test administration are we to believe?

test-retest reliability
a check of a test's consistency found by correlating the results of a test taken by the same subjects at two different times

The type of reliability with which we are usually concerned is **test-retest reliability.** As its name suggests, test-retest reliability involves administering a test to the same group of subjects on two different occasions. Scores on the two administrations are then correlated with each other. Correlation will tell us directly if the test in question is reliable. <u>If the correlation coefficient approaches zero, the test may be declared unreliable. Acceptable levels of reliability are indicated by correlation coefficients that approach +1.00.</u>

<u>Test-retest reliability makes good sense when we are trying to measure consistent and stable characteristics, such as intelligence or extroversion.</u> Test scores should be consistent because we assume that what we are measuring is itself reliable and consistent over time. What happens if the characteristic we are trying to measure is known (or suspected) to change over time? Consider trying to develop a test for anxiety. If we realize nothing else about it, we recognize that how anxious we are changes from week to week, from day to day, and even from hour to hour. That is, one's level of anxiety may not be reliable.

So if we do write a test to measure anxiety, test-retest reliability will not be a sensible criterion to use in evaluating our test. A person may get a very high score today, right before midterm exams, and a very low score just a few days later after having learned that she did well on all her exams. In such cases, we do not abandon the criterion of consistency and reliability altogether, however. There are two alternatives to test-retest reliability.

One thing we might do is make up two forms of our test. They will be very much alike in virtually every detail; they will ask the same sorts of questions about the same behaviors, but in slightly different ways. We will then ask you to take both forms of the test. Your score, or your reactions, should be essentially the same on both alternate forms if our test is reliable.

At the very least, we should expect any psychological test to demonstrate internal reliability. That is, we should require that the test be consistent from beginning to end. We might correlate the scores on items from the first half of the test with scores on the second half of the test. We might correlate scores on the odd-numbered items with scores on the even-numbered items. Such a measure would yield a **split-half reliability** score and would tell us if there is consistency *within* the test, even if consistency over time is irrelevant.

What is reliability and how do we measure the reliability of psychological tests?

Validity. When people worry about the usefulness of a test, they are usually concerned with its **validity.** Measures of validity tell us the extent to which a test actually measures what it claims to be measuring.

We determine a test's *reliability* by correlating the test with itself (at a later time, with test-retest reliability, or at the same time, with alternate forms or split-half reliability). We determine a test's *validity* by correlating test scores with some other, independent measure, or *criterion*. As it happens, there are a number of different types of validity.

One of the most practical types of test validity is **predictive validity**. Here, a psychological test or assessment technique is used to predict some future behavior. The criterion is something that will or will not happen in the future. Does this test of extroversion predict which college students are most likely to join sororities or fraternities? Does this aptitude test predict who will do well in college and who will not? Does this typing test predict who will do well working with a word processor and who will not? Does this clinical assessment predict whether or not this subject is likely to injure himself or herself or others in the future?

Establishing a test's predictive validity is a matter of correlation once again. The test in question is administered to a large group of subjects. All subjects are later measured on the independent criterion, and test scores are correlated with criterion scores. Now you find out if, in fact, those who earn high test scores, for example, also earn good grades in college courses. You now find out, for example, if those who get high scores on your extroversion test do, in fact, tend to join sororities and fraternities. (Notice here that determining the validity of a test requires that we have a good, reliable, and valid criterion to correlate the test with.)

If a psychological test is well correlated with other established tests that purport to measure the same characteristic(s), then the test is said to have **concurrent validity**. If you generate a new technique to measure test anxiety that is not at all correlated with any of the well-established techniques already available that measure test anxiety, we may have to suggest that your technique lacks concurrent validity.

One additional form of validity ought to be mentioned here because it is relevant for students taking classroom exams. It is **content validity,** which is the extent to which a test adequately samples the behaviors that it claims to be testing. For example, you may be told that you are to be given an exam covering all of learning and memory. The test is to be made up of 50 multiple-choice items. You might be more than a little upset if you were to find

split-half reliability
a check on the internal consistency of a test found by correlating one part of a test with another part of the same test

validity
in testing, the extent to which a test measures what it claims to be measuring

predictive validity
the extent to which a test can be used to predict future behaviors

concurrent validity
the extent to which the scores on a test are correlated with the scores on other tests claiming to measure the same characteristic

content validity
the extent to which a test provides an adequate and fair sample of the behaviors being measured

that 48 of the 50 items on the test deal only with Pavlovian classical conditioning. You would claim that the test was not fair. It would lack validity because it does not measure what it claims to measure. In this case, it would lack content validity because the content of the test does not cover a broad range of material on learning and memory. Content validity is usually determined by the judgment of content area experts.

BEFORE YOU GO ON   What are predictive, concurrent, and content validity? How is each of these measured?

Norms.   Let's say that you have just filled out an objective, paper-and-pencil questionnaire, designed to measure the extent to which you are extroverted or introverted. You know that the test is a reliable and valid instrument. You are told that you scored a 50 on the test. So what? What does a score of 50 mean? It doesn't necessarily mean that you answered 50 percent of the items correctly, because this is a test of typical performance and there are no correct or incorrect answers. Does a 50 mean that you are extroverted, introverted, or neither?

The point is that if you don't have a basis of comparison, any one test score by itself is meaningless. You need to compare your score of 50 with the scores of other people like yourself who have already taken the test. Results of a test taken by a large group of subjects whose scores can be used to make comparisons are called **norms**.

You may discover by checking with the norms that a score of 50 is indeed quite average and indicative of neither extreme extroversion nor extreme introversion. On the other hand, a 50 may be a very high score, indicating extroversion, or a very low score, indicating introversion. An aptitude test score of 134 sounds pretty good until you discover that the average score was 265 and that scores in the norms range from 115 to 360. If the norms tell you that the average score on this test is only 67 and that scores tend to range between 30 and 140, then your score of 134 would be a very good score indeed.

The usefulness of a test, then, often depends on the adequacy of the norms that are used to make comparisons or judgments about any one test score. If the extroversion-introversion test you took had been previously administered to only 40 or 50 high school students to compile its norms, it would hardly provide an adequate measure of the extent of *your* extroversion or introversion. The scores that make up norms should be drawn from subjects similar to those who are going to be tested later—and the more the better.

So writing a good psychological test is not as easy as it may at first appear. Writing a series of questions and deciding on acceptable answers may be relatively simple, but the rest takes considerable time and effort. Our focus in the rest of this chapter will be on the techniques and tests that psychologists use to assess personality and intelligence. As we explore this area we should keep in mind as students—and as consumers of psychological tests—the three major criteria for good tests: reliability, validity, and adequate norms.

norms
results of a test taken by a large group of subjects whose scores can be used to make comparisons or give meaning to new scores

PERSONALITY ASSESSMENT

In this section, we will summarize four ways to measure or assess an individual's personality: behavioral observations, interviews, paper-and-pencil tests, and projective techniques. Before we do so, we should review just what it is we are trying to assess, and why we generally want to make such assessments.

As we saw earlier, personality is a very difficult concept to define. Common to most definitions is the notion that there are characteristics of an individual that remain fairly consistent over time and over many (if not all) situations. Many of these characteristics can also be used to describe how one person is different from others. It is further reasoned that if we know which characteristics are typical of an individual, we can use that knowledge to make specific predictions about his or her behaviors or mental processes. The key, then, is to find those characteristics of a person that can be reliably and validly measured.

If we can find those characteristics, what then? Why do we bother? There are three major motives that lie behind the measurement of personality. One is very practical, at least in a clinical sense, and involves making diagnoses. One of the first questions that a psychologist in a clinical setting may ask is "What is wrong with this person?" In fact, the basic question—again, one of diagnosis—may be, "*Is* there anything wrong with this person?" (Burisch, 1984). There are two related issues here: (1) how can assessment techniques help us to determine the extent to which the behaviors, feelings, or cognitions of an individual are abnormal, and if so, in what way; and (2) what relationships exist among assessment, treatment, and outcome (Hayes et al., 1987)?

A second use for personality assessment is in theory-building, where there are a number of interrelated questions: Which personality traits can be measured? How may such traits be organized within the person? Which measured traits are most important for describing a person's personality? For personality trait theorists, this is obviously *the* purpose for constructing personality tests.

A third general purpose for personality assessment involves the question of whether a measured personality trait or characteristic can be used to predict some other, independent behavior. This concern has practical implications—particularly in vocational placement. For example, if we know that Joe X is, in fact, dominant and extroverted, does that knowledge tell us anything about his leadership potential? Which characteristics are best associated with success as a plant manager? What sorts of personality traits best describe a successful astronaut, police officer, or secretary?

In brief, personality assessment has one of three goals: clinical diagnosis, theory building, and/or behavioral prediction. These three goals often interact. A clinical diagnosis is often made in the context of a particular theoretical approach and is often used to predict possible outcomes, such as which therapy technique may be most appropriate for a given diagnosis.

Behavioral Observation

behavioral observation
the personality assessment technique in which one draws conclusions about an individual on the basis of observations of his or her behaviors

As people develop their own impressions of the personalities of friends and acquaintances, they do so largely by relying on **behavioral observation.** As its name suggests, this approach involves drawing conclusions about an individual's personality on the basis of observations of his or her behaviors. We judge Dan to be bright because he was the only one who knew the answer to a question in class. We feel that Pam is submissive because she always seems to do whatever her husband demands.

As helpful as our observations may be to us, there are real problems with the casual unstructured, uncontrolled observations that we normally make. Because we have only observed a small range of behaviors in a small range of settings, we may be guilty of overgeneralizing when we assume that the same behaviors will show up in new, different situations. Dan may never again know the answer to a question in class. Pam may be giving in to her husband only because she knows that we are there. That is, the behaviors we happen to observe may not be typical at all.

Nonetheless, behavioral observation can be an excellent source of information, particularly when the observations being made are purposeful, careful, and structured—as opposed to the casual observations that people usually make. It is commonly a part of any clinical assessment. The clinical psychologist may note any number of behaviors of a client as being potentially significant—style of dress, manner of speaking, gestures, postures, and so on.

Let's consider an example. A small child is reportedly having trouble at school, behaving aggressively, starting fights, and being generally disruptive. One thing a psychologist may do is visit the school and observe the child's behaviors in the natural setting of the classroom. It may be that the

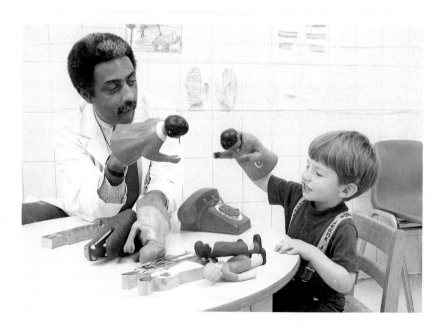

Behavioral observation involves drawing conclusions about an individual's personality on the basis or his or her behaviors. Role-playing is one technique psychologists use to gain insights about a child's behavior.

FIGURE 8.4
A graphic rating scale such as this might be used by an employer in evaluating employees or potential employees. It could also be used by psychologists studying behavior.

Poor   Superior

Dependability				
Requires prodding and supervision	Needs occasional prodding	Steady, responsible worker	Needs little supervision; uses own judgment	Self-starter; needs no supervision
Personal relations				
Rude; causes trouble	Inconsiderate; unkind	Relations with others usually good	Helpful; kind; polite	Well liked; good social skills
Poise				
Nervous; ill at ease	Easily upset; tense	Average poise and self-assurance	Self-assured	Composed; handles crises well

child does behave aggressively and engage in fighting behavior, but only when the teacher is in the room. Otherwise, the child is quite pleasant. It may be that the aggressive behavior of the child is primarily a ploy to get the teacher's attention.

In an attempt to add to her original observations, a psychologist may use *role-playing* as a means to collect more information. Role-playing is a matter of acting out a given life situation. "Let's say that I'm a student, and that you're the teacher, and that it's recess time," the psychologist says to a child. "Let's pretend that somebody takes a toy away from me, and I hit him on the arm. What will you do?"

Some observational techniques are supplemented with some sort of *rating scale* (an example is provided in Figure 8.4). Rating scales provide many advantages over casual observation. For one thing, they focus the attention of the observer on a set of specified behaviors to be observed. Rating scales also yield a more objective measure of a sample behavior. Using rating scales, one can arrange to have behaviors observed by a number of raters. If a number of raters are involved in the observation of the same behaviors (say, children at play in a nursery school), you can check on the reliability of the observations. That is, if all five of your observers agree that Timothy engaged in "hitting behavior" on the average of five times per hour, the consistency (or reliability) of that assessment adds to its usefulness.

How is behavioral observation used to assess personality?   BEFORE YOU GO ON

Interviews

We can find out some things about people by watching them. We can also gain insight about some aspects of their personality by simply asking them questions about themselves. In fact, the **interview** "remains the most important instrument of clinical assessment" (Korchin & Schuldberg, 1981). It is

interview
the personality assessment technique involving a conversational interchange between an interviewer and a subject; used to gain information about the subject

also "one of the oldest and most widely used, although not always the most accurate, of the methods of personality assessment" (Aiken, 1984, p. 296).

The basic data of the interview are what people say about themselves, rather than what they do. The interview is not, strictly speaking, a measurement technique, because the results of interviews are usually impressionistic and not easily quantifiable (although some interview techniques are clearly more structured and objective than others). The interview is more a technique of discovering generalities than specifics.

Test → A major advantage of the interview is its flexibility. The interviewer may decide to drop a certain line of questioning if it seems to be producing no useful information and to pursue some other area of questioning. Unfortunately, there is scant evidence that unstructured interviews have much reliability or validity. For example, in discussing interviews used to assess personality characteristics of job applicants, Tenopyr (1981) calls the history of validity for the interview "dismal." She says that the employment interview, "despite various innovations over the years, has never been consistently shown to improve selection" (p. 1123).

As is the case for observational techniques, there is considerable variety in the degree to which interviews may be unstructured or structured. In the latter type of interview, there are a specific set of questions to be asked in a prescribed order. The structured interview, then, becomes more like a psychological test to the extent that it is objective, standardized, and asks about a particular sample of behavior.

BEFORE YOU GO ON Cite one advantage and one disadvantage of the interview as a technique of personality assessment.

Paper-and-pencil Tests

We've seen that observational and interview techniques barely qualify as psychological tests. They are seldom as standardized or as objective as we would like them to be. In this section, we'll focus on one of the most commonly used objective tests designed to assess personality: the **Minnesota Multiphasic Personality Inventory,** or the **MMPI** for short. The test is referred to as "multiphasic" because it measures a number of different personality dimensions with the same set of items.

Minnesota Multiphasic Personality Inventory (MMPI)
a paper-and-pencil inventory used to assess a number of personality dimensions

The MMPI was designed to help in the diagnosis of persons with mental disturbances and, hence, is not a personality test in the sense of identifying personality traits. The test was first made available just as World War II began and immediately became very popular. It is, no doubt, the most researched test in all of psychology, and remains one of the most commonly used (Lubin et al., 1984). However, the MMPI does have its critics. Cronbach (1984, p. 483) calls the test "long and inefficient," and claims that "A number of items are outdated, and the dimensions used in summarizing responses are—to put it mildly—relics of an antiquated psychiatry."

The MMPI is composed of more than 550 statements to which a subject responds "true" or "false." The statements cover feelings, attitudes, physical symptoms, and past experiences. What makes the MMPI somewhat different is the method used to choose items to include in the inventory and the inclusion of validity scales.

In constructing the MMPI, the authors simply made up a large list of items to which a subject could respond "true" or "false." The authors generated items with no particular theory of personality in mind. They just made up items. The potential test items were then administered to subjects who had already been diagnosed as belonging to some psychiatric category: paranoid, schizophrenic, or depressed, for example. The items were also given to approximately 700 control group subjects who had no psychiatric diagnosis; they were taken to be normal. If any one item were answered by normals and subjects with psychiatric problems in the very same way, the item obviously did not discriminate normals from abnormals and was dropped as a potential item. Items were included only if they discriminated, or differentiated, among the different groups of subjects and patients responding to them.

Because of the way in which it was constructed, the MMPI is called a *criterion referenced* test. That means that each item on the test is referenced to one of the criterion groups—either normals or patients with a particular diagnosis. Some of the items appear quite sensible. "I feel like people are plotting against me," seems like the sort of item that paranoids would call "true," while normals would tend to respond "false." Many items, however, are not so obvious. "I like to visit zoos," is not an MMPI item, but it might be if subjects of one diagnostic group respond to the item differently from the way other subjects do. What the item looks like or what the item may actually mean is irrelevant. The only thing that matters is if subjects of different groups respond differently to the item. We should also add that no one will (or can) make a diagnosis of psychological disorder on the basis of a subject's response to just a few items. What matters is one's *pattern* of responding to a large number of items. The different clinical scales for the MMPI are presented in Figure 8.5.

FIGURE 8.5
MMPI scales and descriptions.
(Based on Aiken, 1970.)

Clinical scales

Scale 1	Hypochondriasis *(Hs)*	Measures excessive somatic concern and physical complaints.
Scale 2	Depression *(D)*	Measures symptomatic depression.
Scale 3	Hysteria *(Hy)*	Measures hysteroid personality features and the tendency to develop physical symptoms under stress.
Scale 4	Psychopathic Deviate *(Pd)*	Measures antisocial tendencies.
Scale 5	Masculinity-Femininity *(Mf)*	Measures sex-role conflict.
Scale 6	Paranoia *(Pa)*	Measures suspicious, paranoid ideation.
Scale 7	Psychasthenia *(Pt)*	Measures anxiety and obsessive behavior.
Scale 8	Schizophrenia *(Sc)*	Measures bizarre thoughts and disordered affect accompanying schizophrenia.
Scale 9	Hypomania *(Ma)*	Measures behavior found in manic affective disorder.
Scale 0	Social Introversion *(Si)*	measures social anxiety, withdrawal, and overcontrol.

Validity scales

Cannot say scale *(?)*	Measures the total number of unanswered items.
Lie scale *(L)*	Measures the tendency to claim excessive virtue or to try to present an overall favorable image.
Infrequency scale *(F)*	Measures a tendency to falsely claim psychological problems.
Defensiveness scale *(K)*	Measures the tendency to see oneself in an unrealistically positive way.

It is clear that the interpretation of one's responses to MMPI items is limited by the validity of those responses. There are a number of factors that might interfere with validity here. Simple fatigue and lack of motivation to respond carefully to more than 500 items is one. Another is the possibility that a person will respond with what he or she believes to be good or socially acceptable answers rather than with responses that truly reflect the subject's personality. In order to monitor such possibilities, four "validity scales" were added to the standard clinical scales of the MMPI.

The *?-scale* checks the number of items left unanswered. Skipping a few items is okay, but leaving too many blank will invalidate the test. The *L-scale,* or lie scale, is made up of a number of items that are sensitive to the attempt to present oneself in an overly positive way. For example, responding "true" to "I always smile at everyone I meet," or "false" to "I sometimes get angry at others," would lead to an overly high score on this scale. In addition, there is a scale that indicates when a subject is trying to put himself or herself in an unfavorable light (agreeing with statements such as, "There is an international plot against me," for example). Finally, there is a validity scale that provides a correction factor to be used in the interpretation of the clinical scales when subjects are being slightly overcritical or overgenerous in evaluating themselves.

Although the MMPI is the most commonly used personality inventory, it is not the only acceptable paper-and-pencil personality test. There are dozens of such tests. *The California Personality Inventory,* or *CPI,* for example, was constructed with the same logic as was used for the MMPI. That is, potential test items were administered independently to subjects known to be different on some personality trait (on the basis of self-reports and the ratings of others who knew them well). If the test item discriminated between the two groups (if each group answered differently), it was included on the final scale. The major difference between the MMPI and the CPI is that the CPI was constructed using only normal subjects, not people who were hospitalized for some psychological problem. The CPI assesses 18 "normal" personality traits, including self-acceptance, dominance, responsibility, and sociability. Because it is designed to measure a number of different traits, it can also be referred to as a multiphasic test.

Some multiphasic tests have been designed in conjunction with a particular personality theory. Cattell's trait theory approach, discussed earlier, investigated a number of potential personality traits and settled on a few basic traits. These traits are what are measured with *Cattell's 16 PF Questionnaire* (where PF stands for personality factors). Analyses of responses on this paper-and-pencil test (of more than 100 statements with which the subject responds "yes" or "no") results in a personality profile. That profile can then be compared with one gathered from a large norm group. Figure 8.2 lists Cattell's 16 personality factors.

Finally, we should mention that there are a number of personality questionnaires or inventories that are designed to measure just one trait and, thus, are not multiphasic. One example is a commonly used test called the Taylor Manifest Anxiety Scale. Taylor began with a very large pool of items—many of them from the MMPI—and asked psychologists to choose those items that they thought would measure anxiety. The 50 items most commonly chosen as indicators of anxiety make up this test, which has gained wide acceptance as a paper-and-pencil indicator of anxiety.

Why was the MMPI constructed?
What does multiphasic mean?
How did the authors of the MMPI try to insure that the
test would be valid?

BEFORE YOU GO ON

Ex. Cat — Dog
word-association

Projective Techniques

A **projective technique** involves asking a subject to respond to ambiguous stimuli. The stimuli involved can be any number of things, as we shall see, and there are clearly no right or wrong answers. The procedure is reasonably unstructured and open-ended. In many ways, the projective technique is more of an aid to interviewing than it is a psychological test (Korchin & Schuldberg, 1981). The basic idea is that because there is, in fact, so little content in the stimulus presented, the subject will *project* some of his or her own self into the response.

projective technique
a personality assessment technique requiring subjects to respond to ambiguous stimuli, thus "projecting" some of their "self" into their responses

Some projective techniques are very simple. Indeed, the word-association technique, introduced by Galton in 1879 and used commonly in psychoanalysis, is a sort of projective technique (although not a test). "I will say a word, and I want you to say the first thing that pops into your head. Do not think about your response; just say the first thing that comes to mind." There certainly are no right answers in this type of procedure. The idea here is that the clinician can gain some insight, perhaps into the problems of a patient, by using this procedure.

Example

A similar technique is the *unfinished sentences* procedure. In this procedure, a sentence is begun, "My greatest fear is that _____," perhaps, and the subject is asked to complete the sentence. Although there are a number of published tests available (such as the *Rotter Incomplete Sentences Blank*), many clinicians prefer to make up their own forms. Again, there are no right or wrong responses, and interpreting responses is rather subjective, but a skilled examiner/interviewer can use these procedures to gain new insights about a subject's personality.

Of all the projective techniques, none is so famous as the **Rorschach inkblot test.** This technique was introduced in 1921 by Hermann Rorschach who believed that people with different sorts of personalities respond differently to inkblot patterns (see Figure 8.6). There are 10 stimulus cards in the test, five are black on white, two are red and gray, and three are multicolored. Subjects are asked to tell what they see in the cards or what the inkblot represents.

very Famous

Rorschach inkblot test
a projective technique in which the subject is asked to say what is seen in a series of inkblots

Scoring of Rorschach responses has become quite controversial. Standard scoring procedures require attending to a number of different factors: what the subject says (content), where the subject focuses attention (location), mention of detail versus global features, reacting to color or open spaces, and how many different responses there are per card. Many psychologists have questioned the efficiency of the Rorschach as a diagnostic instrument. Much of what it can tell an examiner may be gained directly. For example, Rorschach responses that include many references to death, dying, and sadness are probably indicative of a depressed subject. One has to wonder if inkblots are really needed to discover such depression. As a psychological test, the Rorschach inkblots seem neither very reliable nor valid. Nonetheless, this test remains a very popular instrument. It is used primarily to aid assessment and the development of subjective impressions.

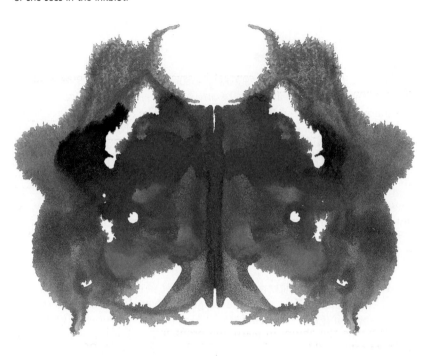

Thematic Apperception Test (TAT)
a projective technique in which the subject is asked to tell a story about a set of ambiguous pictures

A projective device we have discussed earlier (in the context of achievement motivation, Chapter 7) is the **Thematic Apperception Test,** or **TAT.** You may recall that this test is made up of a series of ambiguous pictures about which a subject is asked to tell a story. The subject is asked to describe what is going on, what led up to this situation, and what the outcome is likely to be.

The test is designed to provide a mechanism to discover the subjects' hidden needs, desires, and emotions, which will be projected into their stories about the pictures. This test is called a *thematic* test because scoring depends largely on the interpretation of the themes of the stories that are told. Although some formal scoring schemes are available, scoring and interpretation are usually quite subjective and impressionistic. It is likely that the TAT remains popular for the same reason as the Rorschach: Psychologists are used to it, comfortable with the data it provides, and willing to accept any source of additional information they can use to make a reasonable assessment or diagnosis.

BEFORE YOU GO ON **What is the essence of a projective technique, the Rorschach and TAT in particular?**

We now turn to another area of psychology closely involved with testing—intelligence. In the Introduction to this book, we pointed out that testing was a major force in the development of modern psychology. From its beginnings with the work of Binet and others, the psychology of intelligence has involved testing. We will keep that in mind as we explore the concept of intelligence, individual differences in intelligence, and how we assess intelligence.

INTELLIGENCE

Intelligence is a troublesome concept in psychology. We all know what we mean when we use the word, but we have a terrible time trying to define intelligence concisely. We wonder if John's failure in school is due to his lack of intelligence or to some other factor, such as an emotional disorder. You may argue that locking one's keys in one's car is not a very intelligent thing to do. We may argue that anyone with any intelligence can see the difference between positive and negative reinforcement.

In this section, we'll do two things. First, we'll briefly consider how we might define intelligence. Then, we'll review variations in intelligence. As you probably already know, there are few concepts in psychology that are as controversial as intelligence. What it is and what it means are issues that have been debated since psychology's earliest days.

Defining Intelligence

Intelligence has been variously defined as the sum total of everything that you know, as the ability to learn and profit from experience, or as one's ability to solve problems and to cope with the environment. Of course, there is nothing wrong with any of these definitions or uses of the term intelligence. The problem is that none seem to say it all. We have gotten into the habit of using intelligence as a general label for so many cognitive abilities that it virtually defies specific definition.

Nonetheless, we should settle on some definition to guide our study through the rest of this chapter. We propose that we accept two definitions, one academic and theoretical, the other operational and practical. For our theoretical definition of **intelligence,** we can do no better than David Wechsler, who defines it as "the capacity of an individual to understand the world about him [or her] and his [or her] resourcefulness to cope with its challenges" (1975, p. 139).

This definition (and others like it) does present some ambiguities. Just what does one mean by "capacity"? What is actually meant by "understand the world"? What if the world never really challenges one's "resourcefulness"? Will such people be less intelligent? What at first reading may seem like a very sensible and inclusive definition of intelligence may, upon reflection, pose even more definitional problems.

Perhaps we ought to follow our advice from the Introduction, where we suggested that defining concepts operationally often helped to overcome such difficulties. We have to be somewhat careful here, but we may operationally define intelligence as that which intelligence tests measure. Notice that using this definition simply side-steps the thorny conceptual problem of coming to grips with the "true" nature of intelligence; it doesn't solve it. But it does what most operational definitions do—it gives a definition we can work with for a while. To use this definition, then, we need to see how intelligence tests work and then how people differ on intelligence.

intelligence
the capacity to understand the world and the resourcefulness to cope with its challenges; that which an intelligence test measures

Our ability to measure one's general intellectual capacity (which we continue to call IQ) is not without limitation. Nonetheless, IQ tests have raised a number of controversial questions that psychologists have attempted to answer. We will see that some of these questions may be of more political importance than scientific importance. We have, in this section, defined intelligence, examined differences in intelligence, and briefly considered those individuals with extreme IQ scores. We now turn to the issue of measuring intelligence.

Assessing Intelligence

The assessment of intelligence has primarily meant one thing in psychology—intelligence tests. What are tests of intelligence? How were they created? How are they administered? Are they valid? Why do different people get different scores on them? These are questions that we will address in this section.

As we shall see, intelligence testing has a long history and now makes use of a rich variety of measuring devices. But it has also created controversy as to whether differences between groups are important or whether they even exist. It has also kept the issue of where intelligence comes from in the forefront of our concern. We begin with the first major attempt to measure the elusive concept we call intelligence.

Alfred Binet

Lewis Terman

The Stanford Binet Intelligence Scale.   Historians of psychology would refer to the work of Alfred Binet (1857–1911) even if he hadn't written the first practical test of general intelligence. He was the leading psychologist in France at the turn of the century. Although he had a law degree, he chose to pursue his interests in psychology. When psychology was first beginning to emerge as a science, Binet worked at the psychology laboratory at the Sorbonne. He studied all sorts of things there: hypnosis, abnormal behaviors, optical illusions, and thinking processes. By far, however, his major concern was with individual differences. In particular, Binet was curious about how people differed in their abilities to solve problems.

It was not surprising then that Binet's expertise was sought on a wide range of educational issues. Of great concern in 1900 were those children in the Paris school system who seemed unable to profit from the educational experiences they were being given. What was the problem? Were they uninterested? Did they have some emotional sickness? Or were they just intellectually unable to grasp and use the material they were being presented? With a number of collaborators, Binet set out to construct a test to measure the intellectual abilities of children.

Binet's first test appeared in 1905 and was revised in 1908. The test was an immediate success. It caught the attention of Lewis M. Terman at Stanford University, who translated it into English and supervised a revision of the test in 1916. (Terman's revision included changing some clearly French questions into items more suitable for American children.) Since 1916, the test has been referred to as the Stanford-Binet and has undergone a number

FIGURE 8.7
The factors tested by the Stanford-Binet, Fourth Edition, arranged in three levels, including a listing of each subtest (after Thorndike et al., 1986).

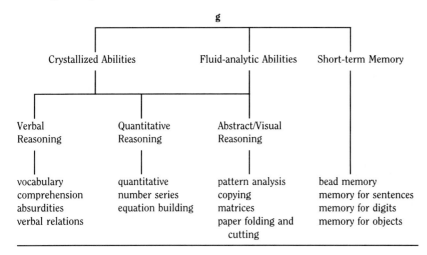

of revisions. A 1937 edition provided two alternate forms of the test, labeled "Form L" and "Form M" (after Terman's initials). Revisions in 1960 and 1972 made few substantive changes, but did update some items and change the scoring scheme. The most recent revision of the Stanford-Binet was published in 1986. This edition—the fourth—made a number of significant changes in the test and in its scoring. So what is this test like?

Although a number of individual items from earlier editions of the Stanford-Binet are still to be found, the 1986 revision of the test is quite different from its predecessors. The test now follows what its authors call a "three-level hierarchical model" of cognitive abilities (Thorndike et al., 1986). As did Binet's original test, the current edition yields an overall test score which reflects **g**, or general intellectual ability. This score is basically what we have all come to think of as a measure of general intelligence, or IQ. The test's authors describe this **g**-factor as "what an individual uses when faced with a problem that he or she has not been taught to solve" (1986, p. 3). One's **g-score** is the highest of the three levels in the model.

Underlying **g** are three second-level factors (see Figure 8.7). *Crystallized abilities* represent those skills required for acquiring and using information about verbal and quantitative concepts to solve problems. They are influenced by schooling and could be called an "academic ability" factor. *Fluid-analytic abilities* are typified by skills needed to solve problems that involve figural or nonverbal types of information. The bases of these skills are less tied to formal schooling. Essentially, they involve the ability to see things in new and different ways. The third factor at the second level of the model is *short-term memory.* Items that test one's ability to hold information in memory for relatively short periods of time can be found on Binet's original test.

The third level of the hierarchy of abilities tested on the new Stanford Binet provide more specific, content-oriented definitions of the factors from

g-score
a measure of one's overall, general intellectual abilities commonly thought of as "IQ."

Pictured here are some of the materials that make up the revised Stanford-Binet test. The fourth edition represents the most signigicant changes made to the test and its scoring.

1. **Vocabulary:** For ages 2–6, provide name and definition of picture or object; for older subjects, define words increasing in difficulty
2. **Bead memory:** String a series of multicolored beads after seeing a picture of the required string
3. **Quantitative:** Complete a series of arithmetic problems, from simple counting to complex word problems
4. **Memory for sentences:** Repeat a series of sentences of increasing complexity
5. **Pattern analysis:** At young ages, match shapes to holes; at older levels, use blocks of different designs to copy patterns of increasing complexity
6. **Comprehension:** Answer questions like "why does the government regulate radio and television broadcasts?"
7. **Absurdities:** Identify what is wrong with picture; For example, a wagon with triangular wheels
8. **Memory for digits:** Repeat a list of digits of increasing length; forward or backward
9. **Copying:** Draw (duplicate) a series of geometric line drawings of increasing complexity
10. **Memory for objects:** Recognize a series of pictures of simple objects presented one at a time from a larger picture displaying many objects
11. **Matrices:** Shown a series of pictures, determine which of a number of alternatives comes next in the series
12. **Number series:** Presented with a series of numbers, determine what number comes next in the series
13. **Paper folding and cutting** Fold and/or cut sheet of paper according to a prescribed pattern
14. **Verbal relations:** Given three words that are alike and a fourth that is different, explain why the three are alike and the fourth is different
15. **Equation building:** Given a series of digits and algebraic signs ($+$, $\times$, $\div$), create a balanced equation

level two. As you can see from Fig. 8.7, at this level crystallized abilities are divided into verbal and quantitative reasoning, fluid analytic abilities are seen as abstract/visual reasoning, and there simply is no ability at this level that corresponds to short-term memory.

At the very base of the hierarchy—and not considered as one of the three levels of cognitive skill—are the 15 subtests that operationally define the structure of the Stanford-Binet test. Figure 8.8 lists each subtest and provides an example item. What all of this means is that the authors of the 1986 revision of the Stanford-Binet acknowledge that a person's measured intelligence should be reflected in more than just one test score. Now, not only can we determine an overall **g**-score, but we can also calculate scores for each factor at each of three levels. In addition, we can calculate scores for any of the 15 subtests, although it is difficult to say that individual subtest scores are very meaningful. It's also unlikely that an examiner would administer all 15 of the subtests to any one subject.

Within each subtest, items are arranged by difficulty, indicated by appropriate age level. Age levels vary from 2 years old to adult (18 years+), although only six subtests have items that are appropriate for all age levels. This means that if you were testing an 8 year old whom you thought had average intellectual abilities, you might start testing for vocabulary, let's say, with the items at the 6-year-old level. You would give credit for the easier, lower age-level items. You would then continue with items of increasing difficulty until your subject failed three out of four at any two consecutive age levels. At this point, there would be no reason to continue testing.

The test manual would then provide you with the data that would allow you to convert your subject's earned score—how many vocabulary items were correctly answered, for example—into a score that compared her performance with that of other children of the same age. You would then make comparisons for each of the factors you tested (see Figure 8.7 again), including the **g** score. When your subject's earned scores are compared to those of others of the same age who have taken the test (the test's *norms,* remember), the resulting score is called a **standard age score** or **SAS.** Standard age scores on the Stanford Binet are computed (in fact, defined) so that an average SAS *always* comes out to be 100. People who do better than average have standard age scores above 100, and those who perform less well than others their age have standard age scores below 100. Figure 8.9 shows how SASs on the Stanford-Binet are distributed for the general population.

Before we go on, let's take a minute to discuss what has happened to the concept of "IQ." IQ, as we noted earlier, is an abbreviation for the term *intelligence quotient.* As you know, a "quotient" is the result you get when you divide one number by another. If one divides 8 by 6, the quotient is 1.25. For the early versions of the Stanford-Binet, the examiner's job was to determine a subject's *mental age* (or *MA*), which was taken to be the age level at which the subject was functioning in terms of intellectual abilities. A subject with the intellectual abilities of an average 8 year old would have an MA of 8. IQ was then determined by dividing the subject's earned mental age by his or her actual age (called *chronological age,* or *CA*). This quotient was then multiplied by 100 to determine IQ, or IQ=MA/CA×100. If an 8-year-old girl has a mental age of 8, that girl would be average, and her IQ would equal 100 (or 8/8×100=1×100). If the 8 year old were above average, functioning with

standard age score (SAS)
a score on an intelligence test by which one's performance is compared to that of others of the same age; average equals 100

FIGURE 8.9
An idealized curve that shows the distribution of scores on the Stanford-Binet Intelligence Scale if the test were taken by a very large sample of the general population. The numbers at the top of the curve indicate the percentage of the population expected to score within the indicated range of scores, that is, 68% score between 85 and 115; 95% score between 70 and 130; and 99% score between 55 and 145.

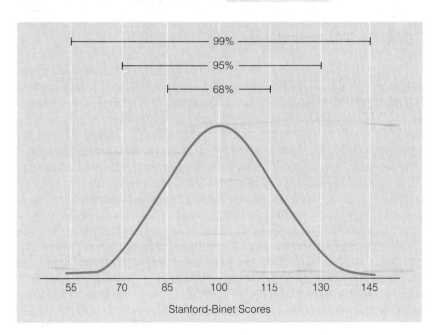

the intellectual abilities of an average 10 year old, then her IQ would be 125 (that's 10/8×100, or 1.25×100). If she were below average, perhaps with the mental abilities of an average 6 year old, then her computed IQ would be 75. Many people are used to the term "IQ" as a measure of one's general intellectual abilities. Because it is a term that is engrained in our vocabulary, *we use "IQ" to stand for a measure of general intelligence,* even though we now report scores as standard scores and no longer compute MAs or calculate quotients.

The Stanford-Binet test has been in use for a long time. There is much to be said for it. It is a well-recognized measure of those behaviors that we commonly label intelligent—at least in an educational or academic sense—and is in that way, at least, a valid instrument. It is also reliable, although we can expect a change in standard scores of as much as eight points on repeated administrations (that is, a score of 100 ought to be thought of as representing a "true" score somewhere between 96 and 104). The Stanford-Binet also has some drawbacks. It is an individual test (one subject and one examiner) and should be administered, scored, and interpreted only by well-trained professionals. The test may take longer than an hour to administer and hence is quite expensive. The latest edition of the Stanford Binet does address two problems found in earlier versions. It is no longer as heavily verbal in its content, and it now yields more than just one overall score.

BEFORE YOU GO ON **Briefly describe the Stanford-Binet Intelligence Scale.**

The Wechsler Tests of Intelligence.   David Wechsler published his first general intelligence test in 1939. Unlike the version of the Stanford-Binet that existed at the time, it was designed for use with adult populations and to reduce the heavy reliance on verbal skills. With a major revision in 1955, the test became known as the *Wechsler Adult Intelligence Scale (WAIS).* The latest revision (now called the WAIS-R) was published in 1981. The WAIS-R is appropriate for subjects between 16 and 74 years of age and is reported to be the most commonly used of all tests in clinical practice (Lubin et al., 1984).

A natural extension of the WAIS was the *Wechsler Intelligence Scale for Children (WISC),* originally published 11 years after the WAIS. After a major revision in 1974, it became known as the WISC-R. The WISC-R is appropriate for testing children between the ages of 6 and 17 (there is some overlap with the WAIS). A third test in the Wechsler series is designed for younger children between the ages of 4 and 6½. It is called the *Wechsler Preschool and Primary Scale of Intelligence,* or *WPPSI.* It was first published in 1967 (and is under revision). There are some subtle differences among the three Wechsler tests, but each is based on the same general logic. Therefore, we'll consider only one, the WAIS-R, in any detail.

The WAIS-R is made up of 11 subtests, or scales. The subtests of the WAIS-R are arranged by the *type* of ability or skill being tested. The subtests are organized into two categories. Six subtests define the *verbal scale,* and five subtests constitute a *performance scale.* Figure 8.10 lists the different subtests of the WAIS-R and describes some of the sorts of items found on each. With each of the Wechsler tests, we can compute three scores: a verbal

The Wechsler tests provide verbal and performance scores that are compared to scores earned by subjects of the same age in the norm group. The Wechsler Intelligence Scale for Children (WISC-R) is a general intelligence test for children between the ages of 6 and 17.

TWO SCALES: PERFORMANCE - VERBAL-

score, a performance score, and a total (or full-scale) score. As with the Stanford-Binet, the total score can be taken as an approximation of **g**, or general intellectual ability.

To administer the WAIS-R, you present each of the 11 subtests to your subject. The items within each subtest are arranged in order of difficulty. You start with relatively easy items—those you are confident that your examinee will respond to correctly—and then you progress to more difficult ones. You stop administering any one subtest when your subject fails a specified number of items in a row. You alternate between verbal and performance subtests. The whole process takes up to an hour and a half.

Each item on each subtest is scored. (Some of the performance items have strict time limits that affect scoring.) You now have 11 scores earned by your subject. As is now the case with the fourth edition of the Stanford-Binet, each subtest score is compared to the score provided with the test's norms appropriate for your subject's age. The WAIS-R was standardized on a large representative sample of nearly 2,000 adults in nine different age groups. How your subject's score compares to the score earned by subjects of the same age in the norm group determines your subject's *standard score* for each of the Wechsler subtests.

As we have already mentioned, the Wechsler tests are very popular instruments for assessing intellectual abilities. In addition to one overall score, these tests provide verbal and performance scores, which may provide useful information about an individual's particular strengths and weaknesses. The Wechsler tests are every bit as "good" as the Stanford-Binet in terms of reliability, validity, and norms.

FIGURE 8.10
The subtests of the Wechsler Adult Intelligence Scale-Revised (WAIS-R)

Verbal Scale

Information	(29 items) Questions designed to tap one's general knowledge about a variety of topics dealing with one's culture; for example, "Who wrote *Huckleberry Finn*?" or "How many nickels in a quarter?"
Digit span	(7 series) Subject is read a series of 3 to 9 digits and is asked to repeat them; then a different series is to be repeated in reverse order.
Comprehension	(16 items) A test of judgment, common sense, and practical knowledge; for example, "Why is it good to have prisons?"
Similarities	(14 pairs) Subject must indicate the way(s) in which two things are alike; for example, "In what way are an apple and a potato alike?"
Vocabulary	(35 words) Subject must provide an acceptable definition for a series of words.
Arithmetic	(14 problems) Math problems must be solved without the use of paper and pencil; for example, "How far will a bird travel in 90 minutes if it flies at the rate of 10 miles per hour?"

Performance scale

Picture completion	(20 pictures) Subject must identify or name the missing part or object in a drawing; for example, a wagon with only three wheels.
Picture arrangement	(10 series) A series of cartoonlike pictures must be arranged in an order so that they tell a story.
Block design	(9 items) Using blocks whose sides are either all red, all white, or diagonally red and white, subject must copy a designed picture or pattern shown on a card.
Object assembly	(4 objects) Free-form jigsaw puzzles must be put together to form familiar objects.
Digit symbol	In a key, each of nine digits is paired with a simple symbol. Given a random series of digits, the subject must provide the paired symbol within a time limit.

For many years, there has been controversy and debate about the use and quality of individually administered intelligence tests, such as the Wechsler tests and the Stanford-Binet. Whether or not the tests are culturally biased, thus favoring one group of subjects over another, whether they truly measure intelligence and not just academic success, and whether test results can be used for political purposes, perhaps as a basis for discrimination, are just some of the questions that keep finding their way into the popular press. A survey of over 600 experts in psychological testing (from a number of disciplines, including education and psychology) indicates considerable agreement about the basic value of intelligence (or IQ) tests (Snyderman & Rothman, 1987). Although the experts suggest that tests may be somewhat biased on racial and socioeconomic grounds, they "believe that such tests adequately measure most important elements of intelligence" (p. 143).

BEFORE YOU GO ON **What are the major features of the Wechsler intelligence scales?**

We have now completed our review of some of psychology's better assessment tools. Next we'll consider what measured intelligence, or IQ, can tell us about group differences.

Group Differences in Intelligence. Recognizing that there are individual differences in intelligence, can't we make any direct statements about differences in IQ in general? Here are those easy questions again. Who are smarter, women or men? Do we become more or less intelligent with age? Are there differences in intelligence between blacks and whites? As you can probably appreciate, simple answers are often misleading and, if interpreted incorrectly, can be dangerous.

One thing we have to ask ourselves is why we care. What motivates our interest in knowing about group differences in IQ? Even the best scientific data can be put to questionable use. Unfortunately, issues of group differences are sometimes raised in order to justify what amounts to social or political ends. Some sexists (male and female), some racists (black and white), and some ageists (young and old) like to point to any observed differences in IQ for groups of individuals to make claims of superiority or inferiority. It is in such cases that clearcut answers can be dangerous.

More commonly, however, reported mean differences in intelligence test scores are simply misleading. Let's imagine for a moment that we have tested two large groups of people—1,000 Umaloos and 1,000 Takatees. On the average, the mean IQ score (measured general intelligence, remember) for Umaloos is found to be 95; for Takatees, it is 110. An appropriate statistical analysis tells me that this observed difference of 15 points is too large to have been expected by chance. Are Takatees smarter than Umaloos? Yes, *on the average* they are—that's what we just discovered. *Test*

Now look at Figure 8.11. Here we find two curves that represent the distributions of IQ scores from our fictitious study. We can clearly see the difference in the averages of the two groups. However, there are some Takatees whose IQs are below the average IQ of Umaloos. And there are Umaloos whose IQs are above the average IQ of Takatees. We may be able to draw

FIGURE 8.11
Hypothetical distributions of IQ scores for two imaginary groups (Umaloos and Takatees). The average IQ for Takatees ($\overline{X}_T$) is higher than that for Umaloos ($\overline{X}_U$), but there is considerable overlap in the two distributions. That is, some Umaloos have IQs that are higher than the average for Takatees (110), and some Takatees have IQs lower than the average for Umaloos (95).

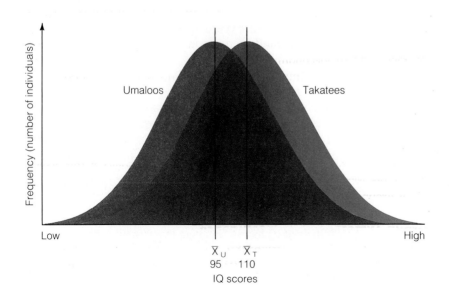

some conclusions about average IQ levels, but making statements about individual Takatees and Umaloos is difficult.

Perhaps the main reason we care about group differences in intelligence (over and above simple curiosity) is the hope that understanding such differences will help us to understand the true nature of intelligence and the factors that influence its development within individuals (Mackintosh, 1986). Being able to demonstrate a significant difference between the average IQs of two groups of individuals in itself tells us nothing about why those differences exist. Are Takatees genetically superior to Umaloos? Maybe, maybe not. Have Umaloos had equal access to the sorts of things that IQ tests ask about? Maybe, maybe not. Are the tests themselves slanted to provide Takatees with an advantage? Maybe, maybe not. Discovering that two identifiable groups of individuals have different average IQ scores usually raises more questions than it answers. But psychologists generally believe that knowledge about differences will be more beneficial in the long run than ignorance (Scarr, 1988).

BEFORE YOU GO ON **If group A and group B have different IQ scores on the average, what may be true about two individuals, one from group A and the other from group B, with regard to intelligence?**

If indeed there are group differences in intelligence, where do they come from? This question is no different from, and has essentially the same answer as the question: Where does intelligence come from? Psychologists aren't sure of the answer to either question but if we are ever to get reasonable answers to them, we need to consider an age-old question in psychology.

Variations in Intelligence

We have defined intelligence from a theoretical perspective and from an operational perspective. Our theoretical definition dealt with individual "capacity" and "resourcefulness" while our operational definition dealt with individual test performance. Both definitions imply that people differ in intelligence. In fact, people differ greatly in intelligence and those differences are what we turn to next.

The Distribution of Intelligence. When we look at the intelligence scores earned by large, random samples of individuals, we find a predictable distribution of scores. The scores are commonly expressed as IQs (*intelligence quotient*—a number which represents intelligence). Keep in mind that there is nothing "magical" about IQ, it is simply a number that tells us where a person is on the distribution of intelligence.

The average IQ score is 100 and most people have scores near that number. More than two-thirds of all IQ scores fall between 85 and 115 and all but 5 percent of IQ scores fall between 70 and 130. Look ahead to Figure 8.9 to see how the distribution of IQ looks—imagine that it represents a group of people arranged according to how they score on an intelligence test. Most of them would be standing on top of each other near the center while those few scoring at the extremes would be a bit more comfortable. It is important to note in Figure 8.9 that the distribution of intelligence is symmetrical. That is, there are equal numbers of people at either end of the distribution. We will come back to that point in a bit.

Most of us are in that crowd in the middle. We are considered to be average or slightly above or below average. For most people in that middle crowd, differences in ability probably depend more on other characteristics such as motivation and personality than on level of intelligence. The ability of two people to do some task or perform a particular job cannot be reliably predicted by their IQ scores if they were 97 and 103 for example. Even larger differences in that middle group are likely to be overshadowed by other individual differences.

To get a better picture of what differences in IQ mean, we should look at the differences between those two equal groups of people at the extremes of intelligence. As you will see next, people at the "tails" of the IQ distribution differ greatly. We can be pretty confident that a person with an IQ score of 69 is very different from one with a score of 131. (Of course, we must always keep in mind that any test score can be inaccurate for a variety of reasons.) First we'll look at the upper extreme, then the lower.

How is intelligence distributed? BEFORE YOU GO ON

The Mentally Gifted.   There are many ways in which a person can be gifted. A United States Office of Education report (1972) defined giftedness as a demonstrated achievement or aptitude for excellence in any one of six areas:

(1) *Psychomotor ability*. This is one of the most overlooked areas in which some individuals can clearly excel. We are dealing here with people of outstanding abilities in skills that require agility, strength, speed, quickness, coordination, and the like.
(2) *Visual and performing arts*. Some people, even as children, demonstrate an unusual talent for arts, music, drama, and writing.
(3) *Leadership ability*. Leadership skills are valued in most societies, and there seem to be individuals who are particularly gifted in this area. This is often true even with very young children. Youngsters with good leadership skills tend to be intellectually bright, but they are not necessarily the smartest of the group.
(4) *Creative or productive thinking*. This area of giftedness has received considerable attention over the past 25 years. Here we are talking about individuals who may be intellectually or academically above average, but, again, not necessarily so. Among other things people with this type of giftedness are able to generate unique and different solutions to problems.
(5) *Specific academic aptitude*. In this case, we are talking about people who have a flair or special ability for a particular subject or two. Someone who is a real whiz in math, history, or laboratory science, without necessarily being outstanding in other academic areas, would fit this category.

Giftedness can be defined as a demonstrated achievement or aptitude for excellence in one of six areas, including leadership. Some people demonstrate leadership ability, even as children.

(6) *Intellectually gifted.* Inclusion in this group is based on scores earned on a general intelligence test, usually a Wechsler test or the Stanford-Binet intelligence scale (both of which will be discussed later in the chapter). It is most likely that when people use the term "mentally gifted," they are referring to individuals who would fit this category—people of exceptionally high IQ. (IQ scores of 130 or above usually qualify for inclusion in this category. Some prefer to reserve the label for those with IQs above 135. In either case, we are dealing with a very small portion of the population—fewer than three percent qualify.)

How can we describe intellectually gifted individuals? Most of what we know about the **mentally gifted** comes directly, or indirectly, from a classic study begun by L. M. Terman in the early 1920s. Terman supervised the testing of more than a quarter of a million children throughout California. Terman's research group at Stanford University focused its attention on those children who earned the highest scores—about 1,500 in all, each with an IQ above 135.

Lewis Terman died in 1956, but the study of those mentally gifted individuals—who were between the ages of 8 and 12 in 1922— still continues. Ever since their inclusion in the original study, and at regular intervals, they have been retested, surveyed, interviewed, and polled by psychologists still at Stanford (Goleman, 1980; Oden, 1968; Sears and Barbee, 1977).

The Terman study has its drawbacks—choosing a very narrow definition of gifted in terms of IQ alone is an obvious one. Failing to control for factors such as socioeconomic level or parents' educational level is another. Nonetheless, the study is an impressive one for having been continued for more than 60 years, if nothing else. What can this longitudinal analysis tell us about people with very high IQs?

Most of Terman's results fly in the face of the common stereotype of the bright child as being skinny, anxious, clumsy, of poor health, and almost certainly wearing thick glasses (Sears & Barbee, 1977). The data just do not support the stereotype. In fact, if there is any overall conclusion that might be drawn from the Terman-Stanford study, it is that, in general, gifted children experience advantages in virtually everything. They are taller, faster, better coordinated, have better eyesight, fewer emotional problems, and tend to stay married longer than average. These findings have been confirmed by others (Holden, 1980). All sorts of obvious things are also true of this sample of bright children, now oldsters. They received much more education, found better, higher-paying jobs, and had more intelligent children than did people of average intelligence. By now, we certainly know better than to overgeneralize. Every one of Terman's children (sometimes referred to as "Termites") did not grow up to be rich and famous and live happily ever after. The truth is that many did, but not all.

mentally gifted
demonstrating outstanding ability or aptitude in a number of possible areas; usually general intelligence where an IQ of 130 is a standard criterion

Test →

BEFORE YOU GO ON

List six ways in which individuals can be considered to be gifted.

Summarize the basic findings of the Terman-Stanford study of intellectually gifted youngsters.

The Mentally Retarded. Intelligence as measured by IQ tests is often used to confirm suspected cases of **mental retardation.** As is the case for the mentally gifted, however, there is more to retardation than IQ alone. The definition provided by the American Association on Mental Deficiency (AAMD) cites three factors to consider: "subaverage general intellectual functioning which originated during the developmental period and is associated with impairment in adaptive behavior" (Grossman, 1973). Let's look at each of these three points.

The IQ cutoff for mental retardation is usually taken to be 70. The AAMD further categorizes mental retardation as follows:

IQ 70–85: *borderline or slow*
IQ 50–69: *mildly mentally retarded*
IQ 35–49: *moderately mentally retarded*
IQ 20–34 *severely mentally retarded*
IQ less than 19: *profoundly mentally retarded*

As you review this list, you need to keep two things in mind. First, these IQ test scores are suggested limits. Given what we know about IQ tests and their reliability, it is ridiculous to claim after one administration of a test that a person with an IQ of 69 is mentally retarded, while someone else with an IQ of 71 is not. Second, diagnosis of mental retardation is not (should not be) made on the basis of IQ score alone.

To fit the definition of mental retardation given above, the cause or the symptoms of the below-average intellectual functioning must show up during the usual period of intellectual development (up to age 18). In many circles, the term "developmentally delayed" is coming to replace the narrower term "mentally retarded." Actual diagnosis may come only after the administration of an IQ test, but initial suspicions generally come from perceived delays in normal developmental or adjustive patterns of behavior.

By making "impairment in adaptive behavior" a part of their definition of mental retardation, the AAMD is acknowledging that there is more to getting along in this world than the intellectual and academic sorts of skills that IQ tests emphasize. Being mentally retarded does not necessarily mean being totally helpless, particularly for those who fall in the categories of more moderate levels of retardation. Of major consideration is (or ought to be) the individual's ability to adapt to his or her environment. In this regard, such skills as the ability to dress oneself, to follow directions, to make change, to find one's way home from a distance, and so on become relevant (Coulter & Morrow, 1978). As it happens, there are a number of psychological assessment devices that try to measure these very skills. Three such instruments are the Vineland Adaptive Behavior Scales (Sparrow et al., 1985), the Adaptive Behavior Scale (Lambert & Windmiller, 1981), and the Adaptive Behavior Inventory (Brown & Leigh, 1986).

Even without a simple, one-dimensional definition, it is clear that the population of retarded citizens is a large one. It is very difficult to obtain exact figures because many individuals who might fit the criteria and be classified as mildly retarded have never been diagnosed as such. Even so, standard estimates indicate that approximately 3 percent of the population at any one time falls within the IQ range for retardation. Two other relevant

mental retardation
a condition indicated by an IQ below 70 that began during the developmental period and is associated with impairment in adaptive functioning

estimates are that approximately 900,000 children with mental retardation between the ages of 3 and 21 years are being served in public schools (Schroeder et al., 1987) and that nearly 200,000 mentally retarded individuals are to be found in community residential facilities, state and county mental hospitals, and nursing homes (Landesman & Butterfield, 1987).

BEFORE YOU GO ON   **How might we best define mental retardation?**

NATURE-NURTURE REVISITED: THE INFLUENCE OF HEREDITY AND THE ENVIRONMENT ON INTELLIGENCE

Are the differences we observe in intelligence due to heredity or to environmental influences? This is one of the oldest and most enduring questions in all of psychology. As reasonable as it may sound, the question does not have a reasonable answer. At least it has no simple, straightforward answer. As we shall see, there is some evidence that intelligence tends to run in families and may be due in part to innate, inherited factors. There are also data (and common sense) that tell us that a person's environment can and does affect intellectual, cognitive functioning. After all these years of scientific investigation, why can't we provide an answer to this question?

Conceptual Problems

When we ask about the origin of intelligence, we have two large conceptual problems (and many smaller ones). We have seen that one difficulty is our inability to define intelligence to everyone's satisfaction. Unable to settle on just one definition, we usually end up relying on intelligence tests to provide operational measures of intelligence, but there continues to be substantial disagreement about the quality and the fairness of our intelligence tests (Mackintosh, 1986).

Our second major problem has to do with the limitations of research design—specifically, the inability to provide adequate controls. Just how might we determine if *any* trait, including intelligence, is experiential (environmental) or genetic (inherited) in origin? In theory, a couple of approaches come to mind. We could take individuals with exactly the same genetic constitution (that is, identical twins) and raise them in different environments. Or we could take people of clearly different genetic constitutions and raise them in identical environments. Either sort of experimental manipulation might prove to be very helpful in separating the two major influences on intelligence.

It doesn't take very long to figure out why such manipulations are not possible—at least with human subjects. How could we ever guarantee that any two persons were raised in identical environments? How can we ever get many more than two subjects at a time who have exactly the same genetic constitution? Even with pairs of subjects, who's to decide what kinds of environments each would be assigned? No matter how important we feel our scientific question is, we cannot simply pluck children out of their homes and then systematically assign them to different environmental conditions just for the sake of an experiment. Nor can we severely deprive children for a few years to see what cognitive abilities might develop without the benefit of a stimulating environment.

What two major problems have inhibited our search for an answer to the heredity vs. environment question with regard to intelligence?   BEFORE YOU GO ON

A Tentative Answer

Before we examine any of the supporting evidence, we can offer a tentative answer to our opening question. Both heredity *and* the environment are critically important in determining intelligence. One's heredity may put limits on what environmental influences can accomplish. Without a nurturing, stimulating environment, even the best of inherited potential may be wasted.

A person does not inherit intelligence. A person inherits genes and chromosomes. These physical entities may very well set limits for the potentials of our intellectual abilities. Some people may be born with the potential, or even the predisposition, to become very intelligent. If the environment does not encourage that predisposition, however, the potential will be wasted. Some individuals may be born with inherited predispositions that severely limit their intellectual growth. Even the best of stimulating environments may be insufficient to raise intellectual functioning above average levels.

Some people are born with the predisposition to become extremely intelligent. This inherited potential must be encouraged and nurtured in a stimulating environment to be fully realized.

The point is that the two, environment and heredity, interact. Each may limit the other. Both are important. This is the point of view that we identified in Chapter 6 as an *epigenetic model* of the interaction of nature and nurture.

What the Data Suggest: The Study of Twins

Maybe we can't all agree precisely on what intelligence is, but we *can* use intelligence test scores as an approximation of an operational definition. Perhaps we can't do the perfectly controlled heredity/environment experiment, but we *can* look at the relationships among the IQs of people with similar and different genetic histories who have been reared in similar and different environments. Such data may be flawed (Mackenzie, 1984, Mackintosh, 1986), but perhaps they can give us some helpful leads.

As you might imagine, studies that examine the correlations of IQ test scores of persons with varying degrees of genetic similarity and those reared in similar and dissimilar environments have been done a number of times. The results of some of the better of these studies are summarized in Figure 8.12. These are oft-cited data, and we ought to be sure that we understand what they mean.

On the left side of the figure, we have a listing of the types of subjects whose IQ scores have been correlated. As you can see, as we go down the list, the genetic similarity between the subjects increases, from unrelated individuals reared apart to identical twins reared together. The graph shows the average (in this case the median) correlation for each of the pairs of groups named under "Subjects." These correlations represent average values from many correlational studies. Quite clearly, such data, drawn from a number of studies conducted at different times, with different subjects, and with different intents, need to be interpreted with great caution. Even with the variability reflected in these data, however, a few general conclusions seem reasonable.

As genetic similarities between subjects increase, correlations also increase. Correlations between the IQ scores of individuals who are unrelated in any biological sense appear quite low. Remembering that fraternal twins are just siblings who happen to be born at about the same time, we find that IQs among family members in general are correlated somewhere near 0.50. When we examine the correlations of IQs of identical twins (whose genetic constitutions are the same, of course), we find very high correlations—as high as those usually reported as reliability coefficients for the IQ tests that were used. It seems quite obvious by inspection that genetic similarity and IQ scores are positively related.

You should also notice another difference in the data presented in Figure 8.12. Regardless of genetic similarity, the correlations for subjects raised together are consistently higher than for subjects raised apart in different environments. We do need to note that children raised apart need not necessarily be reared in significantly different environments, and being raised together does not guarantee that environments are identical. What these differences do suggest is that environmental influences also affect IQ scores. As you can see, we are drawn to the conclusion we made earlier. Even

The correlation of IQ scores of identical twins is very high (even when the twins are raised apart) due to identical genetic constitutions.

FIGURE 8.12
Correlations of IQ test scores as a function of genetic and environmental similarity. Vertical lines indicate average (median) correlations, and horizontal lines indicate the range of correlations from many different studies reviewed by Erlenmeyer-Kimling and Jarvik (1963).

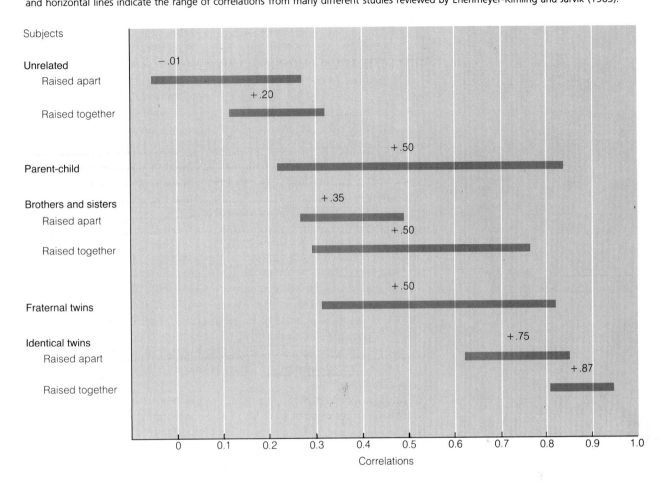

though we are looking at grouped data, and even though many factors are left uncontrolled, inheritance clearly influences intelligence as measured by IQ test scores, but so does the environment.

A more recent survey of similar literature (Bouchard & McGue, 1981) draws the same general conclusion. After reviewing 111 studies, the authors concluded that genetic similarity is related to intercorrelations of IQ test scores. Identical twins produce IQ score correlations fully 20 points higher, on the average, than that found for fraternal twins. Again, however, we need to caution that identical twins are often treated in similar ways (dressed alike, for instance) even more so than are fraternal twins.

Additional insight can be gained by examining the IQs of adopted children. This sort of research also focuses on correlational data. Are the IQs of adopted children more strongly correlated with the IQs of their biological parents (showing a genetic influence) or with the IQs of their foster or adoptive parents (environmental influence)? Once again, the data appear

Adopted children share higher IQ with biological parents than with foster. (correlations)

clearcut, but their interpretation is not. With large groups of subjects, correlations between the IQs of children and their biological parents are significantly higher (around 0.48) than when correlations are computed between the IQs of children and their adoptive parents (around 0.20). This seems to imply that changing environments cannot significantly lessen the relationship between the IQs of biological parents and their offspring, but we'd better not make any snap judgments.

Social agencies do not arrange adoption placements in order to satisfy psychologists' needs for adequate experimental control. What we don't know in most of these studies of adopted children is the degree to which the home environments of the adoptive and the biological parents are the same or different. One study (Scarr & Weinberg, 1976) reports very large increases in IQ scores for children from low socioeconomic backgrounds who were placed with families at a higher socioeconomic level. In this study, adoptive parents were of significantly higher educational level than were biological parents. Here, the environment did appear to have a major impact on IQ.

The same researchers, two years later (Scarr & Weinberg, 1978), reported another investigation in which socioeconomic status was controlled, at least to some degree. In this study, the researchers concerned themselves only with correlations between the IQs of children and their biological or adoptive parents if the socioeconomic level of both types of parent was approximately equal. The idea, of course, was to minimize environmental factors that could be attributed to social class differences. In these conditions, with an additional environmental factor controlled, there was a much stronger relationship between a child's IQ and that of its biological parents than that of its adoptive parents. These results once again show support for the role of inheritance.

To review, the perfect experiment, or correlational study, to determine the relative importance of heredity and the environment has not yet been done. In fact, there is an argument that suggests that it cannot be done. (There is also a compelling argument that there is no reason to even try such research in the first place if the only aim is to apportion the relative influence of heredity and environment. What is needed is to focus on the specific determinants of what we call intelligence [Mackenzie, 1984].) Here's how British psychologist N. J. Mackintosh puts it: "The possibility that there might be some genetic differences for IQ between different social or ethnic groups is usually thought to be a question of considerable social significance. It is certainly one which can be made by people of ill will. But it is not a question of any great scientific interest. Scientifically, it would be much more valuable to have a greater understanding of the nature of human intelligence; and if that seems a hopelessly ambitious goal, then we might settle for an increase in our understanding of whatever it is that IQ tests measure" (1986, pp. 9–10). From the data that we have at present, there is evidence that can be used to justify almost any rationale: that one (nature) or the other (nurture) or both are important. It does seem that, in general, IQ is strongly affected by genetic predispositions. At the same time, it is true that IQ can be influenced or modified by the environment. The more extreme the differences in environments, the greater the resulting differences in IQ.

In general, what has the study of twins and adopted children told us about the relative importance of heredity and the environment in determining intelligence as measured by IQ tests?

BEFORE YOU GO ON

Using psychological tests as measuring instruments is a difficult business. We sometimes have considerable difficulty providing a solid definition of the very characteristic we are attempting to measure. Using a somewhat circular logic, we often fall back to our psychological tests to provide us with operational definitions of concepts that are difficult to define otherwise. Hence, "anxiety" becomes a score on an anxiety questionnaire, and "intelligence" becomes a score on an IQ test.

Psychological tests of high quality are particularly difficult to construct. They must demonstrate reliability and validity and have adequate norms, whether we are dealing with personality assessment or intellectual assessment. In this chapter, we have reviewed some of psychology's better assessment tools and related them to the theories which try to explain individual differences in personality and intelligence. As to where personality and intelligence come from we cannot say as yet. What psychology can offer now are theories and descriptions of how people differ. We trust the fast moving pace of psychological research will provide better answers some day.

SUMMARY

What is a theory of personality?

A theory of personality is a series of related assumptions that, through logic and reason, lead to testable hypotheses that can be used to describe an individual and to differentiate one individual from others. / 333

What are the three levels of consciousness proposed by Freud?

Freud proposed that at any time we are only aware, or *conscious*, of a few things; some ideas or memories are accessible in our *preconscious*, while others may be accessed only with great difficulty—these are in our *unconscious* mind. / 334

According to Freud, what are the three structures of personality, and by what principle does each operate?

Three structures of personality according to Freud are the inborn, instinctive *id*, which operates on a *pleasure principle*, seeking immediate gratification; the *ego*, or sense of self, which operates on a *reality principle*, mediating needs in the context of the real world; and the *superego*, or sense of morality or conscience, which operates on an *idealistic principle*. / 336

Briefly review Freud's five psychosexual stages of development.

Freud believed that one's personality developed through five stages: the oral stage (birth to 1 year), the anal stage (ages 1–3), the phallic stage (ages 3–5), the latency stage (ages 6–puberty), and the genital stage (from puberty on). / 337

Briefly summarize the contributions of Adler, Jung, and Horney to the psychoanalytic approach to personality.

Adler, Jung, and Horney each parted with Freud on theoretical grounds, while remaining basically psychoanalytic in their approaches to personality. For Adler, social influences mattered much more than Freudian instincts. Jung was less biological, more positive, and expanded on Freud's view of the unconscious mind. Horney also rejected the notion of instinctual impulses and discussed instead the notion of basic anxiety and how one reacts to it as the molder of one's personality. / 339

Specify a contribution to the notion of personality contributed by Watson, Skinner, Dollard and Miller, Bandura, and Rotter.

A number of psychologists have argued that personality can be approached through an examination of learning principles and observable behavior. Watson first emphasized focusing on behavior and abandoning mental concepts. Dollard and Miller attempted to explain personality development in terms of learning theory and habits. Skinner emphasizes the notion of reinforcement and the consequences of one's behaviors. Bandura stresses the role of observation and social learning in the formation of personality. And Rotter believes that one's appraisal of control over behavior is an essential part of personality. / 342

Briefly summarize the humanistic/phenomenological approach to personality as epitomized by Rogers and Maslow.

The theories of Rogers and Maslow are alike in many ways, both emphasizing the integrity of the self and the positive power of personal growth and development and both denying the negativity and biological basis of Freudian theory and the sterility of behaviorism. / 345

What is a personality trait?

What are the major traits that influence personality, according to Allport, Cattell, and Eysenck?

A personality trait is a characteristic and distinctive way in which one individual may differ from others. According to Allport, there are two kinds of traits: *common* and *personal,* the former found in virtually everyone, the latter unique just to some individuals. Cattell also feels that there are two kinds of traits: *surface traits,* which are readily observable, and *source traits,* from which surface traits evolve. Eysenck, on the other hand, believes that one's personality can be described somewhere among the intersections of three major dimensions: *extroversion-introversion, stability-instability,* and *psychoticism.* / 348

Define measurement.

What is a psychological test?

What is the difference between personality assessment and intellectual assessment?

Measurement involves assigning numbers to some characteristic of interest according to rules or some agreed upon system. A psychological test is an *objective* (not open to multiple interpretation), *standardized* (adminis-tered and scored in the same way) *measure of a sample* (we cannot measure all behaviors) *of behavior* (because behavior is all we can measure). Personality assessment provides a measure of one's personality or affect in the sense of describing one's typical behavior, whereas intellectual assessment involves measuring one's cognitive abilities and aptitudes in the sense of describing one's maximum, or best, performance. / 351

What is reliability, and how do we measure the reliability of psychological tests?

Reliability means consistency or dependability. With psychological tests, we measure reliability by administering the same test to the same people at different times (test-retest reliability) or we check the internal consistency of the test by comparing scores on some items with scores on other items (split-half reliability). / 353

What are predictive, concurrent, and content validity?

How is each of these measured?

Predictive validity tells us if a test predicts what it claims to predict. To measure it, test scores are correlated with some other, independent criterion measured after the test has been taken. Concurrent validity tell us if the test under consideration is at least correlated with other tests that claim to measure the same thing. Content validity is the extent to which a test is composed of a fair and representative sample of the material or characteristic being tested. / 354

In the context of psychological testing, what are norms, and for what purpose are they used?

Test norms are scores on the test earned by a large number of subjects, similar to those for whom the test has been designed. It is against the standard of these scores that an individual's test score can be compared. / 355

What are the basic goals of personality assessment?

Personality assessment can be used for a number of reasons, including (1) making a clinical diagnosis about the presence and/or nature of a psychological disorder, (2) as a tool in building a theory of personality in order to see which traits are associated with others, and (3) for behavioral prediction in attempting to assess what someone might do in the future. / 356

SUMMARY continued

How is behavioral observation used to assess personality?

One tries to draw conclusions about personality on the basis of the observations of behaviors. Behaviors should be observed in a variety of settings. Observations should be as objective as possible and may involve the use of behavioral rating scales to check reliability. / 357

Cite one advantage and one disadvantage of the interview as a technique of personality assessment.

The major advantage of the interview technique is its flexibility. The interviewer may pursue avenues of interest, while abandoning lines of questioning that are not fruitful. Unfortunately, there is very little data to support the notion that interviewing is a valid technique for most uses. / 358

Why was the MMPI constructed?

What does multiphasic mean?

How did the authors of the MMPI try to insure that the test would be valid?

The MMPI was originally designed (1941) as an aid to psychological diagnosis. As a multiphasic instrument, it measures a number of different personality traits during the same administration of the test. Validity of a sort was built into the test when the authors only used items that discriminated between subjects of different diagnostic categories. They also included items that assess such things as trying to present one's self in an unrealistically positive manner and simply not paying attention while taking the test. / 361

What is the essence of a projective technique, the Rorschach and TAT in particular?

With a projective technique, the assumption is that in responding to an ambiguous stimulus (inkblots with the Rorschach, pictures with the TAT), subjects will project some of their selves, perhaps even unconscious aspects of their selves, into their responses. / 362

Provide a theoretical and an operational definition of intelligence.

In theory, we may define intelligence as has David Wechsler: "the capacity of an individual to understand the world about him or her and his or her resourcefulness to cope with its challenges." An operational definition of intelligence would be "that which an intelligence test measures." / 364

Briefly describe the Stanford-Binet Intelligence Scale.

The Stanford-Binet is the oldest of the tests of general intelligence (commonly called "IQ"). The test is individually administered. Its most recent, 1986, revision provides an overall score, as well as sub-scores for a number of abilities that are assumed to underlie general intelligence. The test is comprised of 15 subtests, each assessing a specific cognitive task, where items are arranged in order by difficulty. Scores on the test, "standard age scores," compare the performance of a subject to that of many others of the same age level. / 368

What are the major features of the Wechsler Intelligence Scales?

The Wechsler Scales are individually administered tests of general intelligence. There are three of them, each appropriate for different age groups, ranging from ages 4 to 74. Each test is made up of a number of subtests of different content. The subtests are grouped together as verbal or performance subtests. Hence, three scores can be determined: an overall score, a score on the verbal subtests, and a score on the performance subtests. Scores on the Wechsler tests are standard scores which compare one's abilities to those of others of the same age. / 370

If group A and group B have different IQ scores on the average, what may be true about two individuals, one from group A and the other from group B, with regard to intelligence?

Mean group differences tell us very little about individual differences. That is, two individuals may have the same IQ score or either may have a score higher than the other. / 372

How is intelligence distributed?

Most people have IQ scores near the middle or average score of 100. There are equal numbers of people at the high and low extremes. / 373

List six ways in which individuals can be considered to be gifted.

Summarize the basic findings of the Terman-Stanford study of intellectually gifted youngsters.

Giftedness can mean a number of things in addition to (1) overall intellectual ability as measured by IQ tests (usually taken to be an IQ in excess of 130 points). Other abilities in which individuals may be gifted include: (2) visual and performing arts, (3) psychomotor, (4) leadership, (5) creative, and (6) specific academic areas. Individuals who are mentally gifted also experience a number of other physical, educational, social, and economic advantages. / 374

How might we best define mental retardation?

Mental retardation should be thought of as indicated by subaverage intellectual functioning (usually indicated by IQ scores below 70), originating during the developmental period (within 18 years), and associated with impairment in adaptive behavior (as well as academic behaviors). / 376

What two major problems have inhibited our search for an answer to the heredity vs. environment question with regard to intelligence?

Two problems that have hindered our search for answers to the heredity vs. environment question have been (1) our failure to adequately define intelligence, and (2) the inability to exercise adequate experimental control over extraneous variables. / 377

In general, what has the study of twins and adopted children told us about the relative importance of heredity and the environment in determining intelligence as measured by IQ tests?

Although we cannot draw any definite conclusions, it seems reasonable to suggest that there are genetic factors that may place limits on one's intellectual potential, but the impact of the environment is needed to exercise such potential because both are ultimately important in determining intelligence as measured by IQ tests. / 381

Chapter Eight
Individual Differences in Personality and Intelligence

REVIEW QUESTIONS

1. Freud based most of his theory of personality on:

a. an empirically validated set of personality assessment techniques.

b. his experience with his patients in his psychiatric practice.

c. the analysis of his dreams.

d. factor analysis.

Freud was, before he began considering theories of personality, a physician who became interested in what were in his time called nervous disorders. His views of human development and personality, therefore, spring from his private practice of analyzing and treating his patients. He also achieved considerable insight through self-analysis. Psychological assessment, empirical and otherwise, as well as factor analysis were to come after Freudian personality theory had been formed. / 334

2. According to Freudian theory, which aspect of one's personality is most often "in touch with reality"?

a. eros.

b. ego.

c. id.

d. superego.

Freud postulated two main instincts that dominated one's personality: eros, the life instinct, and thanatos, the death instinct. With regard to

personality structure, Freud claimed three aspects: The id was base and instinctively striving. The superego was the conscience, or sense of morality. (Both the id and superego operated on an unconscious level.) The ego was conscious and in touch with reality. It was forced to mediate conflicts between the strivings of the id and the morality of the superego, and had to mediate between each of these unconscious forces and reality. / 335

3. Those psychologists, exemplified by Watson and Skinner, who would take a behavioristic view of personality, would argue that one's personality:

a. reflects one's learning history.

b. does not exist in any useful sense.

c. is largely biologically based in the workings of the nervous system.

d. depends mostly on how one views oneself and others.

The fact that both Watson and Skinner devoted much of their research to studying the psychology of learning should serve as a major hint for this item. Behavioral psychologists don't really deny the existence of personality as a useful concept in psychology. They just argue that one's personality is simply a compilation of one's learning history, or reinforcement history. The phenomenological view that what matters most in personality is how one views oneself and others is

associated with the humanistic/phenomonological approach to personality, not to the learning/behavioral approach. / 339

4. When we say that a psychological test is, or should be, *standardized,* we mean that:

a. results of the test should not be open to multiple interpretations.

b. the test should ultimately result in a numerical score.

c. everyone should take the test under the same circumstances.

d. the items should represent the characteristic being tested.

In fact, each of these alternatives addresses a point that is relevent to psychological tests. Tests should be objective—not open to multiple interpretation. They should be measures—resulting in a numerical score of samples of behaviors that represent the characteristic being tested. But, to say that a test is standardized means that the test will be administered according to the same rules and processes for all the persons taking the test. / 350

5. Dr. O'Dwyer has constructed a new test that supposedly measures one's ability to do well in statistics courses. He gives the test to a class of introductory psychology students at the

beginning of the term and again one month later. We may assume that he is doing so in order to establish the test's:

a. reliability.

b. concurrent validity.

c. norms.

d. content validity.

The procedure described here is the one that a test designer would follow to establish the test's reliability. The process being used establishes what we call "test-retest" reliability. Concurrent validity is reflected in the extent to which a test is correlated with other, existing tests that measure the same characteristic. Content validity has to do with the extent to which the test provides an adequate sample of the behaviors being measured. Neither of these can be determined from Dr. O'Dwyer's procedures. Norms are test scores that can be used as a basis of comparison, and perhaps (if the test proves to be reliable and valid) scores from this group of subjects will be part of the norms. But establishing norms does not seem to be the major concern in this item. / 352

6. During the course of a day-long psychological evaluation process, Betsy is asked to describe what she sees when she is shown a series of inkblots on cards. She is taking the _____, which is a(n) _____ test.

a. MMPI; criterion referenced.

b. WAIS-R; individually administered intelligence.

c. Rorschach; projective.

d. Cattel 16PF; paper-and-pencil.

For this item, the first term in the answer should fill the first blank, and the second term should fill the second blank. Actually, the pairings in all of the alternatives are correct. That is, the MMPI *is* a criterion referenced test, the WAIS-R *is* an individual intelligence test, and the Cattel 16PF *is* a paper-and-pencil test. But the correct answer here describes the Rorschach, a projective test in which one is asked to describe a series of inkblots. / 359

7. Which of the following statements concerning mental retardation is *false*?

a. Mental retardation is defined solely in terms of measured IQ.

b. The IQ cutoff for mental retardation is usually 70.

c. The extent to which a person can adapt to his or her environment is in many ways independent of IQ scores.

d. Approximately 3 percent of the population of the U.S. qualifies as mentally retarded.

The American Association on Mental Deficiency (AAMD) reminds us that retardation reflects not only low IQ scores (usually below 70), but also impairment of adaptive behaviors

(which can be independently assessed) and onset during the developmental period. So alternative (a) is not true. Alternative (d), sadly enough, is true. / 375

8. The major differences between the Stanford-Binet and the Wechsler tests of intelligence is that:

a. Wechsler tests yield three IQ scores and the Stanford Binet yields only one.

b. the Stanford-Binet is individually administered, while the Wechsler tests are group tests.

c. the Wechsler tests have separate tests for different age levels, while the Stanford-Binet fits all ages.

d. the Wechsler tests are both reliable and valid, while the Stanford-Binet is neither reliable nor valid.

Both the Stanford Binet and the Wechsler tests are equally reliable and valid as measures of intelligence. Both are individually administered tests, and now with the latest revision of the Stanford-Binet, both instruments yield a number of subscale scores in addition to an overall IQ score. The correct answer is that the Wechsler tests are really a series of three tests, each very much alike, but each designed for different age groups, while the same form of the Stanford-Binet is used for all age groups. / 364

Chapter Nine

Abnormal Psychology

Why We Care

Definition and Classification
  Defining Abnormality
  The Classification of Abnormal Reactions
    The *DSM* Series
    Problems with Classification and Labeling
    On "Insanity"

Anxiety-based Disorders
  Anxiety Disorders
    Phobic Disorder
    Panic Disorder
    Generalized Anxiety Disorder
    Obsessive-compulsive Disorder
  Somatoform Disorders
    Hypochondriasis
    Conversion Disorder
  Dissociative Disorders
    Psychogenic Amnesia
    Psychogenic Fugue
    Multiple Personality

Personality Disorders

Psychotic Disorders
  Organic Mental Disorders
    Degenerative Dementia of the Alzheimer Type
    Substance-induced Organic Mental Disorders
  Mood Disorders
    Depression and Mania
    Biological Factors in Depression
    Psychological Factors in Depression
  Schizophrenia
    Process and Reactive Schizophrenia
    DSM-III-R Types of Schizophrenia
    Hereditary Factors in Schizophrenia
    Biochemical Factors in Schizophrenia
    Psychological and Social Factors in Schizophrenia

Iris *really* doesn't want to get out of bed this morning. She had another rough night—tossing and turning and getting very little sleep. She's been overly tired for weeks. Her main problem is that she feels nervous, anxious, and apprehensive, but doesn't know why. She's been yelling at the children and nagging her husband. Iris realizes that her outbursts have not been justified, but she can't seem to stop them. She has a whole day ahead of her. Nothing *has* to be done, but she just can't decide what to do. Should she go shopping? Play tennis? Clean the house? Sit by the pool? No, none of these options seems worth the effort. Once again, Iris doesn't want to do anything today. She's afraid she'll be too nervous.

Without warning, Mark's hands have become paralyzed. From the wrist down, there is a total loss of voluntary control and feeling. Mark's tensely distorted hands can be held over a candle flame and he will not withdraw them, apparently feeling no pain. There seems to be no impairment at all in his forearms, upper arms, or shoulders. There is no known medical or physiological explanation for Mark's symptoms. What people who know Mark well find most difficult to understand is his apparent lack of

concern about his new handicap. He attributes his paralysis and loss of feeling to "the will of God" and shows no visible anger, regret, or remorse.

Carol was found this morning wandering around in the central business district of a large northeastern city. She was ill-dressed for the cold winds and low temperatures. Her behavior seemed aimless, and she was stopped by a police officer who

---

Without warning, Mark's hands have become paralyzed. There is no known medical or physiological explanation . . .

---

asked if he could be of assistance. It soon became apparent that Carol did not know where she was. The officer took her to a nearby hospital. It was discovered that she had no recollection of where she had been or what she had been doing for the past 5 weeks. She had no idea how she got to the city in which she was found (350 miles from where she lived). To Carol, the last 5 weeks seem never to have happened.

Harold had been suffering from insomnia and fatigue for several weeks, he felt worthless and even considered suicide. But a short time later, he was in surprisingly and increasingly high spirits and claimed he had invented a wonder drink that would outsell Coke and Pepsi. He also said it would cure cancer and bring him the Nobel prize. Somehow, Harold talked the neighborhood bank into a $10,000 loan for his venture, but his family soon found that he had given considerable amounts to strangers whom he referred to as "business associates," after meeting them in bars. He had been spending most of his nights in bars, since he was tireless despite only two or three hours of sleep a night. Then, just as suddenly, Harold decided his ideas were not realistic. This made him feel guilty and sad. He began to think he had failed in his one chance to make good and began thinking about suicide again.

George has the appearance of a person who has dressed hurriedly: disheveled hair, partially unbuttoned shirt. When he talks he either looks down or off into space, seemingly not focusing on anything. He is spending his third day as an in-patient at a community mental health center. His parents brought him to the center when he unexpectedly returned from college, went into his room, and refused to come out because "voices" were telling him not to. He claimed that he come home because his "voices told him to." He had apparently neither bathed nor shaved for days. It took considerable coaxing to get him from his room. A check with college officials revealed that George had not attended classes for the past 3 weeks. He is obviously a very disturbed individual.

Iris, Mark, Carol, Harold, and George have something in common: They each have a psychological or mental disorder. Clearly, their symptoms are quite different; each would be diagnosed and classified as having a different disorder. In this chapter, we'll be reviewing these and other disorders.

Why We Care

In this chapter we begin a discussion of abnormal psychology—the study of psychological disorders of behavior and mental activity. Psychological or mental disorders are much more common than we would like to think. It is impossible to know with certainty exactly how many people are suffering from some form of psychological disorder, but we do have a general idea.

In 1984, the National Institute of Mental Health (NIMH) began to release preliminary findings from the largest study yet attempted of the prevalence of mental health problems. (In this context, prevalence means the number of active cases identified during a given period—here, 6 months.) This ongoing study is massive in scope (about 17,000 community residents have been interviewed in depth). In many respects, the results are both astounding and frightening.

The NIMH study reports that approximately 43 million adult Americans were suffering from some sort of psychological disorder when the survey was taken. That's about 19 percent of the adult population!

These data become all the more impressive when we consider the very large number of people who were not included in the survey. The study dealt only with adults, leaving uncounted the many children and adolescents who qualify as mentally disordered. Recent studies indicate that percentages may be very much the same for children and adolescents as they are for adults. For example, David Offord and his associates (1987) report a prevalence of disorder rate of 18.1 percent for children 4 to 16 years old. Another large study, focusing only on 11 year olds (Anderson et al., 1987), reports that 17.6 percent of the children they tested had a diagnosable disorder; and more than half of their sample had more than one disorder at the time.

In addition, 13 percent of those originally selected to be in the NIMH sample simply refused to be interviewed, so we don't know if they should be included among the disordered or not. Individuals with psychosexual disorders were not included; homeless people were not included; individuals who were institutionalized were not included. Alcoholics and alcohol abusers—perhaps another 10 to 11 million Americans (Mayer, 1983)—were not included in the NIMH data. It seems that as large and carefully done as the NIMH study is, its estimates are very conservative.

Statistics such as these are impressive; they are also impersonal. It is difficult to conceptualize what it really means to say that more than 43 million American adults are suffering from a mental disorder. It seems unlikely that we can be exempt from intimate, personal contact with someone who has a psychological disorder, and *that* is why we care.

In this chapter we'll begin our discussion by considering matters of definition. In no area of psychology are definitional issues as critical as they are in considering psychological disorders. Related to defining abnormality in general are the issues of classifying and labeling various disorders, and we'll review the implications of classification systems before we turn our attention to specific disorders. Having tackled some large theoretical issues, we'll begin a brief description of some of the more common or typical psychological disorders. To even begin to describe all of the known, identifiable psychological disorders is well beyond the scope of our needs. The intent in this chapter is to provide you with an idea of what some of the psychological disorders are like.

In the first half of this chapter we'll cover some of the anxiety disorders, somatoform disorders, dissociative disorders, and personality disorders. Then we'll introduce some disorders that are more disruptive and discomforting.

It is probably inappropriate, and in a sense, unfair, to classify some disorders as being more or less severe or debilitating than others. To the person who is experiencing the disorder, and to those who care about that person, *any* psychological disorder can seem severe and debilitating. But the disorders we'll cover in the second half of this chapter—organic mental disorders, mood disorders, and schizophrenia—are so severe as to frequently require hospitalization. People suffering from these disorders may have difficulty dealing with the demands of everyday life and often lose contact with the real world as the rest of us know it.

DEFINITION AND CLASSIFICATION

We all have a basic idea of what we mean by such terms as *abnormality*, *mental illness*, or *psychological disorder*. The more we think about abnormality and what it means, however, the more difficult it becomes to define. In this section, we'll do two things: we'll generate a working definition of *abnormal* from a psychological perspective, and we'll consider the implications that follow from defining disorders in terms of specific symptoms and then classifying and labeling those disorders.

Defining Abnormality

Defining what we mean by abnormal in psychology is not easily done. In order to be complete, our definitions often tend to get rather complicated. Here's the definition we'll use: **abnormal** means statistically uncommon, maladaptive cognitions, affect, and/or behaviors that are at odds with social expectations and that result in distress and discomfort. That's quite a long definition, but to be useful, it must include each of these points. Let's now briefly review them one at a time.

One way to think about abnormality is to take a literal or *statistical* approach. Literally, *abnormal* means "not of the norm" or "not average." Using this approach, any behaviors or mental processes that are rare should be considered abnormal, and in a literal, statistical sense, of course, they are. The major flaw with this approach, however, is that it would label the behaviors of Michael Jordan, Itzhak Perlman, and Barbara Walters as abnormal. In a statistical sense, they *are* abnormal; there are few others who do what these people do; yet (as far as we know), none of these people is psycholog-

abnormal
statistically uncommon, maladaptive cognitions, affect, and/or behavior that are at odds with social expectations and that result in distress or discomfort

What is considered abnormal or deviant behavior in one society may be quite normal in another. Cultures vary in many respects, including styles of dress. This Arab woman's layered clothing is a sharp contrast to the way these Bororo tribesmen of West Africa are dressed.

ically disordered. As it happens, most of the psychological disorders we'll consider *are* uncommon or unusual in a statistical sense, but that alone is not enough.

The reactions of people who are suffering from a psychological disorder are not only statistically uncommon, but they are also *maladaptive.* Thoughts, feelings, and behaviors are such that the individual does not function as well as he or she could without the disorder. There is some degree of impairment here. In other words, behavior is "abnormal *if* it is maladaptive, that is, *if* it interferes with functioning and growth, *if* it is self-defeating" (Carson et al., 1988, p. 9).

Another observation reflected in our definition is that abnormality may show itself at a number of different levels of functioning. That is, a person may engage in abnormal *behaviors,* have abnormal *cognitions* (thoughts, perceptions, and beliefs), experience abnormal *affect* (emotional reactions or feelings), or demonstrate any combination of these.

Any definition of abnormality should acknowledge social and/or cultural expectations. What may be clearly abnormal and disordered in one culture may be viewed as quite normal, if not commonplace, in another. In some cultures, crying and wailing at the funeral of a total stranger is considered to be strange or deviant; in others, it is common. In some cultures, to claim that you have been communicating directly with dead ancestors would be taken as a sign of severe disturbance; in others, it would be treated as a great gift. The social context we are talking about here need not be so dramatic. Even in your own culture, behaviors that are appropriate, or at least tolerated, in one situation—say, a party—may be judged to be quite inappropriate in another context—say, a religious service.

Yet one other issue needs to be addressed when we define psychological abnormality: psychological disorders involve distress or discomfort. People whom we consider to be abnormal are, in some way, suffering. They are experiencing emotional distress. But not all people with psychological disturbances feel the distress themselves. In fact, they might be quite happy in their own way. The likelihood is, however, that such individuals are the source of distress and discomfort to others around them, friends and family who care and worry about them.

So, as complex as it is, we can see that there is a reason for each of the points in our definition of abnormal: behaviors or mental processes that are statistically uncommon, at odds with social expectations, and result in distress or discomfort.

Now that we have a sense of what abnormal is, let's be sure that we understand a few things that it is *not.* (1) Abnormal and normal are not two separate and distinct categories. They may be thought of as endpoints on some dimension that we can use to describe people, but there is a large gray area between the two where distinctions get fuzzy. (2) Abnormal does not mean dangerous. True, some people diagnosed as having a mental disorder *may* do great violence to themselves and/or to others, but most people with psychological disorders are not dangerous at all. (3) Abnormal does not mean bad. People who suffer from psychological disorders are not necessarily bad people, or weak people, in any evaluative sense. They may do bad things, and bad things may have happened to them, but it is certainly not in psychology's tradition to make moral and ethical judgments about good and bad.

Laurie Dann, who went on a rampage in Winnetka, Illinois in May 1988 shooting six children and killing one of them in their classroom before fatally shooting herself, had a long history of abnormal behavior. Hers is a fascinating case that illustrates the difficulty of understanding why a pattern of behaviors develops or what we can do about them even if we can give those behaviors a name.

BEHAVIORS
COGNITIONS
AFFECT

Predisposing - ALL TYPES
genetic social
(STRESSORS)
(clouds)

Precipitating - causes it to reach
Breaking point

The Classification of Abnormal Reactions

One way of dealing with psychological abnormality is to consider each individual psychological disorder separately, in terms of how that disorder is to be diagnosed. Indeed, **diagnosis** is the act of recognizing a disorder (or disease) on the basis of the presence of particular symptoms. This approach involves describing the symptoms of specific disorders as completely as possible and then organizing or classifying disorders in some systematic way.

Systems of classification are quite common in science and are not at all new in psychology. In 1883, Emil Kraepelin published the first significant classification scheme for mental disturbances. It was based on the notion that each disorder had its own collection of symptoms (called a *syndrome*) and its own cause (at that time thought to be biological or organic). Some of Kraepelin's views have been found to be incorrect, but he clearly demonstrated the value of classifying psychological disorders in a systematic way.

The *DSM* Series.   In 1952, the American Psychiatric Association published a classification scheme for mental disorders. The book in which the scheme was presented was called the *Diagnostic and Statistical Manual of Mental Disorders.* In an ordered way, it listed the symptoms of 60 known disorders. Sixteen years later, a second version was published, referred to as the *DSM-II.* The *DSM-II* rearranged some classifications and expanded some categories and compressed others, but it still listed 145 types and subtypes. The third edition of the *Diagnostic and Statistical Manual,* or *DSM-III,* was written by a large committee of psychologists and psychiatrists and was published in 1980. The *DSM-III* included 230 separate entries that each constitute some form of psychological disorder.

Even before its publication, the *DSM-III* had attracted controversy. Classifying more than 200 behavioral patterns as disordered seemed to many to be going overboard. In May of 1983, yet another group was assembled to revise the third edition of the *Diagnostic and Statistical Manual.* In 1987, the *DSM-III-R* was published.

The *DSM-III-R* is the system of classification most widely used in all mental health fields. We will follow the general outline of the *DSM-III-R* in this chapter on abnormal psychology. Figure 9.1 presents a partial listing of the disorders listed in the *DSM-III-R* and shows subtypes for each major category of disorder.

We should note that the *DSM-III-R* is more than just an organized listing of disorders in terms of their symptoms. The *DSM-III-R* recommends that the diagnosis of a disorder be sensitive to (1) any physical illnesses or ailments that are present, (2) the amount of stress the individual has been under recently, and (3) the level of adaptive functioning that the individual has been able to manage over the past three years. The manual attempts to avoid any reference to the **etiology,** or causes, of disorders. It is meant to be objective, to describe as completely as possible, and to theorize as little as possible.

There are many advantages to having a single, if still imperfect, classification scheme for psychological disorders. The major advantage, of course,

diagnosis
the act of recognizing a disorder or a disease on the basis of the presence of particular symptoms

Emil Kraepelin

(handwritten notes) Collecting various patterns of systems.
sydromes –
Bilogical or ORGANIC IN NATURE

PRIOR TO DSM
ORGANIC VIEW
Some physical cause to mental Disorders

INORGANIC
No organic DO NOT KNOW WHAT causes could be environmental

Neuroses Psychoses
(No split from reality) Hall
Dillusio
Split from reality

etiology
the cause or predisposing factors of a disturbance or disorder

FIGURE 9.1

A sample of the DSM-III classification of psychological disorders (Remember, these are labels, see text for descriptions)

Type of disorder	Subtype (examples)
Disorder usually first evident in infancy, childhood, or adolescence	a. mental retardation b. attention deficit with hyperactivity c. separation anxiety d. eating disorders e. gender identity disorder
Organic mental disorders	a. Alzheimer's disease b. substance induced disorders c. organic hallucinations
Psychoactive substance use disorders	a. alcohol abuse and dependence b. drug abuse and dependence c. nicotine dependence
Schizophrenic disorders	a. schizophrenia (one of five varieties)
Delusional disorders	a. paranoia (one of six varieties)
Mood disorders	a. depression b. bipolar disorders
Anxiety disorders	a. phobias b. panic disorder c. obsessive-compulsive disorder
Somatoform disorders	a. conversion disorder (hysterical neurosis) b. hypochondriasis
Dissociative disorders	a. psychogenic amnesia b. fugue c. multiple personality
Sexual disorders	a. paraphilias b. sexual dysfunctions
Impulse control disorders	a. pathological gambling b. pyromania c. kleptomania
Personality disorders	a. schizoid b. histrionic c. paranoid d. narcissistic e. compulsive f. antisocial g. passive-aggressive

is communication. If we mean one thing when we use the term "phobia" and you mean something quite different, we can't hold a very reasonable conversation about your patient's phobia. If we all agreed on, say, the *DSM-III-R's* definition, we would at least be using the term in the same way. A related advantage is that if we can develop a reliable way of classifying disorders, we can begin thinking about how we might most effectively prescribe appropriate treatment or therapy. We can't leave the impression that there is only one treatment that is most suitable for each of the diagnostic categories of the *DSM-III-R*. As we'll see in the next chapter on treatment and therapy, that is far from the case, but it certainly makes sense that we be able to classify disorders before we can treat them. However, classification can cause difficulties.

Problems with Classification and Labeling.   As useful as it is to have a system for classifying psychological disorders, we must also recognize that there are problems associated with any such scheme. First, applying labels to people may be convenient, but it is often dehumanizing. It is occasionally difficult to remember that Sally Jones is a complex and complicated human being with a range of feelings, thoughts, and behaviors, and not just a "paranoid schizophrenic." In response to this concern, the *DSM-III-R* refers only to disordered behaviors and patterns of behaviors, not to disordered people. That is, it refers to paranoid reactions, not to individuals who are paranoid, or to persons with anxiety, not anxious persons.

A second problem inherent in classification and labeling is that it is so easy to fall into the habit of believing that labels *explain,* when clearly they don't. Being able to reliably and accurately diagnose and label a pattern of behaviors does not explain those behaviors. It does not tell us why such a behavior pattern developed or what we can or should do about it now.

Third, labels often create negative and lasting stigmas about people (for example, Piner & Kahle, 1984). Part of our definition of abnormal was the notion of statistical rarity. We tend to shy away from those who are different, strange, and unusual. To learn that someone is labeled as "psychologically disordered" often carries with it a wide range of negative reactions, and the labels often stick long after the disorder has been treated and the symptoms are gone.

One final consequence of diagnostic labeling is that the brunt of the issue tends to fall on the individual. It is the individual who has psychological disorders in thought, affect, or behavior; it is never the group, the family, or the society of which the person is a part. Systems of classification tend to focus on the person and not on the larger context in which individuals live (Gorenstein, 1984; Szasz, 1960, 1982).

On "Insanity."   So far we have used terms such as *mental disorder, behavior disorder,* and *psychological disorder* interchangeably. We shall continue to do so because the differences between such terms are of no real consequence. There is one term, however, with which we need to exercise particular care, and that's **insanity.**

Insanity is not a psychological term. It is a legal term. It does have to do with psychological functioning, but in a rather restricted sense. Definitions of insanity vary from state to state, but to be judged as insane usually requires evidence to demonstrate that a person did not know or fully understand the consequences of his or her actions at a given time, could not discern the difference between right and wrong, and was unable to exercise control over his or her actions. A related issue has to do with whether or not a person is in enough control of his or her mental and intellectual functions to understand courtroom procedures and aid in his or her own defense. If one is not, one may be ruled "not competent" to stand trial for his or her actions, whatever his or her actions may have been.

Gladys Burr is a tragic example of the dangers of labeling. In 1936, Burr's mother committed her to an institution because of "personality problems." She was 29 years old at the time and was declared mentally retarded. During the years 1946 to 1961, IQ tests given to her revealed that she was of normal intelligence. Despite these findings supported by several doctors, she remained institutionalized until 1978. She was then released and awarded financial compensation after 42 years of unnecessary commitment.

No psychological Term Legal

insanity
a legal term for diminished capacity and inability to tell right from wrong

Having discussed in a general way the problems of defining abnormality and classifying psychological disorders, it's time to turn our attention to specific disorders. We won't cover all of the disorders listed in the *DSM-III-R*. Instead, we'll choose those disorders that are either reasonably common or are unusual in their pattern of symptoms.

BEFORE YOU GO ON   What is the *DSM-III-R*?

What are some of its advantages and disadvantages?

ANXIETY-BASED DISORDERS

As we've seen, *anxiety* is another term that is difficult to define. On the other hand, everyone seems to know what anxiety is; everyone has experienced anxiety and recognizes it as being unpleasant. We shall define **anxiety** as a general feeling of apprehension or dread accompanied by predictable physiological changes—increased muscle tension, shallow rapid breathing, cessation of digestion, increased perspiration, and drying of the mouth. Thus, anxiety involves two levels of reaction: subjective feelings (for example, dread/fear) and physiological responses (for example, rapid breathing). Anxiety is the definitional characteristic of all the anxiety-based disorders, even though, as we shall see, in some cases the anxiety is not clearly observable. The anxiety-based disorders used to be called *neuroses*. The term *neurosis* is no longer used as a label in the *DSM-III-R*, but it is still in common use, even among mental health professionals.

Anxiety-based disorders are among the most common of all the psychological disorders. The 1984 NIMH study reports very high rates: from 7 to 15 percent with "one or more of the several anxiety diagnoses" (Freedman, 1984). Other studies indicate that these figures may be underestimates. If we were to consider just the disorders listed in this section, we would find prevalence rates in excess of 20 percent of the population, or nearly 50 million people (Reich, 1986; Turns, 1985). In any case, percentages of this sort still do not convey the enormity of the problem. We need to remind ourselves that we are talking about real individuals—people like us all. In this section, we'll consider three subtypes of anxiety-based disorders: anxiety disorders, somatoform disorders, and dissociative disorders.

Anxiety Disorders

As we've said, in some anxiety-based disorders the underlying anxiety is not clearly visible or noticeable. Such is not the case with what the *DSM-III-R* calls *anxiety disorders*. The major symptom here is, indeed, real, felt anxiety, often coupled with what is called "avoidance behavior," or the attempt to resist or avoid the stimulus situation that produces the anxiety reaction. We'll consider four subtypes of anxiety disorder: phobic disorder, panic disorder, generalized anxiety disorder, and obsessive-compulsive disorder.

Phobic Disorder.   The essential feature of a **phobic disorder** (or phobia) is a persistent fear of some object, activity, or situation that leads a person to consistently avoid that object, activity, or situation. Implied in this definition is the notion that the fear is intense enough to be disruptive or

anxiety
a general feeling of apprehension or dread accompanied by predictable physiological changes

phobic disorder
an intense, irrational fear that leads a person to avoid the feared object, activity, or situation

A job as a construction worker, laboring high above a city, would be out of the question for an individual afflicted with acrophobia, a fear of high places. Following the idea of avoidance, a person with agoraphobia, a fear of open places, would never participate in a crowd-filled activity, such as this fiftieth anniversary celebration of the Golden Gate Bridge.

debilitating. It is also implied that there is no real threat involved in the stimulus that gives rise to a phobic reaction; that is, the fear is unreasonable, exaggerated, or inappropriate.

Let's look at that the other way around. There are a number of things in this world that are life-threatening and downright frightening. If, for example, you are walking in the downtown center of a large city late at night and three huge thugs dragging bicycle chains and holding knives approach you, you are likely to feel an intense reaction of fear. Such a reaction is not phobic because it is not irrational.

Similarly, there are few of us who truly enjoy the company of large numbers of bees. Just because we don't like bees and would rather they not be around does not qualify us as having a phobic disorder. What is missing here is *intensity* of response. People who do have a phobic reaction to bees (called mellissaphobia) will often refuse to leave the house in the summertime for fear of encountering a bee, become genuinely upset and nervous at the buzzing sound of any insect, fearing it to be a bee, and may become uncomfortable simply reading a paragraph, such as this one, about bees.

There are many different types of phobias. Most are named after the object or activity that is feared. Figure 9.2 lists some of the most common phobic reactions. Most phobias involve a fear of animals—although such phobias are not the type for which people most commonly seek treatment (Costello, 1982). In many such cases, the person with a phobic disorder may be successful simply avoiding the source of his or her fear and may never seek treatment. So long as one's phobia does not have an impact on one's day-to-day adjustment, treatment or therapy is not necessary. Sometimes, however, avoiding the source of one's phobia is virtually impossible. Fortunately, the **prognosis** (the prediction of the future course of a disorder) is quite good for phobic disorders. That is, therapy for persons with a phobia is likely to be successful.

One of the most commonly treated varieties of phobia is **agoraphobia,** which literally means "fear of open places." The fear here is not just reserved

FIGURE 9.2
A sample of phobic reactions

Phobia	Is a fear of
Acrophobia	High places
Agoraphobia	Open places
Algophobia	Pain
Astrophobia	Lightning and thunder
Autophobia	One's self
Claustrophobia	Small, closed places
Hematophobia	Blood
Monophobia	Being alone
Mysophobia	Dirt or contamination
Nyctophobia	The dark
Pathophobia	Illness or disease
Pyrophobia	Fire
Thanatophobia	Death and dying
Xenophobia	The unknown
Zoophobia	Animals

prognosis
the prediction of the future course of an illness or disorder

agoraphobia
a phobic fear of open places, of being alone, or of being in public places from which escape might be difficult

Anxiety-based Disorders **399**

for those occasions in which one stands in the middle of a large open field, however. The diagnosis is used for people who have an exaggerated fear of being alone or of leaving their house to venture forth into the world where they may be trapped in an unpleasant or embarrassing situation. Such people want to avoid crowds, streets, stores, and the like. They essentially establish for themselves a safe home base and may, in extreme cases, refuse to leave it altogether.

BEFORE YOU GO ON   **What are the essential characteristics of a phobic disorder?**

Panic Disorder.   In phobic reactions, there is always a specific stimulus that brings about an intense fear response, and we have people who take steps to avoid the stimulus of their phobias. For a person suffering from **panic disorder,** the major symptom is a sudden, often unpredictable attack of anxiety, or a panic attack. These attacks may last for a few seconds or for hours and involve "the sudden onset of intense apprehension, fear, or terror, often associated with feelings of impending doom" (*DSM-III-R*, 1987, p. 236). The subjective experience is similar to the fear of the phobic reaction, except that there is no particular stimulus to bring it on. The panic attack is unexpected. It just happens. And because it just happens, without warning, a complication of this disorder is that the individual soon begins to fear the next attack and the loss of control that it will bring. Panic attacks are not uncommon among people under stress. It is possible that you know from your own experience what such an attack feels like, but to qualify as a psychological disorder, such attacks must have occurred at a rate of at least four within a four-week period and be accompanied by a number of physiological symptoms (such as chest pain, hot and cold flashes, sweating, or trembling). As it happens, most people who are diagnosed as having a panic disorder are also agoraphobic. The reverse is also true: most cases of agoraphobia are seen as complications of a panic disorder.

panic disorder
a disorder in which anxiety attacks suddenly and unpredictably incapacitate; there may be periods free from anxiety

BEFORE YOU GO ON   **What defines a panic disorder?**

free floating

Generalized Anxiety Disorder.   Yet another disorder in which felt levels of anxiety are the major symptom is the **generalized anxiety disorder.** Here we have unrealistic, excessive, and persistent worry or anxiety. The anxiety may be very intense, but it is also quite diffuse, meaning that it does not seem to be brought on by anything specific in the person's environment. The anxiety just seems to come and go (or come and stay) without reason or warning. People with this disorder are almost always in some state of uneasiness. If they are not experiencing a particularly high level of anxiety at the moment, they may be afraid that they soon will be. Although people with this disorder can often continue to function in social situations and on the job, they may be particularly prone to drug and alcohol abuse.

What is most difficult for people to understand about generalized anxiety disorder (and panic disorder, too) is that those with the disorder usually have no good explanations for their feelings of anxiety. When most of us are anxious, we generally know *why* we're anxious: there's an exam coming up on Wednesday and we're not prepared; the boss wants to see us in his or her office; the dentist recommends having a root canal immediately, and so on.

generalized anxiety disorder
persistent, chronic, and distressingly high levels of unattributable anxiety

Unlike people without the disorder, people suffering from generalized anxiety disorder are usually unable to give a good explanation for their feelings, which may, in turn, increase their feelings of anxiety.

In many cases, persons with anxiety disorders cannot specify with any degree of certainty why it is that they are experiencing their anxiety. That in itself is often enough to make someone even more anxious.

Describe generalized anxiety disorder, and contrast it with panic disorder.

BEFORE YOU GO ON

Obsessive-compulsive Disorder.   In a way, we have three disorders here: an obsessive disorder, a compulsive disorder, and the combination—an obsessive-compulsive disorder. Obsessive disorders are characterized by recurrent **obsessions**—ideas or thoughts that involuntarily and constantly intrude into one's awareness. Generally speaking, the obsessions are pointless or groundless thoughts (most commonly of violence, contamination, or doubt). As is the case with many psychological disorders, we have all experienced something like the major symptom of this disorder—obsessive thoughts. Worrying throughout the first few days of a vacation if you really did remember to turn off the stove would be an example. Have you ever awakened to a clock radio that was playing some particular song? As you take your morning shower, the lyrics keep coming to mind. Even as you get dressed, you hear yourself humming the same song. There you are, driving to work, still thinking about that same song. You have the feeling that "I can't get that song out of my head!" Imagine having a thought or an image like that constantly interrupting, constantly coming to mind whenever you weren't consciously focusing your attention on something else, day after day. As much as you try to ignore or fight off the thoughts, they keep popping into your awareness. Such thoughts would be anxiety-producing to say the least. To qualify as a symptom of this psychological disorder, obsessions must be disruptive; they must be shown to interfere with normal functioning. They are also time-consuming and are the source of severe distress.

obsessions
ideas or thoughts that involuntarily and persistently intrude into awareness

In fact, one explanation for obsessions claims that they *are* serving a purpose. They are acting as (inappropriate) defense mechanisms against some repressed, anxiety-producing idea, desire, or memory. If you were to think about whatever you have repressed, you would experience extreme anxiety. So, whenever your mind "relaxes" and the repressed event might pop into awareness, your mind defends or protects itself by having you focus on your obsession instead.

Compulsions are constantly intruding acts or behaviors. Like obsessions, they too are repetitive. Again, from your own experience, have you ever found yourself walking along on a sidewalk, carefully avoiding the cracks in the pavement? Have you ever checked an exam's answer sheet to see that you've *really* answered all of the questions and then checked it again, and again, and again? To do so is a compulsive sort of response. It serves no real purpose in itself, and it provides no genuine sense of satisfaction, although it is done very conscientiously. The most commonly reported compulsions involve hand washing and counting behaviors. The person recognizes that these behaviors serve no useful purpose, but cannot stop them. It is as if she or he engages in these pointless behaviors to prevent some other (more anxiety-producing) behaviors from taking place.

compulsions
constantly intruding, stereotyped, and essentially involuntary acts or behaviors

Although we all may have experienced similar sorts of reactions, the truly obsessive-compulsive reaction is often very debilitating and the source of great distress. In extreme cases, a particular obsession or compulsion may come to exert a great influence on a person's entire life.

Notice that we often use "compulsive" in an inappropriate way when we refer to someone being a compulsive gambler, a compulsive eater, or a compulsive practical joker. What is usually inappropriate about the use of the term *compulsive* in such cases is that although the individual engages in habitual patterns of behavior, he or she gains pleasure from doing so. The compulsive gambler enjoys gambling; the compulsive eater loves to eat. Such people may not enjoy the ultimate consequences of their actions, but they feel little discomfort about the behaviors themselves. To qualify as a truly compulsive behavior requires that the behavior not be the source of pleasure and be recognized as being senseless.

Important

BEFORE YOU GO ON **In the context of anxiety-based psychological disorders, what is an obsession, and what is a compulsion?**

Somatoform Disorders Types

(body)

somatoform disorders
psychological disorders that reflect imagined physical or bodily symptoms or complaints

psychosomatic disorders
disorders with actual physical symptoms (rashes, ulcers, and the like) thought to be caused by psychological factors such as stress

"Soma" means "body." Hence, all of the **somatoform disorders** in some way or another involve physical, bodily symptoms or complaints. What makes these *psychological* or *mental* disorders is that in each case, there is no known medical or biological cause for the symptoms.

We should point out that **psychosomatic disorders** are *not* somatoform disorders. With the somatoform disorders, there is no actual physical damage or tissue involvement; the symptoms are psychological. With the psychosomatic disorders, there *is* physical damage, as in skin rashes, respiratory ailments, or ulcers. What makes these disorders *psycho*somatic is that their basic cause is psychological (stress-related) in nature. Here we'll review just two of the somatoform disorders: one quite common in medical practice—hypochondriasis; the other quite rare, but rather dramatic—conversion disorder.

hypochondriasis
a mental disorder involving the fear of developing some serious disease or illness

very common

Hypochondriasis. **Hypochondriasis** is the appropriate diagnosis for someone preoccupied with the fear of developing or having some serious disease. Such people (called "hypochondriacs") are unusually aware of every ache and pain and tend to diagnose their own symptoms as being indicative of some terrible physical disorder. They tend to read popular magazines devoted to health issues, and they usually feel free to diagnose their own ailments. The catch is that they have no medical disorder, illness, or disease. However, they constantly seek medical attention and will not be convinced of their good health despite the best of medical opinion and reassurance.

A person with occasional chest pains, for example, may diagnose his own condition as cancer of the heart. Even after numerous physicians reassure him that his heart is perfectly fine and that he has no signs of cancer, the patient's fears are not put to rest. "They are just trying to make me feel better by not telling me, because they know, as I do, that I have cancer of the heart and am going to die soon."

It's not too difficult to imagine why someone would develop the symptoms of hypochondriasis. If the individual comes to believe that he or she (and the disorder is found equally in men and women) has contracted some serious disease, three possible problems might be solved: (1) The person now has a way to explain otherwise unexplainable anxiety. "Well, my goodness, if you had cancer of the heart, you'd be anxious too." (Remember, this disorder is one we're calling anxiety-based.) (2) The illness may be used to excuse the person from those activities that he or she finds anxiety producing. "As sick as I am, you don't possibly expect me to go to work, do you?" (3) The illness or disease may be used as a way to gain attention or sympathy. "Don't you feel sorry for me, knowing that I have such a terrible disease?"

Conversion Disorder. Although **conversion disorder** is "rare," its symptoms are quite striking. Here we find an individual with a "loss or alteration in physical functioning that suggests physical disorder, but that instead is apparently an expression of a psychological conflict or need. The symptoms are not intentionally produced and cannot be explained by any physical disorder" (*DSM-III-R*, 1987, p. 257). The loss in physical functioning is typically of great significance: paralysis, blindness, and deafness are classic examples. As hard as it may be for most people to believe, the symptoms are not imaginary; they are quite real in the sense that the person cannot see, hear, or feel. What makes the disorder psychological is that there is no known medical explanation for the symptoms. In some cases, medical explanations even run contrary to the symptoms. For example, one symptom sometimes found in conversion disorder is called *glove anesthesia,* in which the hands lose all feeling and become paralyzed. As it happens, it is physically impossible to have such a paralysis and loss of feeling in the hands alone; normally there would be some paralysis in the forearm, upper arm, and shoulder, as well. Actual paralysis, of course, must follow neural pathways.

One of the most remarkable secondary symptoms of this disorder (which occurs only in some patients) is known as *la belle indifference*—a seemingly inappropriate lack of concern over one's condition. Persons with this disorder seem to feel quite comfortable with and accepting of their infirmity. Here are people who are demonstrably blind or paralyzed who show very little concern over their condition.

This particular disorder holds an important position in psychology's history. This was the disorder that most intrigued Sigmund Freud in his clinical practice and ultimately led him to develop a new method of therapy, which we now call *psychoanalysis* (see Chapter 10). This disorder was apparently known to the Greeks, who named it "hysteria," a name that is still sometimes applied, as in hysterical blindness, for example. It was the Greek view that the disorder was to be found only in women and that it reflected a disorder of the uterus, or "hysterum," hence the name hysteria. The notion was that the disease would leave the uterus, float through the body, and settle in the eyes, hands, ears or whatever other part of the body was affected. Of course, this notion is no longer considered valid, although the potential sexual basis for the disorder was one of the aspects that caught Freud's attention.

The vast array of over-the-counter medicines available testifies to the preoccupation of many Americans with their health. Taken to extremes, this preoccupation with aches and pains can lead to hypochondriasis.

conversion disorder
the display of a (severe) physical disorder for which there is no medical explanation; often accompanied by an apparent lack of concern on the part of the patient

RARE NOW WAS COMMON
hysterical BlinDNess

Freud developed
Psychoanalysis
to treat Conversion

How do somatoform disorders differ from psychosomatic disorders?

Describe hypochondriasis and conversion disorder.

BEFORE YOU GO ON

Dissociative Disorders (3) types

(handwritten annotations: "(3)", "3 types")

To *dissociate* means to become separate from or to escape. The underlying theme of disorders classified as **dissociative disorders** is that in some way a person dissociates or escapes from some aspect of life or personality that is seen as the source of stress, discomfort, or anxiety (which, again, justifies our classifying them as anxiety-based disorders). These mental disorders are statistically quite "rare," but they are also quite dramatic and are often the subject of novels, movies, and television shows. We will briefly discuss three dissociative disorders: psychogenic amnesia, psychogenic fugue, and multiple personality.

Psychogenic Amnesia. *Psychogenic* means "psychological in origin," and *amnesia* refers to a loss of memory. Thus, **psychogenic amnesia** is an inability to recall important personal information that is too extensive to be explained by ordinary forgetfulness. It is usually the case that what is forgotten is some traumatic incident and some or all of the experiences that led up to or followed the incident. As you might suspect, there is no identifiable, medical explanation for the loss of memory. As you might also suspect, there is a large range of the type and extent of the forgetting associated with psychogenic amnesia. In some cases, a person may lose entire days and weeks at a time; in other cases, only specific details cannot be recalled. Not surprisingly, cases of this disorder tend to be more common in wartime when traumatic experiences are more common.

Psychogenic Fugue. Occasionally, amnesic forgetfulness is accompanied by a physical change of location. That is, the person finds himself or herself in a strange and different place, with no reasonable explanation for how he or she got there. When this dimension is added, we have a disorder known as **psychogenic fugue.** For example, we may find someone wandering around a Florida beach dressed in a three-piece suit. The person has no idea of how or why he or she got there or where he or she is.

Both psychogenic amnesia and fugue are, in their own way, not unlike some of the somatoform disorders in that they may involve an escape from stressful situations. In conversion disorders, for example, a person may escape from stress by taking on the symptoms of a major physical disorder. Here, escape is more literal. People escape by simply forgetting altogether, or they avoid conflict and stress by psychologically or physically "running away."

Multiple Personality. Perhaps the most important fact to recognize about the disorder called **multiple personality** is that it is listed here as an anxiety-based dissociative disorder and *not* as "schizophrenia." The major symptom of multiple personality is "the existence within the individual of two or more distinct personalities or personality states" (*DSM-III-R*, 1987, p. 269). It is also important to recognize that the disorder is extremely rare. Carson et al. (1988) claim that only slightly over 100 verified cases have been reported in psychiatric and psychological records. For unknown reasons, however, the incidence of this strange disorder seems to be on the increase.

The very idea of split personality—of two or more personalities inhabiting the same person—is difficult for most of us to imagine. Perhaps it

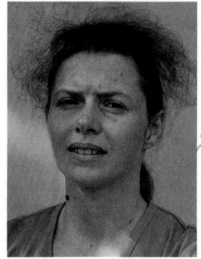

This woman, dubbed "Jane Doe," was found incoherent and near death in Florida in 1980. She was suffering from psychogenic amnesia and was unable to remember her name, her past, and how to read and write. After extensive publicity, a couple from Roselle, Illinois came forward and identified Jane Doe as their daughter who had moved to Florida and had been missing since 1976. Despite the certainty of the couple, Jane Doe was never able to remember her past.

psychogenic fugue
a condition of amnesia accompanied by unexplained travel or change of location

multiple personality
the existence within one individual of two or more distinct personalities, each of which is dominant at a particular time

Multiple personality disorder is one of the most intriguing disorders to consider. It is difficult to imagine as many as 16 separate personalities, each with its own capabilities, living in one human being. One such woman is Sybil, whose artwork illustrates how distinct one personality is from the other. The piece on the right was done by the more home-loving Mary in contrast to the one on the left, done by Peggy, an angry, fearful personality.

would help to contrast this disordered reaction with a pattern of behavior that is typical of all of us. We all change our behaviors and, in some small way, our personalities every day, depending on the situation in which we find ourselves. We do not act, think, or feel exactly the same way at school as we do at work, or at a party, or at church. We change and modify our reactions to fit the circumstances. In a way, then, we are not exactly the same people at a party that we are at work. At a party, you may be a person who is carefree, uninhibited, happy, and filled with pleasant thoughts. At work, you may be a different person: reserved, quiet, serious, and concentrating on the task at hand. You do not have a multiple personality because you act differently in different situations. There are three major differences between multiple personality disorders and the behavior patterns just noted.

The main difference is one of degree. For a person with a multiple personality disorder, the change in personality is usually dramatic, complete, and extreme. We are not dealing with a person who slightly alters his or her behaviors; we are dealing with two or more distinct personalities (about half the reported cases show more than 10 distinct personalities (*DSM-III-R*, 1987)). A second difference is that when most people alter their behaviors, feelings, or thinking, they do so as an appropriate response to the context of their environment. That is, they change in reaction to the situation in which they find themselves. Such is not the case for a person with this dissociative disorder where changes in personality usually take place without warning, predicted by no particular environmental cue. The third major difference has to do with control. When people change their behaviors, they usually do so consciously and intentionally. Individuals with a multiple personality disorder can neither control nor predict which of their personalities will be dominant at any one time.

What is the defining symptom of the dissociative disorders?   **BEFORE YOU GO ON**

PERSONALITY DISORDERS

All of the psychological disorders we have reviewed so far, and those we'll consider in the last half of this chapter, are disorders that seem to afflict people who previously were quite normal and undisturbed. In most cases, we can remember a time when the person did not show the symptoms of his or her disorder. That is much harder to do with the **personality disorders** because persons with these disorders have a long-standing history of symptoms. Personality disorders are "enduring patterns of perceiving, relating to, and thinking about the environment and oneself [that are] inflexible and maladaptive" and cause either impaired functioning or distress (*DSM-III-R*, 1987). Significantly, these maladaptive and distressful personality traits have existed for a considerable period of time. In other words, the problems are long-standing ones that are usually identifiable by the time an individual is an adolescent.

The *DSM-III-R* lists 11 different personality disorders, organized into three groups or clusters. Cluster 1 includes disorders in which the individual can be characterized as being odd or eccentric in some way. Cluster 2 includes disorders in which the individual appears overly dramatic, emotional, or erratic, and where behaviors are quite impulsive. Cluster 3 adds the dimension of anxiety or fearfulness to the standard criteria for personality disorder.

We have already mentioned that there is no clear distinction between behaviors (and affects and cognitions) that can be called "normal" and those

personality disorders
enduring patterns of perceiving, relating to, and thinking about the environment and one's self that are inflexible and maladaptive

The case of Ferdinand Waldo Demara Jr., called the "great imposter" in the 1950s illustrates one type of personality disorder. For years, Demara assumed numerous identities including a Navy doctor in Korea, a deputy prison warden, and a Catholic monk. He is now a minister living at an interfaith monastery in central Missouri.

that can be classified as "disordered." There is no set of psychological disorders for which this observation is more pertinent than personality disorders. It is often very difficult indeed for a psychologist to diagnose someone as having a personality disorder, rather than just being a little strange. Remember that being strange or eccentric *in itself* is insufficient reason to make a diagnosis of disorder. There need to be some symptoms that indicate distress or discomfort and some indication that the person's strangeness or eccentricity is in some way maladaptive or interferes with functioning in the world.

The prognosis, or prediction of likely outcome, is usually quite poor for personality disorders. These maladaptive patterns of behavior have often taken a lifetime to develop. Changing them is very difficult. Figure 9.3 summarizes the 11 personality disorders that are listed in the *DSM-III-R*.

What are the defining characteristics of the personality disorders?   BEFORE YOU GO ON

When most people think about psychology, their first thoughts generally deal with abnormal psychology—the psychological disorders and their treatment. As we have seen so far, the concept of abnormality in psychology is a very complex, multidimensional one. Even so, we've seen that psychological disorders are much more common than any of us care to think about. Applying labels indicative of abnormality or disorder to a person's reactions can have widespread consequences, and needs to be done only with great care. We've seen that psychologists also take great care making sure that only a person's affect, cognitions, or behaviors—*and not the person*—are labeled as disordered.

We have briefly considered two classes, or types, of psychological disorders. In the first type, the anxiety-based disorders, there runs a common thread of anxiety—high levels of discomforting anxiety that impair normal functioning. Usually, individuals with these anxiety-based disorders can generate no good reason or explanation for why they feel as they do. We then looked at the personality disorders, which are characterized by life-long patterns of inflexible and maladaptive patterns of behavior. These disorders are often difficult to diagnose and are equally difficult to treat. The pain and suffering caused by the anxiety-based and personality disorders alone are widespread, touching the lives of tens of millions of Americans.

PSYCHOTIC DISORDERS

The disorders we'll introduce next tend to be more disruptive and discomforting and have poorer prognoses than those we just reviewed. Most forms of the disorders we'll cover now are those that can be classified as **psychotic disorders.** That is usually taken to mean two things: a gross impairment in functioning (difficulty dealing with the demands of everyday life) and a gross impairment in reality testing (a loss of contact with the real world as the rest of us know it). As a result, persons with these disorders frequently require hospitalization.

The term *psychosis,* or psychotic disorder, is not a specific classification in the *Diagnostic and Statistical Manual of Mental Disorders (DSM-III-R)* of

psychotic disorders
psychological disorders that involve gross impairment in functioning and a loss of contact with reality

FIGURE 9.3
Notes on the personality disorders as listed in the *DSM-III-R*

CLUSTER I disorders of "odd" or "eccentric" reactions

Paranoid personality disorder—an extreme sensitivity, suspiciousness, envy, and mistrust of others; interprets the actions of other people as deliberately demeaning or threatening; the attitude of suspicion is not justified; shows a restricted range of emotional reactivity, and avoidance of intimacy; humorless; rarely seeks help; examples*: a person who continuously and without justification accuses a spouse of infidelity and believes that every wrong number was really a call from some secret enemy; or a student who constantly believes that professors are "out to get him," thus justifying poor grades.

Schizoid personality disorder—an inability to form and a marked indifference to interpersonal relationships; little involvement in social affairs; appears "cold and aloof"; often involves excessive daydreaming; examples: the "loner" who never joins any groups or social clubs or shows any interest in doing so; the person who lives, as he or she has for years, alone in a one-room flat in a poor part of town, venturing out only to pick up a social security check and to buy a few necessities at the corner store.

Schizotypal personality disorder—experiences long-standing oddities or eccentricities in thought, perception, speech, or behavior; tends to be very egocentric; although basic contact with reality is usually maintained, there are occasional exceptions; example: the oddly dressed person with a strong belief in ESP and in her or his unique ability to foretell the future.

CLUSTER II disorders of dramatic, emotional, or erratic reactions

Antisocial personality disorder—a history of disregard for the rights and property of others; early signs include lying, truancy, stealing, fighting, resisting authority, and general irresponsibility; an inability to maintain a job is common; demonstrates poor parenting skills; a strong tendency toward impulsive behaviors with little regard for the consequences of that behavior; examples: the person who first steals a car and then drives it down an alley, knocking over garbage cans for the fun of it, *and* who has a history of such impulsive behaviors.

Borderline personality disorder—(as its name suggests, there is no dominant pattern of deviance here) sometimes there is impulsivity; sometimes instability of mood; a pattern of extensive uncertainty about many important life issues; temper tantrums are not uncommon and often appear unprovoked; example: a woman who has three unsuccessful marriages, no close friends, attended four different colleges, and can't keep a job much more than a few months because she hasn't figured out what she wants to do "when she grows up," yet she feels constantly "bored with life."

Histrionic personality disorder—overly dramatic, reactive, and intensely expressed behavior; very lively, tending to draw attention to one's self; tends to "overreact" to matters of small consequence; seeking of excitement and avoiding of routine; a tendency for dependency on others with otherwise poor interpersonal relations; example: a woman sho spends an inordinate amount of time on her appearance, calls almost everyone "darling," seems to be constantly asking for feedback on how she looks, such as "Don't you just *love* this new outfit?" and describes virtually all of her experiences as being "wonderful!" and "vastly outstanding!" even when such an experience is finding detergent on sale at the supermarket.

Narcissistic personality disorder—a grandiose exaggeration of self-importance; displays a need for attention or admiration; tendency to set unrealistic goals; maintains few lasting relationships with others; in many ways, a "childish" level of behavior; example: someone who always wants to be the topic of conversation and shows a lack of interest in saying anything positive about someone else, who seems to believe that no one has ever had a vacation as stupendous as his or understood an issue as clearly as he and will do whatever it takes to get others to compliment him.

CLUSTER III disorders involving anxiety and fearfulness

Avoidant personality disorder—is the name suggests, being oversensitive to the possibility of being rejected by others; an unwillingness to enter into relationships for fear of rejection; devastated by disapproval; there remains, however, a desire for social relations—that is, does not enjoy being alone; example: a man with few close friends who seems to date only women who are much older and less attractive than he and has worked in the same position for years, never seeking a job change or promotion; he hardly ever speaks up in public, occasionally attends meetings and social gatherings, but never participates.

Dependent personality disorder—individual allows and seeks others to dominate and assume responsibility for actions; poor self-image and a lack of confidence; sees self as stupid and helpless, deferring to others; example: a woman whose husband commonly abuses her, particularly when he's been drinking, and although she has from time to time reported the abuse, she refuses to take an active role in finding treatment for him and refuses to leave him, saying that it is "her place" to do as he says, and that if she does not please him, she deserves to be beaten.

Obsessive-compulsive personality disorder—a pervasive pattern of perfectionism and inflexibility; a restricted ability to show love, warmth, or tender emotions; an over-concern for rules and regulations and doing things in a prescribed way; become anxious about "getting the job done," but not about being compulsive in doing so; rigid and "stiff"; example: a man who takes pride in his work to the exclusion of most other social interactions, who will simply not settle for "good enough" no matter how much others may goad him, and who seems insensitive to the fact that others want to be done with the job and to move on to other things; he may retie his tie 10 or 12 times until the ends match exactly.

Passive-aggressive personality disorder—resistance to the demands of others; is passive and indirect; tendency toward procrastination, dawdling, stubbornness, inefficiency, and "forgetfulness"; often tend to be "whiners, moaners, and complainers"; example: the grandmother who, when asked to join the family on a trip to the store, says, "No, I'll stay here. You go." Then, as the family gets ready to leave, she says, "Sure, go ahead; go without me. I never get to go anywhere. I just stay here all day staring at these walls." Then she is invited once again to join the group and responds, "No, you go ahead, I'll stay here and wax the kitchen floor."

---

*Remember that to be classified as a personality disorder, these behaviors or symptoms must be of relatively long-standing, generally beginning in childhood or adolescence.

the American Psychiatric Association (1987). The term (rather like *neurosis*) has come to mean so many different things that it has lost some of its usefulness. It is still quite clear, however, that at least some of the symptoms of the disorders we'll examine in the last half of this chapter qualify as being psychotic—involving a loss of contact with reality and a gross impairment in functioning.

As was the case for the disorders we have discussed so far, we will again see that psychological disturbances often have an impact on each of three levels of functioning: behavior, cognition, and/or affect. We'll begin by taking a brief look at a grouping of disorders that is often classified as psychotic: organic mental disorders. Then we'll discuss two of the major psychotic disorders: mood and schizophrenic disorders.

What criteria are used to classify a symptom or a disorder as psychotic?   **BEFORE YOU GO ON**

Organic Mental Disorders

The name we use for this collection of psychological disorders tells us what they have in common: a disordering of behavior or mental processes the etiology (cause) of which involves some organic brain function. As the *DSM-III-R* points out, it is assumed that in some way or another, brain function is involved in *all* the mental disorders. "Differentiation of Organic Mental Disorders as a separate class does not imply that nonorganic mental disorders are somehow independent of brain processes. On the contrary, it is assumed that all psychological processes, normal and abnormal, depend on brain function" (APA, 1987, p. 98). Here, however, a specific brain function can be implicated as causing the psychological symptoms.

Our approach to organic mental disorders is a little different from the generally descriptive approach we have used so far. Any diagnosis, and resulting labeling, of **organic mental disorders** depends on two interacting factors: (1) an organic mental **syndrome,** which is a collection of psychological symptoms (and is simply descriptive, without regard to cause), and (2) a statement of the known etiology of the syndrome. In other words, a particular syndrome, or group of symptoms, may be associated with drug abuse *or* with senility. Even though the symptoms are the same, they are caused by different factors, and in such cases, we have two, separate disorders. So that we can have the proper vocabulary available, some of the major (and most common) organic mental syndromes are presented in Figure 9.4. You'll need to have these syndromes in mind as we review some of the organic mental disorders.

Organic mental disorders are usually divided into three subgroupings on the basis of their cause. One category is something of a catch-all for disorders that seem to be clearly organic in origin, but where the specific agent or cause is simply not known. The second includes a number of specific disorders where each is associated with the ingestion of some drug (these are called *substance-induced organic mental disorders*). The third category includes those disorders that seem to be caused by abnormal aging processes of the brain. The most common disorder in this category is associated with Alzheimer's disease, and it is with Alzheimer's that we begin.

organic mental disorders
disorders characterized by any of the organic mental syndromes and a known organic cause of the syndrome

syndrome
a collection of psychological symptoms used to describe a disorder

FIGURE 9.4
Defining Terms: The Major Organic Brain Syndromes and Symptoms
(Adapted from *DSM-111-R*, 1987.).

Delirium	a clouded state of consciousness; a lessening of one's awareness; difficulty in maintaining attention; accompanied by disturbances of thought; poor sleep habits; disorientation and confusion; episodes do not last long, a week or so at the most; someone who is delirious cannot seem to relate what is happening now to what has happened in the past.
Dementia	a marked loss of intellectual abilities; attention is unaffected, but use of memory is poor and deteriorates; memory losses may be minor at first and progress to virtual total loss of memory judgment and impulse control may also be adversely affected; person is not delirious.
Amnestic syndrome	impairment of memory occurring in normal state of consciousness; attention and other intellectual skills and abilities remain intact.
Delusions	defined as a false personal belief; the belief is firmly held regardless of what others may say; there are many types, including delusions of being controlled, grandiose delusions, and delusions of persecution; basically coming to believe firmly in something that is clearly not true.
Hallucinations	defined as sensory perception without external stimulation of the relevant sensory organ: hallucinations may occur in any sense, but some are more associated with some causes than others—LSD and visual, alcohol and auditory, for example.
Intoxication	major feature is the impairment of behavior and mental processes following the use of a drug: specific symptoms depend on the nature of the drug used; intoxication may involve any and all of the syndromes listed above; common changes involve disturbance in perception, attention, thinking, judgment, and emotional control.
Withdrawal	a set of symptoms that follow the reduction or cessation in intake of a drug previously used to reach a state of intoxication; particular symptoms depend on drug that has been used; any of the above listed syndromes may be involved in withdrawal.

degenerative dementia
a marked loss of intellectual and cognitive abilities that worsens with age

Degenerative Dementia of the Alzheimer Type. As the name **degenerative dementia** implies, the major syndrome of this disorder is dementia (see Figure 9.4). It is also degenerative, meaning that the symptoms tend to gradually worsen over time. A gradual, progressive deterioration of one's intellectual functioning is the most common symptom associated with Alzheimer's disease. Problems of recent memory mark the early stages of the disease—for example, "Did I take my pills this morning?" Mild personality changes soon follow—apathy, less spontaneity, withdrawal (perhaps in an attempt to hide one's symptoms from others). Consider the following description from a publication of the National Institute of Mental Health (Cohen, 1980), "As the disease progresses, problems in abstract thinking or in intellectual functioning take place. The individual may begin to have trouble with figures when working on bills, with understanding what is being read, or with organizing the day's work. Further disturbances in behavior, such as being agitated, irritable, quarrelsome, and less neat in appearance, may also be seen at this point. Later in the course of the disease, the afflicted may become confused or disoriented about what month or year

Written reminders can help Alzheimer's victims lead a relatively normal life. In the early stages, they can remember how to do things once they are reminded to do them at all. Later on, they may lose the ability to do even simple tasks.

it is and be unable to describe accurately where they live or to name correctly a place being visited. Eventually they may wander, not engage in conversation, become inattentive and erratic in mood, uncooperative, incontinent with loss of bladder and bowel control, and in extreme cases, totally incapable of caring for themselves."

Alzheimer's disease is not something new. It was first described in 1907 by Alois Alzheimer and was thought to be an inevitable process of aging (often referred to incorrectly as *senile psychosis*). It is not a normal, natural, or necessary part of growing old. Among other things, we are discovering more and more cases of Alzheimer's in persons considerably younger than age 65. Estimates are that two to three million Americans are afflicted with Alzheimer's disease, and over 100,000 of these die each year (Hostetler, 1987; Mace & Rabins, 1981; Wurtman, 1985). In terms of percentages, it is believed that 5 to 6 percent of persons over the age of 65 develop the disease. There are now nearly 30 million Americans in that age bracket, and, as we all know, that number is ever-increasing.

Although the major symptoms of Alzheimer's disease are clearly psychological in nature, we must remember that it *is* a physical disease caused by abnormal changes in brain tissue. Alzheimer's can only be diagnosed with certainty by an autopsy, when microscopic analyses indicate the presence of the disease. At autopsy there are four clear signs of Alzheimer's disease. One is a collection of *tangles*—a "spaghetti-like jumble of abnormal protein fibers" (Butler & Emr, 1982). A second sign is the presence of *plaques*— basically waste material, degenerated nerve fibers that wrap around a core of protein. A third sign is the presence of a number of small cavities filled with fluid and debris. The fourth sign is an indication of atrophy, or shrunken structures, in the brain. There are two problems we need to mention here: (1) each of these signs can be found in a normal brain (seldom more than one at a time, however), and (2) we don't know what causes these signs in the first place. In fact, with regard to causes, about all we have to offer are theories and hypotheses—some more promising than others. Richard Wurtman (1985), after reviewing the literature, suggests that there are seven different models used to explain Alzheimer's disease. Each is very complex, and each suggests a different type of treatment. These models of Alzheimer's disease are summarized in Figure 9.5.

(handwritten in margin, top left: reread)

FIGURE 9.5
Seven Models Used to "Explain" Alzheimer's Disease
(After Wurtman, 1985)

1. The genetic model points to the fact that the disease does run in families. Although there may be a genetic basis for the disease, we don't know what it is or where to look for it.

2. The abnormal protein model, because proteins are obviously involved in tangles and plaques, searches for these abnormal proteins and tries to determine where they come from.

3. The infectious agent model focuses its search to see if the brain abnormalities associated with Alzheimer's might be caused by some (probably low-grade) infection.

4. The toxin model suggests that there is evidence that salts of the metal aluminum are acting as a poison, or toxin, and are thus bringing on the symptoms of the disease.

5. The blood flow model returns us to the once popular idea that the symptoms of the disease are caused by a reduced blood flow and lack of oxygen to important areas of the brain.

6. The acetylcholine model, which is no doubt the most popular at the moment, points to a decrease in activity in a brain enzyme that normally produces a very important neurotransmitter, acetylcholine. Acetylcholine levels are measurably low in Alzheimer's disease patients.

7. The elephant model combines the elements of all the others, suggesting that each may be correct, depending upon one's point of view and methodology. [It is Wurtzman's belief that *this* is the most viable model, that none of the above explanations will prove to be sufficient, and that all are, in some way, involved in Alzheimer's disease.]

Substance-induced Organic Mental Disorders.   In Chapter 3 we discussed some of the more common psychoactive drugs and noted their effects on consciousness. As we suggested, if these drugs or chemicals are used long enough, or in large enough doses or quantities, they may cause lasting damage to the central nervous system and produce a wide range of psychological reactions that we can classify as disordered. In this section, we'll take a look at some of the more commonly abused substances that produce organic mental disorders, and we'll indicate which of the syndromes listed in Figure 9.4 are most likely to be associated with such abuse.

As you can tell from a careful examination of Figure 9.1, the *DSM-III-R* has a category of psychological disorders that is related to this one, called "psychoactive substance use disorders." The various instances of these disorders involve the misuse or abuse of some psychoactive substance that may lead to tolerance for or dependence on the substance, lack of control over the use of the substance, and maladaptive behavioral changes that are associated with more or less regular use of the substance. What's missing here, of course, is the known physical or organic damage that is part of the definition of organic mental disorders.

A psychoactive substance is one that has some effect on the user's psychological functioning. *Alcohol* is one of the most commonly used of such substances and certainly ranks as the most commonly abused. It is estimated that between 10 and 15 percent of adult Americans are alcohol abusers (Mayer, 1983; National Council on Alcoholism, 1979). If the abuse of alcohol is left unchecked, damage to the central nervous system may result, and *(handwritten in margin: Important →)* then we would have a person with a substance-induced organic disorder.

Virtually everyone over the age of 21 has had some experience with alcohol. The majority of the population has experienced at least one bout with alcohol intoxication. No other drug carries with it as much potential for the development of a long-term disorder as does alcohol. Its use and abuse are costly almost beyond measure. Nearly $600 million in federal funds are spent each year on alcohol-related actions (Nathan, 1983). Over $30 billion of lost productivity each year in the United States is attributed to alcohol-related problems (Quayle, 1983). Dollar figures become meaningless when compared to the personal and family losses that can be attributed to the mental disorders brought on by the abuse of alcohol, particularly when we consider that, in the United States, "10% of drinkers consume 50% of the total amount of alcohol consumed" (*DSM-III-R,* 1987, p. 173).

The abuse of barbiturates and other *sedative* drugs leads to three possible diagnosable mental disorders. The first is a disorder of use: intoxication, which includes many of the same symptoms as alcohol intoxication—impaired judgment, interference with mental functioning, slurred speech, lack of bodily coordination, unstable mood, irritability, and the like. The other two disorders present themselves during withdrawal and include such symptoms as nausea, weakness, anxiety, depressed mood, tremors, and (within one week after one stops taking the drug) delirium and/or amnestic syndrome.

The *opiate* drugs—called "Opioids" in the *DSM-III-R*—or narcotics (including heroin) give rise to two possible mental disorders when abused, one from taking the drug, the other when drug use stops. Symptoms of opiate intoxication include apathy, constriction of the pupil of the eye, euphoria, drowsiness, and impaired attention or memory. Withdrawal from heavy opiate use leads to a number of mental and physical symptoms, including dilated pupils, insomnia, weakness, diarrhea, hallucinations, or delusions.

Abuse of *cocaine* is related to four organic mental syndromes as listed in Figure 9.4. When use of cocaine is heavy enough to begin to cause physical, tissue damage, we can see evidence of intoxication, withdrawal, delirium, and/or delusions.

Prolonged or excessive use of *amphetamines* (stimulants) may lead to a range of possible disorders, from intoxication (including agitation, elation, talkativeness, and so on) to delirium, to delusional disorders, to severe disorders associated with withdrawal (including disturbed sleep, fatigue, and increased dreaming). As we shall see later, the wide range of symptoms induced by amphetamine use has provided scientists with an insight to one of the possible causes of a major psychotic disorder, schizophrenia.

Obviously, there are other substances that are psychoactive and can be abused, including PCP (or phencyclidine), which may cause delirium, the hallucinogens (such as LSD), which may cause hallucinations, delusions, and/or disorders of affect, and cannibis drugs (such as marijuana and hashish), which may cause intoxication disorders or delusions. In fact, the *DSM-III* and its recent revision list nicotine (withdrawal) and caffeine (intoxication) among the drugs associated with organic mental syndromes. The list of disorders that are substance-induced is a long one, and the symptoms and syndromes associated with each disorder can be very severe and debilitating. There is no way to avoid the obvious conclusion: Psychoactive drugs are dangerous.

Although we recognize the harmful effects and potential for long-term problems alcohol carries with it, the tendency to treat the matter lightly is still prevalent throughout our culture.

Hallucinogens:
  PCP
  LSD

Depressant:
  Alcohol
  Opiates - heroin
  Barbiturates

Stimulant:
  Cocaine
  Nicotine
  Caffeine
  Amphetamines

←Important

What are some of the syndromes associated with organic mental disorders?

What gives rise to these symptoms?

Mood Disorders

1. Depression
2. Mania
3. Bipolar - manic-depression

mood disorders
disorders of affect or feeling; usually depression; less frequently mania and depression occurring in cycles

The **mood disorders** (which were called "affective disorders" until the publication of the *DSM-III-R*) clearly demonstrate some disturbance in one's emotional behaviors or feelings. We have to be a little careful here. Almost all psychological disorders have some impact on one's mood or affect. With mood disorders, however, the intensity or extremeness of mood is the primary, major symptom.

Another thing we must recognize is that we have all felt some degree of extreme mood. At some time in our lives we have all felt really depressed, and there may have been times when we have felt the elevated, heightened, euphoria typical of mania. These extremes of mood have not severely impaired our functioning for very long, however. Furthermore, when we *are* very depressed or happy we know why. We can attribute our depression or our mania to something that has happened to us—a close friend or relative has died, we've won a large prize, we've failed to get an expected promotion, or we've been chosen worker of the year.

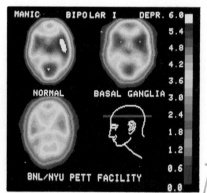

The top two PET scans show manic/bipolar I and depression compared to the third scan of a normal brain. *Important*

Depression and Mania. Mood disorders are defined in terms of extremes of mood, and there is no doubt that depression is the more common of the two extremes. Depression is usually found alone, whereas mania almost never is—it is associated with episodes of depression. Listed under the mood disorder category are a number of specific disorders that are differentiated in terms of such criteria as length of episode, severity of affect, and whether or not there is a known organic basis for the symptoms. The basic symptom here, however, is either depression, mania, or a combination of the two.

Seligman (1975) is credited as having first named depression "the common cold of mental illness." The *DSM-III-R* (1987) claims depression to be twice as likely in women as in men (9 to 26 percent of females and 5 to 12 percent of males are likely to have at least one depressive episode). The 1984 study of the National Institute of Mental Health also recognizes depression as a prevalent disorder, suggesting that at any one time, approximately 1 person in 20 (of their sample) "had suffered a major depressive episode" (NIMH, 1984, p. 952). The symptoms of depression are summarized in Figure 9.6.

Mania is a condition of mood that cannot be maintained for long. It's altogether too tiring to stay extremely manic for an extended time. Remember, people are very rarely ever manic without showing interspersed periods of depression. Because such people swing back and forth between these two extremes of mood (with episodes of normal affect interspersed), they are said to have a *bipolar disorder*, commonly referred to as manic-depression. Figure 9.7 lists some of the major defining characteristics of a manic reaction.

Having listed the major symptoms of the mood disorders and noted that depression is more common than mania, let's now consider *why* people become depressed. Where does depression come from?

FIGURE 9.6
Common Symptoms of Depression

1. Persistently unpleasant mood—feeling sad, blue, depressed, hopeless, low, down-in-the-dumps, irritable, and so on

2. Loss of pleasure or interest in all or almost all usual activities or pastimes

3. Poor appetite or weight loss (not due to dieting)

4. Insomnia

5. Agitation or slowing of motor behavior

6. Decrease in sexual activity and sexual drive

7. Loss of energy—fatigue

8. Feelings of worthlessness—self-reproach, inappropriate guilt feelings

9. Diminished ability to think—real or complained of indecisiveness

10. Recurrent thoughts of death—ideas of suicide, wishes to be dead, actual suicide attempts

The answers we find to the question "What causes depression?" depend in large measure on where and how we look for such answers. It seems most likely that depression is caused by a number of different, but potentially interrelated causes. Some of them are biological, others are more psychological. Next we'll briefly consider some of the factors that seem to influence the development of depression.

Biological Factors in Depression. Bipolar mood disorder is not very common in the general population. Anyone chosen at random would have less than a one half of 1 percent chance of developing the symptoms of the disorder. The chances of developing the symptoms rise to 15 percent if a brother, sister, or either parent ever had the disorder. This 15 percent figure seems to be true for fraternal twins, too. If, however, one member of a pair of identical twins has the disorder, the chances that the other twin will be diagnosed as having the disorder jump to more than 70 percent (Allen,

FIGURE 9.7
Common Symptoms of Mania

1. Elevated mood—feelings are expansive, euphoric, or irritable

2. Increase in activity—socially, at work, or sexually; or physical restlessness; participation in multiple activities, all at the same time

3. More talkative than usual

4. Racing thoughts—ideas come quickly to mind

5. Decreased need for sleep

6. Distractibility—attention easily drawn to unimportant or irrelevant matters

7. Lack of appreciation of possible dangers of behaviors—for example, shopping sprees, sexual indiscretions, foolish investments, reckless driving, and so on

(At least three of these should have occurred over a period of at least three weeks.)

An Amish community in Pennsylvania proved to be an ideal setting to use for a study of bipolar mood disorders. Being able to follow genetic history for all of the residents enabled researchers to find a link between present and past generations and the occurrence of bipolar mood disorder.

1976). What all this means, of course, is that there is excellent evidence that there is a genetic, or inherited, predisposition for the bipolar mood disorder. The data are not quite as striking for the unipolar mood disorder (depression only), where the similar data for identical twins is 40 percent and 11 percent for fraternal twins. We can suspect, however, that there is some sort of genetic basis to the disorder.

Considerable attention in the popular press was recently given to a study by researchers who examined the occurrence of bipolar mood disorders in a community of more than 1200 Old Order Amish in Pennsylvania (Egeland et al., 1987). Because excellent records were available, the researchers were able to trace the genetic history of everyone in the community. They found 32 cases of bipolar mood disorder, and for each and every case, evidence of the same disorder was found in previous generations. More than that, the researchers also identified *the specific gene* (a dominant gene on chromosome 11) that, as they put it, "confers a strong predisposition to manic depressive disease" (p. 783).

It is one thing to find a genetic basis for a disorder and yet another to specify the biological mechanisms that then produce its symptoms. Attention has been focused on a number of neurotransmitters that seem to directly influence mood. Collectively they are referred to as *biogenic amines* and include such known transmitter substances as serotonin, dopamine, and norepinephrine. The major breakthrough in this research came when it was discovered that a drug (reserpine) used to treat high blood pressure also produced symptoms of depression. It was then discovered that reserpine depleted the brain's normal level of norepinephrine, and the search for neurotransmitter involvement in affective disorders was on (Bennett, 1982).

One current theory is that depression is caused by a reduction in the biogenic amines, and that mania is caused by an overabundance of these chemicals. It remains to be seen what produces these biochemical imbalances in some people and not others—perhaps an inherited predisposition.

Stress causes changes in the neurotransmitters in the brain. One change is an increase in biogenic amines (Anisman & Zacharko, 1982). If these substances are overstimulated by prolonged stress, perhaps their supply becomes depleted in the long run, leading to symptoms of depression. Even in those cases of depression that seem to occur without any striking or unusual stressors, we may again suspect that a genetic predisposition makes some people highly susceptible to the biochemical changes that accompany stress in any degree. The theory seems logical, but as yet there is insufficient evidence for us to draw any firm conclusions.

Psychological Factors in Depression.   Learning theorists have attributed depression to a number of experiential phenomena, including most importantly, a lack of effective reinforcers. Given a history of making responses without earning reinforcement, an individual may simply tend to stop responding and become quiet, withdrawn, passive, and, in many ways, depressed. Some people, lacking ability to gain (or earn) reinforcers, simply respond less often to environmental cues. They enter into a long, generalized period of extinction, which ultimately leads to depression. On the other hand, we must acknowledge research that suggests that the ineffectiveness of reinforcers in some people's lives is more a result of their depression than a cause of it. That is, *because* someone is depressed, he or she may find less reinforcement for their responses to the world about them (Carson & Carson, 1984).

Other theorists (most notably a psychiatrist, Aaron Beck, 1967, 1976) argue that although depression is displayed as a disorder of affect, its causes may be largely cognitive. Some people, the argument goes, tend to think of themselves in a poor light; they believe that they are, in many ways, ineffective people. They tend to blame themselves for a great many of their failures, whether deservedly so or not. Facing life with such negative attitudes about one's self tends to foster even more failures and self-doubt, and such cycles then lead to feelings of depression.

To be sure, there are other views about the causes of depression, including some psychoanalytic views that depression is a reflection of early childhood experiences that lead to anger that is directed inward. In brief, we do not yet understand the causes of mood disorders. We can conclude that depression probably stems from a combination of genetic predispositions, biochemical influences, learning experiences, situational stress, and cognitive factors. Which of these is more, or most, important remains to be seen.

**How are the mood disorders defined?   BEFORE YOU GO ON
What do we know about their prevalence and their causes?**

Schizophrenia

schizophrenia
complex psychotic disorders
characterized by impairment of
cognitive functioning, delusions and
hallucinations, social withdrawal,
and inappropriate affect

[handwritten margin notes: Late Adolescents / complex disorder / Delusions / Retreat from reality / Hugollination]

We now turn to what many consider to be the ultimate psychological disorder: **schizophrenia.** In many ways, schizophrenia is "the most devasting, puzzling, and frustrating of all mental illnesses" (Bloom et al., 1985). Schizophrenia is the label given to a number of specific disorders, all of which have a distortion of reality and a retreat from others, accompanied by disturbances in perception, thinking, affect, and behavior.

One of the things that qualifies schizophrenia as the ultimate psychological disorder is that it seems to involve virtually every aspect of living. The possible range of symptoms is so great that it is nearly impossible to specify just which symptoms are basic or fundamental and which are secondary.

Let's simply list some of the symptoms that are commonly associated with schizophrenia. For one thing, there is usually a disturbance of thinking. In fact, schizophrenia always involves delusions and hallucinations in some phase of the illness. As reflected in their delusions, schizophrenics come to believe strange and unusual things that are simply not true. The delusions of the schizophrenic tend to be bizarre, inconsistent, and clearly unsupportable. Perceptions are often distorted, most commonly with auditory hallucinations (hearing voices). Distortions of time are not uncommon. Sometimes a minute seems to last for hours or hours seem to race by in a matter of seconds. Schizophrenics may engage in a number of unusual behaviors, typically ritualized, stereotyped, and meaningless.

One of the most obvious behavioral consequences of schizophrenia is found in language behavior. Some schizophrenics make up words (called *neologisms*) as they talk. A person with schizophrenia once told one of us (Gerow) at great length and with great animation about a "rogaritz" and what that "rogaritz" was going to do with a tree once it caught it. Others may use actual English words, but mix them up and use them inappropriately (in "word salads"). As an example, here's the response of a severely disturbed schizophrenic to the question, "Why are people who are born deaf usually unable to talk?" "When you swallow in your throat like a key it comes out, but not a scissors. A robin too, it means spring" (from Marengo & Harrow, 1987, p. 654).

It is also common to find that affect is involved in schizophrenia. Most commonly, we encounter *flattened affect,* meaning that a person shows no particular emotional response of any kind to external stimuli. Less commonly there is the inappropriate affect of the psychotic: giggling and laughing or crying and sobbing for no apparent reason.

We need to make two things clear. First, as unsettling as this list of symptoms may be, the average patient with schizophrenia does not present the picture of the crazed, wild, lunatic that is often depicted in movies and on television. Day in and day out, the average schizophrenic patient is usually quite colorless, socially withdrawn, and of very little danger. Although there are exceptions to this rule of thumb, it is particularly true when the schizophrenic patient is under treatment and/or under medication. Their "differentness" may be frightening, but people who are schizophrenic are seldom any more dangerous than anyone else.

Second, when literally translated, schizophrenia means "split of the mind." This term was first used by a Swiss psychiatrist, Eugen Bleuler, in 1911. The split that Bleuler was addressing was a split of the mind of the

These drawings show the varying levels of progress by a patient with paranoid schizophrenia. The first picture was chosen from a magazine for the patient to copy from. The second picture shows a first attempt at copying the picture. Note the overall visual distortion and difficulty in using colors and letters. The therapist came to learn that this patient was experiencing visual distortion with other things and, consequently, fear. The third picture, showing vast improvement, was done after the patient had undergone therapy.

schizophrenic from the real world and the social relationships that the rest of us enjoy. Never has the term been used to describe a multiple or split personality of the Dr. Jekyll and Mr. Hyde variety. Such disorders do occur, but they are rare, and we have already seen that they are classified as a variety of dissociative disorder.

Schizophrenia tends to occur around the world at approximately the same rate: 1 percent of the population at any point in time. This figure has been stable for many years. The 1984 NIMH survey revealed about 1 percent of their sample to have symptoms of schizophrenia, with about half of these individuals actively in treatment for the disorder (NIMH, 1984). It is a common claim that schizophrenic patients fill more than half of the hospital beds in mental or psychiatric hospitals in this country (Bloom et al., 1985). Once again, however, the statistics are difficult to deal with on a personal level. We are certainly talking about very large numbers of persons, many of whom will be treated and will recover, while many others will spend the rest of their lives in and out of institutions under rather constant care and supervision. Let's now consider some of the ways in which this collection of disorders can be classified.

What are the major symptoms of schizophrenia? **BEFORE YOU GO ON**

Process and Reactive Schizophrenia. Until now, we have classified varieties of disorders in terms of specific, defining symptoms. With schizophrenia, there is at least one distinction that is not made on the basis of the *nature* of symptoms, but on the basis of their *onset*. We use the term **process schizophrenia** to describe schizophrenic symptoms that have developed gradually, usually over a period of years. It is usually only in retrospect, after the diagnosis of schizophrenia has been made, that we realize that

process schizophrenia
schizophrenia in which the onset of the symptoms is comparatively slow and gradual

Psychotic Disorders **419**

there has been a long history of symptoms that have gradually worsened to the point where intervention is required, treatment sought, and a diagnosis made.

reactive schizophrenia
schizophrenia in which the onset of the symptoms is comparatively sudden

Reactive schizophrenia, on the other hand, is the term we use for the sudden onset of schizophrenic symptoms. Here we have a clinical picture of someone who was, by all accounts, quite normal and well adjusted, but who suddenly showed signs of having a psychotic break.

As we have found to be the case in other situations, we should not consider "reactive" and "process" as two separate and distinct varieties of schizophrenia. Rather, we should view them as poles, or extremes, of a dimension that can be used to describe the nature of the onset of schizophrenic symptoms.

Important →

The significance of this distinction is that there is reason to believe that the prognosis for schizophrenia can be, at least to some degree, based on the nature of its onset—the more toward the *process* variety, the worse the prognosis, and the more toward the *reactive* type of onset, the better the prognosis.

***DSM-III-R* Types of Schizophrenia.** The revised edition of the *Diagnostic and Statistical Manual of Mental Disorders* lists five categories or types of schizophrenia. All of these types share many of the same symptoms of disorganized cognition, inappropriate affect, and strange behavior, but each has a particular symptom or cluster of symptoms that makes it different. The types of schizophrenia listed in the *DSM-III-R* are summarized in Figure 9.8.

BEFORE YOU GO ON **What characterizes the following varieties or types of schizophrenia: process vs. reactive, catatonic, disorganized, paranoid, undifferentiated, and residual?**

FIGURE 9.8
Types of schizophrenia (from Carson et al., 1988).

Undifferentiated type	A pattern of symptoms in which there is a rapidly changing mixture of all or most of the primary indicators of schizophrenia. Commonly observed are indications of perplexity, confusion, emotional turmoil, delusions of reference, excitement, dreamlike autism, depression, and fear. Most often, this picture is seen in patients who are in the process of breaking down and becoming schizophrenic. However, it is also seen when major changes are occurring in the adjustive demands impinging on a person with an already-established schizophrenic psychosis. In such cases, it frequently foreshadows an impending change to another primary schizophrenic subtype.
Paranoid type	A symptom picture dominated by absurd, illogical, and changeable delusions, frequently accompanied by vivid hallucinations, with a resulting impairment of critical judgment and erratic, unpredictable, and occasionally dangerous behavior. In chronic cases, there is usually less disorganization of behavior than in other types of schizophrenia, and less extreme withdrawal from social interaction.
Catatonic type	Often characterized by alternating periods of extreme withdrawal and extreme excitement, although in some cases one or the other reaction predominates. In the withdrawal reaction there is a sudden loss of all animation and a tendency to remain motionless for hours or even days in a single position. The clinical picture may undergo an abrupt change, with excitement coming on suddenly, wherein the individual may talk or shout incoherently, pace rapidly, and engage in uninhibited, impulsive, and frenzied behavior. In this state, the individual may be dangerous.
Disorganized type	Usually occurs at an earlier age than most other types of schizophrenia, and represents a more severe disintegration of the personality. Emotional distortion and blunting typically are manifested in appropriate laughter and silliness, peculiar mannerisms, and bizarre, often obscene, behavior.
Residual type	Mild indications of schizophrenia shown by individuals in remission following a schizophrenic episode.

The genetic predisposition for schizophrenia is well illustrated by the Genain quadruplets, shown here celebrating their 51st birthday in 1981. All four women experienced a schizophrenic disorder of varying severity, duration, and outcome—facts that may suggest an environmental role in schizophrenia.

Hereditary Factors in Schizophrenia.   Schizophrenia is obviously a complex set of disorders. There is even some disagreement about how to define the disorder. (In one study, a sample of schizophrenics was reduced by more than half when the researchers imposed the *DSM-III* criteria rather than those from the *DSM-II* to define their subjects [Winters et al., 1981].) As you might suspect, our bottom-line conclusion on the cause of schizophrenia is going to be tentative and multidimensional. Although we don't know what causes the disorder, we do have a number of interesting ideas to consider. One of these is that schizophrenia tends to run in families (Kessler, 1980; Rosenthal, 1970). The data are not as striking as they are for the affective disorders, but it is clear that one is at a higher risk of being diagnosed as schizophrenic if there is a family history of the disorder.

Adult children of schizophrenics are significantly more likely to develop schizophrenia than are adult children of nonschizophrenic parents. If one parent is schizophrenic, his or her child is 10 to 15 times more likely to develop schizophrenia as an adult, and when both parents are schizophrenic, their children are about 40 times more likely to develop this illness (Cornblatt & Erlenmeyer-Kimling, 1985; Erlenmeyer-Kimmling, 1968). The risk of becoming schizophrenic is 4 to 5 times greater for an identical twin than it is for a fraternal twin if the other member of the twin pair has the disorder. Remember that the odds of being diagnosed as schizophrenic are, in the general population, about 1 in 100. For those who are identical twins of schizophrenics, the odds jump to nearly 1 in 2 (Bloom et al., 1985). It is also true that when adopted children become schizophrenic, it is much more likely that schizophrenia will be found among members of that person's biological family than his or her adoptive family (Bootzin & Acocella, 1984). Some of these data (from Nicol & Gottesman, 1983) are presented in Figure 9.9. We need to remember, once again, that such data do not mean that schizophrenia is directly inherited. Notice, for example, that nearly half of the identical twins of schizophrenics never do develop the disorder. It is more reasonable to say that such data suggest that one may inherit a pre-

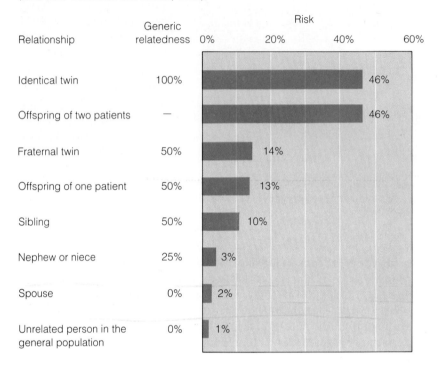

FIGURE 9.9
Lifetime risks of developing schizophrenia are largely a function of how closely an individual is genetically related to a schizophrenic and not a function of how much their environment is shared.
(Data from Gottesman and Shields, 1982).

Relationship	Generic relatedness	Risk
Identical twin	100%	46%
Offspring of two patients	—	46%
Fraternal twin	50%	14%
Offspring of one patient	50%	13%
Sibling	50%	10%
Nephew or niece	25%	3%
Spouse	0%	2%
Unrelated person in the general population	0%	1%

disposition to become schizophrenic. This distinction may be somewhat subtle, but it is an important one, recalling our many earlier discussions about not drawing cause-and-effect conclusions from correlational data.

Biochemical Factors in Schizophrenia. Dopamine is a neurotransmitter substance found in every human brain. The role of this particular neurotransmitter in schizophrenia has recently come to light from several different lines of research.

For one thing, we know that the abuse of amphetamines often leads to the development of many symptoms also found in schizophrenia. We also know that amphetamines are chemically very similar to dopamine and may actually cause an increase in dopamine levels in the brain. Logic then leads us to wonder if perhaps schizophrenic symptoms are caused by excess amounts of dopamine.

Some support for this view comes from examining the workings of various antipsychotic drugs that actually reduce schizophrenic symptoms. Apparently, drugs that alleviate schizophrenic symptoms commonly block receptor sites for dopamine in the brain (Snyder, 1980). If reducing the effectiveness of dopamine by blocking its activity at the synapse can control schizophrenic symptoms, might we not assume that these symptoms are caused by dopamine in the first place?

The arguments for this hypothesis appear compelling, but they are far from certain. There are a number of problems that are difficult to deal with. For one thing, there is little evidence that schizophrenics have elevated levels of dopamine in their brains (Karoum et al., 1987). Even so, there may be a heightened sensitivity in the brains of schizophrenics to what dopamine is present (perhaps more receptor sites for dopamine). In other words, schizophrenics may not have more dopamine than do nonschizophrenics; they may use more of what they have, thus creating psychotic symptoms. Again, this may sound reasonable, but there is little direct evidence to support such a conclusion. For another thing, not all antipsychotic medications have their effects by blocking dopamine receptor sites. It is also troublesome that when drugs *are* effective, their effects generally take a few weeks to show up. If the effect of the drugs on receptor sites is immediate, why isn't the effect on symptoms immediate also? Finally, we have a "chicken-and-egg" problem with this dopamine hypothesis. Even if dopamine were shown to be related to schizophrenic symptoms, we should still have to ask if there is a direct *causal* relationship. That is, do increased levels of dopamine cause schizophrenic symptoms, or does the disorder of schizophrenia cause elevated dopamine levels? We can note in passing that we have the same chicken-and-egg problem with a number of very interesting findings concerning brain structure and schizophrenia. For example, the brains of many patients with schizophrenia have abnormally large ventricles (cavities or openings that contain cerebrospinal fluid) (Andreasen et al., 1982), and recent evidence suggests a lack of balance between the two hemispheres of the brain (Gur et al., 1987; Reveley et al., 1987). Even if these differences in the brains of schizophrenics and nonschizophrenics are confirmed, we don't know if we're dealing with causes or effects.

Psychological and Social Factors in Schizophrenia. It may be that genetic and/or biochemical factors predispose a person to develop the symptoms of schizophrenia. What sorts of events or situations tend to turn such predispositions into reality for the schizophrenic? To this question, our answers are very sketchy indeed. One of the standard views (Lidz, 1965, 1973) is that schizophrenia develops as a response to early experiences within the family unit. The early family experiences of people who later develop schizophrenic symptoms often seem qualitatively different from those who do not become schizophrenic. Factors that have been isolated include such things as inefficient or improper means of communication within the family. That is, there seems to be an inability or unwillingness to share feelings and emotions or to talk openly about problems and conflicts. Early childhood experiences of schizophrenics seem filled with conflict, anxiety, doubt, and emotional tension. There also seems to be an unusually high incidence of double messages and double binds being presented to children who later tend to become schizophrenic. For example, a mother may tell her child that she becomes upset when everyone forgets about her birthday and then turn around and scold the child for spending lunch money to buy a birthday present. Parents who communicate something like, "We want you to be independent and show responsibility, but so long as you live in this house, you'll do things the way we say, no questions asked," are certainly delivering a double message to their child.

One psychiatrist coined the term "schizophrenogenic mother" to describe patterns of mothering behaviors that are cold, aloof, and generally unaffectionate. Attributing such qualities to mothers alone, however, is not supported by the evidence. Fathers may show "schizophrenogenic" behaviors also. Hostile parent-child relationships that lack spontaneous displays of love, affection, and positive regard are commonly found in the early childhood experience of schizophrenics, but, once again, we should not overinterpret. Many people raised in such homes never develop any schizophrenic symptoms, and many schizophrenics were reared in normal homes with families who were loving and accepting. It is certainly not uncommon to find one child from a family developing schizophrenia, while another reared in the same home environment never develops any schizophrenic symptoms. There seems no doubt that one's family atmosphere and learning history *can* be a factor in schizophrenia. That such psychosocial factors might be the only factors involved seems very unlikely.

We will save our discussion of the treatment of the psychological disorders until the next chapter. One treatment method for schizophrenia involves the use of medication to reduce the symptoms of the disorder. Largely because of the introduction of antipsychotic medications, the outlook for patients with schizophrenia is not nearly as dismal as it was just 25 years ago. We may estimate now that nearly one third of all persons diagnosed as schizophrenic will recover (be symptom-free for at least five years). About one-third will be at least partially recovered and may assume, at least to some degree, the normal responsibilities of adaptive living in society. It still remains, however, that nearly one third of all patients diagnosed as schizophrenic will never recover to the point where they will be freed from institutionalization or daily supervision (Bloom et al., 1985).

BEFORE YOU GO ON **Describe some of the factors that have been implicated as possible causes of schizophrenic symptoms.**

In this section, we have briefly reviewed some of the psychological disorders that can be classified as psychotic because they demonstrate symptoms of gross impairment of functioning and a loss of contact with reality. In these disorders, we commonly find delusions and/or hallucinations. Although each of these disorders may have genetic or biochemical bases, such is necessarily the case for the grouping of disorders referred to as organic mental disorders. It is a distortion of affect, usually extreme depression, that marks the mood disorders. Schizophrenia is actually a set of disorders that to some degree involves impairment of all areas of functioning: affect, cognition, and behavior. The prevalence of these disorders is staggering. Millions of people are, at this moment, suffering from one of the disorders we have discussed here. In the next chapter, we will consider what can be done to help, to alleviate the symptoms, and to provide relief to those who suffer the pain of the psychological disorders.

SUMMARY

How do we define psychological abnormality?

In the context of psychological disorders, we take abnormal to mean statistically uncommon maladaptive behaviors, cognitions, and/or affect that are at odds with social expectations and that result in distress and discomfort. / 395

What is the *DSM-III-R?*

What are some of its advantages and disadvantages?

The *DSM-III-R* is the revised third edition of the *Diagnostic and Statistical Manual of Mental Disorders,* the "official" classification scheme for psychological disorders as determined by a large committee of psychologists and psychiatrists. The major advantage of this system is that it provides one standard label and cluster of symptoms for that label that all mental health practitioners can use; it is an aid in communication. It does have its limitations, however. It includes nearly 250 separate entries, which some believe to be too many. On the other hand, there are deviations from social norms that are not included in the manual. Such schemes should not be used to confuse description with explanation; the *DSM-III-R* does the former, not the latter. / 398

What are the essential characteristics of a phobic disorder?

By definition, a phobic disorder is typified by an intense, persistent fear of some object, activity, or situation which is in no real sense a threat to the individual's well-being; in brief, it is an intense, irrational fear. / 400

What defines a panic disorder?

The defining symptom of a panic disorder is a sudden, often unpredictable attack of intense anxiety, called a panic attack. These attacks may last for seconds or for hours and are often associated with feelings of impending doom. Unlike phobic reactions, there is no particular stimulus to prompt the attack. / 400

Describe generalized anxiety disorder, and contrast it with panic disorder.

Panic disorders and generalized anxiety disorders are alike in that their major defining characteristic is a high level of anxiety that cannot be attributed to any particular source. The major difference between the two is that for the generalized anxiety disorder, the felt anxiety is chronic, persistent, and diffuse. In the panic disorder, however, there may be periods

during which the person is totally free from feelings of anxiety; the anxiety occurs in acute debilitating attacks. / 401

In the context of anxiety-based psychological disorders, what is an obsession, and what is a compulsion?

An obsession is an idea or thought that constantly intrudes on one's awareness. A compulsion, on the other hand, is a repeated and stereotyped behavior or act that constantly intrudes on one's behavior. / 402

How do somatoform disorders differ from psychosomatic disorders?

Describe hypochondriasis and conversion disorder.

By definition, each of the somatoform disorders reflects some physical or bodily symptom or complaint. In each case, however, there is no known biological or medical cause for the complaint. Psychosomatic disorders, on the other hand, do involve actual physical, tissue damage, perhaps caused by or worsened by psychological factors such as stress. In hypochondriasis, a person lives in fear and dread of contracting some serious ill-

Chapter Nine
Abnormal Psychology

SUMMARY continued

ness or disease, when there is no medical evidence that such fears are well founded. In conversion disorder, there is an actual loss or alteration in physical functioning that is often dramatic, such as blindness or deafness, and that is not under voluntary control. This suggests a physical disorder but has no medical basis. / 403

What is the defining symptom of the dissociative disorders?

Dissociative disorders are marked by a retreat or escape from (a dissociation with) some aspect of one's personality. It may be a matter of an inability to recall some life event (amnesia), sometimes accompanied by unexplained travel to a different location (fugue state). In some very rare cases, certain aspects of one's personality become so dissociated that we may say that the person suffers from multiple personality, where two or more personalities are found in the same individual. / 405

What are the defining characteristics of the personality disorders?

Personality disorders are enduring patterns of perceiving, relating to, and thinking about the environment and one's self that are inflexible and maladaptive. These are essentially lifelong patterns of response and may be classified as being odd, eccentric, dramatic, erratic, or fearful. / 407

What criteria are used to classify a symptom or a disorder as psychotic?

To qualify as psychotic, a symptom or disorder should display a gross impairment of functioning and a loss of contact with reality. Impairment and loss of reality may be evidenced in thinking, affect, or behavior. / 409

What are some of the syndromes associated with organic mental disorders?

What gives rise to these symptoms?

The organic mental disorders may display any of a number of different syndromes, including delirium, a clouded state of consciousness and lessening of awareness; dementia, a marked loss of intellectual abilities, including memory, judgment, and impulse control; amnestic syndrome, an impairment of memory with no other intel-

lectual deficit; delusions, firmly held false personal beliefs; hallucinations, perceptions without sensory stimulation; intoxication, the impairment of behavioral and mental processes following the use of a drug; and withdrawal, any of the above symptoms that follow the cessation of intake of a drug. These syndromes arise through some form of brain dysfunction or damage, sometimes due to a problem with the aging process, as in Alzheimer's disease, or to the abuse of chemical substances such as alcohol, sedatives, opiates, cocaine, or amphetamines. / 414

How are the mood disorders defined?

What do we know about their prevalence and their causes?

Disturbances of affect can be found in many psychological disorders. In the mood disorders, a disturbance in mood or feeling is the prime, and occasionally only, major symptom. Most commonly, we find the disorder to be one of depression alone; less commonly we find mania and depression occurring in cycles. Depression is a common disorder, affecting as many as 20 percent of all women and 10 percent of all men at some time in their lives. The disorder seems to have a strong basis in heredity. Neurotransmitters (biogenic amines) such as serotonin and dopamine have been implicated in depression. Psychological explanations tend to focus on the learned ineffectiveness of reinforcers and cognitive factors, such as a poor self-image, as models for explaining the causes of depression. / 417

What are the major symptoms of schizophrenia?

Schizophrenia is a label applied to a number of disorders that all seem to involve varying degrees of cognitive impairment (delusions, hallucinations, disturbances of thought, and the like), social isolation, and disturbances of affect and behavior. / 419

What characterizes the following varieties or types of schizophrenia: process vs. reactive, catatonic, disorganized, paranoid, undifferentiated, and residual?

Process schizophrenia is the term used when symptoms tend to develop slowly and gradually, whereas we call those cases in which symptoms arise suddenly reactive schizophrenia. The latter has a better prognosis than the former. Catatonic schizophrenia is characterized by catatonia (states of physical impassivity) and/or extreme excitement. Disorganized schizophrenia is marked by a more severe disintegration of personality, with emotional distortions, inappropriate laughter, and bizarre behaviors. Paranoid schizophrenia is characterized by delusions, usually absurd and illogical. Undifferentiated schizophrenia involves a variety of psychotic symptoms, none of which dominate, and residual schizophrenia indicates a mild form of the disorder following a schizophrenic episode. / 420

Describe some of the factors that have been implicated as possible causes of schizophrenic symptoms.

Although we certainly do not know the causes of schizophrenia, three lines of investigation have produced hopeful leads. (1) There seems to be little doubt of at least a genetic predisposition for the disorder. Although schizophrenia is not inherited, it does tend to run in families. (2) Research on biochemical correlates of schizophrenia have localized the neurotransmitter dopamine as being involved in the production of schizophrenialike symptoms, although dopamine's role in the disorder is now being questioned. (3) It also seems reasonable to hypothesize that early childhood experiences, particularly those involving parent-child interactions and communications, may also predispose one toward schizophrenia. / 424

Chapter Nine
Abnormal Psychology

REVIEW QUESTIONS

1. Of the following definitional aspects of abnormality, which is *least* central or *least* important when we consider abnormality in psychology?

a. maladaptive affect, behavior, and/or cognitions.

b. statistically not average or not of the norm.

c. maladaptation.

d. distress and/or discomfort.

What makes this a difficult item is that it is asking you to make a value judgment. In fact, each of these alternatives raises a point that is mentioned as part of our definition of abnormality in psychology. Of these choices, the least important consideration in psychology is the notion of statistical rarity or uncommonness. True, psychological disorders are not to be considered average, or acceptable, but although the word "abnormal" literally implies statistical rarity, the other aspects listed here are more important, or salient, in our consideration of what is abnormal in psychology. / 393

2. Of the following, which is *not* considered in the DSM-III-R?

a. the diagnosis of mental disorders on the basis of symptoms.

b. whether or not physical diseases or ailments are present.

c. the cause of the disorder being described.

d. the amount of stress experienced recently.

As a classification system for psychological or mental disorders, the *DSM-III-R* lists hundreds of different disorders, considering for each the major symptoms involved, the amount of stress the individual has experienced, the length of time the symptoms have been evidenced, and whether or not there is some associated physical disease or ailment. The *DSM-III-R* purposefully avoids any reference to the causes or etiology of the disorders that it lists and classifies. / 395

3. The term *insanity* comes to us from:

a. the *DSM-III-R*.

b. the legal profession and the courts.

c. the earliest days of classification of psychological disorders.

d. Freud's reference to the unconscious mind.

There are many many terms that are used to classify and identify and label symptoms of psychological disorders. Some are listed "officially" in the *DSM-III*, revised edition, some are holdovers to earlier versions of classification systems (such as neurosis). The term *insanity*, however, is a technical term defined by the legal system and the courts and is not found in the *DSM-III-R*. / 397

4. Mary Ellen has an intense and irrational fear of elevators. She will not even enter an elevator and cannot be persuaded to do so. She is most likely suffering from:

a. generalized anxiety disorder.

b. phobic disorder.

c. panic disorder.

d. obsessive-compulsive disorder.

All of the disorders listed in these alternatives involve a discomforting amount of felt anxiety. The aspect of Mary Ellen's symptoms that indicate that she is suffering from a phobic disorder is that there is a specific object of her fear—elevators, coupled with the observation that her fear is intense and irrational. The actual feelings of a panic disorder attack may be very similar to those of a phobic attack, but there is no known object that produces the reaction in a panic disorder. / 398

5. **Which of the following disorders is *least* associated with the other three; that is, which does not belong?**

a. psychogenic amnesia.

b. obsessive disorder.

c. fugue.

d. multiple personality.

At issue here is the observation that psychogenic amnesia, fugue states, and multiple personality disorders are all considered (or classified) as dissociative disorders in which some aspect of personality becomes separate or dissociated from the self. All of these are basically anxiety related, as is the obsessive disorder, but the obsessive disorder is not dissociative. / 404

6. **The phenomenon known as "la belle indifference" is associated with which of the following disorders?**

a. conversion disorder.

b. hypochondriasis.

c. nervous breakdown.

d. schizophrenia.

"La belle indifference" is the term used to describe the apparent lack of concern that a person with conversion disorder has about his or her physical manifestation of the disorder. With hypochondriasis there is considerable concern over symptoms of a physical disease that does not exist. There is no such thing (at least technically) as a nervous breakdown—the term is popularly used to describe any number of anxiety-based disorders. Schizophrenia is a psychotic disorder for which "la belle indifference" is irrelevant. / 403

7. **Abuse of which of the following drugs accounts for more cases of substance-induced organic mental disorders than the other three?**

a. cocaine.

b. sedatives.

c. amphetamines.

d. alcohol.

This is a straightforward item. Each of the drugs listed here, if abused, can and does cause an organic mental disorder. There is no doubt, however, that alcohol is the most abused of all psychoactive drugs. / 412

8. **Of the following symptoms—all of which have been associated with schizophrenia—which is, virtually by definition, the most common?**

a. flattened affect.

b. the ability to maintain strange postures for unusually long periods of time.

c. hallucinations and delusions.

d. sudden onset.

Hallucinations and delusions are found to some extent in virtually every case of schizophrenia, to the point where they may be considered definitional symptoms. Although the affect of the schizophrenic is typically inappropriate, flattened affect is only one way of demonstrating that inappropriateness. The ability to maintain strange postures for very long time periods is a symptom of the catatonic schizophrenic but is not a typical symptom. Sudden or gradual onset (reactive or process) is an important determinant of prognosis in schizophrenia, where sudden onset is generally associated with more favorable prognoses. Unfortunately, this is not the "most common" of these symptoms. / 418

Chapter Ten

Treatment and Therapy

Why We Care

A Historical Perspective

Biomedical Treatments of Psychological Disorders
Psychosurgery
Electroconvulsive Therapy
Drug Therapy
Antipsychotic Drugs
Antidepressant Drugs
Antianxiety Drugs

Psychotherapy
Psychoanalytic Techniques
Freudian Psychoanalysis
Post-Freudian Psychoanalysis
Evaluating Psychoanalysis
Humanistic Techniques
Client-centered Therapy
Evaluating Humanistic Therapies
Behavioral Techniques
Systematic Desensitization
Flooding and Implosive Therapy
Aversion Therapy
Contingency Management and Contingency Contracting
Modeling
Evaluating Behavior Therapy
Cognitive Techniques
Rational-emotive Therapy
Cognitive Restructuring Therapy
Group Approaches
Choosing a Therapist
Who Provides Psychotherapy?
How Do I Choose the Right Therapist?

Barbara is an 18-year-old freshman at City Community College. Still living at home with her parents and two younger brothers, she is having difficulty dealing with the demands on her time. She has a full-time job at a restaurant and is trying to manage four classes at college. The pressures of home, school, and work seem to be making Barbara uncharacteristically anxious and depressed. She is falling behind in her school work, performing poorly at her job, and is finding life at home almost unbearable. On the recommendation of her psychology instructor, Barbara has been seeing a counselor at the Student Services Center. She has had six visits there with a psychotherapist. Let's listen in on the first few minutes of their seventh session:

Psychotherapist: Good morning, Barbara; how do you feel today?

Barbara: [snapping back quickly] Good lord, can't you ever say anything but "how do you feel today?" I feel fine, just fine.

P: You sound angry.

B: [in a sarcastically mocking tone] "You sound angry today."

P: [silence]

B: Well I'm not angry, so there.

P: Um, hmm.

B: Well, maybe a little angry.

P: So you feel "a little angry"?

B: Yeah, so I'm angry. Big deal. '

B So what of it? Is there something wrong with being angry?

P: Of course not.

B: You'd be angry too.

P: Oh?

B: My old man threatened to kick me out of the house last night.

P: He threatened you?

B: He said that if I didn't get my act together and shape up, he'd send me packing. God

---

B: They *never went to college. What do* they *know?*
P: *You feel that your parents can't appreciate your problems?*

---

knows where I'd go, but if he pulls that crap on me one more time, I'll show him. I will leave.

P: Would you like to leave?

B: Yes! No! No, I don't really want to. It's just that nobody cares about me around there. They don't know how hard it is trying to work and go to school and everything, ya' know?

P: [nods]

B: *They* never went to college.

What do *they* know? They don't know what it's like.

P: You feel that your parents can't appreciate your problems?

B: Damn right! What do they know? They've never tried to work and go to college at the same time.

P: They just don't know what it's like.

B: Right. Of course it's not really their fault, I suppose. They've never been in this situation. I suppose I could try to explain it to them.

P: You mean that it might be helpful to share with them how you feel about this, that it's hard for you, and maybe they'll understand?

B: Yeah! That's a good idea! I'll do that. At least I'll try. I don't want to just whine and complain all the time, but maybe I can get them to understand what it's like. Boy, that would help—just to have somebody understand and maybe be on my side once in awhile instead of on my case all the time. That's a good idea. Thanks.

This dialogue is no doubt idealized, yet it reflects a number of principles of one approach to psychotherapy that we will examine later in this chapter. We'll return to this interchange when we discuss client-centered therapy.

Why We Care

In our last chapter, we reviewed a rather long list of psychological disorders. We also noted that such disorders are, unfortunately, far from rare experiences. Tens of millions of Americans are afflicted with psychological disturbances, from mild disorders that involve excessive anxiety to devastating disorders of schizophrenia and other psychotic reactions. In this chapter, we look at what can be done to help people suffering from psychological disorders.

The basic notion that such persons *should* be treated humanely is less than 200 years old. The acceptance of active intervention to improve the quality of life of persons suffering from mental disorders is even more recent than that. In many ways, we can claim that the humane treatment of persons with psychological problems is a twentieth-century phenomenon. To begin this chapter we'll take a brief look at the history of treatment for psychological disorders. We care about this history because it provides us with some insight as to why, even today, so many people have strong negative attitudes and beliefs about those with psychological disorders.

The first half of this chapter will be devoted to those types of treatment that generally fall outside the realm of psychology—medical or physical treatments. We'll examine psychosurgery and shock therapies, but will concentrate on the use of drugs and chemicals to control and treat the symptoms of mental illness. The use of drugs in the management of psychological disorders has been hailed as one of the major scientific discoveries of the twentieth century.

In the second half of this chapter we'll consider the psychological treatments of mental disorders known as psychotherapy. We'll examine psychoanalytic (or Freudian) techniques, humanistic techniques, behavioral techniques, cognitive techniques, and group approaches to psychotherapy. We'll also provide some practical advice on choosing a psychotherapist.

A HISTORICAL PERSPECTIVE

The history of the treatment of psychological disorders is not a pleasant one. By today's standards, therapy—in the sense of doing something humane to improve the condition of a person in psychological distress—does not even seem like an appropriate term to describe the way in which most disordered persons were treated in the past.

Mental illness is certainly not a new phenomenon. Even the earliest of written records from the Babylonians, Egyptians, and ancient Hebrews clearly describe a variety of cases that we now recognize as psychological disorders (Murray, 1983). Many of the names, or labels, have changed, of course. By the seventeenth century, words such as *melancholia, delirium, delusion, hallucination,* and *mania* were established as medical terms to describe the insane or demented. How individuals with such disorders were treated followed the prevailing view of what caused the disorder.

The ancient Greeks and Romans believed that people who were depressed, irrational, manic, intellectually retarded, or who experienced hallucinations and delusions had in some way offended the gods. In some cases, individuals were simply viewed as being temporarily out of favor with the gods, and it followed that their condition could be improved through religious ritual and prayer. More severely disturbed patients were seen as being physically possessed by evil spirits. These cases were more difficult, often impossible, to cure. The aim of ancient therapists was to exorcise the evil spirits and demons that had inhabited the mind and soul of the mentally deranged. Such treatment was seldom successful, and many unfortunate people died as a direct result or were killed outright when treatment failed. Treatment was left in the hands of the priests who were, after all, thought to be skilled in the ways and means of spirit manipulation.

There were those in ancient times who had a more reasonable view of psychological disorders (that is, by today's standards). Among them was Hippocrates (460 to 377 B.C.), who believed that mental disorders had physical causes, not spiritual ones. He identified epilepsy as being a disorder of the brain, for example. Some of his views were incorrect (that hysteria is a disorder of the uterus, for instance), but at least he attempted (without much success) to demystify mental illness. The impact of enlightened scientists, such as Hippocrates, was slight and short lived.

The Middle Ages (A.D. 1000 to 1500) was a period in history during which the oppression and persecution of the mentally ill were at their peak. During this period, it was the prevailing view that psychologically disordered people were bad people, under the spell of the devil and evil spirits. These people brought on their own grief, and there was no hope for them, except that they save their immortal souls and confess their evil ways and wickedness.

For hundreds of years, from the fourteenth century well into the eighteenth century, the attitude toward those who were mentally ill continued to be that they were in league with the devil or that they were being punished

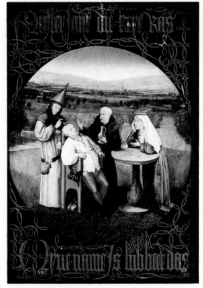

This painting by Hieronymus Bosch depicts one of the measures used on the mentally ill in the Middle Ages. Here, people believing that stones were the cause of this patient's insanity attempt to remove them by boring a hole in his head.

for evil thoughts and deeds. They were seen as witches who could not be cured except through confession and denunciation of their evilness. When such confessions were not forthcoming, the prescribed treatment was torture. If torture failed to evoke a confession, death was the only recourse; often it was death by being burned at the stake.

A large volume, the *Malleus Maleficarum* (The Witches Hammer), was written by two priests, with the blessing of the Pope, in 1478. It described in great detail the symptoms of witches and how witches were to be interrogated so as to ensure a confession. The techniques described in *Malleus* comprise a catalog of the most horrible of tortures. It has been estimated that between the early fourteenth and mid-seventeenth centuries, nearly 200,000 to 500,000 "witches" were put to their death (Ben-Yehuda, 1980). Martin Luther has been quoted as suggesting (in 1540) that a mentally retarded boy be suffocated because he was a captive of the devil and "simply a mass of flesh without a soul" (Tappert, 1967).

When the insane were not tortured or immediately put to death for their strange behaviors and thoughts, they were institutionalized in asylums. The first asylum was probably St. Mary of Bethlehem Hospital in London, given over to "fools" and "lunatics" in 1547. The institution became known as Bedlam (apparently a cockney mispronunciation of Bethlehem). It was a terrible place. Inmates were tortured, poorly fed, or starved to death. To remove the "bad blood" from their systems (thought to be a cause of their melancholy or delirium), some were regularly led to bleeding chambers, where a small incision was made in a vein in the calf of their legs so that their

Associating mental illnesses with witchcraft was an attitude that flourished during the fifteenth and sixteenth centuries. Goya's painting entitled *The Witches Sabbath* reflects the popular preoccupation of the times.

This view of Bedlam is from Hogarth's *Rake's Progress*. In the eighteenth century, it was considered entertaining to visit Bedlam to view the lunatics, as the two ladies of fashion shown here are doing.

blood would ooze into leather buckets. There was no professional staff at Bedlam. The keepers, as they were called, could make some extra money by putting their charges on view for the general public. Going down to see the lunatics of Bedlam became an established entertainment for the nobility. Those inmates who were able were sent into the streets to beg, wearing signs that identified them as "fools of Bedlam."

It would be comforting to think that Bedlam was an exception, an aberration, but it was not. In the eighteenth and nineteenth centuries (and often well into the twentieth century), institutions like Bedlam were commonplace. Philippe Pinel (1745–1826) was a French physician who, in the midst of the French Revolution (on April 25, 1793), was named director of an asylum for the insane in Paris. Here, in Pinel's own words, is the scene he discovered upon taking over (Shipley, 1961):

> *On my entrance to the duties of that hospital, every thing presented to me the appearance of chaos and confusion. Some of my unfortunate patients labored under horrors of a most gloomy and desponding melancholy. Others were furious, and subject to the influence of a perpetual delirium. . . . Symptoms so different, and all comprehended under the general title of insanity. . . . The halls and the passages of the hospital were much confined, so arranged as to render the cold of winter and the heat of summer equally intolerable and injurious. The chambers were exceedingly small and inconvenient. Baths we had none, though I made repeated applications for them; nor had we extensive liberties for walking, gardening or other exercises. So destitute of accommodations, we found it impossible to class our patients according to the varieties and degrees of their respective maladies.*

We know of Pinel today largely because of an act of courage and com-

Philippe Pinel's deep concern for the people living in the inhumane conditions of asylums during the French Revolution is depicted in this painting. Here, he is shown ordering the removal of chains and shackles from hospital inmates.

Benjamin Rush

father of US psychiatry

Dorothea Dix

nurse

Clifford Beers

First father of me

passion. The law of the period required that the inmates in the asylum be chained and confined. On September 2, 1793, Pinel ordered the chains and shackles removed from about 50 of the inmates of his "hospital." He also allowed them to move freely about the institution and its grounds. This humane gesture produced surprising effects: The conditions of the patients, in many cases, improved markedly. Pinel continued to treat those in his care with kindness and respect, demonstrating complete cures for some of them. Unfortunately, we cannot report that Pinel's humane treatment became the norm and spread through France and the rest of the world. It did not, but the tide did begin to turn late in the 1700s. Pinel's unchaining of the insane and his personal belief in moral treatment for the mentally ill can be viewed as the beginning of a very gradual enlightenment concerning mental illness, even though Pinel's successes did not lead to broad, sweeping reforms.

In the United States, three people stand out as pioneers of reform for the treatment of the mentally ill and retarded. The first is Benjamin Rush ① (1745–1813), who is considered to be the founder of American psychiatry, having published the first text on the subject of mental disorders in this country in 1812. Although many of the treatments recommended by Rush strike us as barbaric today (he was a believer in bleeding, for example), his general attitudes were comparatively humane. He was largely responsible for transporting the moral consideration of the mentally ill to America.

The second person we should mention is Dorothea Dix (1802–1887). Dix ② was a nurse. In 1841, she took a position at a women's prison and was appalled at what she saw. Included among the prisoners, and treated no differently, were hundreds of persons who were clearly mentally retarded and/or mentally ill. Despite her slight stature and her own ill health, she entered upon a crusade of singular vigor. She went from state to state campaigning for reform in prisons, mental hospitals, and asylums.

One of the ironic outcomes of Dix's crusade was that many state governments did agree that the mentally ill should not be housed in prisons, and large state-run institutions and asylums were built. Although they began operation in the tradition of moral treatment, they often became no more humane or moral in their treatment than Bedlam had been.

In this brief historical sketch, one other name deserves mention: Clifford ③ Beers. Beers was a graduate of Yale University who was institutionalized in a series of hospitals or asylums. It seems likely that he was suffering from what we now call a mood disorder. Probably in spite of his treatment, rather than because of it, Beers recovered and was released, in itself an unusual occur-

Although Benjamin Rush advocated more humane treatment of the mentally ill, he did retain some of the beliefs and treatments of the time, including "the tranquilizer," a chair he invented to control unruly patients.

rence. He wrote a book about his experience, *A Mind That Found Itself*, in 1908. The book became a bestseller and is often cited as providing the stimulus for a reform that we identify as the mental health movement.

Since the early 1900s, progress in providing help for the mentally ill has been slow and unsteady. World War I and the Depression severely reduced the monies available to support state institutions for mental patients. Within the past 50 years, conditions have improved immeasurably, but there is yet a long way to go. We are still fighting a prejudice against persons suffering from psychological disorders. Perhaps we shouldn't be surprised that even today we can find such prejudices and the fears that arise from them. Our history suggests that until very recently, the prevailing understanding of the psychologically disturbed was that they were bad people, possessed by demons and devils, unable to control their behaviors and thoughts and unable to be cured. The only recourse was to separate the mentally ill from everyone else.

BEFORE YOU GO ON Briefly trace the history of the treatment of persons with psychological disorders.

BIOMEDICAL TREATMENTS OF PSYCHOLOGICAL DISORDERS

As we have seen in our brief review of the history of the treatment of psychological disorders, biological and medical approaches can be traced to ancient times. By definition, treatments that are medical in nature are not those that psychologists use. To perform surgery, administer shock treatments, or prescribe medication requires a medical degree. Psychologists are often involved in biomedical approaches to treatment, however. Psychologists may recommend medical treatment and refer a client or patient to the care of a physician or psychiatrist (a person with a medical degree who specializes in mental disorders). The treatment alternatives that psychologists use, called psychotherapies, will be the subject of the second half of this chapter.

Here we'll review three types of biomedical treatment: psychosurgery, which was quite common just 50 years ago, but is now quite rare; shock treatment, which is used less frequently now than it was 20 years ago, but is far from uncommon; and chemotherapy, the use of psychoactive drugs, which is the newest and one of the most promising developments in the treatment of mental illness.

Psychosurgery

psychosurgery
a surgical procedure designed to affect one's psychological or behavioral reactions

prefrontal lobotomy
a psychosurgical technique in which the prefrontal lobes of the cerebral cortex are severed from lower brain centers

Psychosurgery is the name we give to surgical procedures (usually directed at the brain) designed to affect psychological or behavioral reactions. Although there are other psychosurgical procedures (to treat chronic pain, epilepsy, or depression, for example), in many ways psychosurgery is synonymous with the procedure called a **prefrontal lobotomy,** or simply, lobotomy (Valenstein, 1980, 1986). This surgery severs the major neural connections between the prefrontal lobes (the area at the very front of the cerebral cortex) and lower brain centers.

The technique was first "successfully" performed in 1935 by a Portuguese psychiatrist, Egas Moniz. For developing this procedure, Moniz was awarded the Nobel Prize in 1949. The logic behind the lobotomy was that the frontal lobes of the cortex influence the more basic emotional centers of the brain (the thalamus and the hypothalamus). Severely psychotic patients were thought to have difficulty in coordinating these two parts of the brain. It was further reasoned that if they were separated surgically, the more depressed, agitated, or violent patients could be brought under control.

The operation often appeared to be successful. Used as a measure of last resort, stories of the remarkable changes it produced in chronic mental patients circulated widely. During the 1940s and 1950s, prefrontal lobotomies were performed with regularity. It's difficult to estimate precisely how many lobotomies were performed just within these two decades, but certainly they numbered in the tens of thousands.

Treating severely disturbed, depressed, and schizophrenic patients has always been difficult. Perhaps we shouldn't be surprised that this relatively simple surgical technique was accepted so widely and uncritically at first. The procedure was often done under local anesthetic in the physician's office. An instrument that looks very much like an ice pick was inserted through the eye socket, on the nasal side, and was pushed up into the brain. A few simple movements of the instrument and the job was done—the lobes were severed. Within hours, the patient would be recovered from the procedure.

It was always appreciated that the procedure was an irreversible one. What took longer to realize was that it often carried with it terrible side-effects. In fact, 1 to 4 percent of the patients receiving prefrontal lobotomies died (Carson et al., 1988). Many of those who survived suffered seizures, memory loss, an inability to plan ahead, and a general listlessness and loss of affect. By the late 1950s, psychosurgery had virtually disappeared. Contrary to common belief, it is not an illegal procedure in this country, although the conditions under which it might even be considered are very restrictive. Prefrontal lobotomies are not done anymore for the simple reason that they are no longer needed. There are other means—with fewer side-effects—that can produce similar beneficial results more safely and reliably.

BEFORE YOU GO ON

What is a prefrontal lobotomy?
Why was it ever used, and why is it not used today?

Electroconvulsive Therapy

As gruesome as the procedures of psychosurgery are, many people find the very notion of **electroconvulsive therapy (ECT),** or shock treatments, even more difficult to deal with. This technique, first introduced in 1938, involves passing an electric current (of between 70 and 150 volts) across a tranquilized patient's head for a fraction of a second. As a result, there is a physical seizure, followed by a short loss of consciousness. The whole procedure takes about five minutes, and it is not pleasant to watch. One of the side-effects of ECT is a (rather protective) memory loss of events just preceding the administration of the shock and for the shock itself.

At first, the treatment was devised to help calm agitated schizophrenics, but it soon became clear that its most beneficial results were for those

electroconvulsive therapy (ECT) a treatment (usually for the symptoms of severe depression) in which an electric current passed through a patient's head causes a seizure and loss of consciousness

Long-term memory loss

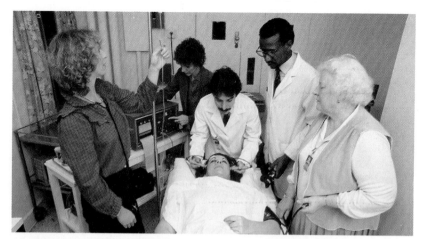
A patient is given electroconvulsive therapy (ECT).

patients suffering from deep depression. It often alleviates the symptoms of depression and, in some cases, has beneficial effects on other psychotic symptoms as well. Virtually all patients (97 percent) receiving ECT give their advised consent to the procedure, and negative side-effects are actually quite rare. For instance, in one study of 99,425 ECT treatments given to 18,627 patients, only two deaths were reported, compared to the death rate for childbirth in the United States which is nearly six times greater (Kramer, 1985). The beneficial effects of ECT are reasonably long-lasting. Many patients remain symptom-free for months. Just why ECT produces the benefits that it does is not fully understood even today.

The poor reputation that ECT has among the general population did not develop without foundation. There *are* horror stories of the negative side effects that can follow abuse of the procedure. It is now recommended that no more than a dozen treatments be given and that these be administered over an extended period of time. There is little doubt that some patients in the past have received hundreds of ECT treatments. In such cases, there has been evidence of brain damage and permanent memory loss.

Even though we do not fully understand how ECT works, and even though it is a treatment that must be used with extreme care, ECT is still very much in practice today. Although the numbers are declining, nearly 100,000 patients receive shock treatments each year, most of them white, middle-and upper-class women (Thompson & Blaine, 1987). Additionally, most ECT patients are far from terrorized by the notion of having an electrical shock delivered to their brain. In one study, 82 percent of the 166 patients surveyed rated ECT as no more upsetting than a visit to the dentist (Sackeim, 1985). With the introduction of psychoactive, antidepressant medications, there is less need to use ECT. Electroconvulsive therapy is generally reserved for (1) patients for whom drug therapies seem ineffective, (2) patients with acute suicidal tendencies (because drugs often take weeks to have their full antidepressant effects), and (3) depressed patients who also suffer from delusions (Kalat, 1984). Some researchers have argued that administering a shock to just one side of the brain (called a *unilateral ECT*) is a safer, yet equally effective procedure with even fewer side effects (Squire & Slater, 1978).

Drug Therapy

As we stated in Chapter 3 in our discussion of consciousness, chemicals that influence psychological functioning have been in use since the beginning of recorded history. Chemicals that have their effect on an individual's cognitions, affect, or behavior are collectively referred to as *psychoactive drugs*. As we have seen, there are many of them, and most are used to artificially produce an altered state of consciousness or awareness. Using drugs effectively to improve the condition of the mentally disordered has been a much more recent development that has been hailed as one of the most significant scientific achievements of the last half of the twentieth century (Snyder, 1984). In this section, we'll examine the three main types of psychoactive drugs used as therapy; the antipsychotic, antidepressant, and antianxiety drugs.

3 types - Psychoactive Drugs

Antipsychotic Drugs.   The first **antipsychotic drug** used in this country was the compound *reserpine*. It is classified as an antipsychotic drug because it does just what its label suggests: it reduces the severity of, and occasionally may even eliminate, psychotic symptoms. As you can imagine, the introduction of the drug in the early 1950s was most welcomed. Unfortunately, reserpine has a number of side-effects that made its use quite dangerous. It does have a calming and settling effect on many severely disturbed patients, but it also lowers blood pressure to dangerous levels. In fact, reserpine (and variants of it), in small doses, is now used to treat chronic high blood pressure.

antipsychotic drugs
chemicals, such as chlorpromazine, that are effective in reducing psychotic symptoms

Treat symptoms Does not provide cure

The real breakthrough in the use of antipsychotic medication came in the mid-1950s with the introduction of a class of drugs known as *phenothiazines*, the first of which was *chlorpromazine*. The major advantage of this drug is that it has all of the benefits of reserpine and virtually none of its side-effects.

← Thorizene

The antipsychotic effects of chlorpromazine were discovered in France in the 1940s. A neurosurgeon, Henri Laborit, was searching for a drug that would calm his patients before surgery. Just before undergoing surgery, patients often feel nervous and anxious. Laborit wanted to help them relax because he knew that if they did, their postsurgery recovery would be improved. A drug company supplied him with chlorpromazine. It worked even better than anyone had expected, and Laborit convinced some of his colleagues to try the drug on their patients, some of whom were suffering from psychological disorders. The experiments met with great success, and by the late 1950s, the drug (with the trade name Thorazine) was widely used both in the United States and in Europe. The drug revolution had begun. With this success in hand, the search for other chemicals that could markedly improve the plight of the mentally ill began in earnest.

Chlorpromazine is not the only antipsychotic drug that is currently being used with success. Most of the other commonly used antipsychotic medications are similar derivatives of the phenothiazines, however. One exception is *lithium,* or lithium salts such as lithium carbonate. Regulating the precise dosage is very difficult, and its side-effects are many and often

Modern psychopharmacology has helped many individuals who would otherwise require hospitalization to live and function in the community. It has also led to earlier discharge for patients who do require hospitalization and has made restraints and locked wards almost nonexistent.

Biomedical Treatments of Psychological Disorders   **441**

quite severe. Nonetheless, lithium salts have been found to be very effective in treating some patients with bipolar mood disorders. The drug occasionally alleviates depression, but seems much more useful in controlling the manic cycle of bipolar disorders. There are those individuals for whom the drug has no beneficial effect, and its prolonged use can lead to convulsions, kidney failure, and other serious reactions.

The effects of the antipsychotic drugs are remarkable and impressive, and they have revolutionized the care of psychotic patients. Nonetheless, they should not be considered as an ultimate solution for disorders such as schizophrenia and the other psychoses. For one thing, there are some patients for whom the drugs either have no effect or have harmful effects. With high dosages or prolonged use, a variety of side-effects emerge that are unpleasant at best: dry mouth and throat, sore muscles and joints, and involuntary muscle tremors are but a few. Although the most effective of the antipsychotic drugs clearly control symptoms, the question is: are they in any sense curing the disorder. Symptom-free patients, who are often released from institutional care to the outside world, soon stop using their medication only to find that their psychotic symptoms return.

BEFORE YOU GO ON   **What are antipsychotic drugs, and what are their effects?**

antidepressant drugs
chemicals, such as MAO inhibitors and tricyclics, that reduce and/or eliminate the symptoms of depression

Antidepressant Drugs.   **Antidepressant drugs** are those that elevate the mood of persons who are feeling depressed. The first effective antidepressant was *iproniazid,* which was originally used in the treatment of tuberculosis. One of the side-effects of the drug was that it made tubercular patients feel cheerful and happy. When tested on depressed patients, it was found to have the same effect. Unfortunately, it was soon discovered that iproniazid causes irreversible liver damage, and its use as an antidepressant was stopped.

The antidepressant medications that are used today are of two major types: *MAO inhibitors* (MAO, or monoamine oxidase, is a chemical found in the brain that reduces levels of two neurotransmitters; MAO *inhibitors* thus increase levels of these neurotransmitters) and *tricyclics.* In fact, there is a wide variety of antidepressant medication presently available, and there are many other chemical compounds under research review. Although no one antidepressant is universally any better than any other, each seems to be particularly effective for certain kinds of individuals (Cole, 1988). That is, an antidepressant drug that has no effect for one person may produce terrible side-effects in another person and yet have remarkably beneficial effects for a third person.

These drugs would be of little use for you if, for example, you were depressed about doing badly on a history exam. They generally require weeks to have their maximum effect and need to be taken on a long-term basis to prevent a recurrence of the depression. Although they elevate the mood of many truly depressed individuals, they have virtually no effect at all on people who are not depressed. That is, they do not produce a euphoric high in people who are already in a pretty good mood.

Of the two types of antidepressants, the tricyclic types (trade names Elavil or Tofranil, for example) are more commonly used. As you might have guessed, the tricyclic drugs do produce unfortunate side-effects in some patients, including intellectual confusion, increased perspiration, and weight gain. Some tricyclics have been implicated as a cause of heart disease. A major problem with the MAO inhibitor drugs is that they require adherence to a strict diet and carefully monitored dosages to have their best effect. They also produce a wide range of more serious side-effects, such as dizziness, sexual impotence, elevated blood pressure, and liver damage to name just a few. Unlike the antipsychotic drugs, however, there is evidence that when these drugs are effective, they may actually bring about long-term cures rather than symptom suppression. In other words, the changes in mood caused by the drugs may outlast the drug itself. The hope and plan is, in fact, to gradually reduce the dosage of the drug over time. For those persons with mood disorders who do not respond to the medications presently available, many other varieties are now being tested, and for such patients, electroconvulsive therapy may be indicated.

What are the two types of antidepressant drugs, and what do they do?

BEFORE YOU GO ON

Antianxiety Drugs.   **Antianxiety drugs,** (or tranquilizers) help to reduce the felt aspect of anxiety. They are the most commonly prescribed of all drugs. One type of antianxiety drug, the *meprobamates* (trade names Miltown or Equanil, for example), is basically a muscle relaxant. When muscular tension is reduced, the patient often reports feeling calm and at ease.

The other major variety of antianxiety drug is the group of *benzodiazepines* (trade names Librium, Valium, and many others). These drugs act on the central nervous system. The impact of these drugs is significant. They help very anxious people feel better. At first, the only side-effects appear to be a slight drowsiness, blurred vision, and a slight impairment of muscle coordination. Unfortunately, the tranquilizing effects of the drugs are not longlasting. Patients can easily fall into a pattern of relying on the drugs to alleviate even the slightest of fears and worries. Soon a dependency and addiction can develop from which withdrawal can be painful. When too much antianxiety medication is taken (an overdose), death may result, and the fact that benzodiazepines and alcohol don't mix has been well-documented. Valium plus alcohol can lead to death.

antianxiety drugs ③
chemicals, such as the meprobamates and benzodiazepines, that alleviate the symptoms of anxiety

✳ Control Symptons — not a cure

Drug treatment
psychotherapy + drugs

What are the common antianxiety drugs, and what are the dangers inherent in their use?

BEFORE YOU GO ON

In summary, we can say that there is great hope that biochemical techniques can be found to suppress (if not eliminate) many severe symptoms associated with psychological disorders. At the moment, however, we should probably remain somewhat cautious. Remember that only 35 years ago it was widely held that prefrontal lobotomies and other forms of psychosurgery would provide the ultimate long-term answer to the question of how to treat psychologically and emotionally disturbed patients. However, scientists are learning more about the chemistry of the nervous system and the delicate balance between brain and behavior. If we remain ever mindful of the harsh and inhumane treatment of the mentally ill that characterized our not-too-distant past, we can now be more cautiously optimistic than ever before.

PSYCHOTHERAPY

psychotherapy
the treatment of mental disorders through psychological means, effecting change in cognitions, affect, and/or behavior

Next, we turn our attention to psychological approaches to treating mental disorders. These approaches are known as **psychotherapy** and are "designed to influence the patient's behavior by psychological means, that is, they seek to persuade the patient to think, feel, or act differently" (Strupp, 1986, p. 128). Because there are so many different varieties of it—literally hundreds—we'll examine only the major forms of psychotherapy.

Different types of therapy often have different goals: some attempt to help the individual gain insight about the true nature of his or her disorder and its underlying cause or causes; some try to help a person develop a stronger sense of self-identity and self-esteem; yet others focus on bringing about lasting and measurable changes in overt behavior. Some forms of psychotherapy are clearly better suited for some problems than they are for others.

The number of people seeking psychotherapy is increasing. Just 30 years ago, only 13 percent of the population sought any kind of psychotherapy in their lifetimes (Meredith, 1986). Now we find that almost 30 percent will have some experience in psychotherapy in their lifetimes. In 1987 alone, "15 million of us will make roughly 120 million visits to mental health professionals—nearly twice as many visits as to internists" (Hunt, 1987, p. 28).

We'll divide our discussion of the major goals and methods of psychotherapy into four main parts: psychoanalytic (or Freudian) techniques, humanistic techniques, behavioral techniques, and cognitive techniques. We'll also examine group approaches to psychotherapy. Finally we'll discuss the different types of professionals who offer psychotherapy and provide some practical advice on choosing a psychotherapist.

Psychoanalytic Techniques

psychoanalysis
the form of psychotherapy associated with Freud, aimed at helping the patient gain insight into unconscious conflicts

We begin our review of the psychotherapies with the procedure called **psychoanalysis.** Psychoanalysis began with Sigmund Freud toward the end of the nineteenth century. Psychoanalysis did not really evolve from Freudian personality theory (see Chapter 8). If anything, the reverse is true. Freud was a therapist first, a personality theorist second. But his technique of therapy and theory of personality sprang forth from the same mind, and they are very much interrelated.

Psychoanalysis is based on a number of assumptions, most of them having to do with the nature of conflict and the unconscious mind. For Freud, one's life is often a struggle to resolve conflicts between naturally opposing forces: instincts for life and instincts for death. The biological, sexual, and aggressive strivings of the id are often in conflict with the superego, which is associated with guilt and overcautiousness. The strivings of the id are also often in conflict with the rational, reality-based ego, which is also called upon to mediate between the id and the superego. Anxiety-producing conflicts that go unresolved are repressed; they are forced out of awareness into the unconscious levels of the mind. Conflicts and anxiety-producing traumas of childhood can be expected to produce symptoms of psychological disturbance later on in life.

According to Freud, the way to truly rid one's self of anxiety is to enter the unconscious, identify the nature of the repressed, anxiety-producing

To help his patients relax, Freud had them lie on this couch while he sat out of view.

conflict, and resolve it as best as possible. The first step is to gain insight into the nature of one's problems, to understand their true nature; only then can problem solving begin. These are the goals of Freudian psychoanalysis: insight and resolution of repressed conflict.

Sigmund Freud died in 1939, but his model for psychotherapy certainly did not die with him. It has been modified (as Freud himself modified it over the years), but it still remains true to the basic thrust of Freudian psychoanalysis. Before we consider how it has changed, let's examine Freudian analysis as Freud practiced it.

Freudian Psychoanalysis. Psychoanalysis with Sigmund Freud was a time-consuming (often five days per week for six to ten years!), often tedious process of self-examination and introspection. Aided by the careful interpretation of the analyst and following the therapist's every suggestion, the patient was to search his or her unconscious mind for inner sources of conflict and stress, which probably were established in childhood. Once identified, the patient's conflicts could then be resolved. A number of procedures and processes were used in this search for repressed conflicts. we'll discuss some of the most important ones in this section.

In 1881, Freud graduated from the University of Vienna Medical School (he had been a student there since 1873). From the start, he was interested in the treatment of what were then called nervous disorders. He went to France to study the technique of hypnosis, which many were claiming to be a worthwhile treatment for many mental disorders. Freud wasn't totally convinced, but when he returned to Vienna, he and a colleague, Josef Breuer, tried hypnosis as a means of treating neurotic disorders, conversion reaction hysteria in particular. They both became convinced that hypnosis itself was of little benefit in treating nervous disorders. What mattered more, they believed, was to have the patient talk—talk about anything and everything. The therapist might occasionally try to guide the talking, but talking by itself seemed therapeutic.

Soon, the method of **free association** became a central procedure of psychoanalysis. Patients were told to say out loud whatever came into their minds. Sometimes the analyst would provide a stimulus word to get a chain of freely flowing associations going. To truly free associate the way Freud would have wanted you to is not an easy task. It often took many sessions for patients to learn the technique. Patients were not to edit their associations. They were to say *whatever* they thought of, and that is not always an easy thing to do. Many people are uncomfortable (at least initially) sharing their private, innermost thoughts and desires with anyone, much less a stranger. Here is where the "Freudian couch" came in. To help his patients relax, he would have them lie down, be comfortable, and avoid eye contact with the analyst. The job of the analyst through all this was to try to interpret the apparently free-flowing and random verbal responses, always looking for expressions of unconscious desires and conflicts.

During the course of talking to a patient, and particularly during periods of free association, the psychoanalyst listens very carefully to what the patient is saying. The analyst also listens to what the patient is *not* saying. Freud believed that **resistance**—the inability or unwillingness to freely discuss some aspect of one's life—was a significant process in analysis. Resistance can show itself in many ways, from simply avoiding the mention of

free association
the procedure in psychoanalysis in which the patient is to express whatever comes to mind without editing responses

resistance
in psychoanalysis, the inability or unwillingness to freely discuss some aspect of one's life

some topic, to joking about small matters as being inconsequential, to disrupting a session when a particular topic comes up for discussion, to missing appointments altogether. The logic here is fairly straightforward. Let's say, for example, that over the last six months you have talked freely about a wide variety of things, including your early childhood memories and all the members of your family—all, that is, except your older brother. Your analyst, noting this possible resistance, suggests that during your next visit, she would like to hear more about your older brother. Then, for the first time since analysis began, you miss your next appointment. You come to the following appointment, but you're 10 minutes late. Your analyst may now suspect that there is some possible problem in your relationship with your older brother. Of course, no problem may exist, but for analysis to be successful, resistances need to be investigated and broken down.

We should not be at all surprised to find that analyzing a patient's dreams is an important part of psychoanalysis. Freud referred to dreams as the "royal road" to the unconscious mind. Freud would often have to train his patients to carefully recall and record their dreams. Then he would have them share the content of their dreams with him. Freud analyzed dreams at two levels: manifest content—the dream as recalled and reported by the patient—and latent content—the dream as a symbolic representation of the contents of the unconscious. The job for the analyst, Freud argued, was to interpret dreams in terms of whatever insights and information they could provide about the true nature of the patient's unconscious mind.

One of the most controversial aspects of Freudian psychoanalysis is his concept of **transference.** Transference occurs when the patient unconsciously comes to view and feel about the analyst in much the same way he or she feels about some other important person in his or her life, usually a parent. As therapy continues over a long period of time, the relationship between analyst and patient does become a complex and often emotional one. If feelings that were once directed toward someone else of significance are now directed toward the analyst, they are more accessible, more easily observed by the analyst, and more readily interpreted and dealt with. Therapists have to guard against doing the same thing themselves—letting their own feelings and past experiences interfere with their neutral and objective interaction with their patients. Failing to do so is called *countertransference*.

— controversial

transference
in psychoanalysis, the situation in which the patient comes to feel about the analyst in the same way he or she once felt about some other important person

BEFORE YOU GO ON Describe the essential nature of Freudian psychoanalysis, defining free association, resistance, dream interpretation, and transference.

Post-Freudian Psychoanalysis.   Early in the twentieth century, Freudian psychoanalysis was the only form of psychotherapy. In the 1940s and 1950s, it was *the* psychotherapy of choice. "Psychoanalytic theory was the dominant force in psychiatry in the postwar period and was embraced by a large number of clinical psychologists. To a certain extent, and for all practical purposes, there was no rival orientation" (Garfield, 1981, p. 176). Recently, psychoanalysis has become a much less common form of psychotherapy, and strict, Freudian-style psychoanalysis is getting very rare indeed. We will see how the Freudian notion of therapy has been changed. But first we should note what hasn't changed.

To still qualify as a psychoanalytic approach, one must hold that the basic aim of therapy is the uncovering of deep-seated, unconscious conflict and that childhood experiences can influence psychological adjustment in adolescence and adulthood. This general statement is about all that unites psychoanalytic approaches to therapy today.

Probably the most significant change since Freud's time is the concern for shortening the length of analysis (for example, Strupp & Binder, 1984). Today we talk about time-limited and short-form analysis, terms that Freud would not have approved of. Today's analyst will also take a more active, directive role than did Freud. The couch as a requirement is usually gone now; the comfort of the patient is what matters, and some patients feel more comfortable pacing or sitting than they do lying on a couch. Another major shift in emphasis is that modern psychoanalysts, although not insensitive to the effects of early childhood experiences, tend to spend more time exploring the present, the here and now.

How is psychoanalysis different today from when it was practiced by Freud?   **BEFORE YOU GO ON**

Evaluating Psychoanalysis.   Although we need to credit psychoanalysis for being the first, and most lasting, psychotherapeutic technique, and although much of the procedure has an undeniable appeal, it is certainly fair to say that the critics have not been kind to psychoanalysis. Some of the arguments brought against psychoanalysis are more telling than others.

Even with the inherent difficulties of doing research on the outcomes of therapy, one might conclude that psychoanalysis has not fared well at all. One of the major blows to psychoanalysis came from Hans Eysenck in 1952, who, after reviewing much of the available research, claimed that there was no evidence that persons treated with psychoanalysis end up any better than persons not treated at all. Many psychoanalysts (and others) yelled foul at Eysenck's evaluation, but a more recent review by Erwin (1980) came to the same conclusion. Joseph Wolpe soon joined in the criticism when he made the following statements about psychoanalysis: "The clinical effectiveness of psychoanalytic therapy has never been established. . . . In actuality, not a single one of the theory's main propositions has ever been supported by scientifically acceptable evidence. . . . But this too is brushed aside. That this happens is a tribute to the expository brilliance with which Freud presented his theories. His writing weaves a magic web from which few can extricate themselves once enmeshed" (Wolpe, 1981, pp. 159–160). The picture is probably not all this bleak nor this one-sided. Some well-controlled studies have shown that psychoanalysis can be an effective form of therapy (Smith et al., 1980). At the very least, we may conclude that claims made against the effectiveness of psychoanalysis are arguable.

On a practical level, we may argue that even with today's briefer approaches, psychoanalysis is a time-consuming and expensive process. When you reflect on what is required in analysis, it is also very obvious that it will be inappropriate for many. It won't be effective for severely disturbed, psychotic patients. It isn't likely to be effective for less intelligent and less insightful or introspective patients.

Humanistic Techniques

There are many different brands of humanistic psychotherapy and their closely allied cousins, the *existential therapies*. What they all have in common is a concern for self-examination and for personal growth and development. The goal of these therapies is not so much to uncover any deep-seated conflicts, but to foster psychological growth, to help one be the best that one can be. Based on the notion that we can all take charge of ourselves and our futures and grow and change, therapy is devised to assist us with that process.

Client-centered Therapy.   Sometimes called Rogerian therapy after its founder, Carl Rogers, **client-centered therapy** is, perhaps, the therapy that best typifies the humanistic approach. As its name suggests, the client is the center of the client-therapist interaction. (Rogers never used the term "patient," and before his death in 1987 began using the term person-centered rather than client-centered to describe his approach to therapy.) For Rogers, therapy provides an opportunity for a person to engage in self-discovery.

What are the characteristics of client-centered therapy? Again, there are many variants, but the following ideas generally characterize a client-centered approach. The focus is on the present, not the past or one's childhood. The focus is on one's feelings or affect, not beliefs or cognitions; that is, you are more likely to hear, "How do you feel about that?" than "What do you think about that?" The therapist will attempt to reflect or mirror—not interpret—how a client is feeling (using statements such as, "You seem angry about that." or "Does that make you feel sad?"). It should be pointed out that assessing the true nature of a client's feelings is not necessarily easy to do. To do so accurately requires that the therapist be an active listener and **empathic,** or able to understand and share the essence of another's feelings. Throughout each session, the therapist will express what is called *unconditional positive regard*. This is the expression of being accepting and noncritical. "I will not be critical." "If that is the way you feel, that is the way you feel." "Anything you say in here is okay." The exchange between client and therapist presented at the beginning of this chapter, is rather typical.

A Rogerian therapist we know was once elated about how well a session with an undergraduate student had gone. When asked why he thought it had gone so well, he said that when the student entered his office and sat down, he asked her how she was feeling and what she'd like to talk about. She said that she didn't want to talk about anything. So the therapist said, "Okay, if you don't want to talk, that's okay too. If you change your mind, I'm right here, and I'm willing to listen." For the next 50 minutes, the two of them sat there, neither doing or saying anything. At the end of their hour, the therapist said, "Well, our time's up. I'll see you next week." The student replied, "Right, see you then." It was the therapist's point of view that the value of this (very quiet) session was that his client had learned something. She had learned that if she didn't want to talk about anything, she didn't have to. That sort of acceptance may then lead her to the realization that if she *did* want to talk about anything (no matter what), that would be okay too.

Evaluating Humanistic Therapies.   Client-centered, nondirective approaches to therapy were at their peak of popularity in the 1960s. This was a period of individualization, of people "doing their own thing," and any

client-centered therapy
the humanistic psychotherapy associated with Rogers, aimed at helping the client grow and change from within

empathic
able to understand and share the essence of another's feelings; to view from another's perspective

Unconditional
Positive
Regard

technique that fostered positive regard and personal growth fit the times very well. As was the case with Freudian analysis, few psychotherapists presently practice a pure form of client-centered therapy. The client/person is still at the center of attention, but newer forms of humanistic therapy attempt to hasten the process by allowing the therapist to become more actively involved.

Also, like psychoanalysis, humanistic therapies, client-centered in particular, will not be effective for many individuals. The technique works best for mild adjustment problems (it will hardly be reasonable to try it with psychotic patients) and for intelligent, sensitive, introspective people.

One problem of evaluating these therapies is that the criteria for success are particularly difficult to measure. How does one manage to get an adequate, reliable picture of someone else's personal growth or ego-strength enhancement? How do we know if therapy has helped someone to be the best they can be? We must usually take the client's word for the quality of changes that have taken place, and there are obvious problems with doing that (for example, having invested considerable time and effort in "becoming," it might be difficult to admit that nothing much happened, even if that were the case).

What are the essential characteristics of client-centered therapy?

BEFORE YOU GO ON

Behavioral Techniques

In a literal sense, there is no one **behavior therapy.** Behavior therapy is more a collection of many specific techniques. What unites these techniques is that they are "methods of psychotherapeutic change founded on principles of learning established in the psychological laboratory" (Wolpe, 1981, p. 159). There are many different principles of learning, and there are many types of psychological disorder to which such methods and principles might be applied. In this section, we will list some of the more prominent applications that have become part of behavior therapy.

behavior therapy
techniques of psychotherapy founded on principles of learning established in the psychological laboratory

Systematic Desensitization.   **Systematic desensitization**—The application of classical conditioning procedures to alleviate extreme feelings of anxiety—is one of the first applications of learning principles to have met with success, and it has experienced lasting acceptance. It was formally introduced by Joseph Wolpe in the late 1950s (Wolpe, 1958), although others had used similar procedures earlier. The procedure is designed to alleviate extreme anxieties, particularly of the sort we find in phobic disorders.

In its standard form, there are three stages involved in systematic desensitization. The first thing the therapist does is instruct the subject to relax totally. There are many ways to go about such training. Some procedures use hypnosis, but most simply have the subject relax one foot, then both feet, then one leg, then both legs, and so on, until the entire body is relaxed—a procedure called *progressive relaxation*. No matter what method is used, this phase generally doesn't take very long, and after a few hours of training at the most, the subject learns how to enter a relaxed state.

The second step is to construct an anxiety hierarchy—a list of stimuli that gradually decrease in their ability to evoke anxiety. The most feared, most anxiety-producing stimulus (the object of the phobia, for example) is

systematic desensitization
the application of classical conditioning procedures to alleviate extreme anxiety in which anxiety-producing stimuli are presented while the subject is in a relaxed state

Joseph Wolpe is shown here conducting systematic desensitization therapy to reduce a client's anxiety. The client, in a relaxed state, is told to vividly imagine the weakest anxiety on her list. If she feels anxious, she in instructed to stop and relax again.

placed at the top of the list. Each item that follows evokes less and less anxiety, until, at the bottom of the list, we find a stimulus that evokes no anxiety at all.

Now treatment is ready to begin. The subject is told to relax completely and think about the item lowest on the anxiety hierarchy. The subject is then instructed to think about the next highest stimulus, and the next, and so on, all the while remaining as relaxed as possible. As progress is made up the list, toward the most anxiety-producing stimulus at the top, the therapist constantly monitors the subject's tension/relaxation level. When anxiety seems to be overcoming relaxation, the subject is told to stop thinking about that item on the hierarchy and to think about an item lower on the list.

The logic here is obvious. A person cannot be relaxed and anxious at the same time—they are incompatible responses. Thus, if we pair a stimulus with relaxation, through classical conditioning it will come to produce a sense of calm, not the incompatible response of tension and anxiety. For most people, the technique works. It works best for those fears or anxieties that are specific, that are associated with easily identifiable, specific environmental stimuli; it works least well for a diffuse, generalized fear (for which hierarchies are difficult to generate).

BEFORE YOU GO ON

Describe the three essential steps of systematic desensitization.

flooding
a technique of behavior therapy in which a subject is confronted with the object of his or her phobic fear while accompanied by the therapist

Flooding and Implosive Therapy.   **Flooding** is another procedure that is aimed at eliminating fears or anxieties based on specific stimuli. Bootzin and Acocella describe flooding as "a cold-turkey extinction therapy" (1984, p. 505). Flooding is referred to as an *in vivo,* or in real life, procedure. In this approach, the subject, accompanied by the therapist, is actually placed in his or her most fear-arousing situation and is prohibited from escaping. For example, someone afraid of heights would be taken to the top of a very tall building or to a very high bridge. Someone afraid of water would be taken out on a large lake or to a nearby swimming pool. There, with the therapist close at hand providing support and encouragement, the subject faces his or her most feared situation, survives (although the session may be terrifying for some), and comes to learn that the fear is irrational.

implosive therapy
a behavior therapy in which one imagines one's worst fears, experiencing extreme anxiety in the safe surroundings of the therapist's office

Implosive therapy is based on the same premise, but involves the use of imagination rather than real-life situations. In implosive therapy, you do not slowly work your way up or down any anxiety hierarchy. You are forced to come to imagine your worst fears, all at once, here and now. The therapist does not try to get the subject to relax. On the contrary, the idea is to experience the full force of anxiety while in the ultimately safe surroundings of the therapist's office. Repeated trials of imagined fears and experienced anxiety paired with the safety and security of the office soon lead to the extinction of the maladaptive fear response.

Although these two techniques do sound somewhat bizarre, and they are definitely not for everyone (some therapists have difficulty dealing with such focused anxiety), they are demonstrably effective and usually require less time than does systematic desensitization.

BEFORE YOU GO ON

Compare and contrast flooding and implosive therapy with systematic desensitization.

Aversion Therapy.   You should recognize **aversion therapy** as another form of conditioning applied to a psychological problem. In aversion therapy, a stimulus that produces a pleasant response is paired with an aversive, painful, unpleasant stimulus until the stimulus becomes unpleasant. For example, every time you put a cigarette in your mouth, a therapist delivers a painful shock to your lip. Every time you take a drink of alcohol a drug given to you previously makes you get violently sick to your stomach. Every time a child molester is shown a slide of a young child, he is shocked.

Now none of these techniques sounds like the sort of thing that anyone would agree to voluntarily. Many people do, however. They volunteer for such treatments for two reasons: (1) aversion therapy is very effective at suppressing a specific behavior, at least for a while, and (2) it is seen as the lesser of two evils—shocks and nausea-producing drugs are not much fun, but subjects see the continuation of their inappropriate behaviors as even more dangerous in the long run.

It is probably aversion therapy more than any other technique that has given behavior therapy a bad reputation among the general public, which often equates behavior therapy with cruel and unusual punishment and mind control. There are a couple of things that we need to recognize here. One is that aversion therapy—in any form—is not commonly practiced. A second reality is that, at best, it tends to suppress certain behaviors for a relatively short time. During that time other techniques may be used in an attempt to bring about a more lasting change in behavior. That is, the techniques of aversion therapy are seldom effective when used alone; they are generally used in conjunction with some other form(s) of therapy.

What is aversion therapy?

Contingency Management and Contingency Contracting. As their names suggest, contingency management and contingency contracting borrow heavily from the learning principles of operant conditioning. The basic idea, of course, is to have the individual come to appreciate the consequences of his or her behaviors. Appropriate behaviors lead to rewards and opportunities to do valued things; inappropriate behaviors lead to aversive stimulation and fewer opportunities.

In many cases, these basic procedures work very well. Their total effectiveness is, as operant conditioning would predict, a function of the extent to which the therapist has control over the situation. If the therapist can control rewards and punishments, which is called **contingency management,** he or she stands a good chance of modifying behavior. As a therapist, you modify behavior by managing the contingencies. *If* a patient (a severely disturbed, hospitalized schizophrenic, for example) engages in the appropriate response (leaving her room to go to dinner), *then* the patient will get something she really wants (an after-dinner cigarette).

Contingency contracting amounts to establishing a token economy of secondary reinforcers. What that means is that the patient is first taught that some token—which may be a checker, a poker chip, a bingo marker, or just a checkmark on a pad—can be saved. When enough tokens are accumulated, they can be cashed in for something of value to the patient. With contracting, the specific token of specific value for a specific behavior is spelled out ahead of time. Because control over the environment of the patient/

aversion therapy ④
a technique of behavior therapy in which an aversive stimulus, such as a shock, is paired with an undesired behavior

Aversion therapy, though not a commonly used technique, is one way to help smokers stop smoking. For a series of sessions, shocks are administered to the smoker. Eventually smoking becomes less desirable and the person will quit his or her habit—at least for a short while.

BEFORE YOU GO ON

Effective in Institutions—

contingency management ⑤
bringing about changes in one's behaviors by controlling rewards and punishers

And Young Children

contingency contracting ⑥
establishing a token economy of secondary reinforcers to reward appropriate behaviors

learner is most complete in such circumstances, this technique is particularly effective in institutions and with young children.

Such a system might work as follows. Mickie's parents have been having trouble getting babysitters for Mickie, who is a real terror of considerable reputation in the neighborhood. Mom and Dad make a deal, a signed contract with Mickie. If he is very good for the sitter, he gets five marbles; if he is bad, he gets none. When Mickie has earned 25 marbles (or stamps, or poker chips, or marks on a record sheet), he can "cash them in" for a toy of his choice. If Mickie's behavior with babysitters improves (and it should), then the marbles are acting as reinforcers, but no doubt only because Mickie has learned the economy for which the marbles are tokens.

Such schemes are often remarkably effective. Perhaps because of their effectiveness, these techniques are offensive to some students. "You're only bribing the child to behave," they claim. There are two counterarguments to this claim. First, bribery is a term that should be reserved for those occasions when someone is reinforced (paid off) for doing something wrong, illegal, or inappropriate, and behaving with babysitters hardly seems inappropriate. Second, our hope is that sooner or later Mickie will come to appreciate the consequences of his appropriate behaviors with babysitters. That is, he will come to learn that behaving himself with babysitters leads to other rewards, such as praise, being allowed to stay up a little later than usual, and so on. In time, appropriate behaviors in the presence of babysitters should become self-sustaining, and the marbles (or tokens) will no longer be necessary.

Modeling.   We have already come to appreciate that learning cannot always be explained readily in terms of classical or operant conditioning. It should be no surprise that some behavior therapy uses learning principles other than those of simple conditioning. **Modeling,** a term introduced by Albert Bandura (1977), involves the acquisition of a new, appropriate response through the imitation of a model. As we saw in Chapter 4, modeling can be an effective means of learning.

In a therapeutic situation, modeling often amounts to having (or allowing) patients to watch someone else perform a certain appropriate behavior, perhaps earning a reward for it (called vicarious reinforcement, you'll recall). Some phobias, particularly those in children, can often be overcome through modeling. A child who is afraid of dogs, for example, will profit from watching another child (which would be more effective than using an adult)

modeling
the acquisition of new responses through the imitation of another who responds appropriately

Bandura uses modeling to help people overcome phobias. By watching other people handle snakes without fear, people can overcome their fears and handle the snakes themselves.

playing with a dog. Assertiveness training involves helping individuals stand up for their rights and come to the realization that their feelings and opinions matter and should be expressed. Such training involves many processes (including direct instruction, group discussions, role-playing, and contingency management) and often relies on modeling to help someone learn appropriate ways to express how they feel and what they think in social situations.

Briefly summarize contingency management, contingency contracting, and modeling as means of psychotherapy.

BEFORE YOU GO ON

Evaluating Behavior Therapy. The most commonly voiced criticism of behavior therapy is that it tends to focus only on the individual's maladaptive behavior and ignores inner matters such as early childhood experiences, subjective feelings, self-esteem, motivational conflict, and personal growth. The behavior therapist claims that such criticisms are unfair on two grounds: (1) Behavior therapists *do* concern themselves with inner states of the individual. If there were not some inner distress, there would be little reason to engage in therapy of any kind. "It is the subjective problem, the complaint, that drives the neurotic patient to seek treatment, no matter of what kind" (Wolpe, 1981, p. 162). (2) Although such matters of deep-seated conflict resolution and personal growth and development are noble aims, there is no scientifically reasonable way to assess progress or achieve a cure using such concepts. The only reasonable alternative is to focus on behaviors and behavior change.

Although there are few quality research reports that behavior therapies are in any general way superior to other forms of psychotherapy, they are certainly every bit as effective in the short- and long-term. Thus, the advantage for the behavior therapies is that they tend to take much less time and, hence, are less expensive than many alternative treatment means.

Cognitive Techniques

Psychotherapists who use cognitive techniques do not deny the importance of a person's feelings or behaviors (in fact, these therapies are often called *cognitive-behavioral*). Rather, they believe that what matters most in the therapeutic session is the subject's set of thoughts, perceptions, attitudes, and beliefs about himself or herself and the environment. The principle here is that to change how one feels and acts, therapy should first be directed at changing how one thinks. As we have seen with other approaches to psychotherapy, there is not just one type of cognitive-behavioral therapy; there are many. We'll examine two: rational-emotive therapy and cognitive restructuring therapy.

Rational-emotive Therapy. Associated with Albert Ellis (1970), **rational-emotive therapy (RET)** has the basic premise that psychological problems arise when a person tries to interpret (a cognitive activity) what happens in the world on the basis of irrational beliefs. Ellis puts it this way, "Rational-emotive therapy (RET) hypothesizes that people largely disturb themselves by thinking in a self-defeating, illogical, and unrealistic manner—especially by escalating their natural preferences and desires into

rational-emotive therapy (RET)
a form of cognitive therapy associated with Ellis, aimed at changing the subject's irrational beliefs or maladaptive cognitions

FIGURE 10.1
Some of the irrational beliefs that lead to maladjustment and disorder. The more rational alternative to these beliefs should be obvious.
(From Ellis, 1970, 1987)

1. One should be loved by everyone for everything one does.
2. Because I strongly desire to perform important tasks competently and successfully, I absolutely must perform them well at all times.
3. Because I strongly desire to be approved by people I find significant, I absolutely must always have their approval.
4. Certain acts are wicked and people who perform them should be severely punished no matter what.
5. It is horrible when things are not the way we want them to be.
6. It is better to avoid life's problems if possible, than to face them.
7. One needs something stronger or more powerful than oneself to rely on.
8. One must have perfect and certain self-control.
9. Because I very strongly desire people to treat me considerably and fairly, they must absolutely do so.
10. Because something once affected one's life, it will always affect it.

Albert Ellis

absolutistic, dogmatic musts and commands on themselves, others, and their environmental conditions" (1987, p. 364). In other words, disturbed behaviors and feelings arise from maladaptive cognitions, which usually are simply unrealistic beliefs about one's self and one's environment.

When compared to client-centered techniques, RET is quite directive. The therapist takes an active role in interpreting the reality or the irrationality of a client's system of beliefs and encourages active change. Therapists often act as role models and make homework assignments for clients that help them bring their expectations and perceptions in line with reality.

To give a very simplified example, refer back to the dialogue between Barbara and her client-centered therapist at the beginning of the chapter. A cognitive therapist might see a number of irrational beliefs operating in this scene, including two that Ellis (1970) claims are very common ones: (1) a person should always be loved for everything they do, and (2) it's better to avoid problems than to face them. These, claims Ellis, are exactly the sort of cognitions that many people hold and that create psychological difficulties (a few others are listed in Figure 10.1). Rather than waiting for self-discovery, which might never come, a cognitive therapist would point out to Barbara that the fact that her parents never went to college and don't understand what it is like to work and go to school at the same time is *their* problem, not hers. Rather than avoiding problems that arise from her parents' lack of appreciation, she needs to either set them straight (trying to do so—pleasantly, of course—might constitute a homework assignment for Barbara) or move out (there are a number of other possibilities, of course).

Cognitive Restructuring Therapy. Along the same lines as rational-emotive therapy is **cognitive restructuring therapy,** as proposed by Aaron Beck (1976). Although the basic ideas and goals are similar, restructuring therapy is much less confrontational and direct than RET.

Beck's assumption is that a great deal of psychological distress stems from a few simple, but misguided beliefs (cognitions, again). According to

cognitive restructuring therapy
a form of cognitive therapy, associated with Beck, in which patients are led to overcome negative self-images and pessimistic views of the future

Aaron Beck's cognitive restructuring therapy has proven successful for treating depression. With the technique, he tries to get the patients to overcome their negative attitudes toward themselves. Beck is shown here with a client.

Beck, people with psychological disorders share certain characteristics. (1) They tend to have very negative self-images. They do not value themselves or what they do. (2) They tend to take a very negative view of life experiences. (3) They overgeneralize. For example, having failed one test, a person comes to believe that there is no way he or she can do college work and withdraws from school and looks for work, even though he or she believes there's little chance that anyone would offer a job to someone who is such a failure and a college drop-out. (4) They actually seek out experiences that reinforce their negative expectations. The student in the above example may apply for a job as a law clerk or as a stockbroker. Lacking even minimal experience, he or she will not be offered either job and, thus, will confirm his or her own worthlessness. (5) They tend to hold a rather dismal outlook for the future. (6) They tend to avoid seeing the bright side of any experience.

In cognitive restructuring, a therapist offers the patient an opportunity to test or demonstrate her or his beliefs. The patient and therapist make up a list of hypotheses based on the patient's assumptions and beliefs and actually go out and test these hypotheses. Obviously, the therapist tries to exercise enough control over the situation so that the experiments do not confirm the patient's beliefs about himself or herself, but will lead instead to positive outcomes. (For example, given the hypothesis, "Nobody cares about me," the therapist need only find one person who does care to refute it.) This approach, of leading a person to the self-discovery that negative attitudes directed toward one's self are inappropriate, has proven very successful in the treatment of depression, although it has been extended to cover a wide range of psychological disorders (Beck, 1985).

Briefly summarize the logic behind rational-emotive therapy and cognitive restructuring therapy. **BEFORE YOU GO ON**

Group Approaches

Many patients profit from some variety of *group therapy*. Group therapy is a general label applied to a variety of situations in which a number of people are involved in a therapeutic setting at the same time. If nothing else, it is clear that group therapy provides an economic advantage over individual psychotherapy—one therapist can interact with a number of people in the same time frame.

In standard forms of group therapy, a number of clients are brought together at one time (under the guidance of a therapist) to share their feelings and experiences. Most groups are quite informal, and no particular form of psychotherapy is dominant. In other words, meeting with people in groups is something that any kind of therapist may do from time to time. There are a number of possible benefits from this procedure, including an awareness that "I'm not the only one with problems." The sense of support that one can get from someone else with psychological problems is occasionally even greater than that afforded by a therapist—a sort of "she really knows from her own experience the hell that I'm going through" logic. And there is truth in the basic idea that getting involved in helping someone else with a problem is, in itself, a therapeutic process. Yet another advantage of group therapy situations is that the person may learn new and more effective ways of "presenting" herself or himself to others.

A group approach that has become quite popular is called **family therapy.** This is a variety of group therapy that focuses on the roles, interdependence, and communication skills of family members. Family therapy is often implemented after one member of a family enters psychotherapy. After discussing the person's problems for a while, other members of the family are invited to join in the therapy sessions.

Underlying this approach are two related assumptions. One is that each individual family member is a part of a *system* (the family unit), and their feelings, thoughts, and behaviors necessarily impact on other family members (for example, Minuchin & Fishman, 1981). Bringing about a change (even a therapeutic one) in one member of the family "system" without involving the other members of the system will not last for long without the support of the others. This is particularly true when the initial problem appears to be with a child or adolescent. We say "appears to be" because we can be confident that other family members have at least contributed to the troublesome symptoms of the child's or adolescent's behavior that prompted the therapy sessions in the first place. A therapist is going to have a terribly difficult time bringing about significant and lasting change in a child whose parents refuse to become involved in therapy.

A second assumption that is often relevant in family therapy sessions is that difficulties within families stem from improper methods of *communication* (for example, Satir, 1967). Quite often, individuals develop false beliefs about the feelings and/or needs of family members. The goal of therapy in such situations, then, is to meet with the family in a group setting to foster and encourage open expressions of feelings and desires. It may be very helpful for an adolescent to learn that her parents are upset and anxious about financial affairs and work-related stress. The adolescent has assumed all along that her parents yelled at her and each other because of something

family therapy
a variety of group therapy focusing on the roles, interdependence, and communication skills of family members

child or adolescent

Family therapy may be used as an alternative to individual therapy or as a continuation of it. By meeting together, families are given an opportunity to express their feelings and resolve their problems under a therapist's guidance.

* Communication –
       is the key

she was doing (remember how egocentric adolescents can be). And the parents didn't want to share their concerns over money with the adolescent for fear that it would upset her.

Evaluating group therapy and family therapy techniques is particularly difficult, and few good reviews of outcome studies are available. In general, there seems to be support for the sorts of group approaches we have briefly outlined here, and there is some indication that family therapy is a better approach for many problems than is individual treatment (Gurman et al., 1986).

Test

What are some advantages of group therapy? BEFORE YOU GO ON

Choosing a Therapist

Throughout these last two chapters, we have repeatedly mentioned the reality that psychological disorders affect many people. As you read these words, tens of *millions* of Americans are in need of, and could profit from treatment for their psychological distress. What if *you* were such a person? What if you were to realize that you were showing the symptoms of a psychological disorder and that psychotherapy would help? Where would you turn; how would you begin?

Who Provides Psychotherapy?   Perhaps the first thing that you would need to do in this hypothertical situation is to realize that many professions are equipped to help, to provide psychotherapy. Let's begin, then, by providing a list of the most common types of mental health providers, as they are sometimes collectively referred to. Please remember that this is a list of generalities; our descriptions will not hold true for each person within a given category. Remember also that because of their training and/or experience, some professionals develop specialties within their fields. That is, some therapists specialize in disorders of children and adolescents; some work primarily with adults; some prefer to work with fami-

Psychoanalysts, like the one pictured above are trained and certified in the methods of Freudian psychoanalysis. A number of professionals, including social workers and licensed counselors are involved in family and group therapy.

lies; some devote their efforts to people with substance and alcohol abuse problems. Finally, you must realize that a psychotherapist can and will use any number of the techniques of therapy we have outlined in this chapter. In other words, few therapists are exclusively behavioral, client-centered, or psychoanalytic in their approach to treatment. Most will try to fit the technique they use to the person and the problem they are dealing with. The following may be considered psychotherapists:

1. The *clinical psychologist* has usually earned a Ph.D. in psychology that provides practical, applied experience, as well as an emphasis on research. The Ph.D. clinician spends a year on internship, usually at a mental health center or psychiatric hospital. The clinical psychologist usually has extensive training in psychological testing (in general, *psychodiagnostics).* Some clinical psychologists have a Psy.D. (pronounced sigh-dee, which is a doctor of psychology, rather than the more common doctor of philosophy degree). Psy.D. programs generally take as long to complete as Ph.D. programs, but emphasize more practical, clinical work and less research.

2. Psychiatry is a specialty area in medicine. In addition to the course work required for an M.D., the *psychiatrist* spends an internship (usually one year) and a residency (usually three years) in a mental hospital, specializing in the care of psychologically disturbed patients. The psychiatrist is the only kind of psychotherapist permitted to use the biomedical varieties of treatment we reviewed in the first half of this chapter.

3. The *counseling psychologist* usually has a Ph.D. in psychology. The focus of study (and the required one-year internship), however, is generally on patients with less severe psychological problems. For instance, rather than spending one's internship in a psychiatric hospital, a counseling psychologist would more likely spend time at a university counseling center.

4. A *licensed professional counselor* will have a degree in counselor education and will have met state requirements for a license to do psychotherapy. Counselors can be found in school settings, but also work in mental health settings, specializing in family counseling and drug abuse.

5. *Psychoanalyst* is a special label given either to a clinical psychologist or a psychiatrist who has also received intensive training (and certification) in the particular methods of (Freudian) psychoanalysis.

6. The terminal degree for *clinical social workers* is generally taken to be the masters degree, although Ph.D.s in social work are becoming more common. Social workers can and do engage in a variety of psychotherapies, but their traditional role has been involvement in family and group therapy.

Psychotherapy may be offered by a number of other professionals and paraprofessionals. Some people practice therapy and counseling with a masters degree in psychology (although because of licensing and certification laws in many states, they may not advertise themselves as psychologists). *Occupational therapists* usually have a masters degree (or, less frequently, a bachelors degree) in occupational therapy, which includes many psychology classes and internship training in aiding the psychologically and physically handicapped. *Psychiatric nurses* often work in mental hospitals and clinics. In addition to their R.N. degrees, psychiatric nurses have special training in the care of mentally ill patients. *Pastoral counseling* is a specialty of many with a religious background and a masters degree in either psychology or educational counseling. The *mental health technician* usually has an associate degree in mental health technology (MHT). MHT graduates are seldom allowed to provide unsupervised psychotherapy, although they may be involved in the delivery of many mental health services.

How Do I Choose the Right Therapist? Realizing that so many different professionals offer psychotherapy, how does one go about choosing one? Many people and agencies can serve as a good resource at this point. Do you have any family or friends who have been in therapy or counseling? What (or whom) do they recommend? If you get no useful information from friends or family, there are many other people you could ask (assuming that your symptoms are not acute and that time is not critical). You might check with your psychology instructor. He or she may not be a psychotherapist, but will probably be familiar with the mental health resources of the community. You might also see if your college or university maintains a clinic or counseling center service for students (if nothing else, this is often an inexpensive route to take). Check with your family physician. Among other things, a complete physical examination may turn up some leads about the nature of your problem. You might talk with your rabbi, priest, or minister. Clergypersons commonly deal with people in distress and, again, are usually familiar with community resources. If there is one in your community, call the local mental health center or mental health association. If you think that you may have a problem, the most important thing is not to give up. Find help. And the sooner the better.

Now let's assume that a psychotherapist has been recommended to you. You have scheduled an appointment. How will you know if you've made a wise choice? To be sure, only you can be the judge of that. Two cautions are appropriate here: (1) Give the therapy and the therapist a chance. By now, surely you recognize that psychological problems are seldom simple and easily solved. (In fact, a therapist who suggests that your problem can be easily solved is probably a therapist to be leery of.) It may take three or four sessions before your therapist has learned (from you) what the exact and real nature of your problem *is*. Most psychological problems have developed over a long period of time. An hour or two per week for a week or two cannot be expected automatically to make everything right again, as if by magic. You should expect progress, and you might expect some sessions to be more helpful than others. To expect a miracle cure is to be unreasonable. (2) On the other hand, you may feel that you have given your therapy every opportunity to succeed. If you have been truly open and honest with your therapist and feel that you are in no way profiting from your sessions, say so. Express your displeasure and disappointment. After careful consideration, be prepared to change therapists. Starting over again with someone new may involve costs in time and effort, but occasionally it is the only reasonable option.

BEFORE YOU GO ON Who may offer psychotherapy?
How does one find an effective psychotherapist?

In general, psychotherapy is an attempt, using psychological means, to bring about a change in the way a person thinks or feels or acts. There are literally hundreds of varieties of such techniques, and we have in this chapter briefly reviewed only a few of the more traditional or classic approaches. Research tells us that psychotherapy—be it psychoanalysis, behavioral, cognitive, humanistic, or some combination—can be effective in helping people who are suffering from psychological distress and discomfort. We cannot yet say that one form of therapy is any more effective than any other for any particular disorder or any particular person. To quote Stiles and his colleagues (1986) on the issue, "Although we know that psychotherapy works, we do not clearly understand how it works. Differently labeled therapies have demonstrably different behavioral contents, yet appear to have equivalent outcomes."

SUMMARY

Briefly trace the history of the treatment of persons with psychological disorders.

In ancient times, and through the Middle Ages, the prevailing view of the mentally ill was that they were possessed by evil spirits or the devil. As a result, treatment was often harsh, involving torture and placement in dungeonlike asylums for the insane, which, in many ways, were worse than prisons. It was not uncommon for the mentally ill, who were often viewed as witches, to be put to death for their evil ways when they did not confess to sins they probably never committed. Throughout history, there have been attempts by compassionate persons to provide humane treatment to the disordered. However, it wasn't until the twentieth century that what we now call the mental health movement began. This movement was started as a campaign to treat the mentally ill with an aim of curing them in the most humane way possible. / 438

What is a prefrontal lobotomy? Why was it ever used, and why is it not used today?

A prefrontal lobotomy is a psychosurgical technique that involves severing the connections between the very front of the cerebral cortex and lower brain centers. It was first used in the mid-1930s and was a common treatment in the 1940s and 1950s. It was used (as a treatment of last resort) be-

cause it was often successful in alleviating the worst of psychotic symptoms. It also produced many mild to severe side-effects, including death. Because of its inherent danger, and because safer, reversible treatments (such as drug therapy) are available today, it is no longer used. / 439

What is ECT? Why is it still being used?

ECT stands for electroconvulsive therapy, commonly called shock therapy. In this treatment, a brain seizure is produced and the patient is rendered unconscious by passing an electric current across his or her head. Upon regaining consciousness, the patient's memory of the treatment is lost. Although there may be negative side-effects, particularly with prolonged or repeated use, the technique is demonstrably useful (for most patients) as a means of reducing or even eliminating severe depression and some other psychotic symptoms. / 441

What are antipsychotic drugs, and what are their effects?

Most antipsychotic drugs are derivatives of the family of drugs called phenothiazines. The most common is chlorpromazine, produced in the 1940s and commonly in use by the mid-1950s to suppress the majority of symptoms associated with psychosis—hallucinations, delusions, disordered thought, inappropriate affect, and the

like. Lithium salts have been found to be useful in treating bipolar mood disorders, mania in particular. Although these drugs reduce the psychotic symptoms in many patients, it is not accurate to say that they cure the disorder, because symptoms often return when drug use is discontinued. / 442

What are the two types of antidepressant drugs, and what do they do?

Two major types of antidepressant drugs are the MAO inhibitors and the tricyclics. Unlike the antipsychotic drugs, these often have long-term beneficial effects, even after the patient stops taking them. They often take weeks to produce their effects, and they do not work for all patients. Long-term use of the drugs may produce a number of potentially harmful or unpleasant side-effects. / 443

What are the common antianxiety drugs, and what are the dangers inherent in their use?

The most common anxiety-alleviating drugs (or tranquilizers) are the meprobamates and the benzodiazepines, including Valium and Librium, which are two of the most commonly prescribed of all drugs in the world. These drugs reduce felt levels of anxiety, generally without producing a total relaxation and loss of intellectual abilities. Unfortunately, there is evidence that persons who use them develop depen-

SUMMARY continued

dencies and addictions to them. Like many psychoactive drugs, even slight overdoses can lead to complications. Excessive overdoses (or use with alcohol) can lead to death. / 443

Describe the essential nature of Freudian psychoanalysis, defining free association, resistance, dream interpretation, and transference.

Freudian psychoanalysis is a psychotherapeutic technique aimed at uncovering repressed conflicts (perhaps developed in early childhood) so they can be successfully resolved. Among other things, the process involves: (1) free association, in which the patient is encouraged to say anything and everything that comes to mind, without editing; (2) resistance, in which a patient seems unable or unwilling to discuss some aspect of their life; taken as a sign that the resisted experiences may be anxiety-producing; (3) dream interpretation, in which one analyzes both the manifest and latent content of dreams for insights into the nature of the patient's unconscious mind; and (4) transference, in which feelings that once were directed at some significant person in the patient's life are directed toward the analyst. / 446

How is psychoanalysis different today from when it was practiced by Freud?

Although the basis of psychoanalysis

has remained unchanged since Freud's day, some changes have evolved. For example, there is now more effort to shorten the duration of analysis; there is less emphasis on childhood experiences and more concern with the here and now. Present-day analysis is also more directive than it was in Freud's day. / 447

What are the essential characteristics of client-centered therapy?

Client-centered therapy, which we associate with Carl Rogers, is based on the belief that people can control their own lives and solve their own problems if they can be helped to understand the true nature of their feelings and problems. It is a procedure of self-discovery and personal growth. The therapist reflects or mirrors the client's feelings, focuses on the here and now, and tries to be empathic, relating to the patient's feelings. Throughout therapy sessions, the therapist provides unconditional positive regard for the client. / 449

Describe the three essential steps of systematic desensitization.

Systematic desensitization is a behavior therapy technique particularly well suited for the treatment of phobic reactions. A subject is first taught to relax. Then an anxiety hierarchy is made, which lists stimuli in order of their capacity to evoke fear or anxiety.

Desensitization is accomplished by gradually presenting more and more anxiety-producing stimuli from the hierarchy while the subject remains in a relaxed state, thus learning to be relaxed in the presence of stimuli that previously evoked anxiety. / 450

Compare and contrast flooding and implosive therapy with systematic desensitization

Flooding and implosive therapy are two rather dramatic forms of behavior therapy that are particularly useful in the treatment of phobias. In flooding, the subject is confronted with the object of her or his fear in person (*in vivo*), accompanied by the therapist. Implosive therapy requires the subject to imagine his or her fears in the most vivid possible way in an effort to increase anxiety to very high levels in the safety and security of the therapist's office. Unlike systematic desensitization, neither procedure is gradual, and neither encourages the subject to remain relaxed; both require the subject to become anxious in order to face and deal with that anxiety. / 450

What is aversion therapy?

Aversion therapy is accomplished by pairing an unwanted behavior with a strongly negative stimulus, such as a shock or nausea-producing drug. It is an effective means of reducing unwanted behaviors (at least temporarily), but should only be thought of as therapy when subjects voluntarily agree to undergo the treatment after recognizing the long-term benefit of submitting to the aversive stimuli. / 451

Briefly summarize contingency management, contingency contracting, and modeling as means of psychotherapy.

Contingency management, contingency contracting, and modeling are three specific applications of accepted learning principles that are used as therapy to increase the likelihood of appropriate behaviors and/or decrease the likelihood of inappropriate behaviors. Contingency management amounts to exercising control over the pattern of rewards that a patient or subject may receive. Contracting usually involves secondary reinforcement and a token economy system in which a subject agrees (by contract) to engage in certain behaviors in order to earn specified rewards. Modeling comes from social learning theory and suggests that persons can acquire appropriate behaviors through the imitation of models, particularly when the models' behaviors are reinforced. / 453

Briefly summarize the logic behind rational-emotive therapy and cognitive restructuring therapy.

Cognitive therapies are designed to alter the way a person perceives and thinks about himself or herself and the environment. Rational-emotive therapy (RET), for example, takes the premise that people with psychological problems are operating on a series of irrational assumptions about the world and themselves. RET is quite directive in its attempts to change people's cognitions. Cognitive restructuring therapy is somewhat less directive, but is based on the same sort of idea as RET. The underlying premise is that people with psychological disorders have developed negative self-images and negative views (cognitions) about the future. Here, the therapist provides opportunities for the patient to test those negative cognitions and discover that everything is not as bad as it may seem. / 455

What are some advantages of group therapy?

There are a number of potential advantages to group therapy. (1) The basic problem may be an interpersonal one and, thus, will be better understood and dealt with in an interpersonal situation. (2) There is value in realizing that one is not the only person in the world with a problem and that there are others who may have even more difficult problems. (3) There is a therapeutic value in providing support for someone else. (4) The dynamics of intragroup communication can be analyzed and changed in a group setting. / 457

Who may offer psychotherapy?

How does one find an effective psychotherapist?

Many different kinds of mental health professionals can be referred to as psychotherapists. These include: clinical psychologists, Ph.D.s or Psy.D.s in psychology with a one-year internship; psychiatrists, M.D.s with an internship and residency in a mental hospital; counseling psychologists, Ph.D.s in psychology specializing in less severe disorders and with an internship in a counseling setting; licensed counselors, often with degrees in education; psychoanalysts, who specialize in Freudian approaches to therapy; clinical social workers, usually with a masters degree; and many others, including pastoral counselors and mental health technicians. Finding a therapist involves questioning local resources, such as family doctors, clergypersons, psychology instructors, or friends who have been in therapy. One can also check the yellow pages or contact a local mental health center or mental health association. Once an appointment has been made, one should avoid making hasty judgments about one's therapist, but after a few visits should be prepared to seek help elsewhere if insufficient progress has been made. / 460

REVIEW QUESTIONS

1. Providing treatment for persons with psychological disorders—the insane or demented—can be traced as far back as:

a. the earliest civilizations of the Egyptians, Babylonians, and Hebrews.

b. the ancient Greeks and Romans.

c. the Middle Ages.

d. Philippe Pinel in the late 1700s.

This is almost a trick item. It is true that Philippe Pinel was probably the first to systematically apply a *humane* style of treatment to the mentally ill, but psychological disorders and (often misguided) treatments of them can be traced back as far as written history, even to the earliest civilizations of the Egyptians, Babylonians, and Hebrews. / 434

2. Which of the following statements concerning psychosurgery is *true*?

a. Prefrontal lobotomies were never very effective.

b. Psychosurgery was most commonly performed in the late 1800s.

c. Nearly one-quarter of the patients receiving prefrontal lobotomies died as a result.

d. Tens of thousands of prefrontal lobotomies were performed in the 1940s and 1950s.

Psychosurgical techniques, prefrontal lobotomies in particular, were quite effective when they were used— mostly in the 1940s and 1950s (having been introduced in 1935). The problem was that the procedures were irreversible and nearly 1 to 4 percent of those receiving prefrontal lobotomies did die (not 1/4, or 25 percent). Hence, the most correct alternative here is d. / 438

3. When it does work, electroconvulsive shock therapy is most effective as a treatment for:

a. schizophrenia.

b. alcoholism.

c. depression.

d. anxiety-based disorders.

Electroconvulsive therapy (ECT) is hardly ever used as a treatment for alcoholism or the anxiety-based disorders. It has sometimes proven effective in reducing some of the affect-related symptoms of schizophrenia, but ECT is a treatment usually associated with chronic, psychotic depression. / 439

4. Of the following psychoactive drugs, which can be useful in directly treating a psychological disorder instead of just suppressing the symptoms?

a. chlorpromazine.

b. MAO inhibitors.

c. valium.

d. reserpine.

Reserpine was the first antipsychotic drug used in this country, followed soon after by chlorpromazine. Although both of these drugs are often effective in suppressing the symptoms of psychosis (reducing hallucination and/or delusions, for example), neither can be said to directly treat the underlying disorder. The same is true of the antianxiety drug, valium: It reduces the symptoms of felt anxiety but does nothing to help the underlying problem that is causing the anxiety. On the other hand, the MAO inhibitors (and tricyclics), the antidepressants, can be said to actually treat the underlying depressive disorder. / 441

5. Of the following approaches to psychotherapy, which is most directly concerned with guiding the patient to achieve insight about the nature of repressed, anxiety-producing conflicts?

a. psychoanalysis.

b. client-centered therapy.

c. contingency management.

d. rational-emotive therapy.

Of the therapeutic techniques listed here, Freudian psychoanalysis is clearly the one that most directly attempts to help the patient gain insight into some anxiety-producing conflict that has been repressed, perhaps from early childhood. Rogers' client-centered approach is more here-and-now oriented and is aimed at fostering self-esteem (as is rational-emotive therapy, where the focus is on inappropriate beliefs, or cognitions). Contingency management attempts to bring about changes in overt behavior with little concern for deep-seated, underlying problems or insight. / 444

6. During six months of psychoanalysis, Carl talks openly and honestly about all aspects of his early childhood experiences and his relationships with close friends and family members—with one exception. He never mentions his sister who is two years older than he. A psychoanalyst might claim that Carl is demonstrating:

a. transference.

b. free association.

c. unconditional positive regard.

d. resistance.

In psychoanalysis, what one cannot or will not talk about may be as significant as what one chooses to discuss. This phenomenon is called resistance. Transference and free association are two aspects of Freudian psychoanalysis, but neither is directly related to resistance, or Carl's behaviors as described in this item. Unconditional positive regard is not even associated with psychoanalysis but with Rogers' client-centered therapy. / 445

7. To be "empathic" means to:

a. treat everyone fairly.

b. be able to understand and share another's feelings.

c. have insight about the true nature of one's repressed conflicts.

d. relax totally.

This is a straightforward vocabulary item that tests to see if you remember the meaning of a term central to the techniques of client-centered therapy. To be empathic means that one is able to understand and share another's feelings. / 448

8. Of the following techniques, which is *least* likely to be used as a treatment for a phobic disorder?

a. aversion therapy.

b. flooding.

c. systematic desensitization.

d. implosion therapy.

No doubt you recognize each of these techniques as being forms of behavior therapy. As such, each is designed to help bring about some relatively permanent change in behavior. The last three alternatives, however, have been expressly designed and are best suited for treating phobic disorders. Aversion therapy is sometimes effective as a means of getting someone to give up a very inappropriate or potentially dangerous behavioral pattern. / 449

Chapter Eleven

Social Psychology

Why We Care

The Social-Psychological Perspective

Attitudes
    The Structure of Attitudes
    The Usefulness of Attitudes
    Attitude Change and Persuasion
        Cognitive Dissonance Theory
        Cognitive Response Theory
        The Source of Persuasive Communication

Attribution Theory

Interpersonal Attraction
    Theories of Interpersonal Attraction
    Factors Affecting Attraction
        Reciprocity
        Proximity
        Physical Attractiveness
        Similarity

Social Influence
    Conformity
        Norm Formation and Conformity
        The Asch Studies
    Obedience to Authority
        Attribution Errors and a Word of Caution
        A Reminder on Ethics in Research
    Bystander Intervention
        A Cognitive Model of Bystander Intervention
        The Bystander Effect: A Conclusion

Other Examples of Social Influence
    Social Impact Theory and Social Loafing
    Social Facilitation
    Decision-making in Groups
    Television and Violent Behavior

In the late 1960s, a third-grade teacher in a small elementary school in Riceville, Iowa, wanted to provide her pupils with a first-hand experience of prejudice. Jane Elliott announced to her students that she had evidence that blue-eyed children were clearly superior to children with brown eyes. As a result, students with brown eyes were declared second-class citizens. They were forced to sit at the back of the classroom. They had to stand at the end of the lunch line, allowing the blue-eyed children first choice; they were not allowed second helpings of food. They were not allowed to use the drinking fountain. The "superior" blue-eyed children were given special privileges, including extra recess time. To make them more visible, brown-eyed children were forced to wear paper collars that identified their lowly status from a distance.

It wasn't long before the children in Ms. Elliott's third-grade class became active participants in her experiment. The classroom performance of the brown-eyed children deteriorated; they performed below their usual levels on a number of academic tasks.

The blue-eyed children performed better than usual. They voluntarily avoided contact with their "inferior" brown-eyed classmates. Fights and arguments broke out. The behavior of the blue-eyed students became aggressive, contemptuous, and occasionally vicious—and all in one day!

With . . . enthusiasm, the brown-eyed children tore off their collars and helped fit the blue-eyed children with collars . . .

The next school day, Ms. Elliott informed the class that she had made a terrible mistake: she had gotten her evidence reversed. It was blue-eyed children who were inferior; the best people were those with brown eyes. With displays of great joy and enthusiasm, the brown-eyed children tore off their offensive collars and helped fit the blue-eyed pupils with paper collars

that identified *them* as inadequate and inferior. Even with their experience of the previous day, the behaviors of the children in the class were exactly the same, only the roles were reversed. Those who just the day before were the objects of prejudice now sat in the front of the class, performed well on classroom tests, rushed to be first in line at lunch time, and treated their blue-eyed classmates very badly.

On the third class day, Ms. Elliott shared her original intent with her pupils and told them that none of what she said the last two days was, in fact, true. The effects of this classroom demonstration were not long-lived. The children could, and did, soon return to their normal behaviors. The artificially-induced prejudice disappeared almost as fast as it had been created. But the experience was a meaningful one for those Iowa third-graders and a significant one for us, too. It tells us a great deal about the irrationality of a prejudice based solely on physical characteristics (Elliott, 1977; Leonard, 1970; Peters, 1971). We will have occasion in this chapter to return to Jane Elliott's classroom demonstration.

Why We Care

Social psychology is the field of psychology that is concerned with how others influence the thoughts, feelings, and behaviors of the individual. Social psychology deals with us as we live—in a social world, interacting with, influencing, and being influenced by others. Social psychologists focus on the person or individual, not on the group *per se* (which is more likely to be the concern of sociologists).

Psychologists in other areas are also interested in social reactions. Developmental psychologists, for example, are interested in how styles of cooperative and competitive play change and develop through the early years of life. Personality psychologists are interested in individual characteristics that affect interpersonal behavior, such as friendliness, aggression, and so on. Learning theorists are interested in how the perception of someone else being rewarded (vicarious reinforcement) affects behavior change. Clinical psychologists have long recognized that social relationships can play an important role in the development of psychological disorders and their treatment. Common to all of these areas is a concern with what people think about themselves and others. How people form these attitudes about the world is a particular concern of social psychologists.

This chapter will cover two major areas in social psychology: (1) first, social cognition, or the perception and evaluation of one's self and other people in social situations, and (2) second, social influence, or how other people affect the psychological reactions of the individual.

Our first task is to examine social cognition. The basic premise here is that we don't necessarily view our social environment solely on the basis of the stimulus information that it presents to us (Higgins & Bargh, 1987). Instead, we have developed a number of cognitive structures and processes (such as attitudes and prejudices) that influence our interpretation of the world around us. These social cognitions influence our reactions to what is going on around us.

We'll begin by discussing the perspective from which social psychologists study behavior and mental processes.

social psychology
the scientific study of how others influence the thoughts, feelings, and behaviors of the individual

We'll spend most of this first half dealing with attitudes—what they are and how they may be changed. We'll discuss attribution theory—how we try to explain our behavior and the behavior of others. We'll review interpersonal (or social) attraction, and consider some factors that influence how and why people are attracted to (or form positive cognitions toward) others.

Then we'll shift from how social forces affect our cognitions, perceptions, and judgments in social situations to how social forces influence our behaviors. It's somewhat artificial to separate thinking from acting since the two processes are intertwined. Later in the chapter, however, we'll focus on overt, directly observable forms of socially influenced behavior. Although they have much in common, we'll consider the processes of influence by conformity and influence through obedience separately. We'll consider the phenomena of bystander apathy and intervention and list some of the factors that determine how, or if, someone will intervene on behalf of someone else. We'll briefly review a number of situations in which social influence is a force in our lives, and we'll end with some comments about television's power as a social influence—particularly as an influence on violence. In each case, the theme will be the same: how the actions of others influence the behavior of the individual.

THE SOCIAL-PSYCHOLOGICAL PERSPECTIVE

Since we are all social organisms, we are, each in our own way, naive social psychologists. Getting along well with other people is considered to be an asset, and those of us who are able to do so easily may be good social psychologists in the sense that we are skilled in predicting the behaviors of others and understanding how others affect us. All of us seem to put a great deal of effort into trying to understand social behavior.

To claim that we are all naive social psychologists has certain implications. On the one hand, it means that social psychology tends to be perceived as interesting and relevant because it deals with familiar, everyday situations that affect us all. On the other hand, it means that many people are willing to accept common sense, personal experience, and even folklore as the basis for explaining and making assumptions about social behavior. Although common sense often may be valid, it is not an acceptable basis for a scientific approach to social behavior. The social psychologist is distinguished, then, by a perspective that relies on experimentation and other scientific research strategies as sources of knowledge about social behavior, even if the results of applying these strategies are contrary to common sense. As we shall see in this chapter, a number of the most influential discoveries in social psychology have been unexpected and counterintuitive.

During the last few years, social psychology has, like many other areas of psychology, taken on a clearly *cognitive* flavor. That is, social psychologists are attempting more and more to understand social behavior by examining the mental structures and processes that are reflected in such behavior.

The results of the experiment third-grade teacher Jane Elliott conducted with her students were visible in the children's drawings as well as in their behavior in class and in their performance on tests. When children were in the "superior" group for a day, their drawings conveyed confidence and happiness such as the one on the left. When the same children were in the less-favored group their drawings reflected feelings of inferiority and anger, such as the drawing on the right by the same student.

To give you a feel for this approach, let's look again at the situation created in Ms. Elliott's third-grade classroom. On the very first day of that experiment, children with blue eyes developed unfavorable ideas about brown-eyed classmates. Pupils with brown eyes were thought of as inferior, lazy, and irresponsible. These cognitions developed without any real test. On the basis of very little actual evidence or data, blue-eyed children were willing to think of all brown-eyed children as inferior. They were willing to ignore their previous experiences and individual differences among their brown-eyed classmates. They mentally came to represent children with brown eyes as inferior. They formed a **stereotype**—a generalized mental representation of members of a group that is based on limited experience and that does not allow for individual differences.

Although this particular example of a stereotype has negative implications because it is based on erroneous information, stereotypes are not necessarily bad. When they are based on accurate information they are useful tools that help us simplify and deal more efficiently with a complex world (Jussim et al., 1987). For instance, assume that your stereotype of law enforcement officers includes the belief (cognition) that they will arrest you for speeding. If you are out on the highway and see a law enforcement vehicle in your rear-view mirror, you'll make sure that your speed is not exceeding the posted limit, regardless of whether you see that vehicle as belonging to a state trooper, a city police officer, or a county sheriff. You won't pause to wonder what that officer is doing out there on the highway until after you have checked your speed. Because you have formed a stereotype, your behavior has become predictable and virtually automatic.

Notice also that once the pupils in Jane Elliott's class developed the idea of superiority and inferiority on the basis of eye color, their behaviors changed accordingly. The students had rather strong notions about how one deals with or reacts to classmates who are "inferior." They are to sit at the back of the class, they are to stand at the end of lunch lines, and they are not to be spoken to in a friendly manner, *because* they are inferior.

Ex. 3rd grade children believe that brown-eyed kids are inferior to blue-eyed

stereotype
a generalized mental (cognitive) representation of someone that minimizes individual differences and is based on limited experience

Ex. Police cars auto, make you check your own speed.

The Social-Psychological Perspective **471**

norms
rules or expectations that guide our behavior in certain social situations by prescribing how we ought to behave

We all develop a complex set of rules or expectations about how to behave that guide and direct our social actions. That is, we have come to know what we are supposed to do in different social situations. These prescriptions or expectations are called social **norms.** Clearly, norms have a cognitive basis (a mental representation) if we are to use them consistently. Like stereotypes, they are cognitions that we may use to help simplify our social world. Because we have developed social norms, we know how we are to act in a wide variety of social situations. Now that we have a sense of what we mean by social cognition, let's explore some areas in social psychology in which this concept has been useful.

BEFORE YOU GO ON What are stereotypes and norms, and in what way are they cognitive?

ATTITUDES

attitude
a relatively stable and general evaluative disposition directed toward some object, consisting of feelings, behaviors, and beliefs

Since the 1920s, a central concern in social psychology has been the nature of attitudes. We'll define **attitude** as a relatively stable and general evaluative disposition directed toward some object; it consists of beliefs, feelings, and behaviors. One component of an attitude, according to this rather traditional definition, is cognitive (beliefs); so in at least one respect, social psychology has nearly always been characterized by a cognitive orientation.

The concept of "evaluative" in this definition refers to a dimension of attitudes that involves notions such as for or against, pro or con, and positive or negative. By "disposition" we mean a tendency or a preparedness to respond to the object of the attitude (actual responding is not necessary). Also notice that by definition, attitudes have objects. We have attitudes *toward* or *about* something. We don't just have good attitudes or bad attitudes in general; we have attitudes about some object.

Anything can be the object of an attitude, whether it is a person, a thing, or an idea. You may have attitudes about this course, the car you drive, your father, the President, or the fast-food restaurant where you occasionally eat lunch. Some of our attitudes are more important than others, of course, but the fact that we do have attitudes toward so many things is precisely the reason why the study of attitudes is so central in social psychology.

Attitudes consist of beliefs, feelings, and behaviors. Thus, if we believe that nuclear arms are dangerous, we may show our beliefs by demonstrating against them.

The Structure of Attitudes

Although many different definitions of attitude have been proposed over the years, most of them suggest that an attitude consists of three components (Chaiken & Stangor, 1987). When we use the term *attitude* in everyday conversation, we most likely are referring to the *affective* component, which consists of our feeling or emotions about the attitudinal object. The *behavioral component* consists of our response or action tendencies toward the object of our attitude. This component includes our actual behaviors and/or our intentions to act should the opportunity arise. The *cognitive* component includes our beliefs or thoughts about the attitudinal object. By now, this notion of three components of affect, behavior, and cognition, or A-B-C, ought to be quite familiar to you.   *of Attitude*

* You must have all 3 ABC to have an attitude

Notice that all three of these components are required to fit our definition (Breckler, 1984). If you believe that brown-eyed children are lazy, you have a belief, not an attitude. If you hate brown-eyed children, you have an emotional reaction, not an attitude. If you make fun of brown-eyed children, you are engaging in behavior, but you do not necessarily have an attitude toward them. Strictly speaking, to say that you have an attitude toward brown-eyed children would require evidence of all three components.

In many cases, the cognitive, affective, and behavioral components of our attitudes are consistent. We think that classical music is relaxing and like to listen to it, so we buy classical music recordings. We believe that a knowledge of psychology will help after we graduate and we enjoy the class, so we plan to sign up for more psychology classes in the future. It is clearly the case, however, that there are a number of occasions when our behaviors are not consistent with our beliefs and our feelings (Ajzen & Fishbein, 1980).

Because our behavior component often does not reflect our feelings or our beliefs, some social psychologists (for example, Fishbein & Ajzen, 1975) prefer to exclude this component; they reserve the term *attitude* to refer only to the fundamental like or dislike for the attitudinal object, that is, the affective component. Others argue that attitude is a two-dimensional concept, involving both affect and cognition (Bagozzi & Burnkrant, 1979; Zajonc & Markus, 1982).

Fishbein and Ajzen, for example, maintain that attitudes *may* lead to behavioral intentions which in turn *may* be correlated with actual behavior. Across a large sample of situations, there should, in fact, be consistency between one's attitude and *most* behaviors. But predicting any single behavior on the basis of one's attitude is very difficult. The basic problem is that one's actual behaviors, particularly in social settings, are subject to many influences over and above one's underlying attitude. A given situation may "overpower" our affective and cognitive components. For example, we may have strong, unfavorable, stereotyped beliefs and negative feelings about someone, yet when we encounter that person at a social gathering, we smile, extend our hand, and say something pleasant.

Our attitudes and behaviors may not always be consistent, especially at social gatherings where we may be friendly and congenial toward someone we have negative feelings about.

What is an attitude and what are its three components?   BEFORE YOU GO ON

The Usefulness of Attitudes

Attitudes are important for a variety of reasons that are readily apparent in everyday life. For example, attitudes may serve as shorthand summaries for a number of our beliefs. Have you ever noticed how quick people are to evaluate the unfamiliar? If a friend tells you that she just bought a new book, saw a new movie, or tried a new restaurant, one of the first things that you will probably want to know is if she liked it or not. Further questioning will probably be required for you to go beyond a general evaluative comment (such as "I didn't like it") and explore the reasons behind the initial reaction. Such probing may reveal that your friend believes the book to be too difficult to understand, the movie to be too corny, or the service in the restaurant to be too slow. In short, we can see that our "attitudes serve as convenient summaries of our beliefs" (Petty & Cacioppo, 1981, p. 8).

social identification function
the observation that attitudes communicate information useful in social evaluation

Attitudes are also useful when they serve a **social identification function** (Greenwald & Breckler, 1984). The attitudes of other people provide useful information about who they are, and, similarly, our attitudes tell others about us. Having information about someone's attitudes allows us to predict that person's behaviors more accurately than we could without such information. It is no accident that people in the process of getting to know one another devote a good bit of time exchanging information about their attitudes. You have probably experienced this social process yourself, perhaps when going on a date with someone for the first or second time. In this situation, don't you usually spend some time discussing the music you like, political preferences, what you enjoy doing in your spare time, and even where you like to go on dates? Many social evaluations are based on likes and dislikes (particularly if they are extreme). Such discussions about likes, dislikes, and attitudes produce information that people use to get to know each other, a process of social identification.

Most people, of course, are aware that providing social information of this sort does influence what others may think of them. Consequently, people often tend to select carefully what information they choose to offer about their own attitudes. Sometimes they may choose to misrepresent their true attitudes completely. In such cases, we say that attitudes can serve an **impression management function** (Chaiken & Stangor, 1987; Goffman, 1959; Snyder, 1974). Obviously, managing someone else's impression of you by providing misleading information about your attitudes will only work for a limited amount of time.

impression management function
the selective presentation or misrepresentation of one's attitudes in an attempt to present one's self in a particular way

BEFORE YOU GO ON   What are some of the functions served by attitudes?

Attitude Change and Persuasion

Much of the social-psychological research on attitudes has been concerned with the very practical questions of when and how attitudes change. A good deal of this research has dealt with conscious, planned attempts to change someone's attitude(s), a process called **persuasion.** In this section, we will examine some of the conditions that lead to attitude change, beginning with an unexpected and counterintuitive finding to which we referred earlier.

persuasion
the process of intentionally attempting to change an attitude

Cognitive Dissonance Theory.   Common sense would seem to suggest that the affective and cognitive components of an attitude will produce behaviors consistent with those feelings and beliefs. In other words, behavior should follow from attitudes, and attitude change should lead to behavior change. In 1957, Leon Festinger proposed just the reverse: that attitudes may follow behavior. Festinger's theory refers to a condition he called **cognitive dissonance.** We know what cognitions are: thoughts, beliefs, perceptions, and the like. Dissonance means discord, discomfort, or distress that is due to things being out of balance or not fitting together well. When our cognitions do not "fit together well," we may find it useful to change our attitudes in order to reduce the unpleasantness of cognitive dissonance.

One example of how this might work that you may be familiar with occurs on the showroom floor of a new car dealer. You may have heard all sorts of negative things about the new model Gazelle X-100s. You've not

cognitive dissonance
the state of tension or discomfort that exists when we hold inconsistent cognitions; we are motivated to reduce dissonance

liked other cars this company has produced, and you're quite prepared not to like the new X-100 either. But there you are on the showroom floor. (You're there because the dealer has offered some incentive—perhaps an AM/FM radio—just for taking a test drive of the new Gazelle X-100.) You soon find yourself under a great deal of pressure to "Give that ol' X-100 a test drive." Clean and polished, it does look pretty sharp. You take it for a test drive, and when you return, you tell the salesperson that you did indeed enjoy the ride and that you were impressed with the X-100's performance. Your salesperson is now close to getting a sale. You've taken an action; you've done something contrary to your original attitude, and cognitive dissonance has been created. ("I thought this car was poor" and "I did enjoy that ride" are two ideas that both exist at the same time and clearly don't lead to the same conclusion.) Getting you to *do* something may have been the first step in getting you to change your attitude about the new Gazelle X-100. When dissonance is created, we may predict that some cognitions will change to reduce the dissonance. Now you may eventually convince yourself that your one ride in the X-100 was a fluke and that by and large, most cars made by this company still aren't very good. Or you may change your attitude about the car maker and the Gazelle X-100 and, to the salesperson's delight, buy the car.

Cognitive dissonance is occurring when you find yourself test-driving and considering a new car that you had previously been against.

What is cognitive dissonance, and how is it relevant to attitude change?

BEFORE YOU GO ON

Cognitive Response Theory.   A theory of attitude change that is more recent than Festinger's, but that is still cognitive in its orientation is one often called *cognitive response theory* (Petty et al., 1981). This theory proposes that the recipient of a persuasive communication (an attempt to change an attitude) is not at all passive. Rather, the person receiving a persuasive message is an active information processor who generates *cognitive responses* or thoughts about the message being received. These cognitive responses can be favorable, agreeing with and supportive of the message. Or they can be unfavorable, disagreeing and counterarguing with the message. This line of reasoning has led researchers to examine variables that may affect persuasion and the cognitive responses that persuasive messages produce. Two interesting variables that have been under study are *message quality* and *distraction.* Let's see what is involved in this sort of research.

Distraction and message quality have been studied experimentally by Petty, Wells, and Brock (1976). In one study, message quality was either high or low; that is, the persuasive speech contained either strong or weak arguments about an attitudinal object. Subjects heard one of these two messages under conditions involving either low or moderate distraction. As Figure 11.1 shows, when the message consisted of strong arguments, agreement with the message was reduced (slightly) when the level of distraction was increased. This occurred, the argument goes, because the distraction interfered with the production of cognitive responses that were in favor of the persuasive message. Increasing distraction had the opposite effect when weak arguments were presented, presumably because the distraction interfered with the listener's ability to think of good counterarguments against the message.

FIGURE 11.1
The extent to which an audience agrees with either strong arguments or weak arguments presented under conditions of low and medium distraction. Note that distraction lowered agreement when strong arguments were used but raised agreement when weak arguments were used.
(After Petty, Wells, & Brock, 1976.)

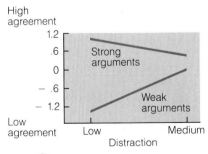

Let's look at an example. Imagine that you are headed for a career in medical research and that you believe very strongly that that research with animals is well-justified because of its ultimate benefit for humankind. You hear that an animal rights group is holding a rally on campus and, mostly out of curiosity, you decide to attend to hear what they have to say about why animals should not be used in medical research. Cognitive response theory says that you will generate counterarguments (cognitions that disagree with those being made) as you listen to the speeches at the rally. Now further assume that there is some very loud construction going on nearby. The noise generated by the construction may interfere with your ability to produce good counterarguments, and you may not be as able to resist the persuasive speeches as you would be without all that background noise. On the other hand, a person who went to the rally already supporting the animal rights group will generate his or her own arguments that agree with the speeches being made. For this person, the construction noise may cause the speeches to be less influential than they would have been otherwise.

Research suggests that cognitive response theory may also be usefully applied to advertising. Advertisers frequently make strong claims about their products and they do not want potential consumers in the audience to counterargue or even begin to question the validity of their claims. Since distractions can interfere with the production of these cognitive responses, distractions would leave the consumer more vulnerable to the persuasive message of the advertiser. Catchy (or loud) music, humor, and novelty are commonly used as ways of creating distraction and, thus, enhancing the effectiveness of the advertising.

The Source of Persuasive Communication. The effectiveness of a persuasive communication is almost always influenced by its source. In general, a highly credible (believable) source will induce more change than will a less credible source. There are probably several factors involved in what we call credibility, but two that seem especially important are expertise and trustworthiness.

A number of studies (Aronson et al., 1963; Hovland & Weiss, 1951, for example) have indicated that the greater the perceived expertise of the communicator, the greater the amount of persuasion that occurs. For example, you would be much more likely to be influenced by Pete Rose (manager of the Cincinnati Reds baseball team) if he is trying to influence your attitudes about baseball than you would be if he were trying to persuade you to buy a certain brand of toaster oven. (Celebrities *are* used to promote products without any apparent expertise on the basis of the following logic: first, you'll recognize them and attend to what they say, and second, their credibility and expertise in some other area [which has brought about their celebrity] will transfer to the product they are selling.)

A second factor likely to enhance a communicator's credibility is a high degree of trustworthiness. Studies by Walster and Festinger (1962) demonstrated that more attitude change resulted when subjects overheard a persuasive communication than when they believed that the communication was directed at them. Trustworthiness and credibility were apparently enhanced by the perceived lack of intent to persuade ("Why should they lie; they don't even know we can hear them?").

We are more likely to be persuaded by communicators we perceive as having expertise and trustworthiness. Often cited as an example is Ronald Reagan, who as a communicator, conveys a high degree of credibility for many people.

Cognitive response theory also speaks to this issue of source credibility. Haas (1981) maintains that persuasive information will be examined (mentally or cognitively) in an attempt to assess its validity, or its truth value. People are simply less likely to question and counterargue information they get from a source they rate as credible; they expect it to be accurate.

Other than cognitive dissonance, what are some factors associated with persuasion?

BEFORE YOU GO ON

ATTRIBUTION THEORY

Another facet of the cognitive orientation that we find in social psychology is the study of what is called **attribution theory.** Social psychologists working with attribution theory are interested in understanding the cognitions we use in trying to explain behavior, both our own and that of others. The question here is "Do we attribute behaviors or events we observe in the world around us to internal or external sources—to personal dispositions or to environmental situations?"

Social psychologists have found it useful to distinguish between two basic types of attributions that we formulate in our own minds as we try to explain the behaviors of ourselves and others: internal and external. This distinction comes down to whether behavior is caused by the person or by the environment. **Internal attributions** explain the source of behavior in terms of some characteristic of the person, often a personality trait or dis-

Behavior
2 Types

attribution theory
the cognitions we generate when we attempt to explain the sources of behavior

internal attribution ①
an explanation of behavior in terms of something (a trait) within the person; a "dispositional attribution"
sometimes called

Attribution Theory **477**

external attribution
an explanation of behavior in terms of something outside the person; a situational attribution ↙

Sometimes called

3 Types of bias (underlined)

fundamental attribution error ①
the tendency to overuse internal attributions when explaining behavior

EX.

just world hypothesis ②
the belief that the world is just and that people get what they deserve

position, and for this reason internal attributions are sometimes called *dispositional attributions.* **External attributions,** on the other hand, explain the sources of behavior in terms of the situation or social context outside the individual; they are referred to as *situational attributions.*

The evidence indicates that people tend to rely on certain types of information when making judgments about the sources of behavior. Imagine, for example, that your best friend shows his temper only when he is with his girlfriend. That information is useful because of its *distinctiveness* (his bad temper only shows up when he's with his girlfriend). As a result, you may take it as a signal of a troubled relationship.

Imagine that you have just received an A on a test in your history class. In this case, you could (and probably would) use information about how well everyone else did on the test before you decide about your own superiority; this kind of information is concerned with *consensus.* If you discover that everyone else also received an A, your explanation of your own behavior (and theirs) might be different from a situation in which you discover that yours is the only A in the class. But before you got too grandiose about your own accomplishment, you might wait for some sign of *consistency* over time lest this one exam be just a fluke and more atypical than usual. In fact, using information about distinctiveness, consensus, and consistency is the basis of one major theory about attributions we make about behavior (Kelley, 1967, 1973). Figure 11.2 shows a few of the ways in which information about distinctiveness, consensus, and consistency may lead one to attribute behavior to internal or external sources.

One currently active area of research deals with the errors we tend to make in our social thinking. One particularly well-documented example of a cognitive bias in the attribution process is called the **fundamental attribution error** (Jones, 1979; Ross, 1977). This bias has to do with the basic tendency when observing others to favor internal, personal attributions for their behavior rather than external, situational explanations. We see a man pick up a wallet that has been dropped on the pavement and race half a block to return it to its true owner. We say, to ourselves, "now there's an honest person." (And we'll probably predict that that person will act honestly in a variety of different situations.) The truth is, however, that the fellow returned the wallet only because he knew that we (and many others) saw him pick it up from the pavement. It may very well be that if no others were around, the wallet would never have been returned. The fundamental attribution error, then, is the tendency to discount situational factors in favor of internal, dispositional factors when we make inferences about the causes of behaviors.

As you might imagine, there are a number of other biases that may lead us to make incorrect attributions about ourselves or others. One is called the **just world hypothesis,** in which people take on the belief that we live in a just world where good things happen to good people and bad things happen to bad people (Lerner, 1965, 1980). It's a sort of "everybody ultimately gets what they deserve" sort of mentality. We see this very bias (we might say fallacy) when we see people claim that victims of rape often "ask for it by the way they dress and act." In fact, even victims of rape themselves sometimes engage in self-blame in an attempt to explain why in the world *they* were singled out for what was in fact a crime in which they were the victim quite by chance and chance alone (Janoff-Bulman, 1979).

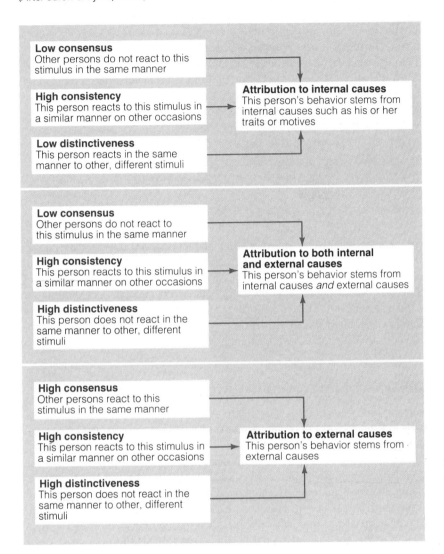

Another attribution error we might mention is the so-called **actor-observer bias** (Jones & Nisbett, 1971; Monson & Snyder, 1977). What we find here is a basic discrepancy between the way we explain our behavior (as actor) and the way we explain someone else's (as observer). What usually happens is that we use external attributions when we talk about why we do things. The basis of our explanation has to do with something about the situation or the environment. "I took that class because the instructor is entertaining." "I date him because he's so caring and considerate." "I went there because the rates were lower than anyplace else." When we explain someone else's behaviors we tend to use internal attributions and refer to characteristics of the person whose behaviors we have been observing. "Oh, he took that class because he's so lazy." "I know that she's dating him only

actor-observer bias ③
overusing internal attributions to explain the behaviors of others and external attributions to explain our own behaviors

Attribution Theory   **479**

because she wants to be seen with an athlete." "He went there because he wanted to show off." That we explain our own behaviors in ways that are different from the ways in which we account for the behaviors of others should not be surprising. For one thing, we have much more information about ourselves and our own past experiences than we do about anyone else. In fact, the more information we have about someone else, the less likely we are to use internal attributions to explain their behaviors. For another thing, in any situation, the actor gets quite a different view of what is happening than does the observer. In other words, the actor and the observer attempt to attribute the cause of behavior on the basis of different information.

BEFORE YOU GO ON   What are the two basic types of attribution?
In what ways can attributions be distorted or biased?

INTERPERSONAL ATTRACTION

You may wonder why interpersonal attraction—a process that clearly involves overt behavior—follows a discussion of social cognition. In addition to behavior, attraction also involves feelings that one person has about another. But attraction also includes beliefs and ideas (cognitions) about some other person. Attraction then can be seen as an attitude—a favorable and powerful attitude at that. In this section, we'll review some of the processes that affect how these particular attitudes are formed.

③ Theories of Interpersonal Attraction

Social psychologists have put forth a number of theoretical models to explain the bases of interpersonal attraction. Let's briefly review three such theories.

 Probably the simplest and most straightforward theory we can call the *reinforcement model* (Clore & Byrne, 1974; Lott & Lott, 1974). This model claims that we tend to be attracted to people we associate with rewards. That is, we learn to like people and become attracted to them through conditioning, by associating them with rewards or reinforcers that are present when they are. We are thus attracted to (have positive attitudes toward) those people we associate with rewarding experiences. It also follows that we'll tend not to be attracted to those we associate with punishment—a sort of "kill the messenger who brings bad tidings" attitude. One implication of this point of view is that you're going to like your instructor more, and seek him or her out for other classes in the future, if you get (or better, earn) a high grade in his or her class than you would if you get a low grade.

 Another popular theory of interpersonal attraction is not quite so direct. It is called the *social exchange model* (Kelley & Thibault, 1978; Thibault & Kelley, 1959). According to this model, what matters most is a comparison of the costs as well as the benefits of establishing or maintaining a relationship. For example, Leslie may judge that Bill is very physically attractive, but that entering into an intimate relationship with him is not worth the grief that she would get from friends and family. On the other hand, if Leslie had just gone through a series of failed relationships with other men who were not physically attractive, she might take a chance on Bill, judging (in her frustration) that he was "worth it." What this theory takes into account then are a number of comparative judgments that individuals make in social situations. Being attracted to someone else is not just a matter of "Is this a good thing?" It's more a matter of, "Is the reward I might get from this relationship worth the cost, *and* what other alternatives exist at the moment?"

A third theoretical approach to interpersonal attraction is called the *equity model,* and it is more an extension of social exchange theory than a departure from it (Greenberg & Cohen, 1982; Walster et al., 1978). Social exchange theory added the notion of cost to that of reward. Equity theory adds the appraisal of rewards and costs of *both* members of a social relationship. That is, you may feel that a certain relationship is worth the effort you've been putting into it, but if your partner in that relationship does not feel likewise, the relationship is in danger. What matters, then, is that both (or all) members of a relationship feel that they are getting a fair deal (equity) from the relationship. Notice two things about this model: (1) Both members of a relationship do not have to share rewards *equally*. What matters is that the ratio of costs to rewards be equitable for both members. (2) If one person were to feel that he or she was getting more from a relationship than was deserved (on the basis of costs and compared to the other member's rewards), the relationship would not be equitable and would be jeopardized. The best relationships are those in which all members receive an equal ratio of rewards to costs.

← Important

We should point out that few people enter into relationships having carefully considered all of the pluses and minuses that these models imply. That is, assessments of reinforcement, or exchange, or equity value are seldom made at a conscious level.

Briefly summarize three theoretical models that account for interpersonal attractions.   **BEFORE YOU GO ON**

Factors Affecting Attraction

We've reviewed three models of interpersonal attraction. Now let's look at some empirical evidence related to attraction. What determines who you will be attracted to? What factors tend to provide the rewards, or the positive reward/cost ratios, that serve as the basis for strong relationships? Here we'll list four of the most common principles of interpersonal attraction.

Reciprocity.   Our first principle is perhaps the most obvious one. Not surprisingly, we tend to value and like people who like us back. Remember that we've already noted, in our discussion of operant conditioning (Chapter 4), that the attention of others is often a powerful reinforcer. This is particularly true if the attention is positive, supportive, and affectionate. In fact, the research indicates that the value of someone else caring for us is particularly powerful when that someone initially seemed to have neutral or even negative attitudes toward us (Aronson & Linder, 1965). That is, we are most attracted to people who like us now, but who didn't originally. The

Proximity leads to liking, which is why teenagers who go to the same school are likely to form friendships.

mere exposure phenomenon
the tendency to increase our liking of people and things the more we see of them

EX.

Physical attractiveness is a powerful influence in interpersonal relationships. Numerous studies have found that physical attractiveness is at least at first, the single most important factor in selecting friends and dates.

logic here is related to attribution. If someone we meet for the first time expresses nothing but positive feelings and attitudes toward us, we are likely to attribute their reaction internally to the way the person is—rather shallow and the sort who just likes everybody. But if someone at first were to express neutral, or even slightly negative, feelings toward us and then were to become more and more positive, we might have a different view of their ability to judge others.

Proximity.   Our second principle suggests that physical closeness, or proximity, tends to produce liking. Sociologists, as well as your own personal experience, will tell you that people tend to establish friendships (and romances) with others with whom they have grown up, worked, or gone to school. Similarly, social psychological studies have consistently found that residents of apartments or dormitories tend to become friends with those other residents living closest to them (Festinger et al., 1950). Being around others gives us the opportunity to discover just who can provide those interpersonal rewards we seek in friendship.

There may be another social-psychological phenomenon at work here called the **mere exposure phenomenon.** A great deal of research, pioneered by Robert Zajonc (1968), has shown with a variety of novel social and non-social stimuli that liking tends to increase with repeated exposure to stimuli. Examples of this phenomenon are abundant in everyday life. Have you ever bought a record album that you have not heard previously, assuming that you will like it because you have liked all the other albums made by this performer? The first time you listen to your new album, however, your reaction may be lukewarm at best, and you may be disappointed in your purchase. Not wanting to feel that you've wasted your money, you play the album a few more times over the next several days. What often happens is that you soon realize that you like this album after all, even more than some of the old ones. The mere exposure effect has occurred, and this commonly happens in our formation of attitudes about other people as well. (If this sounds a bit like our earlier discussion of cognitive dissonance, you're right on the mark. We can't imagine having repeated contacts with someone we don't particularly like (that would be dissonant), so we find that we like them after all.) Apparently there is some truth to the adage that familiarity breeds liking, not contempt.

Physical Attractiveness.   Our physical appearance is one personal characteristic that we cannot easily hide. It is always on display in social situations, and it communicates something about us. People are aware of the role of appearance in nonverbal, interpersonal communication and may spend many hours each week doing whatever can be done to improve the way they look.

The power of physical attractiveness in the context of dating has been demonstrated in a classic study directed by Elaine Walster (Walster et al., 1966). University of Minnesota freshmen completed a number of psychological tests as part of an orientation program. Couples of these freshmen were then randomly matched for dates to an orientation dance, during which they took a break and evaluated their assigned partners. This study allowed researchers the possibility of uncovering intricate, complex, and subtle facts about attraction, such as which personality traits might tend to mesh in such a way as to produce attraction. As it turned out, none of these complex factors, so carefully controlled for, was important. The effect of physical attractiveness was so powerful that it wiped out all other effects. For both men and women, the more physically attractive their date, the more they liked the person and the more they wanted to go out again with that individual.

Numerous studies of physical attractiveness followed this one. Some of these studies simply gave subjects a chance to pick a date from a group of several potential partners (usually using descriptions and pictures). Not surprisingly, subjects almost invariably selected the most attractive person available to be their date (Reis el al., 1980).

You may have noticed, however, that in real life we seldom have the opportunity to request a date without at least the possibility of being turned down. When experimental studies began to build in the possibility of rejection, an interesting effect emerged: Subjects stopped picking the most attractive candidate from a group and started selecting partners whose level of physical attractiveness was more similar to their own. This behavior has been called the **matching phenomenon,** and it is an effect that has been verified by naturalistic observation studies (Walster & Walster, 1969).

Ex. ↓

matching phenomenon
the tendency to select partners whose level of physical attractiveness matches our own

The positive effects of physical attractiveness can be found in many social situations. Studies (for example, Dion et al., 1972; Vaughn & Langlois, 1983) suggest that attractive persons are assumed to have other desirable characteristics as well. Such persons—both men and women—are routinely judged to be more intelligent, to have happier marriages, to be more successful in their careers and social lives, and so on. This effect of overgeneralizing is referred to as the **physical attractiveness stereotype.**

Ex. ↓

physical attractiveness stereotype
the tendency to associate desirable characteristics with a physically attractive person, solely on the basis of attractiveness

Some research has indicated that there may be serious implications involved in the application of this stereotype. For instance, Anderson and Nida (1978) have shown that the same piece of work (in this case an essay) will be evaluated more favorably when a physically attractive person is thought to have produced it. Similarly, a study by Clifford and Hatfield (1973) found fifth-grade teachers to judge attractive children as more intelligent. Another study (Dion, 1972) found that women who were asked to recommend punishment for a child who had misbehaved were more lenient when the child was judged to be physically attractive.

4) *#1 reason why people stay together*

Similarity. There is a large body of research on the relationship between similarity and attraction, but the findings are consistent, and we can summarize them briefly. Much of this research has been done by Donn Byrne and his colleagues (for example, Byrne, 1971). It indicates that there is a very positive relationship between liking and the proportion of attitudes held in common. To put it simply, the more similar another person is to you, the more you will tend to like that person (Buss, 1985; Davis, 1985; Rubin, 1973).

Perhaps you know a happily married couple for whom this sweeping conclusion does not seem to fit. At least some of their behaviors seem to be quite dissimilar, almost opposite. Perhaps the wife appears to be the one who makes most of the decisions while the husband simply seems to follow orders. It may very well be the case, however, that this apparent dissimilarity in behavior exists only on the surface. There may be an important similarity that makes for a successful marriage here: both have the same idea of what a

The more similar another person is to you, the more you will tend to be like that person. Our friends tend to be people who share our attitudes and who like to do the things we like to do.

marriage should be like—wives decide and husbands obey. In such a case, the observed differences in behavior are reflecting a powerful similarity in the view of the roles of married couples.

That similarity enhances interpersonal attraction makes sense in light of the reinforcement theory of attraction we described earlier. Agreement with our attitudinal positions is reinforcing, it confirms that we were right all along. And, by definition, people who are similar to us tend to agree with us. Similarity is probably the glue that—over the long haul—holds together romances and friendships.

BEFORE YOU GO ON   **What are four determinants of interpersonal attraction, and how do they have the effect that they do?**

So far, we've addressed some of the important issues related to social cognition—perception and evaluation in a social context. We've spent most of our time on attitudes, which are largely cognitive in nature, but which also involve affect and action tendencies directed toward some object or event. We've seen that attitudes provide a number of adaptive functions for us, helping us to judge others and to present ourselves to others as we would like to be judged. We've also reviewed the ways in which we theorize, or develop cognitions, about the sources of the behaviors we see around us. It is clear that in many instances, our attributions are made in error. We ended with a discussion of interpersonal attraction, trying to find explanations (attributions again) for why some people get along so well with each other and some do not.

SOCIAL INFLUENCE

To function efficiently in the social world—the world of people, not just things—often depends on the accurate interpretation of information we get from others. Our perception of the world around us is often unclear and ambiguous; when it is, we tend to rely on others for assistance. Much of the time, other people provide useful cues as to how we should respond. The actions of others can provide useful guidelines for our own behaviors; sometimes others actually tell us what to do. Sometimes, however, the social cues we get from others are ambiguous, and we may misinterpret the situation and act inappropriately. At still other times, we may be so confused by the messages we get from other people that we do nothing at all, and that can be inappropriate, too.

What we are saying here is that much of human behavior is influenced by others. In fact, people are so accustomed to this process of social influence that much of the time it escapes awareness. You probably did not consider just why you happened to walk on the right side of the sidewalk the last time you were downtown shopping, or why you quietly took a place at the very end of the line the last time you bought tickets for a movie, or why you applauded and cheered at the last concert you attended. Nevertheless, all of these behaviors were shaped by social influence. In this section, we'll consider several forms of socially influenced behavior.

Conformity

One of the most obvious and direct forms of social influence occurs whenever we modify our behavior (under perceived pressure to do so) so that it is consistent with the behavior of others, a process referred to as **conformity.** Often this means that we follow some norm or standard that prescribes how we should act in a given situation. Although we often tend to think of conformity in a negative way, to conform is natural and often desirable. Conformity helps to make social behaviors efficient.

Norm Formation and Conformity.   Some of the earliest research to demonstrate the power of conformity was performed by Muzafer Sherif (1936). Sherif used the perceptual phenomenon called the **autokinetic effect** to show how social norms can develop and induce conformity in ambiguous circumstances. If a person is seated in a completely darkened room and a small spot of light is projected on the wall, within a few moments the light will appear to move. This compelling, illusory movement is not at all regular—the light seems to dart from place to place. When asked to estimate how far the light moves, people vary widely in their judgments, which may range from a few inches to several feet (remember that the light is actually stationary). Sherif first asked people to make independent judgments about the apparent movement of the light—they were alone in the testing room. Then, in each of several sessions that took place on different days, Sherif asked his subjects to make their judgments with other subjects present in the room. The others were also asked to estimate how far the light moved.

As a result of the group experience, each participant adjusted his or her judgments to match the estimates of others. That is, over the course of the study, the judgments of members of a group of subjects converged, and the end result was agreement within the group as to how far the light had moved. A norm had emerged to guide behavior in this ambiguous situation, and the individuals in the study conformed to that norm.

The Asch Studies.   The results of the demonstrations by Sherif may not be all that surprising. After all, the situation was completely ambiguous. The subjects had had no prior experience with the autokinetic effect, and there were no cues to guide their judgments—at least until the other subjects entered the picture. How might people respond to group pressure when the reality of the situation is much clearer?

Solomon Asch (1951, 1956) initially believed that people are not very susceptible to social pressure when the social situation is clear cut and unambiguous. Asch hypothesized that subjects would behave independently of group pressure whenever there was little question that their own judgments were accurate, and he developed an interesting technique for testing his hypothesis.

A subject in Asch's procedure would join a face-to-face group seated around a table. In his original study, the group consisted of seven people. Unknown to the real subject, however, six individuals were actually confederates of the experimenter. The experimenter explained that the study dealt

conformity
changing one's behavior (under perceived pressure) so that it is consistent with the behavior of others

autokinetic effect
an illusion in which a stationary spot of light in a dark room appears to move

ambiguous

unambiguous

Asch was wrong

The type of stimuli used in Asch's conformity experiment. Subjects are to say which of the three lines on the right (A, B, or C) equals the line on the left. Associates of the experimenter will occasionally make incorrect choices.

*— After consistently disagreeing with the other subjects in Asch's study, the lone dissenter begins to doubt his judgment and looks again at the card, even though the correct answer is obvious.

with the ability to make perceptual judgments. The participants would be doing nothing more than deciding which of three lines was the same length as a standard line (see Figure 11.3). The experimenter would show each set of lines to the group and then go around the table collecting responses from each member of the group. In fact, the only real subject was always the last one to respond.

It is important to note that each of the 18 judgments the subjects were asked to make involved unambiguous stimuli. The correct answer was always obvious. However, on 12 of the 18 trials, the confederates gave a unanimous, but *incorrect* answer. Now what should the subjects do? How should they resolve this conflict? Their own experience told them what the right answer was, but the group was saying something else. Should they trust the judgments of the others, or should they trust their own perceptual ability?

The results of his initial study surprised Asch, because they did not confirm his original hypothesis. Across all of the critical trials (when confederates gave "wrong" answers), conformity occurred 37 percent of the time. That is, subjects responded with an incorrect answer that agreed with the majority on more than one third of the critical trials. Even more striking is that 75 percent of Asch's subjects conformed to the group pressure at least once.

In subsequent studies, Asch tried several variations of his original procedure. In one experiment, he varied the size of the unanimous, incorrect majority. As you might now expect, the level of conformity increased as the size of the majority increased (leveling off at about three or four people). Subjects gave an erroneous judgment only 4 percent of the time when only one incorrect judgment preceded their own. In another study, Asch found that conformity decreased to 10 percent when there was one dissenter among the six confederates who voiced an accurate judgment before the subjects gave theirs. In short, when the subjects had at least some small social support for what their eyes had told them, they tended to trust their own judgment. Recent experiments have demonstrated that the minority opinion (say one dissenter in an Asch-type procedure) can have significant effects on conformity if that minority position is maintained consistently (for example, Moscovici et al., 1969; 1985).

BEFORE YOU GO ON   Briefly describe the methodology and the basic findings of the Sherif and Asch conformity studies.

Obedience to Authority

Although the subjects in Asch's studies obviously took the procedure seriously, the consequences of either conforming or maintaining independence were rather trivial. At worst, Asch's subjects might have experienced some discomfort as a result of voicing their independent judgments. There were no external rewards or punishments for their behavior. Stanley Milgram (1933–1984) a social psychologist at Yale University, went one step beyond Asch's procedure. Milgram's research has become among the most famous

Extreme, unquestioning obedience to authority can have negative consequences. Consider concentration camp commander Franz Hoessler whose blind obedience to Hitler's decrees led to the brutal murder of millions of innocent people.

and controversial in all of psychology. His experiments pressured subjects to comply with the demand of an authority figure—a demand that was both troubling and unreasonable (Milgram, 1963, 1965, 1974).

milgram

The original impetus for Milgram's research was his interest in the extreme obedience to Nazi authority displayed by many German military personnel during World War II. Milgram wondered whether the mass executions and other forms of cruelty perpetrated by the Nazis might reflect something about the German character. The original goal of his research was to determine if people of different nationalities differ in the degree to which they will obey a request to inflict pain on another person. Milgram's research procedure was designed to serve as a basis for making such comparisons.

All of the studies carried out in this series involved the same basic procedure. Subjects arrived at the laboratory to find that they would be participating with a second person (once again, a confederate of the experimenter). The experimenter explained that the research was an investigation of the effects of punishment on learning, and that one person would serve as a teacher while the other would act as learner. These two roles were "randomly" assigned by a rigged drawing in which the actual subject was always assigned the role of teacher. The subject watched as the learner was taken into the next room and wired to electrodes that would be used for delivering punishments in the form of electric shocks.

Ex. Fig. 11.4 pg. 488

The teacher then received his or her instructions. First, he or she was to read to the learner a list of four pairs of words. Then the teacher would read the first word of one of the pairs, and the learner was to supply the second word. The teacher sat in front of a rather imposing electric shock generator

FIGURE 11.4

A shock generator apparatus of the sort the teacher would use to punish the learner in Stanley Milgram's research on obedience. In the photo on the bottom, the subject is given a sample shock.

(see Figure 11.4) that had 30 switches, each with its voltage level labeled. From left to right, the switches increased by increments of 15 volts, ranging from 15 volts to 450 volts. Verbal labels were also printed under the switches on the face of the generator. These ranged from "Slight" to "Moderate" to "Extreme Intensity" to "Danger: Severe Shock." The label at the 450-volt end simply read "XXX."

As the task proceeded, the learner periodically made errors according to a prearranged schedule. The teacher had been instructed to deliver an electric shock for each incorrect answer. With each error, the teacher was to move up the scale of shocks on the generator, giving the learner a more potent shock with each new mistake. (The learner, remember, was part of the act, and no one was actually receiving any shocks.)

Whenever the teacher hesitated or questioned whether he or she should continue, the experimenter was ready with one of several verbal prods, such as "Please continue," or "The experiment requires that you continue." If the subject protested, the experimenter would become more assertive and offer one of his or her alternative prods: "You have no choice; you must go on," he or she might say. The degree of obedience—the behavior of interest to Milgram—was determined by the level of shock at which the teacher refused to go further.

Milgram was astonished by the results of his first study, and the results continue to amaze students of psychology more than 20 years later. Twenty-six of Milgram's 40 subjects—65 percent—obeyed the experimenter's demands and went all the way to the highest shock value and closed all the switches. In fact, *no subject* stopped prior to the 300-volt level, the point at which the learner pounded on the wall of the adjoining room in protest. One later variation of this study added voice feedback from the learner, who delivered an increasingly stronger series of demands to be let out of the experiment. The level of obedience in this study was still unbelievably high as 25 of 40 subjects, or 62.5 percent, continued to administer shocks to the 450-volt level.

It is important to note that the behavior of Milgram's subjects did not at all indicate that they were unconcerned about the learner. The subjects experienced genuine and extreme stress in this situation. Some fidgeted, some trembled, many perspired profusely. A number of subjects laughed nervously. In short, the people caught in this rather unusual situation showed obvious signs of conflict and anxiety. Nevertheless, they continued to obey the orders of the authoritative experimenter even though they had good reason to believe that they might well be harming the learner.

Milgram's first study was performed with male subjects ranging in age from 20 to 50. A later replication of the study using adult women as subjects produced precisely the same results: 65 percent of the subjects obeyed fully. Other variations of the basic procedure, however, uncovered that several factors could reduce the amount of obedience. Putting the learner and teacher in the same room, or having the experimenter deliver his or her orders over the telephone, for example, reduced obedience markedly. Another variation produced an interesting parallel to one of the Asch studies we discussed: When the shocks were delivered by a team consisting of the subject and two disobedient confederates, full obedience dropped to only 10 percent.

Attribution Errors and a Word of Caution.   When one first hears about these rather distressing results, there is a tendency for many people to think that Milgram's obedient subjects were cold, callous, unfeeling, unusual, or even downright cruel and sadistic people. Nothing could be further from the truth. As we have already mentioned, the participants in this research were truly troubled by what was happening. If you thought that Milgram's subjects must be strange or different, perhaps you were a victim of what we identified earlier as an *attribution error.* That is, you were willing to attribute the subjects' behavior to (internal) personality characteristics instead of recognizing the powerful situational forces at work.

Attributing such personality characteristics to the teachers is particularly understandable in light of the unexpected nature of the results. A number of psychologists in commenting on this research have suggested, in fact, that the most significant aspect of Milgram's findings is that they *are* so surprising to us. As part of his research, Milgram asked people (including a group of psychiatrists and a group of ministers) to predict what they would do under these circumstances, and he also asked them to predict how far others would go before refusing the authority. Needless to say, respondents in both cases predicted very little obedience, expecting practically no one to proceed all the way to the final switch on the shock generator.

We have already suggested that people tend to rely on others for help in determining social reality when ambiguity is present. The research procedures of Asch and Milgram created conflict for those subjects who tried to define the situations in which they found themselves. Asch created a discrepancy between what the subject perceived as true and what others said was true. In much the same way, Milgram created a discrepancy between what the subject felt was the right and proper thing to do and what an authority figure said must be done. The situation was probably made even more difficult for Milgram's subjects by the tendency that we have to accept perceived authority without questioning it. From very early in life, we are conditioned to obey our parents, teachers, police officers, and the like. We often tend to trust others when faced with tasks of resolving conflicts such as those presented in these two classic studies.

A Reminder on Ethics in Research.   In reading about Milgram's research, it should have occurred to you that subjecting participants to such a stressful experience might be considered morally and ethically objectionable. Milgram himself was quite concerned with the welfare of his subjects. He took great care to **debrief** them after each session had been completed. That is, he informed them that they had not really administered any shocks and explained why deception had been necessary. It is, of course, standard practice in psychological experiments to conclude the session by disclosing the true purpose of the study and alleviating any anxiety that might have arisen.

Milgram reported that the people in his studies were generally not upset over having been deceived and that their principal reaction was one of relief when they learned that no electric shock had, in fact, been used. Milgram also indicated that a follow-up study performed a year later with some of the same subjects showed that no long-term adverse effects had been created by his procedure.

debriefing
explaining to a subject, after an experiment has been completed, the true nature of the experiment, making sure that there are no lasting negative consequences of participation

Despite these precautions, Milgram was severely criticized for placing people in such an extremely stressful situation. Indeed, one of the effects of his research was to establish in the scientific community a higher level of awareness of the need to protect the well-being of human research participants. It is probably safe to say that because of the extreme nature of Milgram's procedures, no one would be allowed to perform such experiments today.

BEFORE YOU GO ON **Briefly describe Stanley Milgram's experimental demonstrations of obedience.**

Bystander Intervention

In March of 1964, a New York City cocktail waitress named Kitty Genovese was brutally murdered in front of her apartment building as she returned from work at approximately 3:30 a.m. Although murders have become somewhat commonplace in our large urban centers, there were some unusual and particularly disturbing circumstances surrounding this incident:

> *For more than half an hour, thirty-eight respectable law-abiding citizens in Queens watched a killer stalk and stab a woman in three separate attacks in Kew Gardens.*
>
> *Twice the sound of their voices and the sudden glow of their bedroom lights interrupted him and frightened him off. Each time he returned, sought her out and stabbed her again. Not one person telephoned the police during the assault; one witness called after the woman was dead* (New York Times, *March 27, 1964).*

This tragic event stimulated public concern and sparked a good deal of commentary in the media. People wondered how the witnesses could have shown such a lack of concern for a fellow human being. Apathy and alien-

Researchers have found that there are many reasons why people should not be expected to get involved in an emergency, including risk of physical injury and legal consequences. Nevertheless, some bystanders will choose to intervene as was the case in the car accident pictured here where passersby pulled a man to safety just before his car went up in flames.

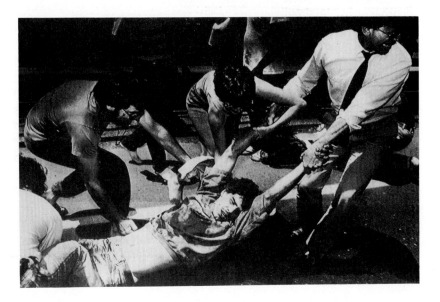

ation were terms frequently used in describing what had happened. One positive outcome of this unfortunate incident was that a program of research was begun to help establish a basic understanding of the social factors that can influence people to intervene or not to intervene in such a situation.

Bibb Latané and John Darley, two social psychologists who at the time were at universities in New York City, were not satisfied that terms such as *bystander apathy* adequately explained what happened in the Genovese case. They were convinced that people's failure to help was not due to internal, dispositional, or personality characteristics of the bystanders. They were convinced that situational factors make such events possible.

Latané and Darley (1970) first pointed out that there are typically several logical reasons why people should *not* be expected to offer help in an emergency. Emergencies tend to happen quickly and without advance warning. Except for medical technicians, firefighters, and a few other select categories of individuals, people generally are not prepared to deal with emergencies when they do arise. In fact, a good predictor of who will intervene in an emergency turns out to be previous experience with similar emergency situations (Huston et al., 1981). By their very nature, emergencies are not commonplace occurrences for most of us. It also goes without saying that the risk of physical injury, as was clearly present in the Genovese case, is an understandable deterrent to helping. Finally, people may fail to help because they genuinely want to avoid the legal consequences that might follow. They simply do not want to get involved.

A Cognitive Model of Bystander Intervention.   Latané and Darley (1968) also suggest that a series of cognitive events must occur before a bystander can intervene in an emergency (Figure 11.5). First, the bystander must *notice* what is going on. A person who is window shopping and thus fails to see someone collapse on the opposite side of the street cannot be expected to rush over and offer assistance. If the bystander notices something happen, he or she still must *interpret* the event as an emergency; perhaps the person who has collapsed is simply drunk and not really having a stroke or a heart attack. The third step involves the bystander deciding that it is his or her (and not someone else's) *responsibility* to do something.

Even if the bystander has noticed something occurring, has interpreted the situation as one calling for quick action, and has assumed responsibility for helping, he or she still faces the decision of what form of assistance to offer. Should he or she attempt to administer first aid; should he or she try to find the nearest telephone; or should he or she simply start shouting for help? As a final step in the process, the person must decide how to implement his or her decision to act. What is the appropriate first aid under the circumstances? Just where can a phone be found? Intervening on behalf of someone else in a social situation is thus seen as a series of cognitive choices.

A negative outcome at any of these cognitive steps of decision-making will lead the bystander to decide not to offer assistance. When one considers the cognitive events necessary for actually helping, along with the many potential costs associated with intervention, it becomes apparent that the deck is stacked against the victim in an emergency. As Latané and Darley have suggested, perhaps we should be surprised that bystanders *ever* offer help.

FIGURE 11.5
Some of the decisions and outcomes involved as a bystander considers intervening.
(After Darley & Latané, 1968.)

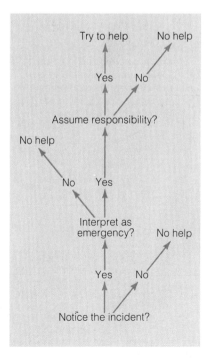

② Bystander Effect

audience inhibition ①
reluctance to intervene and offer
assistance in front of others

pluralistic ignorance ②
a condition wherein the inaction of
others leads each individual in a
group to interpret a situation as a
nonemergency, thus leading to
general inactivity

↑
EX₁

Although tragedies such as the Kitty Genovese murder do not happen every day, hundreds of media reports involving the same sort of scenario have appeared in the 25 years since that event. Rather ironically, it is the very presence of others that leads to this disturbing social-psychological phenomenon (Cunningham, 1984; Shotland, 1985). There seem to be a number of psychological processes that account for what we might call the *social inhibition of helping,* or *bystander effect.* We'll review three such processes (Latané & Darley, 1970; Latané & Nida, 1981).

The first process is called **audience inhibition.** It refers to our tendency to be hesitant to do things in front of others, especially when the others are strangers. We tend to be concerned about how others will evaluate us (a point we will return to later). In public, no one wants to do anything that might appear to be silly, incompetent, or improper. The bystander who intervenes risks embarrassment if he or she blunders. That risk is greater when the number of people present is larger.

Imagine that you are the one who steps out of a crowd to assist an unconscious man slumped against a wall. You might feel rather foolish if, as you turn him on his back to administer CPR, a couple of empty wine bottles were to roll out from under his coat. Simple audience inhibition, then, may frequently be sufficient to prevent intervention in an emergency.

Emergencies tend to be ambiguous: Is the raggedly dressed man who has collapsed on the street ill or drunk? Is the commotion in a neighboring apartment an assault or a family quarrel that's just a little out of hand? As we have already seen, when social reality is unclear, we turn to others for clues.

While a person is in the process of getting information from others, he or she will probably try to remain calm and collected, behaving as if there is no emergency. Everyone else, of course, is doing the very same thing, showing no outward sign of concern. The result is that each person is led by the others to think that the situation is really not an emergency after all. This second psychological process that contributes to the bystander effect is called **pluralistic ignorance.** The group is paralyzed, in a sense, and the phenomenon can be interpreted as a type of conformity—conformity to the inaction of others.

This process was demonstrated clearly in a classic experiment by Latané and Darley (1968, 1970). Columbia University students reported to a campus building to participate in an interview. They were sent to a waiting room and were asked to complete some preliminary forms. While they did so, white smoke began to billow through a vent in the wall. After six minutes (the point at which the procedure was terminated if the "emergency" had not been reported), there was enough smoke in the room to interfere with breathing and prevent seeing across the room.

When subjects were alone in the waiting room, 75 percent of them emerged to report the smoke. However, when two passive confederates were in the room with the subject, only 10 percent responded. People who reported the smoke did so quickly. Those from the groups who failed to do so generated all sorts of explanations for the smoke: steam, vapors from the air conditioner, smog introduced to simulate an urban environment, and even "truth gas." In short, the subjects who remained unresponsive had been led by the inaction of their peers to conclude just about anything other than the obvious—that something was wrong.

In the Kitty Genovese murder, it was terribly clear that an emergency was in progress; there was very little ambiguity about what was happening. Furthermore, the 38 witnesses were not in a face-to-face group that would allow social influence processes such as pluralistic ignorance to operate. Latané and Darley thus suggested that a third important process is necessary to complete the explanation of bystander behavior.

This process is referred to as **diffusion of responsibility.** A single bystander in an emergency situation must bear the full responsibility for offering assistance, but the witness who is part of a group shares that responsibility with other onlookers. The greater the number of other people present, the smaller is each individual's personal obligation to intervene.

diffusion of responsibility ③
the tendency to allow others to share in the obligation to intervene

Latané and Darley devised a clever demonstration of this phenomenon. In this study, college students arrived at a laboratory to take part in a group discussion of some of the personal problems they experienced as college students in an urban environment. To reduce the embarrassment of talking about such matters in public, each group member was isolated in his or her own cubicle and could communicate with the others through an intercom system. Actually there were no other group members, only tape-recorded voices. Thus, there was only one subject in each group, and the perceived size of the group could be easily manipulated to see whether diffusion of responsibility would occur.

The first person to speak mentioned that he was prone to seizures when under pressure, such as when studying for an exam. The others, including the actual subject, then took turns talking for about 10 minutes about their problems. A second round of discussion then began with the seizure-prone student who, shortly after he started talking, began to suffer one of his seizures.

Just as in the Genovese incident, it was obvious that something was wrong. As the "victim" began stammering, choking, and pleading for help, the typical subject became quite nervous—some trembled, some had sweaty palms. This study had another feature in common with the Genovese episode: Subjects could not be sure if any other bystanders (members of the group) had taken any action. (In fact, remember, there were no others.)

As expected, the likelihood of helping decreased as the perceived size of the group increased. Eighty-five percent of those in two-person groups (subject and victim) left the cubicle to report the emergency to the experimenter. When the subject thought that he or she was in a three-person group, 62 percent responded. Only 31 percent of the participants who believed that they were in a six-person group took any step to intervene. The responsibility for reporting the seizure was clearly divided (diffused) among those thought to be present.

Incidentally, diffusion of responsibility does come in forms that are less serious in their implications. Those of you with a few siblings can probably recall times at home when the telephone has rung five or six times before anyone has made a move to answer it, even though the entire family was there at the time. And some of you have probably been at parties where the doorbell went unanswered with thinking that "someone else will get it."

The Bystander Effect: A Conclusion. The situational determinants of helping behavior continued to be a popular research topic for social psychologists throughout the 1970s. Many of these studies included a manipulation of the size of the group witnessing the event that created the need for help in the first place. Latané and Nida (1981) reviewed some 50 studies involving nearly 100 different comparisons between helping alone and in groups. Although these experiments involved a wide range of settings, procedures, and participants, the social inhibition of helping (the bystander effect) occurred *in almost every instance*. Latané and Nida combined the data from all of these studies in a single statistical analysis. Their conclusion: There is very little doubt that a person is more likely to help when he or she is alone rather than in a group. In other words, the bystander effect is a remarkably consistent phenomenon, perhaps as predictable as any phenomenon in social psychology.

BEFORE YOU GO ON

What effect does the presence of others have on a person's willingness to help in an emergency?

What are audience inhibition, pluralistic ignorance, and diffusion of responsibility in the context of bystander and helping behavior?

OTHER EXAMPLES OF SOCIAL INFLUENCE

We have just reviewed in some detail how being a part of a group can alter one's behavior. Since a great deal of our behavior does occur in groups, group influence is an important topic in social psychology. In this section, we'll briefly survey a few additional examples of behavioral phenomena that occur in groups.

Social Impact Theory and Social Loafing

Latané has gone on from his studies of bystander behavior to suggest that other social behaviors also show diffusion effects (Latané, 1981; Latané & Nida, 1980). In fact, this idea has become a major cornerstone of Latané's theory of social impact.

Latané has proposed a **psychosocial law** that seems to predict the extent to which group size influences the behavior of individuals in that group. Fundamentally, this law specifies that each person that is added to a group has less impact on a target individual than the previous person to join the group. In terms of helping in an emergency, for example, this means that adding one other bystander besides yourself to the situation should decrease significantly your likelihood of responding. If, however, you are in a group of 49 bystanders, a fiftieth person would have little effect on the chances of your helping. This law can be usefully applied to almost all of the phenomena of social influence we have reviewed so far.

The data from a typical diffusion of responsibility experiment also support this logic. An idealized graph of the relationship between group size and the likelihood of individual intervention is presented in Figure 11.6. For

Important

psychosocial law
the view that each person who joins a social situation adds less influence than did the previous person to join the group

example, tipping in restaurants follows such a pattern. Freeman and his colleagues (1975) found that tipping declined systematically with increases in the size of the dining party. On the average, people eating alone left about a 19 percent tip, while those dining in groups averaged only about 13 percent of the total check.

Similarly, Latané, Williams, and Harkins (1979) have identified an effect they call **social loafing,** which refers to the tendency to work less (decrease one's individual effort) as the size of the group in which one is working becomes larger. Their studies had participants shout or clap as loud as possible, either in groups or alone. If individuals were lead to believe that their performance could not be identified, they invested less and less effort in the task as group size increased. Other studies (for example, Petty et al., 1977) have used more cognitive tasks, such as evaluating poetry. The results tend to be consistent: When people can hide in the crowd, their effort (and hence their productivity) declines. Notice that although social loafing is a widespread phenomenon, it not always predicted when one works in a group setting. It is only likely to occur if one's individual performance cannot be identified, or if the individual has no particular stake in the outcome of the performance. Indeed, there are some situations in which social influence actually facilitates behavior.

Social Facilitation

Many years ago, a psychologist by the name of Norman Triplett (1898) was struck by his observation that bicycle riders competing against other cyclists outperformed those racing against a clock. He then performed what is considered to be the first laboratory experiment in social psychology. Triplett had children wind a fishing reel as rapidly as possible. They engaged in this task either alone or with another child alongside doing the same thing. Just as he had noticed in his records of bicycle races, Triplett found that the children worked faster when another child was present. We now know that such an effect sometimes occurs not only with coactors (others engaged in the same task), but also if a person performs in front of an audience. When the presence of others improves an individual's performance on some task, we have evidence of what is called **social facilitation.**

Numerous studies of these phenomena were performed early in the twentieth century, but with a puzzling inconsistency in their results. Sometimes social facilitation would occur; but on other occasions, just the opposite would occur. Sometimes people actually performed more poorly in the presence of others than they did alone, an effect we call **social interference.** In fact, the inconsistency in these findings was so bewildering that most psychologists eventually gave up investigating social facilitation.

In 1965, Robert Zajonc resurrected the topic of social facilitation by providing a plausible interpretation for the lack of consistency in social facilitation effects. In his examination of the research, Zajonc noticed that social facilitation occurred whenever the behavior under study was simple, routine, or very well learned (such as bicycle riding or winding a fishing reel). Social interference, on the other hand, tended to occur whenever the behavior involved was complex or not well practiced. Zajonc suggested that

social loafing
the tendency for a person to work less hard when part of a group in which everyone's efforts are pooled

---

FIGURE 11.6
The psychosocial law applied to helping. This theoretical curve predicts the likelihood that someone will help in an emergency. As the number of fellow bystanders increases, the likelihood of helping behavior drops rapidly. (After Latané, 1981.)

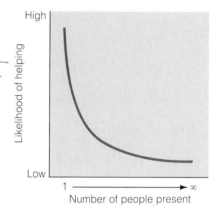

social facilitation
improved performance due to the presence of others *Competeing against a person is better than competeing against a clock*

social interference
impaired performance due to the presence of others

Because of social facilitations, we perform better when we are in the presence of others. Bicycle racers ride faster when racing against other riders than when racing against the clock.

the presence of others creates increased *arousal,* which in turn energizes the dominant (most likely) response under the circumstances. When the dominant response is correct, as with a simple, well-practiced task, social facilitation occurs. When the dominant response is incorrect, as with a complex task or one with which we have had little practice, the result is social interference.

You may have experienced this effect yourself if you have ever tried to acquire a skill at a sport that is totally new to you. Whereas skilled athletes tend to perform better in front of audiences, the novice tends to do better when alone. (There is evidence that even skilled athletes don't always perform better in front of audiences, sometimes "choking" in front of home crowds during important games (Baumeister, 1985).) You may have experienced (as a novice, that is) the frustration of finding it difficult even to hit a golf ball or tennis ball when there are others standing nearby watching you.

As an overall conclusion, we may safely assume that social interference and social loafing are more common phenomena than is social facilitation. Although there are occasions in which coworkers or an audience may enhance the individual's performance, the presence of others is more likely to inhibit it.

BEFORE YOU GO ON   **What can we conclude concerning the effects of social influence on the quality of an individual's performance?**

Decision-making in Groups

Many of the decisions that we face in our daily lives are the sort that must be made in groups. Committees, boards, family groups, and group projects for a class are only a few of many possible examples. There is logic in the belief that group efforts to solve problems should be superior to the efforts of individuals. One might reason that problem solving ought to be more effective in a group because individuals can pool resources. Having more people available should necessarily mean having more talent and knowledge available. It also seems logical that the cohesiveness of the group might contribute to a more productive effort (and for some groups and some problems, this is exactly the case). But by now we know better than to assume that simply because a conclusion is logical that it is necessarily true. In this section, we'll look briefly at two curious phenomena that can occur in the process of group decision-making.

When he was a MIT graduate student in industrial management, James Stoner gave subjects in his research a series of dilemmas to grapple with (Stoner, 1961). The result of each decision would be a statement of how much risk the fictitious character in the dilemma should take. To his surprise, Stoner found that the decisions rendered by groups were generally much riskier than those that the individual group members had made prior to the group decision. Stoner called this move away from conservative solutions a *risky shift*. For example, a number of doctors, if they were asked individually, might express the opinion that a patient's present problem (whatever it may be) could be handled with medication and a change in diet. If these very same doctors were to get together to discuss the patient's situation, they might very well end up concluding that what was called for here was a new and potentially dangerous (risky) surgical procedure.

Several hundred studies later, we now know that this effect can occur in the opposite direction as well (for example, Moscovici et al., 1985). In other words, the "risky shift" is simply a specific case of a more general **group polarization** phenomenon. The process of group discussion usually leads to an enhancement of the beliefs and attitudes of the group members that existed before the discussion began. The group process pushes members further in the direction in which they leaned initially. One explanation for group polarization suggests that open discussion gives group members an opportunity to hear persuasive arguments they have not previously consid-

Many of the decisions we face daily are the sort that are best made in groups, whether committees, boards, or family groups.

group polarization
the tendency for members of a group to give more extreme judgments following a discussion than they gave initially

The successful resolution to the Cuban missile crisis in 1962 demonstrated President John F. Kennedy's efforts to avoid the elements of groupthink that might have led to negative results. Recognizing past examples of faulty decision making with the Bay of Pigs incident, Kennedy chose to set up steps to consider the situation and all possible alternatives in a complete manner. The result was the Russians removed their missiles from Cuba, while the United States agreed to refrain from invading Cuba.

ered, leading to a strengthening of their original attitudes. Another possibility is that after comparing attitudinal positions with one another, some group members feel pressure to catch up with other group members who have more extreme attitudes.

Irving Janis (1972, 1983) has described a related phenomenon of social influence he calls **groupthink.** Janis maintains that this style of thinking emerges when group members are so interested in maintaining harmony within the group that differences of opinion are suppressed. It is especially likely to occur in cohesive groups. Alternative courses of action are not considered realistically and the frequent result is a poor decision. Janis has analyzed several key historical events—including the Pearl Harbor and the Bay of Pigs invasions and the escalation of the Vietnam War—in terms of the operation of groupthink. Each of these situations involved a cohesive decision-making group that was relatively isolated from outside judgments, a directive leader who supplied pressure to conform to his position, and an illusion of unanimity.

Before you conclude that decision-making in a group or social situation always leads to negative consequences, let us point out that there are circumstances in which groups are more efficient than individuals working alone. As we implied above, groups are useful when problems are complex and require skills and abilities that are more likely to be found in a number of different individuals working together. Group decision making can also serve to identify errors that individuals might not identify.

groupthink
a style of thinking of cohesive groups concerned with maintaining agreement to the extent that independent ideas are discouraged

BEFORE YOU GO ON How does social influence affect decision-making in groups?

Television and Violent Behavior

One type of social behavior that has attracted the attention of psychologists for a long time is aggressive behavior. Aggression is usually taken to refer to behaviors that are intended to harm or hurt another. **Violence,** then, is a form of aggression in which one purposively does physical harm to another. (The implication, of course, is that aggression in general may lead to psychological as well as physical harm.) The research literature on the nature of and the forces that influence violent behaviors is extensive. In this section, we'll focus on just one aspect of the nature of violent behavior: the extent to which it is socially influenced by television programming.

violence
behavior with the intent to do physical harm to another

The basic question of research in this area is simple: Does television viewing have an influence on the violent behaviors of viewers? By now, you are well aware that such simple questions seldom have simple answers. In this particular case, however, we do seem to have a simple and direct answer: Yes, watching violence on television does have an effect on violent behaviors, particularly for children.

There is certainly no doubt that television viewing is a popular pastime among children. This was expressed in a particularly disturbing way in a review article by Robert Liebert of the State University of New York at Stoney Brook. Liebert's assertion is that "the average child born today will by the age of 15 have spent more time watching television than going to school" (1986, p. 43)!

Is watching television related to increased violence? "In the simplest terms, only three possibilities exist in this equation. (1) Television has no significant relationship to aggressive behavior. (2) Television reduces aggressive behavior. (3) Television increases aggressive behavior. Almost all the studies reviewed in the past decade support the third possibility. No studies of any consequence support the second possibility" (Rubenstein, 1983).

Television violence seems to have an effect (again, particularly but not exclusively on children) in two ways: direct imitation and desensitization. The direct imitation aspect of television's influence follows nicely from the work of Albert Bandura (for example, 1973), which we reported earlier in Chapter 4. Many studies have shown that aggressive and violent behaviors increase almost proportionally with viewing violence on television (for example, Eron, 1982; Huesmann & Malamuth, 1986). What may be equally disturbing is evidence that even if one does not directly engage in violent behaviors after watching violence on TV, one's *tolerance* (or insensitivity) increases. This is, in a sense, a sort of perceptual adaptation. At first, scenes of great physical violence may be very upsetting and objectionable, but after repeated exposures, one adapts and becomes more accepting (for example, Linz et al., 1984; Singer & Singer, 1981).

Is there anything we can do (perhaps as parents) to mitigate the effects of violence on television. Here are three practical suggestions (from Liebert, 1986): (1) Restrict overall TV viewing time. (This is clear and obvious, but often difficult to manage.) (2) Selectively encourage some programming and discourage others. (It's generally quite easy to predict which shows are most likely to contain a high dose of violence—generally cartoons and crime shows.) (3) Watch TV with children, taking advantage of every opportunity to discuss the long-term ramifications of violence and your personal disapproval of such behaviors. (Remember Bandura's research indicating that children are more likely to imitate those who are rewarded for their behaviors than they are to imitate those whose behaviors lead to disapproval.)

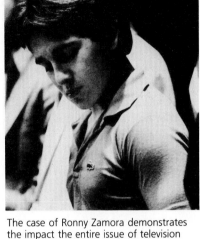

The case of Ronny Zamora demonstrates the impact the entire issue of television violence and its effects are having on our society. Fifteen-year-old Zamora was found guilty of murdering an elderly woman. Although attorneys for Zamora were unable to convince a jury that he was a TV addict who was unable to separate reality from make-believe, studies indicate that there is a correlation between television violence and aggressive behaviors.

Is viewing violence on television related to violent and aggressive behaviors of the viewer?

BEFORE YOU GO ON

We are social animals, and our behaviors as well as our feelings and cognitions are often influenced by those around us in our social environments. We have discussed some of the results of group influence, and a number of them have been unfavorable: leading people not to help someone else in need, to exert less effort, to perform poorly, to think inefficiently, or to act aggressively. At the same time, groups are a major part of social life, and some goals simply cannot be reached alone, without group membership. It is important to realize that effective group performance can be fostered by good morale, healthy communication, sound leadership, and teamwork that is accomplished through the appropriate division of responsibility. Hopefully, an awareness of the possible negative consequences of group activity and the conditions that produce them will enable us to counter obstacles to group productivity and satisfaction.

SUMMARY

What are stereotypes and norms, and in what way are they cognitive?

Both stereotypes and norms are sets of ideas or beliefs (that is, cognitions) that we form about our social world. Stereotypes are generalized mental representations that we have of other people and are often based on very little information. Norms are learned expectations or rules that guide and influence our behaviors in social situations. / 472

What is an attitude and what are its three components?

An attitude is an evaluative disposition (positive or negative) directed toward some object. An attitude consists of feelings (affect), behaviors, and beliefs (cognition). Although the affective and cognitive components of attitudes are often consistent with each other, behavior may be inconsistent with the other two major components. / 473

What are some of the functions served by attitudes?

Attitudes can guide our behaviors and summarize the beliefs we hold. They also serve a social identification function; that is, they tell others about us and the attitudes of others give us useful information about them. When we carefully select the attitudinal information we make available to others, we say that an impression management function is being served. / 474

What is cognitive dissonance, and how is it relevant to attitude change?

Cognitive dissonance is an unpleasant state of tension that may occur when we behave in a fashion inconsistent with the affective component of an attitude. Because we are motivated to reduce dissonance, we may do so by changing our attitudes so that they become consistent with the way we behave. / 475

Other than cognitive dissonance, what are some factors associated with persuasion?

The quality of the arguments involved in a persuasive communication and one's ability to form supportive or counterarguments are likely to affect the degree of persuasion by influencing the cognitive responses that the communication produces. Those communicators perceived as being expert or trustworthy are seen as credible sources of information and, hence, are more persuasive. / 477

What are the two basic types of attribution?

In what ways can attributions be distorted or biased?

Attributions are cognitions we develop to explain the sources of the behaviors we see in our social worlds. The two basic types of attribution are internal and external. An internal attribution finds the source of behavior within the person and is sometimes called a dispositional attribution. An external attribution finds the source of behavior to be outside the person and is sometimes called a situational attribution.

The *fundamental attribution error* leads us to overuse internal attributions in explaining the behavior of others, and our own behavior. Those persons who hold to the *just world hypothesis* are likely to believe that good things happen to good people and bad things only happen to bad people who in some way deserve their misfortune. The *actor-observer* bias refers to the tendency to use external attributions to explain our own (as actor) behaviors, while using internal attributions to explain the behaviors of others (as observer). / 480

Briefly summarize three theoretical models that account for interpersonal attractions.

The *reinforcement model* claims simply that we tend to be attracted to those we associate with rewards or reinforcers. The *social exchange model* adds the notion of cost to the equation, claiming that what matters in interpersonal relationships is the ratio of the benefits received to the costs invested in those relationships. The *equity model* suggests that both (or all) members of a relationship assess a benefit/cost ratio and the best, most stable relationships are those in which the ratio is nearly the same (equitable) for both (or all) parties, no matter what the value of the benefits for any one member of the relationship. / 481

What are four determinants of interpersonal attraction, and how do they have the effect that they do?

The principle of *reciprocity* states that we tend to like people who like us back. This is the most straightforward example of interpersonal attraction being based on a system of rewards. *Proximity* promotes attraction by means of the mere exposure phenomenon: being near another person on a frequent basis gives us the opportunity to see what that other person has to offer. We also tend to be attracted to people who we judge to be *physically attractive*. Finally, the principle of *similarity* suggests that we tend to be attracted to others who we believe are similar to ourselves. / 484

Briefly describe the methodology and the basic findings of the Sherif and Asch conformity studies.

Sherif used the autokinetic phenomenon (a very ambiguous situation) to explore the emergence of norms in groups. Over several days of judging how far a light moved, subjects adjusted their own estimates in the direction of estimates made by others. In the Asch studies, people made simple judgments about unambiguous perceptual stimuli—the length of lines. On some trials, confederates answering before the actual subject gave clearly incorrect judgments. Although there were situations in which yielding to perceived group pressure could be lessened, Asch's subjects followed suit and yielded to the pressure of the group surprisingly often. / 486

Briefly describe Stanley Milgram's experimental demonstrations of obedience.

Subjects in Milgram's experiments were lead to believe that they were administering more and more potent shocks to another subject in what was presented as a learning task. Whenever they hesitated to deliver shocks, an authority figure, the experimenter, prodded them to continue. All subjects obeyed to some degree and nearly two-thirds delivered what they thought was the highest voltage of shock, even over the protests of the learner. The individuals who obeyed in Milgram's experiments were neither cruel nor inhumane. Rather, the experimenter created a powerful social situation that made it very difficult to refuse the authority figure's orders. / 490

SUMMARY continued

What effect does the presence of others have on a person's willingness to help in an emergency?

What are audience inhibition, pluralistic ignorance, and diffusion of responsibility in the context of bystander and helping behavior?

Research data tell us that the likelihood that someone will intervene on the behalf of another in an emergency situation are lessened as a function of how many others (bystanders) are present at the time. A number of factors have been proposed to account for this phenomenon. *Audience inhibition* is the term we use to describe the hesitancy to intervene in front of others, perhaps for fear of embarrassing one's self. *Pluralistic ignorance* occurs when other bystanders lead one to think (by their inactivity) that nothing is really wrong in an ambiguous emergency situation. *Diffusion of responsibility* causes a member a group to feel less obligated to intervene (less responsible) than if he or she were alone. Each of these processes tends to discourage bystander helping and each is more likely to operate as the number of persons present increases. / 494

What can we conclude concerning the effects of social influence on the quality of an individual's performance?

The data suggest that as group size increases, social loafing increases. That is, one is less likely to invest full effort and energy in the task at hand as member of group than he or she would if working alone. It is also the case that the quality of one's performance also tends to suffer when one works in a group, a phenomenon called social interference. On the other hand, when tasks are simple or well rehearsed, performance may be enhanced, a process called social facilitation. / 496

How does social influence affect decision-making in groups?

There are some advantages to problem solving in a group setting. With proper leadership and communication, the combined expertise present in a group may provide better solutions and provide a better check on errors than we might find if individuals worked independently. On the other hand, *group polarization*—the tendency of group discussion to solidify and enhance preexisting attitudes—and *groupthink*—the unwillingness to promote an unpopular view in front of others in a group—operate to detract from group decision-making. / 498

Is viewing violence on television related to violent and aggressive behaviors of the viewer?

There has been a great deal of research on this issue, and the answer seems to be yes. Following the logic of Bandura's social learning theory of imitating models, there is a positive relationship between the viewing of aggression on TV and subsequent aggressive behaviors. In addition, a constant diet of violence on television seems to desensitize the viewer to the negative aspects of violence. / 499

REVIEW QUESTIONS

1. In spite of considerable evidence to the contrary, Paula believes that UFOs really do exist. We may surely conclude that Paula has:

a. positive affect concerning UFOs.

b. cognitions about UFOs.

c. an attitude toward UFOs.

d. an evaluative disposition with regard to UFOs.

In order to have an attitude about UFOs (or anything else), Paula would have to demonstrate affect, or feelings, about them—a tendency to respond in a certain way concerning UFOs, and cognitions, or beliefs, about UFOs. According to the statement made in this item, we can only be sure that Paula has a cognition (a belief) concerning UFOs. We don't know if she has any feelings (affect) or would tend to act in any way to UFOs, so we cannot claim that she has an attitude toward UFOs. / 472

2. Of the following, which component of an attitude is *least* likely to be consistent with the others?

a. affect.

b. evaluation.

c. cognition.

d. behavior.

In most cases, how we feel about an attitudinal object is consistent with our beliefs and our actual behaviors. If any component is likely to be inconsistent with the others, it will usually be our actual behaviors. For example, even if you don't like a particular restaurant and believe the food and service there to be poor, you might still choose to eat there if everyone else you were with decided that restaurant was where they wanted to go for lunch. / 473

3. When we use information about someone else's attitudes to form an impression of them, we say that attitudes are serving a _____ function.

a. social identification.

b. conflict resolution.

c. impression management.

d. stereotyping.

This is a straightforward definition item in which you are asked to recognize that the social identification funciton function of attitudes involves our use of knowledge about the attitudes of others to form impressions of them. Actually, alternatives (b) and (c) can be considered nonsense alternatives, or "fillers," having no relevance to the item at all. Impression management *is* a function of attitudes, but it involves presenting our own attitudes to others to mange their impression of us. / 473

Chapter Eleven
Social Psychology

REVIEW QUESTIONS continued

4. Considering all of the discussion of attitude change research presented in the text, which is the most reasonable conclusion?

a. It is easier to change how someone feels about an attitudinal object than it is to change what they actually do.

b. The more extremely one holds an attitude, the easier it will be to change that attitude.

c. It is easier to change someone's attitude by making extreme and ridiculous claims than by arguing reasonably.

d. Attitude change is generally more successful if one first focuses on changing cognitions, letting affect and behavior change follow.

This lengthy item needs to be read very carefully. Each of the first three alternatives is false. In fact, in each case, the opposite of the statement is true, which means that the fourth alternative is the best choice here. Remember the headings used in this section? The focus was on cognitive dissonance, cognitive response theory, and changing beliefs through persuasive communication--clearly a focus on the cognitive aspects or components of attitudes. / 474

5. The fundamental attribution error involves:

a. judging others more negatively than we judge ourselves.

b. believing that we are more affected by dispositional factors than situational factors.

c. thinking that someone who is good at one thing will necessarily be good at other things as well.

d. explaining behaviors of others in terms of internal attributes rather than external situations.

Here again is a definitional item, where the last alternative provides the best definition of the fundamental attribution error, even though the other alternatives may be distortions of attributions as well. / 478

6. Each of the following observations concerning interpersonal attraction is true _except_ that:

a. the reciprocity principle claims that we tend to value and like people who like us back.

b. the more we are exposed to someone—or something—the more likely we will be attracted.

c. in real life, dating partners are usually chosen to be the most physically attractive of those available.

d. men and women have very similar preferences for the characteristics they look for in a mate.

The first thing you should realize about this item is that it is basically asking you to identify the statement that is _false_. There is little doubt that physical attractiveness is an important factor in interpersonal relationships. However, in real life—where rejection is a real possibility—people tend to choose dating partners whose level of attractiveness is much like their own. This is called the matching phenomenon and is further evidence for the observation that interpersonal attraction is most often based on perceived similarity. / 481

7. In Milgram's experiments on obedience:

a. subjects were threatened with shocks if they did not obey.

b. males showed significantly more obedience than did females.

c. all of the subjects administered shocks that they believed were hurting another person.

d. his failure to debrief his subjects led to the widespread criticism of Milgram's procedures.

In Milgram's classic studies, all of the subjects administered shocks that they were led to believe caused significant pain to another person. None of those who administered the "shocks" was threatened to do so in any way. All of the subjects felt anxiety and discomfort in the experiment, and all were thoroughly debriefed when it was over. Milgram's first experiment used only male subjects. When he replicated the study later using female subjects, he found virtually identical results. / 486

8. Being led by others in a group to believe that an emergency situation is not really an emergency at all is an example of:

a. pluralistic ignorance.

b. bystander intervention.

c. audience inhibition.

d. diffusion of responsibility.

There are many possible explanations for why bystanders sometimes fail to intervene in an emergency situation, including diffusion of responsibility and audience inhibition. The situation described in this item, however, is an example of a phenomenon called pluralistic ignorance. / 492

Chapter Twelve

Applied Psychology

Why We Care

Industrial-organizational Psychology
Fitting the Person to the Job
Defining "Good Work"—The Job Analysis
Picking People Who Can Do Good Work
Training People to Do Good Work
Motivating People to Do Good Work
Fitting the Job to the Person
Job Satisfaction
Job Satisfaction and Work Behaviors
Quality Circles: An Example of Fitting the Job to the Person
Worker Safety

Psychology and Health
Personality and Physical Health
Psychological Interventions and Physical Health

Stress
Stressors: The Causes of Stress
Frustration-induced Stress
Conflict-induced Stress
Life-change-induced Stress
Reactions to Stress
The General Adaptation Syndrome
Reacting to Stress with Learning
Reacting to Stress with Aggression
Reacting to Stress with Defense Mechanisms

PSYCHOLOGICAL PREPARATION GIVES WORLD-CLASS ATHLETES AN ADVANTAGE—In addition to training their bodies to the peak of athletic perfection, Olympic athletes are also spending time training their minds to improve their performance. Sports psychologists have become an integral part of many amateur and professional athletes' training programs. "Physical preparation is no longer enough if you want to be a winner," said one track star.

THE STRESS OF OVERCROWDING MAKES CITY LIFE UNBEARABLE FOR SOME, CHALLENGING FOR OTHERS—Conditions of overcrowding have long been known to have adverse effects on rats, and it is usually assumed that people living in crowded urban settings suffer similar negative consequences. Recent research suggests that the crowded conditions of city life may also have benefits and may provide a sort of support for the individual that is not found elsewhere.

HELP FOR DIABETICS FOUND IN BEHAVIOR MODIFICATION AND BIOFEEDBACK TECHNIQUES— Diabetes is a disease that affects nearly 10 million Americans. At the moment, there is no cure for diabetes, but its symptoms can be treated and its progress arrested through the careful administration of insulin and by effecting changes in the patient's style of life. The psychological techniques

Recent research suggests that the crowded conditions of city life may . . . have benefits and may provide . . . support for the individual that is not found elsewhere.

of biofeedback and behavior modification recently have been demonstrated to be of significant value in helping patients monitor their own glucose levels (so the patient knows how much insulin to take and when to take it) and in actually reducing the need for medication.

PSYCHOLOGISTS URGE CAUTION IN ACCEPTANCE OF EYEWITNESS TESTIMONY—American courts have long relied heavily on the value of eyewitness testimony, particularly in criminal cases. Psychologists point out that many factors may lead to a distortion of the perception of reality and the memory of events, particularly in emotional and stress-laden situations. Basically irrelevant characteristics of the witness may also affect jury deliberations.

HOW AN INFANT CRIES MAY PROVIDE EARLY DIAGNOSIS OF DEVELOPMENTAL PROBLEMS

SEAT-BELT USE CAN BE INCREASED THROUGH PROGRAMS OF PSYCHOLOGICAL INTERVENTION

BEING THE HOME TEAM MAY NOT ALWAYS BE AN ADVANTAGE

CHRONIC PAIN CAN BE LESSENED BY BEHAVIORAL MEANS

THE SHAPE OF A ROOM DETERMINES ITS PERCEIVED SIZE

PSYCHOLOGISTS ARGUE FOR NEW STRATEGIES IN THE FIGHT AGAINST DRUNK DRIVING

PATIENTS WITH ORGAN
TRANSPLANTS REQUIRE HELP
WITH PSYCHOLOGICAL
ADJUSTMENTS

QUALITY CIRCLES HELP
AMERICAN INDUSTRY

PSYCHOLOGISTS QUESTION USE
OF EMPLOYMENT INTERVIEWS

TYPE-A PERSONALITY MAY BE
DANGEROUS TO YOUR HEALTH

These headlines are fictitious. The
stories they represent, however,
are real. Each provides an example
of recent interventions by
psychologists into the world of
social problems. Together they
provide just a glimpse of the sorts
of applications of psychological
principles to real life problems
that are becoming more and more
common. In this chapter, we'll
examine some of these issues of
applied psychology.

Why We Care

One of the themes we have maintained throughout this
text is that psychology has many applications in everyday
life. We have noted, right from the start, that one of the
major goals of psychology is to apply what we have learned
about our subject matter in the real world. Most commonly,
we think first of applying psychology in the context of diagnosis and therapy for psychological disorders. We also think
about applying principles of learning and memory to
improve education and child rearing. We have seen how the
scientific study of behavior and mental processes can be
brought to bear on many of the problems we face from day
to day.

In this chapter, we will focus even more directly on the
application of psychological principles to real-world events
and issues. First, we'll see how some of the ways our understanding of affect, behavior, and cognition can be applied
in the workplace. Then we'll examine the relationships
between psychological variables and health and the role of
stress in health.

INDUSTRIAL-ORGANIZATIONAL PSYCHOLOGY

I/O psychology
industrial-organizational psychology; specializing in the study of affect, behavior, and cognition in the workplace

ABC in workplace

We begin with an examination of **industrial-organizational (I/O) psychology.** Industrial-organizational psychologists specialize in the study of affect, behavior, and cognitions in the workplace. In large measure, psychologists in this field are concerned with applying psychological principles in order to improve the effectiveness and efficiency of business and industrial organizations. That does not mean, of course, that I/O psychologists are "company people," concerned only with the best interests of management. The I/O psychologist cares about the workplace in general, and that includes a consideration of workers' needs, as well as management's needs.

Industrial-organizational psychology is one of the fastest growing of psychology's specialty areas. More than 2,500 members of the American Psychological Association belong to its Division for Industrial and Organizational Psychology (Zedeck, 1987). Most I/O psychologists are employed by business and governmental agencies (approximately 67 percent), while about 30 percent are employed in academic settings. The remainder work either in private consulting firms or in hospital and human services settings (Stapp & Fulcher, 1983).

We'll examine just two of the major thrusts of I/O psychology. First, we'll discuss how best to fit the right person to a given job. This will entail a brief discussion of what we mean by "doing a good job," followed by a consideration of how we can best select, train, and/or motivate an individual to do that good job. Then, we'll examine how best to fit the job to the person, which will involve examining such matters as the quality of work life, job satisfaction, and safety in the workplace. Each of the issues raised here is relevant and meaningful to anyone who has ever entered the world of work.

Fitting the Person to the Job

It is generally to everyone's advantage to have the best available person assigned to any particular job. Employers benefit from having workers who are well-qualified and well-motivated to do their work. Employees also benefit from being assigned tasks that they enjoy and that are within the scope of their talents and abilities. When one of the authors of this text was a college student, a summer job required that he fill in for another employee and drive a large truck loaded with milk from a dairy in upstate New York to various locations in New York City. That he ever got that milk delivered had more to do with youthful enthusiasm and good luck than anything else. It no doubt took him twice as long as the regular driver to make the deliveries, and, to say the least, he didn't enjoy spending the better part of a summer's day being lost in New York City with a truck filled with milk. He was clearly not the best worker for the task.

What is involved in getting the best person to do a job? The relevant issues from the perspective of the I/O psychologist are personnel selection, training, and motivation. That is, one way to get a person to do good work is to *select* and hire a person who already has the ability and the motivation to do that work. On the other hand, we may choose to *train* people so that they acquire the ability to do good work. We may also have to face the task of *motivating* people with ability to do good work. These are the processes we examine in this section. Notice, however, that before we can begin selecting, training, or motivating someone for a job, we need to understand the nature of the job itself. We have to define what we mean by "a good job" before we can fit a person to it. So let's start with the job analysis.

Defining "Good Work"—The Job Analysis. Assume that you are an industrial-organizational psychologist hired by a company to help them select a manager for one of their retail stores in a local shopping center. You could not begin to tell the company what sort of person they were looking for until you had a full description of the job this new manager was to do. In general terms, you would have to know the duties and responsibilities of a store manager for this company. Then, you could translate that job description into a set of measurable characteristics that a successful store manager would possess. In other words, you would begin your selection efforts by doing a **job analysis.** A job analysis is a process that results in a complete and specific description of a job, including the personal qualities required to do it well.

Typically, writing a complete job analysis is a two-step process. The first step involves compiling a complete description of what a person in that job is expected to do. There are many sources of information that a job analyst might use to generate such a description. Most companies have official job descriptions for their employees, but these are usually stated in general terms, such as "supervise workers in the store; maintain acceptable levels of sales; prepare payrolls; monitor inventory; schedule work loads," and the like.

To be useful, a job analysis must be more specific in describing the actual *behaviors* engaged in by someone in a given position. Does a store manager have to know how to operate the cash register and inventory control devices? Does the manager deal with the sales staff on a one-to-one basis or in groups? Are interactions with employees informal and hit-and-miss or are there regularly scheduled, formal meetings that need to be organized? To what extent is the store manager responsible for employee training and development? Will the store manager be involved in labor negotiations? Clearly this list of questions can be a long one. The underlying concern at this level of analysis is, "On a day-to-day basis, just what does a store manager do?"

Valuable information can be gained through careful observation. It is always advisable for the job analyst to spend some time watching a person actually performing the job being analyzed. A good deal of information can be accumulated through questionnaires and interviews with other store managers or with supervisors of store managers. There are many standardized instruments available to help at this level of analysis.

Once duties and responsibilities have been delineated, the second step requires that these be translated into terms of measurable personal characteristics. That is, one determines the **performance criteria** required to do a job well. The goal is to generate a list of characteristics that a person in a given position should have in order to do that job as well as possible.

There are a number of different areas that might be explored at this point. Smith (1976), for example, distinguishes between what she calls "hard" criteria and "soft" criteria. The former come from available data and are objective—salary, number of units sold, number of days absent, and the

job analysis
a complete and specific description of a job, including the qualities required to do it well

One of the most important roles of the industrial-organizational psychologist is to help employers make the best possible personnel selections. The first step is doing a job analysis to get a complete description of a job and the personal qualities required to do it well.

performance criteria
specific behaviors or characteristics that a person should have in order to do a job as well as possible

like. Soft criteria required some degree of subjective judgment—sense of humor, congeniality, creativity, and the like. Let's use an academic example. Suppose your psychology department wants to give an award to its outstanding senior. Some of the criteria that determine which student has done a good job, and is worthy of the award may be hard—senior standing, a certain grade-point average, a minimum number of psychology classes, and so on. But some criteria may be soft. The department may want to give this award to a student only if she or he is well known to many of the faculty, has impressive communication skills, or has been active in the Psychology Club. These criteria require the judgment of those making the award. Indeed, most job analyses involve consideration of both hard and soft criteria.

Remember that the basic task here is to find the best available person to do a job as well as possible. if we are not fully aware of the demands of a job and have not translated those demands into specific performance criteria, we'll have difficulty ever determining if we have found the right person. In other words, we need to build in procedures early on by which our selection, training, or motivation program can be evaluated (Dunnette & Borman, 1979). Once a job analysis has been completed—once we know what an applicant will be expected to do on the job *and* once we have translated those tasks into measurable criteria—we are ready to begin designing an assessment process.

BEFORE YOU GO ON   **What is involved in doing a job analysis?**

Picking People Who Can Do Good Work.   As you might imagine, a wide variety of techniques and sources of information are available to the employer for screening and evaluating applicants for any given position. If the job analysis has been done properly, the psychologist has a complete list of those duties and characteristics in which the employer is interested. The task now is to find the person who best reflects those characteristics. In this section, we'll briefly examine some specific selection techniques.

Some useful information can be gleaned from a well-constructed *job application form*. An application form can serve three useful functions. (1) It can be used as a rough screening device. Some applicants may be denied simply because they do not meet some basic requirement for the job, such as a minimal education level or specified job experience. (2) It can supplement and/or provide cues for interviewing. Bits of data from application forms can be pursued later during in-depth interviews. (3) It provides biographical data (called *biodata*), including educational and work history, that may be useful in making direct predictions about a candidate's likelihood of success. Some I/O psychologists list biographical information of the sort that can be uncovered on job application forms as the best source of data for predicting success on the job (Baley, 1985; Muchinsky, 1987).

An integral part of many selection procedures will be the *employment interview*. We have already commented (Chapter 8) on the inherent dangers of relying too heavily on information gained through interviews. Unstructured interviews in particular are subject to many sources of error. Nonetheless, the interview is the most widely used employee selection procedure in this country (Arvey & Campion, 1982; Thayer, 1983). This is true in spite of the fact that results of validity studies for interviews are "dismal" and that

Interview – most widely used

"despite various innovations over the years, [the interview] has never been consistently shown to improve selection" (Tenopyr, 1981, p. 1123). For one thing, interviews, by their very nature, involve the interaction of two people—the interviewer and the person being interviewed. As a result, the biases of the interviewer, conscious or unconscious, may influence the results of an employment interview (Cash & Kilcullen, 1985).

There is evidence of considerable individual differences in interviewer skill. That is, some interviewers consistently obtain more useful (valid) information than others (for example, Thayer, 1983; Zedeck et al., 1983). Training interviewers to be sensitive to personal biases can also improve the validity of the technique, but such training is expensive. According to Cronbach, "In employment practice, interviews have several functions and surely will continue to be used. The best general advice is to make sure that interviewer judgments are not given excessive weight in selection" (1984, p. 406).

Beyond the application form and the interview, personnel selection often involves the administration and interpretation of *psychological tests.* Many tests are narrow in their application and are designed to assess only one specific characteristic of the applicant (finger dexterity, for example, which a job analysis may indicate to be very relevant for an assembly-line worker in an electronics plant). Other tests are more general, assessing a number of different skills and abilities. Tests of intelligence and/or certain personality characteristics may be called for, particularly when evaluating candidates for managerial or supervisory positions. There are literally hundreds of published paper-and-pencil tests designed to measure a variety of traits or characteristics, from typing skills, to mechanical aptitude, to leadership style, to motivation for sales work, to critical thinking skills. Some popular tests of general traits or abilities are being modified to focus more sharply on work-related applications (for example, Gough, 1985). An I/O psychologist involved in personnel decisions will know about these tests and recommend specific instruments for specific selection tasks.

From time to time, it is necessary to construct one's own test to assess some unique or special ability not measured by available instruments. A form of testing commonly found in employment settings is called *situational testing,* in which applicants are given the opportunity to role-play the task they may be hired to do. If you were going to hire someone to work at the counter of your dry cleaning business, for instance, you might ask an applicant how he or she would respond to an irate customer whose suit was damaged in cleaning. Actually role-playing the part of an angry customer while the applicant plays the part of employee might provide very useful information.

Some large corporations use what is called an **assessment center** approach to select management personnel. This approach provides evaluators with opportunities to observe applicants in a number of social situations and under stress. The assessment center was first introduced during World War II as a device for selecting candidates for the Office of Strategic Services, known today as the CIA. It wasn't until the 1960s that this approach was widely used for selecting and promoting executives in business and industry, although the first application was by AT&T in the mid-1950s (Bray et al., 1974). Assessment centers are now very popular. "The research question

The interview remains an integral part of the employee selection process, though studies reveal that biases on the part of the interviewer may influence the results.

assessment center *Very Popular*
a personnel selection procedure in which persons are tested, interviewed, and observed in a number of (stressful) situations by a team of evaluators

seems not to be whether to use assessment centers but how to understand what goes on in them, how to evaluate the results, and how to make them better" (Guion & Gibson, 1988).

The assessment center procedure involves an intensive period of evaluation, usually lasting three or four days. A number of applicants (usually 6 to 12) for a position are brought together with executives of the company and a team of psychologists. In addition to batteries of standard paper-and-pencil tests and interviews, the applicants are given a number of situational tests in which their behaviors in situations similar to those they might encounter on the job can be observed. One assessment center method is called the **in-basket technique.** Here, applicants are provided with a number of tasks, memos, and assignments of the sort they might encounter in a typical day at the office (as previously determined through a job analysis). They can then be observed as they attempt to sort out and deal with the imaginary issues they find in the in-basket.

Assessment centers provide an approach to selecting key persons in a business who often must function in social and stressful situations. Unfortunately, evaluating the assessment center process seems to lead to mixed reviews. The bulk of the data seem to suggest that the approach is a valid one (for example, Hinrichs, 1976; Saal & Knight, 1988). Others argue that the technique may be useful for predicting such general outcomes as who gets promoted or who gets large salaries, but it is not very useful in making specific predictions with regard to specific behaviors (for example, Hunter & Hunter, 1984; Zedeck & Cascio, 1984).

It may not always be practical or possible to find people who have precisely the abilities and motivation for doing the kind of work we are looking for. It may be that issues facing an organization are issues of training and/or motivating workers to do good work. Let's first look at training.

in-basket technique
an assessment technique requiring applicants to respond to a variety of situations that might be encountered in a typical workday

BEFORE YOU GO ON   **What are some of the sources of information that can be used in making personnel decisions?**

Training People to Do Good Work.   The training and development of employees is one of the major concerns of business and industry. The cost of training in business (and government) runs into billions of dollars every year. New York University psychologists Raymond Katzell and Richard Guzzo (1983) reviewed more than 200 experimental studies that dealt with psychological approaches to improving productivity and concluded that, "Training and instruction activities represent the most frequently reported approach to productivity improvement during 1971–1981" (p. 469). Typically, training programs have been found to be successful in a variety of organizational settings, with various types of personnel, and as indicated by a number of productivity criteria, including quantity and quality of work, cost reduction, turnover, accident reduction, and absenteeism (Katzell & Guzzo, 1983).

In the context of industrial/organizational psychology, **training** is taken to mean "a systematic intentional process of altering behavior of organizational members in a direction which contributes to organizational effectiveness" (Hinrichs, 1976). This definition implies that training is an activity

training
a systematic and intentional process of altering the behaviors of employees to increase organizational effectiveness

intended by an organization to increase the skills or abilities of employees to do the job to which they have been assigned. Training implies a systematic intervention, as opposed to a hit-or-miss approach to instruction.

Developing a successful training program is a complex, multifaceted enterprise. Let's review some of the steps involved in designing and implementing a training program. Our discussion is based on the system proposed by Goldstein (1980, 1986) and is summarized in Figure 12.1. You might want to follow along in this flow-chart of the major aspects of designing a training program.

Training programs are usually designed to address some need within the organization. So, one of the first things you will have to do is a complete assessment of instructional needs. In many ways, a needs assessment in this context is very much like a job analysis in personnel selection. There are a number of basic questions that must be raised and answered at this critical stage. Just what is the problem that training is supposed to solve? Is production down? Is there a new product that salespeople need to know about? Is the accident rate getting too high? The first stage of assessing instructional needs will be to state the general goals of your training program. At this point, a very difficult question to face is whether or not a training program is the best solution for a given problem. In fact, the most crucial decision to be made about training is the extent to which it is really needed, or required, as opposed to desired (Latham, 1988).

The second step requires translating these general goals into actual training objectives. At this stage, general statements of outcomes will no

Retraining employees to learn new skills and procedures will help keep worker motivation high and will also help industries stay abreast of new technologies.

FIGURE 12.1
A flow-chart diagram of the steps involved in planning and conducting a training program.
(Adapted from Goldstein, 1984.)

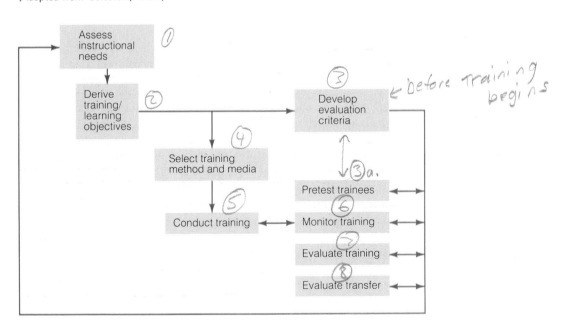

longer suffice. Now you need *specific* statements of what you expect the training program to accomplish. Just precisely what do you want trainees to know (or be able to do) at the end of the training session that they do not know (or do not do) now? Your training program will usually be evaluated in terms of these specific learning or behavioral objectives.

With your objectives in mind, but before you begin actual training, you will want to specify criteria by which your training can be evaluated when it is over. Clearly, your criteria for evaluating your program will be closely related to the needs and objectives of the program. For your program evaluation to be effective, it is important to list now—before training begins—how you will evaluate outcomes (Latham, 1988). There are many factors you might want to consider here. Did the trainees develop the skills and acquire the information you intended? How did the trainees feel about the program? Did the training program have an impact on the organizational needs that prompted the training in the first place? To assist in this evaluation, you might want to consider designing a pretest procedure to assess your trainees in terms of their present skill or information level. Such pretesting may provide a means of determining the impact of your program.

After you have determined the criteria for assessing outcomes, you now turn your attention to how you will go about the actual training. Given what you know about your needs and objectives and what you know about your employees, what will be the most efficient type of training mechanism you can use to reach your specified goals?

There are many different methods that might be used in a training program. In some cases, bringing workers together for what amounts to classroom instruction works well. On the other hand, there are situations in which assembling large numbers of workers would be unrealistic. Automobile manufacturers, for example, can hardly be expected to have all car salespeople report to the home office for instruction on improvements in the new models of cars they will be selling. Occasionally, training has to go to the worker—in the form of printed material, audio cassettes, videotaped programs, or live presentations by a trainer—rather than having the worker go to the training.

In any case, as designer of a training program, you will have many decisions to make about the methods you will use in your training program. Should you use "live" instructors, or should information be presented in the form of some media: print, audiotapes, videotapes, videodiscs, and the like? Should training be formalized and time-limited, or can trainees be allowed to work individually, at their own pace? Will there need to be hands-on experience? Will training be done in groups or will it be individually oriented? Will on-the-job training be efficient or disruptive? Can the job be simply simulated for the purposes of training (called *vestibule training*)? As you can see, your options are many, and all should be considered, because some are clearly more effective than others for certain kinds of training. Too many trainers fall into the habit of using only one or two techniques for a range of different needs and objectives. For example, televised instruction may be very useful to point out a few new features of an automobile to a salesperson, but quite ineffective as a means of training a service person how to repair a new electronic ignition system. By and large, simply presenting information is less effective than demonstrating it, and involving one's audience as participants (a so-called hands-on approach) is most effective.

Having decided on a training technique, you are ready to begin. If you have worked through the procedures outlined so far, you will find that actually conducting the training will be much easier than if you did not take the time to do so. We should add, of course, that you will continually monitor the effectiveness of the training program as it runs its course (check again with Figure 12.1). Even the best of plans sometimes need to be adjusted during actual training.

When you have finished your training program, you are ready to consider (again) what may be the most difficult part of training and development. You must evaluate the success of your training. Now you need some measure of the extent to which your training transfers to the actual job in the workplace, thus meeting the organizational needs that prompted the training originally.

There are many difficulties involved in doing quality evaluations of training programs, and we need not review them all here. We will only make these three observations:

(1) Training programs can be evaluated at a number of different levels. You may ask participants to rate *how they feel about* or evaluate the program. You may try to measure *how much has been learned* (perhaps with a formal testing before and after training). You may assess the extent to which the training has produced *behavioral changes*. Or you may go right to the bottom line and ask about *increases in profit or productivity* (from Kirkpatrick, 1976).

(2) Training programs that do not include ways and means of evaluating short- and long-term effectiveness will generally be of little value. Sadly enough, very few training programs are well-evaluated. Many seem to be taken simply on faith or face value because of their logical appeal (for example, Schultz & Schultz, 1986).

(3) The greater the effort put into the assessment of needs, job analysis, performance criteria, and the establishment of training objectives at the beginning of a training project, the easier it will be to evaluate the program when it is over.

List some of the factors that need to be considered in the design and implementation of a training program.   BEFORE YOU GO ON

Motivating People to Do Good Work.   Let's review for a moment. Our major concern in this section is fitting the person to the job—finding someone to do good work. The first step in that process involves carefully delineating just what is meant by a good job. To this end, one does a job analysis and lists specific performance criteria for the job. An employer can then go through the process of selection, trying to locate the best person for the job—a person who already has all the skills and motivation to do the job well. An alternative is to train a present employee to do good (or better) work. There remains an important consideration. There still may be some-

Motivation to do quality work can reach creative proportions as in this television assembly plant. Here, signs of encouragement were posted by workers themselves.

thing missing: the motivation to do good work. Being able to do a job well and wanting to do a job well are two different matters. Notice, too, that issues of training and motivation are generally continuous, ongoing concerns. People change, and jobs change. Seldom will one training program or one attempt to motivate employees be sufficient over the long term.

As you can imagine, I/O psychologists have long been interested in how to motivate employees to do their best work. When we talk about work motivation, we are referring to three interrelated processes: *arousing* (getting the worker to do any task), *directing* (getting the worker to do the task we want done), and *sustaining* (keeping the worker at the task). As you can also imagine, there are no simple answers to questions about how to motivate workers to do a particular job and stick with it. What we have are theoretical approaches to motivation in the workplace. We'll briefly review a few of the more popular approaches.

The **expectancy theory** of work motivation has found popularity among industrial-organizational psychologists. The approach has been around for many years and has been modified by many theorists, but it is best associated with Victor Vroom (1964). Part of the appeal of this approach is that it is highly cognitive. Expectancy theory says that workers behave rationally and logically, making decisions based on their beliefs, judgments, and expectations.

Vroom's expression of his theory is quite complex, but what it amounts to is that: (1) workers have expectations about the relationship between work behaviors and the likelihood that certain outcomes will occur, and (2) outcomes have different psychological values.

There are a number of implications here for employers concerned about motivating their employees to do good work. For one thing, they should see

motivational
Approaches

expectancy theory ①
the view that workers make logical choices to do what they believe will result in their attaining outcomes of highest value

very popular
among I-O Psychologists

(reward system
positive reinforcement)

if the outcomes that follow good work are truly valued by the workers. For example, in one company doing good work is rewarded by recognition with a plaque and a free trip awarded at the annual company dinner. (The company dinner is also viewed by management as a reward for a profitable year.) Now what if most of the workforce found company dinners to be a huge bore, plaques to be an embarrassment, and free trips a nuisance (arranging for transportation, babysitters, and so on). What if the employees would rather have a cash bonus or longer coffee breaks? That is, what if the employees actually believed that there was little value in what the company thought were rewards?

Another implication of this theory is that it is very important for workers to understand the relationship between their behaviors and outcomes. Simply put, workers need to know what to expect will happen if they behave in a certain way. Which behaviors lead to positive outcomes, and which lead to negative outcomes? Why should an employee work very hard, put in overtime, and take work home on the weekend if he or she has little or no reason to believe that such behaviors will lead to valued rewards? You may recognize the basic thrust of these arguments as being directly related to our discussion of basic learning principles in Chapter 4 (particularly those which covered operant conditioning).

Another approach to work motivation that has received support is called **equity theory,** and it is associated with J. Stacy Adams (1965). Equity theory is also cognitive in nature, claiming that what matters most to workers is their perception of the extent to which they are being treated fairly compared to fellow workers in similar work situations.

equity theory the view that workers are motivated to match their inputs and outcomes with those fellow workers in similar positions

In Adams' view, workers make a number of social comparisons (or cognitive judgments). First, they judge how much they are getting from the organization compared to what they are putting into it. That is, the worker judges the extent to which effort, skill, education, experience, and so on (inputs) are being rewarded by salary, fringe benefits, praise, awards, and the like (outcomes). Then, this ratio of inputs and outcomes is compared with a ratio from some other, similarly placed employee (called a "significant other" in this context). If the relationship is perceived as being approximately the same, or equitable, the worker will not be motivated to change. If, however, there is a perceived inequity compared to the inputs and outcomes of a fellow worker, then changes are predicted. The worker may increase or decrease inputs (work longer or shorter hours; take fewer or more breaks) or try to effect change in outcomes (ask for a raise). Notice that what matters most here is not the absolute value of what a worker gains for his or her efforts. What does matter is the perception of equity—what they gain in comparison to others. A worker will be much more willing to maintain effort (input) and take a cut in pay (outcome) if that worker believes that everyone else in the company is taking a similar cut in pay.

For example, a worker convinced of being underpaid—compared to other workers doing similar jobs—may either demand more money or invest less effort in the job. On the other hand, equity theory predicts that a worker convinced of being overpaid will either refuse some of his or her salary or invest added effort in the job. There is considerably more research support for the former prediction than for the latter (Locke, 1976; Middlemist & Peterson, 1976; Mowday, 1983).

Attention to establishing goals has been the centerpiece of a number of approaches to worker motivation, particularly that of Edwin Locke (1968). This approach, too, has a cognitive basis, assuming that workers are best motivated to perform a task for which the goals are clearly and specifically detailed. In order for goal-setting to have a positive influence on a worker's behavior on a task, two things are necessary. First, the goal must be clear. The employee must have a good *awareness* of what he or she is working for. Second, the employee must *accept* the goal as something worth working for.

The role of goal-setting in motivating workers has received considerable research interest. Here are some general conclusions. (1) Difficult, but achievable goals tend to increase productivity more than do easy goals. The issue here seems to hinge on the acceptance of goals as being worthwhile. Goals that are too easy to reach may simply fail to require any change in performance. At the same time, goals that are perceived as being *too* difficult and beyond the abilities of workers are not likely to be very useful. (2) Specific goals are better than general ones. Simply telling workers to "do better" or "do your best" provides little information about what is expected of them. (3) Feedback that informs workers of their progress toward established goals is important in maintaining motivated behaviors. Feedback delivered soon after a targeted response is made is more effective than delayed feedback. For example, acknowledging safety belt use (or nonuse) when people first enter their cars (with a buzzer, bell, or light) is going to be more effective in increasing safety belt use than waiting for the long-term feedback of either surviving a collision or not (for example, Geller et al., 1985; Geller et al., 1987). (4) Although there may be logic in the prediction that goals set by employers and employees working together are more effective than goals established by employers alone, the evidence suggests that this is not necessarily the case. Again, what matters most is that the employee be aware of specific goals and accept those goals as reasonable (Locke et al., 1981).

As you can well imagine, there are many other approaches to work motivation. Some refer directly to motivational concepts we introduced back in Chapter 7 when we discussed motivation in general. That is, some approaches stress the importance of workers' needs (as in Maslow's theory about a hierarchy from basic physiological needs to needs to self-actualize). Some approaches stress the importance of principles of behavior change through operant conditioning procedures and attention to the consequences of behavior, reinforcers, and punishers (an approach called "organizational behavior management" when applied in work environments).

Here's a brief summary of our discussion. Workers will tend to be well motivated to do a good job if:

(1) Clear and specific goals are established and accepted.
(2) The goals that employers set match workers' expectations and needs.
(3) Workers see clearly the relationship between their on-the-job performance and accepted outcomes.
(4) Workers judge the outcomes that follow from their efforts as being in line with those earned by fellow workers making similar efforts.
(5) Workers are given feedback about the nature of their work.

Now let's shift our emphasis slightly from a concern about finding and fitting the person to the job to the issue of fitting the job to the person. In large measure, our interest here is with what we call job satisfaction. What can be done to make jobs more satisfying? What is the result of doing so?

Briefly summarize some of the factors that affect the motivation of workers to do a good job.   BEFORE YOU GO ON

Fitting the Job to the Person

To this point, we've been taking the perspective of an employer. We have asked what an employer can do to find and/or fit the best person for a given task. In this section, we'll change our point of view ever so slightly and consider the world of work from the perspective of the worker. There are two major issues here. The first has to do with job satisfaction. We'll define the concept, and then we'll see if job satisfaction is correlated with any job performance measures. The second issue has to do with the design of work and the workplace. How can jobs be designed to maximize such factors as employee safety and health?

point of view from worker

Job Satisfaction.   **Job satisfaction** refers to the attitude that one holds toward one's work—"a pleasurable or positive emotional state resulting from the appraisal of one's job or job experiences" (Locke, 1976). Although we may talk about job satisfaction in general terms, it is clear that an employee's degree of satisfaction can vary considerably for different aspects of the job itself. As you know from your own work experience, you might be quite happy with your physical working conditions, very unhappy with base salary, pleased with the availability of fringe benefits, satisfied with the level of challenge provided by the job, very dissatisfied with relationships with coworkers, and so on. In fact, there may be as many sources of job satisfaction and/or dissatisfaction as there are aspects to one's job.

job satisfaction
an attitude; a collection of feelings about one's job or job experiences

A great deal of research has looked for relationships between job satisfaction and personal characteristics of workers. Let's summarize some of that research very briefly. (1) There is a rather strong correlation between overall satisfaction and age. Younger workers tend to be most dissatisfied with their jobs in general and the actual work itself in particular (Rhodes, 1983). (2) Data on sex differences in job satisfaction tend to be inconsistent. By and large, however, sex differences are quite small (Sauser & York, 1978) and virtually nonexistent when pay, tenure, and education are controlled (Hulin & Smith, 1964). (3) Racial differences in job satisfaction consistently have been shown to be small, with whites having more positive attitudes about their jobs than nonwhites (Weaver, 1980). (4) Satisfaction is positively related to the perceived level or status of one's job or occupation, where those of lowest rank tend to be filled by least satisfied workers (King et al., 1982). Of course, the real issue here for the I/O psychologist is to determine *why* these differences in job satisfaction occur or do not. All we have listed here are results of correlational studies that tell us nothing about cause and effect. The focus of attention now is on the question of why older, white workers in high status jobs tend to be more satisfied with their lot than younger, black workers in low status jobs.

← *Important*

quality of work life (QWL)
a group of factors concerning one's work that influence one's attitude toward one's job

Recently, I/O psychologists have become interested in a concept somewhat broader than job satisfaction called **quality of work life**, or **QWL**. QWL is a difficult concept to define concisely, but may be taken to include such factors as: (1) a sense of respect from supervisors; (2) employee security (the future of the job); (3) income adequacy and equity (present and future); (4) a sense of self-esteem, challenge, and independence; (5) opportunities for social interaction; (6) a sense of making a real contribution; (7) a relationship between life on the job and life off the job, and (8) active participation in decision making (from Davis & Cherns, 1975; and Levine et al., 1984). The major concern of I/O psychology in this area has been to develop strategies to improve the quality of work life within an organization (Beer & Walton, 1987; Lawler, 1982; Tuttle, 1983).

It is sometimes difficult to remember that concerns about the welfare of workers, much less their satisfaction with any part of their job, is relatively new in the history of work. Concern for the quality of work life first began to take hold only about 50 years ago (Hoppock, 1935; Mayo, 1933). Before then, workers were often viewed by the organizations that hired them not so much as people, but as pieces of machinery—chosen, hired, and minimally trained to do a particular (often narrowly defined) task (Latham, 1988). Many companies now employ industrial-organizational psychologists whose main charge is to recommend changes in organizational structure that will best facilitate worker satisfaction and improve the quality of work life. Is this recent emphasis on the well-being of workers motivated only by humane considerations? Or is there research support for the hypothesis that increased worker satisfaction leads to increased productivity and increased profitability?

New →

BEFORE YOU GO ON   **What is meant by job satisfaction and quality of work life?**

Job Satisfaction and Work Behaviors.   There is a certain logic to the assertion that the happy worker is a productive worker—that increased job satisfaction necessarily will be reflected in increased worker productivity. For the last 50 years, many managers and executives have assumed, without question, a causal relationship between satisfaction and productivity. In many ways, satisfaction and productivity *may* be related, but the relationship is not a simple one and is at best a weak one (Iaffaldano & Muchinsky, 1985). In fact, research on job satisfaction often refutes the contention that increased performance *necessarily* results from increased satisfaction (Howell & Dipboye, 1982). Over and over, we find contradictory evidence, which among other things reflects the difficulties involved in agreeing on good operational definitions for both quality of work life and worker productivity (Hartman et al., 1986). The only conclusion we can safely draw about these two variables is that in some instances they may be correlated. Cause-and-effect statements are out of the question.

The lack of a strong, consistent relationship between satisfaction and productivity may not be that difficult to explain. Some workers may hate their present jobs, but work very hard at them so that they may be promoted to some other position that they believe they will prefer. Some individuals may be very satisfied with their present positions simply because expectations for productivity are very low—if demands for productivity increase, satisfaction may decrease, at least in this situation. *Increasing productivity may have the effect of increasing satisfaction,* rather than vice versa. A well-motivated employee, who wants to do her very best at her job, will be pleased to enter a training program to improve her on-the-job efficiency. Doing the job better leads to pride and an overall increase in satisfaction for this worker; for another, the same training program may be viewed as a ploy on management's part to make life miserable for the worker.

We shouldn't give the impression that job satisfaction is not consistently or meaningfully related to *any* work behavior. There is evidence that job satisfaction measures can be used to aid the prediction of which workers are likely to be absent from work and which are likely to quit (what Saal and Knight (1988) call "withdrawal behaviors"). As it happens, job satisfaction is not the best predictor of absenteeism (marital status, age, and size of one's work group are better (Watson, 1981)), but the correlations are at least reasonably consistent (Porter & Steers, 1973). The relationship between dissatisfaction with one's job and turnover seems to be even stronger, although the relationship may not be direct. That is, dissatisfaction may be an important contributing factor, but it is only one of a number of variables that can be used to explain why one leaves a job. (Many times people are forced to quit their jobs for reasons that have nothing at all to do with the job or the employer—illness and family concerns, for example.) Nonetheless, the logic that persons who are most unhappy with their work are the ones likely to leave it does have research support (Mobley, 1977; Muchinsky & Tuttle, 1979).

BEFORE YOU GO ON

Briefly summarize the relationship between job satisfaction and job productivity.

Quality Circles: An Example of Fitting the Job to the Person. Quality circles (QC) are small groups of 4 to 12 employees who voluntarily meet on a regular basis (generally once a week) to discuss problems related to the quality of the products or services they work with. The assumption is that these group discussions of production problems will lead to practical solutions (Gibson, 1982). It is then further assumed that quality circle participation will lead to increased productivity, job satisfaction, cost savings, and profitability. Notice that the major emphasis on "quality" in quality circle is on the quality of products or services, not on the quality of work life. The basic idea behind quality circles was discussed in American I/O psychology for many years before, but their actual use began in Japan soon after World War II. Even so, QCs were not transported to Western corporations until the recession of the late 1970s. Since then, the idea has caught on like wild fire, and can be found operating in nearly half of all large corporations in the United States (Rice, 1984; Yager, 1981).

Only recently have industrial-organizational psychologists begun to study QCs to see if they really do bring about all of the positive changes that their proponents claim. The results of these studies give us what we might describe as a condition of cautious optimism (Lawler & Mohrman, 1985; Marks, 1986; Rafaeli, 1985). Probably the most consistent evidence that has come from research on quality circles is that they *do not* have a great impact on overall job satisfaction. QCs *do* have a positive impact on workers' per-

quality circles (QC)
small groups of employees that voluntarily meet on a regular basis to discuss problems of production

Quality circles, introduced by the Japanese after World War II but only recently adopted by American firms, are small groups of employees who meet regularly to discuss problems related to their products or services. With careful planning at the time they are set up, quality circles can improve productivity.

ception of personal influence. The longer a worker is a member of a quality circle, the greater influence that worker feels he or she has in the group and the company. The impact of quality circles on productivity is quite inconsistent. Those studies that do suggest that QCs have a positive impact on productivity caution that most improvements are rather narrowly confined to the focus of the particular QC.

The general conclusion with regard to quality circles is that they may be of some value in increasing job satisfaction, but will probably be of little value in (directly) increasing job productivity. An important variable seems to be the care and planning that go into setting up quality circles in the first place. As I/O psychologist Mitchell Marks says, "QC's can improve employee productivity and have a limited impact on morale and work satisfaction but only when programs are backed by sufficient training and genuine management commitment to them" (1986, p. 46).

BEFORE YOU GO ON **What are quality circles, and how do they affect productivity and job satisfaction?**

Worker Safety.   In this section, we'll review one of the oldest concerns of industrial-organizational psychologists: safety in the workplace. The statistics on industrial accidents are impressive. One compelling example is provided by Schultz and Schultz (1986, p. 445) who claim that during the peak years of the Vietnam War (1966–1970), more Americans were killed in industrial accidents than in combat. Looked at from a different perspective, accidents in the workplace cost the United States well over $50 billion a year in lost wages, insurance and medical expenses, and property loss (DeReamer, 1980). The challenge is clear: increase the safety of the workplace. But how? Here we list three approaches that I/O psychologists have explored (after Landy, 1985).

1. *The Engineering Approach.* This approach attempts to reduce acci- ← "Best"
dents through the design and implementation of safe equipment
and procedures. Of the three approaches, this one has been most
successful in a wide range of applications. Examples abound. All
automobiles now sold in this country are required to have a (third)
stop light positioned at eye level. This requirement evolved from a
safety study done with taxi cabs in San Francisco in a successful
attempt to reduce rear-end collisions (Voevodsky, 1974). Complex
control panels are engineered with safety in mind, so that the
most critically important dials, meters, buttons, and switches are
in clear view and easy to read and interpret. Work areas are designed so that there is adequate illumination, sufficient space to
move about, and so that scrap materials and trash can be readily
removed. Heavy equipment is designed so that it can only be operated in a reasonably safe way. (One of your authors once had a job
using a large paper cutter that could easily cut through hundreds
of sheets of paper with one thrust of a huge, very sharp blade. It
took two hands to activate that blade; one moved a lever from
right to left, while the other hand moved a second lever down-
ward. There was no way that the operator could lower the blade
through a stack of paper and cut a finger at the same time.)

   Engineering approaches to accident prevention may involve the
scheduling of work time as well as the design of machinery and
equipment. There is ample evidence of a positive relationship between fatigue and accidents. Scheduling work time (reducing overtime work, for example) to minimize fatigue seems to improve
safety (Durham, 1979).

2. *The Personnel Approach.* This approach is based on the popular
notion that some people are more "accident prone" than others, or
that at least there are some personality traits that are consistently
related to high incidences of accidents. If this were true, then safety could be improved by not hiring those applicants who are prone
to accidents. The problem is that the basic notion is not true. After many years of trying to identify characteristics of persons likely
to behave in dangerous ways, psychologists are about to give up
the search. There just don't seem to be people who are—in general—any more accident prone than anyone else. (Which, of course,
may reflect our inability to adequately assess such a trait.) There
still is some obvious sense to this approach that relates to a number of points we raised in the first section of this chapter. The less
well qualified a person is for a job, the less well-trained, or the less
well-motivated, the more likely it is that that person will have an
accident—particularly if the job is an inherently dangerous one.
You wouldn't want to send an employee with poor coordination
and balance to work high above the ground on scaffolding, for
example.

3. *The Industrial-social Approach.* This point of view takes the rather
strange sounding position that workers often need to be motivated
to work safely. At first you might think that anyone in his or her
right mind would want to work safely and avoid being in an acci-

dent. And you might be right. But does the worker know *specifically* what constitutes safe behaviors? Does the worker know that the employer *values* safe work and that safe work will rewarded? If such is not the case, workers may take "shortcuts" and "cut corners," working too quickly—and too dangerously—if they believe that the only rewards are for amount of work or size of output. This approach suggests that employers must make sure that workers are trained in safe ways to do their job (Levine, 1983) and that they realize that safe behaviors are valued (Zohar, 1980). What matters most, as we have seen before, is clearly establishing safety goals, providing feedback to workers, and reinforcing those who attain stated goals.

BEFORE YOU GO ON   **What are three approaches to improving safety, and is there any evidence that they are effective?**

We have been able to only scratch the surface of what industrial-organizational psychologists do in their attempt to apply basic principles of psychology to the world of work. We have focused on just two interrelated issues. First, we considered how employers can best fit a person to a given job. This process involves a number of subprocesses, such as doing a complete job analysis, specifying performance criteria by which personnel can be evaluated for a given job, using a number of techniques to select the best person for a job, and training or motivating a person to do the best job. Then we turned our attention to the worker in an organization, looking at such issues as job satisfaction and the quality of work life and how these are related to productivity. We also reviewed some of the approaches that I/O psychologists have taken to improve the safety of the workplace. Next, we'll look at health psychology and the role of stress in physical health.

PSYCHOLOGY AND HEALTH

health psychology
the field of applied psychology that studies psychological factors affecting physical health and illness

Health psychology is a field of applied psychology that is just over ten years old, although the issues involved have been of general concern for a very long time. **Health psychology** is the study of psychological or behavioral factors affecting physical health and illness. Involving psychologists in the medical realm of physical health and well-being is based on at least four assumptions:

1. Certain behaviors increase the risk of certain chronic diseases.
2. Changes in behaviors can reduce the risk of certain diseases.
3. Changing behaviors is often easier and safer than treating many diseases.
4. Behavioral interventions are comparatively cost effective (Kaplan, 1984).

In this section, we'll look at the role of psychologists in the understanding, treatment, and prevention of physical disease.

Personality and Physical Health

Is there a relationship between aspects of a person's personality and that person's state of physical health? Can psychological evaluations of an individual be used to predict physical as well as psychological disorders? Is there such a thing as a "disease-prone personality"? Our response is very tentative, and the data are not all supportive, but for the moment we can say, "Yes, there does seem to be positive correlation between some personality variables and physical health."

One recent review applied a statistical reanalysis to the data of 101 previously published research articles. The goal was to look for relationships between personality (depression, anger/hostility, anxiety, aggression, extroversion) and physical disease (coronary heart disease, asthma, ulcers, arthritis, headaches). The strongest associations were those that predicted coronary heart disease (CHD), although depression, anxiety, and anger/hostility were each associated to some degree with all of the physical components studied (Friedman & Booth-Kewley, 1987). On the basis of their analysis, the authors argued that there is sufficient (albeit weak) data linking some personality variables with some physical diseases to "argue for a key role for psychological research on the prevention and treatment of disease" (p. 539).

When we talk about relating personality variables to physical diseases, what commonly comes to mind is the **Type A behavior pattern (TABP)** and its relationship to coronary heart disease (CHD). The Type A behavior pattern refers to a competitive, achievement-oriented, impatient individual who generally is working at many tasks at the same time, is easily aroused, and is generally hostile or angry (Friedman & Rosenman, 1959; Rosenman et al., 1964). Coronary heart disease (CHD) is a label given to a number of physical symptoms, including chest pains (angina pectoris) and heart attacks (myocardial infarction), caused by a build-up of materials (for example, cholesterol) that block the supply of blood to the heart. For nearly 20 years—from the early 1960s to the early 1980s—study after study seemed to show a clear relationship between CHD and behaviors typical of the Type A personality (Jenkins, 1976; Rosenman et al., 1975; Wood, 1986). A review panel of the National Institute of Heath declared the Type A behavior pattern an independent risk factor for heart disease (NIH Panel, 1981). It all seemed quite clear. Find people who demonstrate the Type A behavior pattern, intervene to change their behaviors, and just see how coronary heart disease rates decline. By now you know to be suspicious when complex problems seem to have such simple solutions.

Beginning in the early 1980s, data began to surface that failed to show a clear relationship between TABP and CHD (Fishman, 1987; Krantz & Glass, 1984; Shekelle et al., 1985; Wright, 1988). Perhaps Type A people were no more at risk for heart disease than anyone else. Perhaps studies that failed to find a relationship between TABP and CHD were seriously flawed. In fact, both of these alternative hypotheses have some evidence to support them. For one thing, the Type A behavioral pattern is, by its nature, quite complex and difficult to diagnose. It seems likely that simple paper-and-pencil inventories—of the sort that have been used in many studies—fail to identify correctly a large number of people with the TABP.

type A behavior pattern (TABP)
a collection of behaviors (competitive, achievement-oriented, impatient, easily aroused, often hostile or angry) often associated with coronary heart disease

People who exhibit the Type A behavior pattern are usually impatient, easily angered, and highly competitive. While many studies support the idea that there is a link between Type A behavior and coronary heart disease, the Type A behavior pattern remains difficult to diagnose.

Concern about the relationship between stress and coronary disease has led many people to undergo testing. A stress test is a way of monitoring a patient's vital signs while he or she walks a treadmill. The test, along with others, will show how the body responds to the stress of physical activity.

It also may be that the TABP, as presently defined, is simply too global a pattern of behaviors. Perhaps there is a subset of behaviors within the constellation of Type A behaviors that does predict coronary disease. This is a hypothesis now under investigation by psychologist Logan Wright, a self-confessed Type A personality, who recently was required to undergo bypass surgery to relieve blockage of his coronary artery. As Wright puts it, ". . . if certain so-called active ingredients, or subcomponents of the TABP are what is really responsible for coronary-prone risk, one would expect to find them to correlate more highly with CHD than does the global Type A pattern itself" (1988, p. 3).

What are Wright's candidates for the most likely active ingredients of the Type A personality? (1) *Time urgency*—concern over wasting precious, small bits of time; shifting lanes while in traffic to gain a car length; (2) *chronic activation*—the tendency to stay alert and aroused and ready all the time; being "fired up" for everything, no matter how mundane; and (3) *multiphasia*—the tendency to have a number of projects all going at once, having many irons in the fire; doing homework and eating while watching TV. Wright cites research to suggest that these components may be worthwhile predictors of coronary heart disease. But the evidence is not conclusive. More work needs to be done. We need more research on adequate diagnosis for Type A behavior patterns. We also need more research on the mechanisms that underlie whatever relationships there may be between TABP and CHD. And we need research on how to bring about psychological changes in individuals that would reduce the likelihood of their contracting any physical disease. Indeed, in many ways, the so-called "active ingredients" of the Type A personality are precisely the characteristics that many people in our society learn to value and to imitate in their quest to "get ahead." As Wright says, ". . . although much Type A functioning may be productive, one *must* still learn to glide" (1988, p. 12). How can psychologists best intervene to help people glide? It is to matters of intervention that we now turn.

Briefly summarize the relationship between the Type A behavioral pattern and coronary heart disease.   BEFORE YOU GO ON

Psychological Interventions and Physical Health

It seems at least possible that some personality characteristics have an influence on the state of one's physical health. As we've seen, the specific traits involved and the nature of that influence are the subject of much debate and continued research. There is no debate and no doubt, however, that certain behaviors do put people at risk for certain physical ailments. Today, the leading causes of death in this country are cardiovascular disorders and cancers. These diseases are caused and maintained by the interaction of a number of factors, including biological, social, environmental, and behavioral influences. Among the latter, such variables as cigarette smoking, nutrition, obesity, and stress have been identified as important risk factors (Krantz et al., 1985). What this means is that for millions of people, factors we may collectively call "life style" are deadly. (Clearly, a "deadly life style" also may involve behaviors that even more directly lead to death, such as excessive alcohol consumption, failure to wear safety belts, or knowingly engaging in other unsafe behaviors at work or play. Our focus here, however, is on behaviors linked to illness and disease.)

One role of the health psychologist is to intervene to bring about changes in dangerous life style behaviors (Matarazzo, 1980; Miller, 1983). Indeed, "7 of the 10 leading causes of death in the United States are in large part behaviorally determined. We believe these unhealthy behaviors can be significantly reduced with help from psychologists" (Heffernan & Albee, 1985, p. 202). Interventions designed to prevent health problems from arising in the first place have been applied to a wide range of behaviors, including smoking, misuse of alcohol, nutrition, physical fitness and exercise, control of stress, high blood pressure control, family planning, immunization, and sexually transmitted diseases (McGinnis, 1985). Psychologists also use behavioral techniques in attempts to promote healthy and safe behaviors such as the wearing of car safety belts (Geller et al., 1987).

Although efforts to effect attitudinal and behavioral change have been moving forward on all these fronts, few have received as much attention as efforts to discourage young people from smoking. Part of the reason for special efforts in this area is that the success rate of programs to persuade smokers to quit smoking have been less than encouraging. Nearly 80 percent of "quitters" relapse within a year. (In fact, most smokers who quit permanently do so without any special program of intervention.) Approaches that use role models and peers to teach specific skills to be used to resist pressures to begin smoking in the first place have been quite successful (for example, Murray et al., 1984).

Health psychologists also intervene to help in the treatment of physical illness and disease. As an example of this sort of work, consider efforts to

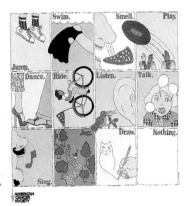

12 THINGS TO DO INSTEAD OF SMOKING CIGARETTES.

Anti-smoking ads such as this one from the American Cancer Society are aimed directly at young people. Studies reveal that quitting on one's own is much more effective in the long-run than specialized programs.

help patients comply with the orders of physicians. Even the best of medical advice will be useless if it is not followed. One estimate (Ley, 1977) suggests that as many as 50 percent of patients fail to follow doctor's orders with regard to taking prescribed medicines. There are many reasons why patients fail to comply with doctors' orders, including lack of good communication between patient and doctor, the financial burden imposed by expensive medications, the extent of disruption of daily routine required to follow the regimen of daily medication, and the lack of clear vision of the advantage of doing so.

Psychologists can assist in improving patient/physician communications concerning medication, and psychologists can assist patients in monitoring their daily medications. For example, many diabetics find it difficult to maintain their daily treatment regimens. A number of strategies have proven useful for this purpose including:

1. *specific assignments* that unambiguously define what is to be done;
2. *skill training* to develop new behaviors relevant to treatment;
3. *cueing* specific behaviors with salient stimuli;
4. *tailoring* the regimen to meet the schedule and particular needs of the patient;
5. *contracts* between patient, therapist, and significant others for prescribed behavior change;
6. *shaping* successive approximations of the desired treatment regimen;
7. *self-monitoring* behaviors relevant to treatment; and
8. *reinforcement* of new desired behaviors (Surwit et al., 1983, p. 260).

Psychologists involved in health psychology, then, are involved in a wide range of activities. Some are investigating the nature of the relationship between psychological variables and the incidence of disease; some look for ways to use psychological methods to help ease the symptoms of physical illness; some seek ways to help people change their attitudes and behaviors in order to become healthier and to prevent health problems; some assist patients in complying with prescribed treatment plans; and still others fill a more traditional role, dealing directly with the psychological and emotional distress that often accompanies the knowledge that one has a serious or life-threatening disorder.

Health psychologists study the psychological and behavioral factors that affect physical health and illness. They may counsel people to change certain behaviors to improve their health.

BEFORE YOU GO ON **What are some of the ways health psychologists intervene to promote physical health?**

STRESS

stress
a complex pattern of reactions to real or perceived threats to one's sense of well-being that motivate adjustment

In this section, we turn our attention to the concept of stress, stressors and our reactions to them. We define **stress** as a complex set of reactions made by an individual under pressure to adapt. It is a general response made to a real or perceived threat to one's well-being that motivates further adjustment. Psychologists suspect that stress is a major cause of physical illness as well as psychological problems. The sources or stimuli for stress are called

stressors. Stressors are the real or perceived threats to one's sense of well-being. In this sense, stress is something that happens inside people, a response to certain circumstances, called stressors.

stressors
real or perceived threats to one's sense of well-being; sources of stress

Stressors: The Causes of Stress

In this first section we'll consider three classes of stressors: frustration, conflict, and life events. In each case we'll provide examples, some of which you may view as quite trivial. We choose such examples to remind ourselves that stress is not necessarily a response to some overwhelming, catastrophic event, such as the death of a loved one.

Frustration-induced Stress. Let us begin with an assumption: *All behavior is goal-directed.* In a way, this is saying that all behavior is motivated. In all of our behavior, we are pushed or pulled toward positive goals and away from negative goals.

Notice that there are a couple of assumptions that we are *not* making here. We are not willing to assume, for example, that you can always tell what goals are directing your behavior. In a real sense, you may not know. We may ask you why you did something: "What was the goal behind that behavior?" Your honest answer may be, "I really don't know." But just because you may not be aware of or able to tell me about the goals that direct your behavior does not mean that our basic assumption is wrong.

Another reality about goals and behavior is that it is often difficult to directly infer one from the other. For example, many people engage in the same behaviors, but for a variety of different reasons—to reach different goals. Many students have registered for a course in introductory psychology this term. Why? In order to reach what goal? There are probably as many reasons as there are students in your class. It is also true that many people share the same goal, but engage in a wide variety of different behaviors in

Nonspecific response = whole body comes into play

When our progress toward a goal is slowed or blocked, we experience frustration. A traffic jam is a prime example.

Three major areas of stressors: (motivated Behavior)

frustration - blocking of motivated behavior

Environmental - things in environment

social

personal

frustration
the blocking or thwarting of goal-directed behavior

0

FIGURE 12.2
A depiction of frustration. A person's goal-directed behavior is being blocked or thwarted.

Ex:

order to reach that goal. For example, a goal for many people is "acquiring lots of money." To reach this end, some work very hard, some take college classes, some rob gas stations, some try to "marry money," and so on.

Our second assumption is this: *Organisms don't always reach all of their goals.* Have you always gotten everything you've ever wanted? Have you always been able to avoid unpleasantness, pain, or sorrow? Do you know anyone who has?

Sometimes we are totally prohibited from ever reaching a certain goal. At other times our progress toward a goal may be slower or more difficult than we would like. In either case, we are being frustrated. **Frustration,** then, is the blocking of goal-directed behavior (see Figure 12.2). The blocking may be either total and permanent or partial and temporary.

Seen in this way, stress that results from frustration is a normal, commonplace reaction. It is a fact of life. It does not imply weakness, pathology, or illness. What will matter most is how individuals react to the frustrations and stressors of their lives. Before we consider adjustments to frustration, let's look at some of its major sources.

To someone who feels the stress that results from frustration, the source of that frustration may be of little consequence. However, in order to respond adaptively to frustration-induced stress, it is helpful to be able to recognize the source of the blocking that is keeping us from our goals. There are basically two types of frustration: environmental and personal.

Environmental frustration implies that the blocking or thwarting of goal-directed behavior is being done by something or someone in the environment. (We should talk about the *source* or origin of frustration, not *fault* or *blame,* which are evaluative terms. All we are trying to do here is describe, not evaluate.)

Losing 25¢ in a coffee vending machine is a simple type of environmental frustration. You want a cup of coffee. Your goal-directed behavior leads you to slip a quarter into the coin slot. Something in your environment—here, a piece of faulty machinery—interferes with your goal-directed behavior and keeps you from reaching your goal. You may want to be outside and find that it's raining. As a result, you may be under some stress because your goal-directed behavior is being thwarted by your environment.

Three-year-old Mindy wants a cookie, but her mother says, "No, it's almost suppertime." Mindy is also being frustrated by her environment, but in a slightly different way. She wants a cookie, and her mother is blocking that motivated behavior. This type of environmental frustration, in which the source of the blocking is another person, is called *social frustration.*

Sometimes we are frustrated not so much because someone or something in our environment is blocking progress toward our goals, but because of some more internal or personal reason *(personal frustration).* Ken fails to make the basketball team simply because he is too short. Someone wanting to be a concert pianist may be frustrated in her attempt to do so because she happens to have short, stubby fingers and can only reach half an octave on the piano keyboard. She may learn to be a good pianist, but she probably won't make it in the world of classical piano. Her frustration is not the fault of people who write piano music or build piano keyboards. Her failure to play some piano music is not her fault, but if she persists in this goal-directed behavior, she will be frustrated, and the source of her frustration will be more personal than environmental.

Ex:

As adults, we seldom encounter stressful situations that result from "per- ←*Important*
sonal frustration anymore. We have gained a useful sense of what we can and
cannot do (occasionally through painful experience). We have changed some
of the goals that we may have had as youngsters because we have recognized
that there are some goals we cannot reach. (We do acknowledge that coming
to grips with personal frustration is not always easy or successful. Many
persons, at least initially, fail in their attempts to overcome frustration-
induced stress.)

What is meant by frustration-induced stress?
Define environmental, social, and personal frustration.

Conflict-induced Stress. It is sometimes the case that we are unable
to satisfy a particular drive or motive because it is in **conflict** with other
drives or motives that are influencing us at the same time. Stress may then
result not from the frustration caused by the blocking of our goal-directed
behaviors, but because our own motivational system is causing a conflict.

With these motivational conflicts, there is always the implication of a
decision or a choice that has to be made. Sometimes the decision is relatively
easy to make; sometimes it is very difficult. In discussing conflict, it is useful
to talk about positive goals or incentives we wish to approach and negative
goals or incentives we wish to avoid. Let's look at some possible stress-
inducing conflicts.

1. *Approach-approach Conflicts.* Conflicts are necessarily unpleasant
and stressful situations. The type of conflict that generally
produces the least amount of stress is the approach-approach conflict (see Figure 12.3). Here an organism is caught between two alternatives, and both of them are potentially reinforcing. If the subject chooses alternative A, he or she will reach a desirable goal. If
alternative B is chosen, a different desirable goal will be attained.
What makes this a conflict is that *both* alternatives are not simultaneously available. It has to be one or the other. A choice has to
be made.

In a way, these can be thought of as simple conflicts, since the
subject ends up with some desired goal no matter which alternative is chosen. For example, if Joanne enters an ice cream shop
with only enough money to buy one dip of ice cream, she may experience a conflict when faced with all the possible flavors she
could choose from. Typical of conflict, we'd probably notice some
vacillation in Joanne's behavior, some swaying back and forth between the two alternatives. But we can assume that this conflict
will eventually be resolved with a choice, and Joanne will at least
walk out of the store with an ice cream cone of one flavor or the
other. Her life might have been easier (less stressful) if the store
provided just one flavor in the first place and she didn't have to
make such choices, but she'll contemplate that possibility with an
ice cream cone in hand.

Sometimes the choices that we are called upon to make are
much more serious than those involving ice cream flavors. What
will be your college major? On the one hand, you'd like to go to
medical school and be a surgeon (that's a positive goal, or incen-

BEFORE YOU GO ON

conflict
a source of stress in which some
goals can be satisfied only at the
expense of others

FIGURE 12.3
A diagram of an approach-approach
conflict. Here, the subject is faced with
two (or more) positive, attractive goals and
must choose from among them.

*me with school
– Major – ?*

tive). On the other hand, you'd like to cultivate your aptitude for music and study composition and conducting at a school of music (also a clear positive incentive). At the moment, you cannot do both. The courses you'd take as a premed student are quite different from those you'd take if you were to follow music as a career path. Both avenues are good, constructive, desirable alternatives, but now, at registration, you have to make a choice; one that may have long-lasting repercussions.

2. *Avoidance-avoidance Conflicts.* Among the most stressful and unpleasant conflicts are those characterized as avoidance-avoidance conflicts (see Figure 12.4). In this type of conflict, a person is faced with a number of alternatives, and each of them is negative or punishing. No matter which way he or she turns, he or she is going to "get burned." Imagine a college dean who has to make a decision. If she chooses Plan A, the faculty may be outraged. If she opts for Plan B, the students may riot. If she does nothing she may get fired. No matter what she chooses, someone is going to be unhappy—yet she has to choose. To be in an avoidance-avoidance conflict is, in a way, to be boxed in so that no matter what you do, the result will be punishing.

We have a number of clichés in the English language that seem to be describing such conflicts: "Caught between the devil and the deep blue sea," "Out of the frying pan, into the fire," "Stuck between a rock and a hard place" are three that come to mind. In each case, we seem to be describing a situation from which a pleasant reprieve seems unlikely.

3. *Approach-avoidance Conflicts.* Good examples of simple approach-avoidance conflicts are not so easy to generate (see Figure 12.5). The problem here is that our subject is considering only one goal. What makes this situation a conflict is that the person would very much like to reach that goal, but, at the same time, would very much like not to. It's a matter of "yes, I'd love to. Well, as a matter of fact, I'd rather not. Well, maybe I would. No. I wouldn't . . . yes . . . no." Typical of conflicts in general, what we see here is vacillation, a swinging back and forth—motivated to approach and, at the same time, motivated to avoid.

It's easy to see how we might set up such a conflict situation for a rat. (In fact, Brown (1948) and Miller (1959) have demonstrated all of these conflicts using rats rather than humans as subjects.) We'd place a nice, attractive pile of food at the end of a runway. We would also arrange to shock the portion of the runway floor around the food. A hungry rat on that runway would be in a true approach-avoidance conflict. It would want to get to the end of the runway to get the food, but it would also want to avoid that same end to avoid getting shocked.

Most of us usually try not to get into approach-avoidance conflicts in the first place. We try to arrange things to "keep our options open," so that we are not faced with just one possibility.

4. *Multiple Approach-avoidance Conflicts.* The type of conflict most commonly found among adult humans is the multiple approach-

FIGURE 12.4
A diagram of an avoidance-avoidance conflict. Here, the subject is faced with two (or more) negative, unattractive goals, and one must be chosen. This is a no-win situation.

FIGURE 12.5
A diagram of a simple approach-avoidance conflict. Here, the subject is faced with but one goal. What puts the subject in conflict is that the goal has both positive and negative features.

avoidance conflict (see Figure 12.6). As its name implies, this type of conflict arises when an individual is faced with a number of alternatives, each one of which is in some way positive and in some way negative at the same time.

EX! Perhaps you and some friends are out shopping on a Saturday morning. You suddenly discover that it's getting late and you're all hungry. Where will you go to lunch? You may have a multiple approach-avoidance conflict here. "We could go to Bob's Diner, where the food is cheap and the service is fast, but the food is terrible. Or we could go to Cafe Olé, where the food is better, but service is a little slower, and the food is more expensive. Or we could go to The Grill, where the service is elegant and the food superb, but the price is very high." Granted this is not an earth-shaking dilemma, but in each case there is a plus and a minus to be considered in making the choice.

Life is filled with such conflicts, and some of them can be severe and very stressful. They may very well encompass questions of the "what shall I do with the rest of my life?" sort. "Should I stay at home and raise the children (+ and −), or should I have a career (+ and −)?" "Should I get married or stay single, or is there another way (again, + and − in each case)?" "Should I work for Company A (+ and −), or should I work for Company B (+ and −)?" Quite clearly, lists like this could go on and on. You might want to reflect on the conflicts you have faced during the past few weeks. You should be able to categorize each of them into one of the four types we have listed here.

Name four types of motivational conflict and provide an example of each.

BEFORE YOU GO ON

③ **Life-change-induced Stress.** It is clear that frustration and conflict are potent sources of stress in our lives and are often unavoidable consequences of being a motivated organism. Psychologists have also attempted to deal with those sources of stress that do not fit neatly into our descriptions of either frustration or conflict. One useful approach has been to look at the changes that occur in one's life as potential sources of stress.

In 1967, Holmes and Rahe published their first version of the Social Readjustment Rating Scale, or SRRS (see also Holmes & Holmes, 1970). The basic idea behind this scale is that stress results whenever our life situation changes. The scale's authors provided subjects with a list of life events that might be potentially stressful. The original list of such events was drawn from the reports of patients suffering from moderate to high levels of stress in their lives. Marriage was arbitrarily assigned a value of 50 stress points (technically called *life change units*). With marriage = 50 as their guide, subjects rated a number of other more-or-less typical life changes in terms of the amount of stress they might provide. Figure 12.7 is a version of the 1970 modification of the original scale.

In a rather direct way, the SRRS gives us a way to measure the stress in our lives. Psychologists have reported a positive correlation between scores on the SRRS and the incidence of physical illness and disease (Rahe &

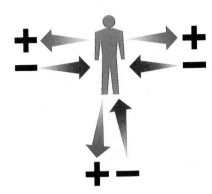

FIGURE 12.6
A diagram of a multiple approach-avoidance conflict. Here, the subject is faced with a number of alternative goals, each of which has positive and negative characteristics, and a choice must be made.

life events

FIGURE 12.7
The Social Readjustment Rating Scale
(From Holmes & Rahe, 1970).

Life event	Mean value
1. Death of spouse	100
2. Divorce	73
3. Marital separation from mate	65
4. Detention in jail or other institution	63
5. Death of a close family member	63
6. Major personal injury or illness	53
7. Marriage	50
8. Being fired at work	47
9. Marital reconciliation with mate	45
10. Retirement from work	45
11. Major change in health or behavior of a family member	44
12. Pregnancy	40
13. Sexual difficulties	39
14. Gaining a new family member (e.g., through birth, adoption, oldster moving in, etc.)	39
15. Major business readjustment (e.g., merger, reorganization, bankruptcy, etc.)	39
16. Major change in financial state (e.g., a lot worse off or a lot better off than usual)	38
17. Death of a close friend	37
18. Changing to a different line of work	36
19. Major change in the number of arguments with spouse (e.g., either a lot more or a lot less than usual regarding child-rearing, personal habits, etc.)	35
20. Taking out a mortgage or loan for a major purchase (e.g., for a home, business, etc.)	31
21. Foreclosure on a mortgage or loan	30
22. Major change in responsibilities at work (e.g., promotion, demotion, lateral transfer)	29
23. Son or daughter leaving home (e.g., marriage, attending college, etc.)	29
24. Trouble with inlaws	29
25. Outstanding personal achievement	28
26. Wife beginning or ceasing work outside the home	26
27. Beginning or ceasing formal schooling	26
28. Major change in living conditions (e.g., building a new home, remodeling, deterioration of home or neighborhood)	25
29. Revision of personal habits (dress, manners, associations, etc.)	24
30. Trouble with the boss.	23
31. Major change in working hours or conditions	20
32. Change in residence	20
33. Changing to a new school	20
34. Major change in usual type and/or amount of recreation	19
35. Major change in church activities (e.g., a lot more or a lot less than usual)	19
36. Major change in social activities (e.g., clubs, dancing, movies, visiting, etc.)	18
37. Taking out a mortgage or loan for a lesser purchase (e.g., for a car, TV, freezer, etc.)	17
38. Major change in sleeping habits (a lot more or a lot less sleep, or change in part of day when asleep)	16
39. Major change in number of family get-togethers (e.g., a lot more or a lot less than usual)	15
40. Major change in eating habits (a lot more or a lot less food intake, or very different meal hours or surroundings)	15
41. Vacation	13
42. Christmas	12
43. Minor violations of the law (e.g., traffic tickets, jaywalking, disturbing the peace, etc.)	11

Arthur, 1978). People with SRRS scores between 200 and 299 have a 50-50 chance of developing noticeable symptoms of physical illness within the next two years. *Eighty* percent of those with scores above 300 may develop physical symptoms within the same time period. The logic is that stress causes illness, particularly cardiovascular disorders. But we must remember what we said back in our first chapter about correlations: They do not tell us about cause-and-effect. After all, some of the SRRS items themselves are related to physical illness or are in some way health related. It may not be a surprise, then, to find scores on this scale related to levels of physical illness.

Richard Lazarus (1981) argues that we ought to focus more of our attention on those causes of stress that are less dramatic than big life changes such as the death of a family member or marriage. What often matters most, at least in the short term, is life's little hassles—the traffic that goes too slowly, the toothpaste tube that splits, ants at a picnic, the cost of an ice cream cone (compared to what it was just a few years ago), and so on.

Important

Part of Lazarus' argument is that big crises or major life change events are often too large to have an impact on us directly. What may cause us to feel stressed are the ways in which these big events produce little changes in our lives. For example, being in jail may mean that one can't watch a favorite TV program. Being retired may mean a lack of access to friendly conversation at coffee break time. A spouse who starts to work may make life a little more difficult; the other spouse may have to cook dinner for the first time. Thus, stress results not so much from the event itself, but from the little hassles it creates. Clearly we could go down the entire list of life events in Figure 12.7 and see that in each case, the event itself is often a collection of small, stress-inducing hassles.

What does the SRRS measure, and how is it related to stress?   **BEFORE YOU GO ON**

Reactions to Stress

So far we have defined stress and reviewed a number of potential stressors— frustration, conflict, and life events that involve making changes. Now we need to consider what someone might do when under stress. How might we respond to stress; that is, what can be done about it? In this sense, we are now treating stress as a motivator, a process that arouses and directs a reaction.

Before we go any further, there is an important point that we need to make. As with so many other things, there are large individual differences in responding *with* stress or *to* stress. What constitutes a stressor, and what an individual may do in response to stress, varies considerably from person to person. Some people fall apart at weddings; others don't find them stressful at all. For some people, even simple choices are difficult to make; for others, choices are not enough—they seek challenges. The variability in stress levels that we see among different people can usually be found within any one individual at different times. You know this from your own experience. On one day, being caught in slow-moving traffic may drive you up the wall. In the very same situation a few days later, you may find that you couldn't care less. So we need to remember that the reactions *of* stress and *to* stress vary from time to time and from person to person. We'll begin this discussion with a view of stress that has found favor in psychology and that serves to remind us of the physiological relationship between stress and other emotions.

① ✗ **The General Adaptation Syndrome.**   In the view of Hans Selye, continued extreme stress presents a challenge to one's physical well-being as well as to one's psychological well-being. Selye claims (1956, 1974) that one's reaction to stress occurs in three stages: alarm, resistance, and exhaustion. Taken together, this pattern of reaction is called the **general adaptation syndrome,** or GAS (see Figure 12.8).

According to the GAS, a person's initial response to stress is *alarm.* Alarm involves rapid and noticeable changes in the sympathetic division of the autonomic nervous system. Consistent with changes that accompany any emotional response, the sympathetic division causes an increase in blood pressure and heart rate, pupilary dilation, a cessation of digestion, and a rerouting of the blood supply to the extremities of the body. The adrenal glands help to mobilize the body's resources, indirectly providing increased levels of blood sugar. All of these reactions are much like those we experience in any extremely emotional situation. This reaction is one that cannot last long. We can seldom maintain an alarm reaction for more than a few minutes, a few hours at the most.

Let's illustrate this process with an example. Imagine a student, Pam, in the midst of a very important semester. Pam is strongly motivated to do well this term in all of her courses. Just past mid-term, she gets word that her father has had a heart attack. She leaves school and rushes home to the hospital. Her father had never been seriously ill before; now he's in the coronary intensive care unit. The shock and disbelief are overwhelming. Pam doesn't know what to do.

In *resistance,* the second stage of the general adaptation syndrome, stress remains present. Pam's father begins to show signs of recovery, but he will be in intensive care for at least another week and will be hospitalized for a long time. There is little that Pam can do to help her father, but she feels that she can't leave to go back to school; and every day that she stays at home, she gets farther behind in her classes.

Pam's bodily resources were first mobilized in the alarm stage. Now the drain on her body's resources continues. This often has negative consequences. If additional stress occurs, Pam will be very vulnerable to physical illness and infection. As she continues to search for ways to reduce and eliminate the stress she is experiencing, Pam's physiological reaction continues to be one of resistance and mobilization: high blood pressure, ulcers, skin rashes, or respiratory difficulties may develop. Pam may appear to be in control, but the reality of her father's condition and the approach of final exams continue to eat away at her, intruding into her awareness.

If Pam cannot find some effective way to deal with her stress, her physiological reaction to the continuing stress in her life may produce a condition of *exhaustion.* In this stage of the GAS, her bodily resources become nearly depleted. She is running out of energy and out of time. If effective means of coping with her father's condition and her college courses are not found, Pam may break down—psychologically and/or physically. Although the resistance stage may last for several months, eventually one's bodily resources become expended. In extreme cases, the exhaustion stage of the general adaptation syndrome may result in death.

As we shall see, the nature of one's reaction to stress depends on many factors. Selye's general adaptation syndrome emphasizes the physiological responses of alarm, resistance, and exhaustion that are made to stress. Stress

general adaptation syndrome (GAS)
a pattern of physiological reactions to stress, including alarm, resistance, and exhaustion stages

FIGURE 12.8
When we are first exposed to stress, our bodily resources are mobilized in an alarm reaction, which raises our resistance above normal levels. Our resistance is maintained at this high level during the stage of resistance. If the stressor remains, resistance may eventually fall below normal levels, depicted here as the stage of exhaustion. (From Selye, 1956.)

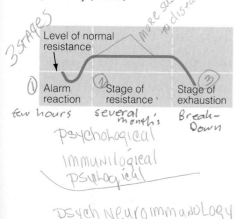

Hans Selye

mobilizes the body's resources to combat real or perceived threats to well-being. We have limited supplies of such resources. The GAS predicts that dire consequences will follow when a person is simultaneously or successively faced with a number of stressful situations. Now let's turn our attention to those reactions to stress that are more psychological in nature.

Name and describe the three stages of the general adaptation syndrome.   BEFORE YOU GO ON

Reacting to Stress with Learning.   One of the most effective ways to deal with stress is to bring about relatively permanent changes in our behaviors as a result of the experience of stress. That is, to learn and adapt in such a way as to reduce or eliminate the source of the stress.

This response makes particularly good sense when we consider frustration-induced stress. Here, our path to a goal is being blocked or thwarted. An adaptive way to handle such stress is to find some new way to reach our goal or to learn to modify our goal (see Figure 12.9).

In fact, a great deal of our everyday learning is motivated by such frustration-induced stress. We have had to learn many new responses as a means of coping with stress. Let's look at a few imaginary examples. Having been frustrated once (or twice) by locking yourself out of your house or car, you have learned to hide a second set of keys somewhere you can easily find them. Having been denied promotion because you didn't have a college degree, you are learning about general psychology on the way toward earning such a degree. Having been caught at home in a blizzard with no cookies in the house, you learned to bake them yourself. Having discovered that you're too short to make the basketball team, you learned to play tennis. You may have learned as a child to get what you wanted from your parents by smiling sweetly and asking politely. In each of these cases, what prompted the learning of new responses or establishing of new goals was stress—stress resulting from frustration.

Learning through experience with stress may also have taught you the value of escape and avoidance (and the usefulness of negative reinforcers). You know how to avoid getting into many motivational conflicts. You try to plan things so as to keep your options open to avoid getting into avoidance-avoidance or approach-avoidance conflicts in the first place. You may have learned that the only sensible thing to do once you are in such a conflict is to escape or to make major changes in what is motivating you.

This is one way in which stress can be seen as a positive force in our lives. If we were never challenged, if we never set difficult goals, if we never faced stressful situations, we would miss out on many opportunities for growth and learning. The stress we experience might be quite unpleasant at the time, but it may produce positive consequences.

How can learning be seen as a reaction to stress?   BEFORE YOU GO ON

Reacting to Stress with Aggression.   It is clear there are many sources and causes of aggression and that one of those causes is frustration. At one time, it was proposed that frustration was *the* major cause of aggression, the so-called **frustration-aggression hypothesis** (Dollard et al., 1939). This point of view claimed that frustration could produce a number of reac-

FIGURE 12.9
Reacting to frustration with learning. If progress towards a positive goal (or away from a negative goal) is blocked, one can learn a new route to reach the same goal, or one can learn to modify the goal so that it can be attained.

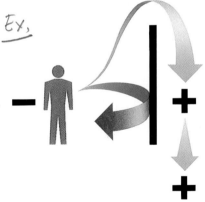

frustration-aggression hypothesis
the view (now discredited) that all aggression stems from frustration

Stress   **539**

Acts of aggression are usually unhelpful but are common reactions to frustration.

tions, including aggression, but that aggression was always caused by frustration. Even though there *are* other sources of aggression (some view aggression as innate and instinctive, while others see it as a response learned through reinforcement or through modeling that need not be stimulated by frustration), stress and frustration remain prime candidates as the cause of a great deal of aggression. It doesn't do much good in the long run, but a flash of aggressive behavior often accompanies the stress of frustration (Berkowitz, 1978; 1982).

There you are in the parking lot, trying to get home from class, and your car won't start. Over and over you turn the ignition key. Frustrated, you swing open your door, get out, kick the front left fender, throw up the hood, and glower at the engine. Being angry and kicking at the car (or yelling at someone who offers to assist) won't help you solve your problem, but such anger and aggression are common reactions to frustration.

BEFORE YOU GO ON

What is the frustration-aggression hypothesis?

Is aggression in any way a healthy response to stress?

Reacting to Stress with Defense Mechanisms.   Stress may occasionally promote positive outcomes. Motivated to overcome stress and the situations that produce it, we may learn new and adaptive responses. It is also clear, however, that stress involves a very unpleasant emotional component. **Anxiety** is a general feeling of tension or apprehension that often accompanies a perceived threat to one's well-being. It is this unpleasant emotional component that often prompts us to learn new responses to rid ourselves of stress.

There are a number of techniques, essentially self-deceptive, that we may employ to keep from feeling the unpleasantness associated with stress. These

anxiety
a general feeling of tension or apprehension accompanied by a perceived threat to well-being

techniques, or tricks we play on ourselves, are not adaptive in the sense of helping us to get rid of stress by getting rid of the source of stress. Rather, they are mechanisms that we can and do use to defend ourselves against the *feelings* of stress. They are called **defense mechanisms.** Freud believed defense mechanisms to be the work of the unconscious mind. He claimed that they are ploys that our unconscious mind uses to protect us (our *self* or *ego*) from stress and anxiety. Many psychologists take issue with Freud's interpretation of defense mechanisms and consider defense mechanisms in more general terms than did Freud, but few will deny that defense mechanisms exist. It *is* true that they are generally ineffective if consciously or purposively employed. The list of defense mechanisms is a long one. Here, we'll review some of the more common defense mechanisms, providing an example of each, to give you an idea of how they might serve as a reaction to stress.

defense mechanisms
techniques, beyond one's conscious control, employed to protect against the feelings of stress

1. *Repression.* The notion of **repression** came up earlier in our discussion of memory. In a way, it is the most basic of all the defense mechanisms. It is sometimes referred to as *motivated forgetting,* which gives us a good idea of what is involved. Repression is a matter of conveniently forgetting about some stressful, anxiety-producing event, conflict, or frustration. Paul had a teacher in high school he did not get along with at all. After spending an entire semester trying his best to do whatever was asked, Paul failed the course. The following summer, while walking with his girlfriend, Paul encountered this teacher. When he tried to introduce his girlfriend, Paul could not remember his teacher's name. He had repressed it. As a long-term reaction to stress, repressing the names of people we don't like or that we associate with unpleasant, stressful experiences is certainly not a very adaptive reaction. But at least it can protect us from dwelling on such unpleasantness.

repression
"motivated forgetting," in which stressful events are forced from awareness and cannot be remembered

2. *Denial.* **Denial** is a very basic mechanism of defense against stress. In denial, a person simply refuses to acknowledge the realities of a stressful situation. When a physician first tells a patient that he or she has a terminal illness, a common reaction is denial; the patient refuses to believe that there is anything seriously wrong.

Other less stressful events than serious illness sometimes evoke denial. Many smokers are intelligent individuals who are well aware of the data and the statistics that can readily convince them that they are slowly (or rapidly) killing themselves by continuing to smoke. But they deny the evidence. Somehow they are able to convince themselves that they aren't going to die from smoking; that's something that happens to other people, and besides, they *could* stop whenever they wanted.

denial
refusing to acknowledge the presence of stressors

3. *Rationalization.* **Rationalization** amounts to making excuses for our behaviors when facing the real reasons for our behaviors would be stressful. The real reason Kevin failed his psychology midterm is that he didn't study for it and has missed a number of classes. Kevin hates to admit, even to himself, that he could have been so stupid as to flunk that exam because of his own actions. As a result, he rationalizes: "It wasn't really *my* fault. I had a lousy

rationalization
generating excuses to explain one's behaviors rather than facing the real (anxiety-producing) reasons for those behaviors

instructor. We used a rotten text. The tests were grossly unfair. I've been fighting the darn flu all semester. And Marjorie had that big party the night before the exam." Now Susan, on the other hand, really did want to go to Marjorie's party, but she decided that she wouldn't go unless somebody asked her. As it happens, no one did. In short order, Susan rationalized that she "didn't want to go to that dumb party anyway"; she needed to "stay home and study."

compensation
a mechanism through which resources are invested in some trait or ability to offset deficits in other traits or abilities

4. *Compensation.* We might best think of **compensation** in the context of personal frustration. This defense mechanism is a matter of overemphasizing some positive trait or ability to counterbalance a shortcoming in some other trait or ability. If some particular goal-directed behavior becomes blocked, a person may compensate by putting extra effort and attention into some other aspect of behavior. For example, Karen, a seventh grader, wants to be popular. She's a reasonably bright and pleasant teenager, but isn't—in the judgment of her classmates—very pretty. Karen *may* compensate for her lack of good looks by studying very hard to be a good student, or by memorizing jokes and funny stories, or by becoming a good musician. Compensation is not just an attempt to be a well-rounded individual. It is a matter of expending *extra* energy and resources in one direction to offset shortcomings in other directions.

fantasy
an escape from stress through imagination and/or daydreaming

5. *Fantasy.* **Fantasy** is one of the more common defense mechanisms used by college students. It is often quite useful. Particularly after a hard day when stress levels are high, isn't it pleasant to sit in a comfortable chair, kick off your shoes, lie back, close your eyes, and daydream, perhaps about graduation day, picturing yourself walking across the stage to pick up your diploma—with honors.

When things are not going well for us, we may retreat into a world of fantasy where everything always goes well. Remember that to engage from time to time in fantasizing is a normal and acceptable response to stress. You should not get worried if you fantasize occasionally. On the other hand, you should realize that there are some potential dangers. You need to be able to keep separate those activities that are real and those that occur in your fantasies. And you should realize that fantasy in itself will not solve whatever problem is causing you stress. Fantasizing about academic successes may help you feel better for awhile, but it is not likely to make you a better student.

projection
seeing in others those very characteristics and/or motives that cause stress in one's self

6. *Projection.* **Projection** is a matter of seeing in others those very traits and motives that cause us stress when we see them in ourselves. Under pressure to do well on an exam, Mark may want to cheat, but his conscience won't let him. Because of projection, he may think he sees cheating going on all around him.

Projection is a mechanism that is often used in conjunction with hostility and aggression. When people begin to feel uncomfortable about their own levels of hostility, they often project their aggressiveness onto others, coming to believe that others are "out to do me harm," and "I'm only defending myself."

7. *Regression.* To employ **regression** is to return to earlier, even childish, levels of behavior that were once productive or reinforced. Curiously enough, we often find regression in children. Imagine a 4 year old who until very recently was an only child. Now Mommy has returned from the hospital with a new baby sister. The 4 year old is no longer "the center of the universe," as her new little sister now gets parental attention. The 4 year old reverts to earlier behaviors and starts wetting the bed, screaming for a bottle of her own, and crawling on all fours in an attempt to get attention. She is regressing.

Many defense mechanisms can be seen on the golf course, including regression. After Doug knocks three golf balls into the lake, he throws a temper tantrum, stamps his feet, and tosses his three-iron in the lake. His childish regressive behavior won't help his score, but it may act as a release from the tension of his stress at the moment.

8. *Displacement.* The defense mechanism of **displacement** is usually discussed in the context of aggression. Your goal-directed behavior becomes blocked or thwarted. You are frustrated, under stress, and somewhat aggressive. You cannot vent your aggression directly at the source of the frustration, so you displace it to a safer outlet. Dorothy expects to get promoted at work, but someone else gets the new job she wanted. Her goal-directed behavior has been frustrated. She's upset and angry at her boss, but feels (perhaps correctly) that blowing her top at her boss will do more harm than good. She's still frustrated, so she displaces her hostility toward her husband, children, and/or the family cat.

Displacement doesn't have to involve hostility and aggression. A young couple discovers that having children is not going to be as easy as they thought. They want children badly, but there's an infertility problem that is causing considerable stress. Their motivation for love, sharing, and caring may be displaced toward a pet, nephews and nieces, or some neighborhood children—at least until their own goals can be realized with children of their own.

regression
a return to earlier, childish levels of previously productive behaviors as an escape from stress

displacement
directing one's motives at some substitute person or object rather than expressing it directly

The list of defense mechanisms provided above is not an exhaustive one. These are among the most common, and this list gives you an idea of what defense mechanisms are like. There are a couple of important points about them that deserve special mention.

First, using defense mechanisms is a normal reaction to stress. You shouldn't be alarmed if you find that many of the defense mechanisms listed here sound like reactions you have used. In moderation, they help us to cope with some of the stresses of life and the frustrations and conflicts that we face from day to day because they reduce levels of felt anxiety. Second, although they are normal, defense mechanisms can be maladaptive. So long as we can defend ourselves against the unpleasant feelings of stress, we will be less motivated to take any direct action to ultimately get rid of that stress. We will be less likely to try to solve those conflicts, remove those sources of frustration, or adapt to those life changes that are causing the stress in the first place. Finally, another possible danger in using defense mechanisms is that the user will lose sight of what is real and what is defensive. Largely because defense mechanisms are employed without our conscious awareness, it sometimes becomes difficult to separate rationalizations from reasons, fantasy from truth, repression from forgetfulness, displaced aggression from real aggression, and so on.

BEFORE YOU GO ON **Define repression, denial, rationalization, compensation, fantasy, projection, regression, and displacement.**
In what ways are these defense mechanisms?

In this chapter, we have reviewed industrial-organizational psychology, health psychology, and the potential threat to health that stress poses. We have seen how to improve the fit between people and jobs, how personality and behavioral factors may be related to physical disease, and how stress is caused and may be managed.

Our sampling of areas in which psychological understanding can be applied to real-life situations was just that—a sampling of major applications. There are a number of other applied fields of psychology, such as environmental psychology, sports psychology, applied developmental psychology, psychology and the law, consumer psychology, the psychology of advertising and marketing, engineering psychology, political psychology, and many others. Psychology is a science, and it is an academic discipline. It is also a field ready and able to be a force of influence and change in the real world.

SUMMARY

What is involved in doing a job analysis?

Doing a proper job analysis involves two things: (1) constructing a complete and specific description of the activities performed by someone in a given position, a listing of those characteristics required to do the job well, and (2) a means of evaluating the performance of a person in that job (performance criteria). This information is accumulated through an inspection of official documents, interviews, questionnaires, and the direct observation of job activities. / 512

What are some of the sources of information that can be used in making personnel decisions?

Once a job analysis has been completed, personnel selection involves compiling a series of assessment tools to measure the relevant characteristics of applicants. Many such tools are available, including application forms, interviews, psychological tests, situational tests, and assessment center approaches. Of these, interviews are of the least value, and the quality of data from assessment centers also has been questioned. / 514

List some of the factors that need to be considered in the design and implementation of a training program.

A number of factors need to be considered in the design and implementation of an employee training program. These include an assessment of the organization's instructional needs (specifically as possible, what training, if any, is required?), the development of specific learning/training objectives, means by which training will be evaluated, and the selection of appropriate methods and media for the actual training. Once training has begun, it should be constantly monitored to see if objectives are being met, and after training has been completed, the program itself should be evaluated, as should the transfer of information and skills from training to actual on-the-job performance. / 517

Briefly summarize some of the factors that affect the motivation of workers to do a good job.

Even workers with ability will not do a good job unless they are motivated to do so. There are many theories to describe what motivates workers. We looked at three approaches. Vroom's *expectancy theory* says that workers develop expectations concerning the relationship between their work behaviors and the likelihood of certain outcomes. They also assign values to different outcomes. They will then be most highly motivated to do those things they see as most likely to earn them valued rewards. Adams' *equity theory* says that what matters most is the perception of fairness or equal reward for equal effort when one's work behaviors are compared with those of a significant other. Locke's *goal setting* approach says that what matters most is that workers be clearly aware of just what they are working for and that they accept that goal as worth the effort. / 521

What is meant by job satisfaction and the quality of work life?

Job satisfaction and quality of work life are complex concepts, usually inferred from interview and questionnaire data. In the broadest sense, job satisfaction is an attitude, a measure of an employee's evaluation of his or her position in an organization. QWL involves many factors, such as feelings about employment conditions, job security, compensation, autonomy, opportunities for social interaction, self-esteem, and participation in the decision-making process. / 522

Briefly summarize the relationship between job satisfaction and job productivity.

Although job satisfaction and productivity may be related, there is very little evidence to suggest that the relationship is a strong one and no evidence to suggest that one causes the other. Interventions designed to increase job satisfaction do sometimes have a positive impact on productivity, but interventions designed to improve production may also increase job satisfaction. Job satisfaction seems most closely related to employee turnover and somewhat less related to absenteeism. / 523

SUMMARY continued

What are quality circles, and how do they affect productivity and job satisfaction?

Quality circles (QCs) are small groups of workers who voluntarily meet regularly to discuss production problems and related issues. The use of QCs may improve productivity, but usually only in the restricted area of the workers' assignments. QCs have virtually no positive impact on job satisfaction in general, but can increase a worker's sense of influence in the group. Many claims of large increases in profits after quality circles were implemented are probably exaggerated. For QCs to work well requires considerable commitment and training on the part of the organization. / 524

What are three approaches to improving safety, and is there any evidence that they are effective?

I/O psychologists have long been interested in making the workplace as accident-free as possible. We looked at three ways of approaching work safety. (1) *Engineering* the job and equipment to be as safe as possible. This is a generally effective process. (2) Looking at *personnel* to identify accident-prone individuals or characteristics. This approach has not been a successful one. (3) *Motivating* workers to work more safely by providing training in specific, safe behaviors and convincing them that safety is valued in the organization. This approach has also been successful. / 526

Briefly summarize the relationship between the Type A behavioral pattern and coronary heart disease.

Many health psychologists believe that there is a relationship between personality variables and physical health; that is, that some psychological traits put one at risk for disease. Since the late 1950s, evidence accumulated that showed a positive relationship between the Type A behavioral pattern, or TABP, (a competitive, achievement-oriented, impatient person who is easily aroused, often angry or hostile, and tends to have many projects all going at once) and coronary heart disease (blockage of major arteries). Recent evidence suggests that only some of the characteristics of TABP (time urgency, chronic activation, and multiphasia) are adequate predictors of coronary heart disease. / 529

What are some of the ways health psychologists intervene to promote physical health?

Reacting to the observation that 70 percent of the leading causes of death in the United States are in large part determined by "life-style" behaviors that put an individual at risk, many health psychologists intervene to try to bring about changes in what might be called "unhealthy behaviors," such as smoking, overeating, not exercising, and the like. Health psychologists also intervene to assist in the actual treatment of physical disease, helping patients to understand and comply with physicians' orders, for example. / 530

What is meant by frustration-induced stress?

Define environmental, social, and personal frustration.

Frustration-induced stress is caused by the blocking or thwarting of goal-directed behaviors. The specific type of frustration that leads to stress is named according to the source of the blocking. If the source of the blocking is something in the environment, we call the frustration *environmental*. If the source of frustration is a person in the environment, we call the frustration *social*. If the source of frustration is from within, from the person himself or herself, we call it *personal*. / 533

Name four types of motivational conflict and provide an example of each.

In an *approach-approach* motivational conflict, an organism is faced with two (or more) attractive goals and must choose among them when all are not available. In an *avoidance-avoidance* conflict, a choice must be made among unpleasant, potentially punishing alternatives. In an *approach-avoidance* conflict, there is but one goal under consideration; in some ways that goal is attractive, while in others it is not—it attracts and repels at the same time. Perhaps the most common conflict is the *multiple approach-avoidance* conflict in which a person is faced with a number of alternatives and each has its own strengths and weaknesses. / 535

What does the SRRS measure, and how is it related to stress?

The SRRS (or Social Readjustment Rating Scale) acknowledges that some of the day-to-day events and life changes that are simply a part of living often act as stressors. The SRRS is an attempt to measure the severity of stress in one's life by having the person indicate how many life change events have recently occurred. Some events are more stress-producing than others. High scores on the SRRS have been correlated with increased incidence of physical illness. / 537

Name and describe the three stages of the general adaptation syndrome.

According to Hans Selye, a reaction to prolonged stress progresses through three stages, a pattern called the general adaptation syndrome. At first, there is the mobilization of the sympathetic division of the ANS in the *alarm* stage as the body prepares to deal with the stress. If the stress is not removed, the body then goes through a stage of *resistance,* when resources continue to be mobilized, but when new stress will be difficult to deal with, and physical illness becomes more likely. If the stress remains, one may finally enter a stage of *exhaustion,* where the body's resources become depleted, adaptation breaks down, and death may result. / 539

How can learning be seen as a reaction to stress?

Learning is defined as a relatively permanent change in behavior that occurs as the result of experience. In many cases, stress (and frustration-induced stress in particular) provides experiences and motivation for learning. We often have to learn new responses to acquire our goals, and sometimes we must learn to modify our goals when attempts to reach them lead to stress. / 539

What is the frustration-aggression hypothesis?

Is aggression in any way a healthy response to stress?

The frustration-aggression hypothesis is the view, first proposed by Dollard, that the blocking or thwarting of goal-directed behaviors (that is, frustration) causes aggression. That is, frustration may produce a number of reactions, but aggression can always be traced to frustration. This view is now seen as overly simplistic, although it is surely the case that some aggression does stem from frustration. Such aggression may momentarily relieve tension, but cannot be viewed as a healthy response because it does nothing to resolve the situation that caused the stress in the first place. / 540

Define repression, denial, rationalization, compensation, fantasy, projection, regression, and displacement

In what ways are these defense mechanisms?

Defense mechanisms protect the individual from the felt emotional component of stress. They do not solve conflicts, nor do they resolve stress, but they lessen the anxiety produced by stress. There are many defense mechanisms, including: (1) repression—unconsciously forgetting an anxiety-producing or stressful experience; (2) denial—refusal to acknowledge the realities of a stressful situation; (3) rationalization—attempts to find excuses for one's behaviors rather than facing the real, anxiety-producing reasons for one's behaviors; (4) compensation—overemphasizing some positive trait to make up for a lacking in some other trait; (5) fantasy—engaging in daydreaming or imaginary thoughts of successes and achievements; (6) projection—seeing in others those traits and motives that cause us stress when we see them in ourselves; (7) regression—retreating to earlier, now less appropriate, behaviors that were productive, or reinforced, in the past; and (8) displacement—directing aggression at some safe outlet rather than at the true source of frustration. / 544

REVIEW QUESTIONS

1. When we set about to have the best person do a given job, the very first thing we have to do is to:

a. select the best person from among those who have applied.

b. do a job analysis to define what doing a good job means.

c. decide how we will motivate a worker to do her or his best job.

d. design a training program so that the worker knows what to do.

Fitting a person to a job may very well involve selection, training and/or motivation, but first we must analyze the job in question so that we have a full understanding of what we are selecting, training, or motivating the employee to do. / 511

2. From the discussion in the text, which of the following would you judge to be the *least* successful aid in finding a good employee?

a. the unstructured interview.

b. the application form.

c. assessment centers.

d. psychological tests.

There is no doubt that each of these techniques has been, and continues

to be, used as an aid in locating the best person for a given job. The least successful of these—according to the research evidence—is the unstructured interview, which many psychologists argue is a waste of time. The well-designed, structured interview administered by a skilled interviewer is much more useful. / 512

3. Once training needs have been assessed, and you know what it is that you want to get across in your training program, what is the *next* step?

a. Choose a technique to deliver the required information.

b. Determine how program outcomes are to be evaluated.

c. Decide where training will be given, and by whom.

d. Motivate workers to attend the training program.

Motivating workers to attend training programs is usually a very simple matter (motivating them to understand and apply what is presented is another matter). Before you begin to decide who will do the training, where it will be given, or which specific technique is to be used, it is generally recommended that you determine just how you will go about evaluating whether or not your program—whatever its final form—has had the desired impact. / 515

4. Adams' position regarding motivating employees claims—among other things—that workers tend to judge how they are rewarded compared to others who they see as doing similar work. This view is called:

a. expectancy theory.

b. the law of effect.

c. goal setting.

d. equity theory.

Psychologists have offered a wide variety of views concerning what motivates people, workers in particular. In fact, each of the alternatives listed here can be correctly associated with worker motivation issues. However, the theory that argues that workers seek fairness in treatment compared to how they see others rewarded is called the equity theory. / 519

5. Which of the following assertions concerning job satisfaction is *true*?

a. Satisfaction is typically found to be unrelated to the status or level of one's job.

b. Women tend to be more satisfied with their jobs than men are.

c. Younger workers tend to be less satisfied with their jobs than older workers are.

d. With considerable consistency, nonwhites are more satisfied with their jobs than whites are.

Of these four statements concerning job satisfaction, only the third is supported by research evidence. That is, higher status is associated with higher satisfaction; there are virtually no sex differences with regard to job satisfaction; and nonwhites are typically less satisfied with their jobs than whites are. / 521

6. Discussions at quality circles are meant to focus on:

a. how workers can get along better with each other on the job.

b. personal problems that have impact on workers' jobs.

c. what the company can do to improve working conditions for the workers.

d. how productivity in the company can be improved.

Clearly, any of these issues *can* be raised in quality circle discussions, but the main focus is typically on what can be done to increase the productivity of those at the QC meeting. This may very well involve "getting along better with others," or "improved working conditions," or "personal problems," but the overall focus is on productivity, which makes the fourth alternative the one of choice for this item. / 523

7. At least some aspects of the so-called *Type A behavior pattern* have been implicated in coronary heart disease. Of the following characteristics, which is most likely to be an "active ingredient," or most dangerous part of the Type A behavior pattern?

a. confused thinking.

b. rather extreme swings of mood.

c. concern over wasting small amounts of time.

d. a tendency to focus on the trivial and the insignificant, while ignoring important matters.

According to Logan Wright, there are three good candidates for the list of "active ingredients" in the Type A behavior pattern: (1) multiphasia—the tendency to have a number of things all going on at the same time; (2) chronic activation—always staying alert, aroused, and ready for action; and (3) time urgency—reflected here in the third alternative—concern over wasting precious, small bits of time. / 528

8. If Joanne stays home and studies tonight, she will probably do well on her exam tomorrow. If she goes to Bob's party, she'll have a good time, but probably fail her exam. Joanne is expressing stress, brought on by a(n)_____conflict.

a. approach-approach

b. avoidance-avoidance

c. approach-avoidance

d. multiple approach-avoidance

The alternatives to this item list the four major motivational conflicts that act as stressors in our lives. Approach-approach conflicts involve having to make a decision among a number of positive alternatives. Avoidance-avoidance conflicts put us in the unpleasant situation of having to choose among negative outcomes. With the simple approach-avoidance conflict, we have but one choice and it is both positive and negative. Joanne is faced with a multiple approach-avoidance conflict; she wants to go to the party (+), but in doing so she'll flunk the exam (−); on the other hand if she studies for the exam and passes it (+), she'll miss out on the party (−). / 533

Statistical Appendix

Why We Care

An Example to Work With

Organizing Data
    Frequency Distributions
    Graphic Representations

Descriptive Statistics
    Measures of Central Tendency
        The Mean
        The Median
        The Mode
    Variability

Inferential Statistics

Some Normal Curve Statistics

Why We Care

Doing research in psychology, or applying psychology, often involves the measurement of some aspect of behavior and/or mental processes. When we measure the affect, cognitions, or behaviors of organisms, the result of our measurement is a set of numbers. Assuming that we have adequately measured what we are interested in, now we have to deal with the numbers we have accumulated. That's where statistics come in.

It's one thing to be able to measure some psychological characteristic and something else again to make sense out of those measurements once they've been made. This is particularly true when we have a very large number of measurements, either made repeatedly on the same individual or on many different subjects. After making our measurements and generating a large number of numbers, we need to be able to summarize and describe our data. We may also want to make decisions on the basis of the numbers we have collected. Statistics help us to summarize, describe, and make judgments about measurements. How they do so will be the principle subject of this Appendix.

Before we go on, we would like to insert a word of caution. We are going to be dealing with numbers and a few simple formulas. Please don't let the numbers make you anxious. Some students find dealing with numbers difficult and think that statistics are not relevant for psychology students. Keep in mind that statistics are *tools,* necessary tools, to help us understand our subject matter. We have long argued that (at this level at least) you don't need to be mathematically sophisticated to appreciate statistics. What is required is a positive attitude and a few arithmetic skills, such as addition, subtraction, multiplication, and division. If you haven't had much math background, just go slowly and think about the issues involved in our discussion. Don't let yourself get bogged down in the numbers.

AN EXAMPLE TO WORK WITH

Statistics involve numbers; when we measure something, we assign it a numerical value, and statistics help us to analyze and understand measurements once we have made them. So that we'll have some numbers to work with, let's consider the following problem.

You and your best friend are both enrolled in the same introductory psychology class this semester. You have just taken your first exam—a 50-item multiple-choice test. Concerned about the possibility of cheating, your instructor provided two forms of your first exam, Form A and Form B. They both covered the same material, of course, but the questions were different on the two forms. By chance, you took Form A of the test, and your friend took Form B. You had studied together, and you thought that you both knew the material equally well. But your score on the test was eight points lower than your friend's. You suspect that perhaps the two forms of your first test were not equally difficult. You believe that your test (Form A) was harder than your friend's (Form B). You ask your instructor for all the grades on the test for both forms. Because of confidentiality, your instructor cannot provide you with names, but does supply you with all the grades from the exam.

There are 100 students in your class who took the first exam. Fifty took Form A and 50 took Form B. When you get the scores from your instructor, you find that they are arranged as follows:

FORM A:

98	86	100	60	94
72	80	78	66	86
92	62	86	96	62
82	86	78	88	84
64	86	68	76	80
86	96	76	72	80
80	82	82	64	78
68	74	98	98	84
66	64	70	90	86
96	92	82	68	92

FORM B:

82	100	90	80	60
72	86	82	88	80
82	76	84	74	84
86	74	78	78	78
78	74	84	80	80
90	84	68	78	86
80	80	80	84	80
76	76	80	82	82
86	74	70	78	76
82	82	80	76	80

What a mess. Just looking at all these numbers doesn't tell you much at all. Arranged as they are, it's difficult to see if either form of the exam yielded higher or lower scores. To answer your original question (was there a difference in performance on the two forms of the exam?), you're going to have to manipulate these numbers somehow. Such manipulations involve statistics. As we'll repeat throughout this Appendix, statistics are tools that we use to help us make sense out of data we have collected. They will be very helpful in analyzing these data. Statistical manipulations are even more useful (even necessary) when we have collected many more than 100 numbers.

ORGANIZING DATA

Let's assume that we have collected the measurements, or data, in which we are interested. Now the task before us is to make some decisions based on those data. The first thing we need to do is to assemble our data, our numbers, in some sensible way so that we can quickly and easily get some idea of what they mean. At very least, we should put our data into the form of a frequency distribution. We might then consider some graphic representation of our data.

Frequency Distributions

Once we have collected a large number of numbers, we seek ways to organize and summarize them to make them useful and meaningful. One of the easiest things to do with our numbers is to arrange them in a **frequency distribution.** As its name suggests, a frequency distribution lists, in order, all of the numbers or scores that we have collected and indicates the frequency with which each occurs.

frequency distribution
an ordered listing of all X-values, indicating the frequency with which each occurs

---

FIGURE A.1

Frequency distributions for our sample data of two forms (A and B) of a classroom exam. Scores, or measurements, are listed in order in the left column, and the frequency with which each occurs is indicated with either a hash mark (/) or a number.

Score	Form A Frequency		Form B Frequency	
100	/	1	/	1
98	/ /	2		0
96	/ / /	3		0
94	/	1		0
92	/ / /	3		0
90	/	1	/ /	2
88	/	1	/	1
86	/ / / / / / /	7	/ / / /	4
84	/ /	2	/ / / / /	5
82	/ / / /	4	/ / / / / / /	7
80	/ / / /	4	/ / / / / / / / / / /	11
78	/ / /	3	/ / / / / /	6
76	/ /	2	/ / / / /	5
74	/	1	/ / / /	4
72	/ /	2	/	1
70	/	1	/	1
68	/ / /	3	/	1
66	/ /	2		0
64	/ / / /	4		0
62	/ /	2		0
60	/	1	/	1
		N = 50		N = 50

Figure A.1 shows two types of frequency distributions for the scores earned on Form A and Form B of the exam we introduced as an example in the last section. One type of frequency distribution indicates each score with a hash mark (/), while the other type simply indicates the frequency of each score with a number. In this figure, we've placed the two frequency distributions side by side. You can easily see, just by inspection of these distributions, that there is a difference between the scores earned on Form A and on Form B of our imaginary classroom exam.

Graphic Representations

It is often helpful to go one step beyond the simple frequency distribution and draw a graph of our data. There have been a number of different graphs used throughout this text. Graphs of frequencies of scores are among the most common types of graphs in psychology. For such a graph, our scores (in general referred to as *X-scores*) are plotted on the horizontal (X) axis of the graph, and frequencies (f) are plotted on the vertical (Y) axis of our graph.

Figure A.2 shows one way to graph frequencies. This sort of bar graph is called a **histogram.** The frequency of each X-score is indicated by the height of the bar above that score. When we have a few X-scores, and when frequencies are not too large, histograms provide clear depictions of our data. The differences between Form A and Form B of the classroom exam are more clearly seen in the two histograms of Figure A.2 than in a simple frequency distribution.

Figure A.3 shows the same data in a simple line graph. The advantage of this sort of graph is obvious: we can easily show both distributions of test scores on the same axes. As is the case with histograms, scores are plotted on the X axis and frequencies are indicated on the Y axis. With line graphs, it is important to provide a key indicating which line represents each group of scores.

histogram
a bar graph; a graphical representation of a frequency distribution

---

FIGURE A.2
Histograms showing the frequency with which scores were earned on Form A and Form B of the classroom exam.

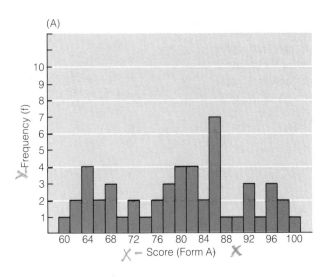
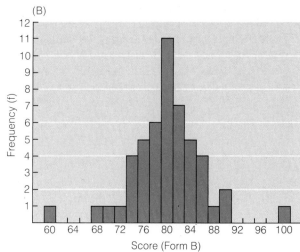

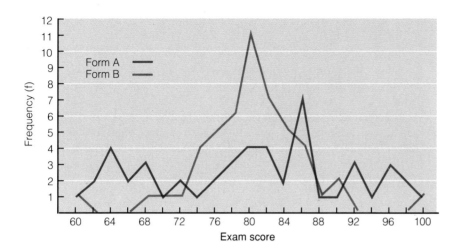

What is a frequency distribution and what is a histogram? **BEFORE YOU GO ON**
What are they used for?

DESCRIPTIVE STATISTICS

Let's continue working with our opening problem. We began with two sets of 50 numbers, scores earned on Form A and Form B of a classroom exam. Our basic question was whether or not these two forms of the same test were really equally difficult. To get started, we put the scores into frequency distributions and then constructed graphs that represented our data. That helped, but there is much more that we can do.

When describing collections or distributions of data, our two major concerns are usually with measures of central tendency and variability. Measures of **central tendency** are statistics that tell us where our scores tend to center. In general terms, measures of central tendency are called *averages*. If we want to know if performance on Form A was better or worse *on the average* than performance on Form B, we would have to compute a measure of central tendency for both distributions of scores. Measures of **variability** are statistics that tell us about the extent of dispersion, or the spread of scores within a distribution. Are scores clustered closely around the average, or are they more variable, deviating considerably from the average? First we'll deal with measures of central tendency, then with variability.

central tendency
a measure of the middle, or average, score in a set

variability
the extent of spread or dispersion in a set or distribution of scores

Measures of Central Tendency

There are three statistics that we can use to represent the central tendency of a distribution of numbers. The most commonly used is the mean. The median and mode are also measures of central tendency, but they are used less frequently.

mean
(X̄), the sum of all X scores (ΣX) divided by N, the number of X scores

The Mean.   When we think about computing the average of a distribution of scores we are usually thinking about computing the **mean**. The mean of a set of scores is their total divided by the number of scores in the set. For example, if Max is 6 feet tall and Ruth is 4 feet tall, their mean height is 5 feet. Four inches of snow yesterday and 2 inches today yields a mean snowfall of 3 inches for the two days ($4'' + 2'' = 6'' \div 2 = 3''$).

So, to compute the mean scores for Form A of our example we add up all the scores and divide by 50 because there are 50 scores in the set. We'd do the very same thing for the scores earned on Form B—add them up and divide by 50.

The mean of a set of numbers is symbolized by $\overline{X}$, read *X bar*. The upper case Greek letter sigma, Σ, stands for "take the sum of whatever follows." We use the symbol X to represent an individual score from a set of scores and N for the number of scores in the set. So the formula for computing a mean looks like this:

$$\overline{X} = \frac{\Sigma X}{N}$$

This is just a fancy shorthand way of expressing what you already know: To find the mean of a set of scores ($\overline{X}$), add the scores (X) together and then divide by the number of scores (N). When we do this for Form A and Form B of our classroom exam example, we find that the mean for both sets of scores is 80. That is $\Sigma X \div N = 80$ for both forms of the exam. In terms of average score (as indicated by the mean), there is clearly no difference between the two forms of the test.

The Median.   Although the mean is generally the central tendency measure of choice, there are occasions when it may not be appropriate. These occasions occur when a distribution includes a few extreme scores. For a simple example, the mean of the numbers 2, 3, 3, 5, 7 is 4 ($\Sigma X = 20$; $N = 5$; so $\overline{X} = 4$). Even on inspection, 4 looks right; it is a value near the middle or center of the set. Now consider the numbers 2, 3, 3, 5, 37. What is their mean? Their sum of these 5 numbers is 50, so their mean equals 10. Here it seems by inspection that the extreme score of 37 is adding too much weight to our measure of central tendency. For a real-life example, imagine computing the average income of a small, working-class community that happened to include two millionaires. The *mean* income of this community would be unduly influenced by just two persons with unusually high incomes.

median
the score of an ordered set above which and below which fall half the scores

In such cases, we might prefer to use the **median** as our measure of central tendency. The median is the value of a set of numbers that divides it exactly in half. There are as many scores above the median as below it. Perhaps you recognize that the median is the same as the 50th percentile of a distribution—50 percent of the scores are higher; 50 percent are lower.

Don't fall for this trick: "What is the median of these test scores: 42, 58, 37, 62, 55?" There is a tendency to want to say "37" because it is in the middle of the list with two scores to the left and two scores to the right. But "37" certainly isn't at the center of these scores; it's the lowest of the five! Before you choose the median, the scores must first be placed in order: 37, 42, 55, 58, 62. *Now* the score in the middle, 55, is the median score, the one that divides the set in half. Whenever we have an even number of scores, there will be no one number in the middle, will there? What is the median of these numbers: 3, 6, 8, 10, 14, 18? What we do here to calculate the mean of the two numbers in the middle (here 8 and 10). So, the median of these six numbers is 9. When we have a large number of scores to deal with, the computation of the median becomes slightly more complicated. We can't always just put our scores in order and identify the median by inspection. But in such cases, the logic is the same, and we have formulas that tell what steps to take to calculate the median. For the two distributions of our example, the median for Form A of the exam is 80; for Form B it is 79.

The Mode. No doubt the easiest measure of central tendency to calculate is the **mode.** The mode is simply the most frequently occurring value in a set or distribution of scores. If you have already constructed a frequency distribution, finding the mode is particularly easy. Just locate the X-value with the greatest frequency and you've found the mode. For many psychological characteristics measured for large numbers of subjects, the mode *does* tend to fall at or near the center of the distribution of scores. For our example problem, the mode of scores earned on Form A is 86 and on Form B the mode is 80.

mode
the most frequently occurring X-value in a set

As it happens, the mode is seldom used as a measure of central tendency. For one thing, computing the mode disregards all of the other values in the distribution. For another, there is no guarantee that the most frequently occurring number will be at (or even near) the middle. Notice also that it is quite possible for a collection of numbers to have two modes (be "bi-modal") or three modes, or more.

Name and define three measures of central tendency. **BEFORE YOU GO ON**

Variability

If we know how two sets of scores, or distributions, differ "on the average," we know a lot. We would know, for instance, that there is no apparent difference in central tendency for the two sets of scores we have been using as an example. There is, however, a second descriptive characteristic of distributions of numbers that may be of interest: their spread, or dispersion, or **variability.**

variability
the extent of spread or dispersion in a set or distribution of scores

It is quite possible to have two sets of scores that have identical means but that, at the same time, are clearly different from each other. This sort of difference can be seen in Figure A.3 and is even more clearly obvious in Figure A.4. In this figure, we can see that most of the scores of distribution A are packed, or clustered, around the mean of the distribution. The scores of distribution B are much more spread out, or variable, even though the mean of this set of scores equals the mean of distribution A.

Imagine for a moment that the two graphs in Figure A.4 represent grades earned by two very large classes. Further imagine that the mean grade for each class is a C. If this is the case, then these graphs tell us that almost everyone in Class A received a C, a C+, or a C−. Some may have received a B− or a D+, but most grades were near the average C. In Class B, on the other hand, there were obviously many more As, Bs, Ds, and Fs than were

Two distributions of X-scores (A and B) that have identical means but clearly different variability.

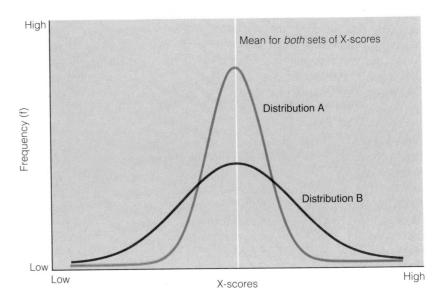

earned by the other class, even though the mean grade for the two classes was a C. So knowing about a distribution's variability is to have some useful information. How shall we represent variability statistically?

One way to measure the spread of scores in a distribution is to use a statistic called the **range.** Range is one of the easiest statistics to calculate. It is found by subtracting the lowest score from the highest. Unfortunately, range (as a measure of variability) simply disregards all the other scores between the highest and lowest. Even when most scores are bunched tightly around the mean, if there are a just a couple of extreme scores, the range will be large. The range would be an inappropriate measure of variability for our example. Scores on both Form A and Form B of the classroom exam range from a high score of 100 to a low score of 60. Thus, the range for both sets of scores is 40 points. An inspection of our Figure A.3, however, indicates that scores on Form A are generally more variable than scores on Form B.

A measure of variability that does take into account all of the scores of a distribution is **standard deviation.** Standard deviation is usually symbolized by **SD.** What it amounts to is a kind of average of the extent to which all the scores in a distribution are different from (deviate from) their mean. Let's go through the procedures that reflect this definition of standard deviation.

The first thing that we need to know is the mean of our distribution ($\overline{X}$). Then we find the difference between each score (X, remember) and the mean ($\overline{X}$). This is a simple process of subtraction, yielding a collection of ($X - \overline{X}$) scores. Because means are by definition, in the middle of distributions, some X-scores will be above the mean (so $X - \overline{X}$ will be a positive number), and some X-scores will be below the mean (so $X - \overline{X}$ will be a negative number). If we then simply add up all of our deviations, $\Sigma(X - \overline{X})$, we will always have a sum of zero. What we do to deal with this complication is simply square each deviation score, so that we have a set of $(X - \overline{X})^2$ scores. Any real

range
the highest score in a distribution, minus the lowest

standard deviation (SD)
a type of average of the deviations of each X score from the mean of the distribution:

$$SD = \sqrt{\frac{\Sigma(X - \overline{X})^2}{N}}$$

The computation of the standard deviation for a small distribution of X-scores.

X-Scores	$X - \overline{X}$	$(X - \overline{X})^2$
12	6.5	42.25
10	4.5	20.25
7	1.5	2.25
6	.5	.25
5	−.5	.25
5	−.5	.25
4	−1.5	2.25
4	−1.5	2.25
1	−4.5	20.25
1	−4.5	20.25
		$\Sigma(X - \overline{X})^2 = 110.50$

$$\Sigma X = 55$$
$$N = 10$$
$$\overline{X} = \Sigma X \div N = 5.5$$

$$SD = \sqrt{\frac{\Sigma(X - \overline{X})^2}{N}} = \sqrt{\frac{110.50}{10}} = \sqrt{11.05} = \underline{3.32}$$

number, even a negative one, that is squared, or multiplied by itself, will yield a positive number. *Now* we add together our squared deviations, $\Sigma(X - \overline{X})^2$. We then find an average by dividing this total by N, the number of scores we are dealing with. In formula form, what we have so far is: $\Sigma(X - \overline{X})^2/N$. This statistic is called *variance*.

In our calculations, we introduced a squaring operation just to get rid of negative numbers. We now reverse that operation by taking the square root of our result (variance). What we end up with then is our formula for standard deviation, and it looks like this:

$$SD = \sqrt{\frac{\Sigma(X - \overline{X})^2}{N}}$$

You may never be called upon to actually compute a standard deviation using this formula. For one thing, even simple hand-held calculators often come with a button that yields a standard deviation value once you've punched in all the X scores. For another, there are simpler computational formulas that provide the same result in fewer, easier steps. But you should appreciate what standard deviations do. They tell us the extent to which scores in a distribution deviate, or are spread from the distribution's mean. We use them often in psychology.

To reinforce our discussion, Figure A.5 depicts the computation of a standard deviation for some simple data. When the procedure is applied to our example data we find that the standard deviation for Form A of the exam is 11.29; for Form B, the SD = 6.18. This result conforms to our observation that the scores on Form A of the test are more variable than those earned on Form B.

INFERENTIAL STATISTICS

inferential statistics
statistical tests that tell us about the significance of the results of experimental or correlational studies

We have already seen that statistics can be used to summarize and describe some of the essential characteristics of large collections of data. Statistics can also be used to guide our decision making concerning the data we have collected. That is, statistics can allow us to make inferences about our data. **Inferential statistics** tell us about the *significance* of the results of our experimental or correlational studies. In general, they tell us the likelihood that the data we have collected might have occurred by chance. Let's use another example, again dealing with means.

For this example, let's say that our concern is with the effects of background music on studying. You want to do an experiment to determine if background music affects study skills. To keep matters simple, let's assume that you have two groups of volunteer subjects. Each group is to try to learn 50 words in a five-minute study session. One group will practice in silence (your control group); the other will have classical music playing in the background (the experimental group). We'll call the first group Group S and the second, Group C. Let's say there are 40 subjects in each group, or N = 40. After each group studies their word lists for five minutes, you test to see how many words have been learned. Then you construct a frequency distribution of your data and compute the means and standard deviations for each set of data. What you discover is that Group S has a mean number of words learned equal to 26.0 and Group C's mean is 28.5. Now what? There's no doubt that 28.5 is larger than 26.0, but the difference is not very large. Is the difference large enough for you to claim that the background music had an effect? We need to backtrack just a little.

Imagine that we had two groups of subjects in a similar experiment, but that both groups received exactly the same treatment. That is, both groups performed the same task under the same conditions. Some dependent variable is measured for both groups (perhaps the number of words that were learned in a five-minute study session). Even though both groups were treated exactly the same, would we expect the mean scores for the two groups to be *exactly* equal? Wouldn't we expect *some* chance variation in scores between the two groups? If we did this same experiment again tomorrow, or next week, would we expect (again) to get exactly the same mean scores, even though experimental conditions remain the same? No. We generally anticipate that simply because of chance factors alone there will be some difference between the scores earned by two different groups of subjects—even if they are doing the same thing under the same conditions. So if mean scores for our two groups turn out to be somewhat different, we aren't surprised; we can attribute the difference to chance. But what if the groups are treated differently? What if the difference in measured responses are large? Can these differences also be attributed to chance? Or do they reflect real, significant differences between the two groups? This is where inferential statistics come in.

Inferential statistics allow us to make probability statements. They help us to determine if observed differences in our descriptive statistics (such as means) are differences due to chance and random factors or reflect some true difference between the groups we have measured. Differences that are not likely to have occurred by chance are called **statistically significant differences.** If the difference between two calculated means is statistically significant, that difference may or may not be *important* or *meaningful,* but we can claim that the difference is not likely to be due to chance.

statistically significant differences differences between descriptive statistics not likely to have occurred by chance if the descriptive statistics were describing the same group

One way to think about statistical significance is in terms of replication. If, for example, two means are found to be significantly different, it is likely that if the measurements were taken over and over again, the same difference in the same direction would show up most of the time. Inferential statistics can be used to judge the statistical significance of any statistic. They can be used to tell us about the probability with which means, or medians, or standard deviations, or proportions, or correlation coefficients are truly different or, rather, are different by chance alone.

Significance is usually stated as a proportion. We talk about means being different at the "0.05 level," for instance. What this means is that the likelihood of our finding a mean difference as large as we did by chance alone is less than 5 in 100. The "0.01 level of significance" is even more conservative. It implies that the difference that we have observed would have occurred by chance—if in fact no real differences exist—less than 1 time in 100.

Let's return now to the example with which we are working in this section and add a small insight to this business of statistical significance. We have reported that the results of an experiment provide us with two mean scores: 26.0 for the group that studied in silence and 28.5 for subjects who studied with classical music in the background. Our interest now is in determining the extent to which these means are statistically different or due to chance factors. As we have implied, there is a statistical test of significance that can be applied to our data to answer this very question. The statistical test is called a *t-test*.

There are three factors that influence a test of significance such as the one that would be applied to our data for this example. One, of course, is the size of the mean difference itself. *Everything else being equal,* the larger the measured difference, the more likely that the difference reflects a real difference and not chance factors. A second factor is the size of the sample, or the number of measurements being tested. *Everything else being equal,* differences based on large numbers of observation are more likely to be significant than the same differences based on fewer observations. The third factor that influences a measure of statistical significance is the variability of the data.

To see why variability (usually standard deviation) matters in determining the significance of difference between means, refer to Figure A.6. On the left hand side of Figure A.6 we see two distributions of X-scores that have different means ($\overline{A}$ and $\overline{B}$). The right side of the figure shows two other distributions that have the very same mean difference ($\overline{C} - \overline{D}$). Because the variability (standard deviations) of distributions A and B are small, it is more likely that their means reflect significant differences than is the case for distributions C and D—even though the actual mean difference is the same in either case. In fact, the formula for the t-test of the significance of the difference between two means includes: (1) the mean difference itself, (2) the size of the groups involved, or N, and (3) the standard deviations of the scores from each group.

The possible outcomes of two experiments. In both cases, the mean differences $(\overline{B} - \overline{A})$ $(\overline{D} - \overline{C})$ are the same, and the Ns are also the same for each distribution. But because the variabilities in (A) are smaller, the difference between A and B is more likely to be significant than is the difference between C and D.

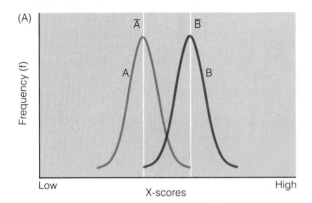

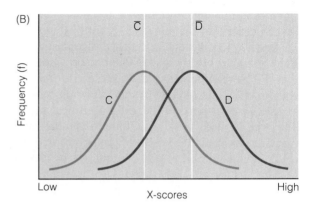

BEFORE YOU GO ON   **What is meant by "test of statistical significance?"**

What does it mean to say that two means, for example, are statistically significant at the 0.01 level?

SOME NORMAL CURVE STATISTICS

normal curve
a commonly found, symmetrical, bell-shaped frequency distribution

As we have suggested in our chapter on personality and intelligence, many of the measurements we make in psychology tend to fall into a similar pattern. Particularly when measurements are made on large numbers of subjects, we commonly find that they fall into a distribution we call the **normal curve** (see Figure A.7). The normal curve is a frequency distribution that is symmetrical and bell-shaped. As you can see, scores that are normally distributed tend to bunch around the mean and become infrequent at the extreme values of X (whatever the X-scores may be). Because this normal distribution of scores does occur so often, we tend to know a lot about the nature of this curve.

The normal curve is simply a graphical representation of a collection of numbers. As such, we can compute the mean and the standard deviation of the scores that make up the distribution. Because the normal distribution is symmetrical, the mean always falls precisely in the middle of the distribution and is coincident with the median and the mode. *That is, there are just as many scores above the mean as there are below it.* We also know how many scores, or what proportion of scores, fall within standard deviation units around the mean. For example, we know that 68 percent of all scores fall between 1 standard deviation below the mean and 1 standard deviation above the mean (see Figure A.7). It is also the case that 95 percent of the cases fall between ±2 standard deviations around the mean. Almost all the cases (about 99 percent) in a normal distribution fall between −3 and +3 standard deviations around the mean. What good is this sort of information? Let's look at an example problem.

The percentage of cases in a normal distribution falling between ± 1 s.d. around the mean (68%), ± 2 s.d. (95%), and ± 3 s.d. (99%). Note that the curve is symmetrical and the mean divides it exactly in half, and that virtually all scores fall between 3 standard deviations below the mean and 3 standard deviations above the mean.

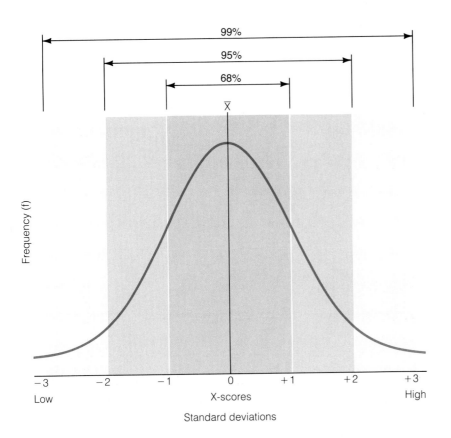

When many people are measured, IQ scores tend to fall in distributions that we may consider to be normal distributions. Figure A.8 depicts a theoretical IQ distribution where, by definition, the mean equals 100 and the standard deviation is equal to 15 IQ points. We might want to know, for instance, what percentage of the population has an IQ score above 100. Well, that's an easy one. Because the mean equals 100, and because the mean divides the distribution exactly in half, 50 percent of the cases fall above 100 and 50 percent of the cases fall below an IQ of 100, so the answer is 50 percent.

What percentage of the population has an IQ score above 115? This takes a little more effort, and following along with Figure A.8 might help. We might work backward. If we know the percentage of cases in the shaded portion of the curve (up to IQ = 115) then the difference between that percentage and 100 will be the percentage who have IQs above 115. We can't determine the shaded percentage by inspection, but we can do so in a few easy steps. Up to the mean fall one-half, or 50 percent of the cases (this we've already established). Now what about that segment between 100 and 115? What we do know (check on Figure A.7 again) is that 68 percent of the cases

A theoretical normal curve of IQ scores. Here we can see, with mean = 100 and s.d. = 15, that 84 percent of the population has an IQ of 115 or less (50% to the mean and 34% from the mean to 1 s.d. above the mean). Thus, only 16 percent have IQs above 115.

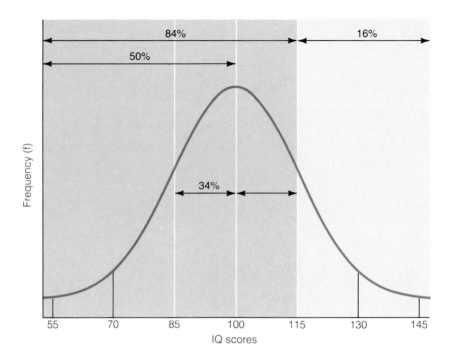

fall between −1 standard deviation and +1 standard deviation. In a normal distribution, the mean divides this segment exactly in half, so that between the mean and 1 standard deviation above the mean 34 percent of the cases are included. (Note that IQ = 115 *is* 1 SD above the mean.) So now we have 50 percent to the mean of 100, and 34 percent from the mean to 115. We add the two together and determine that 84 percent of the cases fall *below* an IQ of 115, so 16 percent must fall above it. Using the same logic, we can convert any score to a percentage or proportion, if we are dealing with a normal curve. To do so for scores that do not fall precisely on standard deviation units above or below the mean involves a slight complication, but the general method is the same as we have indicated here. What percentage of the population (in accord with our Figures A.7 and A.8) have earned IQ scores above 130? (The answer is 2.5 percent. Can you see where that comes from?)

BEFORE YOU GO ON

What is a normal curve?

In a normal curve, what percentage of the cases fall between ±1, ±2, and ±3 standard deviations around the mean?

Statistical Appendix

SUMMARY

What is a frequency distribution and what is a histogram?

What are they used for?

As its name suggests, a frequency distribution is a way of organizing collected data by listing all scores (X-values) in order and indicating the frequency with which each occurs. A histogram is a bar graph that represents the frequency with which X-values occur by the height of a bar over each X-value. Both histograms and frequency distributions help us to summarize data so that we may make some determinations about its nature by visual inspection. / 555

Name and define three measures of central tendency.

There are three measures of central tendency, or average: (1) the *mean* ($\overline{X}$), the sum of X-scores divided by the number of scores, that is, $\overline{X} = \Sigma X/N$; (2) the *median,* the score above which and below which fall 50 percent of the scores, and (3) the *mode,* the most frequently occurring score in the distribution. / 557

What is the formula for standard deviation, and of what is it a measure?

The standard deviation (SD) is a measure of the spread, or dispersion, of the scores in a distribution. It is, essentially, the average of the extent to which each score in the distribution deviates from its mean. The formula for standard deviation is:

$$SD = \sqrt{\frac{\Sigma(X - \overline{X})^2}{N}} \quad / 560$$

What is meant by "test of statistical significance"?

What does it mean to say that two means, for example, are statistically significant at the 0.01 level?

A test of statistical significance tells us about the likelihood that an observed descriptive statistical difference might have occurred by chance. For example, to say that the difference between two means is "statistically significant at the 0.01 level" means that if there were no real difference between the groups from which the

means came, the likelihood of discovering a mean difference as large as the one observed is less than 1 in 100. / 562

What is a normal curve?

In a normal curve, what percentage of the cases fall between ±1, ±2, and ±3 standard deviations around the mean?

The normal curve depicts data often encountered in psychology when large numbers of measurements are made. It is a graph of frequencies of scores that is symmetrical and bell-shaped. Within 1 standard above the mean and 1 standard deviation below the mean fall 68 percent of all the cases measured. Between ±2 SDs around the mean fall 95 percent of all cases, and 99 percent of all cases fall between −3 SD and +3 SD around the mean. / 564

REVIEW QUESTIONS

1. In a histogram, X-scores are plotted on the:

a. ordinate.

b. horizontal axis.

c. Y-axis.

d. vertical axis.

When we graph a frequency distribution—with a histogram or a line graph—frequencies are indicated on the vertical Y-axis, while X-scores are indicated on the horizontal X-axis. / 554

2. Which measure of central tendency is most appropriate for a distribution of scores that includes a few extreme scores?

a. the mean.

b. the average.

c. the median.

d. the mode.

The median is the statistic of choice for indicating central tendency when our collection of scores includes a few extreme scores (which are unduly reflected in the mean). *Average* is a term that may be used to refer to the mean, median, *or* mode, but is most commonly taken to be the mean. / 556

3. Standard deviation is:

a. the squared deviations of averages from two distributions.

b. a measure of central tendency.

c. the sum of all scores, divided by the number of scores in the distribution.

d. the square root of variance.

Standard deviation is a measure of variability, found by taking the square root of the average of squared deviations of all X-scores from the mean—which is really what variance is. So standard deviation is the square root of variance. / 558

4. In a normally distributed distribution of test scores with a mean of 100 and a standard deviation of 10, nearly two-thirds of all test scores will fall between:

a. 100 and 150.

b. 80 and 100.

c. 90 and 110.

d. 70 and 130.

Given what we know about the normal curve, we find that 68 percent of all scores fall between one standard deviation below the mean and one standard deviation above the mean. In this case, with the mean = 100 and standard deviation = 10, we know that 68 percent of the cases fall between 100 ± 10, or between 90 and 110. / 562

Glossary

References

Acknowledgments

Name Index

Subject Index

Glossary

A

abnormal statistically uncommon, maladaptive cognitions, affect, and/or behavior that are at odds with social expectations and that result in distress or discomfort (p. 393)

accommodation in Piaget's theory, the changing or revising of existing schemas in response to new experiences (p. 248)

accommodation the process in which the ciliary muscles change the shape of the lens in order to focus a visual image (p. 75)

acquired immune deficiency syndrome (AIDS) a deadly STD caused by a virus (the HIV) that destroys the body's natural immune system (p. 307)

acquisition the process in classical conditioning in which the strength of the CR increases with repeated pairings of the CS and UCS (p. 146)

acquisition the process in operant conditioning in which the rate of a reinforced response increases (p. 158)

action potential the difference in electric charge between the inside and outside of a neuron when it fires (p. 39)

actor-observer bias overusing internal attributions to explain the behaviors of others and external attributions to explain our own behaviors (p. 479)

addiction an extreme dependency, usually accompanied by symptoms of tolerance and painful withdrawal (p. 127)

adolescence the developmental period between childhood and adulthood, often begun at puberty and ending with full physical growth—generally between the ages of 12 and 20 (p. 256)

adolescent egocentrism self-centered cognitions plus the belief that one is the center of others' attention (p. 262)

adrenal glands located on the kidneys, part of the ANS especially involved in emotional reactions (p. 320)

affect the feelings or mood that accompany an emotional reaction (p. 7)

affirmative concepts concepts defined by the presence of one particular attribute (p. 219)

ageism discrimination or negative stereotypes about someone formed solely on the basis of age (p. 271)

agoraphobia a phobic fear of open places, of being alone, or of being in public places from which escape might be difficult (p. 399)

all-or-none principle the observation that a neuron will either fire and generate a full impulse or it will not fire at all (p. 39)

alpha activity an EEG pattern associated with quiet relaxation and characterized by slow wave cycles of 8 to 12 per second (p. 115)

androgen the male sex hormones produced by the testes (p. 300)

antianxiety drugs chemicals such as the meprobamates and benzodiazepines, that alleviate the symptoms of anxiety (p. 443)

antidepressant drugs chemicals, such as MAO inhibitors and tricyclics, that reduce and/or eliminate the symptoms of depression (p. 442)

antipsychotic drugs chemicals, such as chlorpromazine, that are effective in reducing psychotic symptoms (p. 441)

anxiety a general feeling of tension or apprehension accompanied by a perceived threat to well-being (pp. 398, 540)

aphrodisiac a substance that, when drunk or eaten, increases sexual arousal; none are known to exist (p. 303)

aqueous humor watery fluid found in the space between the cornea and the lens that nourishes the front of the eye (p. 75)

arousal one's level of activation or excitement; indicative of a motivational state (p. 286)

assessment center a personnel selection procedure in which persons are tested, interviewed, and observed in a number of (stressful) situations by a team of evaluators (p. 513)

assimilation in Piaget's theory, taking in new information and fitting it into existing schemas (p. 248)

association areas those areas in the frontal, parietal, and temporal lobes that are neither sensory nor motor in function where cognitive activity is assumed to take place (p. 56)

attitude a relatively stable and general evaluative disposition directed toward some object, consisting of feelings, behaviors, and beliefs (p. 472)

attribution therapy the cognitions we generate when we attempt to explain the sources of behavior (p. 477)

audience inhibition reluctance to intervene and offer assistance in front of others (p. 492)

autokinetic effect an illusion in which a stationary spot of light in a dark room appears to move (p. 485)

autonomic nervous system (ANS) those neurons that activate the smooth muscles and the glands (pp. 44, 320)

axon the long taillike extension of a neuron that carries an impulse away from the cell body toward the synapse (p. 36)

axon terminals the series of branching end points of an axon where one neuron communicates to the next in a series (p. 38)

B

baseline design a method in which subjects' performance with an experimental treatment is compared with performance without that treatment (p. 25)

basilar membrane a structure within the cochlea that vibrates and thus stimulates the hair cells of the inner ear (p. 88)

behavior any action or reaction of an organism that can be observed and measured (p. 5)

behavior therapy techniques of psychotherapy founded on principles of learning established in the psychological laboratory (p. 449)

behavioral observation the personality assessment technique in which one draws conclusions about an individual on the basis of observations of his or her behaviors (p. 356)

behaviorism the school of psychology (associated with Watson and Skinner) that focuses on the observable, measurable behavior of organisms (p. 12)

blindspot the region of the retina, containing no photoreceptors, where the optic nerve leaves the eye (p. 76)

brain stem a portion of the brain just above the spinal cord comprised of the medulla and the pons (p. 49)

brightness the psychological experience associated with a light's intensity or wave amplitude (p. 68)

British empiricism the school of thought that focuses on the source of mental processes and claims they are learned through experience (p. 7)

C

case history an intensive, retrospective, and detailed investigation of certain aspects of one (or a few) individual(s) (p. 19)

category clustering at recall, grouping words together into categories even if they are presented in a random order (p. 198)

cell body the largest mass of a neuron, containing the cell's nucleus; may receive neural impulses (p. 36)

central nervous system (CNS) those neurons in the brain and spinal cord (p. 43)

central tendency a measure of the middle, or average, score in a set (p. 555)

cerebellum a spherical structure at the lower rear of the brain that is involved in the coordination and smoothing of muscular activity (p. 50)

cerebrum the large, convoluted outer covering of the brain that is the seat of cognitive functioning and voluntary action (p. 53)

ciliary muscles small muscles attached to the lens that control its shape, and focusing capability (p. 75)

classical conditioning learning in which an originally neutral stimulus comes to evoke a new response after having been paired with a stimulus that reflexively evokes that same response (p. 144)

client-centered therapy the humanistic psychotherapy associated with Rogers, aimed at helping the client grow and change from within (p. 448)

closure the Gestalt principle or organization that claims that we tend to perceive incomplete figures as whole and complete (p. 103)

cochlea part of the inner ear where sound waves become neural impulses (p. 88)

cognitions the mental processes of "knowing"—of thinking, attending, perceiving, remembering, and the like (p. 7)

cognitive dissonance the state of tension or discomfort that exists when we hold inconsistent cognitions; we are motivated to reduce dissonance (p. 474)

cognitive processes the mental activities that involve forming and using cognitions (p. 216)

cognitive psychology the subfield in psychology that studies the nature of cognitions and their formation (p. 13)

cognitive restructuring therapy a form of cognitive therapy, associated with Beck, in which patients are led to overcome negative self-images and pessimistic views of the future (p. 454)

compensation a mechanism through which resources are invested in some trait or ability to offset deficits in other traits or abilities (p. 542)

compulsions constantly intruding, stereotyped, and essentially involuntary acts or behaviors (p. 4)

concept a mental event used to represent a category or class of events or objects (p. 217)

concrete operations stage in Piaget's theory, the stage (ages 7–12 years) characterized by the formation of concepts, rules, and ability to solve conservation problems (p. 251)

concurrent validity the extent to which the scores on a test are correlated with the scores on other tests claiming to measure the same characteristic (p. 353)

conditioned response (CR) in classical conditioning, the learned response (for example, salivation) evoked by the CS after conditioning (p. 145)

conditioned stimulus (CS) in classical conditioning, an originally neutral stimulus (for example, a tone) that, when paired with a UCS comes to evoke a new response (a CR) (p. 144)

conditioning demonstrated by a relatively permanent change in behavior that occurs as the result of practice or experience (p. 143)

cones photosensitive cells of the retina that operate best at high levels of illumination and are responsible for color perception (p. 75)

conflict a source of stress in which some goals can be satisfied only at the expense of others (p. 533)

conformity changing one's behavior (under perceived pressure) so that it is consistent with the behavior of others (p. 485)

conjunctive concepts concepts that are defined by "and" rules; that is, having all attributes of the concept (p. 218)

consciousness our awareness or perception of the environment and of our own mental processes (p. 114)

conservation the understanding that changing something's form does not change its essential character (p. 251)

content validity the extent to which a test provides an adequate and fair sample of the behaviors being measured (p. 353)

contingency contracting establishing a token economy of secondary reinforcers to reward appropriate behaviors (p. 451)

contingency management bringing about changes in one's behaviors by controlling rewards and punishers (p. 451)

continuity the Gestalt principle of organization that claims that a stimulus or a movement will be perceived as continuing in the same smooth direction as first established (p. 103)

continuous reinforcement schedule (CRF) a reinforcement schedule in which each and every response is followed by a reinforcer (p. 165)

contrast the extent to which a stimulus is in some physical way different from other surrounding stimuli (p. 97)

control group those participants in an experiment who do not receive any experimental treatment or manipulation (p. 25)

conversion disorder the display of a (severe) physical disorder for which there is no medical explanation; often accompanied by an apparent lack of concern on the part of the patient (p. 403)

cornea the outermost structure of the eye that protects the eye and begins to focus light waves (p. 73)

corpus callosum the network of nerve fibers that sends impulses between the two hemispheres of the cerebrum (p. 57)

correlation a largely statistical technique used to determine the nature and degree of R-R relationships (p. 19)

correlation coefficient a number (r) that indicates the nature (positive/negative) and the strength of the relationship between measured responses (p. 20)

cross-laterality the principle that, in general, sensory and motor impulses to and from the brain cross from the left side of the body to the right side of the brain, and vice versa (p. 55)

D

death instincts (thanatos) those inborn impulses proposed by Freud that compel one toward destruction, including aggression (p. 335)

debriefing explaining to a subject, after an experiment has been completed, the true nature of the experiment, making sure that there are no lasting negative consequences of participation (p. 489)

decibel scale a scale of our experience of loudness in which 0 represents the absolute threshold and 140 is sensed as pain (p. 85)

defense mechanisms techniques, beyond one's conscious control, employed to protect against the feelings of stress (p. 541)

degenerative dementia a marked loss of intellectual and cognitive abilities that worsens with age (p. 410)

delta wave an EEG wave pattern (.5 to 3 cycles per second) indicative of deepening levels (stages 3 and 4) of sleep (p. 116)

dendrite a branchlike extension of a neuron's cell body, where most impulses are received by the neuron (p. 36)

denial refusing to acknowledge the presence of stressors (p. 541)

dependence a state in which drug use is either necessary or believed to be necessary to maintain functioning at some desired level (p. 127)

dependent variables those responses measured in an experiment whose values are hypothesized to depend upon manipulations of independent variable (p. 22)

depressants those drugs (such as alcohol, opiates, heroin, and barbiturates) that slow or reduce nervous system activity (p. 129)

diagnosis the act of recognizing a disorder or a disease on the basis of the presence of particular symptoms (p. 395)

diffusion of responsibility the tendency to allow others to share in the obligation to intervene (p. 493)

discrimination the phenomenon in classical conditioning in which an organism learns to make a CR in response to only one CS, but not to other stimuli (pp. 148, 166)

disjunctive concepts concepts defined by "either/or" rules, that is, either having some attributes or others (p. 219)

displacement directing one's motives at some substitute person or object rather than expressing it directly (p. 543)

dissociative disorders disorders in which one separates from or dissociates from aspects of one's personality (p. 404)

distributed practice rehearsal in which practice is done in segments with rest intervals interspersed (p. 212)

double-blind technique a protection against bias in which neither subjects nor the experimenter collecting and/or analyzing the data is told the hypothesis (p. 26)

drive a state of tension resulting from a need that arouses and directs an organism's behavior (p. 287)

duplicity theory of vision the theory that rods and cones have different functions (p. 76)

E

eardrum the outermost membrane of the ear that is set in motion by the vibrations of a sound; transmits vibrations to the ossicles (p. 88)

ego that aspect of personality that encompasses the sense of "self"; in contact with the real world, operates on the reality principle (p. 335)

egocentric seeing everything from one's own point of view; unable to appreciate someone else's perspective (p. 250)

elaborative rehearsal a mechanism for processing information into LTM that involves the meaningful manipulation of the information to be remembered (p. 195)

electroconvulsive therapy (ECT) a treatment (usually for the symptoms of severe depression) in which an electric current passed through a patient's head causes a seizure and loss of consciousness (p. 439)

electroencephalogram (EEG) an instrument used to measure and record the electrical activity of the brain (p. 115)

electromyogram (EMG) an instrument used to measure and record muscle tension/relaxation (p. 115)

emotion a reaction involving subjective feelings, physiological response, cognitive interpretation, and behavioral expression (p. 315)

empathic able to understand and share the essence of another's feelings; to view from another's perspective (p. 448)

encoding the active process of putting information into memory (p. 186)

encoding specificity principle the hypothesis that we can only retrieve what we have stored and that how we retrieve information depends on how we encoded it (p. 203)

endocrine system a series of glands that secrete hormones directly into the bloodstream (p. 44)

epigenetic model the point of view that developmental processes emerge based on genetic programming interacting with experiences with the environment (p. 240)

epinephrine (adrenalin) a hormone produced by the adrenal glands that is involved in emotional activity, mostly affecting heart activity (p. 320)

episodic memory in LTM, where life events and experiences are stored (p. 197)

equity theory the view that workers are motivated to match their inputs and outcomes with those fellow workers in similar positions (p. 519)

erogenous zones areas of the body which, when they are stroked, lead to sexual arousal (p. 302)

escape conditioning a form of operant conditioning in which an organism learns to escape, thus earning negative reinforcement (p. 161)

estrogen the female sex hormones, produced by the ovaries (p. 300)

etiology the cause of predisposing factors of a disturbance or disorder (p. 395)

expectancy theory the view that workers make logical choices to do what they believe will result in their attaining outcomes of highest value (p. 518)

experiment a series of operations used to investigate relationships between manipulated and measured events, while others are controlled (p. 21)

experimental group those participants in an experiment who receive treatment or manipulation; there may be more than one group in an experiment (p. 25)

experimental neurosis a condition of anxiety and agitation evidenced by subjects that are required to make too fine a discrimination in a classical conditioning task (p. 148)

external attribution an explanation of behavior in terms of something outside the person; a situational attribution (p. 478)

extinction the process in operant conditioning in which the rate of a response decreases as reinforcers are withheld (p. 159)

extinction the process in classical conditioning in which the strength of the CR decreases with repeated presentations of the CS alone (p. 146)

extraneous variables those factors in an experiment that need to be controlled or eliminated so as not to affect the dependent variable (p. 22)

extrinsic control external, environmental processes that exercise control over our behaviors or that motivate us (p. 312)

F

family therapy a variety of group therapy focusing on the roles, interdependence, and communication skills of family members (p. 456)

fantasy an escape from stress through imagination and/or daydreaming (p. 542)

figure-ground relationship the Gestalt psychology principle that stimuli are selected and perceived as figures against a ground or background (p. 97)

flashbulb memories particularly clear, detailed, vivid, and easily retrieved memories from one's episodic memory (p. 205)

flooding a technique of behavior therapy in which a subject is confronted with the object of his or her phobic fear while accompanied by the therapist (p. 450)

formal concepts concepts with relatively few, well-defined attribute values and clearly defined rules to relate them (p. 218)

formal operations stage in Piaget's theory, the stage (ages over 12 years) characterized by abstract, symbolic reasoning (p. 252)

fovea the region at the center of the retina, comprised solely of cones, where acuity is best in daylight (p. 76)

free association the procedure in psychoanalysis in which the patient is to express whatever comes to mind without editing responses (p. 445)

frequency distribution an ordered listing of all X-values, indicating the frequency with which each occurs (p. 553)

frontal lobes the largest of the cerebral lobes in front of the central fissure and above the lateral fissure (p. 54)

frustration the blocking or thwarting of goal-directed behavior (p. 532)

frustration-aggression hypothesis the view (now discredited) that all aggression stems from frustration (p. 539)

functionalism the school of psychology that studies the function of the mind and consciousness as they help the organism adapt to the environment (p. 10)

fundamental attribution error the tendency to overuse internal attributions when explaining behavior (p. 478)

G

g-score a measure of one's overall, general intellectual abilities commonly thought of as "IQ" (p. 365)

gate-control theory the theory of pain sensation that argues that there are brain centers that regulate the passage of pain messages from different parts of the body to the brain (p. 95)

general adaptation syndrome (GAS) a pattern of physiological reactions to stress, including alarm, resistance, and exhaustion stages (p. 538)

generalization the process by which a response that was reinforced in the presence of one stimulus appears in response to other, similar stimuli (pp. 147, 166)

generalized anxiety disorder persistent, chronic, and distressingly high levels of unattributable anxiety (p. 400)

genes the basic structures of heredity that determine, in part, one's development (p. 240)

genital herpes (Herpes Type II) the most common STD; a skin infection in the form of a rash or blisters in the genital area (p. 307)

gestalt whole, totality, configuration, or pattern; the whole (gestalt) is seen as more than the sum of its parts (p. 10)

gonorrhea an STD caused by a bacterial infection of moist tissues in the genital area (p. 306)

group polarization the tendency for members of a group to give more extreme judgments following a discussion than they gave initially (p. 497)

groupthink a style of thinking of cohesive groups concerned with maintaining agreement to the extent that independent ideas are discouraged (p. 498)

growth spurt a marked increase in both height and weight that marks the onset of adolescence (p. 258)

H

hair cells the receptor cells for hearing, located in the cochlea, stimulated by the vibrating basilar membrane, they send neural impulses to the temporal lobe of the brain (p. 88)

hallucinations perceptual experiences without sensory input; that is, perceiving that which is not there or not perceiving that which is there (p. 124)

hallucinogens those drugs (such as LSD) whose major effect is the alteration of perceptual experience and mood (p. 131)

health psychology the field of applied psychology that studies psychological factors affecting physical health and illness (p. 526)

hemispheres the two halves of the cerebral cortex that are separated by a deep fissure running from front to back (p. 54)

hertz (Hz) the standard measure of sound wave frequency that is the number of wave cycles per second (p. 85)

histogram a bar graph; a graphical representation of a frequency distribution (p. 554)

homeostasis a state of balance or equilibrium among internal, physiological conditions (p. 292)

homosexuals those persons who are sexually attracted to and aroused by members of their own sex (p. 304)

hormones a variety of chemical compounds, secreted by endocrine glands, carried through the bloodstream (p. 44)

hue the psychological experience associated with a light's wavelength (p. 69)

humanism the school of psychology (associated with Maslow and Rogers) that focuses on the person (self) as the central matter of concern (p. 13)

hypnosis an altered state of consciousness characterized by an increase in suggestibility, attention, and imagination (p. 123)

hypochondriasis a mental disorder involving the fear of developing some serious disease or illness (p. 402)

hypothalamus a small structure at the base of the brain involved in many drives, including thirst, hunger, sex, and temperature regulation (pp. 52, 295)

hypothesis a tentative proposition or explanation that can be tested and confirmed or rejected (p. 5)

I

id that instinct aspect of personality that seeks immediate gratification of impulses; operates on the pleasure principle (p. 335)

idealistic principle governs the superego; opposed to the id, seeks adherence to standards of ethics and morality (p. 335)

identity crisis the struggle to define and integrate one's sense of self, and what one's attitudes, beliefs, and values should be (p. 261)

implosive therapy a behavior therapy in which one imagines one's worst fears, experiencing extreme anxiety in the safe surroundings of the therapist's office (p. 450)

impression management function the selective presentation or misrepresentation of one's attitudes in an attempt to present one's self in a particular way (p. 474)

in-basket technique an assessment technique requiring applicants to respond to a variety of situations that might be encountered in a typical workday (p. 514)

incentives external stimuli that an organism may be motivated to approach or avoid (p. 290)

independent variables those events in an experiment manipulated by the experimenter that are hypothesized to produce changes in responses (p. 22)

inferential statistics statistical tests that tell us about the significance of the results of experimental or correlational studies (p. 560)

inferiority complex the Adlerian notion that as children we develop a sense of inferiority in dealing with our environment; needs to be overcome to reach maturity (p. 338)

insanity a legal term for diminished capacity and inability to tell right from wrong (p. 397)

insomnia the chronic inability to get to sleep and to get an adequate amount of sleep (p. 115)

instinctive drift the tendency of behaviors that have been conditioned to eventually revert to more natural, instinctive behaviors (p. 168)

instincts unlearned, complex patterns of behavior that occur in the presence of particular stimuli (p. 287)

intellectual assessment the measurement of intelligence, ability, or aptitude, one's "best performance" (p. 350)

intelligence the capacity to understand the world and the resourcefulness to cope with its challenges; that which an intelligence test measures (p. 363)

intermittent reinforcement schedules reinforcement in which responses are not reinforced every time they occur (p. 165)

internal attribution an explanation of behavior in terms of something (a trait) within the person; a dispositional attribution (p. 477)

interneurons nerve cells within the brain or spinal cord (p. 38)

interview the personality assessment technique involving a conversational interchange between an interviewer and a subject; used to gain information about the subject (p. 357)

intrinsic control internal, personal processes that control and/or motivate our behaviors (p. 312)

introspection a technique in which one examines one's own mental experiences and describes them in the most fundamental, basic way (p. 9)

I/O psychology industrial-organizational psychology specializing in the study of affect, behavior, and cognition in the workplace (p. 510)

iris the colored structure of the eye that reflexively opens or constricts the pupils (p. 73)

J

job satisfaction an attitude; a collection of feelings about one's job or job experiences (p. 521)

just world hypothesis the belief that the world is just and that people get what they deserve (p. 478)

K

kinesthetic sense the position sense that tells us the position of different parts of our bodies and what our muscles and joints are doing (p. 94)

L

language a large collection of arbitrary symbols that have significance for a language-using community and that follow certain rules of combination (p. 224)

latent content the underlying meaning of a dream, thought to be symbolically representative (p. 118)

learned helplessness a condition in which a subject does not attempt to escape from a painful or noxious situation after learning in a previous, similar situation that escape is not possible (p. 163)

learning demonstrated by a relatively permanent change in behavior that occurs as the result of practice or experience (p. 142)

lens the structure behind the iris that changes shape to focus visual images in the eye (p. 74)

lesion a cut or wound made on neural tissue to study the impact of the destruction of specific brain areas (p. 51)

levels of processing model of memory the view that there is but one memory, but that information can be processed within that memory at different degrees, levels, or depths (p. 187)

libido the energy that activates the life (sexual) instincts (largely of the id) (p. 335)

life instincts (eros) those inborn impulses proposed by Freud that compel one toward survival, including hunger, thirst, and sex (p. 335)

light a radiant energy that can be represented in wave form with wavelengths between 380 and 760 nanometers (p. 68)

limbic system a collection of small structures that are involved in emotional and motivational reactions (pp. 51, 321)

locus of control a general belief that what happens is either under our control (internal locus) or a matter of chance and environmental factors (external locus) (p. 338)

long-term memory (LTM) a type of memory with virtually unlimited capacity and very long, if not permanent, duration (p. 193)

loudness the psychological experience correlated with the intensity, or amplitude, of a sound wave (p. 84)

M

maintenance rehearsal a process of rote repetition, (attending again) to keep information in STM (p. 191)

malleus, incus and, stapes (collectively, ossicles) three small bones that transmit and intensify sound vibrations from the eardrum to the oval window (p. 88)

manifest content the literal content of a dream as it is recalled by the dreamer (p. 118)

mantra a soft word or sound chanted repeatedly to aid the meditation process (p. 125)

massed practice rehearsal in which there is no break in one's practice (p. 212)

matching phenomenon the tendency to select partners whose level of physical attractiveness matches our own (p. 483)

meaningfulness the extent to which information to be retrieved evokes associations with material already in one's memory (p. 206)

mean (X̄), the sum of all X scores (ΣX) divided by N, the number of X scores (p. 556)

measurement the assignment of numbers to some characteristic of interest according to rules or some agreed upon system (p. 349)

median the score of an ordered set above which and below which fall half the scores (p. 556)

meditation the focusing of awareness in order to arrive at an altered state of consciousness and relaxation (p. 125)

medulla an area of the brain stem that monitors reflex functions such as respiration and heart rate and where cross-laterality begins (p. 49)

memory the cognitive ability to encode, store, and retrieve information (p. 186)

menarche a female's first menstrual period, often taken as a sign of the beginning of adolescence (p. 258)

mental images pictures of visual representations in one's mind (p. 207)

mental processes activities of consciousness not normally observable by others, including cognitions and affect (p. 6)

mental retardation a condition indicated by an IQ below 70 that began during the developmental period and is associated with impairment in adaptive functioning (p. 375)

mental set a predisposed (set) way to perceive something; an expectation (p. 101)

mentally gifted demonstrating outstanding ability of aptitude in a number of possible areas; usually general intelligence where an IQ of 130 is a standard criterion (p. 374)

mere exposure phenomenon the tendency to increase our liking of people and things the more we see of them (p. 482)

metamemory in LTM our stored knowledge of how our own memory systems work; directs LTM searches (p. 197)

method of loci the mnemonic device that mentally places information to be retrieved at a series of familiar locations (loci) (p. 208)

Minnesota Multiphasic Personality Inventory (MMPI) a paper-and-pencil inventory used to assess a number of personality dimensions (p. 358)

mnemonic devices strategies for improving retrieval that take advantage of existing memories in order to make new material more meaningful (p. 206)

mode the most frequently occurring X-value in a set (p. 557)

modeling the acquisition of new responses through the imitation of another who responds appropriately (p. 452)

monochromatic literally "one colored"; a pure light made up of light waves all of the same wavelength (p. 71)

mood disorders disorders of affect or feeling; usually depression; less frequently mania and depression occurring in cycles (p. 414)

morpheme the smallest unit of meaning in a language (p. 227)

motivation the process of arousing and directing behavior (p. 285)

motor area that portion at the very back of the frontal lobe in which are found the centers that control voluntary movement (p. 55)

motor neurons nerve cells carrying impulses away from the brain or spinal cord toward the muscles and glands (p. 38)

multiple personality the existence within one individual of two or more distinct personalities, each of which is dominant at a particular time (p. 404)

multistore model of memory the view that there are three separate and distinct types (or stores) of memory, each with its own manner of processing information (p. 187)

myelin a white, fatty covering on some axons that protects and increases the speed of the neural impulse (p. 37)

N

nanometer (nm)   the unit of measurement of the wavelength of light, equal to one millionth of a millimeter (p. 69)

narrative chaining   the mnemonic device of relating words together in a story, thus making them more meaningful (p. 207)

natural concepts   the "fuzzy" sorts of concepts that occur in real life, with ill-defined attributes and/or rules (p. 220)

naturalistic observation   the method of observing and noting behaviors as they occur naturally (p. 16)

nature-nurture controversy   a long-standing discussion in psychology over the relative importance of one's heredity and one's environment as shapers of development (p. 240)

need   a lack or shortage of some biological essential resulting from deprivation (p. 287)

need for affiliation   the need to be with others and to form relationships and associations (p. 311)

need for competence   the need to meet the challenges (large and small) provided by one's environment (p. 311)

need for power   the (learned) need to be in control of events or persons, usually at another's expense (p. 311)

need to achieve (nAch)   the (learned) need to meet or exceed some standard of excellence in performance (p. 309)

negative reinforcer   a stimulus that increases the rate of a response when that stimulus is removed after the response is made (p. 161)

neo-Freudians   those theorists of the psychoanalytic school who have taken issue with some parts or Freudian theory, including Adler, Jung, and Horney (p. 337)

neonate   the newborn child from birth through the first two weeks (p. 242)

network models   organizational schemes that describe the relationships among meaningful units stored in semantic memory (p. 199)

neural impulse   sudden, reversible change in the electrical charges within and outside a neuron that travel from dendrite to axon when neuron is fired (p. 39)

neural threshold   the minimum amount of stimulation required to produce a neural impulse within a neuron (p. 39)

neuron   a nerve cell that is the basic building block of the nervous system; transmits neural impulses (p. 36)

neurotransmitters   chemical molecules released at the synapse that, in general, either excite or inhibit neural impulse transmission (p. 41)

norepinephrine   a hormone secreted by the adrenal glands; involved in emotional arousal (p. 320)

normal curve   a commonly found, symmetrical, bell-shaped frequency distribution (p. 562)

norms   results of a test taken by a large group of subjects whose scores can be used to make comparisons or give meaning to new scores (p. 354)

norms   rules or expectations that guide our behavior in certain social situations by prescribing how we ought to behave (p. 472)

nuclei   nervous system structures made up of collections of cell bodies (p. 49)

O

object permanence   the realization that objects that are not physically present are not gone forever and may still reappear (p. 250)

observer bias   a problem in observational methods that occurs when an observer's motives and/or expectations interfere with objectivity (p. 16)

obsessions   ideas or thoughts that involuntarily and persistently intrude into awareness (p. 401)

occipital lobes   the lobes of the cerebrum at the back of the brain (p. 54)

operant   behavior(s) that operate on the environment to produce reinforcement or punishment (p. 155)

operant conditioning   changing the rate of a response on the basis of the consequences that result from the response (p. 155)

operational definition   a definition given in terms of the operations used to measure or create the concept being defined (p. 6)

optic nerve   the fiber of many neurons that leaves the eye and carries impulses to the occipital lobe of the brain (p. 75)

organic mental disorders   disorders characterized by any of the organic mental syndromes and a known organic cause of the syndrome (p. 409)

overlearning   the practice or rehearsal of material over and above what is needed to just barely learn it (p. 210)

P

panic disorder   a disorder in which anxiety attacks suddenly and unpredictably incapacitate; there may be periods free from anxiety (p. 400)

parasympathetic division   (of ANS) those neurons involved in the maintenance of states of calm and relaxation (pp. 44, 320)

parietal lobes   the lobes of the cerebrum behind the frontal lobes, in front of the occipital lobes, and above the lateral fissure (p. 54)

peg word method   the mnemonic device of forming interactive visual images of materials to be learned and items previously associated with numbers (p. 208)

perception   the cognitive process of selecting, organizing, and interpreting stimuli (p. 68)

performance criteria   specific behaviors or characteristics that a person should have in order to do a job as well as possible (p. 511)

peripheral nervous system (PNS)   those neurons not located in the brain or spinal cord; that is, those in the periphery (p. 43)

personality   relatively enduring and unique traits (including affects, behaviors, and cognitions) that can be used to characterize an individual in different situations (p. 332)

personality assessment   the measurement of affect, or personality characteristic; one's "typical behaviors" (p. 350)

personality disorders   enduring patterns of perceiving, relating to, and thinking about the environment and one's self that are inflexible and maladaptive (p. 406)

persuasion   the process of intentionally attempting to change an attitude (p. 474)

phenomenological   an approach that emphasizes one's perception and awareness of events as being more important than the events themselves (p. 342)

phobic disorder   an intense, irrational fear that leads a person to avoid the feared object, activity, or situation (p. 398)

phoneme   the smallest unit of sound in the spoken form of language (p. 226)

photoreceptors   light-sensitive cells (cones and rods) of the retina that convert light energy into neural energy (p. 75)

physical attractiveness stereotype   the tendency to associate desirable characteristics with a physically attractive person, solely on the basis of attractiveness (p. 483)

pinna   the outer ear that collects and funnels sound waves into the auditory canal toward the eardrum (p. 88)

pitch   the psychological experience that corresponds to sound wave frequency and gives rise to high (treble) or low (bass) sounds (p. 86)

plasticity   a term describing the variability involved in expressing genetic predispositions (p. 241)

pleasure principle   the impulse of the id to seek immediate gratification to reduce tensions (p. 335)

pluralistic ignorance   a condition wherein the inaction of others leads each individual in a group to interpret a situation as a nonemergency, thus leading to general inactivity (p. 492)

pons   an area of the brain stem forming a bridge between the brain and spinal cord that plays a role in monitoring sleep-wake cycles (p. 50)

positive reinforcer   a stimulus that increases the rate of a response when that stimulus is presented to an organism after the response is made (p. 160)

pragmatics   the study of how context affects the meaning of linguistic events (p. 228)

predictive validity the extent to which a test can be used to predict future behaviors (p. 353)

prefrontal lobotomy a psychosurgical technique in which the prefrontal lobes of the cerebral cortex are severed from lower brain centers (p. 438)

preoperational stage in Piaget's theory, the stage (ages 2–6 years) of cognitive development characterized by symbol formation, but without rules, and egocentric thinking (p. 250)

primary colors red, green, and blue; those colors (of light) from which all others can be produced (p. 81)

primary reinforcers stimuli (usually biologically or physiologically based) that increase the rate of a response with no previous experience required (p. 164)

proactive interference the inhibition of retrieval of recently learned material caused by material learned earlier (p. 215)

procedural memory in LTM, where learned S-R associations and skilled patterns of responses are stored (p. 196)

process schizophrenia schizophrenia in which the onset of the symptoms is comparatively slow and gradual (p. 419)

prognosis the prediction of the future course of an illness or disorder (p. 399)

projection seeing in others those very characteristics and/or motives that cause stress in one's self (p. 542)

projective technique a personality assessment technique requiring subjects to respond to ambiguous stimuli, thus "projecting" some of their "self" into their responses (p. 361)

prototype the member of a concept or category that best typifies or represents that concept or category (p. 221)

proximity the Gestalt principle of organization that claims that stimuli will be perceived as belonging together if they occur together in space or time (p. 102)

psychoactive drug a chemical that has an effect on psychological processes and consciousness (p. 127)

psychoanalysis the form of psychotherapy associated with Freud, aimed at helping the patient gain insight into unconscious conflicts (p. 444)

psychoanalytic the approach to personality associated with Freud and his followers that relies on instincts and the unconscious as explanatory concepts (p. 333)

psychogenic amnesia a psychologically caused inability to recall important personal information (p. 404)

psychogenic fugue a condition of amnesia accompanied by unexplained travel or change of location (p. 404)

psycholinguistics the science that studies the cognitive processes involved in the use and acquisition of language (p. 224)

psychological test an objective, standardized measure of a sample of behavior (p. 350)

psychology the scientific study of behavior and mental processes (p. 4)

psychosocial law the view that each person who joins a social situation adds less influence than did the previous person to join the group (p. 494)

psychosomatic disorders disorders with actual physical symptoms (rashes, ulcers, and the like) thought to be caused by psychological factors such as stress (p. 402)

psychosurgery a surgical procedure designed to affect one's psychological or behavioral reactions (p. 438)

psychotherapy the treatment of mental disorders through psychological means, effecting change in cognitions, affect, and/or behavior (p. 444)

psychotic disorders psychological disorders that involve gross impairment in functioning and a loss of contact with reality (p. 407)

puberty the stage of physical development at which one becomes capable of sexual reproduction (p. 258)

publicly verifiable the agreement (verifiability) of observers (public) that an event did or did not take place (p. 5)

punishment the administration of a punisher, which is a stimulus that decreases the rate of probability of a response that precedes it (p. 165)

pupil the opening in the iris that changes size in relation to the amount of light available and emotional factors (p. 73)

Purkinje shift the phenomenon of perceived levels of relative brightness changing as a function of level of illumination (p. 79)

Q

quality circles (QC) small groups of employees that voluntarily meet on a regular basis to discuss problems of production (p. 523)

quality of work life (QWL) a group of factors concerning one's work that influence one's attitude toward one's job (p. 522)

R

random assignment the selection of members of a population in such a way that each has an equal opportunity to be assigned to any one group (p. 25)

range the highest score in a distribution, minus the lowest (p. 558)

rational-emotive therapy (RET) a form of cognitive therapy associated with Ellis, aimed at changing the subject's irrational beliefs or maladaptive cognitions (p. 453)

rationalization generating excuses to explain one's behaviors rather than facing the real (anxiety-producing) reasons for those behaviors (p. 541)

reactive schizophrenia schizophrenia in which the onset of the symptoms is comparatively sudden (p. 420)

reality principle governs the ego; arbitrating between the demands of the id, the superego, and the real world (p. 335)

recall a measure of retrieval in which an individual is provided with the fewest possible cues to aid retrieval (p. 210)

recognition a measure of retrieval in which an individual is required to identify material previously learned as being familiar (p. 202)

reflex an unlearned, automatic response that occurs in the presence of specific stimuli (p. 144)

refractory period during the process of the human sexual response, that period following orgasm during which arousal in the male is not possible (p. 304)

regression a return to earlier, childish levels of previously productive behaviors as an escape from stress (p. 543)

reinforcer a stimulus that increases the rate of the response that it follows (p. 160)

relational concepts concepts defined in terms of their comparative relation to other concepts (p. 220)

relearning a measure of memory in which one notes the improvement in performance when learning material for a second time (p. 203)

reliability consistency or dependability; in testing, consistency of test scores (p. 352)

REM sleep rapid eye movement sleep during which vivid dreaming occurs, as do heightened levels of physiological functioning (p. 117)

repression "motivated forgetting" in which stressful events are forced from awareness and cannot be remembered (p. 541)

resistance in psychoanalysis, the inability or unwillingness to freely discuss some aspect of one's life (p. 445)

responses any observable or measurable actions or reactions of an organism (p. 16)

resting potential the difference in electric charge between the inside and outside of a neuron when it is at rest (p. 39)

reticular activating system (RAS) a network of nerve fibers extending from the brain stem to the cerebrum that's involved in one's level of arousal (p. 51)

retina layers of cells at the back of the eye that contain the photosensitive rod and cone cells (p. 75)

retrieval the process of locating, removing, and using information that is stored in memory (p. 186)

retroactive interference the inhibition of retrieval of previously learned material caused by material learned later (p. 214)

rods photosensitive cells of the retina that are most active in low levels of illumination and do not respond differentially to different wavelengths of light (p. 75)

Rorschach inkblot test a projective technique in which the subject is asked to say what is seen in a series of inkblots (p. 361)

R-R relationships   statements of correlation, telling us how and the extent to which two sets of responses are related to each other (p. 16)

S

sample   the portion of a larger population chosen for study (p. 18)

saturation   the psychological experience associated with the purity of light wave, where the most saturated lights are monochromatic and the least saturated are white light (p. 71)

schemas   in Piaget's theory, one's organized mental representations of the world (p. 248)

schizophrenia   complex psychotic disorders characterized by impairment of cognitive functioning, delusions and hallucinations, social withdrawal, and inappropriate affect (p. 418)

science   an organized body of knowledge gained through application of scientific methods (p. 4)

scientific law   a statement about one's subject matter thought to be true, based upon evidence (p. 15)

scientific methods   systematic procedures involving observation, description, control, and replication to gain knowledge (p. 4)

secondary reinforcers   stimuli that increase the rate of a response because of their being associated with other reinforcers; also called conditioned, or learned, reinforcers (p. 164)

semantic memory   in LTM, where vocabulary, facts, simple concepts, rules, and the like are stored (p. 196)

semantics   the study of the meaning of words and sentences (p. 227)

sensation   the process of receiving information from the environment and changing that input into nervous system activity (p. 67)

sensorimotor stage   in Piaget's theory, the stage (ages 0–24 months) in which the child comes to know about the world by sensing and doing (p. 249)

sensory adaptation   a condition in which there is a reduction in the level of sensation as a function of exposure to a constant stimulus (p. 92)

sensory areas   those areas of the cerebral cortex that receive impulses from our sense receptors (p. 55)

sensory memory   the type of memory that holds large amounts of information registered at the senses for very brief periods of time (p. 188)

sensory neurons   nerve cells carrying impulses from receptor cells toward the brain or spinal cord (p. 38)

set point   a normal, optimum level (or value) of equilibrium or balance among physiological or psychological reactions (p. 292)

sexually transmitted diseases (STDs)   contagious diseases that are usually transmitted through sexual contact (p. 306)

shaping   a procedure of reinforcing successive approximations of a desired response until the desired response is made (p. 158)

short-term memory (STM)   a type of memory with limited capacity (7 + − 2 bits of information) and limited duration (15–20 seconds) (p. 189)

similarity   the Gestalt principle of organization that claims that stimuli will be perceived together if they share some common characteristic(s) (p. 102)

single-blind technique   a protection against bias in which the subjects are not aware of the hypothesis of the experiment (p. 25)

sleep spindles   very brief, high-amplitude peaks in EEG pattern, found in stage 2 sleep (p. 116)

social facilitation   improved performance due to the presence of others (p. 495)

social identification function   the observation that attitudes communicate information useful in social evaluation (p. 474)

social interference   impaired performance due to the presence of others (p. 495)

social learning theory   the theory that learning takes place through observation and imitation of models (p. 172)

social loafing   the tendency for a person to work less hard when part of a group in which everyone's efforts are pooled (p. 495)

social psychology   the scientific study of how others influence the thoughts, feelings, and behaviors of the individual (p. 469)

somatic nervous system   sensory and motor neurons outside the CNS that serve the sense receptors and skeletal muscles (p. 44)

somatoform disorders   psychological disorders that reflect imagined physical or bodily symptoms or complaints (p. 402)

spinal cord   a mass of interconnected neurons within the spine that conveys impulses to and from the brain and is involved in some reflex behaviors (p. 45)

spinal reflex   an automatic involuntary response to a stimulus that involves sensory neurons sending impulses to the spinal cord (p. 47)

split-brain procedure   the surgical procedure of separating the functioning of the two cerebral hemispheres by destroying the corpus callosum (p. 57)

split-half reliability   a check on the internal consistency of a test found by correlating one part of a test with another part of the same test (p. 353)

spontaneous recovery   the phenomenon in operant conditioning in which a previously extinguished response returns after a rest interval (p. 159)

spontaneous recovery   the phenomenon in classical conditioning in which a previously extinguished CR returns after a rest interval (p. 147)

S-R relationships   cause and effect statements relating stimuli to the responses they produce (p. 21)

standard age score (SAS)   score on an intelligence test by which one's performance is compared to that of others of the same age; average equals 100 (p. 367)

standard deviation (SD)   a type of average of the deviations of each X-score from the mean of the distribution:

$$SD = \sqrt{\frac{\Sigma(X - \bar{X})^2}{N}}$$

(p. 558)

state-dependent memory   the hypothesis that retrieval can be affected by the extent to which one's state of mind at retrieval matches one's state of mind at encoding (p. 205)

statistically significant differences   differences between descriptive statistics not likely to have occurred by chance if the descriptive statistics were describing the same group (p. 561)

stereotype   a generalized mental (cognitive) representation of someone that minimizes individual differences and is based on limited experience (p. 471)

stimulants   those drugs (such as caffeine, cocaine, and amphetamines) that increase nervous system activity (p. 128)

stimulus   any event or energy that produces a response or reaction in an organism (p. 22)

storage   the process of holding encoded information in memory until the time of retrieval (p. 186)

stress   a complex pattern of reactions to real or perceived threats to one's sense of well-being that motivate adjustment (p. 530)

stressors   real or perceived threats to one's sense of well-being; sources of stress (p. 531)

structuralism   the school of psychology interested in the structure or elements of the mind or consciousness (p. 9)

subjective organization   the tendency for subjects to impose some order on their recall of randomly presented events or items (p. 199)

superego   that aspect of personality that refers to ethical or moral considerations; operates on the idealistic principle (p. 335)

survey   a means of collecting data (observations) from large numbers of subjects, either by interview or by questionnaire (p. 18)

sympathetic division   division of the ANS that becomes involved during emotional states (pp. 44, 320)

synapse   the location where an impulse is relayed from one neuron to another by chemical neurotransmitters (p. 41)

synaptic cleft   the space between the presynaptic membrane of one neuron and the postsynaptic membrane of the next neuron (p. 41)

syndrome   a collection of psychological symptoms used to describe a disorder (p. 409)

synesthesia   a condition of cross-sensory experience—seeing sounds, hearing colors, tasting odors, and the like—associated with hallucinogen use (p. 132)

syntax   the rules that govern how the morphemes of a language may be combined to form meaningful utterances (p. 227)

syphilis   an STD caused by a bacterial infection which may pass through four stages, ultimately resulting in death (p. 307)

systematic desensitization   the application of classical conditioning procedures to alleviate extreme anxiety in which anxiety-producing stimuli are presented while the subject is in a relaxed state (p. 449)

T

taste buds   the receptors for taste located in the tongue (p. 90)

temporal lobes   the lobes of the cerebrum located at the temples (p. 54)

test-retest reliability   a check of a test's consistency found by correlating the results of a test taken by the same subjects at two different times (p. 352)

thalamus   the final sensory relay station that projects sensory fibers to their proper location in the cerebrum and that may be involved in regulating sleep-wake cycles (p. 53)

thematic apperception test (TAT)   a projective personality test requiring a subject to tell a series of short stories about a set of ambiguous pictures (pp. 309, 362)

theory   a collection of related assumptions that are used to explain some phenomenon and that lead, through logical reasoning, to testable hypotheses (p. 332)

theta waves   on EEG pattern characterized by slow wave cycles of 3 to 7 per second (p. 115)

timbre   the psychological experience related to wave purity by which we differentiate the sharpness, clearness, or quality of a tone (p. 87)

tolerance   in using a drug, a state where more and more of the drug is required to produce the same desired effect (p. 127)

training   a systematic and intentional process of altering the behaviors of employees to increase organizational effectiveness (p. 514)

traits   distinguishable, relatively enduring ways in which individuals may differ (p. 345)

transference   in psychoanalysis, the situation in which the patient comes to feel about the analyst in the same way he or she once felt about some other important person (p. 446)

tremors   involuntary, trembling, jerky movements that are usually associated with damage in the cerebellum (p. 51)

type A behavior pattern (TABP)   a collection of behaviors (competitive, achievement-oriented, impatient, easily aroused, often hostile or angry) often associated with coronary heart disease (p. 527)

U

unconditioned response (UCR)   in classical conditioning, a response (for example, salivation) reliably and reflexively evoked by a stimulus (p. 144)

unconditioned stimulus (UCS)   in classical conditioning, a stimulus (for example, food powder) that reflexively and reliably evokes a response (the UCR) (p. 144)

V

validity   in testing, the extent to which a test measures what it claims to be measuring (p. 353)

variability   the extent of spread or dispersion in a set or distribution of scores (pp. 555, 557)

vestibular sense   the position sense that tells us about balance, where we are in relation to gravity, acceleration, or deceleration (p. 94)

violence   behavior with the intent to do physical harm to another (p. 498)

vitreous humor   the thick fluid behind the lens of the eye that helps keep the eyeball spherical (p. 75)

W

wave amplitude   a characteristic of wave forms (the height of the wave) that indicates intensity (p. 68)

wavelength   a characteristic of wave forms that indicates the distance between any point on a wave and the corresponding point on the next cycle of the wave (p. 69)

white light   a light of the lowest possible saturation, containing a mixture of all visible wavelengths (p. 72)

white noise   a sound composed of a random assortment of all wave frequencies from the audible spectrum (p. 87)

withdrawal   a negative, painful reaction that may occur when one stops taking a drug (p. 127)

References

A

Adams, G. R. (1977). Physical attractiveness, personality and social reactions to peer pressure. *Journal of Psychology, 96,* 287–296.

Adams, G. R. & Gullotta, T. (1983). *Adolescent life experiences.* Monterey, CA: Brooks/Cole.

Adams, J. A. (1980). *Learning and memory: An introduction.* Homewood, IL: Dorsey.

Adams, J. S. (1965). Inequity in social exchange. In L. Berkowitz (Ed.), *Advances in experimental social psychology.* New York: Academic Press.

Agnew, H. W., Webb, W. B., & Williams, R. L. (1964). The effects of stage 4 sleep deprivation. *Electroencephalography and clinical neurophysiology, 17,* 68–70.

Aiken, L. R. (1984). *Psychological testing and assessment.* Boston: Allyn and Bacon.

Ajzen, I. & Fishbein, M. (1980). *Understanding attitudes and predicting social behavior.* Englewood Cliffs, NJ: Prentice-Hall.

Allen, B. P. (1987). Youth suicide. *Adolescence, 22,* 271–290.

Allen, M. G. (1976). Twin studies of affective illness. *Archives of General Psychiatry, 33,* 1476–1478.

Allport, G. W. & Odbert, H. S. (1936). Trait-names: A psycho-lexical study. *Psychological Monographs, 47,* Whole No. 211.

American Psychiatric Association. (1980). *Diagnostic and statistical manual of mental disorders* (3rd ed., Revised). Washington, DC: American Psychiatric Association.

American Psychiatric Association. (1987). *DSM-III-R: Diagnostic and statistical manual of mental disorders* (Revised). Washington, DC: American Psychiatric Association.

Amoore, J. E. (1970). *Molecular basis of odor.* Springfield, IL: C. C. Thomas.

Anastasi, A. (1982). *Psychological testing* (5th ed.). New York: Macmillan.

Anderson, J. C., Williams, S., McGee, R., & Silva, P. A. (1987). *DSM-III* disorders in preadolescent children. *Archives of General Psychiatry, 44,* 69–76.

Anderson, J. R. (1980). *Cognitive psychology and its implications.* San Francisco: Freeman.

Anderson, J. R. (1980). On the merits of ACT and information-processing psychology: A response to Wexler's review. *Cognition, 8,* 73–88.

Anderson, R. & Nida, S. A. (1978). Effect of physical attractiveness on opposite- and same-sex evaluations. *Journal of Personality, 46,* 401–413.

Andreasen, N. C., Olsen, S. A., Dennert, J. W., & Smith, M. R. (1982). Ventricular enlargement in schizophrenia: Definition and prevalence. *American Journal of Psychiatry, 139,* 291–196.

Andrew, R. J. (1963). Evolution of facial expression. *Science, 142,* 1034–1041.

Anisman, H. & Zacharko, R. M. (1982). Depression: The predisposing influence of stress. *The Behavioral and Brain Sciences, 5,* 89–137.

Aronson, E. (1984). *The social animal.* San Fransisco: Freeman.

Aronson, E. & Linder, D. (1965). Gain and loss of esteem as determinants of interpersonal attractiveness. *Journal of Personality and Social Psychology, 1,* 156–171.

Aronson, E., Turner, J. A., & Carlsmith, J. M. (1963). Communicator credibility and communication discrepancy as a determinant of opinion change. *Journal of Abnormal and Social Psychology, 67,* 31–36.

Arvey, R. D. & Campion, J. E. (1982). The employment interview: A summary and review of recent research. *Personnel Psychology, 35,* 281–322.

Asch, S. E. (1951). The effects of group pressure upon the modification and distortion of judgment. In H. Guetzkow (Ed.), *Groups, leadership and men.* Pittsburgh: Carnegie.

Asch, S. E. (1956). Studies of independence and conformity: I. A minority of one against a unanimous majority. *Psychological Monographs: General and Applied, 70,* (Whole No. 416), 1–70.

Aserinsky, E., & Kleitman, N. (1953). Regularly occurring periods of eye mobility and concomitant phenomena during sleep. *Science, 118,* 273–274.

Atkinson, J. W. & Feather, N. T. (Eds.) (1966). *A theory of achievement motivation.* New York: Wiley.

Atkinson, J. W. & Litwin, G. H. (1960). Achievement motive and test anxiety conceived as motive to approach success and motive to avoid failure. *Journal of Abnormal and Social Psychology, 60,* 27–36.

Atkinson, R. C. (1975). Mnemotechnics in second-language learning. *American Psychologist, 30,* 821–828.

Atkinson, R. C. & Shiffrin, R. M. (1968). Human memory: A proposed system and its control processes. In K. W. Spence & J. T. Spence (Eds.), *The psychology of learning and motivation: Advances in research and theory.* New York: Academic Press.

B

Babor, T. F., Berglas, S., Mendelson, J. H., Ellinboe, J., & Miller, K. (1983). Alcohol, affect and the disinhibition of behavior. *Psychopharmacology, 80,* 53–60.

Baddeley, A. D. (1966). Short-term memory for word sequences as a function of acoustic, semantic and formal similarity. *Quarterly Journal of Experimental Psychology, 18,* 362–365.

Bagozzi, R. P. & Burnkrant, R. E. (1979). Attitude organization and the attitude-behavior relationship. *Journal of Personality and Social Psychology, 37,* 913–929.

Baley, S. (1985). The legalities of hiring in the 80s. *Personnel Journal, 64,*112–115.

Bandura, A (1965). Influence of models' reinforcement contingencies on the acquisition of imitative responses. *Journal of Personality and Social Psychology, 1,* 589–595.

Bandura, A. (1973). *Aggression: A social learning analysis.* Englewood Cliffs, NJ: Prentice-Hall.

Bandura, A. (1976). Modeling theory: Some traditions, trends and disputes. In W. S. Sahakian (Ed.), *Learning: Systems, models, and theories.* Chicago: Rand McNally.

Bandura, A. (1977). *Social learning theory.* Englewood Cliffs, NJ: Prentice-Hall.

Bandura, A. (1978). The self-system in reciprocal determinism. *American Psychologist, 33,* 344–358.

Bandura, A., Ross, D., & Ross, S.A. (1963). Imitation of film-mediated aggressive models. *Journal of Abnormal and Social Psychology, 66,* 3–11.

Barber, T. F. X. (1972). Suggested (hypnotic) behavior: The trance paradigm vs. an alternative paradigm. In E. Fromm & R. E. Shorr (Eds.), *Hypnosis: Research developments and perspectives.* Chicago: Aldine-Atherton.

Baumeister, R. F. (1985). The championship choke. *Psychology Today, 19,* 48–52.

Baumrind, D. (1978). Parental disciplinary patterns and social competence in children. *Youth & Society, 9,* 239–276.

Beck, A. T. (1967). *Depression: Clinical, experimental, and theoretical aspects.* New York: Harper & Row.

Beck, A. T. (1976). *Cognitive therapy and the emotional disorders.* New York: International Universities Press.

Beck, A. T. (1985). Theoretical perspectives on clinical anxiety. In A. H. Tuma & J. D. Maser (Eds.), *Anxiety and the anxiety disorders.* Hillsdale, NJ: Lawrence Erlbaum.

Beckman, L. J. & Houser, B. B. (1982). The consequences of childlessness on the social-psychological well-being of older women. *Journal of Gerontology, 37,* 243–250.

Beecroft, R. (1966). *Classical conditioning.* Goleta, CA: Psychonomic Press.

Beer, M. & Walton, A. E. (1987). Organization change and development. *Annual Review of Psychology, 38,* 339–367.

Bell, A. P., Weinberg, M. S., & Hammersmith, S. K. (1981). *Sexual preference: Its development in men and women.* Bloomington, IN: Indiana University Press.

Bennett, T. L. (1982). *Introduction to physiological psychology.* Monterey, CA: Brooks/Cole.

Bennett, W. (1980). The cigarette century. *Science, 80,* 36–43.

Benson, H. (1975). *The relaxation response.* New York: Morrow.

Ben-Yehuda, N. (1980). The European witch craze. *American Journal of Sociology, 86,* 1–31.

Berkowitz, L. (1978). Whatever happened to the frustration-aggression hypothesis? *American Behavioral Scientist, 21,* 691–708.

Berkowitz, L. (1982). Aversive conditions as stimuli to aggression. *Advances in Experimental Social Psychology, 15,* 249–288.

Berlyne, D. E. (1960). *Conflict, arousal, and curiosity.* New York: McGraw-Hill.

Berlyne, D. E. (1971). *Aesthetics and psychobiology.* New York: Appleton-Century-Crofts.

Bernstein, I. (1978). Learned taste aversion in children receiving chemotherapy. *Science, 200,* 1302–1303.

Berscheid, E. & Walster, E. (1978). *Interpersonal attraction.* Reading, MA: Addison-Wesley.

Birdwhistell, R. L. (1952). *Introduction to kinesics.* Louisville, KY: University of Louisville Press.

Birren, J. E. (1983). Aging in America: Roles for psychology. *American Psychologist, 38,* 298–299.

Bloom, F. E., Lazerson, A., & Hotstadter, L. (1985). *Brain, mind, and behavior.* New York: W. H. Freeman.

Bootzin, R. R. & Acocella, J. R. (1984). *Abnormal psychology: Current perspectives* (4th Ed.). New York: Random House.

Boring, E. G. (1930). A new ambiguous figure. *American Journal of Psychology, 42,* 109–116.

Bouchard, T. J. & McGue, M. (1981). Familial studies of intelligence: A review. *Science, 212,* 1055–1059.

Bourne, L. E., Dominowski, R. L., & Loftus, E. F. (1979). *Cognitive processes.* Englewood Cliffs, NJ: Prentice-Hall.

Bousfield, W. A. (1953). The occurrence of clustering in the free recall of randomly arranged associates. *Journal of General Psychology, 49,* 229–240.

Bower, G. H. (1970). Imagery as a relational organizer in associative learning. *Journal of Verbal Learning and Verbal Behavior, 9,* 529–533.

Bower, G. H. (1972). Mental imagery and associate learning. In L. W. Gregg (Ed.), *Cognition in learning and memory.* New York: Wiley.

Bower, G. H. (1981). Mood and memory. *American Psychologist, 36,* 129–148.

Bower, G. H. & Clark, M. C. (1969). Narrative stories as mediators for serial learning. *Psychonomic Science, 14,* 181–182.

Bower, G. H., Monteiro, K. P., & Gilligan, S. G. (1978). Emotional mood as a context for learning and recall. *Journal of Verbal Learning and Verbal Behavior, 17,* 573–587.

Bower, G. H. & Springston, F. (1970). Pauses as recoding points in letter series. *Journal of Experimental Psychology, 83,* 421–430.

Bray, D. W., Campbell, R. J., & Grant, D. L. (1974). *Formative years in business: A long-term AT&T study of managerial lives.* New York: Wiley.

Breckler, S. J. (1984). Empirical validation of affect, behavior, and cognition as distinct components of attitude. *Journal of Personality and Social Psychology, 47,* 1191–1205.

Breland, K. & Breland, M. (1961). The misbehavior of organisms. *American Psychologist, 16,* 681–684.

Broadbent, D. E. (1958). *Perception and communication.* London: Pergamon Press,

Brody, E. M. (1981). Women in the middle and family help to older people. *Gerontologist, 21,* 471–480.

Brody, E. M. (1985). Parent care as a normative family stress. *Gerontologist, 25,* 19–29.

Brown, J. (1958). Some tests of the decay theory of immediate memory. *Quarterly Journal of Experimental Psychology, 10,* 12–21.

Brown, J. I. (1973). *The Nelson-Denny Reading Test.* Boston: Houghton Mifflin.

Brown, J. S. (1948). Gradients of approach and avoidance responses and their relation to motivation. *Journal of Comparative and Physiological Psychology, 41,* 450–465.

Brown, L. & Leigh, J. E. (1986). *Adaptive behavior Inventory (ABI).* New York: Slosson Educational Publications.

Brown, R., & Kulik, J. (1977). Flashbulb memories. *Cognition, 5,* 73–99.

Bruner, J. S., Goodnow, J. J., & Austin, G. A. (1956). *A study of thinking.* New York: Wiley.

Buckhout, R. (1975). Nearly 2000 witnesses can be wrong. *Social Action and the Law, 2,* 7.

Burisch, M. (1984). Approaches to personality inventory construction. *American Psychologist, 39,* 214–227.

Buss, D. (1985). Human mate selection. *American Scientist, 73,* 47–51.

Buss, D. M. (1984). Evolutionary biology and personality psychology. *American Psychologist, 39,* 1135–1147.

Buss, D. M. & Barnes, M. (1986). Preferences in human mate selection. *Journal of Personality and Social Psychology, 50,* 559–570.

Butler, R. & Lewis, M. (1981). *Aging and mental health.* St. Louis: C. V. Mosby.

Butler, R. N. & Emr, M. (1982). SDAT research: Current trends. *Generations, 7,* 14–18.

Byrne, D. (1971). *The attraction paradigm.* New York: Academic Press.

Byrne, D., & Clore, G. L. (1970). A reinforcement model of evaluative responses. *Personality. An International Journal, 1,* 103–128.

C

Campos, J. J. (1976). Heart rates: A sensitive tool for the study of emotional development. In L. Lipsitt (Ed.), *Developmental psycholobiology: The significance of infancy.* Hillsdale, NJ: Erlbaum.

Campos, J. J., Langer, A. & Krowitz, A. (1970). Cardiac responses on the visual cliff in prelocomotor human infants. *Science, 170,* 196–197.

Cannon, W. B. (1932). *The wisdom of the body.* New York: Norton.

Carson, R.C. (1983). The schizophrenias. In H. E. Adams & P. B. Sutker (Eds.), *Comprehensive handbook of psychopathology.* New York: Plenum.

Carson, R. C., Butcher, J. N., & Coleman, J. C. (1988). *Abnormal psychology and modern life* (8th ed.). Glenview, IL: Scott, Foresman.

Carson, T. P. & Carson, R. C. (1984). The affective disorders. In H. E. Adams & P. B. Sutker (Eds.), *Comprehensive handbook of psychopathology.* New York: Plenum.

Cash, T. F., & Kilcullen, R. N. (1985). The eye of the beholder: Susceptibility to sexism and beautyism in the evaluation of managerial applicants. *Journal of Applied Social Psychology, 15,* 591–605.

Cattell, R. B. (1973). Personality pinned down. *Psychology Today, 7,* 40–46.

Cattell, R. B. (1979). *Personality and learning theory. The structure of personality in its environment* (Vol. 1). New York: Springer.

Cermak, L. S. & Craik, F. I. M. (Eds.), (1979). *Levels of processing in human memory.* Hillsdale, NJ: Erlbaum.

Chaiken, S. & Strangor, C. (1987). Attitudes and attitude change. *Annual Review of Psychology, 38,* 575–630.

Cherry, C. (1953). Some experiments on the recognition of speech with one and two ears. *Journal of the Acoustical Society of America, 25,* 975–979.

Chilman, C. S. (1980). Parent satisfactions, concerns, and goals for their children. *Family Relations, 29,* 339–346.

Chomsky, N. (1957). *Syntactic structures.* The Hague: Mouton.

Clifford, B. R. & Lloyd-Bostock, S. (Eds.), (1983). *Evaluating witness evidence: Recent psychological research and new perspectives.* Norwood, NJ: Ablex.

Clifford, M. M. & Hatfield, E. (1973). The effect of physical attractiveness on teacher expectation. *Sociology of Education, 46,* 248–258.

Clore, G. L. & Byrne, D. (1974). A reinforcement-affect model of attraction. In T. L. Huston (Ed.), *Foundations of interpersonal attraction.* New York: Academic Press.

Cohen, G. D. (1980). *Fact sheet: Senile dementia (Alzheimer's disease)* [No. (ADM) 80–929]. Washington, DC: (NIMH) Center for Studies of the Mental Health of the Aging.

Cohen. L. R., DeLoach, J. & Strauss, M. (1978). Infant visual perception. In J. Osofky (Ed.), *The handbook of infant development.* New York: Wiley.

Colby, A. & Kohlberg, L. (1984). Invariant sequence and internal consistency in moral judgment stages. In W. M. Kurtines & J. L. Gewitz (Eds.), *Morality, moral behaviors, and moral development.* New York: Wiley.

Cole, J. O. (1988). Where are those new antidepressants we were promised? *Archives of General Psychiatry, 45,* 193–194.

Collins, A. M., & Quillian, M. R. (1969). Retrieval time from semantic memory. *Journal of Verbal Learning and Verbal Behavior, 8,* 240–247.

Collins, G. R. (1982). Research links violent juvenile behavior to abuse. *Justice Assistance News, 3,* 3–4.

Colt, C. H. (1983). Suicide in America. *Harvard magazine,* Sept/Oct.

Conger, J. J. & Peterson, A. C. (1984). *Adolescence and youth: Psychological development in a changing world.* New York: Harper & Row

Conrad, R. (1963). Acoustic confusions and memory span for words. *Nature, 197,* 1029–1030.

Conrad, R. (1964). Acoustic confusions in immediate memory. *British Journal of Psychology, 55,* 75–84.

Cooper, L. A. & Shepard, R. N. (1973). Chronometric studies of the rotation of mental images. In W. G. Chase (Ed.), *Visual information processing.* New York: Academic Press.

Cornblatt, B. A. & Erlenmeyer-Kimling, L. (1985). Global attention deviance as a marker of risk for schizophrenia: Specificity and predictive validity. *Journal of Abnormal Psychology, 94,* 470–486.

Costa, P. T., & McCrae, R. R. (1980). Still stable after all these years: Personality as a key to some issues in adulthood and old age. In P. B. Baltes & O. G. Brim Jr. (Eds.), *Life-span development and behavior.* New York: Academic Press.

Costello, C. G. (1982). Fears and phobias in women: A community study. *Journal of Abnormal Psychology, 91,* 280–286.

Coulter, W. A. & Morrow, H. W. (Eds.) (1978). *Adaptive behavior: Concepts and measurements.* New York: Grune & Stratton.

Craik, F. I. M. (1970). The fate of primary memory items in free recall. *Journal of Verbal Learning and Verbal Behavior, 9,* 143–148.

Craik, F. I. M. & Lockhart, R. S. (1972). Levels of processing: A framework for memory research. *Journal of Verbal Learning and Verbal Behavior, 11,* 671–684.

Craik, F. I. M. & Tulving, E. (1975). Depth of processing and the retention of words in episodic memory. *Journal of Experimental Psychology: General, 104,* 268–294.

Cratty, B. J. (1970). *Perceptual and motor development in infants and children.* New York: Macmillan.

Cronbach, L. J. (1984). *Essentials of psychological testing* (4th ed.). Cambridge, MA: Harper & Row.

Crooks, R. & Baur, K. (1987). *Our sexuality* (3rd ed.). Menlo Park, CA: Benjamin/Cummings.

Cunningham, S. (1984). Genovese: 20 years later, few heed stranger's cries. *APA Monitor, 15,* 30.

Curran, D. K. (1987). *Adolescent suicidal behavior.* Washington: Hemisphere.

D

Darley, J. M. & Latané, B. (1968). Bystander intervention in emergencies: Diffusion of responsibility. *Journal of Personality and Social Psychology, 8,* 377–383.

Darwin, C. (1872). *The expression of emotion in man and animals.* New York: Philosophical Library (reprinted in 1955 and 1965 by the University of Chicago Press, Chicago.)

Darwin, C. T., Turvey, M. T., & Crowder, R. G. (1972). An auditory analogue of the Sperling partial report procedure: Evidence for brief auditory storage. *Cognitive Psychology, 3,* 255–267.

Datan, N., Rodeheaver, D., & Hughes, F. (1987). Adult development and aging. *Annual Review of Psychology, 38,* 153–180.

Davidson, J. M., Smith, E. R., Rodgers, C. H., & Bloch, G. J. (1968). Relative thresholds of behavioral and somatic responses to estrogen. *Physiology and Behavior, 3,* 227–229.

Davis, K. (1985). Near and dear: Friendship and love compared. *Psychology Today, 19,* 22–30.

Davis, L. E. & Cherns, A. B. (1975). *The quality of working life: Vol. 1. Problems, prospects and the state of the art.* New York: The Free Press.

DeCasper, A. J. & Fifer, W. P. (1980). Of human bonding: Newborns prefer their mother's voice. *Science, 208,* 1174–1176.

Dement, W. C. (1960). The effect of dream deprivation. *Science, 135,* 1705–1707.

Dement, W. C. (1974). *Some must watch while some must sleep.* San Francisco: Freeman.

Dement, W.C. & Kleitman, N. (1957). The relation of eye movements during sleep to dream activity: An objective method for the study of dreaming. *Journal of Experimental Psychology, 53,* 339–346.

DeReamer, R. (1980). *Modern safety and health technology.* New York: Wiley.

Diamond, M. & Karlen, A. (1980). *Sexual decisions.* Boston: Little, Brown.

Dion, K. K. (1972). Physical attractiveness and evaluations of children's transgressions: *Journal of Personality and Social Psychology, 24,* 207–213.

Dion, K. K., Berscheid, E., & Walster (Hatfield), E. (1972). What is beautiful is good. *Journal of Personality and Social Psychology, 24,* 285–290.

Dollard, J., Doob, L., Miller, N., Mowrer, O. H., & Sears, R. R. (1939). *Frustration and aggression.* New Haven, CT: Yale University Press.

Domjan, M. (1987). Animal learning comes of age. *American Psychologist, 42,* 556–564.

Duffy, E. (1962). *Activation and behavior.* New York: Wiley.

Duke, P. M., Carlsmith, J. M., Jennings, D., Martin, J. A., Dornbusch, S. M., Gross, R. T., & Siegel-Gorelick, B. (1982). Educational correlates of early and late sexual maturation in adolescence. *Journal of Pediatrics, 100,* 633–637.

Dunham, R. B. (1979). Job design and redesign. In S. Kerr (Ed.) *Organizational behavior.* Columbus, OH: Grid.

Dunnette, M. D. & Borman, W. C. (1979). Personnel selection and classification systems. *Annual Review of Psychology, 30,* 477–525.

E

Edwards, C. P. (1980). The comparative study of the development of moral judgment and reasoning. In R. L. Munroe, R. Munroe & B. B. Whiting (Eds.), *Handbook of cross-cultural human development.* New York: Garland.

Egeland, J. A., Gerhard, D. S., Pauls, D. L., Suddex, J. N., Kidd, K. K., Allen, C. R., Hostetter, A. M., and Housman, D. E. (1987). Bipolar affective disorders linked to DNA markers on chromosome 11. *Nature, 325,* 783–787.

Eich, J. E., Weingartner, H., Stillman, R. C., & Gillan, J. C. (1975). State-dependent accessibility of retrieval cues in the retention of a categorized list. *Journal of Verbal Learning and Verbal Behavior, 14,* 408–417.

Eisdorfer, C. (1983). Conceptual models of aging. *American Psychologist, 38,* 197–202.

Ekman, P. (1972). Universals and cultural differences in facial expression of emotion. In J. K. Cole (Ed.), *Nebraska Symposium on Motivation.* Lincoln, NB: University of Nebraska Press, 207–283.

Ekman, P. (1973). Cross-cultural studies in facial expression. In P. Ekman (Ed.), *Darwin and facial expressions: A century of research in review.* New York: Academic Press.

Ekman, P., Friesen, W. V., O'Sullivan, M., Diacoyanni-Tarlatzis, I., Krause, R., Pitcairn, T., Scherer, K., Chan, A., Heider, K., LeCompte, W. A., Ricci-Bitti, P. E., & Tomita, M. (1987). Universals and cultural differences in the judgment of facial expressions of emotion. *Journal of Personality and Social Psychology, 53,* 712–727.

Ekman, P. Levenson, R. W., & Friesen, W. V. (1983). Autonomic nervous system activity distinguishes among emotions. *Science, 221,* 1208–1210.

Elkind, D. (1967). Egocentrism in adolescence. *Child Development, 38,* 1025–1034.

Elkind, D. (1981). *Children and adolescents: Interpretive essays on Jean Piaget.* New York: Oxford University Press.

Elkind, D. (1984). *All grown up and no place to go.* Reading, MA: Addison-Wesley.

Elkind, D. & Bowen, R. (1979). Imaginary audience behavior in children and adolescents. *Developmental Psychology, 15,* 38–44.

Ellis, A. (1970). *Reason and emotion in psychotherapy.* New York: Lyle Stuart.

Ellis, A. (1987). The impossibility of achieving consistently good mental health. *American Psychologist, 42,* 364–375.

Ellis, L. & Ames, M. A. (1987). Neurohormonal functioning and sexual orientation: A theory of homosexuality-heterosexuality. *Psychological Bulletin, 101,* 233–258.

Ericsson, K. A. & Chase, W. G. (1982). Exceptional memory. *American Scientist, 70.* 607–615.

Erikson, E. H. (1963). *Childhood and society.* New York: Norton.

Erikson, E. H. (1968). *Identity, youth and crisis.* New York: Norton.

Erienmeyer-Kimling, L. (1968). Studies on the offspring of two schizophrenic parents. In D. Rosenthal & S. S. Kety (Eds.), *The transmission of schizophrenia.* New York: Pergamon Press, 65–83.

Eron, L. D. (1982). Parent-child interaction, television violence, and aggression in children. *American Psychologist, 37,* 197–211.

Erwin, E. (1980). Psychoanalytic therapy: The Eysenck argument. *American Psychologist, 35,* 435–443.

Eysenck, H. J. & Eysenck, S. B. G. (1976). *Psychoticism as a dimension of personality.* London: Hodder & Stoughton.

F

Fantz, R. L. (1961). The origin of form perception. *Scientific American, 204,* 66–72.

Fantz, R. L. (1963). Pattern vision in newborn infants. *Science, 140,* 296–297.

Fast, J. (1970). *Body language.* New York: M. Evans.

Festinger, L. (1957). *A theory of cognitive dissonance.* Stanford, CA: Stanford University Press.

Festinger, L., Schacter, S., & Back, K. (1950). *Social processes in informal groups: A study of human factors in housing.* New York: Harper.

Fishbein, M. & Ajzen, I. (1975). *Belief, attitude, intention, and behavior: An introduction to theory and research.* Reading, MA: Addison Wesley.

Fisher, S. & Greenberg, R. P. (1977). *The scientific credibility of Freud's theories and therapy.* New York: Basic Books.

Fishman, J. (1987). Type A on trial. *Psychology Today, 21,* 42–50.

Flavell, J. H. (1971). What is memory development the development of? *Human Development, 14,* 272–278.

Flavell, J. H. (1982). On cognitive development. *Child Development, 53,* 1–10

Flavell, J. H. (1985). *Cognitive development.* Englewood Cliffs, NJ: Prentice-Hall.

Flavell, J. H. & Wellman, H. M. (1977). Metamemory, In R. V. Kail & J. H. Hagen (Eds.), *Perspectives on the development of memory and cognition.* Hillsdale, NJ: Erlbaum.

Flexser, A. J. & Tulving, E. (1982). Priming and recognition failure. *Journal of Verbal Learning and Verbal Behavior, 21,* 237–248.

Flynn, J. P., Vanegas, H., Foote, W., and Edwards, S. (1970). Neural mechanisms involved in a cat's attack on a rat. In R. E. Whalen, R. F. Thompson, M. Verzeano, and N. M. Weinberger (Eds), *The neural control of behavior.* New York: Academic Press.

Ford, M. R. & Lowery, C. R. (1986). Gender differences in moral reasoning: A comparison of justice and care orientations. *Journal of Personality and Social Psychology, 4,* 777–783.

Forisha-Kovach, B. (1983). *The experience of adolescence.* Glenview, IL: Scott, Foresman.

Frankenberg, W. K. & Dodds, J. B. (1967). The Denver Developmental Screening Test. *Journal of Pediatrics, 71,* 181–191.

Freedman, D. X. (1984). Psychiatric epidemiology counts. *Archives of General Psychiatry, 41,* 931–934.

Freeman, S., Walker, M. R., Borden, R., & Latané, B. (1975). Diffusion of responsibility and restaurant tipping. Cheaper by the bunch. *Personality and Social Psychology Bulletin, 1,* 584–587.

Freud, S. (1955). *The interpretation of dreams.* (orig. pub. 1900). New York: Basic Books.

Friedman, H. S. & Booth-Kewley, S. (1987). The "disease-prone personality: "A meta-analytic view of the construct. *American Psychologist, 42,* 539–555.

Friedman, M. & Rosenman, R. (1959). Association of specific overt behavior pattern with blood and cardiovascular findings. *Journal of the American Medical Association, 169,* 1286.

Friedman, M. I. & Stricker, E. M. (1976). The physiological psychology of hunger: A physiological perspective. *Psychological Review, 83,* 409–431.

Friedman, S. (1972). Habituation and recovery of visual response in the alert human newborn. *Journal of Experimental Child Psychology, 13,* 339–349.

G

Gallagher, J. J. & Ramey, C. T. (1987). *The malleability of children.* Baltimore: Paul H. Brookes.

Garbarino, J. (1985). *Adolescent development: An ecological perspective.* Columbus, OH: C. E. Merrill.

Garcia, J., Ervin, F. R., & Koelling, R. A. (1966). Learning with prolonged delay of reinforcement. *Psychonomic Science, 5,* 121–122.

Garfield, S. L. (1981). Psychotherapy: A 40-year appraisal. *American Psychologist, 36,* 174–183.

Gazzaniga, M. S. & LeDoux, J. E. (1978). *The integrated mind.* New York: Plenum.

Geller, E. S., Bruff, C. D., & Nimmer, J. G. (1985). "Flash for Life": Community-based prompting for safety belt promotion. *Journal of Applied Behavioral Analysis, 18,* 309–314.

Geller, E. S., Rudd, J. R., Kalsher, M. J., Streff, F. M., & Lehman, G. R. (1987). Employer-based programs to motivate safety belt use: A review of short-term and long-term effects. *Journal of Safety Research, 18,* 1–17.

Gelman, D., Doherty, S., Joseph, N., & Carroll, G. (1987 Spring). How infants learn to talk. *Newsweek: On Health.*

Gelman, R. (1978). Cognitive development. *Annual Review of Psychology, 29,* 297–332.

Gemberling, G. A. & Domjan, M. (1982). Selective associations in one-day old rats: Taste toxicosis and texture-shock aversion learning. *Journal of Comparative and Physiological Psychology, 96,* 105–113.

Gerow, J. R. & Murphy, D. P. (1980). The validity of the Nelson-Denny Reading Test as a predictor of performance in introductory psychology. *Educational and Psychological Measurement, 40,* 553–556.

Gibson, E. & Walk, R. D. (1960). The visual cliff. *Scientific American, 202,* 64–71.

Gibson, E. J. (1987). Introductory essay: What does infant perception tell us about theories of perception? *Journal of Experimental Psychology: Perception and performance, 13,* 515–523.

Gibson, E. J. (1988). Exploratory behavior in the development of perceiving, acting and the acquiring of knowledge. *Annual Review of Psychology, 39,* 1–41.

Gibson, P. (1982). *Quality circles: An approach to productivity improvement.* New York: Pergamon.

Gilligan, C. (1982). *In a different voice.* Cambridge, MA: Harvard University Press.

Glenn, N. D. & Weaver, C. N. (1981). The contribution of marital happiness to global happiness. *Journal of Marriage and the Family, 43,* 161–168.

Goffman, E. (1959). *The presentation of self in everyday life.* New York: Doubleday.

Gold, P. E. (1987). Sweet memories. *American Scientist, 75,* 151–155.

Goldstein, I. L. (1980). Training in work organizations. *Annual Review of Psychology, 31,* 229–272.

Goldstein, I. L. (1986). *Training in organizations.* Pacific Grove, CA: Brooks/Cole.

Goleman, O. (1980). 1,528 little geniuses and how they grew. *Psychology Today, 14,* 28–53.

Gough, H. G. (1985). A work orientation scale for the California Psychological Inventory. *Journal of Applied Psychology, 70,* 505–513.

Gorenstein, E. E. (1984). Debating mental illness. *American Psychologist, 39,* 50–56.

Gottlieb, G. (1970). Conceptions of prenatal development, In L. R. Aronson, E. Tobach, D. S. Lehrman, & J. S. Rosenblatt (Eds.), *Development and evolution of behavior,* San Francisco: Freeman.

Greenberg, J. & Cohen, R. L. (Eds.) (1982). *Equity and justice in social behavior.* New York: Academic Press.

Greenwald, A. G. & Breckler, S. J. (1984). To whom is the self presented? In B. R. Schlenker (Ed.), *The self and social life.* New York: McGraw-Hill, 126–145.

Grinspoon, L. (1977). *Marihuana reconsidered* (2nd ed.). Cambridge, MA: Harvard University Press.

Gross, R. T. & Duke, P. M. (1980). The effect of early vs. late maturation on adolescent behavior. *The Pediatric Clinics of North America, 27,* 71–77.

Guilford, J. P. (1959). *Personality.* New York: McGraw-Hill.

Guion, R. M. & Gibson, W. M. (1988). Personnel selection and placement. *Annual Review of Psychology, 39,* 349–374.

Gur, R. E., Resnick, S. M., Alavi, A., Gur, R. C., Caroff, S., Dann, R., Silver, F. L., Saykin, A. J., Chawluk, J. B., Kushner, M., & Reivich, M. (1987). Regional brain function in schizophrenia. *Archives of General Psychiatry, 44,* 119–125.

Gurman, A. S., Kniskern, D. P., & Pinsof, W. M. (1986). Research on the process and outcome of marital and family therapy. In S. L. Garfield & A. E. Bergin (Eds.), *Handbook of psychotherapy and behavior change* (3rd ed.). New York: Wiley.

H

Haas, R. G. (1981). Effects of source characteristics on cognitive responses and persuasion. In R. E. Petty, T. M. Ostrom & T. C. Brock (Eds.), *Cognitive responses in persuasion.* Hillsdale, NJ: Erlbaum.

Hall, G. S. (1905). *Adolescence.* New York: Appleton.

Hall, W. G. & Oppenheim, R. W. (1987). Developmental psychobiology, *Annual Review of Psychology, 38,* 91–128.

Harlow, H. F. (1932). Social facilitation of feeding in the albino rat. *Journal of Genetic Psychology, 41,* 211–221.

Harris, B. (1979). What ever happened to little Albert? *American Psychologist, 34,* 151–160.

Harris, L. & Associates (1975), (1981), (1983), *The myth and reality of aging in America.* Washington, DC: The National Council on Aging.

Harris, P. L. (1983). Infant cognition. In P. H. Mussen (Ed.), *Handbook of child psychology,* Vol. II. New York: Wiley.

Harter, S. (1978). Effectance motivation reconsidered: Toward a developmental model. *Human Development, 21,* 34–64.

Hartman, S., Grigsby, D. W., Crino, M. D., & Chhokar, J. (1986). The measurement of job satisfaction by action tendencies. *Educational and Psychological Measurement, 46,* 317–329.

Havighurst, R. J. (1972). *Developmental tasks and education* (3rd ed.). New York: D. McKay.

Haynes, S. G., McMichael, A. J. & Tyroler, H. A. (1978). Survival after early and normal retirement. *Journal of Gerontology, 33,* 872–883.

Hebb, D. O. (1955). Drives and the C.N.S. (conceptual nervous system). *Psychological Review, 62,* 243–254.

Heffernan, J. A. & Albee, G. W. (1985). Prevention perspectives. *American Psychologist, 40,* 202–204.

Heidbreder, E. (1946). The attainment of concepts. *Journal of General Psychology, 24,* 93–108.

Higgins, E. T. & Bargh, J. A. (1987). Social cognition and social perception. *Annual Review of Psychology, 38,* 369–426.

Hilgard, E. R. (1975). Hypnosis. *Annual Review of Psychology, 26,* 19–44.

Hilgard, E. R. (1978). Hypnosis and Consciousness. *Human Nature.* January, 42–49.

Hilgard, E. R. & Hilgard, J. R. (1975). *Hypnosis in the relief of pain.* Los Altos, CA: W. Kaufman.

Hinrichs, J. R. (1976). Personnel training. In M. Dunnette (Ed.), *Handbood of industrial and organizational psychology.* Chicago: Rand McNally

Hobson, J. A. (1977). The reciprocal interaction model of sleep cycle control: Implications for PGO wave generation and dream amnesia. In R. R. Drucker-Colin & J. L. McGaugh (Eds.), *Neurobiology of sleep and memory* (pp. 159–183). New York: Academic Press.

Hobson, J. A. & McCarley, R. W. (1977). The brain as a dream state generator: An activation-synthesis hypothesis of the dream process. *American Journal of Psychiatry, 134,* 1335–1348.

Holden, C. (1980). A new visibility for gifted children. *Science, 210,* 879–882.

Holinger, P. C. (1978). Adolescent suicide: An epidemiological study of recent trends. *American Journal of Psychiatry, 135,* 754–756.

Holmes, D. S. (1984) Meditation and somatic arousal reduction: A review of the experimental evidence. *American Psychologist, 39,* 1–10.

Holmes, D. S. (1985). To meditate or to simply rest, that is the question: A response to the comments of Shapiro. *American Psychologist, 40(6),* 722–725.

Holmes, T. H. & Rahe, R. H. (1967). The social readjustment rating scale. *Journal of Psychosomatic Research, 11,* 213–218.

Holmes, T. S. & Holmes, T. H. (1970). Short-term intrusions into the life-style routine. *Journal of Psychosomatic Research, 14,* 121–132.

Hoppock, R. (1935). *Job satisfaction.* New York: Harper & Row.

Hörmann, H. (1986). *Meaning and context.* New York: Plenum.

Horner, M. S. (1969). Women's will to fail. *Psychology Today,* March, 3, 36.

Hostetler, A. J. (1987). Alzheimer's trials hinge on early diagnosis. *APA Monitor, 18,* 14–15.

Houston, J. P. (1986). *Fundamentals of learning and memory* (3rd ed.). New York: Harcourt Brace Jovanovich.

Hovland, C. I. & Weiss, W. (1951). The influence of source credibility on communication effectiveness. *Public Opinion Quarterly, 15,* 635–650.

Howard, D. V. (1983). *Cognitive psychology.* New York: Macmillan.

Howell, W. C., & Dipboye, R. L. (1982). *Essentials of industrial and organizational psychology.* Homewood, IL: Dorsey Press.

Hubel, D. H (1979). The brain. *Scientific American, 241,* 45–53.

Huesmann, L. R. & Malamuth, N. M. (Eds.) (1986). Media violence and antisocial behavior. *Journal of Social Issues, 42.*

Hughes, J., Smith, T. W., Kosterlitz, H. W., Fotergill, L. A., Morgan, G. A., & Morris, H. R. (1975). Identification of two related peptides from the brain with potent opiate antagonist activity. *Nature, 258,* 577–579.

Hulin, C. L. & Smith, P. C. (1964). Sex differences in job satisfaction. *Journal of Applied Psychology, 48,* 88–92.

Hull, C. L. (1943). *Principles of behavior.* New York: Appleton-Century-Crofts.

Hunt, M. (1987). Navigating the therapy maze. *The New York Times Magazine,* August 30, 1987, 28–31, 37, 44, 46, 49.

Hunter, J. E. & Hunter, R. F. (1984). Validity and utility of alternative predictors of job performance. *Psychological Bulletin, 96,* 72–98.

Huston, T. L., Ruggiero, M., Conner, R., & Geis, G. (1981). Bystander intervention into crime: A study based on naturally occurring episodes. *Social Psychology Quarterly, 44,* 14–23.

I

Iaffaldano, M. T. & Muchinsky, P. M. (1985). Job satisfaction and job performance: A meta-analysis. *Psychological Bulletin, 97,* 251–273.

Izard, C.E. (1972). *Patterns of emotions: A new analysis of anxiety and depression.* New York: Academic Press.

J

Jacobs, B. L. (1987). How hallucinogenic drugs work. *American Scientist, 75,* 386–392.

Jacobs, B. L. & Trulson, M. E. (1979). Mechanisms of action of LSD. *American Scientist, 67,* 396–404.

James, W. (1890): *Principles of psychology.* New York: Holt.

James, W. (1892). *Psychology: Briefer course.* New York: Holt.

James, W. (1904). Does consciousness exist? *Journal of Philosophy, 1,* 477–491.

Janis, I. L. (1972). *Victims of groupthink.* Boston: Houghton-Mifflin.

Janis, I. L. (1983). *Groupthink: Psychological studies of policy decisions and fiascos* (2nd ed.). Boston: Houghton Mifflin.

Janoff-Bulman, R. (1979). Characterological versus behavioral self-blame: Inquiries into depression and rape. *Journal of Personality and Social Psychology, 37,* 1798–1809.

Jenkins, C. D. (1976). Recent evidence supporting psychological and social risk factors for coronary disease. *New England Journal of Medicine, 294,* 987–994; 1033–1038.

Jenkins, J. G. & Dallenbach, K. M. (1924). Oblivescence during sleep and waking. *American Journal of Psychology, 35,* 605–612.

Johnson, E. S. (1978). Validation of concept-learning strategies. *Journal of Experimental Psychology, 107,* 237–265.

Johnson, M. K. & Hasher, L. (1987). Human learning and memory. *Annual Review of Psychology, 38,* 631–668.

Jones, E. E. (1979). The rocky road from acts to dispositions. *American Psychologist, 34,* 107–117.

Jones, E. E. & Nisbett, R. E. (1971). *The actor and the observer: Divergent perceptions of behavior.* Morristown, NJ: General Learning Press.

Jones, H. E. (1971). Physical maturing among girls as related to behavior. In M. C. Jones, N. Bayley, J. W. Macfarlane, & M. P. Honzik (Eds.), *The course of human development.* Waltham, MA: Xerox Publishing.

Jones, M. C. (1957). The careers of boys who were early or late maturing. *Child Development, 28,* 113–128.

Jones, M. C. (1965). Psychological correlates of somatic development. *Child Development, 36,* 899–911.

Julien, R. M. (1985). *A primer of drug action* (4th ed.). San Francisco: Freeman.

Jussim, L., Coleman, L. M., & Lerch, L. (1987). The nature of stereotypes: A comparison and integration of three theories. *Journal of Personality and Social Psychology, 52,* 536–546.

K

Kahn, S., Zimmerman, G., Csikszentmihalyi, M., & Getzels, J. W. (1985). Relations between identity in young adulthood and intimacy at midlife. *Journal of Personality and Social Psychology, 49,* 1316–1322.

Kalat, J. W. (1984). *Biological psychology* (2nd ed.). Belmont, CA: Wadsworth.

Kalish, R. A. (1976). Death and dying in a social context. In R. H. Binstock & E. Shanas (Eds.), *Handbook of aging and the social sciences.* New York: Van Nostrand.

Kalish, R. A. (1982). *Late adulthood: Perspectives on human development.* Monterey, CA: Brooks/Cole.

Kalish, R. A. (1985). *Death, grief, and caring relationships.* Monterey, CA: Brooks/Cole.

Kalish, R. A. & Reynolds, D. K. (1976). Death and dying in a social context. In R. H. Binstock & E. Shanas (Eds.), *Handbook of aging and the social sciences.* New York: Van Nostrand.

Kamin, L. (1968). Attention-like processes in classical conditioning. In M. Jones (Ed.), *Miami symposium on the prediction of behavior: Aversive stimulation.* Miami: University of Miami Press.

Kamin, L. (1969). Predictability, surprise, attention, and conditioning. In R. Church & B. Campbell (Eds.), *Punishment and aversive behaviors.* New York: Appleton-Century-Crofts.

Kaplan, H. S. (1979). *Disorders of sexual desire.* New York: Simon & Schuster.

Kaplan, R. M. (1984). The connection between clinical health promotion and health status. *American Psychologist, 39,* 755–765.

Karoum, F., Karson, C. N., Bigelow, L. B., Lawson, W. B., & Wyatt, R. J. (1987). Preliminary evidence of reduced combined output of dopamine and its metabolites in chronic schizophrenia. *Archives of General Psychiatry, 44,* 604–607.

Katchadourian, H. (1977). *The biology of adolescence.* San Francisco: Freeman.

Katzell, R. A. & Guzzo, R. A. (1983). Psychological approaches to productivity improvement. *American Psychologist, 38,* 468–472.

Keating, D. P. (1980). Thinking processes in adolescents. In J. Adelson (Ed.), *Handbook of adolescent psychology.* New York: Wiley.

Keesey, R. E. & Powley, T. L. (1986). The regulation of body weight. *Annual Review of Psychology, 37,* 109–133.

Keesey, R. E. & Powley, T. L. (1975). Hypothalamic regulation of body weight. *American Scientist, 63,* 558–565.

Keith, P. M. (1983). A comparison of the resources of parents and childless men and women in very old age. *Family Relations, 32,* 403–409.

Kelley, H. H. (1967). Attribution theory in social psychology. In D. Levine (Ed.), *Nebraska symposium on motivation.* Lincoln, NB: University of Nebraska Press.

Kelley, H. H. (1973). The process of causal attribution. *American Psychologist, 28,* 107–128.

Kelley, H. H. & Thibaut, J. W. (1978). *Interpersonal relations: A theory of interdependence.* New York: Wiley-Interscience.

Kelley, K. (1985). Sex, sex guilt, and authoritarianism: Differences in responses to explicit heterosexual and masturbatory slides. *The Journal of Sex Research, 21,* 68–85.

Kelly, C. & Goodwin, G. C. (1983). Adolescent's perception of three styles of parental control. *Adolescence, 18,* 567–571.

Kermis, M. D. (1984). *The psychology of human aging.* Boston: Allyn & Bacon.

Kessler, S. (1980). The genetics of schizophrenia: A review. In S. J. Keith & L. R. Mosher (Eds.), *Special report: Schizophrenia.* Washington, DC: U. S. Government Printing Office.

Kett, J. F. (1977). *Rites of passage: Adolescence in America from 1790 to the present.* New York: Basic Books.

Kientzle, M. J. (1946). Properties of learning curves under varied distributions of practice. *Journal of Experimental Psychology, 36,* 187–211.

Kiester, E. Jr. (1980). Images of the night: The physiological roots of dreaming. *Science 80, 1* (4), 36–43.

Kimble, G. A. (1981). Biological and cognitive constraints on learning. In L. T. Benjamin (Ed.), *The G. Stanley Hall Lecture Series,* Vol. 1. Washington, DC: American Psychological Association.

King, M., Murray, M. A., & Atkinson, T. (1982). Background, personality, job characteristics, and satisfaction with work in a national sample. *Human Relations, 35,* 119–133.

Kinsbourne, M. (1982). Hemispheric specialization and the growth of human understanding. *American Psychologist, 37,* 411–420.

Kinsey, A. C., Pomeroy, W. B., & Martin, C. E. (1948). *Sexual behavior in the human male.* Philadelphia: Saunders.

Kinsey, A. C., Pomeroy, W. B., Martin, C. E., & Gebhard, P. H. (1953). *Sexual behavior in the human female.* Philadelphia: Saunders.

Kirkpatrick, D. L. (1976). Evaluation of training. In R. L. Craig (Ed.) *Training and development handbook* (2nd ed.). New York: McGraw-Hill.

Kleitman, N. (1963). Patterns of dreaming. *Scientific American, 203,* 82–88.

Knittle, J. L. (1975). Early influences on development of adipose tissue. In G. A. Bray (Ed.), *Obesity in perspective.* Washington, DC: U. S. Government Printing Office.

Kohlberg, L. (1963). Moral development and identification. In H. W. Stevenson (Ed.), *Child Psychology.* Chicago: University of Chicago Press.

Kohlberg, L. (1969). *Stages in the development of moral thought and action,* New York: Holt.

Kohlberg, L. (1981). *Philosophy of moral development.* New York: Harper & Row.

Kohlberg, L. (1985). *The psychology of moral development.* San Francisco: Harper & Row.

Kohut, H. (1977). *The restoration of self.* New York: International Universities Press.

Kolata, G. (1987). What babies know, and noises parents make. *Science, 237,* 726.

Korchin, S. J. & Schuldberg, D. (1981). The future of clinical assessment. *American Psychologist, 36,* 1147–1158.

Kramer, B. A. (1985). Use of ECT in California, 1977–1983. *The American Journal of Psychiatry, 142,* 1190–1192.

Krantz, D. S. & Glass, D. C. (1984). Personality, behavior patterns, and physical illness: Conceptual and methodological issues, In W. D. Gentry (Ed.), *Handbook of behavioral medicine.* New York: Guilford, 38–86.

Krantz, D. S., Grunberg, N. E., & Baum, A. (1985). Health psychology. *Annual Review of Psychology, 36,* 349–383.

Krueger, W. C. F. (1929). The effect of overlearning on retention. *Journal of Experimental Psychology, 12,* 71–78.

Kübler-Ross, E. (1969). *On death and dying.* New York: Macmillan.

Kübler-Ross, E. (1981). *Living with death and dying.* New York: Macmillan.

L

Labov, W. (1973). The boundaries of words and their meanings. In C. J. N. Bailey & R. W. Shuy (Eds.), *New ways of analyzing variations in English.* Washington, DC: Georgetown University Press.

Lambert, N. M. & Windmiller, M. (1981). *AAMD Adaptive behavior scale.* Wilmington, DE: Jastak.

Landers, S. (1987). AIDS: behavior change yes, test no. *American Psychological Association Monitor, 18*(11), 28–29.

Landy, F. J. (1985). *Psychology of work behavior.* Homewood, IL: Dorsey Press.

Lanetto, R. (1980). *Children's conceptions of death.* New York: Springer.

Langer, S. K. (1951). *Philosophy in a new key.* New York: The New American Library.

Lasky, R. E. & Kallio, K. D. (1978). Transformation rules in concept learning. *Memory and Cognition, 6,* 491–495.

Latané, B. (1981). The psychology of social impact. *American Psychologist, 36,* 343–356.

Latané, B. & Darley, J. M. (1968). Group inhibition of bystander intervention in emergencies. *Journal of Personality and Social Psychology, 10,* 215–221.

Latané, B. & Darley, J. M. (1970). *The unresponsive bystander: Why doesn't he help?* New York: Appleton-Century-Crofts.

Latané, B. & Nida, S. (1980). Social impact theory and group influence: A social engineering perspective. In P. B. Paulus (ED.), *Psychology of group influence.* Hillsdale, NJ: Erlbaum.

Latané, B. & Nida, S. (1981). Ten years of research on group size and helping. *Psychological Bulletin, 89,* 308–324.

Latané, B., Williams, K., & Harkins, S. (1979). Many hands make light the work: The causes and consequences of social loafing. *Journal of Personality and Social Psychology, 37,* 822–832.

Latham, G. P. (1988). Human resource training and development. *Annual Review of Psychology, 39,* 545–582.

Lauer, J. & Lauer, R. (1985). Marriages made to last. *Psychology Today, 19,* 22–26.

Lawler, E. E. (1982). Strategies for improving the quality of work life. *American Psychologist, 37,* 486–493.

Lawler, E. E. & Mohrman, S. A. (1985). Quality circles after the fad. *Harvard Business Review,* 65–71.

Lazarus, R. S. (1981). Little hassles can be hazardous to your health. *Psychology Today, 15,* 58–62.

Leahey, T. H. & Harris, R. J. (1985). *Human learning.* Englewood Cliffs, NJ: Prentice-Hall.

Lempers, J. D., Flavell, E. R., & Flavell, J. H. (1977). The development in very young children of tactile knowledge concerning visual perception. *Genetic Psychology Monographs, 95,* 3–53.

Leon, G. R. & Roth, L. (1977). Obesity: Psychological causes, correlations and speculations. *Psychological Bulletin, 84,* 117–139.

Leonard, J. M. & Whitten (1983). Information stored when expecting recall or recognition. *Journal of Experimental Psychology, 9,* 440–455.

Lerner, M. J. (1965). The effect of responsibility and choice on a partner's attractiveness following failure. *Journal of Personality, 33,* 178–187.

Lerner, M. J. (1980). *The belief in a just world.* New York: Plenum.

Lerner, R. M. (1978). Nature, nurture, and dynamic interactionism. *Human Development, 21,* 1–20.

Levine, H. Z. (1983). Safety and health programs. *Personnel, 3,* 4–9.

Levine, M. F., Taylor, J. C., & Davis, L. E. (1984). Defining quality of work life. *Human Relations, 37,* 81–104.

Levinson, D. J. (1978). *The seasons of a man's life.* New York: Ballantine.

Levinson, D. J. (1986). A conception of adult development. *American Psychologist, 41,* 3–13.

Levinson, D. J., Darrow, C. M., Klein, E. B., Levinson, M. H., & McKee B. (1974). *The seasons of a man's life.* New York: Knopf.

Levinthal, C. F. (1983). *Introduction to physiological psychology* (2nd ed.). Englewood Cliffs, NJ: Prentice-Hall.

Ley, P. (1977). Psychological studies of doctor-patient communication. In S. Rachman (Ed.), *Contributions to medical psychology* (Vol I), Oxford: Pergamon.

Lidz, T. (1973). *The origin and treatment of schizophrenic disorders.* New York: Basic Books.

Lidz, T., Fleck, S., & Cornelison, A. R. (1965). *Schizophrenia and the family.* New York: International University Press.

Liebert, R. M. (1986). Effects of television on children and adolescents. *Developmental and Behavioral Pediatrics, 7,* 43–48.

Lindsley, D. B., Bowden, J., & Magoun, H. W. (1949). Effect upon EEG of acute injury to the brain stem activating system. *Electroencephalography and Clinical Neurophysiology, 1,* 475–486.

Linz, D., Donnerstein, E., & Penrod, S. (1984). The effects of long-term exposure to violence against women. *Journal of Communication, 34,* 130–147.

Locke, E. A. (1968). Toward a theory of task motivation and incentives. *Organizational Behavior and Human Performance, 3,* 157–189.

Locke, E. A. (1976). The nature and causes of job satisfaction. In M. D. Dunnette (Ed.), *Handbook of industrial and organizational psychology.* Chicago: Rand McNally.

Locke, E. A., Shaw, K. N., Saari, L. M., & Latham, G. P. (1981). Goal setting and task performance: 1969–1980. *Psychological Bulletin, 90,* 124–152.

Loftus, E. F. (1984). The eyewitness on trial. In B. D. Sales & A. Alwork (Eds.), *With liberty and justice for all.* Englewood Cliffs, NJ: Prentice-Hall.

Loftus, E. F. & Loftus, G. R. (1980). On the permanence of stored information in the human brain. *American Psychologist, 35,* 409–420.

Long, P. (1986). Medical mesmerism. *Psychology Today, 20(1),* 28–29.

Lott, A. J. & Lott, B. E. (1974). The role of reward in the formation of positive interpersonal attitudes. In T. L. Huston (Ed.), *Foundations of interpersonal attraction.* New York: Academic Press.

Lubin, B., Larsen, R. M., & Matarazzo, J. D. (1984). Patterns of psychological test useage in the United States: 1935–1982. *American Psychologist, 39,* 451–454.

Lugaresi, E., Medori, R., Montagna, P., Baruzzi, A., Cortelli, P., Lugaresi, A., Tinuper, P., Zucconi, M., & Gambetti, P. (1986). Fatal familial insomnia and dysautonomia with selective degeneration of thalamic nuclei. *New England Journal of Medicine, 315,* 997–1003.

Luh, C. W. (1922). The conditions of retention. *Psychological Monographs,* Whole No. 142.

M

Mace, N. L. & Rabins, P. V. (1981). *The 36-hour day.* Baltimore, MD: The Johns Hopkins University Press.

Mackenzie, B. (1984). Explaining race differences in IQ: The logic, the methodology, and the evidence. *American Psychologist, 39,* 1214–1233.

Mackintosh, N. J. (1986). The biology of intelligence? *British Journal of Psychology, 77,* 1–18.

Maharishi, Mahesh Yogi. (1963). *The science of living and art of being.* London: Unwin.

Maier, S. F. & Seligman, M. E. P. (1976). Learned helplessness: Theory and evidence. *Journal of Experimental Psychology, 105,* 3–46.

Maki, R. H. & Swett, S. (1987). Metamemory for narrative test. *Memory and Cognition, 15,* 72–83.

Mandler, G. (1980). Recognizing. The judgment of previous occurrence. *Psychological Review, 87,* 252–271.

Manning, M. L. (1983). Three myths concerning adolescence. *Adolescence, 18,* 823–829.

Marcia, J. (1976). Identity six years after: A follow-up study. *Journal of Youth and Adolescence, 5,* 145–160.

Marengo, J. T. & Harrow, M. (1987). Schizophrenic thought disorder at follow-up. *Archives of General Psychiatry, 44,* 651–659.

Marks, M. L. (1986). The question of quality circles. *Psychology Today, 20,* 36–38, 42–46.

Martin, G. B. & Clark, R. D. (1982). Distress crying in neonates: Species and peer specificity. *Developmental psychology, 18,* 3–9.

Martindale, C. (1981). *Cognition and consciousness.* Homewood, IL: Dorsey Press.

Maslow, A. H. (1943). A theory of human motivation. *Psychological Review, 50,* 370–396.

Maslow, A. (1954). *Motivation and personality.* New York: Harper.

Maslow, A. H. (1970). *Motivation and personality* (2nd ed.). New York: Harper and Row.

Massaro, D. W. (1975). *Experimental psychology and information processing.* Chicago: Rand McNally.

Masters, W. & Johnson, V. (1979). *Homosexuality in perspective.* Boston: Little, Brown.

Masters, W., Johnson, V., & Kolodny, R. C. (1987). *Human sexuality* (3rd ed.). Glenview, IL: Scott, Foresman/Little Brown.

Matarazzo, J. D. (1980). Behavioral health and behavioral medicine: Frontiers for a new health psychology. *American Psychologist, 35,* 807–817.

Mayer, W. (1983). Alcohol abuse and alcoholism. *American Psychologist, 38(10),* 1116—1121.

Mayo, E. (1933). *The human problems of an industrial civilization.* Cambridge, MA: Harvard University Press.

McCann, I. L. & Holmes, D. S. (1984). Influence of aerobic exercise on depression. *Journal of Personality and Social Psychology, 46,* 1142–1147.

McCarley, R. W. & Hoffman, E. (1981). REM sleep, dreams, and the activation-synthesis hypothesis. *American Journal of Psychiatry, 138,* 904–912.

McClelland, D. C. (1958). Risk-taking in children with high and low need for achievement. In J. W. Atkinson (Ed.), *Motives in fantasy, action, and society.* Princeton, NJ: Van Nostrand.

McClelland, D. C. (1975). *Power: The inner experience.* New York: Irvingston-Halstead-Wiley.

McClelland, D. C. (1982). The need for power, sympathetic activation, and illness. *Motivation and Emotion, 6,* 31–41.

McClelland D. C. (1985). *Human motivation.* Glenview, IL: Scott, Foresman.

McClelland, D. C., Atkinson, J. W., Clark, R. A., and Lowell, E. L. (1953). *The achievement motive.* New York: Appleton-Century-Crofts.

McCloskey, M. & Zaragoza, M. (1985), Misleading postevent information and memory for events: Arguments and evidence against memory impairment hypotheses. *Journal of Experimental Psychology: General, 114,* 1–16.

McCrae, R. R. & Costa, P. T. (1984). *Emerging lives, enduring dispositions: Personality in adulthood.* Boston: Little, Brown.

McDougall, W. (1908). *An introduction to social psychology.* London: Methuen.

McGaugh, J. L. (1983). Hormonal influences on memory. *Annual Review of Psychology, 34,* 297–323.

McGinnis, J. M. (1985). Recent history of federal initiatives in prevention policy. *American Psychologist, 40,* 205–212.

McGraw, K. O. (1987). *Developmental psychology.* San Diego: Harcourt Brace Jovanovich.

McKim, W. A. (1986). *Drugs and behavior.* Englewood Cliffs, NJ: Prentice-Hall.

Meer, J. (1986). The reason of age. *Psychology Today, 20*, 60–64.

Meltzoff, A. N. & Moore, M. K. (1977). Imitation of facial and manual gestures by human neonates. *Science, 198*, 75–78.

Melzack, R. (1973). *The puzzle of pain*. London: Penguin.

Melzack, R. & Wall, P. D. (1965). Pain mechanisms: A new theory. *Science, 150*, 971–979.

Meredith, N. (1986 June). Testing the talking cure. *Science 86* 7(5), 30–37.

Middlemist, R. D. & Peterson, R. B. (1976). Test of equity theory by controlling for comparison of worker's efforts. *Organizational Behavior and Human Performance, 15*, 335–354.

Milgram, S. (1963). Behavioral studies of obedience. *Journal of Abnormal and Social Psychology, 67*, 371–378.

Milgram, S. (1965). Some conditions of obedience and disobedience to authority. *Human Relations, 18*, 57–76.

Milgram, S. (1974). *Obedience to authority*. New York: Harper & Row.

Miller, B. C. & Sollie, D. L. (1980). Normal stress during the transition to parenthood. *Family Relations, 29*, 459–465.

Miller, G. A. (1956). The magical number seven, plus or minus two: Some limits on our capacity for processing information. *Psychological Review, 63*, 81–96.

Miller, G. A., Galanter, E., & Pribram, K. H. (1960). *Plans and the structure of behavior*. New York: Holt, Rinehart and Winston.

Miller, N. E. (1944) Experimental studies of conflict. In J. M. Hunt (Ed.), *Personality and the behavior disorders*. New York: Ronald Press, 431–465.

Miller, N. E. (1959). Liberalization of basic S-R concepts: Extensions to conflict behavior, motivation, and social learning. In S. Koch (Ed.), *Psychology: A study of a science* (Vol. 2). New York: McGraw-Hill.

Miller, N. E. (1983). Behavioral medicine: Symbiosis between laboratory and clinic. *Annual Review of Psychology, 34*, 1–31.

Minami, H. & Dallenbach, K. M. (1946). The effect of activity upon learning and retention in the cockroach. *American Journal of Psychology, 59*, 682–697.

Minuchin, S. & Fishman, H. C. (1981). *Family therapy techniques*. Cambridge, MA: Harvard University Press.

Mobley, W. H. (1977). Intermediate linkages in the relationship between job satisfaction and employee turnover. *Journal of Applied Psychology, 62*, 237–240.

Money, J. (1987). Sin, sickness, or status? Homosexual gender identity and psychoneuroendocrinology. *American Psychologist, 42*, 384–399.

Monson, T. C. & Snyder, M. (1977). Actors, observers, and the attribution process. *Journal of Experimental Social Psychology, 13*, 89–111.

Morris, C. W. (1946). *Signs, language, and behavior*. New York: Prentice-Hall.

Moruzzi, G. (1975). The sleep-wake cycle. *Reviews of Physiology, 64*, 1–165.

Moruzzi, G. & Magoun, H. W. (1949). Brain stem reticular formation and activation of the EEG. *Electroencephalography and Clinical Neurophysiology, 1*, 455–473.

Moscovici, S., Lage, E., & Naffrechoux, M. (1969). Influences of a consistent minority on the responses of a majority in a color perception task. *Sociometry, 32*, 365–380.

Moscovici, S., Mugny, G., & Avermaet, E. (Eds.) (1985). *Perspectives on minority influence*. Cambridge: Cambridge University Press.

Mowday, R. T. (1983). Equity theory predictions of behavior in organizations. In R. M. Steers & L. W. Porter (Eds.), *Motivation and work behavior* (3rd ed.). New York: McGraw-Hill.

Muchinsky, P. M. (1987). *Psychology applied to work* (2nd ed.). Chicago: Dorsey Press.

Muchinsky, P. M. & Tuttle, M. L. (1979). Employee turnover: An empirical and methodological assessment. *Journal of Vocational Behavior, 14*, 43–77.

Murray, D. J. (1983). *A history of western psychology*. Englewood Cliffs, NJ: Prentice-Hall.

Murray, D. M., Johnson, C. A., Luepker, R. V., & Mittlemark, M. B. (1984). The prevention of cigarette smoking in children: A comparison of four strategies. *Journal of Applied Social Psychology, 14*, 274–288.

Murray, H. A. (1938). *Explorations in personality*. New York: Oxford.

N

Nathan, P. E. (1983). Failures in prevention: Why we can't prevent the devastating effect of alcoholism and drug abuse. *American Psychologist, 38*, 459–467.

National Council on Alcoholism (1979). *Facts on alcoholism*. New York.

National Institute of Mental Health (1984). Epidemiologic Catchment Area Program. *Archives of General Psychiatry, 41*, 931–1011.

National Institute of Mental Health (1984). The NIMH epidemiologic catchment area program. *Archives of General Psychiatry, 41*, 931–1011.

National Institutes of Health, Review Panel on Coronary Prone Behavior and Coronary Heart Disease (1981). Coronary-prone behavior and coronary heart disease: A critical review. *Circulation, 63*, 1199–1215.

Newby, R. W. (1987). Contextual areas in item recognition following verbal discrimination learning. *Journal of General Psychology, 114*, 281–287.

Newman, B. M. & Newman, P. R. (1984). *Development through life: A psychosocial approach*. Homewood, IL: Dorsey.

Nickerson, R. S. & Adams, M. J. (1979). Long-term memory for a common object. *Cognitive Psychology, 11*, 287–307.

Nicol, S. E. & Gottesman, I. I. (1983). Clues to the genetics and neurobiology of schizophrenia. *American Scientist, 71*, 398–404.

Nisbett, R. E. (1972). Hunger, obesity, and the ventromedial hypothalamus. *Psychological Review, 79*, 433–453.

O

Oden, G. C. (1987). Concept, knowledge, and thought. *Annual Review of Psychology, 38*, 203–227.

Oden, M. H. (1968). The fulfillment of promise: 40-year follow-up of the Terman gifted group. *Genetic Psychology Monographs, 77*, No. 1, 3–93.

Offer, D. & Offer, J. (1975). *From teenage to young manhood*. New York: Basic Books.

Offord, D. R., Boyle, M. H., Szatmari, P., Rae-Grant, N. I., Links, P. S., Cadman, D. T., Byles, J. A., Crawford, J. W., Blum, H. M., Byrne, C., Thomas, H., & Woodward, C. A. (1987). Ontario child health study. *Archives of General Psychiatry, 44*, 832–836.

Olton, D. S. (1978). Characteristics of spatial memory. In S. H. Hule, H. F. Fowler, & W. K. Honig (Eds.), *Cognitive processes in animal behavior*. Hillsdale, NJ: Erlbaum.

Olton, D. S. (1979). Mazes, maps, and memory. *American Psychologist, 34*, 583–596.

Olton, D. S. & Samuelson, R. J. (1976). Remembrance of places passed: Spatial memory in rats. *Journal of Experimental Psychology: Animal Behavior Processes, 2*, 96–116.

Orne, M. (1969). Demand characteristics and the concept of quasi controls. In R. Rosenthal & R. Rosnow (Eds.), *Artifact in behavioral research*. New York: Academic Press.

Oswald, I. (1980). Sleep as a restorative process: Human clues. In P. S. McConnell, G. J. Boer, H. J. Romijn, N. E. van de Poll, & M. A. Carner (Eds.), *Adaptive capabilities of the nervous system*. Amsterdam: Elsevier.

P

Parker, E. S., Birnbaum, I. M., & Noble, E. P. (1976). Alcohol and memory: Storage and state dependency. *Journal of Verbal Learning and Verbal Behavior, 15*, 691–702.

Pavlov, I. (1927). *Conditioned reflexes*. Oxford: Oxford University Press.

Pavlov, I. (1928). *Lectures on conditioned reflexes: The higher nervous activity of animals.* (Vol. I) translated by H. Gantt. London: Lawrence and Wishart.

Peck, M. (1982). Youth suicide. *Death education, 6*, 29–47.

Petersen, A. & Taylor, B. (1980). The biological approach to adolescence: Biological change and psychological adaptation. In J. Adelson (Ed.), *Handbook of adolescent psychology*. New York: Wiley.

Peterson, L. R. & Peterson, M. J. (1959). Short-term retention of individual verbal items. *Journal of Experimental Psychology, 58*, 193–198.

Petty, R. E. & Cacioppo, J. T. (1981). *Attitudes and persuasion: Classic and contemporary approaches*. Dubuque, IA: Wm. C. Brown.

Petty, R. E., Harkins, S. G., Williams, K. D., & Latané, B. (1977). The effects of group size on cognitive effort and evaluation. *Personality and Social Psychology Bulletin, 3*, 579–582.

Petty, R. E., Ostrow, T. M., & Brock, T. C. (1981). *Cognitive responses in persuasive communications: A text in attitude change*. Hillsdale, NJ: Erlbaum.

Petty, R. E., Wells, G. L. & Brock, T. C. (1976). Distraction can enhance or reduce yielding to propaganda: Thought disruption versus effort justification. *Journal of Personality and Social Psychology, 34*, 874–884.

Piaget, J. (1932/1948). *The moral judgment of the child*. Glencoe, IL: Free Press.

Piaget, J. (1954). *The construction of reality in the child*. New York: Basic Books.

Piaget, J. (1967). *Six psychological studies*. New York: Random House.

Piner K. E. & Kahle, L. R. (1984). Adapting to the stigmatizing label of mental illness: Foregone but not forgotten. *Journal of Personality and Social Psychology, 47*, 805–811.

Pines, M. (1983). Can a rock walk? *Psychology Today, 17*, November, 46–54.

Pion, G. (1986). Employment settings: Job focus shifts to service, policy. *APA Monitor, 17*(1), 25.

Pittman, T. S. & Heller, J. F. (1987). Social motivation. *Annual Review of Psychology, 38*, 461–489.

Plutchik, R. (1980a). *Emotion: A psychoevolutionary synthesis*. New York: Harper and Row.

Plutchik, R. (1980b). A language for the emotions. *Psychology Today*, February, 68–78.

Porter, L. W. & Steers, R. M. (1973). Organizational, work, and personal factors in employee turnover and absenteeism. *Psychological Bulletin, 80*, 151–176.

Posner, M. I & Keele, S. W. (1968). On the genesis of abstract ideas. *Journal of Experimental Psychology, 77*, 353–363.

Posner, M. I. & Keele, S. W. (1970). Retention of abstract ideas. *Journal of Experimental Psychology, 83*, 304–308.

President's Commission on Mental Health (1978). *Report to the President*. Washington, DC: U. S. Government Printing Office.

Pressley, M., Levin, J. R., & Delaney, H. D. (1982). The mnemonic keyword method. *Review of Educational Research, 52*, 61–91.

Q

Quayle, D. (1983). American productivity: The devastating effect of alcoholism and drug abuse. *American Psychologist, 38*, 454–458.

R

Rafaeli, A. (1985). Quality circles and employee attitudes. *Personnel Psychology, 38*, 603–615.

Rahe, R. H. & Arthur, R. J. (1978). Life changes and illness reports. In K. E. Gunderson & R. H. Rahe (Eds.), *Life stress and illness*. Springfield, IL: Thomas.

Rappaport, D. (1951). The autonomy of the ego. *Bulletin of the Menninger Clinic, 15*, 113–123.

Rechtschaffen, A. (1971). The control of sleep. In W. A. Hunt (Ed.), *Human behavior and its control*. (pp. 75–92). Cambridge, MA: Schenkman.

Reich, J. (1986). The epidemiology of anxiety. *The Journal of Nervous and Mental Disease, 174*, 129–136.

Reinke, B. J., Ellicott, A. M., Harris, R. L., & Hancock, E. (1985). Timing of psychological changes in women's lives. *Human Development, 28*, 259–280.

Reis, H. T., Nezlek, J., & Wheeler, L. (1980). Physical attractiveness in social interaction. *Journal of Personality and Social Psychology, 38*, 604–617.

Rescorla, R. A. (1968). Probability of shock in the presence and absence of CS in fear conditioning. *Journal of Comparative and Physiological Psychology, 66*, 1–5.

Rescorla, R. A. (1987). A Pavlovian analysis of goal-directed behavior. *American Psychologist, 42*, 119–129.

Rescorla, R. A. & Wagner, A. R. (1972). A theory of Pavlovian conditioning. In A. A. Black & W. F. Prokasky (Eds.), *Classical conditioning II*. New York: Appleton-Century-Crofts.

Rest. J. R. (1983). Morality. In J. Flavell & E. Markman (Eds.), *Handbook of child development: Cognitive development*. New York: Wiley.

Reveley, M. A., Reveley, A. M., & Baldy, R. (1987). Left cerebral hemisphere hypodensity in discordant schizophrenic twins. *Archives of General Psychiatry, 44*, 625–632.

Revusky, S. H. & Garcia, J. (1970). Learned associations over long delays. In G. H. Bower & J. T. Spence (Eds.), *The psychology of learning and motivation: IV*. New York: Academic Press.

Rhodes, S. R. (1983). Age-related differences in work attitudes and behaviors: A review and conceptual analysis. *Psychological Bulletin, 93*, 328–367.

Rice, B. (1984). Square holes for quality circles. *Psychology Today, 18*, 17.

Roche, A. F. & Davila, G. H. (1972). Late adolescent growth in stature. *Pediatrics, 50*, 874–880.

Rodin, J. (1981). Current status of the internal-external hypothesis of obesity. What went wrong? *American Psychologist, 36*, 361–372.

Rosch E. (1973). Natural categories. *Cognitive Psychology, 4*, 328–350.

Rosch, E. (1975). Cognitive representations of semantic categories. *Journal of Experimental Psychology: General, 104*, 192–253.

Rosch, E. (1978). Principles of categorization. In E. Rosch & B. B. Lloyd (Eds.), *Cognition and categorization*. Hillsdale, NJ: Erlbaum.

Rosch, E. H. (1973). Natural categories. *Cognitive Psychology, 4*, 328–350.

Rose, S. A. & Blank, M. (1974). The potency of context in children's cognition: An illustration through conservation. *Child Development, 45*, 499–502.

Rosenman, R. H., Brand, R. J., Jenkins, C. D., Friedman, M., Strauss, R., & Wurm, M. (1975). Coronary heart disease in the Western Collaborative Group Study: Final follow-up experience of 8½ years. *Journal of the American Medical Association, 233*, 872–877.

Rosenman, R. H., Friedman, M., Strauss, R., Wurm, M., Kositchek, R., Hahn, W., & Werthessen, N. T. (1964). A predictive study of coronary heart disease. *Journal of the American Medical Association, 189*, 15–22.

Rosenthal, D. (1971). *Genetics of psychopathology*. New York: McGraw-Hill.

Ross, L. D. (1977). The intuitive psychologist and his shortcomings: Distortions in the attributional process. In L. Berkowitz (Ed.), *Advances in experimental social psychology* (Vol. 10). New York: Academic Press.

Rossi, A. S. (1980). Aging and parenthood in the middle years. In P. B. Baltes & O. G. Brim Jr. (Eds.), *Lifespan development and behavior* (Vol. III). New York: Academic Press.

Rotter, J. B. (1982). *The development and application of social learning theory: Selected papers*. New York: Praeger.

Rowe, J. W. & Kahn, R. L. (1987). Human aging: Usual and successful. *Science, 237*, 143–149.

Rubenstein, E. A. (1983). Television and behavior. *American Psychologist, 38*, 820–825.

Rubin, Z. (1973). *Liking and loving. An invitation to social psychology*. New York: Holt, Rinehart, & Winston.

S

Saal, F. E. & Knight, P. A. (1988). *Industrial/Organizational psychology.* Pacific Grove, CA: Brooks/Cole.

Sackeim, H. A. (1985). The case for ECT. *Psychology Today, 19,* 36–40.

Samuelson, F. J. B. (1980). Watson's Little Albert, Cyril Burt's twins, and the need for a critical science. *American Psychologist, 35,* 619–625.

Satir, U. (1967). *Conjoint family therapy.* Palo Alto, CA: Science and Behavior Books.

Sauser, W. J. & York, C. M. (1978). Sex differences in job satisfaction: A reexamination. *Personnel Psychology, 31,* 537–547.

Scarr, S. (1988). Race and gender as psychological variables. *American Psychologist, 43,* 56–59.

Scarr, S. & Weinberg, R. A. (1976). IQ test performance of black children adopted by white families. *American Psychologist, 31,* 726–739.

Schacter, S. (1971). Some extraordinary facts about obese humans and rats. *American Psychologist, 26,* 129–144.

Schaie, K. W., & Willis, S. L. (1986). *Adult development and aging* (2nd ed.). Boston: Little, Brown.

Schneider, A. M. & Tarshis, B. (1986). *Physiological psychology* (3rd ed.). New York: Random House.

Schultz, D. P. & Schultz, S. E. (1986). *Psychology and industry today.* New York: Macmillan.

Schultz, R. & Alderman, D. (1974). Clinical research and the "stages of dying." *Omega, 5,* 137–144.

Schwartz, B. (1984). *Psychology of learning and behavior* (2nd ed.). New York: Norton.

Scott, K. G. & Carran, D. T. (1987). The epidemiology and prevention of mental retardation. *American Psychologist, 42,* 801–804.

Sears, P. S. & Barbee, A. H. (1977). Career and life satisfaction among Terman's gifted women. In J. Stanley et al. (Eds.), *The gifted and the creative: Fifty-year perspective.* Baltimore: Johns Hopkins University Press.

Seligman, M. E. P. (1975). *Helplessness: On depression, development and death.* San Francisco: W. H. Freeman.

Selye, H. (1956). *The stress of life.* New York: McGraw-Hill.

Selye, H. (1974). *Stress without distress.* Philadelphia: Lippincott.

Selye, H. (1976). *The stress of life* (Rev. ed.). New York: McGraw-Hill.

Shaffer, M. (1983). *Life after stress.* New York: Knopf.

Shapiro, D. H., Jr. (1985). Clinical use of meditation as a self-regulation strategy: Comment on Holmes's conclusions and implications. *American Psychologist, 40(6),* 719–722.

Shekelle, R. B., Hulley, S. B., Neaton, J. D., Billings, J. H., Borhani, N. O., Gerace, T. A., Jacobs, D. R., Lasser, N. L., Mittlemark, M. B., & Stamler, J. (1985). The MRFIT behavior pattern study II. Type A behavior and incidence of coronary heart disease. *American Journal of Epidemiology, 122,* 559–570.

Sherif, M. (1936). *The psychology of social norms.* New York: Harper & Row.

Shertzer, B. (1985). *Career planning* (3rd ed.). Boston: Houghton-Mifflin.

Shipley, T. (1961). *Classics in psychology.* New York: Philosophical Library.

Shotland, R. L. (1985). When bystanders just stand by. *Psychology Today, 19,* 50–55.

Siegel, S. (1979). The role of conditioning in drug tolerance and addiction. In J. D. Keehn (Ed.), *Psychopathology in animals: Research and clinical implications.* New York: Academic Press.

Siegel, S. (1983). Classical conditioning during drug tolerance, and drug dependence. In *Recent advances in alcohol and drug problems* (Vol. 7, pp. 207–246). New York: Plenum.

Siegel, S. (1986). Environmental modulation of tolerance: Evidence from benzodiazepine research. In H. H. Frey, W. P. Koella, W. Froscher, & H. Meinardi (Eds.), *Tolerance to beneficial and aversive effects of antiepileptic drugs.* New York: Raven, 89–100.

Siegler, R. S. (1983). Five generalizations about cognitive development. *American Psychologist, 38,* 263–277.

Silverman, L. H. (1976). Psychoanalytic theory. "The reports of my death are greatly exaggerated." *American Psychologist, 31,* 621–637.

Singer, J. L. & Singer, D. G. (1981). *Television, imagination, and aggression: A study of preschoolers.* Hillsdale, NJ: Lawrence Erlbaum.

Skinner, B. F. (1938). *The behavior of organisms: A behavioral analysis.* New York: Appleton-Century-Crofts.

Skinner, B. F. (1956). A case history in the scientific method. *American Psychologist, 11,* 221–233.

Skinner, B. F. (1983). Intellectual self-management in old age. *American Psychologist, 38,* 239–244.

Skinner, B. F. (1984). *A matter of consequence.* New York: A. Knopf.

Skinner, B. F. (1987). What ever happened to psychology as the science of behavior? *American Psychologist, 42,* 780–786.

Skolnick, A. (1978). *The intimate environment* (2nd ed.). Boston: Little, Brown.

Slobin, D. I. (1979). *Psycholinguistics.* Glenview, IL: Scott, Foresman.

Smith, M. L., Glass, G. V., & Miller, T. I. (1980). *The benefits of psychotherapy.* Baltimore: Johns Hopkins University Press.

Smith, P. C. (1976). Behavior, results, and organizational effectiveness: The problem of criteria. In M. D. Dunnette (Ed.), *Handbook of industrial and organizational psychology.* Skokie, IL: Rand McNally.

Smith, S. (1979). Remembering in and out of context. *Journal of Experimental Psychology: Human Learning and Memory, 5,* 460–471.

Snarey, J. (1987). A question of morality. *Psychology Today, 21,* 6–8.

Snyder, M. (1974). The self-monitoring of expressive behavior. *Journal of Personality and Social Psychology, 30,* 526–537.

Snyder, S. H. (1980). *Biological aspects of mental disorder.* New York: Oxford University Press.

Snyder, S. H. (1984). Medicated minds. *Science 84,* November, 141–142.

Snyderman, M. & Rothman, S. (1987). Survey of expert opinion on intelligence and aptitude testing. *American Psychologist, 42,* 137–144.

Spanos, N. P. & Barber, T. F. X. (1974). Toward convergence in hypnosis research. *American Psychologist, 29,* 500–511.

Sparrow, S. S., Balla, D. A., & Cicchetti, D. U. (1985). *Vineland adaptive behavior scales.* Circle Pines, MN: American Guidance Service.

Sperling, G. (1960). The information available in brief visual presentations. *Psychological Monographs, 74,* Whole No. 498.

Sperling, G. (1963). A model for visual memory tasks. *Human Factors, 5,* 19–31.

Sperry, R. (1982). Some effects of disconnecting the cerebral hemispheres. *Science, 217,* 1223–1226.

Sperry, R. W. (1968). Hemispheric disconnection and unity in conscious awareness. *American Psychologist, 23,* 723–733.

Springer, J. P. & Deutsch, G. (1981). *Left brain, right brain.* San Francisco: W. H. Freeman.

Squire, L. R. & Slater, P. C. (1978). Bilateral and unilateral ECT: Effects on verbal and nonverbal memory. *American Journal of Psychiatry, 135,* 1316–1320.

Standing, L. (1973). Learning 10,000 pictures. *Quarterly Journal of Experimental Psychology, 25,* 207–222.

Standing, L., Conezio, J., & Haber, R. N. (1970). Perception and memory for pictures: Single-trial learning of 2500 visual stimuli. *Psychonomic Science, 19,* 73–74.

Stapp, J. & Fulcher, R. (1983). The employment of APA members: 1982. *American Psychologist, 38,* 1298–1320.

Stern, L. (1985). *The structures and strategies of human memory.* Homewood, IL: Dorsey Press.

Sternbach, R. A. (Ed.) (1978). *The psychology of pain.* New York: Raven.

Stiles, W. B., Shapiro, D. A., & Elliott, R. (1986). "Are all psychotherapies equivalent?" *American Psychologist, 41,* 165–180.

Stinnett, N., Walters, J., & Kaye, E. (1984). *Relationships in marriage and family* (2nd ed.). New York: MacMillan.

Stoner, J. A. F. (1961). *A comparison of individual and group decisions involving risk*. Unpublished master's thesis; Massachusetts Institute of Technology, Cambridge, MA.

Storandt, M. (1983). Psychology's response to the graying of America. *American Psychologist, 38,* 323–326.

Strupp, H. H. (1986). Psychotherapy: Research, practice, and public policy (How to avoid dead ends). *American Psychologist, 41,* 120–130.

Strupp, H. H. & Binder, J. L. (1984). *Psychotherapy in a new key.* New York: Guliford Press.

Suler, J. R. (1985). Meditation and somatic arousal: A comment on Holmes's review. *American Psychologist, 40(6),* 717.

Surwit, R. S., Feinglos, M. N., & Scovern, A. W. (1983). Diabetes and behavior. *American Psychologist, 38,* 255–262.

Szasz, T. (1982). The psychiatric will: a new mechanism for protecting persons against "psychosis" and psychiatry. *American Psychologist, 37,* 762–770.

Szasz, T. S. (1961). *The myth of mental illness.* New York: Harper & Row.

T

Tanner, J. M. (1981). Growth and maturation during adolescence. *Nutrition Review, 39,* 43–55.

Tappert, H. T. (1967). *Luther's works, Volume 54: Table Talk.* Philadelphia: Fortress Press.

Tenopyr, M. L. (1981). The realities of employment testing. *American Psychologist, 36,* 1120–1127.

Termine, N., Hrynick, T., Kestenbaum, R., Gleitman, H., & Spelke, E. S. (1987). Perceptual completion of surfaces in infancy. *Journal of Experimental Psychology: Perception and performance, 13,* 524–532.

Thayer, W. P. (1983). Industrial/organizational psychology: Science and application. In C. J. Scheirer & A. M. Rogers (Eds.), *The G. Stanley Hall Lecture Series* (Vol. 3). Washington: American Psychological Association.

Thibaut, J. W. & Kelley, H. H. (1950). *The social psychology of groups.* New York: Wiley.

Thompson, C. I. (1980). *Controls of eating.* Jamaica, NY: Spectrum.

Thompson, C. P. (1982). Memory for unique personal events: The roommate study. *Memory and Cognition, 10,* 324–332.

Thompson, D. M. & Tulving, E. (1970). Associative encoding and retrieval: Weak and strong cues. *Journal of Experimental Psychology, 86,* 255–262.

Thompson, J. W. & Blaine, J. D. (1987). Use of ECT in the United States in 1975 and 1980. *American Journal of Psychiatry, 144,* 557–562.

Thorndike, A. L., Hagen, E. P., & Sattler, J. M. (1986). *The Stanford-Binet Intelligence Scale (4th ed.): Technical Manual.* Chicago: Riverside.

Thorndike, E. L. (1911). *Animal intelligence.* New York: Macmillan.

Tiedeman, D. V. & O'Hara, R. P. (1963). *Career development: Choice and adjustment.* New York: College Entrance Examination Board.

Tilley, A. J. & Empson, J. A. C. (1978). REM sleep and memory consolidation. *Biological Psychology, 6,* 293–300.

Tobin-Richards, M., Boxer, A., & Peterson, A. C. (1984). The psychological impact of pubertal change: Sex differences in perceptions of self during early adolescence. In J. Brooks-Gunn & A. C. Peterson (Eds.), *Girls at puberty: Biological, psychological and social perspectives.* New York: Plenum.

Tolman, C. W. (1969). Social feeding in domestic chicks: Effects of food deprivation of nonfeeding companions. *Psychonomic Science, 15,* 234.

Tolman, E. C. (1932). *Purposive behaviorism in animals and men.* New York: Appleton-Century-Crofts.

Tolman, E. C. & Honzik, C. H. (1930). Introduction and removal of reward and maze performance in rats. *University of California Publications in Psychology, 4,* 257–275.

Triplett, N. (1898). The dynamogenic factors in pacemaking and competition. *American Journal of Psychology, 9,* 507–533.

Tucker, D. M. (1981). Lateral brain function, emotion, and conceptualization. *Psychological Bulletin, 89,* 19–46.

Tulving, E. (1962). Subjective organization in free recall of "unrelated" words. *Psychological Review, 69,* 344–354.

Tulving, E. (1972). Episodic and semantic memory. In E. Tulving & W. Donaldson (Eds.), *Organization of memory.* New York: Academic Press.

Tulving, E. (1985). How many memory systems are there? *American Psychologist, 40(4),* 385–398.

Tulving, E. (1986). What kind of a hypothesis is the distinction between episodic and semantic memory? *Journal of Experimental Psychology: Learning, Memory and Cognition, 12,* 307–311.

Tulving, E. & Thompson, D. M. (1973). Encoding specificity and retrieval processes in episodic memory. *Journal of Experimental Psychology: Learning, Memory, and Cognition, 8,* 336–342.

Turkington, C. (1985). Endorphins: Natural opiates confer pain, pleasure, immunity. *APA Monitor, 16(9),* 17–19.

Turner, J. S. & Helms D. B. (1987). *Lifespan development.* New York: Holt, Rinehart & Winston.

Turns, D. M. (1985). Epidemiology of phobic and obsessive-compulsive disorders among adults. *American Journal of Psychotherapy, 39,* 360–370.

Tuttle, T. C. (1983). Organizational productivity. A challenge for psychologists. *American psychologist, 38,* 479–486.

U

Underwood, B. J. (1957). Interference and forgetting. *Psychological Review, 64,* 49–60.

United States Surgeon General's Report. (1979). *Healthy people.* Washington, DC: U. S. Government Printing Office.

V

Valenstein, E. S. (Ed.) (1980). *The psychosurgery debate: Scientific, legal, and ethical perspectives.* San Francisco: Freeman.

Valenstein, E. S. (1986). *Great and desperate cures.* New York: Basic Books.

Vaughn, B. E. & Langlois, J. H. (1983). Physical attractiveness as a correlate of peer status and social competence in preschool children. *Developmental Psychology, 19,* 561–567.

Verillo, R. T. (1975). Cutaneous sensation. In B. Scharf (Ed.), *Experimental sensory psychology.* Glenview, IL: Scott, Foresman.

Voevodsky, J. (1974). Evaluations of a deceleration warning light for reducing rear-end automobile collisions. *Journal of Applied Psychology, 59,* 270–273.

Vroom, V. (1964). *Work and motivation.* New York: Wiley.

W

Wallace, R. K. & Benson, H. (1972). The physiology of meditation. *Scientific American, 226,* 85–90.

Walster, E., Aronson, V., Abrahams, D., & Rottman, L. (1966). Importance of physical attractiveness in dating behavior. *Journal of Personality and Social Psychology, 4,* 508–516.

Walster, E. & Festinger, L. (1962). The effectiveness of "overheard" and persuasive communications. *Journal of Abnormal and Social Psychology, 65,* 395–402.

Walster, E. & Walster, G. W. (1969). The matching hypothesis. *Journal of Personality and Social Psychology, 6,* 248–253.

Walster, E., Walster, G. W., & Berschied, E. (1978). *Equity: Theory and research.* Boston: Allyn & Bacon.

Watson, C. J. (1981). An evaluation of some aspects of the Steers and Rhodes model of employee attendance. *Journal of Applied Psychology, 66,* 385–389.

Watson, J. B. (1925). *Behaviorism*. New York: Norton.

Watson, J. B. (1926). What is behaviorism? *Harper's Monthly Magazine, 152,* 723–729.

Watson, J. B. & Raynor, R. (1920). Conditioned emotional reactions. *Journal of Experimental Psychology, 3,* 1–14.

Watson, M. W., & Amgott-Kwan, T. (1984). Development of family-role concepts in school-age children. *Developmental Psychology, 20,* 953–959.

Waugh, N.C. & Norman, D. A. (1965). Primary memory. *Psychological Review, 72,* 89–104.

Weaver, C. N. (1980). Job satisfaction in the United States in the 1970s. *Journal of Applied Psychology, 65,* 364–367.

Webb, W. B. (1974). Sleep as an adaptive response. *Perceptual and Motor Skills, 38,* 1023–1027.

Webb, W. B. (1975). *Sleep, the gentle tyrant.* Englewood Cliffs, NJ: Prentice-Hall.

Webb, W. B. (1981). The return of consciousness. In L. T. Benjamin, Jr. (Ed.), *The G. Stanley Hall Lecture Series.* (Vol. I). Washington, DC: American Psychological Association.

Wechsler, D. (1975). Intelligence defined and undefined: A relativistic reappraisal. *American Psychologist, 30,* 135–139.

Weil, A. T., Zinberg, N., & Nelson, J. M. (1968). Clinical and psychological effects of marijuana in man. *Science, 162,* 1234–1242.

Werner, H. & Kaplan, E. (1950). Development of word meaning through verbal context: An experimental study. *Journal of Psychology, 29,* 251–257.

West, M. A. (1985). Meditation and somatic arousal reduction. *American Psychologist, 40(6),* 717–719.

White, R. W. (1959). Motivation reconsidered: The concept of competence. *Psychological Review, 66,* 297–333.

White, R. W. (1974). Strategies of adaptation: An attempt at a systematic description. In G. V. Coelheo, D. A. Hamburg, & J. E. Adams (Eds.), *Coping and adaptation.* New York: Basic Books.

Wickens, D. D. (1973). Some characteristics of word encoding. *Memory and cognition, 1,* 485–490.

Wilkes, J. (1986). Conversation with Ernest R. Hilgard: A study in hypnosis. *Psychology Today, 20(1),* 23–27.

Winick, M. (1981). Food and the fetus. *Natural History, 88,* 38–44.

Winter, D. G. and Stewart, A. J. (1978). The power motive. In H. London and J. E. Exner, Jr. (Eds.), *Dimensions of personality.* New York: Wiley.

Winters, K. C., Weintraub, S., & Neale, J. M. (1981). Validity of MMPI code types in identifying DSM-III schizophrenics, unipolars, and bipolars. *Journal of Consulting and Clinical Psychology, 49,* 486–487.

Winton, W. M. (1987). Do introductory textbooks present the Yerkes-Dodson Law correctly? *American Psychologist, 42,* 202–203.

Wollen, K. A., Weber, A., & Lowry, D. H. (1972). Bizarreness versus interaction of mental images as determinants of learning. *Cognitive Psychology, 3,* 518–523.

Wolpe, J. (1958). *Psychotherapy by reciprocal inhibition.* Stanford, CA: Stanford University Press.

Wolpe, J. (1981). Behavior therapy versus psychoanalysis. *American Psychologist, 36,* 159–164.

Wood, C. (1986). The hostile heart. *Psychology Today, 20,* 10–12.

Wright, L. (1988). The Type A behavior pattern and coronary artery disease. *American Psychologist, 43,* 2–14.

Wurtman, R. J. (1985). Alzheimer's disease. *Scientific American, 247,* 62–74.

Y

Yager, E. G. (1981). The QC explosion. *Training and Development Journal, 35,* 98–105.

Yates, F. A. (1966). *The art of memory.* Chicago: University of Chicago Press.

Yerkes, R. M. & Dodson, J. D. (1908). The relation of strength of stimulus to rapidity of habit-formation. *Journal of Comparative Neurology and Psychology, 18,* 459–482.

Z

Zadeh, L. (1965). Fuzzy sets. *Information and Control, 8,* 338–353.

Zajonc, R. B. (1965). Social facilitation. *Science, 149,* 269–274.

Zajonc, R. B. (1968). Attitudinal effects of mere exposure. *Journal of Personality and Social Psychology,* Monograph supplement, *9,* 1–27.

Zajonc, R. B. & Markus, H. (1982). Affective and cognitive factors in preferences. *Journal of Consumer Research, 9,* 123–131.

Zedeck, S. (1987). *The science and practice of industrial and organizational psychology.* Pamphlet prepared for the Society for Industrial and Organizational Psychology, Inc. College Park, MD.

Zedeck, S. & Cascio, W. F. (1984). Psychological issues in personnel decisions. *Annual Review of Psychology, 35,* 461–518.

Zedeck, S., Tziner, A., & Middlestadt, S. E. (1983). Interviewer validity and reliability: An individual analysis approach. *Personnel Psychology, 36,* 355–370.

Zilbergeld, B. & Evans, M. (1980). The inadequacy of Masters and Johnson. *Psychology Today, 14,* 28–43.

Zohar, D. (1980). Safety climate in industrial organizations: Theoretical and applied implications. *Journal of Applied Psychology, 65,* 96–102.

Zuckerman, M., Buchsbaum, M. S., & Murphy, D. L. (1980). Sensation seeking and its biological correlates. *Psychological Bulletin, 88,* 187–214.

Zuckerman, M., Eysenck, S., & Eysenck, H. J. (1978). Sensation seeking in England and America: Cross-cultural, age, and sex comparisons. *Journal of Consulting and Clinical Psychology, 46,* 139–149.

Acknowledgments

Credits for photographs, illustrations, and quoted material not given on the page where they appear are listed below.

PHOTO AND ILLUSTRATION CREDITS

Positions of the photographs are indicated in the abbreviated form as follows: top (t), bottom (b), center (c), left (l), right (r). All photographs not credited are the property of Scott, Foresman.

Cover and Chapter Openers: Illustrations by Guy Billout

Introduction

0   Illustration by Guy Billout; originally appearing in THE ATLANTIC MONTHLY
8   (t, b) The Granger Collection, New York (c) The Bettmann Archive
9   (t) The Bettmann Archive (b) The Granger Collection, New York
10   (t) The Granger Collection, New York (b) The Royal College of Surgeons of England, Darwin Museum, Down House, Kent
11   UPI/Bettmann Newsphotos
12   (t) Historical Pictures Service, Chicago (b) Courtesy B. F. Skinner
13   (both) The Bettmann Archive
14   (t) National Portrait Gallery, London (b) The Bettmann Archive
17   Rick Friedman/Black Star
23   Hank Morgan/Rainbow

Chapter 1

32   © 1988 Illustration by Guy Billout for Scott, Foresman and Company
37   Fig. 1.2. Manfred Kage/Peter Arnold, Inc.
58   (t) Don Smetzer/Click/Chicago (b) Rick Berkowitz/The Picture Cube

Chapter 2

64   Illustration by Guy Billout; originally appearing in THE ATLANTIC MONTHLY
72   Fig. 2.5. (r) Courtesy Munsell Color, Baltimore, Maryland
84   Fig. 2.14. MacMillan Science Co., Inc.
95   REPRINTED FROM PSYCHOLOGY TODAY MAGAZINE Copyright © 1987 American Psychological Association
99   Charles Feil/Stock, Boston
100 Spencer Grant/The Picture Cube

Chapter 3

110 Illustrations by Guy Billout; originally appearing in THE ATLANTIC MONTHLY
116 Fig. 3.1. (r) Christopher Springmann
118 (l) DREAMSTAGE Scientific Catalog Copyright © 1977 J. Allan Hobson and Hoffman-La Roche Inc. (r) Louis Psihoyos
121 Patrick Ward/© 1984 DISCOVER PUBLICATIONS, INC.
123 Mimi Forsyth/Monkmeyer
126 Michael O'Brien/Archive
129 Jon Feingersh/Stock, Boston
130 Campbell & Boulanger/Click/Chicago
132 Collection of Ronald K. Siegel
133 Jon Feingersh/Click/Chicago

Chapter 4

138 © 1988 Illustration by Guy Billout for Scott, Foresman and Company
142 John Running/Stock, Boston
143 Paul Damien/Click/Chicago
145 From the film *The Function of the Brain (Behavior of Animals and Humans)*
149 John Eastcott & Eva Momatiuk/The Image Works
150 (both) From J. B. Watson's 1919 film *Experimental Investigation of Babies*
151 Vloo/Stockphotos, Inc.
156 The Granger Collection, New York
166 Hank Morgan/© 1985 DISCOVER PUBLICATIONS, INC.
168 Animal Behavior Enterprises, Inc.
169 Courtesy Department of Psychology, University of California, Berkeley
173 REPRINTED FROM PSYCHOLOGY TODAY MAGAZINE Copyright © 1986 American Psychological Association
174 Fig. 4.10. Courtesy Albert Bandura

Chapter 5

182 © 1988 Illustration by Guy Billout for Scott, Foresman and Company
190 Mark Antman/The Image Works
191 Jean-Claude Lejeune
192 Bob Daemmrich/The Image Works
194 Ken Heyman/Archive
195 (both) Wide World
197 Charles Gupton/Southern Light
198 C. Bryan Jones/Taurus Photos, Inc.
206 Hugh Rogers/Monkmeyer
209 (both) From *Congestorium Artificia Memoriae* by Johannes Romberch, Venice, 1553
221 (l) Nina Lisowski

224   Burk Uzzle/Archive
225   Milt & Joan Mann/Cameramann International, Ltd.
229   Stacy Pick/Stock, Boston

Chapter 6

236   © 1988 Illustration by Guy Billout for Scott, Foresman
       and Company
241   Per Sundstrom/© 1982 DISCOVER PUBLICATIONS, INC.
242   Elizabeth Crews
244   George Goodwin/Monkmeyer
246   Fig. 6.4. Enrico Ferorelli/Dot
247   (t) Courtesy David Linton (b) Enrico Ferorelli/Dot
249   Yves De Braine/Black Star
250   Fig. 6.6. George Zimbel/Monkmeyer
253   Bonnie Schiffman/ONYX
261   Bob Daemmrich
266   Michael Weisbrot
268   Elizabeth Crews
269   Sidney Harris
270   John Anderson/Click/Chicago
272   (t) David Lissy/Southern Light (b) Bob Daemmrich/Stock,
       Boston

Chapter 7

282   Illustration by Guy Billout; originally appearing in THE
       ATLANTIC MONTHLY
287   Dr. E. R. Degginger
289   (1) Francis de Richemond/The Image Works (r) Anthony
       Jalandoni/Monkmeyer
290   Alan Carey/The Image Works
291   Billy E. Barnes/Stock, Boston
292   Daniel L. Feicht/Cedar Point, Inc.
295   (1) Douglas Corry/DPI (r) Brian Parker/Tom Stack &
       Assoc.
299   John Anderson/Click/Chicago
300   Nancy Sheehan/The Picture Cube
302   Gil Dupuy
305   Michael D. Sullivan/TexaStock
310   Fig. 7.5. Reprinted by permission of the publishers from
       THEMATIC APPERCEPTION TEST by Henry A. Murray,
       Cambridge, Mass.: Harvard University Press, Copyright
       © 1943 by the President and Fellows of Harvard
       College; © 1971 by Henry A. Murray.
311   Charles Harbutt/Archive
312   Bob Daemmrich
315   (1) Peter Marlow/Magnum (r) Ellis Herwig/Stock, Boston
317   Fig. 7.8. (1) George H. Harrison (r) Animals Animals/John
       Chellman
318   Fig. 7.9. From *Darwin and Facial Expression: A Century
       of Research in Review,* edited by Paul Ekman. Academic
       Press, 1973. By permission of Dr. Paul Ekman, Ed
       Gallob, and Dr. Silvan Tomkins.
319   Fig. 7.10. From *Darwin and Facial Expression: A Century
       of Research in Review,* edited by Paul Ekman. Academic
       Press, 1973. By permission of Dr. Paul Ekman.

Chapter 8

328   © 1988 Illustration by Guy Billout for Scott, Foresman
       and Company
336   (t) Eve Arnold/Magnum (b) Ken Robert Buck/The Picture
       Cube
337   (b) Historical Pictures Service, Chicago
338   (t) The Bettmann Archive (b) Association for the
       Advancement of Psychoanalysis of the Karen Horney
       Psychoanalytic Institute and Center, New York
340   Elizabeth Crews
342   Courtesy Julian B. Rotter
343   Brian Seed/Click/Chicago
344   (1) Independence Historical Park Collection, Eastern
       National Park and Monument Association (r) Courtesy
       Franklin D. Roosevelt Library
345   Sidney Harris

346   (t) Courtesy Harvard University News Office (b) Jeff
       Dunn/Stock, Boston
350   Michael Weisbrot
356   Michal Heron/Monkmeyer
364   (t) Historical Pictures Service, Chicago (b) Courtesy
       Stanford University News and Publications Service
365   Riverside Publishing Company, Chicago, IL, © 1986
369   Ray Stott/The Image Works
377   Elizabeth Crews/The Image Works
378   Dave Schaefer/The Picture Cube

Chapter 9

388   © 1988 Illustration by Guy Billout for Scott, Foresman
       and Company
393   (1) Victor Englebert (r) Rick Smolan
394   Wide World
395   The Granger Collection, New York
397   Wide World
399   (1) Charles Harbutt/Archive (r) Wide World
400   Owen Franken/Stock, Boston
404   Susan Greenwood/Gamma-Liaison
405   (1) Courtesy Cornelia B. Wilbur, M. D. (r) Courtesy
       Cornelia B. Wilbur, M. D. Prints available from
       Dr. Cornelia B. Wilbur, P. O. Box 21731, Lexington,
       KY 40502
406   UPI/Bettmann Newsphotos
411   (both) Ira Wyman/Sygma
413   Charles Gatewood/The Image Works
414   Brookhaven National Laboratory & New York University
       Medical Center
416   Obremski/The Image Bank
419   (all) Al Vercoutere, Malibu, California
421   NIMH

Chapter 10

430   © 1988 Illustration by Guy Billout for Scott, Foresman
       and Company
434   Scala/Art Resource, NY
435   (t) Scala/Art Resource, NY (b) The Metropolitan Museum
       of Art, Harris Brisbane Dick Fund, 1932
436   Bulloz
437   (tl, tc) Historical Pictures Service, Chicago (tr) Brown
       Brothers (b) National Library of Medicine
440   Andy Freeberg
441   Louis Fernandez/Black Star
444   Historical Pictures Service, Chicago
450   Courtesy Dr. Joseph Wolpe
451   Lester Sloan/Woodfin Camp & Assoc.
452   (all) Courtesy Albert Bandura
454   UPI/Bettmann Newsphotos
455   REPRINTED FROM PSYCHOLOGY TODAY MAGAZINE
       Copyright © 1985 American Psychological Association
457   (1) Paul L. Meredith/Click/Chicago (r) Bohdan
       Hrynewych/Stock, Boston

Chapter 11

466   © 1988 Illustration by Guy Billout for Scott, Foresman
       and Company
471   (both) Courtesy Mrs. Jane Elliott and ABC Television
472   Burk Uzzle/Archive
473   Marcia Weinstein
475   Richard Younker
477   Michael Evans/The White House
482   (t) Don Smetzer/Click/Chicago (b) Charles
       Gupton/Southern Light
483   Ethan Hoffman/Archive
486   William Vandivert
487   Courtesy World Federation of Bergen-Belsen Associations
488   Fig. 11.4. Copyright 1965 by Stanley Milgram. From the
       film OBEDIENCE, distributed by the New York
       University Film Division and the Pennsylvania State
       University, PCR
490   Wide World

496 Jean-Claude Lejeune
497 (t) Jon Feingersh/Stock, Boston (b) Carl Mydans, LIFE
MAGAZINE © 1962 Time Inc.
499 UPI/Bettmann Newsphotos

Chapter 12

506 Illustration by Guy Billout; originally appearing in THE
ATLANTIC MONTHLY
515 Jim Pickerell/Click/Chicago
518 Brian Seed/Click/Chicago
524 REPRINTED FROM PSYCHOLOGY TODAY MAGAZINE
Copyright © 1986 American Psychological Association
527 © Joel Gordon 1983
528 Charles Harbutt/Archive
529 Courtesy American Cancer Society
531 Bob Daemmrich
538 © Laszlo
540 Charles Biasiny-Rivera

LITERARY, FIGURES, AND TABLES

Chapter 1

45 Fig. 1.6. From *Fundamentals of Neurology,* 4th Edition
by Ernest Gardner. Copyright © 1963 by W. B. Saunders
Company. Reprinted by permission.

Chapter 3

116 Fig. 3.1 "EEG patterns of human sleep stages" from
Current Concepts™: The Sleep Disorders by Peter Hauri,
PhD. Copyright © 1982 by The Upjohn Company,
Kalamazoo, Michigan. Reprinted by permission.
119 Fig. 3.2 "Typical sleep pattern of a young adult" from
Current Concepts™: The Sleep Disorders by Peter Hauri,
PhD. Copyright © 1982 by the Upjohn Company,
Kalamazoo, Michigan. Reprinted by permission.

Chapter 4

171 Fig. 4.8 "Introduction and Removal of Reward, and Maze
Performance in Rats" by E. C. Tolman and C. H. Honzik,
from *University of California Publications in Psychology*
Volume IV 1928–1931. Reprinted by permission.
171 Fig. 4.9 "Mazes, Maps, and Memory" by David S. Olton,
from *American Psychologist* (July, 1979). Copyright ©
1979 by the American Psychological Association, Inc.
Reprinted by permission of the author.

Chapter 5

190 Fig. 5.1 "Short-term Retention of Individual Verbal
Items" by Lloyd R. Peterson and Margaret J. Peterson,
from *Journal of Experimental Psychology* (September,
1959), the American Psychological Association. Reprinted
by permission of the authors.
200 Fig. 5.2 From "Retrieval Time From Semantic Memory"
by Allan M. Collins and M. Ross Quillian, from *Journal of
Verbal Learning and Verbal Behavior* 8, 1969. Reprinted
by permission of Academic Press, Inc. and the author.
204 Fig. 5.4 From "Long-term Memory for a Common
Object" by Raymond S. Nickerson and Marilyn Jager
Adams, *Cognitive Psychology*, 11, © Copyright 1979
Academic Press. Reprinted by permission.
207 Fig. 5.5 from "Narrative Stories as Mediators for Serial
Learning" by Gordon H. Bower and Mical C. Clark, from
Psychonomic Science, 1969, Volume 14(4). Copyright ©
1969 by Psychonomic Journals, Inc. Reprinted by
Permission.
207 Fig. 5.6 From "Mnemotechnics in Second-Language
Learning" by Richard C. Atkinson, from *American
Psychologist* Volume 30, August 1975, Number 8.
Published by the American Psychological Association.
Reprinted by permission of the author.
208 Fig. 5.7 From "Bizareness versus Interaction of Mental
Images as Determinants of Learning" by Keith A. Wollen,
Andrea Weber, and Douglas H. Lowry, from *Cognitive
Psychology,* 1972. Copyright © 1972 by Academic Press,
Inc. Reprinted by permission.
208 Fig. 5.8 From *Plans and the Structure of Behavior* by
George A. Miller, Eugene Galanter, and Karl H. Pribram
(Holt, Rinehart and Winston 1960). Reprinted by
permission of the authors.
210 Fig. 5.9 From "The Conditions of Retention," by C. W.
Luh, from *Psychological Monographs.* Psychological
Review, Co., 1922.
211 Fig. 5.10 From "Properties of Learning Curves under
Varied Distribution of Practice" by Mary J. Kientzle, from
Journal of Experimental Psychology 36 (June, 1946).
Published by the American Psychological Association,
Inc. Reprinted by permission of the author.
213 Fig. 5.11 Hiroshi Minami and Karl M. Dallenbach, "The
Effect of Activity Upon Learning and Retention in the
Cockroach." *The American Journal of Psychology.*
January 1946.
213 Fig. 5.11 From "Obliviscence During Sleep and Waking"
by John G. Jenkins and Karl M. Dallenbach, from
American Journal of Psychology. Copyright © 1946,
1974 by the Board of Trustees of the University of
Illinois. Reprinted by permission of the University of
Illinois Press.
220 Fig. 5.14 From *New Ways of Analyzing Variation in
English* by Charles-James N. Bailey and Roger W. Shuy,
Editors. Copyright © 1973 by Georgetown University.
Reprinted by permission.
222 Fig. 5.15 "Cognitive Representations of Semantic
Categories" by Eleanor Rosch, from *Journal of
Experimental Psychology: General* (September, 1975).
Copyright © 1975 by the American Psychological
Association, Inc. Reprinted by permission of the author.

Chapter 6

244 Fig. 6.2 From *The First Two Years,* by Mary M. Shirley.
Reprinted by permission of University of Minnesota Press.
245 Fig. 6.3 Bryant J. Cratty, *Perceptual and Motor
Development in Infants and Children,* Copyright © 1979,
p. 212. Reprinted by permission of Prentice-Hall, Inc.,
Englewood Cliffs, N.J.
259 Fig. 6.10 Figure 8 from "Standards from Birth to
Maturity for Height, Weight, Height Velocity, and Weight
Velocity: British Children, 1965" by J. M. Tanner, R. H.
Whitehouse, and M. Takaishi from *Archives of Diseases
in Childhood,* Vol. 41, October 1966. Copyright © 1966
by the British Medical Association. Reprinted by
permission of the British Medical Journal and the
authors.
260 Fig. 6.11 Two figures from "Growing Up" by J. M.
Tanner from *Scientific American,* September 1973,
Volume 229, Number 3. Copyright © 1973 by *Scientific
American,* Inc. All rights reserved.
264 Fig. 6.12 From "Youth Suicide: Predispositions,
Predictors, and Precipitating Events" by B. P. Allen from
Adolescence, 22, 1987. Copyright © 1987 by Libra
Publishers, Inc. Reprinted by permission.
267 Fig. 6.13 "Human Mate Selection" by David M. Buss,
from *American Scientist* (January–February, 1985).
Reprinted by permission of American Scientist.

Chapter 7

316 Figs. 7.6 & 7.7 From "Language for the Emotions" by
Robert Plutchik from *Psychology Today,* February 1980,
p. 73 and graph on p. 74. Copyright © 1980 by American
Psychological Association. Reprinted by Permission from
Psychology Today.
318 Fig. 7.9 From "Cross-Cultural Studies of Facial

Expressions from *Darwin and Facial Expression: A Century of Research in Review* edited by Paul Ekman. Copyright © 1973 by Academic Press, Inc. Reprinted by permission of Academic Press, Inc. and the author.

Chapter 8

330, 331 "Are You Naturally Sexy" by Barry Cooper, from *Womans World Advertising Supplement*. March 13, 1984. Reprinted by permission of *Womans World*.

348 Fig. 8.3 From *The Inequality of Man* by H. J. Eysenck. Copyright © 1973 by Hans J. Eysenck. Reprinted by permission of Educational & Industrial Testing Services.

359 Fig. 8.5 Table "Descriptions of MMPI scales and simulated items" from *Psychological Testing and Assessment* by Lewis R. Aiken. Copyright 1943, renewed © 1970 by the University of Minnesota. Reprinted by permission.

365, 366 Figs. 8.7 & 8.8 Reprinted with permission of The Riverside Publishing Company from the *Stanford-Binet Intelligence Scale Guide for Administering and Scoring the Fourth Edition* by R. L. Thorndike, E. P. Hagen and J. M. Sattler. The Riverside Publishing Company, 8420 W. Bryn Mawr Avenue, Chicago, IL 60631.

370 Fig. 8.10 Reproduced by permission from the manual of the Wechsler Adult Intelligence Scale-Revised. Copyright © 1981, 1955 by The Psychological Corporation. All rights reserved. Reprinted by permission of The Psychological Corporation.

379 Fig. 8.12 From "Genetics and Intelligence: A Review" by L. Erlenmeyer-Kimling and L. F. Jarvik, from *Science* Vol. 142, pp. 1477–1479, Fig. 1, 13 December 1963. Copyright © 1963 by the American Association for the Advancement of Science. Reprinted by permission of the publisher and author.

Chapter 9

408 Fig. 9.3 From *Diagnostic and Statistical Manual of Mental Disorders, Third Edition.* pp. 307–329. Washington, D.C., American Psychiatric Association. Copyright © 1980. Used with permission.

420 Fig. 9.8 Types of Schizophrenia from *Abnormal Psychology and Modern Life*, Eighth Edition by Robert C. Carson, James N. Butcher and James C. Coleman. Copyright © 1988, 1984, 1950 Scott, Foresman and Company.

422 Fig. 9.9 From "Clues to the Genetics and Neurobiology of Schizophrenia" by Susan E. Nicol and Irving I. Gottesman, *American Scientist*, Vol. 71, No. 4, July–August 1983. Copyright © 1983 by Sigma Xi, The Scientific Research Society, Inc. Reprinted by permission.

Chapter 10

436 From "Treatise on Insanity" by Phillippe Pinel from *Classics in Psychology*. Copyright © 1961 by Philosophical Library, Inc. Reprinted by permission.

454 Fig. 10.1 From *Reason and Emotion in Psychotherapy by Albert Ellis* (New York: Citadel, 1962) and *A New Guide to Rational Living* by Albert Ellis and Robert A. Harper (North Hollywood, CA: Wilshire Books, 1975). Copyright © by the Institute for Rational-Emotive Therapy.

Chapter 11

475 Fig. 11.1 From "Distraction Can Enhance or Reduce Yielding to Propaganda: Thought Disruption Versus Effort Justification" by Richard E. Petty, Gary L. Wells, and Timothy C. Brock from *Journal of Personality and Social Psychology* Vol. 34, No. 5, November, 1976. Copyright © 1976 by American Psychological Association. Reprinted by permission.

479 Fig. 11.2 From *Social Psychology: Understanding Human Interaction*. Fourth Edition, by Robert A. Baron and Donn Byrne, page 59. Copyright © 1984, 1981, 1977, 1974 by Allyn and Bacon, Inc. Reprinted by permission.

490 From "37 Who Saw Murder Didn't Call the Police" by Martin Gansberg from *The New York Times,* March 17. 1964. Copyright © 1964 by The New York Times Company. Reprinted by permission.

491 Fig. 11.5 From "When Will People Help In A Crisis?" by John M. Darley and Bibb Latané from *Psychology Today*. Copyright © 1968 by American Psychological Association. Reprinted by permission from *Psychology Today*.

Chapter 12

515 Fig. 12.1 From *Training: Program Development and Evaluation,* by I. L. Goldstein. Copyright © 1974 by Wadsworth Publishing Company, Inc. Reprinted by permission of Brooks/Cole Publishing Company, Monterey, California.

536 Fig. 12.7 Reprinted with permission from *Journal of Psychosomatic Research* Volume 11, 1967, by T. H. Holmes and R. H. Rahe, "The Social Readjustment Rating Scale," pp. 213–218.

538 Fig. 12.8 Figure 3 from "The Three Phases of General Adaptation Syndrome" (p. 39) in *Stress Without Distress* by Hans Selye, M.D. (J. B. Lippincott Co.). Copyright © 1974 by Hans Selye, M.D. Reprinted by permission of Harper & Row, Publishers, Inc.

Name Index

A

Acocella, J. R., 421, 450
Adams, G. R., 258
Adams, J. A., 187
Adams, J. S., 519
Adams, M. J., 203
Adler, A., 337–338
Agnew, H. W., 121
Aiken, L. R., 358, 359
Ajzen, I., 473
Albee, G. W., 529
Alderman, D., 274
Allen, B. P., 264, 265
Allen, M. G., 415–416
Allport, G., 346
Alzheimer, A., 411
Ames, M. R., 306
Amgott-Kwan, T., 223
Amoore, J. E., 91
Anderson, J. C., 391
Anderson, J. R., 192
Anderson, R., 483
Andreasen, N. C., 423
Andrews, R. J., 317
Angell, J., 10
Anisman, H., 417
Aristotle, 8
Aronson, E., 476, 481
Aronson, V., 482
Arthur, R. J., 535, 536
Arvey, R. D., 512
Asch, S., 485–486
Aserinsky, E., 117
Atkinson, J. W., 187, 309, 310
Atkinson, R. C., 207
Atkinson, T., 521
Austin, G. A., 223

B

Babor, T. F., 130
Baddeley, A. D., 193
Bagozzi, R. P., 473
Baley, S., 512
Bandura, A., 142, 169, 172, 341, 342, 452, 499

Barbee, A. H., 374
Barber, T. F. X., 123
Bargh, J. A., 469
Barnes, M., 267
Baron, R. A., 479
Baumeister, R. F., 496
Baumrind, D., 264
Baur, K., 302
Beck, A. T., 417, 454, 455
Beckman, L. J., 268
Beer, M., 522
Beers, C., 437
Bell, A. P., 306
Bennett, T. L., 36, 128, 133, 300, 417
Bennett, W., 128
Benson, H., 125
Ben-Yehuda, N., 435
Berkeley, G., 7, 8
Berkowitz, L., 540
Berlyne, D. E., 292
Bernstein, I., 154
Binet, A., 14, 364
Birdwhistell, R. L., 317
Blaine, J. D., 440
Blank, M., 253
Bleuler, E., 418
Bloom, F. E., 36, 418, 419, 421, 424
Blum, H. M., 391
Bogen, J., 57
Booth-Kewley, S., 527
Bootzin, R. R., 421, 450
Boring, E. G., 104, 105
Borman, W. C., 512
Bouchard, T. J., 379
Bourne, L. E., 217
Bousfield, W. A., 198
Bower, G. H., 192, 205, 207, 208
Bray, D. W., 513
Breckler, S. J., 473
Breland, K., 167
Breland, M., 167
Broadbent, D. E., 98
Brody, E. M., 271
Brown, J., 190
Brown, J. I., 19
Brown, J. S., 534

Brown, L., 375
Brown, R., 205
Bruner, J. S., 223
Buckhout, R., 195
Burisch, M., 355
Burnkrant, R. E., 473
Buss, D. M., 267, 333, 483
Butler, R. N., 274, 411
Byrne, D., 479, 480, 483

C

Campion, J. E., 512
Campos, J. J., 246
Cannon, W. B., 292
Carson, R. C., 394, 404, 417, 420, 439
Carson, T. P., 417
Cash, T. F., 513
Cattell, R. B., 346–347
Cermak, L. S., 187
Chaiken, S., 472
Chase, W. G., 192
Cherns, A. B., 522
Cherry, C., 98
Chilman, C. S., 268
Chomsky, N., 228
Clark, M. C., 207
Clark, R. D., 246
Clifford, B. R., 195
Clifford, M. M., 483
Clore, G. L., 480
Coates, T., 308
Cohen, G. D., 410
Cohen, L. R., 245
Cohen, R. L., 481
Colby, A., 255
Cole, J. O., 442
Collins, A. M., 199, 200
Collins, G. R., 264
Colt, C. H., 264
Conezio, J., 193
Conger, J. J., 257, 259
Conrad, R., 192
Cooper, L. A., 193
Cornblatt, B. A., 421
Costa, P. T., 265

Costello, C. Q., 399
Coulter, W. A., 375
Craik, F. I. M., 187, 196, 205
Cronbach, L. J., 350, 358, 513
Crooks, R., 302
Cunningham, S., 492
Curran, D. K., 264

D

Dallenbach, K. M., 213
Dann, L., 394
Darley, J. M., 491, 492, 493
Darwin, C. T., 10, 14, 188, 317
Davidson, J. M., 300
Davila, G. H., 258
Davis, K., 483
Davis, L. E., 522
DeCasper, A. J., 246
Dement, W. C., 115, 117, 118, 120, 121
DeReamer, R., 524
Dewey, J., 10, 12
Diamond, M., 305
Dion, K. K., 483
Dipboye, R. L., 522
Dix, D., 437
Dodson, J. D., 293
Dollard, J., 340–341, 342, 539
Domjan, M., 152, 153, 174
Duffy, E., 292
Duke, P. M., 259, 260
Durham, R. B., 525

E

Edwards, C. P., 255
Eich, J. E., 205
Eisdorfer, C., 271
Ekman, P., 317, 318
Elkind, D., 262
Elliott, J., 468, 471
Ellis, A., 453, 454
Ellis, L., 306

Empson, J. A. C., 119
Emr, M., 411
Ericsson, K. A., 192
Erikson, E. H., 246, 261, 265, 266, 268, 271, 273
Erlenmeyer-Kimling, L., 421
Eron, L. D., 499
Erwin, E., 447
Eysenck, H., 348, 447

F

Fantz, R., 247, 248
Fast, 317
Feather, N. T., 310
Fechner, G., 8
Festinger, L., 474, 476, 482
Fifer, W. P., 246
Fishbein, M., 473
Fisher, S., 339
Fishman, H. C., 456
Fishman, J., 527
Flavell, J. H., 197, 253
Flexser, A. J., 204
Flynn, J. P., 321
Ford, M. R., 256
Forisha-Kovach, B., 256
Freedman, D. X., 398
Freeman, S., 495
Freud, S. 14, 19, 118, 119, 253, 254, 303, 333, 337, 339, 403, 444–445, 447, 541
Friedman, H. S., 527
Friedman, M. I., 298, 527
Friedman, S., 247
Fulcher, R., 510

G

Galanter, E., 208
Gallagher, J. J., 241
Galton, F., 14, 361
Garbarino, J., 257
Garcia, J., 153
Garfield, S. L., 446
Gazzaniga, M. S., 57
Geller, E. S., 520, 529
Gelman, R., 18, 253
Gemberling, G. A., 153
Genovese, K., 490, 492, 493
Gerow, J. R., 20
Gibson, E. J., 245, 246, 523
Gibson, W. M., 514
Gilligan, C., 256
Glass, D. C., 527
Glass, G. V., 447
Glenn, N. D., 266
Gold, P. E., 205
Goldstein, I. L., 515
Goleman, O., 374
Goodnow, J. J., 223
Goodwin, G. C., 264
Gorenstein, E. E., 397
Gottesman, I. I., 421
Gottlieb, G., 240
Gough, H. G., 513
Greenberg, J., 481
Greenberg, R. P., 339

Grinspoon, L., 133
Gross, R. T., 259, 260
Grossman, H. J., 375
Guilford, J. P., 345
Guion, R. M., 514
Gullota, T., 258
Gur, R. C., 423
Gurman, A. S., 457
Guzzo, R. A., 514

H

Haas, R. G., 477
Haber, R. N., 193
Hall, G. S., 261
Hall, W. G., 241, 245
Harkins, S., 495
Harlow, H. F., 299
Harris, B., 151, 273
Harris, P. L., 253, 271, 273
Harris, R. J., 205
Harrow, M., 418
Harter, S., 312
Hartley, D., 7
Hartman, S., 522
Hasher, L., 196
Hatfield, E., 483
Havighurst, R. J., 270
Hayes, J. R., 355
Haynes, S. G., 273
Hebb, D. O., 292
Heffernan, J. A., 529
Heidbreder, E., 223
Heller, J. F., 313
Helmholtz, H. von, 8, 81
Helms, D., 268
Hering, E., 82, 83
Higgins, E. T., 469
Hilgard, E. R., 123, 124
Hilgard, J. R., 123, 124
Hinrichs, J. R., 514
Hippocrates, 434
Hobson, J. A., 117, 119
Hoffman, E., 122
Hoffman, M., 306
Holden, C., 374
Holinger, P. C., 264
Holmes, D. S., 126, 266
Holmes, T. H., 535
Holmes, T. S., 535
Honzik, C. H., 169
Hoppock, R., 522
Hörmann, H., 227
Horney, K., 338–339
Hostetler, A. J., 411
Houser, B. B., 268
Houston, J. P., 202
Hovland, C. I., 476
Howard, D. V., 228
Howell, W. C., 522
Hubel, D. H., 36
Huesmann, L. R., 499
Hughes, J., 96
Hulin, C. L., 521
Hull, C. L., 287
Hume, D., 7
Hunt, M., 444
Hunter, J. E., 514
Hunter, R. F., 514
Huston, T. L., 491

I

Iaffaldano, M. T., 522
Izard, C., 316

J

Jacobs, B. L., 131
Jacobs, D. R., 527
James, W., 9–10, 113, 114, 287, 315
Janis, I., 498
Janoff-Bulman, R., 478
Jefferson, T., 344
Jenkins, C. D., 527
Johnson, E. S., 223
Johnson, M. K., 196
Johnson, V., 300, 301, 302, 303, 304, 305, 308
Jones, E. E., 478
Jones, H. E., 259
Jones, M. C., 261
Julien, R. M., 128, 133
Jung, C., 338
Jussim, L., 471

K

Kahle, L. R., 397
Kahn, R., 273
Kahn, S., 266
Kalat, J. W., 440
Kalish, R. A., 272, 274
Kallio, K. D., 222
Kamin, L., 153
Kaplan, E., 217
Kaplan, H. S., 302
Karlen, A., 305
Karoum, F., 423
Katzell, R. A., 514
Keele, S. W., 223
Keesey, R. E., 298
Keith, P. M., 268
Kelley, H. H., 478, 480
Kelley, K., 303
Kelly, C., 264
Kermis, M. D., 271
Kessler, S., 421
Kett, J. F., 257
Kiester, E. Jr., 117
Kilcullen, R. N., 513
Kimble, G. A., 160
King, M., 521
Kinsbourne, M., 57
Kinsey, A., 302, 304
Kirkpatrick, D. L., 517
Kleitman, N., 117
Knight, P. A., 514
Koffka, K., 97
Kohlberg, L., 246, 254, 255, 256
Köhler, W., 97
Kohut, H., 339
Kolata, G., 246
Korchin, S. J., 357, 361
Kraepelin, E., 395
Kramer, B. A., 440

Krantz, D. S., 527, 529
Kübler-Ross, E., 274
Kulik, J., 205

L

Laborit, H., 441
Labov, W., 220, 221
Lambert, N. M., 375
Landers, S., 309
Landy, F. J., 524
Lanetto, R., 274
Langer, S. K., 224
Langlois, J. H., 483
Lasky, R. E., 222
Latané, B., 491, 492, 493, 494, 495
Latham, G. P., 515, 516, 520, 522
Lauer, J., 267
Lauer, R., 267
Lawler, E. E., 522, 523
Lazarus, R. S., 537
Leahey, T. H., 205
LeDoux, J. E., 57
Leigh, J. E., 375
Lempers, J. D., 253
Leon, G. R., 299
Leonard, J. M., 203, 468
Lerner, M. J., 478
Lerner, R. M., 240
Levine, M. F., 522
Levinson, D. J., 265, 266, 268, 270
Levinthal, C. F., 296, 321
Lewis, M., 274
Ley, P., 530
Lidz, T., 423
Liebert, R. M., 498, 499
Linder, D., 481
Lindsay, P. H., 70
Lindsley, D. B., 51
Linz, D., 499
Litwin, G. H., 310
Lloyd-Bostock, S., 195
Locke, E. A., 10, 11, 519, 520, 521
Locke, J., 7, 93, 222
Lockhart, R. S., 187, 196
Loftus, E. F., 194, 195, 217
Loftus, G. R., 195
Long, P., 124
Lott, A. J., 480
Lott, B. E., 480
Lowery, C. R., 256
Lowry, D. H., 208
Lubin, B., 358
Lugaresi, A., 53
Luther, M., 435

M

Mace, N. L., 411
Mackenzie, B., 378, 380
Mackintosh, N. J., 372, 376, 378
Magoun, H. W., 51
Maier, S. F., 163

Maki, R. H., 197
Malamuth, N. M., 499
Mandler, G., 202
Manning, M. L., 257
Marengo, J. T., 418
Marks, M. L., 523, 524
Markus, H., 473
Marschark, M., 207
Martin, G. B., 246
Martindale, C., 193
Maslow, A. H., 13, 287, 289, 290, 344–345, 520
Massaro, D. W., 188
Masters, W., 300, 301, 302, 303, 304, 305, 308
Matarazzo, J. D., 358, 529
Mayer, W., 130, 392, 412
Mayo, E., 522
McCann, I. L., 266
McCarley, R. W., 119, 122
McClelland, D. C., 309, 310, 311
McCloskey, M., 195
McCrea, R. R., 265
McDougall, W., 287
McGaugh, J. L., 205
McGee, R., 391
McGinnis, J. M., 529
McGraw, K. O., 240
McGue, M., 379
McKim, W. A., 128, 129
Meer, J., 272
Meltzoff, A. N., 248
Melzack, R., 95
Meredith, N., 444
Middlemist, R. D., 519
Milgram, S., 486–490
Miller, B. C., 268
Miller, G. A., 192, 208
Miller, N. E., 340–341, 342, 529, 534, 539
Miller, T. I., 447
Minami, H., 213
Minuchin, S., 456
Mobley, W. H., 523
Mohrman, S. A., 523
Money, J., 304, 305, 306
Moniz, E., 439
Moore, M. K., 248
Morris, C. W., 224
Morrow, H. W., 375
Moruzzi, G., 51, 53
Moscovici, S., 486, 497
Mowday, R. T., 519
Muchinsky, P. M., 512, 522, 523
Murphy, D. P., 20
Murray, D. J., 434
Murray, D. M., 529
Murray, H. A., 309, 521

N

Newby, R. W., 204
Newman, B. M., 266
Newman, P. R., 266
Nickerson, R. S., 203
Nicol, S. E., 421
Nida, S. A., 391, 492, 494
Nisbett, R. E., 298, 299
Norman, D. A., 70, 187

O

Odbert, H. S., 346
Oden, G. C., 220
Oden, M. H., 374
Offer, D., 257
Offer, J., 257
Offord, D., 391
O'Hara, R. P., 268
Olton, D. S., 142, 169, 170
Oppenheim, R. W., 241, 245
Orne, M., 124
Oswald, I., 122

P

Parker, E. S., 205
Pavlov, I., 141, 144, 146, 148
Peck, M., 264
Peters, W. A., 468
Peterson, A. C., 257, 259, 261
Peterson, L. R., 190
Peterson, R. B., 519
Petty, R. E., 473, 475, 495
Piaget, J., 246, 248, 249, 250, 251, 252, 254, 255
Pinel, P., 436, 437
Piner, K. E., 397
Pines, M., 253
Pion, G., 3
Pittman, T. S., 313
Plutchik, R., 316
Porter, L. W., 523
Posner, M. I., 223
Powley, T. L., 298
Pressley, M., 207
Pribram, K. H., 208

Q

Quayle, D., 413
Quillian, M. R., 199, 200

R

Rabins, P. V., 411
Rafaeli, A., 523
Rahe, R. H., 535–536
Ramey, C. T., 241
Rappaport, D., 339
Raynor, R., 150–151
Rechtschaffen, A., 120
Reich, J., 398
Reinke, B. J., 265
Reis, H. T., 483
Rescorla, R. A., 152
Rest, J. R., 255
Reveley, M. A., 423
Revulsky, S. H., 153
Reynolds, D. K., 274
Rhodes, S. R., 268, 521
Rice, B., 523
Robins, E., 306
Roche, A. F., 258
Rodin, J., 299

Rogers, C., 13, 343–344, 448
Roosevelt, E., 344
Rorschach, H., 361
Rosch, E., 221
Rose, S. A., 253
Rosenman, R. H., 527
Rosenthal, D., 421
Ross, D., 172
Ross, L. D., 478
Ross, S. A., 172
Rossi, A. S., 270
Roth, L., 299
Rothman, S., 370
Rotter, J., 341–342
Rowe, J. W., 273
Rubenstein, E. A., 499
Rubin, Z., 483
Rush, B., 437

S

Saal, F. E., 514, 523
Saghir, M. T., 306
Samuelson, F. J. B., 150
Satir, V., 456
Sauser, W. J., 521
Scarr, S., 372, 380
Schachter, S., 299, 482
Schaie, K. W., 268
Schneider, A. M., 121
Schuldberg, D., 357, 361
Schultz, D. P., 517, 524
Schultz, R., 274
Schultz, S. E., 517, 524
Schwartz, B., 148, 153
Sears, P. S., 374
Seligman, M. E. P., 163, 414
Selye, H., 321, 538
Shaffer, M., 266
Shapiro, D. H., Jr., 126
Shekelle, R. B., 527
Shepard, R. N., 193
Sherif, M., 485
Shertzer, B., 268
Shiffrin, R. M., 187
Shipley, T., 436
Siegel, S., 154
Siegler, R. S., 248
Silver, F. L., 423
Silverman, L. H., 339
Singer, D. G., 499
Singer, J. L., 499
Skinner, B. F., 12, 155, 156, 165, 167, 168, 271, 341, 342
Skolnick, A., 268
Slater, P. C., 440
Slobin, D. I., 228
Smith, M. L., 447
Smith, P. C., 511, 521
Smith, S., 204
Snarey, J., 255
Snyder, S. H., 422, 441
Snyderman, M., 370
Sollie, D. L., 268
Spanos, N. P., 123
Sparrow, S. S., 375
Sperling, G., 188
Sperry, R., 57, 321
Springston, F., 192
Squire, L. R., 440

Standing, L., 193, 194
Stangor, C., 472
Stapp, J., 510
Steers, R. M., 523
Stern, L., 223
Sternbach, R. A., 96
Stewart, A. J., 311
Stiles, W. B., 460
Stinnett, N., 266
Stoner, J. A. F., 497
Storandt, M., 271
Stricker, E. M., 298
Strupp, H. H., 444
Suler, J. R., 126
Surwit, R. S., 530
Swett, S., 163
Szasz, T., 397

T

Tanner, J. M., 258, 259
Tappert, H. T., 435
Taylor, J. C., 522
Tenopyr, M. L., 358, 513
Terman, L. M., 14, 364, 374
Termine, N., 245
Thayer, W. P., 512, 513
Thibault, J. W., 480
Thompson, C. I., 299
Thompson, C. P., 205
Thompson, D. M., 204
Thompson, J. W., 440
Thorndike, A. L., 365
Thorndike, E. L., 156, 157, 161
Tiedeman, D. V., 268
Tilley, A. J., 119
Tobin-Richards, M., 261
Tolman, E. C., 142, 169, 170, 299
Triplett, N., 495
Tucker, D. M., 321
Tulving, E., 187, 196, 199, 204, 205
Turkington, C., 96
Turner, J., 268
Turner, J. A., 476
Turns, D. M., 398
Tuttle, M. L., 523
Tuttle, T. C., 522

U

Underwood, B. J., 202, 215

V

Vaughn, B. E., 483
Verillo, R. T., 94
Voevodsky, J., 525
Vroom, V., 518

W

Walk, R., 246
Wall, P. D., 95

Wallace, R. K., 125
Walster, E., 476, 481, 482, 483
Walster, G. W., 481, 483
Walton, A. E., 522
Watson, J. B., 11, 12, 113, 150–151, 339–340, 523
Watson, M. W., 223
Waugh, N. C., 187
Weaver, C. N., 266, 521
Webb, W. B., 114, 115, 121, 122, 127
Weber, A., 208
Wechsler, D., 363
Weil, A. T., 133
Weinberg, R. A., 380
Weiss, W., 476

Wellman, H. M., 197
Werner, H., 217
Wertheimer, M., 10, 97
West, M. A., 126
White, R. W., 311
Whitten, J. M., 203
Wickens, D. D., 193
Wilkes, J., 123
Williams, K., 495
Williams, R. L., 121
Williams, S., 391
Willis, S. L., 268
Windmiller, M., 375
Winter, D. G., 310, 311
Winters, K. C., 421
Winton, W. M., 293

Wolfe, D., 306
Wollen, K. A., 208
Wolpe, J., 447, 449, 453
Wood, C., 527
Woodward, C. A., 391
Wright, L., 527, 528, 529
Wundt, W., 8, 9, 10, 113, 315
Wurtman, R. J., 411–12
Wyatt, R. J., 423

Y

Yager, E. G., 523
Yates, F. A., 208

Yerkes, R. M., 293
York, W. J., 521
Young, T., 81

Z

Zacharko, R. M., 417
Zadeh, L., 220
Zajonc, R., 473, 482, 495–496
Zaragoza, M., 195
Zedeck, S., 510, 513, 514
Zilbergeld, B., 302
Zimmerman, G., 266
Zohar, D., 526

Subject Index

A

Abnormal psychology, 388–424
Abnormal reactions, classification of, 395–398
Abnormality: anxiety-based disorders, 398–405; classifications of, 395–398; definition of 393–394; personality disorders, 406–424; statistical approach to, 393–394
Acceptance, 274
Accommodation, 75, 248–249
Achievement motivation, 309–310
Acquired immune deficiency syndrome (AIDS), 306, 307–309
Acquisition, in classical conditioning, 146; in operant conditioning, 158
Action potential, 39
Actor-observer bias, 479
Acuity, 76
Addiction, 127
Adolescence, 256–262; cognitive and social development in, 261–265; and egocentrism, 262–263, 457; growth spurt in, 258; physical changes in, 258–261; and suicide, 264–165
Adrenal glands, 320
Adulthood, 265–274; early, 266–269; late, 271–275; middle, 269
Advertising, and cognitive response theory, 476
Affect, 7
Affective disorders, 414. *See also* Mood disorders
Affiliation motivation, 311
Affirmative concepts, 219
Age, satisfaction and, 521
Ageism, 271–272; myth of, 273
Aggression, 346; reacting to stress with, 539–540
Aggressiveness, 346
Agoraphobia, 399–400
Alarm, as stress response, 538
Alcohol, 130, 412–413, 451
All-or-none principle, 39
Alpha activity, 115
Alzheimer's disease, 409–412
American Association on Mental Deficiency (AAMD), 375
American Psychological Association (APA): Division for Industrial and Organizational Psychology, 510; ethical guidelines of, 26; use of surveys, 18

Amnesia, psychogenic, 404
Amnestic syndrome, 410
Amphetamines, 128, 129, 413; abuse of, 422
Amygdala, 52
Anal stage, 336
Analgesics, 96, 130
Androgens, 258, 300, 302
Anger, 274
Animals: classical conditioning of, 144; operant conditioning of, 167–168; research on, 27
Antianxiety drugs, 443
Antidepressant drugs, 442–443
Antipsychotic drugs, 441–442, 443
Antisocial personality disorder, 408
Anxiety, 398, 540; operational definition of, 6
Anxiety-based disorders, 398–405; anxiety disorders, 392, 398–405; conversion disorder, 403; dissociative disorders, 404–405; generalized anxiety disorder, 400–401; hypochondriasis, 402–403; multiple personality, 404–405; obsessive-compulsive disorder, 401–402; panic disorder, 400; phobic disorder, 398–400; psychogenic amnesia, 404; psychogenic fugue, 404; somatoform disorders 402–403
Aphrodisiac, 303
Applied psychology, 506–544
Approach-approach conflicts, 533–534
Approach-avoidance conflicts, 534
Aqueous humor, 75, 77
Arousal, 286, 302, 496; theories on, 292–293
Assessment center, 513–514
Assimilation, 248
Association areas, of cerebral cortex, 54, 56–57
Athletics, purposive behaviorism in, 172
Attention, 97
Attitudes, 472–477; changes in, 474–477; structure of, 472–473; usefulness of, 473–474
Attribute-rule approach, to concepts, 217–218
Attribution errors, 489
Attribution theory, 477–480
Audience inhibition, 492
Audition, 84
Authoritarian style, of parenting, 263
Authority, obedience to, 486–490
Autonomic nervous system (ANS), 44; and

emotions, 319, 320; parasympathic division of, 44, 320; sympathetic division of 44, 320
Average, 555
Aversion therapy, 451
Avoidance-avoidance conflicts, 534
Avoidance conditioning, 162–163
Avoidant personality disorder, 408
Axon, 36, 38
Axon terminals, 38, 41

B

Balance, motivation based on, 292–293
Barbiturates, 131, 413
Bargaining, and death, 274
Base rate, 156
Baseline design, 25
Basilar membrane, 88
Bedlam, 436
Behavior, study of, 5–6, 35
Behavior modification, 508
Behavioral/learning approach, 339–342; evaluation of, 342–345
Behavioral observation, 356–357
Behavioral techniques: aversion therapy, 451; contingency contracting, 451–452; contingency management, 451–452; evaluation of, 453; flooding, 450; implosive therapy, 450; modeling, 452–453; systematic desensitization, 449–450
Behaviorism, 11–12
Benzodiazepines, 443
Bias, overcoming in experiments, 25–26
Binet-Simon test, 14
Biofeedback techniques, 508
Biogenic amines, 416
Biological drive, 300
Biological factors, in depression, 415–417
Biomedical treatments, 438–443; antianxiety drugs, 443; antidepressant drugs, 442–443; antipsychotic drugs, 441–442; drug therapy, 441–443; electroconvulsive therapy (ECT), 439–440; psychosurgery, 438–439
Bipolar cells, 75
Bipolar disorder, 414
Blindspot, 76
Body language, 317
Borderline personality disorder, 408

Brain: center of, 48; cerebral cortex 53–59; cerebellum, 50–51; and emotions, 319, 321–322; hypothalamus, 52–53; limbic systems, 51–52; lower centers of, 48–53; reticular activating system, 51; thalamus, 53
Brain stem, 48–50
Brain syndromes, major organic, 410
Brightness, 68–69
British empiricism, 7–8
Bystander apathy, 491
Bystander intervention, 490–494; cognitive model of, 491–493

C

Caffeine, 128, 413
California Personality Inventory (CPI), 360
Camouflage, 98
Cardinal trait, 346
Career choice, in adulthood, 268–269
Case histories, 19
Catatonic type, of schizophrenia, 420
Category clustering, in long-term memory, 198
Cattell's 16 PF Questionnaire, 360
Causality, 249
Cause and effect, 16
Cell body, 36
Centers for Disease Control, 307
Central nervous system (CNS), 43
Central tendency, 555; measures of, 555–557
Central traits, 346
Cerebellum, 50
Cerebral cortex, 48, 53–59; association areas in, 54, 56–57; motor areas in, 54, 55; hemispheres of, 54, 57–59; role of, in emotions, 321–322; sensory areas in, 54, 55
Cerebral hemispheres, 54, 57–59
Chemical senses, 89–91
Childhood: cognitive and social development in, 246–256; physical and motor development in, 242–245; sensory and perceptual development in, 245–246
Chlorpromazine, 441–442
Chronological age (CA), 367
Chronic activation, 528
Chunking, 192
Ciliary muscles, 75
Classical conditioning, 141, 143–155; acquisition, 146; discrimination, 147–148; and drug addiction, 154–155; extinction, 146–147; generalization, 147–148; Pavlov's experiments on, 145–146; recent developments in, 152–154; significance of, 149–152; spontaneous recovery, 147
Classifications, problems with, 397
Client-centered therapy, 448–449
Clinical psychologist, 15, 458, 469
Clinical social workers, 458
Closure, in perceptual organization, 103–104
Cocaine, 128–129, 413
Cochlea, 88
Cognitions, 7, 229
Cognitive development: in adolescence, 261–265; in childhood, 246–256; Piaget's theory of, 248–253; stages of, 274
Cognitive dissonance theory, 474–475
Cognitive map, 170–172

Cognitive model, of bystander intervention, 491–493
Cognitive processes, 216; and concepts, 216–223
Cognitive psychology, 13
Cognitive response theory, 475–476, 477
Cognitive restructuring therapy, 454–455
Cognitive techniques: cognitive restructuring therapy, 454–455; rational-emotive therapy (RET), 453–454
Cognitive theories, 175
Collective monologues, 251
Collective unconscious, 338
Color-blindness, 78, 83
Color vision, 81–84
Common traits, 346
Communication, 456; persuasive, 476–477
Compensation, 542
Competency motivation, 311–313
Compulsions, 401–402
Concept(s), 216–218; affirmative, 219; attribute-rule approach to, 217–218; concept of, 216–218; conjunctive, 218–219; disjunctive, 218–219; formation of, 222; in the laboratory, 218–219; natural, 220–222; in the real world, 220–222; relational, 220
Concrete operations stage, 251–252
Concurrent validity, 353
Conditioned response, 145
Conditioned stimulus (CS), 144; selection of 152–153; time interval between unconditional stimulus and, 153–154
Conditioning, 143, 175; avoidance, 162–163; escape, 161–164
See also Classical conditioning; Operant conditioning
Conditioning trial, 145
Cones, 75, 77–81
Conflict-induced stress, 533–535
Conflicts: approach-approach, 533–534; approach-avoidance, 534; avoidance-avoidance, 534; multiple approach-avoidance, 534–535
Conformity, 485–486; Asch studies on, 485–486; and norm formation, 485
Conjunctive concepts, 218–219
Consciousness, 113; altering with drugs, 127–133; and hypnosis, 123–124; levels of, in psychoanalytic theory, 334; and meditation, 125–127; nature of, 114; and sleep and dreams, 115–121
Conservation, 251
Content validity, 353–354
Context, effects of, 203
Contiguity, in perceptual organization, 102
Contingency contracting, 451–452
Contigency management, 451–452
Continuity, 103
Continuous reinforcement (CRF) schedule, 165
Contrast, in perceptual selectivity, 97–99
Control, exercising, in experiments, 24
Control Group, 25
Control variables, 22
Conversion disorder, 403
Cornea, 73
Coronary heart disease (CHD), 527
Corpus callosum, 57
Correlation coefficient, 20
Correlational study, 19–21; in twin studies, 380
Counseling psychologist, 15, 458
Countertransference, 446

Crack, 129
Criterion referenced test, 359
Cross-laterality, 55, 58
Crystallized abilities, 365
Cutaneous senses, 92–93

D

Dark adaptation, 78
Data, organizing, 553–555
Death, dealing with, 272, 274
Death instinct, 335, 338
Debriefing, 489
Decibel scale, 84
Decision-making, in groups, 496–498
Defense mechanisms, 541; reacting to stress with, 540–544
Deficiency needs, 345
Delirium, 410
Delta wave, 116
Delusions, 410; in schizophrenia, 418
Dementia, 410
Democratic style, of parenting, 263
Dendrites, 36
Denial, 274, 541
Dependence, 127
Dependent memory, 205
Dependent personality disorder, 408
Dependent variables, 22
Depressants, 129–131
Depression, 274, 414–415; biological factors in, 415–417; common symptoms of, 415; psychological factors in, 417
Deprivation studies, of sleep, 120–121
Descriptive statistics, 555–559
Development, and nature-nurture controversy, 238, 240–241, 376–381
Developmental psychologists, 469
Developmental psychology, 236–275
Diagnosis, 395
Diagnostic and Statistical Manual of Mental Disorders, 395–397, 398, 403, 404–405, 406–407
Diffusion of responsibility, 493
Diminishing returns phenomenon, 211
Discrimination: in classical conditioning, 148; in neonates, 247–248; in operant conditioning, 166–167
Disjunctive concepts, 219
Disorganized type, of schizophrenia, 420
Displacement, 543
Dispositional attributions, 478
Dissociative disorders, 392, 404–405
Distributed practice, 212
Dopamine, 129, 416, 422–423
Dorsal, 46
Double-blind technique, 26
Dreams, 115, 117; Freud on, 119; latent control of, 118; manifest content of, 118; reasons for, 118; and REM sleep, 117–120. See also Sleep
Drinking behavior, 296–297
Drive(s), 287; learned, 288; motivation based on, 287–288, 294; primary, 288; secondary, 288
Drive-reduction, Hull's theory of, 287–288
Drug addiction, and classical conditioning, 154–155
Drugs; altering consciousness with, 127–133; depressants, 129–131; hallucinogens, 131–132; marijuana, 133; stimu-

lants, 128–129; as therapeutic agents, 128, 441–443
Dual-center theories, 297
Duplicity theory of vision, 77–81; evidence to support, 78–81

E

Ear, role of, in hearing, 88–89
Eardrum, 88
Eating, 297–299
Ego, 335
Ego identity, 273
Egocentrism: in adolescence, 262–263, 457; in childhood, 250
Elaborative rehearsal, 205
Elavil, 442
Electra complex, 336
Electric stimulation, 55
Electroconvulsive therapy (ECT), 439–440
Electroencephalogram (EEG), 115
Electromyogram (EMG), 115
Emotion(s), 286, 313; classification of, 315–316; conditioning of, 149–152; definition of, 314–315; nature of, 313–316; outward expressions of, 316–318; physiological aspects of, 319–322; studying, 314
Empathic listening, 448
Employment interview, 512–513
Empty nesting, 273
Encapsulated nerve endings, 92
Encoding: amount and distribution of practice, 209–212; effects of context, 203–205; overlearning, 209; and rehearsal, 203–212; scheduling practice for, 211–212; strategies that guide, 205–209
Encoding specificity principle, 203–204
Endocrine system, 44
Endorphins, 96
Engineering approach, to worker safety, 525
Environment, influence of, on intelligence, 376–381; and nature-nurture controversy, 238, 240–241, 376–381; and sexuality, 306
Environmental frustration, 532
Epigenetic model of development, 240
Epinephrine, 129, 320
Episodic memory, 197
Equanil, 443
Equilibrium, motivation based on, 292–293
Equity model, 481
Equity theory, of work motivation, 519
Erogenous zones, 302
Eros, 335
Escape conditioning, 161–164
Estrogen, 258, 300, 302
Ethics, in psychological research, 26–27, 489–490
Etiology, 395
Evolution, 14
Evolutionary perspective, of sleep, 122
Evolutionary theory, 10
Excitement, in the human sexual response, 302–303
Exhaustion, as stress response, 538
Existential therapies, 448
Expectancy theory, of work motivation, 518–519
Expectations, in perceptual selectivity, 101

Experiences, in perceptual selectivity, 101–102
Experimental group, 25
Experimental methods, 21–26; in psychological research, 9–10
Experimental neurosis, 148
External attributions, 478
External locus of control, 342
Extinction: in classical conditioning, 146–147; in operant conditioning, 158–159
Extraneous variables, 22
Extrinsic control, 312
Extroversion-introversion dimension, 348
Eye, role of, in vision, 73–77
Eyewitness testimony, acceptance of, 508

F

Facial expressions, and emotion, 317–318
Factor analysis, 347
Failure, fear of, 310
Family: influence of in adolescence, 263–264; and marriage, 266–268
Family therapy, 456
Fantasy, 542
Fears. See Phobic disorders
Fertility cycle, 300
Figure-ground relationship, 97
Flashbulb memories, 205
Flattened affect, 418
Flooding, 450
Fluid analytic abilities, 365
Formal concepts, 218
Formal operations stage, 252
Fovea, 76
Free association, 445
Free nerve endings, 92
Frequency distributions, 553–554
Freudian psychoanalysis, 333–337, 445–446
Frontal lobe, 54
Frustration, 532
Frustration-aggression hypothesis, 539–540
Frustration-induced stress, 531–533
Fugue, psychogenic, 404
Functionalism, 10, 11
Fundamental attribution error, 478

G

Ganglion cells, 75
Gate-control theory, of pain, 95–96
General adaptation syndrome, 538–539
Generalization: in classical conditioning, 147–148; in operant conditioning, 166–167
Generalized anxiety disorder, 400–401
Genes, 240
Genital herpes, 307
Genital stage, 337
Gestalt, 10–11
Gestalt psychology, 10–11, 97
Goal-setting, role of, 520
Gonorrhea, 306–307
Graphic representations, 554–555
Group polarization, 497–498
Groups, decision-making in, 496–498
Groupthink, 498
Growth hormone production, during sleep, 122

Growth needs, 345
Growth spurt of early adolescence, 258
Gustation, 67, 89, 90

H

Habituation, 144
Hair cells, 88
Hallucinations, 124, 410; negative, 124; in schizophrenia, 418
Hallucinogens, 131–132
Hands-on approach, 517
Hashish, 133, 413
Health, and psychology, 526–530
Health psychology, 526
Hearing, 67; role of ear in, 88–89; sounds as stimulus for, 84–88
Hemispheres, cerebral, 54, 57–59
Heredity, influence of, on intelligence, 376–381; nature and nurture controversy, 238, 240–241, 376–381; and schizophrenia, 421–422
Heroin, 130–131
Hertz, 85
Heterosexuality, 304–305
Hidden observer, 124, 127
Hippocampus, 52
Histogram, 554
Histrionic personality disorder, 408
Homeostasis, 292, 294, 298
Homosexuality, 304–306
Hormones, 44
Hue, 69
Human immunodeficiency virus (HIV), 308
Human motivation, theory of, 13
Human sexual response, 301
Humanism, 13
Humanistic/phenomenological approach, 342–345; evaluation of, 345–348
Humanistic techniques, 448–449; evaluation of, 448–449
Hunger, 297–299
Hypnosis, 123–125; hidden observer in, 124, 127
Hypnotherapy, 112
Hypochondriasis, 402–403
Hypothalamus, 52–53, 295; in drinking behavior, 296–297; in eating behavior, 297–298; and emotions, 321, 322; and temperature control, 294–295
Hypothesis, 5; testing of, 223
Hysteria, 403

I

Id, 335
Idealistic principle, 335
Identity crisis, 261
Identity formation, in adolescence, 261–262
Impulse, 39–40; transmission of, 41–43, 49
Implosive therapy, 450
In-basket technique, 514
Incentives, 290–291; motivation theory based on, 290
Incus, 88
Independence, 265
Independent variables, 22
Industrial-organizational (I/O) psychology, 510–526; employee selection, 512–514; fitting job to the person, 521–526; fitting

person to the job, 510–521; job analysis, 511–512; job satisfaction, 521–523; motivation of employees, 517–521; quality circles, 523–524; training of employees, 514–517; worker safety, 524–526
Industrial-social approach, to worker safety, 525–526
Inferential statistics, 560–562
Inferiority complex, 338
Information: representation of, in long-term memory, 198–201; representation of, in short-term memory, 192–193
Insanity, 397
Insomnia, 115
Instinctive drift, 168
Instincts, 287; in psychoanalytic theory, 334–335; motivation based on, 287
Instrumental conditioning, 155
Intellectual assessment, 14, 350, 364–376; Stanford-Binet Intelligence Scale, 364–368; Wechsler tests for intelligence, 368–370
Intelligence, 363–364; definition of, 363–364; distribution of, 372–373; group differences in, 370–372; influence of heredity and environment on, 376–381; twin studies of, 378–381; variations in, 372–376
Intelligence quotient (IQ), 367
Intensity, 98
Interdependence, 265
Interference, and inhibition of retrieval, 212–216
Internal attributions, 477–478
Internal locus of control, 342
Interneurons, 38
Interpersonal attraction, 480–484; factors affecting, 481–484; theories of, 480–481
Interviews, 357–358
Intoxication, 410
Intrinsic control, 312
Introspection, 9
Iproniazid, 442
Iris, 73–74

J

Job, fitting person to, 523–524
Job analysis, 511–512
Job application form, 512
Job satisfaction, 521, 522–523
Just world hypothesis, 478

K

Key word method of study, 207–208
Kinesthetic sense, 94

L

La belle indifference, 403
Labeling, problems with, 397
Laboratory, concepts in, 218–220
Language: definition of, 223–226; and morphemes, 227; and phonemes, 226; and pragmatics, 228–229; and semantics, 227;
and speech behaviors, 51, 56, 58; and speech sounds, 226–227; structure in, 226–229; syntax of, 227–228
Latency stage, 336
Latent content of dreams, 118
Latent learning, 169–170
Lateral geniculate body, 83
Law of effect, 161
Learned helplessness, 163
Learning, 141, 340; application of conditioning and cognitive theory to, 175–176; classical conditioning in, 143–155; definition of, 142–143; discrimination, 166–167; generalization, 166–167; operant conditioning in, 155–159, 169–174; punishment, 165; reacting to stress with, 539; reinforcement, 160–165
Learning theorists, 469
Left hemisphere, 59
Lens, 74–75
Lesions, 51
Levels of processing model of memory, 187
Libido, 335
Librium, 443
Licensed professional counselor, 458
Life change-induced stress, 535–537
Life change units, 535
Life instincts, 335
Light, 68–72; wave amplitude of, 68–69; wave length of, 69–71; wave purity in, 71–72
Limbic system, 51–52; and emotions, 321, 322
Linguistic intuitions, 228
Lithium, 441–442
Lobes and localization, 54
Locus of control, 341–342
Long-term memory (LTM), 193–201; encoding in, 195–196; representation of information in, 198–201; types of, 196–198
Loudness, 84–85
LSD (lysergic acid diethylamide), 131–132, 413

M

Maintenance rehearsal, 191
Malleus, 88
Malleus Maleficarum, 435
Mania, 414–415; common symptoms of, 415
Manic-depression, 414
Manifest content, of dreams, 118
Mantra, 125
MAO inhibitors, 442, 443
Marijuana, 133, 413
Marriage and family, 266–268
Massed practice, 212
Matching phenomenon, 483
Mean, 556
Measurement, 349
Median, 556
Medication, 530
Meditation, 125–127
Medulla, 49
Mellissaphobia, 399
Memory, 186–187; and eyewitness testimony, 508; flashbulb, 205; and hypnosis, 124–125; long-term, 193–201; measuring retrieval from, 201–203; models of, 187; in neonates, 247; sensory, 188–189;
short-term, 189–193; state-dependent, 205
Menarche, 258
Mental age (MA), 367
Mental health technician, 459
Mental images, 207
Mentally gifted, 373–374
Mentally retarded, 375–376
Mental measurements, 14
Mental processes, study of, 6–7
Mental set, 101
Meprobamates, 443
Mere exposure phenomenon, 482
Mescaline, 131
Metamemory, 197–198
Metaneeds, 345
Methadone, 131
Method of loci, 208
Microsleep, 121
Miltown, 443
Minnesota Multiphasic Personality Inventory (MMPI), 358–360; clinical scales for, 359
Mnemonic devices, 206–209
Mode, 557
Modeling, 172–174, 452–453
Monochromatic, 71
Mood disorders, 414–417; depression, 414–417; mania, 414
Moral development, Kohlberg's theory of, 254–256; stages of, 275
Morpheme, 227, 229
Morse code, 226
Motion, 98
Motion sickness, 94
Motivated forgetting, 541
Motivation, 285, 286, 510, 517–521; achievement, 309–310; competency, 311–313; cyclical nature of, 284–285; in I/O psychology, 510, 517–521; in perceptual selectivity, 101; physiologically based, 294–299; power, 311; psychologically based, 309–313; theories of, 286–293
Motor areas, of the cerebral cortex, 54, 55
Motor development, in childhood, 242–243; stages of, 274
Motor neurons, 38
Multiphasia, 528
Multiphasic tests, 360
Multiple approach-avoidance conflicts, 534–535
Multiple personality, 404–405
Multistore model of memory, 187
Myelin, 37, 38, 47

N

Nanometer (nm), 69
Narcissistic personality disorder, 408
Narrative chaining, 207
National Council on Alcoholism, 412
National Institute of Mental Health (NIMH), 391, 414
Natural concepts, 220–222
Naturalistic observation, 16–18
Nature-nurture controversy, 238, 240–241, 376–381
Need(s), 287; hierarchy of, 289–290, 344–345
Need for affiliation, 311
Need for competence, 311
Need for power, 311
Need to achieve (nAch), 309

Negative afterimages, 83
Negative reinforcer, 161–163
Nelson Denny Reading Test, 19
Neo-Freudians, 337
Neologisms, 418
Neonate, 242–243; cognitive abilities of, 247–248; reflexes, 243
Nerve cells, 34
Nervous systems, 43; autonomic, 44, 319, 320; central, 43; peripheral, 43–44; somatic, 44
Network models, of long-term memory, 199–201
Neural impulses, 36, 39; transmission of, 42–43
Neural threshold, 39
Neuron, 36; function of, 39–40; structure of, 36–37; and transmission of impulses, 42–43
Neurotransmitters, 41, 129, 131; role of, 42
Nicotine, 128, 413
Norepinephrine, 129, 320, 416, 417
Normal curve, 562
Normal curve statistics, 562–564
Norms, 472; formation of, and conformity, 485; on a psychology test, 354
NREM sleep, 117
Nuclei; 49

O

Object permanence, 250
Observational learning, 173
Observational methods: in accessing personality, 357–358; in psychological research, 16–21
Observer bias, 16–17
Obsessions, 401
Obsessive-compulsive disorder, 401–402, 408
Occipital lobe, 54
Occupational therapists, 459
Oedipus complex, 336
Office of Strategic Services, 513
Olfaction, 53, 89–91
Operant conditioning, 140, 141, 155–159; acquisition, 158; definition of, 155–156; extinction, 158–159; factors influencing, 167–174; procedures of, 156–157; shaping, 157–158; spontaneous recovery, 159
Operational definition, 6
Opiates, 130, 413
Opponent-process theory, 82
Optic nerve, 75
Oral stage, 336
Organic mental disorders, 409–412
Orgasm, in the human sexual response, 303
Orienting reflex, 144
Ossicles, 88
Oval windows, 88
Overcrowding, effects of, 508
Overlearning, 209–211
Overweight, 299

P

Pain, 67, 94–96; gate control theory of, 95–96; and hypnosis, 124; sensation of, 96
Panic disorder, 400

Paper-and-pencil tests, 358–360
Paradoxical sleep, 120
Paranoid personality disorder, 408
Paranoid type, of schizophrenia, 420
Parasympathetic division, of automatic nervous system, 44, 320
Parenting styles, 263–264; and development of schizophrenia, 423–424
Parietal lobe, 54
Passive-aggressive personality disorder, 408
Past experience, 101–102
Pastoral counseling, 459
PCP (phencyclidine), 413
Peg word method, 208
Perception(s), 8, 67, 68; and Gestalt psychology; in schizophrenia, 418–419
Perceptual organization, 102; personal factors, 104–105; stimulus factors, 102–104
Perceptual selectivity, 96; and Gestalt psychology, 97; personal factors, 100–102; stimulus factors, 97–100
Performance criteria, 511
Peripheral nervous system (PNS), 43–44
Peripheral retina, 77
Permissive style of parenting, 263
Personal fables, 262
Personal factors: in perceptual organization, 104–105; in perceptual selectivity, 100–102
Personal frustration, 532
Personality, 332–333; behavioral/learning approach to, 339–342; development of, 336–337; humanistic/phenomenological approach to, 342–345; multiple, 404–405; and physical health, 527–529; psychoanalytic approach to, 333–339; structure of, 335; trait approach to, 345–349
Personality assessment, 330–332, 350, 355–362; behavioral observation, 356–357; interviews, 357–358; paper-and-pencil tests, 358–360; projective techniques, 309–310, 311, 361–363
Personality disorders, 392, 406–407; antisocial personality disorder, 408; avoidant personality disorder, 408; borderline personality disorder, 408; dependent personality disorder, 408; histrionic personality disorder, 408; narcissistic personality disorder, 408; obsessive-compulsive personality disorder, 408; paranoid personality disorder, 408; passive-aggressive personality disorder, 408; schizoid personality disorder, 408; schizotypal personality disorder, 408
Personality psychology, 333
Personal traits, 346
Personal unconscious, 338
Personnel approach, to worker safety, 525
Personnel selection, 510
Persuasion, 474
Persuasive communication, source of, 476–477
Phallic stage, 336
Phenothiazines, 441
Philosophy, roots of psychology in, 7–8
Phobic disorder, 398–400
Phonemes, 229
Photoreceptors, 75
Physical attractiveness, and interpersonal attraction, 482–483
Physical attractiveness stereotype, 483
Physical dependence, 127
Physical development: in adolescence, 258–261; in childhood, 242–243

Physical health: and personality, 527–529; and psychological interventions, 529–530
Physiological aspects, of emotion, 319–322
Physiological needs, 290
Pinna, 88
Pitch, 86
Plaques, 411
Plasticity, 241
Plateau, in the human sexual response, 303
Pleasure principle, 335
Pluralistic ignorance, 492
Pons, 50
Position senses, 93–94
Positive reinforcers, 160–161
Postsynaptic membrane, 41
Power motivation, 311
Pragmatics, 228–229
Predictive validity, 353
Prefrontal lobotomy, 438–439
Prejudice, irrationality of, 468
Preoperational stage, 250–251
Pressure, 67
Presynaptic membrane, 41
Primary colors, 81–82
Primary reinforcers, 163–164
Proactive interference, 215
Probability statements, 560–561
Procedural memory, 196
Process schizophrenia, 419–420
Prognosis, 399
Progressive relaxation, 449
Projection, 542
Projective test, 309
Prototypes, 221, 222
Proximity: and interpersonal attraction, 482; in perceptual organization, 102–103
Psychiatric nurses, 459
Psychiatrist, 458
Psychiatry, 458
Psychoactive drugs, 127, 413, 441
Psychoanalysis, 14–15, 334, 403; evaluation of, 339–342, 447; Freudian, 333–337, 445–446; post-Freudian, 337–339, 446–447
Psychoanalyst, 458
Psychodiagnostics, 458
Psychogenic amnesia, 404
Psychogenic fugue, 404
Psycholinguistics, 224, 229
Psychological, 127
Psychological interventions, and physical health, 529–530
Psychological preparation, 508
Psychological principles, application of, 509
Psychological research, 551; descriptive statistics in, 555–559; ethical considerations in, 26–27, 489–490; experimental methods in, 21–26; frequency distributions, 553–554; graphic representations, 554; inferential statistics, 560–561; and laboratory concepts, 218–220; measures of central tendency, 555–557; normal curve statistics, 562–564; observational methods in, 16–21; organization of data in, 553–554; variability, 557–559
Psychological test(s), 14, 331–332, 513; criteria for good, 351–354; for intellectual assessment, 364–372; in I/O psychology, 513–514; nature of, 349–354; norms in, 354; for personality assessment, 309–310, 311, 355–362; reliability of, 352–353; in twin studies, 381; validity of, 353–354; working definition of, 350–351
Psychologists, studies of, 5–7

Psychology, abnormal, 388–424); applications of, 13–15; cognitive, 13, 175–176; definition of, 4–7; developmental, 236–275; and ethics, 26–27; experimental, 9–10; functional, 12; Gestalt, 10–11, 97; goals of, 15; and health, 526–530; history of, 7–15; and humanism, 13; industrial-organizational, 510–526; reasons for studying, 3–4; research methods in, 16–26; as a science, 2, 4–5; social, 469–499; subject matter of, 5–7
Psychosis, 407, 409
Psychosocial development: Erikson's theory of, 253–254; stages of, 275
Psychosocial law, 494
Psychosomatic disorders, 402
Psychosurgery, 438–439
Psychotherapy, 13, 444–460; aversion therapy, 451; behavioral techniques, 449–453; client-centered therapy, 448; cognitive restructuring therapy, 454–455; cognitive techniques, 453–455; contingency contracting, 451–452; contingency management, 451–452; flooding, 450; Freudian psychoanalysis, 445–446; group approaches, 456–457; humanistic techniques, 448–449; implosive therapy, 450; modeling, 452–453; post-Freudian psychoanalysis, 446–447; psychoanalytic techniques, 444–447; rational-emotive therapy (RET), 453–454; sources of, 457–460; systematic desensitization, 449–450
Psychotic disorders, 407, 409–413; degenerative dementia of the Alzheimer type, 410–412; depression, 414–415; mania, 414–415; mood disorders, 414–417; organic mental disorders, 409–412; substance-induced organic mental disorders, 412–413
Psychoticism dimension, 348
Puberty, 258
Punishment, 159, 165; and observational learning, 173; vicarious, 174. See also Reinforcement
Pupil, 73
Purkinje shift, 79–81

Q

Quality circles, 523–524
Quality of work life (QWL), 522

R

Racial differences, in job satisfaction, 521
Random assignment, 25
Range, 558
Rating scale, 357
Rational-emotive therapy (RET), 453–454
Rationalization, 541–542
Reactive schizophrenia, 420
Reality principle, 335
Rebound effect, 121
Recall, 201
Reciprocity, and interpersonal attraction, 481–482
Recognition, 202
Reflex, 144

Refractory period, 39, 304
Regression, 543
Reinforcement: and locus of control, 342; and observational learning, 173; scheduling of, 164–165; vicarious, 174. See also Punishment
Reinforcement model, 480
Reinforcer: definition of, 160; negative, 161–163; positive, 160–161; primary, 163–164; secondary, 163–164
Relational concept, 220
Relaxation, 126
Relearning, 203
REM sleep, 117, 118, 119
Repetition, in perceptual selectivity, 99–100
Repression, 541
Reserpine, 416–417, 441
Residual type, of schizophrenia, 420
Resistance, 445–446; as stress response, 538
Resolution, in the human sexual response, 303–304
Responses, 16
Resting potential, 39
Restorative perspective, of sleep, 121–122
Reticular activating system (RAS), 51
Retina, 75–77
Retirement, 273
Retrieval: and encoding, 203–212; inhibiting, 212–216; measurement of, 201–203
Retroactive interference, 214
Reversible figures, 97
Right hemisphere, 58, 59
Risky shift, 497
Rod-cone break, 79
Rods, 75, 77–81
Rogerian therapy, 448
Role-playing, 357
Rorschach inkblot test, 361–362
Rotter Incomplete Sentences Blank, 361
R-R relationships, 16, 19, 20, 22

S

Safety needs, 290
Saliva, 89
Sample, 18
Saturation, 71
Schemas, 248
Schizoid personality disorder, 408
Schizophrenia, 413, 418–424; biochemical factors in, 422–423; DSM-III-R types of, 420; hereditary factors in, 421–422; process, 419–420; psychological and social factors in, 423–424; reactive, 420
Schizotypal personality disorder, 408
Science, roots of psychology in, 8
Scientific law, 15
Scientific methods, 4–5
Secondary dispositions, 346
Secondary reinforcers, 163–164
Sedative drugs, 413
Self-actualization, 290, 344
Semantic memory, 196–197
Semantics, 227, 228
Senile psychosis, 411
Sensation, 67
Sensorimotor stage, 249–250
Sensory adaptation, 93
Sensory areas, of cerebral cortex, 54, 55
Sensory development, in childhood, 245–246

Sensory memory, 188–189
Sensory neurons, 38
Septum, 52
Serotonin, 131, 416
Set point, 292, 298
Sex differences, in job satisfaction, 521
Sex drives, 299–309
Sexual behavior, 299–309
Sexual response, 301–304
Sexually Transmitted Diseases, 306–309
Sexual preference, 304
Shaping, in operant conditioning, 157–158
Short-term memory (STM), 189–193, 365; capacity of, 192; duration of, 190–191; measurement of, on Stanford Binet, 365; representation of information in, 192–193
Significant other, 519
Similarity: and interpersonal attraction, 483–484; in perceptual organization, 103
Single-blind technique, 25
Situational attributions, 478
Situational testing, 513
Skin senses, 92–93
Skinner box, 156, 167
Skinnerian conditioning, 155
Sleep, 115; deprivation studies of, 120–121; evolutionary perspective of, 122; functions of, 120–122; NREM, 117; regulation of, 50; REM, 117–120; restorative perspective of, 121–122; stages of, 115
Sleep spindles, 116
Smell, 53, 89–91
Smoking, 128; and use of hypnotherapy, 112–113
Social cognition, 469
Social development: in adolescence, 261–264; in childhood, 246. See also Cognitive development
Social exchange model, 480
Social facilitation, 495–496
Social frustration, 532
Social impact theory, 494–495
Social influence, 484–499; bystander intervention, 490–494; conformity, 485–486; obedience to authority, 486–490; social facilitation, 495–496; social impact theory, 494–495; social loafing, 495, 496
Social inhibition of helping, 492
Social interference, 495, 496
Social learning, 172–74
Social learning theory, 172
Social loafing, 495, 496
Social-psychological perspective, 470–472
Social psychology, 469–499; and attitudes, 472–477; and attribution theory, 477–480; and interpersonal attraction, 480–494; and social influence, 484–499
Social Readjustment Rating Scale (SRRS), 535–536
Somatic arousal, 125
Somatic nervous system, 44
Somatic relaxation, 126
somatoform disorders, 392
Sound, 84–88; wave amplitude of, 84–85; wave frequency of, 85–87; wave purity in, 87–88
Sound waves, 84
Source traits, 347
Speech: and damage to brain, 51, 56, 58; sounds in, 226–227
Spinal cord, 34, 45; function of, 46–48; structure of, 45–46

Spinal reflexes, 47–48
Split-brain procedures, 57–58
Split-half reliability score, 353
Spontaneous recovery, in classical conditioning, 147; in operant conditioning, 159
Sports psychologists, 508
S-R relationships, 21–22
Stability-instability dimension, 348
Standard age score (SAS), 367
Standard deviation, 558, 561
Stanford-Binet Intelligence Scale, 14, 364–368
Stapes, 88
State-dependent memory, 205
Statistical approach, to abnormality, 393–394
Statistically significant differences, 561
Statistics, 552–53; descriptive, 555–559; inferential, 560–561; normal curve, 562–564
Stereochemical theory, 91
Stereotype, 471
Stimulants, 128–129, 413, 422
Stimulus, 22
Stimulus factors, in perceptual organization, 102–104; in perceptual selectivity, 97
Storage, 186
Stress, 530–543; and aggression, 539–540; causes of, 531–537; and changes in neurotransmitters, 417; conflict-induced, 533–535; and defense mechanisms, 540–544; frustration induced, 531–533; and learning, 539; life-change-induced, 535–537; reactions to, 537–543
Stressors, 531–537
Structuralism, 9–10
Studying, key word method of, 207
Subjective organization, in long-term model, 199
Substance-induced organic mental disorders, 409, 412–413
Suicide, teenage, 264–265
Superego, 335
Surface traits, 347
Surveys, 18
Sympathetic division, of automatic nervous system, 44, 320
Synapse, 41
Synaptic cleft, 41
Syndrome, 395, 409
Synesthesia, 132
Syntax, 227–228
Syphilis, 307
Systematic desensitization, 449–450

T

Tachistoscope, 206
Taste, 67, 89, 90
Taste buds, 90
Taylor Manifest Anxiety scale, 360
Teenage suicide, 264–265
Television, and violent behavior, 498–499
Temperature, 67, 92; regulation of, 294–296
Temperature spots, 93
Temporal lobe, 54
Test-retest reliability, 352
Thalamus, 53
Thanatos, 335
THC (tetrahydrocannabinol), 133
Thematic apperception test (TAT), 309–310, 311, 362
Theory, 332
Therapist, choosing a, 457–460
Theta waves, 115–116
Thirst, 296–297
Thorazine, 441
Threshold, 78
Timbre, 87
Time urgency, 528
Tip-of-the-tongue phenomenon (TOT), 184
Tofranil, 442
Tolerance, 127
Touch, 67, 92
Training, of employees, 510, 514–517
Trait approach, 345–348; evaluation of, 349
Traits, 345
Transcendental meditation, 125
Transference, 446
Treatments: biomedical, 438–443; historical perspective of, 434–438
Tremors, 51
Trichromatic theory, 81
Tricyclics, 442–443
T-test, 561
Twin studies, 378–380; and depression, 415–416; and schizophrenia, 421–422
Type A behavior pattern (TABP), 527, 528 ingredients of the, 528

U

Unconditional positive regard, 448
Unconditioned response (UCR), 144
Unconditioned stimulus (UCS), 144; and time interval between conditional response and, 153–154
Undifferentiated type, of schizophrenia, 420

V

Valium, 443
Variability, 557–559; measures of, 555
Variances, 559
Ventral, 46
Vesicles, 41
Vestibular sacs, 94
Vestibular sense, 94
Vestibule training, 516
Vicarious punishment, 174
Vicarious reinforcement, 174
Violent behavior, and television, 498–499
Vision, 67; color, 81–84; duplicity theory of, 77–81; light as stimulus for, 68–72; role of eye in, 73–77
Visual cliff, 246
Vitreous humor, 75

W

Wave amplitude: of light, 68–69; of sound, 84–85
Wave frequency, of sound, 85–87
Wavelength: of light, 69–71
Wave purity: of light, 71–72; of sound, 87–88
Wechsler Adult Intelligence Scale (WAIS), 368–369
Wechsler Intelligence Scale for Children (WISC), 368
Wechsler Preschool & Primary Scale of Intelligence (WPPSI), 368
Wechsler tests for intelligence, 368–370; scales in, 368–369
White light, 72, 87
White noise, 87
Withdrawal, 127, 128, 410
Work behaviors, and job satisfaction, 522–523
Worker safety, 524–526; engineering approach to, 525; industrial-social approach to, 525–526; personnel approach to, 525
Working memory, 189

Z

Zero correlation coefficient, 20